The Sino-Soviet Conflict

The Sino-Soviet Conflict

A Global Perspective

Edited by HERBERT J. ELLISON

UNIVERSITY OF WASHINGTON PRESS
Seattle and London

Copyright © 1982 by the University of Washington Press
Printed in the United States of America

All rights reserved. No part of this book may be reproduced or transmitted in any form or by any means, electronic or mechanical, including photocopy, recording, or any information storage or retrieval system, without permission in writing from the publisher.

Library of Congress Cataloging in Publication Data
Main entry under title:

The Sino-Soviet conflict.

    Papers presented at a conference sponsored by the Center for Contemporary Chinese and Soviet Studies of the University of Washington and held at the Battelle Research Center, Seattle, Oct. 30–Nov. 1, 1980.
    Includes index.
    1. China—Foreign relations—Soviet Union—Congresses. 2. Soviet Union—Foreign relations—China—Congresses. 3. World politics—1975–1985—Congresses. I. Ellison, Herbert J. II. University of Washington. Center for Contemporary Chinese and Soviet Studies.

DS740.5.S65S56   327.51047   81–51279
ISBN 0-295-95854-5   AACR2
ISBN 0-295-95873-1 (pbk.)

Contents

Foreword   SENATOR HENRY M. JACKSON   vii

Acknowledgments   xi

Maps   xii, xiii

Introduction   HERBERT J. ELLISON   xv

PART 1. THE PARTNERS TO THE CONFLICT

Internal Politics: China and the Soviet Union

The Background in Chinese Politics   KENNETH LIEBERTHAL   3

The Soviet Perspective   SEWERYN BIALER   29

Foreign Affairs and Security

China's Agonizing Reappraisal   JONATHAN D. POLLACK   50

Soviet Foreign and Security Problems and Policies   PAUL H. BORSUK   73

Economic Problems and Policies

The Economic Background and Implications for China   DWIGHT PERKINS   91

The Economic Background and Implications for the USSR   HENRY W. SCHAEFER   112

Part 2. International Repercussions of the Dispute

The Global Impact

International Politics and
the Sino-Soviet Dispute WILLIAM E. GRIFFITH 131

The Challenge of the "New Internationalism" KEVIN DEVLIN 146

The Regional Impact: Northeast and Southeast Asia

The Impact of the Sino-Soviet Dispute
on Northeast Asia DONALD C. HELLMANN 172

The Impact of the Sino-Soviet Dispute
on Southeast Asia DOUGLAS PIKE 185

The Regional Impact: South Asia and the Middle East

The Impact of the Sino-Soviet Dispute
on South Asia WILLIAM J. BARNDS 206

The Sino-Soviet Interaction
in the Middle East BETTIE M. AND OLES M. SMOLANSKY 240

The Regional Impact: Europe

The Impact of the Sino-Soviet Dispute
on Eastern Europe TROND GILBERG 268

The Impact of the Sino-Soviet Dispute
on Western Europe JOAN BARTH URBAN 295

Part 3. Overview and Assessment

Perspectives

Alternative Western Views of the
Sino-Soviet Conflict DONALD W. TREADGOLD 325

The Sino-Soviet Dispute in the 1970s:
An Overview HARRY GELMAN 355

Prospects for the 1980s HUGH SETON-WATSON 372

Index 388

Contributors 409

Foreword

For many years, I have believed that the triangular relationship of the United States, China, and the Soviet Union is of critical importance for Americans. How we manage this relationship will profoundly affect the prospects of peace for the remainder of this century and on into the next. It is for this reason that I am especially pleased to see scholarly attention returning to the policy issues raised by the Sino-Soviet dispute and our relation to it. In this regard, we face difficult and complex decisions in the years ahead, and policy makers need the perspective and reflections that the scholarly community can offer.

This volume, focusing as it does on the development of the Sino-Soviet dispute, does much to clarify what Americans have been slow to accept: China and the Soviet Union are fundamentally different countries, with different ambitions and different allies, and different intentions toward us. Our interests with respect to each of them, therefore, do differ, and the way that we deal with each of them will be distinctive.

The impressive gains in Soviet strategic power in the 1970s and the invasion of Afghanistan have reawakened the Western world and reminded our peoples of the fundamental mentality of the Soviet Union in its foreign policy. Long ago I took my clues on how the Soviets might behave, were they to achieve such strategic gains, from the beloved historian, Professor Philip Mosely of Columbia University. Back in 1967, before a Senate Committee I was chairing, he warned: "In any future period in which it might attain either nuclear equality or nuclear superiority, however that may be measured in terms of the ratio between offensive and defensive systems, we would be prudent to assume that Soviet policy would be tempted to undertake a more extensive, more acute, and more dangerous range of risks in order to pursue its declared long-range ambition to reshape the world according to its own dogma."

How right Phil was. Its increasingly favorable strategic nuclear position allows Moscow to pursue probes abroad, directly or by proxies, to expand its influence and power. Like popularity in politics, strategic advantage may be difficult to define, but when it shifts, those who gain it and those who lose it are bound to be sensitive to the change. Today, American diplomacy does not enjoy the comfortable freedom of action that it experienced in the past, and the element of uncertainty in crisis situations is now more serious.

As I see it, a robust strategic equivalence with the Soviet Union is essential for an effective American foreign policy—one which will ensure our national security and the safety of other free nations.

As many of the articles in this volume demonstrate, a central set of issues is raised by the problem of dealing with China in the context of the Sino-Soviet dispute. How do we treat the Sino-Soviet dispute with its ramifications on China's northern and southern borders? What kind of security relations do we really wish to have with the People's Republic of China? How do we handle closer and improving relations with China without unnecessarily feeding Soviet anxiety about China? What should be our arms-sale policy with China? Do we envision China's strengths as supplementary to or as a substitute for United States power in the Pacific? What are the implications of the Soviet build-up for the United States defense posture in the Western Pacific? How do we handle our new ties with China in ways that reinforce our old ties in the area and do not disrupt them? These concerns are hard upon us in the light of Moscow's invasion of Afghanistan and the diversion of the United States forces from the Pacific to the Middle East and the Indian Ocean areas.

The Sino-American relationship has come a long way. Even before the Afghan crisis, it was clear that our China policy was entering a new stage. Full normalization of relations is now a reality. We have seen the admission of China to the United Nations, President Nixon's visit and the Shanghai Communiqué, the establishment of liaison offices, the lifting of the ban on direct trade with China, cultural and scholarly exchanges, visits by government leaders, the normalization of relations and exchange of ambassadors, and the coming into force of the United States–China Trade Agreement providing for the extension of most-favored-nation treatment and access to official credits.

Today Sino-American relations are fully advanced, inclusive, and, indeed, complex. On the one hand, China is a developing nation that looks to us as a source of strength in order to counterbalance the strength of the Soviets, their present principal adversary. They want from us technology, capital, and expertise to accelerate their modernization. We, on the other hand, are a developed country that looks to China as a counterweight to the Soviet Union, a potentially significant source of stability in Asia, and a likely and attractive market. No wonder there are difficult choices of policy to be considered in our relations with China. The relatively easy-to-do things have been done. Where do we go from here? We are at a kind of watershed in China policy. It turns out that policy makers in both the Executive Branch and Congress have more questions than answers. For decisions that have to be made they have run out of the road maps that guided them intellectually over the past decade.

We are in a period of fateful decisions, not easy decisions like resistance when you are attacked. In fact, we confront a protracted, complicated, costly effort which alone can ensure the future of freedom. It is for this reason that I warmly welcome the appearance of this collection of papers by distinguished experts on the subject, and, above all, I welcome the renewed interest in the study of Sino-Soviet relations that this conference volume bespeaks.

SENATOR HENRY M. JACKSON *June 1981*

Acknowledgments

An effort such as this volume, and the conference that contributed so much to it, inevitably owes its success to the efforts and cooperation of many people. I am indebted to Professor William Griffith of M.I.T. for his help in planning the conference topics. I am also indebted to the conference session chairmen whose direction of the discussion contributed so much to the critical evaluation of the papers which became the chapters of this book— to Professor Paul Brass, Dr. Raymond Garthoff, Mr. Samuel Blair Griffith II, Professor Herbert Levine, Dr. Sidney Ploss, Professor John Reshetar, Professor Robert Scalapino, and Professor James Townsend. I should like also to give special thanks to those conference participants from abroad who added so much to those same evaluations, especially to Dr. Dieter Heinzig and Dr. Joachim Glaubitz from the Federal Republic of Germany, to Professor Takashi Inoguchi from Japan, and to Mr. Hua Di from the People's Republic of China. And I am grateful to many colleagues and staff of the School of International Studies, especially the director, Professor Kenneth Pyle, Dr. Lawrence Lerner, and Mrs. Beverly Weiss; and to colleagues working with our new Center for Contemporary Chinese and Soviet Studies who gave much helpful support and advice.

I should also like to thank the following individuals and organizations whose generous donations made this project financially possible: Battelle Memorial Institute; The Boeing Company; Mr. Edward E. Carlson; John Deere Foundation; Mr. and Mrs. George P. Duecy; Mr. Stanley D. Golub; Mrs. Maxwell Hamilton; Senator Henry M. Jackson; Kaiser Family Foundation; Mr. Henry Kotkins, Sr.; Dr. Haakon Ragde; Rainier National Bank; Mr. and Mrs. Walter E. Schoenfeld; John L. Scott, Inc.; United Airlines Foundation; and United Technologies Corporation.

HERBERT J. ELLISON, Chairman
Center for Contemporary Chinese and Soviet Studies
School of International Studies
University of Washington

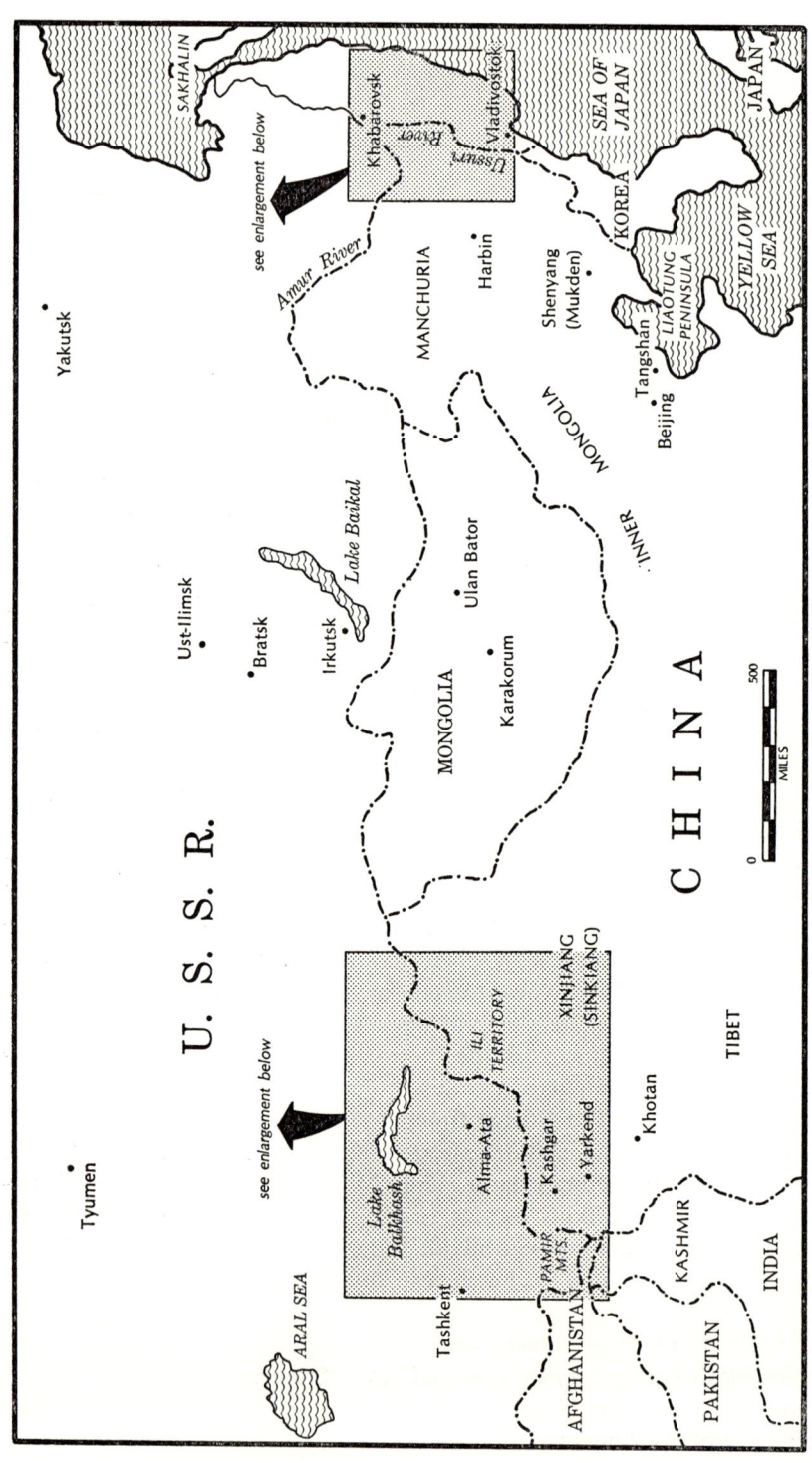

Sino-Soviet borderlands

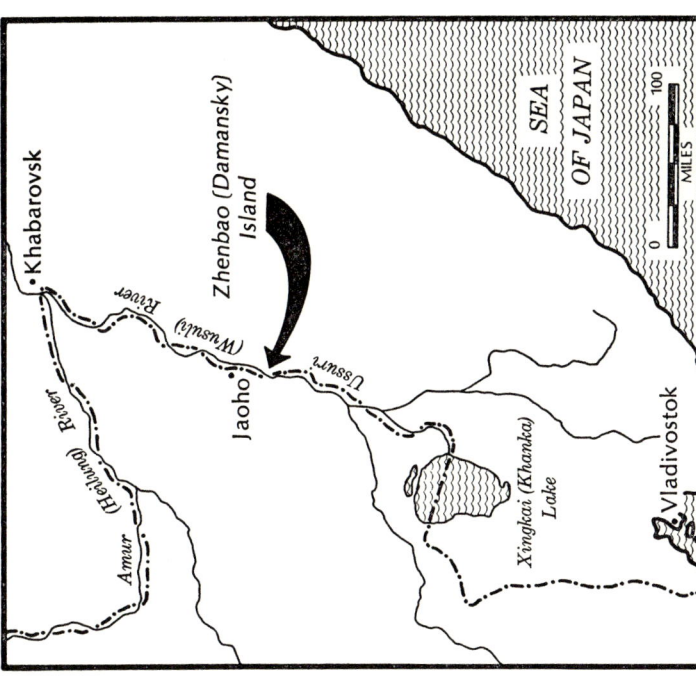

The Amur-Ussuri boundary between China and the U.S.S.R. The arrow points to Zhenbao Island, one of the riverine islands involved in the 1969 border conflict. (Courtesy of *Problems of Communism*)

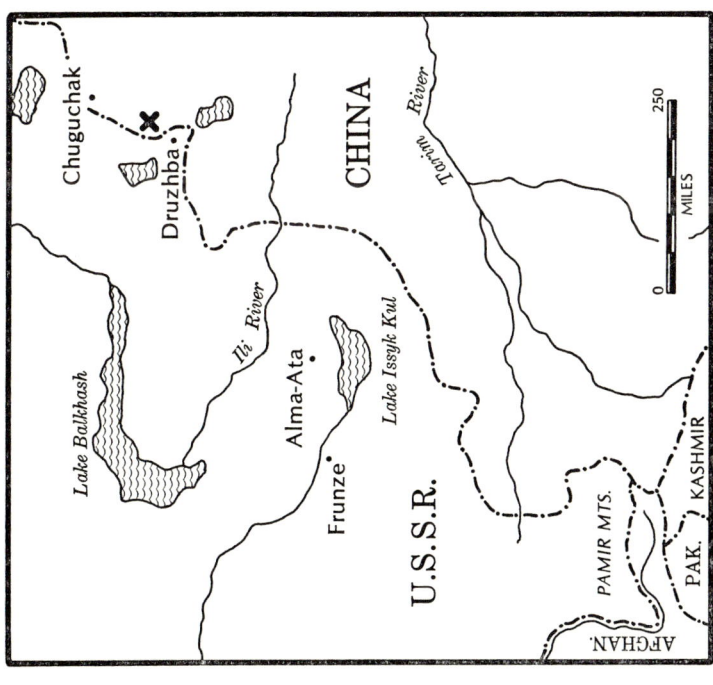

The disputed frontier between China's westernmost province of Xinjiang (Sinkiang) and Soviet Central Asia. "X" marks the area where an armed clash took place on August 13, 1969. (Courtesy of *Problems of Communism*)

Introduction

Few developments have had greater impact on the international politics of our era than the Sino-Soviet conflict. From modest beginnings in the 1950s, it has steadily broadened in scope and importance. Intitially affecting mainly the partners to the dispute, its influence soon extended to the world communist movement, to diplomatic relations of the two states in developing countries, and finally to global politics, where it became a central issue in the confrontation of the superpowers in the 1970s and 1980s. A conflict that seemed at the start to be based on minor and manageable irritations has become a tense diplomatic military confrontation, a major foreign policy concern of both countries, and the central concern for China. It is the purpose of the present volume to explore the complexities of the conflict, and its international repercussions, within the rapidly changing international scene of the 1970s, and to project the likely trends of the 1980s.

From its earliest beginnings, the Sino-Soviet conflict revealed a mix of national interests and communist ideology. Since the participants were leaders of communist parties, the dispute inevitably found expression in ideological language, though the real significance of ideological concerns has diminished over time. And beneath the polemics lay not only the special concerns and perspectives of historic nations but the competing claims of their communist party leaders within an international movement. During the 1950s and 1960s, when the dispute developed rapidly into an open break, a central issue implied in the Chinese attacks on Soviet foreign policy was strategic: how is communist revolution to be pursued? This was hardly a new question in the history of communism. Nor was the second major issue, this one the basis of Chinese criticisms of Soviet domestic policy:

what are the proper institutions and policies for a communist society? What had changed was the context of interparty relations within which these questions were debated, and only as the debate progressed did the scope and implications of the change become clear.

From the Bolshevik Revolution to the Second World War the Soviet leadership gave the authoritative and binding answers to such questions. The Russian (later Soviet) Communist Party set the organizational and ideological terms for admission to the new Communist International (Comintern) at its founding in 1919, and Moscow decided all the major questions of leadership and policy for those parties during the interwar years. But even in that period of Soviet dominance China had been different. The collapse of the Soviet-designed united front with the Kuomintang in 1927, and the failure of urban revolutionary efforts, were followed by the creation of Mao Zedong's communist rural base—a revolutionary resistance enclave within which the communists built a state administration and an army. Tempered in the long resistance struggle against the Nationalist government and the invading Japanese, a period during which its leadership grew accustomed to making most of its own decisions, the Chinese party emerged politically victorious and independently powerful in 1949.

Neither Lenin nor Stalin had taken well to independence in fellow communists, domestic or foreign. Lenin's domination of the non-Russian communist leaders in the reconquered borderlands of the old Russian Empire set the pattern to which Stalin gave final form in the 1924 Constitution of the USSR. It was essentially the same centralism, guaranteeing organizational and ideological control to Moscow, that Lenin built into the Comintern. Stalin moved forward operationally in the 1920s and 1930s to impose his will on the world communist movement with the same force that he applied internally. And he showed himself no less determined or harsh in the postwar period.

But before the war Stalin had dealt with communist leaders struggling for power. Communists in power—particularly when they had gained power by means of their own administrative and military organization, as had Tito and Mao—had both independent minds and means. The Soviet-Yugoslav break in 1948 was an abortive Soviet effort to compel obedience; Stalin apparently thought that condemnation and expulsion from the Cominform would bring a Stalin-loyalist revolt against Tito in his own party. And Khrushchev in his turn, deeply rooted in the tradition of Soviet domination, and in spite of his condemnation of Stalin's handling of Tito, also assumed Soviet primacy in interparty relations.

In contrast to Tito, Mao initiated both the dispute and the eventual break with the Soviets. The Soviets had criticized Tito's policies, but Mao criticized Soviet domestic and foreign policies. With Stalin gone, Mao clearly regarded himself as senior to Khrushchev. His charges that the Soviets feared U.S. power and had abandoned the serious pursuit of revolution, and his attachment of the dread label "revisionist" to Soviet domestic policies, were stinging rebukes. But more than that, the very act of offering them implied that Beijing was Moscow's equal as a center of ideological authority.

During Khrushchev's first visit to Beijing in October 1954, the Soviets and Chinese signed a number of important political and economic agreements granting concessions to China. Yet they refused to reduce the ties binding Mongolia to the Soviet Union, or to allow significant expansion of Chinese control in North Korea. Clearly there were important Sino-Soviet differences over policy in Northeast Asia. But the rapid deterioration of mutual relations during the succeeding two years had other causes—Khrushchev's reconciliation with Tito (whose brand of communism Mao regarded as revisionist), his pursuit of improved relations with the United States, and his disturbing criticisms of Stalin at the Twentieth Congress of the CPSU in February 1956.

The differences appeared greatly to diminish in the aftermath of Soviet military intervention against the Hungarian Revolution the following November. Khrushchev's policy toward Tito, and the easy acceptance of "different roads to socialism," had borne bitter fruit. Khrushchev now welcomed Mao's endorsement of his attacks on Tito and revisionist national communism at the Moscow conference of communist parties in November 1957. But though Mao asserted on the eve of the conference, "The socialist camp must have one head, and that head can only be the USSR,"[1] the new rapport was short-lived. Within a year Khrushchev and his colleagues "sensed [that Mao] had aspirations to be the leader of the world Communist movement."[2]

Meanwhile, new issues aggravated the relationship—Moscow's condescending criticism of the Chinese Great Leap Forward in 1958 and cautious detachment in the Sino-American conflict during the Quemoy crisis, and the Chinese feeling that the Soviets gave too limited aid to their economic and military development. The Soviet cancellation in June 1959 of the Sino-Soviet agreement on atomic cooperation in effect since 1957, followed by Khrushchev's visit to the United States, seemed to confirm the Chinese charges that the Soviets sought accommodation rather than revolutionary confrontation with the United States.

At the meeting of the Romanian Communist Party in Bucharest in June 1960 Khrushchev attempted to mobilize support against the Chinese, but the effort failed. The Moscow meeting of communist parties in November

---

1. Strobe Talbott, ed., *Khrushchev Remembers: The Last Testament* (Boston: Little, Brown, 1974), p. 254.
2. Ibid., p. 261.

brought an ideological compromise: Beijing accepted the possibility of varied roads to socialism and the avoidability of war, while Moscow acknowledged the ideological acceptability of achieving revolutionary power either by bomb or by ballot. But mutual reproaches continued, thinly disguised as Muscovite attacks on Albanian "dogmatism" and Chinese attacks on Yugoslav "revisionism." Following Premier Zhou Enlai's abrupt departure from the Twenty-Second Congress of the CPSU in October 1961—a protest against Khrushchev's attacks on Chinese policies through the Albanian surrogate—the Sino-Soviet recriminations came into the open and became rapidly more inflammatory.

Relations deteriorated steadily from late 1961 to Khrushchev's fall from power in October 1964. A Moscow meeting of Chinese and Soviet party leaders in July 1963 failed to achieve positive results, and during the following year the exchanges included bitter personal attacks on Mao and Khrushchev. Khrushchev scheduled a meeting of representatives of twenty-five communist parties for December 1964, apparently aiming to settle scores with Mao. After Khrushchev's removal Brezhnev postponed the conference until March 1965, hoping for an improvement in relations. But the meeting was boycotted by the Chinese and their supporters, and the Soviets turned to other means of isolating the Chinese within the communist community—strengthening their ties with Mongolia, North Korea, and North Vietnam, and seeking to build a pro-Soviet party to compete with the pro-Chinese communist party in Japan.

During the late 1960s, the years of the Vietnamese War and the Cultural Revolution, the Sino-Soviet relationship became progressively more strained. Soviet students and diplomatic personnel were expelled from China during 1966, and the Soviets expelled Chinese students in October of that year. Soviet attacks on Chinese policy, suspended since Khrushchev's retirement, were now aggressively resumed. The Chinese were accused not only of splitting the movement but of weakening national liberation efforts and playing into the hands of the imperialists. In March 1969 the border conflict erupted violently near the confluence of the Amur and Ussuri rivers, an area where intermittent disputes had festered for a decade.

As the 1960s ended it was clear not only that the Soviets were taking a variety of initiatives to contain the Chinese challenge but that some of these measures were further aggravating an already embittered relationship. The most threatening of the Soviet responses was the steady military build-up along the Chinese border during the late 1960s. To the fifteen Soviet divisions stationed along the Chinese border in 1967 the Soviets had added another fifteen by 1970, and these forces were vastly better equipped than their Chinese counterparts. The presence of such forces, combined with stern military warnings to the Chinese, tended to strengthen the already forceful impression made on the Chinese by the Soviet invasion of Czechoslovakia in August 1968, an action they had vigorously denounced along with the Brezhnev Doctrine that justified it.

The Soviets continued their efforts to isolate China both within the communist movement and by conventional diplomatic initiatives. The former effort, focused on the Moscow Conference of World Communist Parties in June 1969, was a conspicuous failure. Although there was little sympathy for Maoist China, particularly in the era of the Cultural Revolution, many party leaders, especially in Europe, were chiefly concerned to reduce Soviet domination of the movement (especially after Czechoslovakia), and found the split a convenient instrument for that purpose. Concentrating their efforts on the states bordering China—Mongolia, North Korea, Vietnam, Laos, Burma, India, Pakistan, and Afghanistan—the Soviets found conventional diplomacy more rewarding. Indeed, the combination of growing Soviet military power and Chinese diplomatic isolation was a grim fact for the leaders to reckon with as China emerged painfully from the period of the Cultural Revolution. For their part the Soviets continued to make overtures to China. Prime Minister Kosygin visited Beijing in September 1969 on his return trip from Hanoi, border negotiations resumed during the following month, and by the end of 1970 the two countries had once again exchanged ambassadors and entered into new trade agreements. But as so often before in the history of the dispute, the Chinese now undertook a bold initiative: in July 1971 it was announced that Secretary of State Henry Kissinger had arrived secretly in Beijing and had arranged for President Richard Nixon to visit China.

The Chinese opening to the United States signaled the beginning of a new era in the history of the Sino-Soviet relationship, one in which the perception of both the issues and the appropriate means of response had changed fundamentally on the Chinese side. During the 1950s and 1960s the Chinese had focused on the strategy of world communist revolution, with particular emphasis on world area priorities and the appropriate diplomatic and internal political alliances. China had advocated an aggressive revolutionary policy in the Third World and a bold confrontation with the United States and its allies and was bitterly disdainful of the peaceful coexistence policy of Khrushchev and his successors with its courting of the United States and of Third World nationalist leaders.

In Mao's view the Soviets were obliged to accept China at least as an equal partner in this global revolutionary enterprise, and to show a willingness to provide the scale of economic development and military (including nuclear weapons) aid that would maximize Chinese effectiveness. When the Soviets failed to respond satisfactorily, Mao's criticism, and his internal policies, became steadily more extreme, particularly in the era of the Cultural Revolution. Lacking the Soviet economic and military resources for the competition, the Chinese were reduced mainly to hurling ideological stones at the Soviet Goliath and to stirring up politically fruitless border incidents. Meanwhile the area of the communist movement, and of international diplomacy, was left largely to the Soviets.

The Chinese decision to reenter this arena opened a new phase of the Sino-Soviet relationship in the 1970s. The fundamental conflict remained, embittered by fifteen years of competition and recrimination. But now the stakes were much larger for both parties, and the general situation more worrying. At the opening of the decade of the 1970s it was clear to the Chinese that the USSR had emerged as a hostile superpower with global ambitions and capacities. The United States no longer threatened China, but was an imperialist power in decline. Hence the Chinese must seek to build a new diplomatic relationship with the United States, Japan, and Europe, and restore severed or neglected ties with fellow communist parties and states. They must seek as well to repair the political, economic, and social disorder inherited from recent years and resume economic growth and technological modernization. Significantly, the shift of policies was undertaken before Mao's death and continued after, shattering Soviet hopes that his demise would create opportunities for Sino-Soviet reconciliation.

From the Soviet point of view the situation also presented challenges and worries. The Chinese were as intractable as themselves on border negotiations. And what might the Chinese attain with their new approach to the industrial democracies, and to other communist parties and states? Relieved of the ideological narrowness and fanaticism that had crippled their economic development, weakened their military capability, and drastically limited their diplomatic options, the Chinese could be a far more formidable competitor than in the 1960s. Moreover, the new flexibility and vigor of Chinese policy appeared in a decade marked by serious economic problems and, from mid-decade onward, growing conflict with the United States over the same Third World adventures that the Chinese denounced. Already approximately 25 percent of Soviet military commitment was to the defense of the Chinese border; what would be the cost of competing with a growing Chinese power, particularly one having close diplomatic ties with major capitalist states?

Such is the background of events that provide the setting for the new phase of the Sino-Soviet conflict in the 1970s. The present volume is the outgrowth of discussions in the new Center for Contemporary Chinese and Soviet Studies at the University of Washington in the summer of 1979. It was generally agreed that the 1970s had brought a new and extraordinarily important stage in the Sino-Soviet conflict, greatly expanding its international impact, and that a group of scholarly specialists could be brought together to write on the main elements of that new phase. After the themes of the proposed study had been outlined, scholarly specialists were asked to prepare papers on these topics, and they were presented at a conference

Introduction xxi

entitled "The Sino-Soviet Conflict: The Seventies and Beyond" sponsored by the Center and meeting at the Battelle Research Center in Seattle from October 30 to November 1, 1980. Another group of specialists was invited to the conference to provide critical review of the papers in preparation for revision and editing for inclusion in the projected volume.

The three major sections of the book correspond to the main themes pursued in the conference. The first section contains three subsections, each a pair of chapters (one for China, one for the USSR) and focusing in turn on these three topics: the domestic political background of the dispute, its foreign affairs and security dimensions, and its connections with the economies of the two states. These chapters provide a close look at Chinese and Soviet internal developments, as well as extensive analysis of the foreign policy and security questions involved in the dispute. They provide a great deal of insight into the important events of the 1970s, including the impact in China of the end of the Cultural Revolution, the course of the Vietnam War, and the dramatic expansion of Soviet power and international ambitions. The revolution in Chinese foreign policy and the Soviet response are closely analyzed. Also a great deal of attention is given to the evidence of continuity and change in Soviet-Chinese images of one another.

The chapters on the Soviet and Chinese economies are chiefly concerned with the economic costs of the dispute, its impact on development plans and trade patterns, and above all trends that might indicate changing relative economic strength of the two states. Dwight Perkins's chapter on the Chinese economy challenges the conventional wisdom about China's present and future economic (hence military) inferiority to the Soviet Union, projecting a rapid change of economic power in China's favor over the next two decades.

The second section of the book places the Sino-Soviet conflict in international perspective, including a chapter on the global impact of the dispute, one on its impact on the international communist movement, and six chapters that deal with the main regions of the world where the Soviets and Chinese have come into competition or conflict: East Asia, Southeast Asia, South Asia, the Middle East, Eastern and Western Europe. This section enables the reader to follow the influence of changing global political circumstances on the dispute, on the one hand, and the impact of the dispute on global and regional politics, on the other. The chapter on the international communist movement, and the regional chapters, provide a sense of the wide repercussions of the dispute on the relations of communist parties around the world, ruling and nonruling, and on a variety of communist revolutionary efforts, particularly in the Middle East, South and East Asia.

The third section of the book aims to do two things. First, it seeks to provide a summary overview of Sino-Soviet relations in the 1970s, so that the complex issues traced in the earlier sections of the book can be reviewed as a whole within the context of the bilateral conflict. The second objective is to place the Western scholarly discussion of the entire conflict into a broad critical perspective in a discussion of "Alternative Western Views of the Sino-Soviet Conflict."

Professor Seton-Watson was asked to provide concluding summary reflections on the conference papers and discussions. Happily he chose to emphasize some very thoughtful reflections. Readers will doubtless find much of interest and stimulation in his analysis of Russian and Chinese attitudes, his speculations about the future role of that considerable portion of the Islamic world that lies between the Soviet Union and China, and his thoughts on the immense significance of the new ties between China and Japan.

HERBERT J. ELLISON *April 1981*

PART 1

The Partners to the Conflict

Internal Politics:
China and the Soviet Union

The Background in Chinese Politics

KENNETH LIEBERTHAL

Since the late 1960s China's domestic politics have taken a dramatic turn, abjuring the radically anarchist policies of the Cultural Revolution in favor of development-oriented priorities that have won kudos from the World Bank, among many others. During the same decade, the People's Republic of China (PRC) has emerged from its diplomatic isolation (as of 1968, China's sole ambassador posted abroad was Beijing's envoy to Cairo) to link up economically, politically, and increasingly militarily with the industrialized countries of the West and Japan along a strongly anti-Soviet axis. To what extent are the domestic and international components of this political sea change interconnected? And in what ways has China's foreign policy—Sino-Soviet relations in particular—both influenced and been shaped by the domestic political arena during the 1970s?

THE BACKGROUND

China specialists typically advise that one needs a historical perspective to fathom contemporary events in the Middle Kingdom. This caution is especially well taken when trying to understand the interaction of domestic and foreign policy. For in a fundamental sense, the international arena has posed the basic questions with which the Chinese revolution has grappled over the past one hundred years. Traditional China had held that the emperor mediated between heaven and earth, and that he therefore in theory ruled all under heaven. The Dragon Throne obviously did not directly control all the people with whom the Han Chinese came in contact, and in fact most dynasties had very active and hardheaded foreign policies to manage the security threats posed by outsiders and to benefit from foreign trade.[1] But the Middle Kingdom took great pains to establish and maintain an elaborate ritualistic framework within which these foreign policies were implemented—a set of rituals that affirmed symbolically the central and superior position of the Dragon Throne itself. Under this ceremonial façade, most trade assumed the form of tribute, and exchange of required gifts often became a device to bribe potentially threatening outsiders. While form and substance thus frequently gave very different clues to underlying power relationships, the form nevertheless was critical in maintaining the basic cosmology that specified the centrality of the Dragon Throne to all civilization.

The political flaw in this cosmology was that it lacked a theology, and therefore its validity depended on actual practice. Once the forms of obeisance could no longer be maintained, in short, the emperor could not claim legitimately to rule all under heaven, and his position in the domestic political system perforce lost an important dimension of its ideological sanction.[2] The industrial revolution in the nineteenth and twentieth centuries created precisely this situation. It produced enormous growth in the power of England, then the Continent, Japan, and America, and they in turn refused to conform to the rituals of obeisance even as they pressed for greater contact with China. This in turn undermined not only one of the traditional bases of the emperor's position in the Chinese polity but also the rationale for the nature of the polity itself. Far-reaching changes almost had to ensue. Chinese society had to reorganize to cope with the Western threat.

By the first decade of the twentieth century, China's leaders and intellectuals had seemingly fully embraced the idea of "sovereignty" as the central goal of the state.[3] Although this in itself represented a significant departure from earlier orthodoxy, it nevertheless left unanswered the question of what combination of domestic and foreign policies could secure that sovereignty. The twentieth century has produced a variety of answers to this critical concern, all of them trying to maintain China's political independence while protecting the society from the corrupting influences and military depredations of the West and Japan. Three significantly different positions have emerged along this common base line during the past eighty years.

1. See the essay by Lien-sheng Yang in John K. Fairbank, ed., *The Chinese World Order* (Cambridge, Mass.: Harvard University Press, 1968), pp. 20–33.
2. As we would define domestic politics. Imperial China recognized a less clear division between domestic and foreign policies.
3. See Mary Wright's introduction in Mary Wright, ed., *China in Revolution: The First Phase, 1900–1913* (New Haven: Yale University Press, 1968).

The first approach might be termed "nativist," for it has looked inward for strength, assuming that China's real power inheres in the ability to weld her people together ideologically around a central set of values. Some have looked to the past for these unifying values. Others (such as Jiang Qing) have sought them in a revolutionary culture. What has been common to all nativists is a burning desire to set China off from the corrupting influence of the outside world and enhance the country's strength via a cultural revival. The source of China's strength, in this conception, lies in the hearts and minds of its people. Any notion that material production and weapons are the major measures of power simply focuses on the wrong set of issues—and very much to China's disadvantage at that.

The second school might be called the "selective modernizers." These are people who have recognized the importance of modern technology and an advanced economy as components of national strength (and therefore of an adequate national security policy) but at the same time have viewed the West's society as inferior and corrupting. They thus have wanted to borrow technology and related resources from the West but to do this in a way that minimizes the cultural and political spillover effects in China. Both Chiang Kai-shek and Mao Zedong fell into this category, as did Yuan Shikai in an earlier age. As these names indicate, the selective modernizers have held power at the top of the Chinese system almost continuously throughout this century.[4] At the same time, their position is one that builds in enormous tensions, for recent Chinese history has shown time and again the tendency of foreign imports to have ripple effects far beyond any initially expected by those who sanctioned their introduction. There has been a tendency for the selective modernizers to become more xenophobic later in their careers, as they have tried to fight a rear-guard action against the unexpected consequences of their earlier initiatives. Thus, Yuan Shikai sought a dynastic restoration in 1916, Chiang Kai-shek launched the New Life Movement in 1936, and Mao Zedong unleashed the Cultural Revolution in 1966.

The third point of view has been put forward by a group best labeled "technology firsters." These people have averred (often implicitly) that China must be willing to change its society to whatever degree necessary to be able to produce, on a continuing basis, the kind of technological dynamism that has in fact been the source of power for her industrialized adversaries. Simply borrowing from abroad is not sufficient, since it leaves the country in a permanently inferior position. And such borrowing does not produce the results intended. The technology firsters clearly share with the selective modernizers a full appreciation of the importance of economic and military modernization as a component of any national security policy.

4. Ci Xi might also be considered a "selective modernizer" after 1901.

As such, people of both groups should be considered "modernizers" in China. But the technology firsters have gone even farther and have been willing to give economic development such high priority that they will make any cultural sacrifices necessary to achieve it. This does not mean that technology firsters would tolerate the complete Westernization of Chinese society. Rather, they have sought some mix of Chinese and Western elements that suits the country's own conditions (including its enormous peasantry) but at the same time produces rapid economic growth. Of all three groups, the technology firsters are probably the most revolutionary in the traditional Marxist sense of the term. At the same time, they have always been the most vulnerable to the charge that they are selling out the national identity in an ill-conceived effort to secure national sovereignty. The Guang Xu emperor became one of the earliest technology firsters, and Deng Xiaoping is certainly the most prominent in China now. Zhou Enlai may well have been a technology firster, but he almost always carefully sculpted his preferences to make them reasonably compatible with those of Mao Zedong.[5]

Chinese politics from the turn of the century to 1976 were dominated by selective modernizers. Although as they advanced in age these individuals tended personally to move closer to the nativists, the center of gravity of Chinese society and politics during the course of the century seems to have been shifting inexorably in the other direction. During the 1970s China underwent a transition at the top that saw power pass from an enfeebled Mao Zedong, who had in his declining years brought uncompromising nativists into the highest councils of power,[6] to one of the most ardent technology firsters in modern Chinese history, Deng Xiaoping. This transition dominated the politics of the decade.

As the above overview indicates, all parties to this struggle conceived of domestic priorities and China's position in the international arena as one integrated set of issues. Put differently, in a country the size of China, unquestionably domestic affairs consumes the thoughts and energies of most people. But the country's history has produced such a central concern with sovereignty and security that the priority its leaders have given to different fundamental domestic goals (economic development, cultural transformation, class struggle, and so forth) has been inextricably bound up with their notions of what will produce the necessary strength internationally to pro-

5. For a similar but not identical attempt to summarize the basic twentieth-century Chinese approaches to ordering their society, see Michel Oksenberg and Steven Goldstein, "The Chinese Political Spectrum," *Problems of Communism*, 23, no. 2 (March–April 1974): 1–13.

6. Here as elsewhere, "nativists" is used interchangeably with "radicals" in discussing the late 1960s and the 1970s in China.

tect China's integrity. These basic perspectives, moreover, often lead to quite different concrete foreign policy choices, as was clearly the case in the 1970s, when precisely these fundamental issues set the terms of reference for both domestic political conflict and debate about Soviet policy in Beijing.

POLITICS OF THE 1970S: THE SETTING

China approached the 1970s with the issues defining the nature and future thrust of the revolution very much up in the air. The Cultural Revolution had by 1968 severely disrupted the civilian party and government administrative structures and had wrought havoc in the society. Virtual civil war flared in numerous locales during the hot summer months in 1967 and 1968, and even the power of arrest and detention had de facto been given to numerous self-defined political groups who used it at times with cruel zeal. The People's Liberation Army (PLA) stood as the one nationally integrated administrative apparatus capable of holding the country together, but the army never seized absolute power in Beijing. Indeed, as of 1968 zealous nativists fully shared with the army the benefits of the revolution from below that Mao Zedong had begun two years earlier. And the nativists with good reason distrusted the military hierarchy.

Within this confused and unsettled context, the Soviet Union invaded Czechoslovakia in August 1968 and quickly thereafter proclaimed a Brezhnev Doctrine that could be used to justify follow-up military action against China (among other socialist countries). In the context of the Soviets' increasing pace of militarization of the Sino-Soviet border during 1966-68, the invasion of Czechoslovakia highlighted the degree to which China's chaos had increased her vulnerability. Internal forces had already been at work to wind down the Cultural Revolution, and indeed since January 1967 the Chinese had been trying to devise structures of political power to run the country. The looming Soviet threat now lent greater urgency to Beijing's search for a means to build new political institutions. In so doing it brought to the fore two stark questions that had bubbled beneath the surface of Chinese politics since 1966: Who will staff the new organs of power when they are formed? What priorities should these organs pursue? The two questions were interrelated, and their answers would determine the victors—and the ultimate victims—of the Cultural Revolution.

The Twelfth Plenum of the Eighth Central Committee met in this context in October 1968, and it in turn called for convening the Ninth Party Congress. The Congress met in a still more tense atmosphere in April 1969 almost directly after two major border clashes between Chinese and Soviet forces at Zhenbao island (called Damansky by the Russians) in early and mid-March. Beijing used these bloody encounters to whip up a war psychosis in the country,[7] from which Lin Biao and his military establishment benefited during the Congress.

Indeed, the Ninth Congress elected a Central Committee and produced a Politburo heavily weighted with military officers.[8] The party constitution it passed set a precedent in the international communist movement by designating by name the successor to the current party chairman (Lin Biao received the nod). And the Congress stressed the need to reestablish order throughout the society.[9] This permitted the army under Lin to carry out what was possibly the bloodiest period of purging in the entire Cultural Revolution. Lin issued General Order Number One, which called for measures that included the physical removal of all people from the area of the capital who could possibly be used by the Russians as a puppet alternative leadership to the Mao-Lin group. Liu Shaoqi died as a result of the harsh conditions of his treatment during this period, as evidently did many other former high-ranking officials. On a mass level, the PLA dispatched millions of former Red Guards to the countryside to "temper themselves in revolution by learning from the poor and lower middle peasants"—which effectively removed these disruptive elements from the politically sensitive cities.

THE LIN BIAO AFFAIR

The four years after the Ninth Party Congress witnessed dramatic changes in China's domestic and foreign policy. In the domestic arena, by 1970 the general orientation toward increasing order and social discipline had spilled over into the economic and educational realms. New policies gave greater priority to economic production. Schools were reopened, and a movement toward more vigorous academic standards took hold. These initiatives in turn required relatively skilled and experienced administrators, and the politics of cadre rehabilitation quickly became one of the most central and explosive issues in the polity.

The shift in the direction of priorities that resembled those of the pre-1966 era naturally jeopardized many Cultural Revolution heroes. Thus, fittingly, the first high-level victim of the new policy drift was Chen Boda, one of the chief theorists of Mao's radical politics. Chen is alleged to have tried to restore a highly dogmatized version of Mao Zedong Thought to center stage in the political arena at a party Central Committee plenum in the late summer of 1970. He clearly felt that this measure was a necessary

---

7. See Thomas W. Robinson, "The Sino-Soviet Border Dispute: Background, Development, and the March 1969 Clashes," *American Political Science Review*, 66, no. 4 (December 1972): 1175–1202.

8. See Donald W. Klein and Lois B. Hager, "The Ninth Central Committee," *China Quarterly*, no. 45 (January–March 1971), pp. 37–56.

9. *Peking Review*, April 30, 1969, pp. 16–39; *Issues and Studies*, March 1970, pp. 92–93.

step in retaining his legitimacy at the top of the system, in that it would enable him to continue to act as one of the high priests who could interpret the sacred doctrine on which the political system relied. But Mao undercut Chen at the plenum, assuming a cloak of modesty and demanding that his own Thought not be blown out of all proportion. Mao asserted that he himself was not a genius and that those who insisted he was one must therefore harbor ulterior motives. Chen's position quickly eroded thereafter, and by the end of 1970 he had been purged. Mao had also clearly served notice that he was shifting the basis of legitimate authority at the top of the Chinese system. Those who had risen because they were close to the Chairman and understood his thinking would now find that they were no longer needed. They would be replaced by people with the programs necessary to fit the new historical demands. Lin Biao, who allegedly worked in league with Chen Boda at the 1970 plenum, took appropriate warning. By the end of 1970 seven of Lin's closest military associates were forced to make self-criticism. Lin began his contingency planning for a coup against Mao, and Mao began to chip away at the organizational bases of Lin's power in anticipation of a showdown in late 1971.[10]

There was substantial disagreement over Sino-Soviet relations among the key participants in this drama, and this debate over foreign policy probably got caught up with the domestic political maneuvering just discussed. In broad terms, three basic views seem to have been brought into the policy debate of the period.[11] The radicals, headed by Jiang Qing, argued against using the United States to counter the menacing Soviet situation. They contended that if given a chance, both superpowers would simply collude to pick the fruits of the Chinese revolution, much as foreign imperialists had throughout the previous century recognized their common interest in having a weak China on which all of them could impose their separate (and sometimes conflicting) demands. Indeed, the radicals adopted a relatively traditional Chinese perspective in playing down the very notion of dealing in state-oriented politics, advocating instead international revolution "from below" based on the universal validity of Mao Zedong Thought.[12]

10. *Chinese Law and Government*, 5, nos. 3–4 (1972–73): 31–42; Michael Y. M. Kau, ed., *The Lin Piao Affair* (White Plains: International Arts and Sciences Press, 1975).

11. These views are taken from the analyses in Thomas Gottlieb, *Chinese Foreign Policy Factionalism and the Origins of the Strategic Triangle* (Santa Monica: Rand R-1902-NA, 1977), and Kenneth Lieberthal, *Sino-Soviet Conflict in the 1970's: Its Evolution and Implications for the Strategic Triangle* (Santa Monica: Rand R-2342-NA, 1978). Significant parts of the radicals' and moderates' positions were not articulated in the Chinese media until 1973–75. This analysis assumes that the people concerned held similar ideas in 1969–72.

12. See Harry Harding, "The Domestic Politics of China's Global Posture,

The radicals, whose perspective was essentially nativist, believed that security from a Soviet attack would derive more from political than from objective military considerations. They held that the Soviets would never be able to conquer and occupy a politically mobilized, uncompromisingly anti-Soviet China. The only possibility for a successful Soviet action against China would be through subversion, where Moscow took advantage of the emergence of a relatively pro-Soviet national leadership in China. The radicals stressed, therefore, the critical importance of continuing political mobilization in China, using mass campaigns to heighten people's awareness of the dangers and to ferret out potentially pro-Soviet cadres before they had a chance to do their damage. The radicals affirmed that China's own economic and military backwardness meant that concentrating on those dimensions of the power equation would be self-defeating, because the country's leaders would thereby calculate their strategy based on an analytical framework that highlighted the country's weakness. This in turn would encourage the very kinds of compromises and policies that would fulfill their prophecy of national capitulation over time. Thus the radicals stressed political virtue and argued against giving priority to economic and military modernization. They believed in continuing a dual adversary strategy, where China drew a clear line between itself and both the United States and the Soviet Union in favor of championing popular revolutionary movements, especially in the Third World. The actual course of China's domestic and foreign policy during 1969–72 bears witness to how weak the radicals' position in the leadership became as the Cultural Revolution wound down. But they remained a potentially important coalition partner nevertheless, and were not completely without influence in the central leadership.

Zhou Enlai took an almost diametrically opposite view on both domestic and foreign policy. Zhou understood well the importance of economic and military resources in gauging a country's national strength. As one of the twentieth century's most skilled diplomats, he also believed in the efficacy of diplomatic maneuver to exploit differences among potential enemies. In 1969, therefore, Zhou argued that China should exploit differences between the United States and the Soviet Union to its own advantage. He also asserted that the Soviet invasion of Czechoslovakia in 1968 and the Sino-Soviet border clashes of March 1969 had made the Soviet Union China's main enemy. In response, the PRC should explore the possibility of détente with the United States. At the same time, Zhou believed, China should turn its attention in domestic affairs to reestablishing an administration that could run the country effectively, giving priority to rapid economic development. This would, of course, require rehabilitating many of Zhou's

---

1973–78," in Thomas Fingar, ed., *China's Quest for Independence: Policy Evolution in the 1970s* (Boulder, Colo.: Westview Press, 1980), pp. 96–98.

former colleagues and subordinates who had been purged during the fury of the Cultural Revolution. It is not clear how Zhou proposed to handle direct relations with the Soviet Union. He may have advocated limited contacts in order to take some of the edge off Sino-Soviet tensions and decrease the chances that the Soviets would attack the PRC. Or he may have advocated a hard line.

This dilemma reflects a debate that seems to have gone on throughout the 1970s within the group that advocated a rapprochement with the United States. The debate (in many ways echoing similar polemics in the United States) concerned how to make the Soviets behave in the international arena. Some argued that the Soviets are inherently aggressive and respect only diplomatic and military strength. They felt that China's search for security must center on trying to contain Soviet expansionism by putting together an anti-Soviet united front that would confront Moscow with both diplomatic and military obstacles to expansionism in any direction. The Soviets, according to this view, understand and respect the language of power, and this containment strategy would, therefore, produce precisely the kind of reasonable Soviet response desired. Compromise, by contrast, would be misread by the Kremlin as a sign of weakness and would actually encourage Soviet aggression. "Give Moscow an inch," according to this reasoning, "and it will take a country."

An alternative view within this group argued that Moscow in fact contained both hawks and doves and that China's policy should be one that did not undercut the doves and favor the hawks. While endorsing an anti-Soviet united front and a generally hard line in bilateral relations, these people argued that Beijing should occasionally appear reasonable and willing to compromise. This would at least enable the doves in Moscow to argue that relatively friendlier people did remain in the Chinese leadership and therefore the Soviet Union should show some restraint so as to bolster the chances of these people in the political succession struggle obviously under way in Beijing. Both the hard-line approach and the somewhat more compromising view toward dealing with the Soviet Union remained in evidence among this group throughout the 1970s, and the available evidence does not make completely clear where Zhou himself stood.

Lin Biao may in many ways have embraced the priorities in domestic policy that Zhou advocated. At least, the major moves in this direction occurred while Lin still retained enormous power, and a secret document purportedly expressing his views lends further credence to this hypothesis.[13] The military procurement budget during Lin's heyday clearly reflects his own keen appreciation of the importance of weapons in gauging a country's

13. The famous "571 Document" circulated after Lin's death. For the text, see Kau, *The Lin Piao Affair*, pp. 81–95.

military strength.[14] Indeed, insofar as Lin and Zhou had differences on domestic budget issues, they probably concerned the question of how much China should spend on the military as opposed to developing other sectors of the economy. Thus in theory there might have been considerable compatibility between Lin's and Zhou's positions as of 1969–70. But in fact the two men viewed each other as mortal enemies. There were two major points of disagreement between them.

First, Lin's forces participated actively in the measures that savaged Zhou's supporters during the Cultural Revolution. Although both Zhou and Lin supported the reestablishment of capable administrative systems as of 1969–70, each was anxious to capture these new systems for his own people. Lin appears to have used the Soviet threat to perpetrate additional reprisals against some of Zhou's allies, and his motivation was probably in large part to keep these people from assuming power in the new governmental and party committees being formed. In foreign affairs, Lin disagreed with Zhou's assessment that the Soviet Union had become the principal enemy and that China should exploit U.S.-Soviet differences via rapprochement with the United States. Rather, Lin seems to have argued that the United States would pose the chief national security threat to China for the foreseeable future and China must act accordingly. The Soviet Union had obviously also become a danger, but one of lesser immediacy.[15] Moscow could be handled by taking a hard line (including appropriate redeployment of Chinese military forces to the north), possibly combined with tactical compromises that would take some of the sting out of the harsh approach.

How did these various perspectives translate into actual coalition politics at the beginning of the 1970's? Lin and the radicals probably worked more together than at odds, even though they stood far apart on both international and domestic political issues. Zhou Enlai maneuvered against them both. That both Lin and Zhou believed in the importance of economic recovery and development meant that this basic policy would certainly be adopted even though the radicals sharply disagreed. At the same time, Lin's and Zhou's forces contended over who should take charge of this effort. Thus staffing problems remained extremely nettlesome. In foreign policy, Mao Zedong was willing to support Zhou Enlai's position against Lin and the radicals on the opening to the United States to the extent that

14. See Sydney H. Jammes, "The Chinese Defense Burden, 1965–1974," in *China: A Reassessment of the Economy: A Compendium of Papers Submitted to the Joint Economic Committee, Congress of the United States, July 10, 1975* (Washington, D.C.: U.S. Government Printing Office, 1975), pp. 463–64.

15. Richard Wich supports this assessment of the rather minimal threat the Soviet Union posed to China at this time. See his *Sino-Soviet Crisis Politics* (Cambridge, Mass.: Harvard Council on East Asian Studies, 1980).

Zhou could demonstrate that this policy was both feasible and potentially effective. Finally, both Lin and the radicals wanted to maintain the primacy of Mao Zedong Thought (ironically, given that Mao was clearly moving away from them), for they were widely regarded as the most authoritative interpreters of this gospel.

These crosscutting cleavages provided the context for China's policies of 1969–71, but tracing causal lines for this period remains difficult. For example, the available evidence strongly suggests that China purposely created a situation on the Sino-Soviet border at the beginning of 1969 that almost certainly would produce a major border incident within a matter of months. Beijing did this by changing the rules of patrolling, and clearly the actual incident that occurred on March 2 had all the signs of a Chinese ambush.[16] But why would China want to provoke a much stronger Soviet adversary into an armed confrontation, inviting almost certain retaliatory action in the ensuing weeks? Three explanations can be advanced. The first is strictly a foreign policy calculus. China was anxious after the Soviet invasion of Czechoslovakia to demonstrate how aggressive the Soviets were and how untrustworthy Moscow could be. Beijing was especially concerned with this because Hanoi had endorsed the Soviet action against Czechoslovakia, thereby raising nightmares in Beijing about possible future Soviet-Vietnamese collaboration at China's expense. Thus China was willing to provoke a border conflict with Moscow—one that the Chinese were fairly confident the Soviets would prove willing to keep under control—in order to heighten worldwide concern about Soviet aggression. Richard Wich has argued this thesis in detail in his new book (see note 15).

A second explanation makes Lin Biao the strategist behind the Chinese provocation. Lin certainly benefited in the short run from the war hysteria that Beijing whipped up in the wake of the border clashes, and it was border forces under PLA control that sparked the conflict in the first place. Thus Lin may have been willing to worsen relations with the Soviet Union and risk a wider conflict in order to dramatize the need for the military under his command to take control during the transitional period of early 1969. The Ninth Congress did in fact convene in the wake of these clashes and, as noted above, greatly enhanced Lin's immediate position.

A third explanation, presented by former CIA analyst Roger Brown, has the border conflict resulting from a Mao-Zhou initiative to help them make the case that the Soviet Union had in fact become China's main enemy and that the country's entire foreign and domestic policy must now be sculpted to take this central strategic fact into account.[17] All three of these explana-

16. Neville Maxwell, "The Chinese Account of the 1969 Fighting at Chenpao," *China Quarterly*, no. 56 (October–December 1973), pp. 734–35.

17. Roger Glenn Brown, "Chinese Politics and American Policy: A New Look at the Triangle," *Foreign Policy*, no. 23 (Summer 1976), pp. 3–23.

tions fit with all the known data, and probably one of them (or some combination of the first with one of the other two) accurately reflects the thinking in Beijing at the time.

After the border clashes, the Soviets tried to bring the crisis under control by submitting it to negotiations—talks that Moscow hoped would provide a forum for working out a more far-reaching accommodation with the Chinese.[18] But China clearly had trouble achieving a consensus to participate in the talks and in fact agreed to do so only in September 1969. In addition, within a week of China's agreeing to formal negotiations, Beijing made clear that it would insist that the "first item" on the agenda be the withdrawal of all military forces from all disputed areas (so that the negotiations would take place "free from any threats").[19] But all the "disputed areas" lay on the Soviet side of the de facto border, and Moscow predictably refused to meet what amounted to a demand for unilateral withdrawal. The border talks stalled over this Chinese demand in 1969 and have never advanced beyond that stage.[20] These Chinese fits and starts during 1969, followed by Beijing's subsequent rigid intransigence, probably reflect the shifting politics of the spring and summer and the fact that the only coalition possible by late September was one based on a hard line toward the negotiations.

During 1970–71 Sino-Soviet tensions remained high and continued to impart a sharp edge to Chinese domestic politics. The conflict between Mao and Lin Biao gradually intensified, with Zhou Enlai the obvious beneficiary. Foreign policy interacted with this domestic political struggle in several concrete ways. First, during 1969–71 the PRC shifted substantial forces from the east and central-south to north China to protect against a possible Soviet invasion.[21] But information released after Lin Biao's demise in September 1971 (see note 13) indicates that by early 1971 Lin was planning a military action to seize power in China, based primarily on forces loyal to him in precisely the military regions from which these troops had been shifted during the previous two years. Mao Zedong revealed quite candidly his own strategy for securing control over the Beijing military region and its forces before any final showdown with Lin.[22] Thus either consciously or

18. *Pravda*, December 22, 1972, in *Current Digest of the Soviet Press*, 24, no. 51 (January 17, 1973): 11–12.

19. *Peking Review*, no. 41, October 10, 1969, p. 4.

20. A full review of the history of the border negotiations is available in Lieberthal, *Sino-Soviet Conflict* (see note 11 above).

21. See Lu Yung-shu, "Preparation for War in Mainland China," in *Collected Documents on Mainland China* (Taipei: Institute for International Relations, 1971), pp. 895–918; and appropriate annual issues of *The Military Balance*.

22. *Zhongfa* (1972), no. 12, in Kau, *The Lin Piao Affair*, pp. 55–66.

by chance the troop changes in China related to the Soviet threat had the effect of reducing the forces potentially available to Lin in a showdown.

China decided in 1971 to reduce substantially its high level of military procurement. This made sense in terms of the technological gap separating the PRC from the Soviets (why pour money into procuring large quantities of out-of-date military hardware?), but it also undercut the portion of the budget of greatest concern to Lin.[23] China's success in establishing an anti-Soviet connection with the United States, made evident in Henry Kissinger's historic visit to Beijing in July 1971, probably provided a major part of the excuse needed to justifiy the cutback in military procurement. The success of the Kissinger visit thus likely contributed to exacerbating tensions between Mao and Lin at the same time that it marked a historic turning point in the strategic triangle. Indeed, one could argue that this visit *created* the strategic triangle, or at least the possibility of triangular politics.

In sum, both Zhou and Lin evidently shared similar concepts of power—and therefore of the need to give priority to creating an economically and militarily strong China. But they disagreed about who should rule China and what foreign country posed the greatest threat to the PRC. The international arena on balance played into Lin's hands in 1969, but affected him adversely on such issues as troop dispositions and military budgets during the following two years. Thus Lin had reason to oppose the opening to the United States on more grounds than simply his conviction that the United States could not be trusted. His domestic political strategy also suffered from China's bold foreign policy course in the wake of the new wave of fear over the Soviet threat after Warsaw pact troops crushed the Prague Spring.

MODERNIZERS AGAINST NATIVISTS

In the short run, the policies already in place at the time of Lin's demise were simply continued in the wake of his fall. The domestic political system continued to focus on the problem of staffing new organs of power, and naturally the military now fared badly in this competition after being stained by its association with Lin's coup attempt.[24] Economic policy continued to evolve in the direction of restoring production systems, and China's foreign trade grew rapidly. The PRC also went on an international buying spree, signing orders for major complete plant purchases beginning in late 1972. This greater involvement with the international market had

23. Jammes, "The Chinese Defense Burden," p. 464.
24. The entire high command was implicated in the coup attempt and purged. On the continuing process of staffing the new organs of power, see Frederick C. Teiwes, *Provincial Leadership in China: The Cultural Revolution and Its Aftermath* (Canberra: Australian National University, 1973).

unquestionably become a more feasible strategy with the signing of the Shanghai Communiqué in February 1972 and with the normalization of Sino-Japanese relations later that year.

But within China, Mao Zedong's health was failing, and at some point during 1972 Zhou Enlai learned that he himself had incurable cancer. By early 1973 at the latest Zhou had become so frail that he could no longer shoulder the enormous burdens of government administration. That spring, Mao therefore brought back to power the most capable administrator purged during the Cultural Revolution—Deng Xiaoping.[25] Deng's reemergence in turn deepened a split that had been growing more ominous during the preceding months—a division that pitted the Cultural Revolution radicals against Zhou and his allies.

Tensions between these forces could well have been expected, given their very different backgrounds and history of adversary relations. The politics of handling the Lin Biao affair, for example, reflected the behind-the-scenes infighting that had taken place during 1972. Lin's name had become anathema when his perfidy was made known, and therefore each side in Beijing's political battles tried to associate the disgraced PLA commander with its opponents. Since Lin had been a major figure in launching the Cultural Revolution and had probably allied with the radicals in 1969–71, Zhou Enlai's forces quickly branded him an "extreme leftist," thereby tainting the remaining radical opposition. But in early 1973 Lin suddenly became someone who was deemed to have been "left in form but right in essence."[26] Obviously a formulation coined by the radicals, this new label implied that Lin in fact shared views associated with Zhou and the increasing numbers of rehabilitated Cultural Revolution victims. Thus by early 1973 succession politics had become more clearly a contest that separated Zhou and the modernizers from Jiang Qing and the nativists. The military had not completely faded from the scene, but the PLA had been disgraced and its power substantially reduced. Now, as the succession unfolded, the army lurked as a potentially important coalition partner rather than as a chief contender. Mao Zedong seemed to hope for a regime that embodied the programs of the modernizers and the sociopolitical conscience of the nativists—a combination that the division in the Politburo ultimately denied to him.

As Zhou's and Jiang Qing's forces squared off, the focus of the debate over foreign policy became more clearly one that conformed to the differences between nativists on the one side and both selective modernizers and technology firsters on the other. The former disagreed with the latter two

---

25. See Deng's recapitulation of these events in the *Washington Post*, August 31, 1980.

26. Maxine Meisner, *Mao's China* (New York: Free Press, 1977), p. 373.

over the very nature of power in the international arena and argued that, since power was inherently political and cultural in nature, economic development could be given lower priority. The nativists also chided those who concentrated on economic development policies for exacerbating tensions in Chinese society (by increasing social stratification, and so forth) and thereby actually *weakening* the country overall. Moreover, giving priority to economic development, argued the radicals, means attracting foreign capital, which in turn required that China act "responsibly" from the point of view of Western leaders in both foreign and domestic affairs. This would, then, create bonds between Chinese leaders and the imperialists— and would inevitably lead to the elimination of the radicals from politics. Through this process, the Chinese revolution would be stolen from within. The radicals advocated an uncompromisingly antagonistic policy toward the Soviet Union in order to provide a continuing focus for Chinese political mobilization and purification around the theme of antirevisionism. The radicals' target thus became Soviet revisionism in general and Moscow's political subversion in particular. Whenever the nativists/radical position strengthened in Beijing during 1973-76, this conception of the Soviet menace loomed larged in the Chinese media.

The modernizers agreed on the need for economic development, although perhaps not on the relative budget priorities to be assigned to the civilian and military sectors. To them, moreover, economic development meant development of political and economic ties with the advanced industrial countries. All of this required that China successfully use rapprochement with the United States to counter the Soviet Union (put differently, that the U.S.-Soviet contention remain a stronger force than Washington's desire for U.S.-Soviet détente in shaping American actions).[27]

Throughout 1973-76 the modernizers had control over the executive departments of the Chinese party and government bureaucracies, and the nativists headed the cultural, educational, and propaganda hierarchies. The former used their power to implement development-oriented domestic and foreign policies (and to rehabilitate increasing numbers of their colleagues who had fallen during the Cultural Revolution), while the latter used the press organs to critique the policies of the modernizers, launch political attacks against them, and leak information so as to disrupt normal procedures of policy planning. The relative balance of power between these groups shifted, partly in response to international and domestic conditions and partly in response to the whims of a very sick and increasingly fickle Mao Zedong. Deng Xiaoping's rehabilitation in March 1973 had exacerbated relations between these contending forces, because the diminutive

---

27. Sources for these views are documented in Lieberthal, *Sino-Soviet Conflict*, pp. 69-94.

"number two person in authority taking the capitalist road" was known as a hardheaded administrator who had suffered grievously during the Cultural Revolution and almost certainly would seek revenge against his tormentors. (Also, one of Deng's sons had been permanently crippled by the Red Guards during the Cultural Revolution.)

In the summer of 1973 the nativists gained strength, probably as a result of three circumstances. The Watergate affair in the United States had mushroomed in the late spring to the point where Beijing realized that President Nixon would not be able to follow through on his promise of full normalization of relations in his second administration. Indeed, Sino-U.S. relations became essentially frozen in mid-1973 and did not witness substantial forward movement until the spring of 1978. Second, the summer of 1973 brought a virtual honeymoon in the Soviet Union's relations with all of the NATO countries. The Vietnamese peace agreement of February 1973 had removed a bitter issue of contention in U.S.-Soviet relations, and the Nixon-Brezhnev summit in June had gone smoothly. The initiation of the Helsinki Conference then put détente and East-West cooperation on the front pages of the international media. This, of course, directly undercut the diplomatic premises of Zhou Enlai's entire strategy of Sino-U.S. rapprochement. Third, Mao Zedong seems to have weighed in to give the nativists a more prominent position in the succession. He evidently was seriously considering the bold stroke of passing on the party chairmanship to the youngest new recruit to the Politburo, Wang Hongwen.[28]

The radicals' new-found strength was evident at the Tenth Party Congress in August 1973. There, for example, Zhou Enlai had to bob and weave in his political report in order to salvage key components of his foreign policy. He conceded to the nativists the general point that the Soviet threat to China was likely to be primarily one of subversion rather than direct military confrontation. Indeed, he announced the new orthodoxy that the Soviets were "making a feint in the East to attack in the West." Zhou warned, nevertheless, against a Soviet "surprise attack" against China, and he used the supposedly increased Soviet threat against Europe to suggest to the Europeans how valuable to them their China ties might be.[29] Following the Tenth Congress, the radicals initiated the "Campaign to Criticize Lin Biao and Confucius" to spell out their critique of Zhou's foreign and domestic policies and to whip up related political activities to drive this critique home.

The general upsurge in radical influence during the winter of 1973–74

---

28. Wang, a member of the subsequently designated Gang of Four, became the third-ranking person in the party at the Tenth Congress in August 1973. He was roughly forty years Mao's junior.

29. *Peking Review*, nos. 35–36, September 7, 1973, pp. 17–25.

resonated in both domestic and foreign policy. Domestically, factional political battles again flared up throughout the country, bringing economic disruption and social disorder in their wake. In Sino-Soviet relations, in January 1974 China captured five alleged Soviet spies in Beijing in an episode that had all the earmarks of an entrapment staged by China's public security organs. The Chinese media gave this incident wide publicity, dramatizing the "subversive" nature of the Soviet threat to the PRC.[30] Then on March 14 a Soviet helicopter strayed over the Chinese border in Xinjiang Province and was captured by Chinese frontier guards and militiamen. Beijing immediately declared the three crew members guilty of espionage and held them incommunicado until the end of 1975. Again, Soviet "subversion" received prominent attention in China's media.[31] During these same months Beijing also launched a combined arms operation to seize control over the Paracel Islands from the South Vietnamese, and the nativists gave this conquest stridently nationalistic play in the media.[32]

The international economy also played into the radicals' hands, as the sharp jump in OPEC prices in late 1973 threw the industrialized world into a recession in 1974. China suddenly found that it could not meet its export targets, and thus it ran a substantial deficit in foreign trade for the first time in more than a decade. The radicals took advantage of this situation to criticize the modernizers' economic and political strategies.

But on balance the radicals overplayed their hand, especially in domestic politics. Zhou's forces not only struck back at the Campaign to Criticize Lin Biao and Confucius with allegorical counterattacks, but also took advantage of the increasing disruption in China's cities to call for a halt to the radical's offensive. On July 1, 1974, the Central Committee issued a document that essentially took the wind out of the sails of the campaign and shifted priorities back to the programs of the modernizers.[33] Preparations soon began for the long-delayed Fourth National People's Congress—a major government (versus party) conclave that would fix a new long-term economic plan and elect a new cabinet.

During the fall of 1974 one of the few indications of possible Chinese flexibility on bilateral relations with the Soviet Union occurred. Beijing sent Moscow a congratulatory telegram on the anniversary of the Oc-

30. See, for example, *Peking Review*, no. 5, February 1, 1974, pp. 14–17.
31. *Peking Review*, no. 13, March 29, 1974, p. 5.
32. *Peking Review*, no. 4, January 25, 1974, pp. 3–4; *Renmin Ribao*, March 16, 1974. This attack on the Paracels also sowed the seeds of future discord with Hanoi, which also laid claim to these islands.
33. Text of this document in *Issues and Studies*, no. 1, 1975, pp. 101–4. For analysis of this document, see Kenneth Lieberthal, *Central Documents and Politburo Politics in China* (Ann Arbor: Center for Chinese Studies, University of Michigan, 1978), pp. 59–63.

tober Revolution that could be read as considerably softer in tone and content than previous communications. But China's use of this telegram to reaffirm publicly that removal of all forces from "disputed areas" must remain the first item on the agenda of negotiations with Moscow called into question the flexibility that could otherwise have been read into the remainder of the telegram. This message possibly represented a compromise between some soft-line modernizers who wanted to hint about improved relations with Moscow and some hard liners among both the modernizers and nativists who opposed that position.[34]

On the domestic side, throughout the fall of 1974 the nativists tried to convince Mao to endorse them for top positions in the new cabinet, but the fickle Chairman sided against them.[35] Thus, when the National People's Congress convened in January 1975, it officially resurrected the "four modernizations" as China's basic economic program and produced a State Council that gave surprisingly few portfolios to members of the nativists' group. Deng Xiaoping became a vice-premier and concurrently chief of staff of the PLA (he had become a vice-chairman of the CCP at a Central Committee plenum the week before the NPC). Zhang Chunqiao fared best among the nativists, capturing positions just below those of Deng in the government, party, and military hierarchies.

Once Deng Xiaoping achieved this position of personal strength in January 1975, he worked rapidly to build a coalition that would support him after the deaths of Mao and Zhou (both could have occurred at almost any time given the age and marginal health of these men). Deng adopted a strategy of providing benefits to each of the major constituencies that he would need. For example, in the late spring and summer he used meetings of the Military Affairs Commission of the party to call for more modernized, depoliticized, highly trained, and leaner armed forces—the kind of military program that would appeal to the commanders of the strategic forces if not to the leaders of the local garrison troops.[36] Then during the course of the summer he commissioned drafts of programmatic documents covering policy on industry, on science and technology (with implications for education), and on party priorities.[37] The resulting policy proposals

34. Telegram text in Peking Radio, November 26, 1974, *Foreign Broadcast Information Service Daily Report—People's Republic of China* (hereafter *FBIS-PRC*), November 7, 1974, p. A-1. For an interpretation that stresses the conciliatory aspects of this telegram, see Harding, "The Domestic Politics of China's Global Posture," pp. 104–5.

35. *Zhongfa* (1976), no. 24, in *Issues and Studies*, 12, no. 9 (September 1977): 99–104.

36. Harry Harding presents the fullest available analysis of these meetings in "The Domestic Politics of China's Global Posture," pp. 114–17.

37. Texts and analysis in Lieberthal, *Central Documents* (see note 33 above).

called for increased contacts with the international community, a purge of those who disrupted discipline, reestablishment of rigorous educational and research establishments, and so forth. In September Deng addressed a major conference on agriculture, at which he tried to skew agricultural policy toward more production-oriented priorities. And there is evidence that in the late fall he planned to take similar initiatives targeted directly on the educational system. In each of these major areas, Deng was appealing to the interests of key sectors—the strategic military commanders, intellectuals, managers, and old-line bureaucrats. He used only slightly veiled language to indicate that he would give short shrift to any radicals who opposed his plans after Mao and Zhou had departed.

Deng's foreign policy preferences run very much along the lines of the hard-line modernizers outlined above. He has repeatedly identified himself with uncompromising anti-Sovietism, asserting that Moscow would misread any compromise as a sign of underlying weakness.[38] But Deng's bid for the succession led him in the closing months of 1975 to support the seemingly biggest concession China had made to the Soviet Union since 1966—that is, the sudden exculpation and release of the Soviet helicopter pilots who had been captured twenty-one months earlier in Xinjiang. Deng's about-face on this issue indicates that some potential coalition partners—probably including Marshal Ye Jianying—were urging him to make this move. It was a gesture almost certainly not fully supported by Mao and strongly opposed by the nativists, and it was made in a way almost guaranteed to undercut the possibility that the Soviets would respond positively to it.[39] Deng has never again shown a disposition to compromise with, or make gestures of good will toward, the Soviet Union.

Deng's frenetic activities of 1975 alarmed the radicals, who clearly had to unseat him or face their own political oblivion. They evidently tried to convince Mao that if Deng was permitted to inherit political power, Mao's works and his name would suffer much as Stalin's had under Khrushchev. For whatever reason, Mao intermittently supported the radicals in a series of attacks they launched against Deng's initiatives throughout the year. This began in the spring with a campaign to study the dictatorship of the proletariat (used as a vehicle to attack the program adopted by the NPC in January), then in the late summer shifted to a campaign based on the classic novel *The Water Margin* (the campaign's theme was that the revolution would be undone if traitorous individuals were allowed to acquire power). Jiang Qing personally challenged Deng at the September confer-

---

38. See, for example, the Deng interviews with foreign correspondents carried in *FBIS-PRC*, September 26, 1977, pp. A 10–11; *FBIS-PRC*, March 23, 1978, pp. A22–24; and the *Washington Post*, September 1, 1980.

39. Lieberthal, *Sino-Soviet Conflict*, pp. 126–33.

ence on agriculture (with a speech that even Mao found unprintable), and by November–December yet another attack—this one targeted on the newly emerging educational policies—was launched. These campaigns did not succeed in stopping the Deng Xiaoping steamroller, but they did raise sharp political questions about his policies and evidently heightened Mao Zedong's own distrust of his probable successor.

Unfortunately for Deng, Zhou Enlai preceded Mao to the grave in 1976. Zhou's death removed Deng's protector, and the radicals pulled out all the stops in trying to unseat their rival for power. Deng gave the oration at Zhou's funeral in January and then dropped from public view. He came under increasing attack—at first oblique and then more direct—through the course of the spring. And on April 5 he was blamed for massive demonstrations staged in honor of Zhou (and quite clearly against Mao) in Tianamen Square and was purged by Mao. Hua Guofeng, who had worked closely with Deng throughout 1975, was now chosen by Mao to replace him.

The infighting over the succession essentially paralyzed China from April until Mao's death in September 1976. The attempts of the radicals to capitalize on Deng's purge through a major campaign to vilify him and his ideas fizzled, but the supercharged political climate produced such disruption that China's economy stagnated and the social situation remained extremely tense. The devastating Tangshan earthquake in late July simply added to the misery. This natural disaster, however, allowed the army to recapture some honor after years of humiliation stemming from the Lin Biao affair, for the army took responsibility for a good part of the relief work carried out in the Tangshan area. Overall, the battle between the nativists and modernizers during these months produced virtual guerrilla warfare throughout China's administrative bureaucracies to the degree that little of substance could be accomplished. Many of the people whom Deng had rehabilitated during 1973–75 now fell again with their patron's disgrace.

Mao's death on September 9 led within a month to the purge of the radicals. In essence, the coalition Deng had put together held, and Hua Guofeng decided that his interests lay more with the modernizers than with their adversaries. The last member to join the coalition was Wang Dongxing, who headed the secret police that provided security for the top political leaders. Wang was too loyal to Mao to be approached while the Chairman lived, but after Mao's death, he evidently recoiled against actions taken by some of the radicals to undercut his power and quickly sided with Hua and Deng's coalition. Wang's troops arrested the radical leaders—now dubbed the Gang of Four—and their key supporters in early October.[40]

40. Kenneth Lieberthal, "Strategies of Conflict in China during 1975–1976," *Contemporary China*, 1, no. 2 (November 1976): 7–14.

AFTER MAO

The tumultuous politics of the 1970s left Mao's immediate successors with an enormously full agenda of issues with which to cope. The major task during the remainder of 1976 and 1977 was to repair the political and economic damage that the years of infighting had produced. This included rehabilitating yet again those who had been purged during the previous year, Deng Xiaoping most notable among them.[41] It also meant trying to foster cooperation and unity while eliminating the most dangerous radicals from their positions throughout the bureaucracies. And of course it required an official critique both of the radicals' activities and of their political views—a critique that could be used to explain China's failings of the previous years without at the same time besmirching the name of Mao himself. Stopgap measures were taken throughout the economy to rehabilitate sector after sector. Numerous national conferences helped provide the central leaders with pertinent economic information and gave them the forums necessary to work out appropriate rehabilitative policies.

During these frenetic months, Beijing clearly had to deal with a crisis of authority. Deep tensions remained among the political survivors, and the prestige of the party as a whole had been severely undermined by the years of murderous infighting and political about-faces. Thus the national leaders tried to be responsive to the demand from virtually every sector for substantial budget allocations. Beijing seemed to lack the authority to say "no."

The Soviet Union quickly tried to test the waters to see if a post-Mao leadership would evince any interest in normalization of Sino-Soviet relations. The Soviet initiatives, however, remained half-hearted (a cessation of anti-China polemics, a symbolic party-to-party telegram congratulating Hua Guofeng on his assumption of the party chairmanship, and a request to renew long-stalled border negotiations). The Chinese leadership, moreover, was too weak, divided, and overwhelmed with domestic problems to tackle a major and potentially divisive foreign policy issue such as a change in Sino-Soviet relations. When the Soviets received no satisfactory response to their efforts, Moscow reverted to the wearily unfriendly position it had adopted in recent years.[42]

China's overall policy since Mao's death has reflected the modernizers' program. There has also been dramatic movement away from the position of the selective modernizers (among whom one should put Hua Guofeng)

---

41. The decision to rehabilitate Deng was adopted in March 1977, and Deng formally returned to power in July 1977.
42. Dieter Heinzig, "PRC–Soviet Relations after Mao," in Jürgen Domes, ed., *Chinese Politics after Mao* (Cardiff: University College, 1979), pp. 269–77.

and toward that of the technology firsters. Domestic policy has focused on economic development, making full use of material incentives to increase production. Restrictions on foreign trade and on general intercourse with the international economy have been relaxed, as the Chinese attempt to attract capital and know-how and to export their goods to a world market. The country has encouraged cooperation among all advanced Western states to join in the cause of containing Soviet communism. More liberal policies toward science and education have encouraged intellectual contacts with the international community that dovetail neatly with these other initiatives.

These priorities became official policy during several important meetings in 1978. The Fifth National People's Congress in February–March adopted an extraordinarily ambitious "ten-year plan" that reflected the large budget promises made to various sectors of China's economy. This congress's deliberations implicitly assumed that China's political and economic institutions would remain essentially unchanged as work shifted toward achieving rapid economic growth.[43] In December 1978 the Third Plenum of the Eleventh Central Committee took a major additional step in declaring that the time for focusing on the evils of the Gang of Four had ended and that henceforth all political as well as economic work must take the four modernizations as China's central task. The Third Plenum continued the policy, in evidence since the purge of the radicals, of rehabilitating (often posthumously) all those who had been purged during the Cultural Revolution for their fidelity to the goals that had by late 1978 again been embraced by the Chinese Communist Party. Finally, the Third Plenum also witnessed the consummation of the negotiations to normalize relations with the United States—a political triumph that added luster to Deng's heady accomplishments in forging an integrated economic and strategic policy during the course of 1978.[44]

China's foreign policy successes with the advanced Western countries during this period created a situation somewhat analogous to that of 1971, in which the People's Liberation Army was made to settle for half a loaf in budget allocations. A debate over the priority to be given to military modernization had been evident in the Chinese media starting as early as the winter of 1976–77, and it was clear that some in the military establishment were making a case for acquisition of weapons and equipment that would provide "quick fix" improvements in military capabilities. In line

43. Congress documents are translated in *FBIS-PRC*, Supplement, March 16, 1978.
44. *Xinhua*, December 23, 1978, in *FBIS-PRC*, December 26, 1978, pp. E1–13. U.S.-Chinese normalization was actually consummated at the end of the month-long Central Work Conference that directly preceded this plenum.

with this, China encouraged Western countries to allow sales of military hardware and technology, with the resulting Chinese window-shopping trips highly publicized abroad. But the predominant opinion in Beijing has maintained that military modernization must be built on the basis of overall upgrading of the civilian economy and must not be allowed to get in the way of that more broad-based effort by preempting precious funds. Deng probably has sanctioned the military purchase missions abroad as a way of further demonstrating, to Moscow's consternation, the strategic dimensions of China's new economic and political ties to the NATO countries.[45] At home, however, he has evidently concluded that China can hold down military spending, since it no longer faces the Soviet Union in isolation. The professional military has had to be satisfied instead with nonbudget concessions, such as granting increased authority to commanders, placing more emphasis on rigorous troop training, and so forth.

Serious problems in early 1979 forced Beijing finally to face up to its budget constraints in many sectors. The fiscally conservative central leadership found itself saddled with a budget deficit. China's brief but fierce Vietnam war of February–March 1979 proved expensive and forced a one-shot increase in defense appropriations. Many bureaucrats, perhaps sensing that their access to the international economy might prove short-lived, concluded import deals that exceeded China's probable ability to pay. And recently commissioned studies on the economy revealed imbalances and structural problems more severe and far reaching than had previously been understood. All of this forced abandonment of the ten-year plan adopted in March 1978 in favor of a new program of economic consolidation and reform. The watchwords now became efficiency and rationality instead of growth and leaps.

This consolidation and reform targeted on pragmatic economic growth has further removed current policy from the Maoist kind of revivalism that had contributed to China's estrangement from the Soviet Union starting in the late 1950s. Indeed, the lowered growth targets have been coupled with institutional and policy reforms so fundamental in scope that they clearly reflect the relatively iconoclastic calculus of the technology firsters. Given China's new approaches in domestic policy, it has become well nigh impossible even for thick-skinned leaders in Beijing to accuse the Soviet Union of revisionism. Thus diatribes against Soviet revisionism have disappeared from the Chinese press. China is, therefore, now in the ideologically anomalous position of forming its foreign policy around the objective of protecting itself against Soviet expansionism ("hegemonism") without being

---

45. See Francis J. Romance, "Modernization of China's Armed Forces," *Asian Survey*, 20, no. 3 (March 1980): 304–10; and the forthcoming article by Christopher Chyba in *Asian Survey*.

able to explain the sources of this aggression in the domestic Soviet political system. Beijing has tacitly admitted, in short, that the Soviet Union has become a dangerously expansionist socialist country.

CONCLUSION

Mao forced China onto a path of development that differed significantly from that in the Soviet Union. With his death, a key obstacle to Sino-Soviet reconciliation has been removed. An integral part of current Chinese domestic policy—the rehabilitation of cadres who held power before the Cultural Revolution—may also contribute to the possibility of improved Sino-Soviet ties. For Mao had been so viscerally anti-Soviet since the mid-1950s that he had undermined the positions of all those leaders who did not fully support his tough stance toward the USSR. While Mao was alive in the early 1970s, therefore, he permitted the rehabilitation of only those Cultural Revolution victims of whose anti-Sovietism he felt confident, like Deng Xiaoping. By 1978–79, however, the rehabilitations had gone beyond this circle to include former leaders who had never been brought back under Mao, some of whose backgrounds suggest they may have held different ideas about Soviet policy. Many of these were rehabilitated only posthumously, like Peng Dehuai and Zhang Wentian. Others, like Chen Yun, now hold powerful positions in Beijing.

Mao Zedong's death, therefore, removed the most persistently anti-Soviet force from Chinese politics. Now China's Soviet policy can again be debated in Beijing without fear that suggesting the idea of a limited (or even a far-reaching) rapprochement will be mistaken for treason. Some evidence suggests that this change in Chinese politics has in fact opened up discussion of a wider range of options in the Forbidden City. The center of gravity, however, remains with hard liners like Deng Xiaoping, who have created an integrated domestic and foreign policy that will cope with the Soviet challenge (as they understand it) even as it furthers China's modernization effort. This policy reaps both economic and military advantages from China's relations with Western countries through stressing the strategic interests that the PRC shares with the NATO countries and Japan. In almost every dimension, it is a strategy that meshes domestic and foreign policies to create a secure, strong, and modern China. This multifaceted interaction of domestic and foreign strategies, as illustrated above, has characterized Chinese politics throughout the past decade.

On balance, the forces favoring rapid economic development are now probably stronger in China than at any previous time. After a century of vacillation the country has, it seems, finally developed a strategy that reflects the challenge it faces from the international arena and will yield it security and strength in the decades ahead. Or has it? The domestic component of this strategy has far-reaching consequences for the distribution of power in the country. By taking maximization of efficiency as its touchstone, it is increasing economic inequality and social stratification, both within locales and on an interregional basis. There is little question that those who fare relatively badly under this set of policies will form a pool of support for those who want to change some of the rules of the game. Perhaps more important, these policies include leading China toward a largely market socialist society, one in which market forces will influence the distribution of investment, size of production, configuration of sales, level of wages, and so forth for much of the economy. This requires a major diminution of the power of the party and government administrative hierarchies, vesting that authority instead in enterprises and other local units. At the same time, the party is being told to limit its interference in economic decisions at all levels of the system, thereby changing its relations with the government. And in all units (including those of the party and the government), pressure is being applied to enforce new performance criteria—criteria that will reward the efficient at the expense of those who are merely loyal. The basis of recruitment to administrative cadre positions is also changing, so that people with good educational backgrounds, the very people previously discriminated against in China, will now monopolize access to these coveted jobs.

These changes will inevitably produce opposition. To date, moreover, Deng Xiaoping and his colleagues have failed to develop the needed moral justification for the controversial initiative they are taking to achieve rapid economic development. Rather, Deng is preaching a mixture of pragmatism ("seek truth from facts and make practice the sole criterion of truth") and Realpolitik (the "dictatorship of the proletariat, socialist road, and sole rule by the Chinese Communist Party" are three of the "guiding principles" for the modernization program). But Chinese history from ancient times to the 1970s provides support for the idea that politics are perceived as operating within a moral framework and that failure to elaborate this framework weakens the force of the strategy being pursued. Should Deng's policies not produce rapid economic growth and security in the international arena, they will lack the moral justification needed to keep them on track.

China faces so many problems that will adversely affect the results of Deng's program that, on balance, the odds favor a considerable retreat from the program itself. Should the country avert both major economic catastrophe and war, the institutional interests being undermined by the current strategy will probably be able to capitalize on shortfalls in results in order to kill many of the institutional reform aspects of the program with the death of a thousand slices. If so, China will remain committed to rapid modernization and will tolerate significant social inequality in order to achieve it. But the economy will continue to be dominated by the major party and government hierarchies, and centralized economic planning will remain a key feature of the system. China will, in short, resemble more closely the present Soviet polity than current policy envisions.

Other possibilities exist. Sino-Soviet military conflict—especially if limited largely to some severely damaging Soviet punishing raids (as it is likely to be)—would probably produce all-out industrialization that resembled more the Stalin than the Brezhnev era. China would adopt taut planning, priority development of defense-related industries, and a virulently nationalist ideology. Or China might experience another upsurge of nativist politics, especially if things go severely wrong with the economy. The center of gravity of the Chinese system has probably moved sufficiently far from this position that any renewal of xenophobic radicalism would prove disruptive but relatively short-lived.

All four of these possibilities for China's future domestic system are compatible with continued anti-Sovietism in Chinese foreign policy. Three of the possibilities (Deng's current program, a Stalin-type mobilization system, and a nativist resurgence) are heavily weighted in favor of just this outcome. This is because the relatively market-oriented economy of the Deng approach is especially compatible with the Western economic system, while the other two systems are inherently antiforeign. The final possibility, a bureaucratically dominated system more like that of the Brezhnev era, would increase the intellectual distance between China and the Western democracies at the same time that its relatively inefficient economy and its administrative approach to economic issues would prove less felicitous to economic cooperation with the West. This system, which is the one most likely to characterize the PRC a decade hence, is therefore also the one that is structurally the most conducive to the possibility of Sino-Soviet rapprochement. But none of these possibilities demand such an outcome, and an amalgam of domestic political interests and different strategic perspectives will continue to shape China's actual foreign policy in the future, as it has in the past.

The Soviet Perspective

SEWERYN BIALER

Sino-Soviet relations were one of the focal points of world politics in the 1970s and will continue to be during the 1980s. While the Soviet-American contest will for the foreseeable future remain the central focus of international relations, the Sino-Soviet conflict influences all aspects of those relations. Yet even though it is significantly influenced by the changing international environment, the Sino-Soviet conflict has an impetus and internal logic of its own.

This chapter is devoted to the analysis of the Sino-Soviet conflict as it evolved in the 1970s, and to its prospects for the 1980s. To the extent that analysis of the Soviet and Chinese sides of the conflict can be disaggregated, this study will focus on Soviet perspectives. A voluminous literature that traces the Sino-Soviet conflict through all its turns and twists in the 1970s is available, so I see no reason to engage in a similar exercise.[1] Instead I would like to examine briefly a limited number of questions that bear on the present and future of the conflict, primarily from the Soviet point of view. First, from the Soviet perspective, what are the nature and goals of Chinese domestic and foreign policy, particularly in the post-Mao period? Second, how can one explain the persistence of the conflict, and why are the Soviets unwilling or unable to meet the basic Chinese demands for its alleviation and normalization of relations? Third, what are the prospects—from the Soviet side—for the evolution of the conflict in the 1980s?

POST-MAO POLICY IN CHINA

Inconsistencies, hesitations, and ambiguities are evident in the Soviet view of the post-Mao internal situation in China, particularly regarding developments during the past two years.[2] This is in contrast to the more

---

1. The most extensive treatment of the Sino-Soviet conflict in the 1970s can be found in the brilliant essay by Kenneth Lieberthal, *Sino-Soviet Conflict in the 1970's: Its Evolution and Implications for the Strategic Triangle* (Santa Monica: Rand R-2342-NA, 1978). Other general overviews are given by Harry Gelman, "Outlook for Sino-Soviet Relations," *Problems of Communism*, 28, no. 5–6 (September–December 1979): 50–66; and Steven I. Levine, "The Unending Sino-Soviet Conflict," *Current History*, 79 (October 1980): 70–75, 104–5.

2. The most authoritative Soviet statement about Chinese internal developments in the post-Mao period can be found in "Kitai: Nekotorye tendentsil

consistent Soviet evaluation of the changes that have taken place in the international activity of the Chinese leadership.[3] Indeed, authoritative Soviet sources emphasize that the new course in China's internal policies is directly linked with Chinese foreign policy changes and its goals are primarily foreign oriented. To use the Soviet terminology, the goal of the Chinese course toward modernization involves the creation—with the help of the United States, Japan, West Germany, and other imperialistic states—of a stronger, more stable military, economic, and scientific-technological basis for accomplishing Great Han (*veliko-khanskikh*) expansionist plans.

According to the Soviets, a qualitative change of a counterrevolutionary nature occurred in the international activities of the Chinese leadership. The title of an editorial in the main theoretical journal of the Soviet Communist Party neatly summarizes the Soviet position: "Beijing: Yesterday—Reserve of Imperialism, Today—Its Ally."[4] The "Chinese Problem" is portrayed by the Soviets as not only encompassing Sino-Soviet relations but also directly threatening the peace and security of nations.

With regard to the states that compose the world communist/socialist system, the Chinese problem finds its expression in the sharpening of an open and direct confrontation with an increasing number of socialist countries and in an attempt to intervene in their internal affairs. This intervention sometimes even takes the form of military action.[5]

With regard to world capitalism, the problem is expressed in an open convergence of Beijing's foreign policy orientation with the anticommunist strategy of imperialism, in the coordination of actions with the most reactionary historical forces, in the open opposition against the world socialist system, against both the national-liberation movements and the developing countries that have a socialist orientation. This finds its expression in various cooperative ventures with the imperialists and in the build-up of China's military and economic potential.

With respect to the developing countries, the problem manifests itself in the increasing economic, political, and military support given by China

---

vnutrennego polozheniia," *Kommunist*, no. 3, February 1980, pp. 95–106. Because of the large volume of Soviet literature devoted to the analysis of China, I will quote only the most authoritative and interesting items.

3. One of the most telling Soviet analyses of the foreign policy of China in the post-Mao period can be found in B. Pyshkov and B. Starostin, "Ot 'Ul'trarevoliutsionnosti' k soiuzu s imperializmom i reaktsiei," *Kommunist*, no. 16, November 1978, pp. 98–109.

4. See "Pekin: Vchera—rezerv imperializma, segodnia—ego soiuznik," *Kommunist*, no. 4, March 1979, pp. 71–84.

5. On Chinese attitudes toward the world socialist system and its allies, see A. Kruchinin and V. Feoktistov, "Kak preemniki Mao voiuiut protiv sotsializma i ego soiuznikov," *Kommunist*, no. 5, March 1978, pp. 89–100.

to reactionary regimes, in the development of good relations with such regimes, and in the help given by China to forces of internal reaction.[6]

The goals and methods of Beijing's present policy are perceived by the Soviets as differing very little from those of imperialist states. If some time ago one could still speak about the desire of the Chinese leaders to exploit the contradictions between the two world systems for their own profit, today the situation is quite different. China has moved from the ideological struggle against the socialist countries to a political, economic, and even military struggle. Viewed in class terms, China's coordination of its activities with those of the imperialists signifies that China has been transformed into a link of the world capitalist system.

The Soviet leadership's view of the internal changes that have taken place following Mao's death and the defeat of the Gang of Four can be expressed as follows: The Chinese leadership, without changing its basic strategic goals, is engaged in broad tactical maneuvers in search of more effective ways to realize its hegemonic plans. Policy changes have been instituted by the Chinese leaders in order to preserve and strengthen their power over the country and the party, to search for more effective ways to transform China into a militaristic superpower, and to attempt to diminish the growing social tension that contributes to the political instability of the "militaristic-bureaucratic" regime.

The maneuvers and changes adopted by the Chinese leadership are portrayed as conforming with and explainable in terms of the goals outlined above. But we are reminded that these developments are taking place under conditions in which China finds itself economically unstable, torn politically by factional struggles, and ideologically confused and chaotic. Economically, the leadership is attempting to redirect the activity of the party, government, and military apparatus not only toward the modernization of agriculture, industry, the military, science and technology, but also toward the improvement of the political system and the revision of existing economic programs. While during the initial post-Mao period this revision consisted of an attempt to proclaim a new Great Leap Forward, at present the center of gravity has switched to the "regulation" of the national economy. Politically, an attempt is being made to increase the effectiveness and efficiency of government. Ideologically, a change has taken place in the attitude toward class struggle, which is no longer proclaimed as the main contradiction in Chinese society. Chinese leaders assert that although the class struggle has not withered away, it should not at the same time be "artificially sharpened." Furthermore, a campaign of selective rephrasing

---

6. See, for example, T. M. Kotova, A. S. Krasil'nikov, and A. V. Pedin, "Gegemonizm Pekina-ugroza svobode i nezavisimosti stran Azii i Afriki," *Narody Azii i Afriki*, no. 4, April 1979, pp. 3–16.

and reinterpretation of some of the slogans and "truths" of Maoism is being conducted according to current needs.

The period following Mao's death and the defeat of the Gang of Four is distinguished by a symmetry between Russian and Chinese views of each other. The ideological substance and formulas that constituted a major part of the struggle between those two countries have declined and even disintegrated. The leadership in both countries is now looking frantically for an ideological underpinning for the conflict. The conflict today is one of national interests, a clash between the two great powers, but both powers derive their integral legitimacy from the communist ideology and need an ideological justification and rationalization for their conflict.

Soviet spokesmen make a major distinction between the official and the popular anti-Maoism in China. They see, on the one hand, maneuvers by the present leadership to readjust Mao's teaching to current needs in order to minimize its impact on Chinese society, and to revise it in the interest of their own power struggles. At the same time, they discern a wave of popular disillusionment with China's Maoist past and a growing sentiment among all strata of the population which endangers not only Mao's heritage but the role of his successors. They tend to be realistic in evaluating the chances of success of this popular wave: they emphasize the strength of the Chinese state's coercive apparatus and of the force of nationalism in keeping this movement under control. Nevertheless, they see this movement as at least delaying the efforts to modernize and stabilize the country.[7]

The general Soviet view on post-Mao China is that the situation has gone from bad to worse. On the one hand, it is grudgingly recognized that Chinese internal policy moved away from the extremes of Maoist "permanent revolution," from the great leaps and cultural revolutions, and that the internal behavior of the Chinese leadership became much more rational and coldly calculating. But from the Soviet perspective this is exactly a change for the worse, because the opponent has become much more formidable. Early hopes following Mao's death that the new-found rationality of the changing Chinese leadership would lead to the tempering of Chinese hostility toward Russia have not been fulfilled. They now see a China that is becoming stronger internationally, and that is moving from absolute faith in the force of revolutionary slogans to faith in what can be accomplished through the process of modernization. This is a China that has abandoned its isolation and Western xenophobia and has increased its activities in the international arena immensely. It is a China that enters into virtual alliances with developed Western countries—particularly the United States—and that, as much as being used as a "card" by the United States against the

---

7. See V. Lazarev, "Antimaoistskoe dvizhenie v KNR," *Kommunist*, no. 8, May 1980, pp. 101–12.

Soviet Union, is itself using the "American card" in its struggle with Russia.

To any independent observer, the current Chinese leadership's significant break with Maoism is beyond question. The consequent change in Chinese internal policies is probably clear to the Soviet leaders also, although they cannot admit it publicly. Instead, their official announcements proclaim a virtual continuity with Maoism in post-Mao China.[8] But there has been a shift in emphasis that is reflected in a partial reversal of their previous argument. While Mao was alive they emphasized that the internal policies of the Chinese leadership were at the source of China's deviation and led, in turn, to its "hegemonistic" foreign policy. Today the focus of their criticism has switched to Chinese foreign policy, now portrayed as anti-Soviet and in search of world domination. A subordinate role is assigned to China's internal policies: they are designed merely to serve and support foreign policy goals.

The Soviets argue that the changes in the method of economic management that were forced on the Chinese leadership by the bankruptcy of their previous efforts do not alter the antisocialist essence of China's economic activity. The absolutely central goal of the modernization program is the accelerated increase of military-economic power. Soviet figures suggest that in 1979 China occupied third place in the world with regard to total military expenditures. While investment in China's national economy declined in absolute figures in that year, direct military expenditures increased by 20 percent. Thus the Soviets reason that the Chinese modernization program is in fact a program of forced militarization.[9]

Despite its new economic policy, the Chinese leadership is seen as having no new "scientifically valid" overall program of economic development. Moreover, some of the changes instituted by the Chinese leadership in the last two years, in both the domestic and international spheres, are shown as proof of a growing danger to China's socialist accomplishments. Today China finds itself at a new, dangerous stage where socialist forms of development are being diluted by the privatization of the economy, by the introduction of elements of market socialism, and especially by the risky decision to enter into joint ventures with capitalist firms. Beijing's decision to create mixed companies is a part of its general political line of allying with imperialism. Previously one could speak about the deformation of the socialist bases of Chinese society as a result of the exploitation of China's economic resources for antisocialist goals. Today one can also speak about

---

8. "Maoism without Mao," *Far Eastern Affairs*, no. 3, 1978, pp. 14–22.

9. An American government publication denies this Soviet assertion, which is clearly used for propaganda reasons. See Central Intelligence Agency, National Foreign Assessment Center, *Chinese Defense Spending, 1965–79*, SR 80-10091, July 1980.

the danger of the growth of spontaneous tendencies toward a private economy in China, about the overall weakening of both the state and the collectivist economic sectors, and about attempts to introduce into China forms of economic activity foreign to socialism and belonging to a market economy.[10]

In its present form the modernization program impels the Chinese leadership to seek support primarily among such groups as skilled workers, rich peasants, the intelligentsia, and remnants of the national bourgeoisie. The urban and rural "poor" cannot, through either their economic or political characteristics, serve the goals of modernization with the necessary effectiveness. Moreover, modernization aimed primarily at the build-up of Chinese military power will not result in the improvement of the masses' material situation.

The Soviets portray the official Chinese line as slavishly consistent with Mao's dicta in deed, while anti-Maoist in appearance to mask an authentic broad and spontaneous anti-Maoist movement developing in China. Soviet hopes lie in the destabilizing potential of this movement, which may even force a change in Chinese policies. These hopes are dampened somewhat by Soviet reminders not to exaggerate the force of the movement in the face of a military-bureaucratic dictatorship engaged in extreme methods of coercion and intimidation.[11] Yet the Soviets caution against underestimating the importance of this movement, especially under present conditions of Chinese instability.

Soviet analysts devote considerable attention to the factional struggle within the top Chinese leadership. According to Soviet views, the divisions within the leadership have not decreased at all as a result of the purge of the Gang of Four: factionalism still fractures China's communist party from top to bottom. It is interesting that in both their published material and in private conversations, Soviet observers see the greatest value of this factionalism for the Soviet Union in its weakening effects on China. They do not contend that any of the factions that are presently fighting each other represent diverse opinions on the basic direction of Chinese policies, particularly foreign policy and especially relations with the Soviet Union. In the Soviet view, the struggle is primarily a fight for personal power and only secondarily involves tactical differences concerning the party's internal policies.

10. V. Akimov and V. Potapov, "Results of the 'Lost Decade' " and "China's Economic Situation," *Far Eastern Affairs*, no. 2, 1979, pp. 53–70; idem, " 'Four Modernisations': Outlines and the Reality," *Far Eastern Affairs*, no. 3, 1979, pp. 52–63.

11. K. Yegorov, "Punitive-Repressive Apparatus in the System of Maoist Dictatorship," *Far Eastern Affairs*, no. 2, 1976, pp. 70–77.

Soviet observers do not ignore the ideological revisions of Maoism that have taken place in China. Yet in their opinion the recent ideological "modification" of Maoism does not change its basic nature. They stress that the revisions reinforce those elements of Maoist ideology that are most hateful to the Soviets—militant great-power nationalism, unbridled hegemonism in foreign policy, and anti-Sovietism and reliance on war and coercion as the key means of solving China's international and domestic problems.

PERSISTENCE OF THE CONFLICT

The conflict between the Soviet Union and the People's Republic of China is intensifying as it enters its third decade. The question arises: why is the conflict so intractable from the Soviet side?

It is important to understand, first, that the conflict has deep historical roots, and that its longevity provides a mechanism for its continuation beyond the foreseeable future. The Soviets have developed a hatred toward, and a lack of confidence in, a China that is consistently able to carry its own weight. In counterdistinction to their dealings with the West, whose leaders they at least are beginning to understand, the Soviet political elite views the Chinese leadership and elite as irrational and unpredictable. And while often insecure and inferior in their dealings with the West, the Soviets display a feeling of superiority and contempt for the Chinese. The deeply inculcated distrust of the Chinese, the attitude that "you can expect only the worst from the Chinese" and that the Chinese understand and react only to superior power, colors the whole perception of the conflict on the Soviet side. And there have developed in various groups of the Soviet bureaucracy powerful vested interests in the conflict. Among the Soviet ideologues the Chinese apostasy is seen both as a danger to Soviet influence in the international leftist and revolutionary movements and as the most powerful device to mobilize Soviet public opinion in support of the state. The military uses the Chinese danger, and lately the developing military alliance between China and the West, as a powerful lever to extract sufficient economic resources for a continuous military build-up.

Second, there are very few countries in the world that have a great past and a great future. China is foremost among them. On the Soviet side, the rational roots of the Sino-Soviet conflict lie in the fact that China will become a superpower in the near future. The Soviet Union, therefore, attempts to prevent—or at least postpone—the process of China's acquiring such status. Thus the Soviets fear not the present but the future. They do not overestimate China's strength and see quite clearly its enormous weaknesses, but they think that in historical perspective now is the time to keep the Chinese down, to teach them "lessons," to isolate them as much as possible, to delay as long as possible their emergence as a superpower.

Third, the Soviet leadership apparently believes that real Soviet concessions in the Sino-Soviet border dispute will encourage only greater demands from China as it grows stronger. They are afraid that even symbolic recognition of Chinese claims of the historical injustice of the Russia-China border treaties will create further claims on Soviet territory in the future— this time more than symbolic ones. Moreover, real border concessions and symbolic recognition of Russian injustice with regard to the contested territories would encourage and raise the hopes of other nations, notably Japan and Romania, who have similar claims on Russia. Major concessions to one communist state that has claims against Russia would also create dangerous precedents in Soviet relations with other communist states. It might lead to an increase in irredentism in Eastern Europe.

Fourth, the Soviet suspiciousness of China, and distrust of Chinese motives, creates an almost insoluble dilemma in responding to a key Chinese demand that would help normalize Soviet-Chinese relations: the Chinese want the Soviets to initiate a large-scale troop withdrawal from the Sino-Soviet border. Such a gesture would constitute a real sign to the Chinese of Soviet sincerity in the effort to normalize relations, and it is only after such troop withdrawals that the Sino-Soviet relationship can improve. On their side, however, the Soviets see their own troop withdrawal from the Chinese border as the final step in the process of normalizing relations with China. In their perception, the process of normalization has to be advanced very far and tested before large-scale troop removals can occur. They fear that the Chinese demand for initial and substantial troop withdrawals deep into Soviet territory is a Chinese trap designed to leave large parts of scarcely inhabited Soviet territory at the mercy of the Chinese, and thus encourage Chinese aggression.

Fifth, one may conclude that the general Soviet attitude toward the normalization of relations with China is logically faulty. If the Soviets believe that China is now weak and may at some point attain a superpower status, the time to make peace with China is now rather than when the opponent is in a better position. This logic, however correct, does not take into consideration two points: (1) the Soviets consider themselves strong today— much stronger than China—and therefore believe that they can outwait China; (2) the Soviets believe that possible developments inside China, for example the failure of the Four Modernizations and particularly the disillusionment with the "American card," will make China more susceptible in the future to Soviet pressures. Other possible internal developments in China that the Soviets are not excluding are an intensification of factional struggle, a weakening of the central government, and an ultimate fragmentation in the wake of internal social and political turmoil. Nobody who knows Chinese history and the confusion that exists currently in China can exclude such possibilities. But even more important is the question of what the Soviets can gain by making major concessions now—what costs are incurred by the improvement of relations with China. The point is that, in Soviet eyes, the prize to be gained by such improvement, at the cost of major concessions, will remain quite limited. The Russians have no illusions with regard to the possibility of restoring an alliance with China. The decline in the intensity of the Sino-Soviet conflict and a measure of normalization in relations with China will not remove the strategic threat that China poses to the Soviet Union. This threat will remain a constant in Soviet calculations and will not visibly lessen the burden that it imposes on Soviet military planning. Most important, such normalization will hardly lead to a Chinese agreement to refrain from strongly opposing, in both word and deed, Soviet expansionist efforts in the Third World, no more than it would lessen the Soviet attempt to expand its power and influence in the global arena. The gain for both sides from normalization of relations, therefore, is really quite limited and illusory.

In one crucial dimension the conflict between China and the Soviet Union is much more dangerous and unpalatable to the Soviet leadership and elite than are conflicts with their capitalist enemies and competitors. The United States and its allies are in sharp conflict and competition with the Soviet Union, but they do not question the legitimacy of the Soviet state. They have long since ceased to pose a threat to the Soviet internal system; they are, rather, reconciled to a process of containing the system within its own imperial boundaries. Even while they are engaged in ideological struggle with the West, the Soviets have no difficulties in presenting the struggle as a contest between two opposing world systems; and in the eyes of the communists themselves, the credentials of the Western powers to question Soviet internal order are rather unimpressive and ineffective. With regard to China the situation is very different, because the Chinese leadership questions the basic legitimacy of the Soviet order; it is engaged in a vociferous campaign regarding the degeneration of the Soviet system, and accuses the Soviet leaders of sins that are anathema to communists.

The powerful challenge to Soviet legitimacy has to be treated seriously, because it comes from a country that underwent an authentic victorious grand revolution, whose leader—regarded as one of the key perpetuators of the Marxist-Leninist tradition—has authority as a theorist unequaled by anyone in the Soviet Union since Stalin. It comes from a communist country with the largest party in the world, which is as adept at using Marxist-Leninist ideology for its own purposes as the Soviet Union is. In the 1920s and 1930s the Soviet leadership faced a challenge to the legitimacy of its internal role from various groups within the Bolshevik party itself, notably from the Trotskyites. We know how seriously the leadership treated this challenge and how forcefully it reacted even though the Trotskyite movement was insignificant compared with the power of the Soviet state. For

Stalin, Trotsky's challenge was a challenge to his own role, and in many respects more dangerous than that of an enemy power. The present Soviet leaders see a resurrection of this challenge in the Sino-Soviet conflict, this time represented not by a tiny splinter group but by a powerful state and party. It is, without any doubt, easier to make peace and achieve a compromise with a clear-cut enemy who belongs to the "other" side than with a power that challenges Soviet primacy and its very legitimating credentials, and which derives from a similar tradition of revolutionary rule.

It is often asserted that the ideological dimension of the Sino-Soviet conflict, which played such an important part in the initial stages of its development, has been almost nullified and that the conflict today is primarily—or only—a clash of national interests and ambitions. There is some truth to this statement. As in many other cases, conflicts do sometimes derive from one set of circumstances and causes, and in the process of their continuation are fed and aggravated by different ones. The causes of the present Sino-Soviet conflict, on both sides, originate above all in sharp competition between one state, the Soviet Union, which has attained the status of global power and now wants to taste, unhindered, the fruits of its achievement, and another power, China, which seeks to maximize its power status in the face of Soviet opposition. Yet one should not neglect the remaining ideological dimension of the conflict. On the Soviet side, those ideological aspects still play an important role—first and foremost because of the threat to Soviet internal legitimacy posed by the Chinese challenge, and second because of the threat created by that challenge to the legitimacy of Soviet international behavior in the eyes of leftist and revolutionary groups. Yet there are other ideological aspects of the conflict that have to be taken into consideration and that touch on the key question of the role of ideology in Soviet and Chinese societies.

Proponents of the theory of the erosion of ideology in the Soviet Union and China confuse the degree to which form and substance are tied together and depend on each other, as well as the extent to which what people believe is connected with what they express,[12] or the extent to which communist ideology has acquired the characteristics not simply of a doctrinal belief system but of a cultural system.[13] In the Soviet Union, and even to a greater degree in China, legitimization of the conflict cannot be attained outside the ideological framework. In both countries the conflict can be

12. For a discussion of the role of ideology in Soviet foreign policy thinking, see Seweryn Bialer, "Sources of Soviet Foreign Policy," in Seweryn Bialer, ed., *Domestic Context of Soviet Foreign Policy* (Boulder, Colo.: Westview Press, 1981), pp. 409–41.

13. For a view of ideology as a cultural system, see Clifford Geertz, "Ideology as a Cultural System," in David E. Apter, ed., *Ideology and Discontent* (New York: Free Press, 1964), pp. 47–76.

expressed verbally only through ideological language. This is the only medium through which the "truths" about the conflict can be brought to the attention of party elites and one's own conduct justified. This is an additional reason for the perpetuation of the conflict in an all-or-nothing atmosphere, on both sides, that leaves relatively little room for maneuvering and compromise on either side. This is also why both countries are now engaged in a frantic and piteous search for consistent ideological explanations that take into consideration the internal changes in each country during the last few years, as well as the changes in their international behavior. On the Soviet side, it finds its expression in the attempt to come to grips with the moderating changes in Chinese internal policies and in a sometimes convoluted effort to show that despite Mao's death and the anti-Mao campaigns, Maoism retains power in China. The Chinese party at its highest levels, in turn, is engaged in a search that will tie expansionist Soviet behavior to the domestic nature of the Soviet system. The Chinese ideologues are not satisfied with the formula that domestically the Soviet Union has become a "regular" capitalist-imperialist state, and they are at a loss to find a suitable replacement for this formula. They are in a quandary because many of the policies that they are now adopting were, and are, in force in the Soviet bloc countries; they are therefore faced with the dilemma of explaining why "what is good for the goose is not good for the gander." They are also engaged in an initial reevaluation of the Stalinist heritage, which bears a resemblance too close for comfort to the trauma of the Cultural Revolution, which they now reject totally.

Anybody who has traveled in the Soviet Union and has engaged in conversation about China with Soviet citizens is struck by the primitiveness and intensity of their views. One has an unavoidable impression that in the Russian popular mind, China looms as a danger of overwhelming proportions. The Soviet citizen will give some lip service to the danger from the "white imperialist," will express his dissatisfaction at a particular policy of the American government, and will voice regret that the Americans do not understand the Russians; but when it comes to the Chinese his deepest feelings are of unconcealed fear, distrust, aversion, and even hatred. In the popular Russian mind there looms the danger of the yellow peril, of the one billion Chinese who are ready without the slightest provocation to move out of their borders in search of living space. There is a clear association in the popular mind between China and Chingis Khan and the Russian suffering under the Tatar-Mongol yoke.[14] Adding the fact that the average

14. Throughout my discussion of the Soviet attitude toward the Chinese, I use the term "Russian" to describe those attitudes. This is not only because I consider that the Russian attitude is the dominant and defining attitude of Soviet policy toward China, but also because I do not think that the attitude of non-

Russian believes that the Chinese are repaying with ingratitude the enormous help that the Russians, in difficult times, gave to the People's Republic of China, and the genuine fear that the Chinese are trying to push the United States into direct confrontation with the Soviet Union, the Soviet vision becomes truly nightmarish.

I must add that in my conversations with members of the intelligentsia and particularly the political experts, the picture of the Chinese, although expressed in somewhat more temperate terms, was not very different. A historian of contemporary Russia, in his postscript to the famous essay by the Soviet dissident Andrei Amalrik, *Will the Soviet Union Survive until 1984?*, depicts Russian feelings toward China in these words:

> China, whether metaphorically perceived as the "yellow menace" or the "red dragon," is in itself an image of menacing power for the Russian reader. Russian racial feeling about "Orientals"—though often repressed, sometimes successfully, and publicly of course unacknowledged—is strong and widespread. It applies to Chinese, to Japanese, to Uzbeks and other Turkic peoples, and it is sometimes passionately reciprocated. No doubt such feelings go back to the days of the Mongol conquest, the Muscovite princely wars for independence, the imperial expansion of Russia and the subjugation and attempted integration of Asiatic populations. Russia's defeat at the hands of the Japanese in 1904 may have played a certain role here. The writer Andrei Bely, for example, had a pathological fear of "Orientals" and used to hide when he saw a slant-eyed face approach on the street. In his great novel, *St. Petersburg*, set on the eve of the Revolution of 1905, the "Orient"—whether represented by Japanese, or merely Japanese fashions among the upper classes, or the Mongol ancestry of the central characters—stands for the forces of destruction. . . .
>
> The "red dragon" image, mentioned earlier, may be understood in two senses. In the traditional sense it refers to the allegorical beast of the Book of Revelation whose appearance in the Roman world will bring time to a

---

Slav nationals in the Soviet Union, particularly the Central Asians, is sympathetic to China. I am fully in agreement with Vernon Aspaturian when he states: "The Central Asian Turks are Moslems and the connection with Chinese culture and civilization is now remote and they are more mid-eastern in their culture and orientation than Far Eastern. They fear being overwhelmed and smothered by the Chinese and do not take great comfort in the treatment their kinsmen receive under Chinese rule. For Central Asians, bad as it may be to many, Russian and Soviet rule is preferable to Chinese, because the Russians do not threaten their national identity in the way they perceive the Chinese would, and the Soviet system allows for far greater cultural, linguistic, and national identity and development than the Chinese approach to multilateralism." Vernon Aspaturian, "The Domestic Sources of Soviet Policy Toward China" (unpublished manuscript, n.d.).

stop. But in a more contemporary sense, it evokes the image of China which the Russian middle class, with its newly acquired amenities and comforts and pretensions to culture, fears most. Driven by what Amalrik calls "the relentless logic of revolution" (he does not attempt to explain either the basis or the thrust of that logic), China reminds the Soviet middle class of the dangerous and overstrained days of Stalinism from which they hoped they had emerged. They fear on the one hand the threat of Chinese expansionism and on the other the possible influence (which may be exerted negatively as well as positively) of the Chinese on their own regime, i.e., the threat of a backsliding into Stalinist militancy at home. Amalrik, indeed, sees contemporary China in a situation that parallels that of the Soviet Union a generation back, and he concludes from this that Peking has inevitably entered a period of expansionist foreign policy.[15]

But how can we be sure what is the view of the Soviet leadership and political elite? It is my deep conviction that the image of the Chinese in the minds of the Soviet leadership and political elite does not differ substantially from the Russian popular image. After all, one has to remember that the Soviet Union has become a country without a separate elite and mass culture. Well before the revolution in Russia and to the present day, society has exhibited a pronounced attitude of "we," the simple, normal people, versus "they," the power holders on all levels, the *nachal'stvo*. Yet the reality and genuineness of this division may conceal a phenomenon no less real and—for questions of interest here—even more significant. It involves a sense of cultural community between "we" and "they," where the "we" represents the working classes. After all, they both come from the same social fabric; they share similar life histories; they resemble one another culturally to an amazing degree, as witness their sentimentalism, basic nationalism, mannerisms, artistic and literary preferences, language, and all the rest. The world of privilege may separate "we" and "they" in Soviet society, but origin and culture unites them. It is in this sense, and only in this sense, that one should understand the observation of a Russian writer, conveyed in a conversation with me, "Our power is a genuinely popular power" (*u nas nastoiashchaia narodnaia vlast'*).

But we also have direct testimony of the Soviet leadership's attitude toward the Chinese from the well-authenticated Khrushchev memoirs. Let us look at some of Khrushchev's views:

> You might say that China is both close to us and far from us. It's close in that it's our next-door neighbor and shares a long border with our country. At the same time, China is far away in that the Chinese have little in

15. Sidney Monas, "Commentary: Amalrik's Vision of the End," in Andrei Amalrik, *Will the Soviet Union Survive until 1984?* (New York: Harper and Row, 1970), pp. 84–85.

common with our people. . . . it's always difficult to know what the Chinese are really thinking. . . . It's impossible to pin these Chinese down. There is, however, one thing I know for sure about Mao. He's a nationalist, and at least when I knew him, he was bursting with an impatient desire to rule the world. His plan was to rule first China, then Asia, then . . . what? There are seven hundred million people in China, and in other countries like Malaysia, about half the population is Chinese. . . . His [Mao's] chauvinism and arrogance sent a shiver up my spine.[16]

It may well be that one of the secondary reasons for Khrushchev's ouster was his inability to control the conflict with China. His successors made an initial effort to repair the damage that they thought Khrushchev had wrought. They were eminently unsuccessful, and they went far beyond Khrushchev's policies in dealing with the Chinese from a position of strength. Khrushchev's successors, now ruling the Soviet Union, came from the same background as he did. There is nothing to suggest that their views on China differ from his. If anything, after the catastrophic experiences of the late 1960s and 1970s, they must be even more bitter and one-sided in their view of the Chinese enemy.

PROSPECTS FOR THE 1980s

What are the prospects for Sino-Soviet relations in the 1980s from the Soviet perspective? I would not like to engage in predictions about the development of those relations. I would rather concentrate on depicting the pressures on the Soviets domestically and internationally that may influence their behavior toward their adversary. There are five sets of circumstances that might affect Soviet behavior in the conflict during the coming decade.

The first concerns Soviet military policy, which is clearly at a crossroads. Before the Soviet Union achieved strategic parity with the United States and possessed a global military reach, its goal was clear, unchanging, and not a matter of significant dispute. Now, however, the basic aims of long-term Soviet military power have been achieved, or, as some Western observers would argue, overachieved. But it seems that the Soviet military build-up continues by the sheer force of inertia and drift. There are no signs that major disputes are taking place regarding the aims of Soviet military policy under the new circumstances, or that an effort is being made to define more clearly what constitutes Soviet security interests. The Soviet military build-up is, to a point, clearly beyond the range of its traditional de-

16. *Khrushchev Remembers*, ed. Strobe Talbott (Boston: Little, Brown, 1970), quotations from pp. 473 and 474, see also pp. 475–78; *Khrushchev Remembers: The Last Testament*, ed. Strobe Talbott (Boston: Little, Brown, 1974), quotation from p. 235, see also pp. 283, 288–89.

fense needs. The change in the East-West military balance evoked a major reaction from the Western alliance, particularly the United States. If counteracted by the Russians, the Western reaction will undoubtedly start a new, major, and uncontrollable arms race. This prospect may initiate a reevaluation of military growth policy among the top Soviet leaders and among the experts who advise them. I am not at all optimistic about the results of such a reevaluation, and I have major doubts whether U.S. policies, with their clear denigration of arms control measures, will have any positive influence here. Yet it seems to me that, for a number of economic and political reasons that will be discussed below, the inertia of Soviet military policy may be broken and the question of its redefinition may enter the Soviet political agenda of the 1980s.

The second set of circumstances concerns the direction of Soviet foreign policy in general. What we have witnessed in recent years, in my opinion, is not a fulfillment of some master plan of expansion, but a foreign policy that exploits targets of immediate opportunity with a relatively low cost and risk. In its ability to relate the tempting options of temporary or partial gains and strategic improvements to its other professed goals of reducing international tensions and conducting a policy of détente with the West, overall Soviet foreign policy demonstrated a very limited coherence. The Soviet leadership has not yet resolved the question of the proper ordering of priorities for Soviet foreign policy in the new situation. One has the impression that the leadership has not thought through what to do in the long run, and how to use their newly acquired capacity for international action.[17] Their policy in this respect may well continue into the 1980s.

The third set of circumstances, and the most important stimulus for change in Soviet policy toward China, will not originate in new political issues but in the policy-making process itself—in the impending turnover of leaders and elites in the 1980s. Lacking a predetermined set of procedures, Soviet successions have always been periods in which unpredictability in the emergence of a new leader with new policy positions is coupled with a situation offering high potential for ferment, for disruption of bureaucratic inertia, and for an opening of the political process. Yet the approaching succession of the 1980s, by combining a number of developments, will create the conditions to compound these disruptive effects. Most important, it almost inevitably will combine the replacement of the top leader with that of the broad core leadership group and a large part of the central elite, and with the beginning of a generational turnover among Soviet elites. Not only will such a turnover be massive, but it will also be

17. See Seweryn Bialer, *Stalin's Successors: Leadership, Stability, and Change in the Soviet Union* (New York: Cambridge University Press, 1980), chap. 14.

compressed into a relatively short time span, a pattern that can be significant in determining the formation of the emergent leadership's behavior and style.[18]

A key question, then, is whether and to what extent this succession and subsequent replacement of large segments of the elite will coincide with the emergence of distinctive political differences between the incoming and outgoing leadership groups. I would like to suggest that such a coincidence will occur, because of the generational change by which a large proportion of the new elite will have entered politics after Stalin's death. The approaching succession, whatever the form and results of its initial stage, will eventually involve a replacement of the top leadership and the central establishment on a scale much greater than the last two successions and will be combined with this increased generational turnover of the political elite. This conjunction of successions, in both the broad and the narrow sense, has no precedent in Soviet history. It will be a political development of long duration and significance.

Equally significant may be the effects of the pressures on the policy-making process created by the forthcoming succession, in combination with the emerging political issues. They may, and in all probability will, lead to a destabilization of the central policy-making system that—in a highly centralized polity such as the Soviet Union—may have very important consequences. The destabilization will involve a breakdown of the consensus among the leadership and elites, the intensification of factional struggles at the top and middle levels of the bureaucracy, possible realignments of existing alliances, the exploitation of policy issues for the accumulation of power by individual leaders and groups, and sharp twists and turns in central policies.

The fourth set of pressures will originate in the Soviet economy. There exists a consensus among students of Soviet economics that in the 1980s the Soviet Union will face grave economic problems.[19] A decline in eco-

18. See Seweryn Bialer, "Succession and Turnover of Soviet Elites," *Journal of International Affairs*, 32, no. 2 (Fall-Winter 1978): 181–200.

19. These tendencies and trends are well presented in *Soviet Economy in a Time of Change: A Compendium of Papers Submitted to the Joint Economic Committee, Congress of the United States, October 10, 1979*, 96th Cong., 1st sess. (Washington, D.C.: U.S. Government Printing Office, 1979), vols. 1 and 2. Several papers by the CIA also provide a basis for an analysis of the Soviet outlook for the 1980s: *Testimony of the DCI dm. Stansfield Turner before the U.S. Congress, Joint Economic Committee, Subcommittee on Priorities and Economy in Government*, 96th Cong., June 26, 1979: National Foreign Assessment Center, *Simulations of Soviet Growth Options to 1985*, ER 79–10131, March 1979; idem, *SOVSIM: A Model of Soviet Economy*, ER 79–10001, February 1979; idem, *Soviet Economic Problems and Prospects*, ER 77–10436U,

nomic growth rates in all sectors will confront the Soviets in the coming decade. Extensive development has reached such limits that the high growth rates of the past are no longer possible. Yet the Soviet system of economic management, pricing, and incentives is ill-prepared to maximize the possibilities for intensive growth. The conditions for a relatively rapid change would require fundamental changes in the economic-political system and are unlikely to be accomplished in the foreseeable future. Among the steps already undertaken by the Soviet government to counteract the declining tendencies of growth, none will have any major impact on the Soviet economy.

The Soviet Union faces other economic problems. It will confront an energy balance unfavorable to its economic growth, as well as disturbing demographic trends. And agriculture, despite the enormous investments of the Brezhnev era, will remain a highly volatile sector, with the unavoidable fluctuations exacerbating the effects on GNP of the decline in growth in other sectors.

In sum, the Soviet Union faces a difficult economic situation in the 1980s. How difficult it will be is a matter of conjecture. According to the worst-case scenarios, it will be a period of low growth intermingled with economic stagnation. But even in the more optimistic scenarios, the Soviet Union will face an economic crunch far more severe than anything it encountered in the 1960s and 1970s.

During the 1980s the Soviet Union will in all probability be unable to pursue a policy in which military expenditures, investments, and consumer spending will all grow steadily and sometimes even rapidly. The general agreement among Soviet leaders and elites made possible by high growth rates in the past will give way to fierce competition, which in a situation of leadership succession can become quite intense. In the context of the present discussion, the most important aspect of the growing Soviet economic difficulties will be the increasing pressure with regard to military expenditures. One should not have any illusions. If the Soviets feel that their security is threatened, they will make any sacrifice necessary to keep up their military strength. Yet the cost will be immeasurably higher than in the past. Soviet economic problems will require enormous investments in renovating technological plants and developing costly energy resources. But throughout the 1960s and 1970s social constraints developed on how much the leadership could depress the growth rate of the standard of living. With

---

July 1977; idem, *Prospects for Soviet Oil Production*, ER 77–10270, April 1977; idem, *USSR: Long Term Outlook for Grain Imports* ER 79–10057, January 1979. A representative nongovernmental study of the prospects for the Soviet economy in the 1980s can be found in Holland Turner, ed., *The Future of the Soviet Economy, 1978–1985* (Boulder, Colo.: Westview Press, 1978).

the abolition of mass terror during the post-Stalinist period, stability of the system and of the compact between the leadership and the broad strata of the population was increasingly based on a steadily growing consumption and on the expectation of the population that such growth would continue. Neither the Soviet leaders nor Western analysts know how the working classes, especially industrial workers, will react to a stagnating standard of living. In light of the events in Poland, the specter of labor unrest must hound the Soviet leadership.

The fifth set of circumstances that might influence Soviet behavior in relation to China concerns Soviet relations with the West, particularly the United States. The initial deterioration and then the crash of détente with the United States in the 1970s does not, in my opinion, signify a momentary aberration in the regulation of tensions between the two superpowers. It is a logical outcome, on the one hand, of growing Soviet danger to vital American interests in the Third World—particularly in the vital Persian Gulf area—and, on the other hand, of the growing American dissatisfaction about the balance of strategic and conventional power between the Soviet Union and the United States. Unless there is a radical change in Soviet military policy and expansionist international behavior, there can be little doubt that in the 1980s we will see a major effort on the part of the United States to redress the global balance of power, a stiffening opposition to Soviet expansion, and the increased likelihood of confrontational politics in U.S.-Soviet relations.

If logic is a guide to policies, all the elements mentioned above should exert pressure in the 1980s on the Soviet Union to regulate and improve its relations with China, especially in light of the latter's increased stability and growing power. One thing is almost certain: during the upcoming succession, the new set of Soviet leaders will again make an effort to present the Chinese with initiatives to regulate their border disputes. The Soviet leaders may even increase the extent of concessions on the deployment of forces along their common border. In other words, the Soviet Union will attempt to achieve a breakthrough in the Sino-Soviet struggle. Yet one has the impression that the concessions will not go far enough and that inertia, deep bitterness, and mutual suspicion will mark the conflict throughout the 1980s.

While there are clear pressures on the Soviet side to normalize relations with China, and under the influence of those pressures the Soviets can offer the Chinese more than they have before, there are no equivalent pressures on the Chinese side. The Chinese welcome the end of détente and are delighted by the stiffening of American resistance to Soviet expansionism and by the planned increase in Western military build-up. Their major concern is to see that the American resistance to the Soviet Union stiffens even further. Under these circumstances, the Chinese can hardly be expected to engage in anything but token negotiations with the Russians. Moreover, the Chinese attach great importance to their newly acquired American connection, and expect major help for Chinese modernization programs. They know very well that this newly developed relationship will be threatened if their position regarding the Soviet Union changes. All in all, despite the pressures that may encourage new Soviet reconciliatory efforts, the overall configuration of the 1980s will make even a partial reconciliation unlikely. More likely is the continuation of conflict, which may be accompanied by increasing tensions, dangerous incidents, and military actions.

One caveat is in order here. If American resolve to oppose the Soviets and change the balance of power does not live up to the promises currently being made by American statesmen, and if the Chinese become disillusioned with the extent and effectiveness of their modernization program, they may become more receptive to Soviet efforts to moderate the conflict. Whether this will happen is anybody's guess.

AMERICAN STRATEGY

Finally, I would like to offer a few thoughts on American policy regarding the Sino-Soviet conflict and the strategic triangle.

First, both the Carter and the Nixon-Kissinger administrations made a major effort to use the "China card" in their relations with the Soviet Union. The Nixon-Kissinger administration used it in a limited, but initially quite successful way in attempting to build détente with the Soviet Union. The Carter administration achieved a major breakthrough in relations with China and attached great importance to Sino-American relations in the containment of the Soviet Union. Indeed, it would be no exaggeration to say that key Carter administration spokesmen considered the use of the "China card" to be their major achievement in the international arena. In my opinion, the utility of the China card in the containment of Soviet expansionism is very restricted. The crucial point here is that the "China card" cannot be used as a substitute for American strength. It is primarily American power, along with the strength of NATO and American ability to persuade its European allies to counteract Soviet expansionism on a global scale, that can be effective in containing the Soviet Union. Without the growth of American strength and the redressing of the balance of power, even the marginal utility of the "China card" will diminish, if for no other reason than the likely Chinese disillusionment with American policy.

Second, American policy makers and experts in international relations sometimes are in sharp disagreement on whether U.S. policy toward the USSR and China should be evenhanded or should tilt toward one or the other. To me the answer to this question is clear: there is no reason why America should be evenhanded in its relations with China and the USSR. The Soviet Union is the United States' main opponent in the international arena; American and Soviet interests are in sharp conflict. Of course, the United States should make every effort to avoid direct confrontation with the Soviet Union. The United States should also seek areas of mutual agreement, for example, on the crucial question of arms control, to a greater extent than was attempted by the Carter administration. Nonetheless, the major effort with regard to the USSR must be directed toward its containment. Such an effort must be rooted in the expectation that if the cost incurred by Soviet expansionism is maximized by U.S. opposition, then the time will come when the Soviet Union will pass its imperial expansionist stage and be willing to participate in the stabilization of a changed world order.

Given China's present stage of development, China and the United States have a partial coincidence of interests, both in containing the Soviet Union and in stabilizing areas of international conflict that provide the Soviets with opportune targets. The instruments available to America and China in this effort supplement each other. A stronger and more stable China is thus in the American interest. Any help that the United States and its allies can give to China in the economic, scientific, and cultural arenas serves American interests.

The third major point concerns U.S. military relations with China. It is my opinion that a military alliance between the United States and China is not in the American interest. Although the United States may directly or indirectly offer economic help to China in order to strengthen its military potential, direct military relations—the arming of China and the coordination of strategic planning—should not be attempted. Little would be gained from such an effort, and a great deal could be lost. Whatever is gained by stiffening Chinese resistance to the Soviet Union will be lost by immensely magnifying Soviet paranoia about China. It is a dangerous illusion to suppose that the arming of China and the formation of a Sino-American military alliance will not lead to Soviet countermeasures, particularly an immediate military build-up. Moreover, such a policy would probably diminish the possibility of reaching agreements with the Soviets in areas of mutual interest, such as arms control. But most important, such a policy multiplies the likelihood of the United States becoming involved in armed conflicts between the Soviet Union or its allies and China. This would not be the first time that a weaker ally would force its major partner into a dangerous military confrontation that is highly undesirable.

This contention requires further elaboration. One has to distinguish between the existence of the Sino-Soviet conflict as a means of promoting U.S. global policies and the possibilities available to the United States of using the conflict as a "card" in its struggle with the Soviet Union. The limitations and dangers of the use of the "China card" by the United States are especially pronounced with regard to the questions of a prospective military alliance with China and large-scale sales of military equipment. First of all, the completion of a formal or even an informal military alliance with China would create the danger of American involvement in military adventures started by the Chinese. It is well known that the Chinese belief in the inevitability of war prescribes local wars with the Soviet Union or its allies as the best course for preventing big wars. One has to take the Chinese prescription seriously and avoid the possibility that the Chinese may initiate a local conflict that will develop into a confrontation between the two superpowers. Thus the United States should strive to contain the Soviets without provoking confrontation.

The United States, while engaged in global competition with the Soviet Union, should also strive to seek areas of partial coincidence of interests, as in the field of arms limitation. In dealing with the Soviets, the prospect of a Sino-American military alliance may act as a positive stimulus to temper Soviet international behavior and encourage negotiations. But the actual formation of such an alliance would exhaust the effectiveness of the "China card." A military alliance between China and the United States could stiffen Soviet resistance, push the Soviets toward more adventurous behavior, and preclude negotiations where American and Soviet interests coincide.

Finally, we do not really know what would be the threshold of possible Soviet military response to a mass arming of China by the United States, and the most that can be said is that this would be a step of incalculable consequences. A military alliance might prove to be the deciding factor that pushes the Soviet Union toward armed preemptive intervention against China. In a world fraught with danger, the United States should refrain from taking steps that unnecessarily exacerbate tensions, the results of which cannot be calculated.

Foreign Affairs and Security

China's Agonizing Reappraisal*

JONATHAN D. POLLACK

With the advantage that hindsight conveniently affords, the 1970s unquestionably emerge as a time of profound transformation in the Sino-Soviet relationship and its effect on the security and foreign policy of the People's Republic of China (PRC). No doubt there is a certain artificiality in demarcating a specific period as coinciding neatly with particular trends in a nation's internal or external policy. Throughout this decade, however, there was pervasive evidence of dramatic change in Chinese assessments of the international situation as a whole and of the PRC's corresponding foreign and security policy objectives. Yet the full dimensions of these changes remain insufficiently appreciated, along with their consequences for both global and regional politics.

A single essay cannot possibly hope to encapsulate, let alone explain, the entirety of this transformation. Nevertheless, we can explore key dimensions of these changes, in particular when China's leaders, however intermittently or cryptically, have revealed some of their underlying political and strategic calculations. The purposes of this essay, therefore, are fourfold: (1) to describe those specific dimensions of the Sino-Soviet relationship that transformed the conflict from its earlier form(s); (2) to indicate those areas of Chinese external policy making that were particularly affected by such changes; (3) to establish the shifting political and stra-

---

* The views expressed in this chapter are entirely my own, and do not represent the opinions of the Rand Corporation or any of its governmental sponsors. My thanks to Steven Levine for his detailed and valuable comments and criticisms of an earlier draft of this essay.

tegic context of the Moscow-Beijing conflict, thereby clarifying its effects on both the Chinese political process and the PRC's relations with various major powers; and (4) to speculate briefly on the likelihood of the Sino-Soviet rivalry undergoing a significant transformation in the coming decade. It is necessary, therefore, to describe first the overall context of the relationship at the close of the 1960s.

SINO-SOVIET RELATIONS IN THE 1960s

By 1970 the Sino-Soviet conflict had flourished openly for a full decade. What had begun in the late 1950s as a somewhat esoteric and highly personalized dispute between Mao and Khrushchev had degenerated by 1963 into a pervasive (and public) name calling over what one of the key Chinese documents in the Sino-Soviet polemics appropriately termed "two diametrically opposed lines" on the issues of war and peace, the proper path to socialist economic development, and the relationship between the communist and capitalist worlds. So construed, there were boundaries to the competition. No matter how rancorous these exchanges, neither party had yet called into question its opposite number's legitimacy as a ruling body. If there was a struggle for predominance within the world communist movement, there was still a presumption of a "socialist camp" whose members' allegiances were worthy of solicitation.

By the mid-1960s, however, various developments in the domestic and external politics of both political systems had greatly widened the scope of the conflict. An increasing number of issues were now raised to the interstate level, including highly sensitive questions of national security. For example, the relatively quiescent Sino-Soviet border issue was by 1964 a matter of public record. Perhaps even more important, the Chinese in 1965 (no doubt at Mao Zedong's personal insistence) chose to reject publicly and pointedly Soviet calls for "united action" in response to growing American military presence in Southeast Asia. Thus Mao had decided to challenge the previously existing "rules of the game" in the Sino-Soviet competition—guidelines which assumed that China and the Soviet Union at least remained uneasy allies, especially in the context of a military threat to a fellow socialist state.[1]

Mao, moreover, deliberately scuttled the opportunity presented by Khrushchev's ouster from power to rectify the grievances of previous years. Emboldened by his indirect role in discrediting Khrushchev within the CPSU leadership, Mao ignored the appeals of the newly installed Soviet leaders to put aside past Sino-Soviet differences. Within weeks of Khru-

1. These issues have been extensively addressed in Richard Wich's study, *Sino-Soviet Crisis Politics: A Study of Political Change and Communication* (Cambridge, Mass.: Harvard Council on East Asian Studies, 1980).

shchev's dismissal from office and following Premier Zhou Enlai's visit to Moscow, a searing editorial in the *People's Daily* declared that Brezhnev and Kosygin were practicing "Khrushchevism without Khrushchev." The former premier's line of "capitulation and treachery" in regard to the United States had not ended with his political passing; indeed, his policies were now considered a structural problem within the Soviet system rather than a function of one man's political idiosyncracies.

Mao's defiance of Soviet overtures, moreover, occurred in the context of increasing threats to Chinese security and at a time when the Chairman had initiated in earnest his efforts to destabilize Chinese internal politics. By implicitly suggesting that revisionism in the Soviet Union and the PRC was a greater threat to the integrity of the Chinese political system than growing U.S. military activity along China's border, Mao had embarked on an audacious course whose consequences are still felt today. Whatever remained of the Sino-Soviet political and military alliance was now being deliberately and openly undermined at the highest levels of the Chinese leadership.

It is not our intention to trace in great detail the process of foreign policy assessment and strategic debate surrounding these events.[2] Undeniably, however, a significant portion of the Chinese Communist Party leadership had concluded that the international situation was on the verge of a far-reaching transformation. While still at an embryonic stage, these changes had the potential to alter fundamentally the direction of world politics, and China's role in the international system. As a major Chinese statement asserted, "A process of great upheaval, great division, and great reorganization is taking place. . . . Drastic divisions and realignments of political forces are taking place on a worldwide scale."[3] The hallmarks of this change (as depicted in PRC writings) were threefold: (1) the increasing fragmentation and dissipation of the power of the West, in particular the passing of unquestioned American predominance ("hegemony") within the "imperialist camp"; (2) the increasing emergence of the Soviet Union as a world power with a greater stake in and affinity for its strategic, political, and military competition with the United States than for its existing

2. For greater detail, see Harry Harding and Melvin Gurtov, *The Purge of Lo Jui-ch'ing: The Politics of Chinese Strategic Planning* (Santa Monica: Rand R-548-PR, 1971); Thomas M. Gottlieb, *Chinese Foreign Policy Factionalism and the Origins of the Strategic Triangle* (Santa Monica: Rand R-1902-NA, 1977); Wich, *Sino-Soviet Crisis Politics*; and Jonathan D. Pollack, *Security, Strategy, and the Logic of Chinese Foreign Policy* (University of California: Institute of East Asian Studies, Policy Studies Monograph, 1981).

3. Editorial Departments of *Renmin Ribao* (*People's Daily*) and *Honggi* (*Red Flag*), *Refutation of the New Leaders of the CPSU on 'United Action'* (Beijing: Foreign Languages Press, 1965), p. 31.

obligations and responsibilities as the leader of the "socialist camp"; and (3) an uneven but unmistakable mobilization of power among the nations subsequently identified as the Third World but then deemed part of what Mao called the "vast intermediate zone" between the imperialist and socialist worlds. The evolution of these trends in the late 1960s did not always accord with Chinese premises or predictions; the degree and duration of U.S. military involvement in Vietnam in particular defied the logic of Chinese strategic assessment. On balance, however, the direction of events (at least as depicted in Chinese writings) tended to confirm these judgments.

To be sure, Chinese leaders were for a time severely divided over these questions. How one depicted the international situation had an immediate relevance to China's foreign policy, military allocations, and the distribution of political power. Thomas Gottlieb, for example, has argued that Defense Minister Lin Biao and others linked to him were far more committed to a "dual adversary" conception of China's relations with the United States and Soviet Union. Lin, Gottlieb further asserts, remained convinced that U.S. military involvement in Vietnam was intended ultimately to threaten and attack China. Zhou Enlai (and presumably Mao Zedong) opposed this view, interpreting U.S. actions in Vietnam as the final, futile gasps of an overcommitted imperialist power in its "deathbed struggle."[4] In Zhou's view, despite American military commitments and deployments throughout East Asia, the U.S. military challenge to China was unmistakably diminishing over time, with a much greater long-term threat to China posed by the growth of Soviet power.

Events in the waning years of the 1960s increasingly confirmed Zhou's judgments. Beginning in late 1965, the USSR slowly began to build up its forces along what had previously been a lightly defended Sino-Soviet border.[5] Soviet calculations in undertaking these actions were no doubt complex. Mao's public airing in 1964 of continuing Chinese grievances on the demarcation of the Sino-Soviet border no doubt constituted one factor. Increasing Chinese xenophobia in the context of the Cultural Revolution further fueled Soviet anxieties. The PRC's rapid breakthroughs in its strategic weapons program were also highly unsettling: Chinese MRBMs were quite possibly directed at Soviet targets. Most significant, however, was that such troop movements reflected an increasing Soviet realization that a long-term Sino-Soviet competition had begun, involving national security as well as issues of history, personality, and ideology. An incremental build-

4. Gottlieb, *Chinese Foreign Policy Factionalism*, sec. 3.
5. Thomas W. Robinson, *The Sino-Soviet Border Dispute: Background, Development, and the March 1969 Clashes* (Santa Monica: Rand RM-6171-PR, 1970), pp. 27–28.

up of forces thus seemed a prudent and necessary step, all the more so as Mao contemptuously defied Soviet overtures in the wake of Khrushchev's ouster, an event the Chairman had undoubtedly welcomed. Equally important, Moscow still hoped to persuade Washington that the world's two leading powers shared a far greater and more serious challenge from a hostile, overpopulated, underdeveloped China than they did from one another.

It is not wholly clear if Soviet decision makers fully appreciated the consequences of injecting an explicitly military dimension into the conflict. Whether intended or inadvertent, however, the militarization of the Sino-Soviet dispute (in conjunction with the events in Czechoslovakia and the Brezhnev Doctrine) altered the Moscow-Beijing relationship at least as profoundly as any of Mao's defiant gestures and actions. Even if one concedes that Soviet planners saw the transfer of troops to the border as a prudent, precautionary, and not unduly provocative step, a comparably benign view of these actions did not necessarily exist in Beijing. For various Chinese leaders, the increasing recognition of a growing, hostile, and superior military force at their northern borders dramatically affected the context and tenor of public debate over strategy and foreign policy.

Much of the residual uncertainty or ambiguity about viewing the USSR as a military threat was removed during the summer and fall of 1968. The Soviet invasion of Czechoslovakia in August and the subsequent articulation of the doctrine of "limited sovereignty" for socialist states raised the very real prospect that China—already wracked by severe internal conflict and still warily assessing U.S. strategy in Vietnam—might also be subject to either intimidation or punitive military attack, perhaps focused on the PRC's incipient nuclear weapons capability. Indeed, in the aftermath of the Czech invasion the USSR was first labeled by Zhou and others as a "social-imperialist state"—that is, socialist in name but imperialist in deeds—capable of initiating a surprise attack against the PRC.[6]

To be sure, for some Chinese leaders, the growth of such a hostile military presence represented an opportunity as much as a problem. Lin Biao's predominance in the CCP hierarchy was given vivid testimony by his designation at the Ninth Party Congress in April 1969 as Mao's constitutionally appointed successor. Furthermore, his followers then possessed enormous strength at the Politburo level and in the ranks of the CCP Central Committee. A threatening external environment in conjunction with a still highly unstable domestic situation strengthened arguments for disproportionate military representation in party councils. Moreover, the existence of yet another threat to China's security provided the Chinese armed forces with a powerful justification for the People's Liberation Army (PLA) to garner an increasing share of the state budget. Notwithstanding the disruptive ef-

6. Wich, *Sino-Soviet Crisis Politics*, pp. 56–60.

fects of the Cultural Revolution on the Chinese economy as a whole (even including the relatively insulated defense industries), Chinese defense expenditure grew very impressively throughout the late 1960s. From the time of Lin's triumph over Chief of Staff Luo Ruiqing in the "strategic debate" of 1965, until his ignominious death in the fall of 1971, China's military budget grew at an average rate of 10 percent per year. Between 1967 and 1971 alone, the growth was more than 60 percent.[7]

Despite such efforts, China's military vulnerability and diplomatic isolation was never greater than in the late 1960s. When significant border clashes occurred in the spring and summer of 1969 at various points along the Sino-Soviet border, the previously unthinkable prospect of full-scale war between the world's two major communist powers became far more real. No matter how one apportions responsibility for initiating these exchanges, the PRC leadership—even those locked in fierce political rivalry with one another—could hardly have viewed the onset of the 1970s with equanimity. The immediate agenda was clear: how was the Soviet threat to be assessed, bilaterally and globally, and what possible opportunities did China have to lessen the trauma and anxiety created by the existence of "new tsars" on China's northern borders?

ASSESSING THE SOVIET CHALLENGE TO CHINA

Although the Soviet Union in the late 1960s began to emerge as the dominant national security problem for Chinese decision makers, it is not enough to assert that an undifferentiated "Soviet threat" compelled the PRC to alter its external policies radically. To begin with, what was the nature of this threat? How severe a challenge did it pose? In what areas was China particularly vulnerable to Soviet pressure? These are all complicated questions, and China's leaders have rarely been able to agree on the answers. Indeed, from the time of Mao's earliest private doubts about the Soviet system and its leaders, discussions of the Soviet issue in relation to Chinese politics and foreign policy grew progressively more complex and diverse.[8] With the passage of time, an increasingly more differentiated view of Soviet institutions and behavior began to emerge, with correspond-

---

7. Central Intelligence Agency, National Foreign Assessment Center, *Chinese Defense Spending, 1965–79*, SR 80-10091, July 1980, pp. 2–3. While estimates on PRC defense expenditure encompass three separate resource categories (investment expenses, operating expenses, and research, development, testing, and evaluation expenses), two-fifths of this overall figure is accounted for by weapons procurement alone, reflecting the new equipment needs created by the growth of the Chinese force structure in the late 1960s.

8. Kenneth Lieberthal, *Mao Tse-tung's Perception of the Soviet Union as Communicated in the Mao Tse-tung Ssu-hsiang Wan Sui! (1969)* (Santa Monica: Rand P-5726, 1976).

ing consequences for defining the dominant issues in the Chinese political process.

The 1970s witnessed significant changes in the number and nature of these concerns. In no sense was the Soviet Union portrayed as a unitary or static challenge. Rather, a composite set of views developed, with various levels of China's leadership more responsive to concerns in some areas than in others. Insofar as Chinese policy debate influenced foreign and security affairs, three major issues predominated in this process: the military dimension, the developmental dimension, and the strategic dimension.[9] Each is defined and discussed separately below, with the period up to the death of Mao providing an appropriate demarcation point.

The Logic of Power. The beginning of an active Soviet military presence along China's northern borders was not the first occasion since 1949 that the PRC had been faced with a hostile and superior armed force directed against China. How and why was a Soviet military threat to China different, especially compared with the long-term American effort to encircle the PRC? In the absence of more revealing or comprehensive official accounts, any reconstruction of the Chinese leadership debate must remain somewhat speculative. But with the knowledge of broader Chinese perspectives on military doctrine and the use of force, as well as Beijing's twenty-year experience in countering U.S. military pressure, certain conclusions can be reached.[10]

For several critical reasons, the Soviet military threat to China was judged qualitatively and quantitatively different and more worrisome than the U.S. political and military presence in East Asia. In numerous respects, America's post-1949 involvement in Asia was more a source of puzzlement and confusion to the PRC than one of outright alarm. Having left the verdict of the Chinese revolution unchallenged in 1949, the Americans reversed course in 1950, choosing to defend the residual Nationalist pres-

---

9. My omission of certain factors (clashes of personality, historical, cultural, and racial factors, etc.) is deliberate. While I do not deny the contribution of such considerations to the evolution of Sino-Soviet tensions, they tend to constitute "constants" rather than variables in the overall equation. Our interest in this essay, therefore, is in identifying those specific policy considerations over which leadership sentiment crystallized, especially insofar as they touched on the realms of foreign and security policy.

10. This discussion draws on studies I have undertaken on Chinese military doctrine and strategic assessment. See, in particular, Jonathan D. Pollack, "China as a Military Power," in Onkar Marwah and Jonathan Pollack, eds., *Military Power and Policy in Asian States* (Boulder, Colo.: Westview Press, 1980), pp. 43–99; *Security, Strategy, and the Logic of Chinese Foreign Policy*; and "The Evolution of Chinese Strategic Thought," in R. J. O'Neill, ed., *New Directions in Strategic Thinking* (London: George Allen and Unwin, 1981).

ence on Taiwan and intervene in Korea. Yet American forces, for all the energy and effort expanded in successive administrations, were committed to a containment rather than rollback strategy. When the United States deployed ground forces—what the Chinese have always correctly viewed as the preeminent, indispensable instrument of invasion and occupation—it was (with the exception of the first year of the Korean War) always along China's periphery, not on the PRC's borders. A major network of U.S. bases was established to ring China, supposedly constraining Beijing from undertaking offensive actions against its noncommunist neighbors, a highly unlikely prospect in view of both the PRC's obvious military limitations and its discernible intentions. Mao in early 1956 described the United States as having "bases everywhere, just like an ox with its tail tied to a post."[11] He therefore argued that in the absence of a clearer political and military purpose, the Americans in time would see the folly of their deployments and return home. The absence of a coherent strategy or design for the U.S. military presence convinced various Chinese strategic analysts that the United States was at best an ineffectual imperial power, dangerous not so much because it deployed military forces abroad, but because U.S. intentions and actions were so unfathomable and unpredictable. Thus Mao and others concluded that, in any extended competition with the United States, Beijing might lose an occasional battle, but could expect ultimately to win the war.

Calculations about Soviet strategy were from the outset far more pessimistic. The quantity, quality, and disposition of Soviet forces deployed against China, while obviously insufficient to subjugate the entire country, were (and are) capable of inflicting great harm, especially against China's industrial heartland. The extensive Soviet familiarity with both the terrain of possible military operations (based on the Manchurian campaign of 1945) and China's force structure and military capabilities was to Moscow's considerable advantage. No matter how distant and attenuated the Eastern Military Districts might be from sources of resupply, over time Soviet logistic capacities could only improve. Unlike the Americans, who relied principally on naval and air assets deployed thousands of miles from home to "contain" China, the Soviets had a distinct geographic advantage. Its soldiers, including a healthy complement of ground forces, were already home, on Soviet soil. Finally, putting aside Mao's almost obsessive suspicions about many of his erstwhile comrades in arms, other Chinese leaders (if not avowedly pro-Soviet) saw a Sino-Soviet military confrontation as an exceptionally worrisome development. The era of polemical exchanges had ceased, and words in any case were cheap. China could no longer run

---

11. Cited in John Gittings, *The World and China, 1922–1972* (New York: Harper and Row, 1974), p. 224.

the risks of gratuitously offending Soviet sensibilities, with the attendant dangers of an attack on Chinese soil.

In a purely military sense, therefore, the escalation of Sino-Soviet tensions and the outbreak of border clashes created a whole new set of issues, constraints, and choices for Chinese planners. How severe was the Soviet military threat to China? Were there upper limits to the number and variety of forces that the USSR might deploy? Could the Soviet threat be ameliorated by political means? And if full-scale war occurred, how did Chinese military commanders intend to fight?

Thus the immediate needs created by the build-up of Soviet forces were threefold: (1) to avoid a larger conflict; (2) to establish the legitimacy of Chinese claims; and (3) to undertake preparatory measures that would convey China's readiness to fight if necessary in defense of its own territory. These objectives were somewhat at cross purposes, given the difficulty of signaling reasonability and a willingness to negotiate while transferring additional forces to the Sino-Soviet border and engaging at times in extremely strident verbal attacks on the USSR, no doubt to strengthen internal resolve.[12] The onset of Sino-Soviet clashes in early 1969, however, imparted an immediacy and urgency to Moscow's supposed territorial designs on the PRC. Even if Chinese statements intermittently still depicted the United States as a greater threat to Chinese and world security, overt military hostilities with the Soviet Union and the rapid build-up of Soviet forces in the early 1970s increasingly commanded the attention of Chinese decision makers.[13] By generally trying to refrain from gratuitously provocative actions with both active and passive defense measures, leaders in the PRC sought to prepare for what only a few years earlier was the remotest of possibilities.

The likelihood and locale of such hostilities were far from certain. Clashes in Xinjiang in the late summer of 1969 and intimations from various quarters that the Soviets might launch a preemptive strike against Chinese nuclear facilities had raised interstate tensions to their highest level since the militarization of the conflict. Yet the Zhou-Kosygin meetings in September and the onset of border negotiations in October suggested a degree of shared interest in defusing hostilities, if not conclusively resolving the issues under dispute.[14]

12. See, for example, the documents in *Down with the New Tsars!* (Beijing: Foreign Languages Press, 1969).

13. Linda D. Dillon, Bruce Burton, and Walter C. Soderlund, "Who Was the Principal Enemy?: Shifts in Official Chinese Perceptions of the Two Superpowers, 1968–1969," *Asian Survey*, 17, no. 5 (May 1977): 456–73; John Garver, "Chinese Foreign Policy in 1970: The Tilt Towards the Soviet Union," *China Quarterly*, no. 82 (June 1980), pp. 214–49.

14. The negotiations are discussed in considerable detail in Kenneth Lieber-

Any evidence of restraint, however, was principally at a verbal level. If the build-up of Soviet forces in the middle and late 1960s had been incremental, Soviet force levels in the early 1970s expanded far more rapidly, surpassing forty divisions by 1973. Although major hostilities did not occur, a much larger and more sophisticated force structure was now being formed, which compelled a Chinese response. Chinese leaders had to await more definitive indications of the probable upper limits on the Soviet force structure, but they also debated the appropriate "mix" of political and military instruments in an overall security equation. While the evidence is not conclusive, it appears that Lin Biao continued to give disproportionate emphasis to the military dimension. The major expansion of Chinese procurement noted earlier (especially in aircraft) continued unabated until Lin's demise in 1971. Indeed a later accusation suggested that Lin's policies had highly deleterious consequences for China's economy as a whole:

> The Lin Biao antiparty clique . . . opposed Chairman Mao's instructions on making still greater efforts to strengthen economic construction in order to strengthen the defense forces. Disregarding the potential of the national economy, it one-sidedly expanded the plan of construction for the national defense industry. As a result, the development of the national economy was impeded and the defense industry was very seriously damaged.[15]

Although one should be wary about *post hoc* accusations, it appears that Lin was far more persuaded than certain other leaders (in particular Mao and Zhou) of the necessity of a highly assertive approach to military strategy.[16] With Lin's death and political disgrace, the impediments to a largely Mao/Zhou-oriented approach to national security were substantially reduced.

In rejecting a more purely military approach, Mao and Zhou recognized that China's vulnerability to Soviet political and military pressure could be reduced by political as well as military means. Indeed, Zhou in May 1973

---

thal, *Sino-Soviet Conflict in the 1970's: Its Evolution and Implications for the Strategic Triangle* (Santa Monica: Rand R-2342-NA, 1978), pp. 8–22; and Harry Gelman, *The Soviet Union and China* (Santa Monica: Rand P-6465, 1980), pp. 13–17.

15. "The Strategic Policy on Strengthening Defense Construction—On Studying Chairman Mao's Dissertation of the Relationship between Economic Construction and Defense Construction," *Guangming Ribao* (*Enlightenment Daily*), January 20, 1977, in *Foreign Broadcast Information Service Daily Report—People's Republic of China* (hereafter *FBIS-PRC*), January 31, 1977, p. E3.

16. A number of these divergent accusations against Lin are presented and discussed in Harry Harding, "The Domestic Politics of China's Global Posture, 1973–78," in Thomas Fingar, ed., *China's Quest for Independence: Policy Evolution in the 1970s* (Boulder, Colo.: Westview Press, 1980), pp. 111–15.

was the first Chinese decision maker to suggest publicly that the possibility of a Soviet suprise attack on the PRC had been deterred.[17] The coincidence of this assertion with an abating growth rate in Soviet troop strength enabled Zhou (echoing Mao) to assert that the Soviet military threat was posed principally to other regions and states. As Zhou suggested in his speech to the Tenth Party Congress in August 1973, China, while "an attractive piece of meat coveted by all," had proven "too tough even to bite," let alone "devour."[18] Moreover, Zhou's views accorded closely with the strategic reassessment then under way (to be discussed in a later section).

Thus Chinese military strategy was one of deterrence, but based on a commitment and readiness to fight, no matter what the disparities in military forces, whether conventional or nuclear. The transfer of front-line Chinese divisions to threatened border areas in the early 1970s indicated that Chinese commanders did not intend to yield key industrial and urban concentrations without significant resistance. By the mid-1970s, about two-thirds of China's infantry divisions had been assigned to the Shenyang and Beijing Military Regions, contiguous to the areas where Soviet forces in East Asia were concentrated.[19] The fact that these units were deployed some distance from the border did not suggest a continuing "people's war" strategy of "luring the enemy in deep" or of trading space for time. Rather their placement conveyed their lack of offensive intentions and capabilities, further revealing the more realistic line of defense that Chinese forces would seek to maintain. No matter what the deficiencies in the mobility, firepower, and other key characteristics of Chinese forces, the PRC's military commanders were clearly prepared to commit large numbers of their best troops to any Sino-Soviet confrontation. Nor was such a "signal" likely to be lost on the Soviet high command.

The Logic of Development. As noted earlier, a pivotal issue in Chinese assessments of the Sino-Soviet relationship concerned the perceived nature of the Soviet challenge. Depending on how leaders depicted a "Soviet threat," a wide range of issues and policies—not to mention the overall allocation of internal political power—would be vitally affected. Thus, for

17. Marquis Childs, "Talking with Chou En-lai," *Washington Post*, May 26, 1973, p. A19.

18. Zhou Enlai, Report to the Tenth National Congress of the Communist Party of China, August 24, 1973, in *The Tenth National Congress of the Communist Party of China Documents* (Beijing: Foreign Languages Press, 1973), pp. 24–25.

19. Statement of Morton I. Abramowitz, deputy assistant secretary of defense, East Asia and Pacific Affairs, April 6, 1976, in *United States–Soviet Union–China: The Great Power Triangle*, Committee on International Relations, House of Representatives (Washington, D.C.: U.S. Government Printing Office, 1976), p. 184.

much of the 1960s, the dominant if not exclusive concern of China's avowedly anti-Soviet leaders (in particular Mao) was the threat that a "revisionist" Soviet leadership posed to the integrity and values of the Chinese revolution. The depiction of Liu Shaoqi as "China's Khrushchev" epitomized these anxieties. Mao's preoccupation with what he saw as the pernicious, inexorable bureaucratization and stratification in the Soviet system fused with his commitment to "self-reliance" in China's economic and political affairs. As a result, policies unduly reminiscent of Soviet approaches to organization, management, and economic development became immediately suspect. Even policies suggesting a preeminent emphasis on industrial growth or scientific, technological, and educational achievement constituted prima facie evidence of illegitimate, revisionist (hence pro-Soviet) leadership tendencies.

If Chinese politics in the late 1960s were characterized by such strident, highly personalized accusations, the quality of political discourse hardly improved in the early and mid-1970s. Any resurrection of China's economic and political system at that time presupposed at least a partial resuscitation of the economic planning apparatus; it also necessitated supplanting political criteria by the goals of economic development and institutional rectification. Adopting such policies did not mean that China's future would be mortgaged to a Soviet-style model of development, or that expanded political, technological, and economic links with the noncommunist world put China's capacity for independent action at risk. But opponents of such efforts could and did attempt to discredit such initiatives by attaching (implicitly or otherwise) a pro-Soviet label to them. By arguing that the Soviet threat remained essentially an ideological one, efforts to redirect the dominant orientation of China's internal and external politics were frequently stymied and on occasion reversed.

Thus a legitimate desire to diminish China's dependence on the outside world was elevated to a virtual fixation by certain leaders, intermittently including Mao himself. By viscerally attacking proponents of policies that would strengthen China's ties with the major powers, China's more dogmatic politicians indirectly but substantially impeded efforts to alter China's foreign policies. One need not accept fully the more extreme attacks by the political left in China—either the surreptitious ones against Zhou Enlai or the subsequent more pointed assaults against Deng Xiaoping—to appreciate the sensitivity of these issues or their centrality to Chinese domestic politics in the 1970s.[20] Later attacks on the Gang of Four have clarified

20. On this issue, see Lieberthal, *Sino-Soviet Conflict in the 1970s*, passim; and Allen S. Whiting, *Chinese Domestic Politics and Foreign Policy in the 1970s* (Ann Arbor: Center for Chinese Studies, Michigan Papers in Chinese Studies, no. 36, 1979), pp. 53–85.

the substantial role it played in the growing paralysis of this period. By labeling various actions intended to modernize China as evidence of either a "slavish devotion to things foreign" or an effort to transfer the supposed ills and evils of the Soviet system to China's economic, political, and institutional landscape, China's more radical leaders assured the PRC's continuing economic and organizational stagnation in relation to a stronger, more developed outside world.

Thus the anticipated consequences of seeking to foster what later became known as a "strong and secure China" to counter Soviet political and military pressure became political issues in their own right. That such changes were anathema to certain elements of the leadership clearly illustrates the complex relation between China's domestic politics and foreign policy. While not among the classic issues of high state policy, they touched on key questions of China's relation to the external world. In a range of policy areas—for example, China's access to and dependence on foreign technology, the extent and terms of foreign trade, and the possible role of foreign capital and expertise in China's industrialization—the Gang of Four was quite clearly prepared to muster its available resources to discredit or otherwise oppose these initiatives. The implications in the context of China's vulnerability to external pressure were clear and considerable. As Minister of Foreign Trade Li Qiang later observed, by "viciously vilifying and hampering our country from trading with second world countries, the 'gang of four' . . . interfere[d] with and undermine[d] the great struggle to oppose the two superpowers . . . particularly Soviet social imperialism."[21] An additional article identifies the Gang of Four's 1976 attacks on the importation of equipment, the export of crude oil, and the purchase of foreign vessels as the third major intervention of the "ultra leftwing foreign policy line" since the Cultural Revolution.[22]

Indeed, recent assertions that Lin Biao and the Gang of Four were "jackals of the same lair" seem in critical respects contrived. The divergence between issues of economic and institutional development and the military considerations discussed in the previous section is quite dramatic. For example, articles produced under the presumed guidance of the Gang of Four attacked the development of a "special war economy" within the Soviet Union and its "calamitous consequences" for the Soviet economy as a

21. Li Qiang, "Distinguish between Right and Wrong in Line and Actively Develop Socialist Foreign Trade," *Hongqi*, no. 10, October 1977, in *FBIS-PRC*, October 20, 1977, p. E4.

22. Zhang Mingyang, "An Analysis of Lin Biao and the 'Gang of Four's' Ultra Leftwing Foreign Policy Line," *Fudan Xuebao (Fudan Journal)*, no. 2, March 1980, in *China Report*, no. 103, pp. 40–51.

whole. Such commentaries were an implicit warning to those organizational interests more inclined to support a greater investment of higher technology for military needs.[23]

Yet the concerns of the political left in China were more visceral than institutional or strategic. Recasting the Sino-Soviet competition into a classic great-power rivalry—thereby stripping the conflict of much of its ideological gloss—severely threatened the left's political and personal prerogatives. Any belief that the Soviet challenge necessitated a fundamental reordering of China's political and economic priorities posed a threat at least as great as that induced by growing Soviet military power. The development of Sino-Soviet relations in the 1970s, therefore, did not respect any neat boundaries between internal and external affairs. Rather, defining the most appropriate means to deal with this threat at home as well as abroad—and for the long as well as the short run—became a pivotal political question in China. It is hardly surprising that conclusive decisions had to await the outcome of the leadership succession struggle of 1976. This conclusion becomes clearer by turning to developments in the realm of Chinese strategic assessment.

The Logic of Strategy. The most profound alterations in the Sino-Soviet conflict in the 1970s concerned the relationship of the rivalry to what the Chinese term "the higher plane of global strategy." A discernible (but highly dynamic) strategic logic pervades Chinese assessments of the international situation as a whole. This topic is far too complicated for an extended discussion in this essay.[24] As noted earlier, however, over the past decade Chinese leaders and strategic analysts alike have assessed and reevaluated the dynamics of world politics in terms of the interplay of three key factors: (1) the retrenchment of American political and military power; (2) the growth and increasing assertiveness of Soviet political and military power and its resultant effects on Soviet-American competition; and (3) the emergence of the Third World as a largely independent political and economic force in the international system. Our focus here is the second issue.

By their own admission, Chinese strategic analysts acknowledge the fre-

23. "Militarization of the Soviet Economy and Its Calamitous Consequences," *Peking Review*, no. 3, January 17, 1975, pp. 8–9. See also Liang Xiao and Cheng Li, "Advance Victoriously Along Chairman Mao's Line in Army Building," *Peking Review*, no. 5, January 31, 1975, especially p. 11. See also Harding, "Domestic Politics."

24. I have considered these questions in greater detail in *Security, Strategy, and the Logic of Chinese Foreign Policy*, and "Chinese Global Strategy and Soviet Power," *Problems of Communism*, 30, no. 1 (January–February 1981): 54–69.

quent and often baffling "twists and turns in the revolutionary process."[25] Any effort to comprehend this strategic logic is further complicated by the frequency with which China's position on various international developments is either unstated or ambiguous. To assert a more vital role for the PRC in international affairs challenges some of the underlying assumptions of its overall strategy. Yet the purported characteristics of the international situation at any given time—for example, the identity of the key actors in world politics, the scope and focus of their political and military ambitions, and the likelihood and locale of the outbreak of war—have direct and immediate implications for Chinese security. And the PRC has made increasing efforts during the 1970s to put together a diverse coalition of states to counter the continued growth of Soviet political and military influence.

At the close of the 1960s, however, Chinese theoretical statements remained predominantly if not exclusively wedded to the notion of "collusion" between the United States and USSR. The world's two major powers were allegedly "working hand in glove" in pursuit of their "common counterrevolutionary interests." The Soviet invasion of Czechoslovakia and alleged Soviet border incursions against China constituted evidence that the Soviets, like the Americans, were an imperialist, aggressive power, neither better nor worse than their erstwhile adversaries. Yet this theoretical logic clashed with actual political and military developments. In relation to PRC security and foreign policy interests, the growth of Soviet political and military power became a progressively more worrisome development for the Chinese leadership than the continuing American military involvement in Southeast Asia. As Thomas Gottlieb has argued, Zhou Enlai and his political allies made a major effort toward the close of the 1960s to undertake an adjustment in China's policy. As events in the early and mid-1970s tended to confirm Zhou's views, official opinion in Beijing increasingly leaned toward an alternative approach to "global strategy."

Inasmuch as a doctrinal compulsion pervades Chinese writings, changes in strategic assessment can be followed in the flow of official documentation. Thus it was not until April 1970 (the centenary of Lenin's birth) that an authoritative PRC statement (a joint editorial in *People's Daily*, *Red Flag*, and *Liberation Army Daily*) took full stock of the portentous changes in Soviet behavior since the ouster of Khrushchev, and placed such changes in the context of the global evolution of Soviet-American relations. Although many antecedents existed for the views expressed in the editorial,

25. Such "twists and turns" are given their most detailed and authoritative presentation in "Chairman Mao's Theory of the Differentiation of Three Worlds Is a Major Contribution to Marxism-Leninism," *Renmin Ribao*, November 1, 1977, in *Peking Review*, no. 45, November 4, 1977, pp. 10–45.

the Soviet Union's emergence as rival and intermittent partner of the United States had never before been so fully or candidly assessed:

> The essence of the Khrushchev-Brezhnev renegade clique's rise to power lies in the transformation of the socialist state created by Lenin and Stalin into a hegemonic social imperialist power. . . .
>
> The Soviet revisionist renegade clique . . . is trying hard to bring a number of these countries [in Asia, Africa, and Latin America] into its sphere of influence in contending with U.S. imperialism for the intermediate zone. . . .
>
> In order to redivide the world, Soviet revisionism and U.S. imperialism are contending and colluding with each other at the same time. . . .
>
> Since Brezhnev came to power, the Soviet revisionist renegade clique has gone farther and farther down the road of militarism. It has taken over Khrushchev's military strategic principle of nuclear blackmail and . . . at the same time redoubled its efforts to expand conventional armaments, comprehensively strengthening its ground, naval, and air forces, and carried out the imperialist "gun-boat policy" throughout the world. . . .
>
> With Soviet revisionist social-imperialism joining the company of world imperialism, the contradictions among the imperialists have become more acute. . . . All countries and people subjected to aggression, control, intervention or bullying by U.S. imperialism and Soviet revisionism are forming the broadest united front.[26]

Having further deemed the Brezhnev Doctrine an "outright doctrine of hegemony," the editorial's authors argued that a reinforcing pattern of Soviet global reach and asserted global interests had begun to develop, with inescapable consequences for the security of China.

Left undetermined in this assessment, however, was the precise balance in degree of threat that the two superpowers posed to the PRC, and the corresponding opportunities and imperatives impinging on China. An authoritative discussion on this issue appeared in *Red Flag* two weeks after Henry Kissinger's secret visit to Beijing in July 1971. According to this evaluation, the competition between the world's two leading imperialist states would provide China with precisely the "breathing space" Beijing so urgently required. Although the article was ostensibly a discussion of CCP strategy in the war of resistance against Japan, the distinctions drawn between "Japanese imperialism which is now committing aggression against China and the imperialist powers which are not doing so now" were only too apparent. The proletariat therefore needed to grasp the opportunities afforded it by the "many contradictions" among the imperialist powers, in

---

26. "Leninism or Social Imperialism?—In Commemoration of the Centenary of the Birth of the Great Lenin," April 21, 1970, in *FBIS–Communist China*, April 22, 1970, pp. A8, 9, 13, 16.

particular the opportunity "to force our principal enemy into a narrow and isolated position." As the article observed without apology, "the tactical principles formulated by Chairman Mao for struggling against the enemy represent a dialectical unity of firm principles and great flexibility." Mao's analysis therefore "still provides good guidance for us to know the present international situation correctly."[27] It hardly required a master dialectician to appreciate and apply these arguments.

Such reasoning characterized the dualistic quality of Chinese security strategy throughout the 1970s. Beijing would seek wherever possible to deflect political and military pressure directed against the PRC, thereby insulating China from the political and military fray. Yet the Chinese would also encourage all efforts to organize a "united front," initially against both the United States and the Soviet Union, but with progressively greater attention to the latter. Zhou Enlai was more closely identified with these early efforts than any other decision maker, though his efforts undoubtedly had Mao's consent and approval. Lin Biao's death and the rapid consolidation of Sino-American relations emboldened Zhou to push forward these efforts in significant ways. As Henry Kissinger has noted, the "American connection" had immediate benefits to China in three specific areas pertaining to the Sino-Soviet competition. It relieved the Chinese of the threat of a two-front war; it compelled the USSR to rethink its calculus with respect to either pressuring or attacking China; and the United States was able to provide the Chinese with the assurance that there would be no joint Soviet-American moves ("collusion") at China's expense—the recurrent nightmare of Chinese strategists.[28] When coupled with the private U.S. pledges to the PRC in November 1971 to provide China with military assistance should Moscow attack Beijing in the context of the Indo-Pakistani war, the "returns" on China's investment in the United States seemed readily apparent.[29]

No attempt will be made in this essay to review the complex course of Sino-American relations between the initial Kissinger-Zhou meetings and the agreement on full diplomatic relations. For our purposes, it is sufficient to note the efforts of the PRC to shore up its own security needs by encouraging others to increase their pressure on the Soviets. This was nowhere more effectively conveyed than by Zhou Enlai at the Tenth Party Congress. Although Zhou still argued that the superpowers "contend as well as col-

27. All these quotations are drawn from "A Powerful Weapon to Unite the People and Defeat the Enemy—A Study of 'On Policy,'" *Hongqi*, no. 9, August 2, 1971, in *Survey of China Mainland Magazines*, no. 711, pp. 1–9.

28. Henry Kissinger, *White House Years* (Boston: Little, Brown, 1979), p. 765.

29. Ibid., pp. 906, 910–11.

lude with each other," competition and antagonism were clearly the dominant characteristics: "Contention is absolute and protracted, whereas collusion is relative and temporary." Not only that, "strategically the key point of their contention is Europe." Any moves toward China were diversionary rather than a serious effort to subjugate China, which, after all, was "too tough even to bite."[30]

Thus the essential logic of PRC policy was to portray China as largely outside the sphere of great-power competition, hence generally immune to pressures and threats from abroad. China did not wish to be exploited to America's advantage in its rivalry with the Soviet Union—pithily described by Mao as "standing on China's shoulders to reach Moscow."[31] But the corollary to such views was a persistent and at times almost strident Chinese effort to attack any suggestions that great-power tensions were decreasing. Soviet-American competition was portrayed as unrelenting and permanent—a reflection of both nations' "hegemonic ambitions," which existed "independent of man's will" and were "bound to lead to world war someday." Conveniently left out of this formulation was the People's Republic. Being neither imperialist in nature nor the "focus of superpower contention," China could stand at the side of various oppressed and threatened nations, but as observer not participant.[32] At least in theory, leaders in Beijing had decided to sit on the mountain and watch the tigers fight.

Zhou had succeeded in fusing his calculations at the diplomatic and strategic level with his objectives in the Sino-Soviet military confrontation. By 1973, Soviet troop deployments appeared to approach their upper limits, although qualitative improvements continued. Earlier in the 1970s, Chinese officials had spoken ominously about the presence of "a million Soviet troops massed on China's borders and threatening China's security." (This, of course, reflected arithmetic license by a factor of two.) Now these "mere million troops" were deemed obviously insufficient to invade and subjugate China. Sino-Soviet war was deterred, if only because no adversary would be so rash or foolish as to repeat Japan's fatal strategic blunder of four decades past. China was buying both time and international breathing space, which (at least theoretically) should have allowed Beijing to turn its attention to the long deferred goals of national economic development, as outlined by Zhou in his address to the National People's Congress in January 1975.[33]

30. Zhou, Political Report, pp. 24–25.
31. Kissinger, *White House Years*, p. 763.
32. See, in particular, Deng Xiaoping's Speech to the Special Session of the U.N. General Assembly, April 10, 1974, in *Peking Review*, Supplement to no. 15, April 12, 1974, pp. 1–5.
33. Zhou Enlai, "Report on the Work of the Government," January 13, 1975, in *Peking Review*, no. 4, January 24, 1975, especially pp. 23–24.

Zhou's inability to consummate these efforts is of course a vast topic in its own right, and will not be explored here. Any attempt to garner support for a comprehensive approach to the Soviet challenge was both complicated and politically risky, since it depended critically on the vicissitudes of both domestic and international politics, the loyalty and support of an aged, fickle, and increasingly senile party chairman, and (by no means least) Zhou's own precarious health. It is apparent, moreover, that the search for an effective Soviet strategy tended to "pull" or "push" leaders in divergent directions. Indeed, in selected areas of strategic assessment—in particular those related to Third World concerns—a predominantly collusionist interpretation of Soviet-American relations was for a time still voiced.

More important, the Chinese assertion of a world of two essentially coequal hegemonic powers was overtaken by events—specifically, the final collapse of South Vietnam. Two weeks after the fall of Saigon a *People's Daily* editorial argued that in the contention for world hegemony, "the later upstarts . . . are leaving no stone unturned in their efforts to replace the U.S. imperialists at a time when the latter are becoming increasingly vulnerable and strategically passive."[34] By strongly implying that the United States was divesting itself of its hegemonic teeth, Chinese analysts had begun yet another revision in their underlying strategic premises. In July a Xinhua correspondent drew analogies between the appeasement of Hitler and similar efforts of "the Brezhnev clique exploit[ing] war fears of certain people and the desire for peace in the West to get its way." Whatever the flaws of the United States, the Soviet Union had become a "far more dangerous" source of a "new world war."[35] As Ren Guping, the most prominent name in the area of Chinese strategic assessment, observed several weeks later, "While one imperialist power has left the scene in defeat, another is taking its place." The Soviet Union had become the "more avaricious" of the two superpowers; in Southeast Asia, Moscow had "jump[ed] at the opportunity of supplanting the United States." The nations of Southeast Asia had to guard against "letting the tiger in through the back door while repulsing the wolf at the front gate. This situation draws the attention of all. . . . Soviet social imperialism . . . poses an even greater danger to the states and peoples in Southeast Asia than decaying U.S. imperialism."[36]

---

34. "Commemorating 30th Anniversary of Victory over German Fascism," *Renmin Ribao*, May 9, 1975, in *Peking Review*, no. 20, May 16, 1975.

35. "The Brezhnev Clique Is Following Hitler's Beaten Track," *Peking Review*, no. 29, July 18, 1975, pp. 4–6.

36. Ren Guping, "Repulse Wolf at the Gate, Guard against Tiger at the Back Door," *Renmin Ribao*, July 29, 1975, in *Peking Review*, no. 32, August 8, 1975, pp. 11–12.

Such assessments no doubt had a certain inexorable logic. The tenor and style of such analysis, of course, became far more fully developed in the context of the events of 1977–78 leading to the normalization of U.S.-Chinese relations. But domestic events in China in the mid-1970s intruded severely on such developments. First Zhou and later Deng Xiaoping had to deal with the persistent obstruction and opposition of the Gang of Four. Jiang Qing and her allies did succeed, albeit temporarily, in blocking Zhou and Deng's efforts to forge a coalition compromising military, economic, strategic, and diplomatic interests.[37] Not until the completion of a major purge and succession crisis did Chinese leaders finally square this largest of circles. We therefore need to turn briefly to those events.

THE LONG ROAD TO THE UNITED FRONT

Mao's death in September 1976 and the abrupt arrest of the Gang of Four only a month later dramatically altered the overall context and direction of Chinese policy making. Foreign and security policy played an important part in these changes. While there have been substantial elements of continuity, major reorientations and new initiatives have also been undertaken. At each of the levels of the Soviet challenge discussed previously, bargains were struck and decisions made, many bearing the unmistakable imprint of Deng Xiaoping. This is not to suggest that events since late 1976 can be viewed exclusively through a "Deng in command" model. But it was Deng far more than anyone else who challenged past policies and encouraged leaders at all levels to "emancipate the mind," as one of his principal political slogans suggested. The less restrained political atmosphere enabled leaders to address previously unmentionable policy questions, with the issues of defense strategy, economic modernization and the acquisition of modern technology from abroad, the likelihood and inevitability of war, and China's overall strategic and diplomatic orientation very much on the agenda. We cannot possibly hope to address all these questions in a few pages. We can, however, indicate how their increasing interconnection provides a political context for evaluating the Sino-Soviet competition not only in the late 1970s but in the next decade as well.

While it is extremely hazardous to identify a single issue as the predominant political question in China, the effort to achieve China's "comprehensive modernization" between now and the year 2000 seems as likely a candidate as any. The relation between the international environment and

---

37. For a more detailed assessment, see Jonathan D. Pollack, "Political Succession and Foreign Policy in China," *Journal of International Affairs*, 32, no. 2 (Fall–Winter 1978): 275–89. For a recent Chinese account, see Zhang Mingyang in *Fudan Xuebao* (see note 22 above).

the consequent imperatives and opportunities for China's internal development has long been a central issue for Chinese leaders.[38] As argued in this essay, the characterization of the international situation has direct relevance for the allocation of political, economic, and institutional resources. For example, if the threat of war involving China is considered modest, agricultural, industrial, and scientific development can proceed less impeded by external threats, with the acquisition of more modern military capabilities deferred to a later date. If armed conflict is deemed possible or even imminent, however, then "preparedness against war" assumes immediate importance, with the tasks of economic construction deferred at least in part to a later date.

As discussed earlier, during the course of the late 1960s and early 1970s, various Chinese leaders intermittently addressed the issue of the likelihood of war and whether and how it might involve China. In the immediate aftermath of the deaths of Zhou and Mao, Soviet intentions toward China again became a question for open debate. For some months, a more urgent quality was apparent in these discussions, with major articles focusing on the threat from the north and the dangers of "surprise attack." These issues had generally been deemphasized since the early 1970s, when Zhou and others had asserted that a Sino-Soviet war was no longer probable and when the Gang of Four severely impeded efforts to accelerate industrial or military modernization. It is difficult to determine whether these altered views reflected a genuine concern that the traumas and uncertainties of the Chinese succession were tempting Moscow to intervene militarily. But the central role of various military leaders in elevating Hua Guofeng to the party chairmanship undoubtedly enabled military officials to address these concerns much more forcefully.

If China could no longer be deemed immune to the possibility of renewed war, then a faster pace was required for defense construction.[39] Various articles written under military aegis were most emphatic in asserting this view. Making effective use of Mao's grandiose statements that "the danger of war was visibly growing" (even though Mao was only speaking of war between major imperialist states, not a war involving China), these spokesmen argued that China was engulfed in a "race against time" to prepare militarily for the outbreak of an "inevitable world war."[40] Others contested

---

38. See, for example, Mao Zedong's April 1956 speech, "On the Ten Major Relationships," in *Peking Review*, no. 1, January 1, 1977, especially pp. 12–14.

39. See, in particular, "The Strategic Policy of Strengthening Defense Construction—On Studying Chairman Mao's Dissertation on the Relationship between Economic Construction and Defense Construction," *Guangming Ribao*, January 20, 1977, in *FBIS-PRC*, January 31, 1977, pp. E1–5.

40. For the most forceful presentation of this argument, see "A Great Call

these views, including some veteran military officials, most notably Zhou's long-time ally, Marshal Ye Jianying. By the summer of 1977 (coincident with Deng's restoration to power) advocates of "development first" had established a predominant position in overall debate, and they have successfully maintained it ever since.[41] Indeed, it was at this time, in Hua Guofeng's political report to the Eleventh Party Congress, that the possibility of delaying the outbreak of the "inevitable world war" was raised for the first time since Zhou Enlai's report to the Tenth Congress: "So long as the people of all countries heighten their vigilance, close their ranks, get prepared and wage unrelenting struggles, they may be able to put off the outbreak of war, or will find themselves in a favorable position when war does break out."[42] Thus, even if, as Hua also contended, the Soviet Union was still "bent on subjugating our country," the appropriate strategy was to emphasize China's long-term scientific, industrial, and technological development, not any sudden—and by implication illusory—"quick fix" to compete with the USSR.[43] In a word, China needed to buy time rather than race against it.

The credibility of this argument rested on China's ability to undertake common—or at least parallel—political efforts with other major states to "oppose Soviet hegemonism" and "frustrate their war schemes." It presupposed an increasingly benign view of the superpower now unambiguously defined as a lesser evil. Hua, quoting Lenin, reminded his colleagues that "the more powerful enemy can be vanquished only by ... making use without fail of every ... 'rift' among the enemies ... and also by taking advantage of every ... opportunity of gaining a mass ally, even though this ally be temporary, vacillating, unstable, unreliable, and conditional."[44] The benefits of forming a quasi alliance with the United States, whose defects in Chinese eyes were glaring and worthy of intermittent public criticism, seemed to outweigh the risks.[45] Irrespective of the likelihood of war,

---

for Accelerating the Revolutionization and Modernization of Our Army," *Jiefangjun Bao* (*Liberation Army Daily*), Editorial, June 5, 1977, in *FBIS-PRC*, June 6, 1977, especially pp. E7–9.

41. For a more extended discussion of these debates, see Jonathan D. Pollack, "China's Changing Polity," paper presented to Workshop on Security and Arms Control in the Pacific, Punalu'u, Hawaii, January 2–7, 1978; and Harding, "Domestic Politics."

42. Hua Guofeng, Political Report to the Eleventh National Congress of the Communist Party of China, August 12, 1977, in *The Eleventh National Congress of the Communist Party of China* (Beijing: Foreign Languages Press, 1977), p. 41.

43. Ibid., pp. 53–54.

44. Ibid., pp. 60–61.

45. For a more detailed discussion, see Jonathan D. Pollack, "The Implica-

the Soviet Union's emergence as a global power coincident with the retrenchment of American power and the militarization of the Sino-Soviet conflict had left China far too weak and vulnerable. Deng and his allies were therefore able to argue that circumstances no longer permitted undue equivocation in pursuing positive, extensive ties with the West. The logic in all three areas—military power, national development, and global strategy—made the case for a "united front" unassailable. There seems little doubt that Deng and those aligned with him genuinely deem their relationship with the United States as one of strategic, long-term significance, rather than one of mere momentary or tactical expedience.

But what of China's long-term relations with the "other superpower"? The future of the Sino-Soviet relationship is of course an extremely complicated question in its own right, so no overall review will be undertaken here.[46] Chinese views and policies seem a good deal more complex and decidedly more ambiguous than is frequently conveyed in the PRC's strategic pronouncements. A division in opinion is apparent in various statements and evaluations. Most depict the Soviet Union as marching inexorably toward global conquest. Other interpretations, however, see the USSR as increasingly beleaguered on various fronts, confronted by insoluble problems in its economy, military deployments and doctrine, and geostrategic position.[47] By this alternative logic, these "fatal flaws" in Soviet strategy and the Soviet inability to "complete their strategic deployments for starting a war" will ultimately compel the CPSU leadership (not unlike the United States a decade ago) to retreat from an overly expansive security role beyond its borders, thereby creating circumstances far more conducive to improved Sino-Soviet relations.[48]

Independent of such considerations however, various long-range Chinese goals could be well served by a diminished urgency to the Sino-Soviet competition. Virtually all PRC assessments pose the threat of Soviet hegemonism as directed principally against states other than China. If the USSR

---

tions of Sino-American Normalization," *International Security*, 3, no. 4 (Spring 1979): 37–57.

46. I have undertaken a preliminary assessment in "Sino-Soviet Relations in Strategic Perspective," in Douglas Stuart and William Tow, eds., *China, the Soviet Union and the West: Strategic and Political Dimensions for the 1980s* (Boulder, Colo.: Westview Press, in press).

47. Compare, for example, Commentator, "The Current Danger of War and the Defense of World Peace," *Hongqi*, no. 11, November 2, 1979, in *FBIS-PRC*, November 27, 1979, pp. A1–7, and idem, "On the Soviet Hegemonists' 'Antihegemonism,'" *Hongqi*, December 2, 1979, in *FBIS-PRC*, December 14, 1979, pp. C1–4.

48. For a more detailed reconstruction of these debates, see Pollack, "Chinese Global Strategy and Soviet Power."

remains preoccupied in a more visible and active way with various areas of instability, China's capacity to pursue its developmental goals in untrammeled fashion will obviously increase. To the extent that Sino-Soviet antagonisms remain bounded, a measure of restraint could well be introduced into the overall competition, to the potential benefit of both powers. Statements from various PRC leaders about China's urgent need for stability and a "long-term peaceful international environment" suggest such concerns. The long-standing rivalry would by no means disappear, but it could be channeled in a way that would enable the PRC to compete more effectively over the longer term.

There is nothing foreordained in this alternative logic, however, any more than ominous Chinese statements about global strategic trends are fixed for the indefinite future. Now as before, time and political opportunity could ultimately prove the decisive factors in the tortuous, complicated evolution of Sino-Soviet relations, both in their dealings with each other and with various other interested parties in Asia and the West.

Soviet Foreign and Security Problems and Policies*

PAUL H. BORSUK

Sino-Soviet relations over the past decade have steadily deteriorated, apparently immune to any moderating impulse. Even before the Soviet in-

* The views expressed in this chapter are solely those of the author. Reference to his employment by the U.S. Central Intelligence Agency is for personal identification only. This material has been reviewed by the CIA to ensure that no classified information has been included. However, such review neither constitutes CIA authentication of this material as factual nor implies CIA endorsement of the author's views.

vasion of Afghanistan the failure of the formal border negotiations, then of the "political talks" in 1979, revealed that the two sides could barely converse, let alone transact major diplomatic business. But can Sino-Soviet relations really be that bad? Also during 1979, Sino-Soviet deterrence withstood a major test during the Sino-Vietnamese war. Perhaps it is true that both sides, despite their seemingly systematic misperceptions of each other, do grasp what is essential to managing their conflict during the 1980s.

This study will argue that a persistent failure on the part of the USSR to identify and acknowledge the interests and constraints that govern the actions of its Chinese adversary may eventually undermine the crucial psychological foundation of mutual deterrence. To be more concise, the subject of this chapter is Soviet antagonism toward China—an antagonism that should be viewed not as a luxury of the emotions or as an excess of cynical propaganda, but as a political fact. Thus, this study will discuss the Soviet image of China that was formed and tested during the 1970s. There can be little doubt that the evolution of that image during the coming decade will greatly affect the prospects for the maintenance and development of a stable deterrent relationship between the Soviet Union and China.

THOUGHTS ON HISTORICAL CONTEXT

At no sacrifice to its usefulness, this essay could easily consist of nothing but historical discussion. Three points, however, stand out. First, Sino-Soviet relations simply lack any coherent tradition. Second, some stipulation of the overall aims of Soviet foreign policy would be helpful to the analysis. Third, the record of the 1950s and 1960s should at least be reviewed before discussing the 1970s and 1980s.

The Absence of Tradition. Though certainly rich and complex, the history of Russian-Chinese relations displays few recurrent patterns or circumstances. Russia and China almost literally stumbled into each other in their earliest contacts, for the most part in territory properly belonging to neither. Well into the twentieth century, their relations were marked by profound ignorance and fear, rampant avarice, deliberate duplicity, intermittent violence, and an inability to identify each other's interests or even to decide whether a regular diplomatic and commercial relationship was necessary at all.

Perhaps more important, even well after 1900 both states were in an advanced condition of decay, unable to demonstrate a sustained ability to repel foreign intrusion either diplomatically or culturally. Both were laboring under heavy burdens of internal weakness and disunity. Both Russia and China, in short, were in need of revolution—and both obtained it, with consequences that shook all of world politics.

Yet their experience of revolution did little to create common ground, or even any widespread grasp of the real issues yet to be resolved between two giant neighbors. Images of Lenin and the October Revolution dominated the world view of a small but vital segment of the Chinese revolutionary intelligentsia, at least for a time, and helped establish the Chinese Communist Party. But these images were little more than fantasies—as were the images that inspired the Comintern stalwarts who overnight became "China hands" in search of the levers of world revolution.[1] The real foundation for Soviet policy toward China had already been laid before 1920, as Moscow hurried to redefine the Karakhan Declaration to suit its more tangible interests.[2]

The historical point most relevant to the contemporary situation might be this: never has a strong, internally united China been required to face a strong, internally united Russia. The challenge facing the USSR and China today is to define a new relationship that reflects the facts of international and domestic life. There is simply no precedent of routine dealings, even as rivals, to build on.

The Central Aims of Soviet foreign policy. The construction of a stable relationship with a strong China is not the only urgent task facing Soviet policy makers in foreign affairs. In broader terms, the absence of clear and acknowledged basic objectives for Soviet foreign policy cannot be sustained much longer in a world of constricting choices.

This essay, of course, will not try to resolve here and now the often intense debate about the basic character of Soviet or Russian foreign policy; in any case, the argument over the "present danger" pertains much more to policy made in Washington than in Moscow. My wish is only to contend that Soviet foreign policy since the failure of the German revolution in the early 1920s has alternately flailed, probed, and stood perfectly still, without any internal agreement on what positive goals this foreign policy was intended to achieve. In short, the birth shock of Soviet foreign policy lasted well into the 1950s. By the start of the 1970s, however, Soviet policy was making discernible progress toward at least tentative resolution of Moscow's ambivalence. The struggle for survival was over, at least in the physical sense. Moscow's realization of this was brought out in the debate preceding the emergence of the USSR's proclaimed "peace policy"—dubbed in the West, perhaps unwisely, "détente"—around the time of the Twenty-fourth Congress of the CPSU in early 1971.

1. For the most comprehensive Soviet treatment of the leading figures in the field of China studies during the 1920s, see V. N. Nikiforov, *Sovetskie istoriki o Kitae* (Moscow: "Nauka," 1972).

2. See Allen S. Whiting, *Soviet Policies in China, 1917–1924* (Stanford: Stanford University Press, 1968), chapter 2. For the most recent Soviet interpretation of the Karakhan Declaration and its contemporary significance, see M. S. Kapitsa, "Vazhnyi dokument iz istorii sovetsko-kitaiskikh otnoshenii," *Problemy Dal'nego Vostoka*, no. 2, 1979, pp. 141–46.

What is—or was—this "peace policy"? Its aims might be sketched as acknowledged military and diplomatic parity with the United States in the presence of expanded economic exchanges, even greater exchanges with an energy-hungry Western Europe and perhaps Japan, leading to the advent of a favorably evolving yet stable status quo both at home and abroad. This bid for cheap security was perhaps unrealizable for many reasons, but to judge by the quality of foreign affairs analysis coming out of Moscow during the period, it was at least intellectually superior to the conceptual vacuum that had underlain Soviet conduct abroad up to that time. One of the prime factors undermining this attempt to establish a coherent and productive foreign policy for the USSR was Washington's willingness to pursue active diplomatic cooperation with China. By the start of the 1980s, a succession of diplomatic options that Moscow seemingly envisioned for use against the spectre of Sino-American entente has been exhausted without apparent result.

Where will this now lead Soviet foreign policy? I would suggest that a certain nostalgia, perhaps unconscious, for the seeming certainty of purpose that guided late nineteenth-century Russian diplomacy within a universally acknowledged international system is likely to be seen in Soviet actions over the next few years. In practical terms, this would entail avoidance of any intense direct relationship with the United States, cultivation of the (Moscow-perceived) balance in Europe, and willingness to act assertively in adjoining parts of Asia—all sustained by a growing sense of Russian national legitimism about the supposed prerogatives of a "great power." The key uncertainty burdening such a neoclassical policy would clearly be the unresolved conflict with China, a problem without precedent in the supposed golden age.

The Record of Sino-Soviet Relations, 1950–70. What is the record of two decades of purported intimacy—ten years of supposedly intimate cooperation succeeded by another ten of intimate conflict—between Moscow and Beijing? What impact have the events of those years had on the development of Sino-Soviet relations in the 1970s? In retrospect, the answer might well be that surprisingly little of note was established during the 1950s and 1960s. The issues that first appeared to unite, then to divide the USSR and China have by now either been pulled inside out or have vanished completely. The USSR might perhaps be granted some indulgence for real outrage over China's settling in with the United States after years of Beijing's excoriation of Khrushchev's "psalm singing" about coexistence.

It may well be that both parties to the misalliance of the 1950s now understand that the breakdown in cooperation under Khrushchev came over one central issue—whether or not China should remain permanently subordinate to the Soviet Union. In presuming that such was the natural state of things, Khrushchev in retrospect appears either grossly naïve or grossly cynical, perhaps both. Yet in view of the policies on East-West nuclear relations that Mao professed to honor at the time, it is hard to imagine that, aside from a few points of tact, Moscow's response to the Chinese challenge could have been different.

During the 1960s, this particular issue was resolved—China could not voluntarily subordinate itself to Soviet authority on any issue at all. Had world events stood still while the USSR absorbed this fact, real diplomacy between the communist giants might have come about. Already, however, the war in Vietnam was introducing the new geopolitical conflict over which of the two states would be the principal actor in East Asia.

Even in the confusion unleashed by the Cultural Revolution, it was clear by the end of the 1960s that the security needs of either state would be met only if the other altered its basic policies and, in essence, its entire self-identification. An advanced stage of direct competition began with the border confrontation of 1969, yet the diplomatic interlude that followed never ceased posing the question of superior versus subordinate. Which of the two would find it impossible to avoid making the first concrete concession which, no matter how slight, would signal the other's victory? It hardly needs to be pointed out that China's strong sense that the USSR would only exploit its advantages of strength constituted a vital element in the transformation of U.S.-Chinese relations.

THE SOVIET IMAGE OF CHINA

The Soviet image of China that formed during the mid-1970s was a startling conceptual mix of the bizarre and the conventional. From 1966 on, Soviet propaganda on China was nourished on a rich diet of outrages and absurdities linked with the Cultural Revolution. Through simple reportage, the anti-Soviet excesses and purported claims on behalf of the power of Mao Zedong Thought spoke for themselves to the Soviet public at large, as well as to various Soviet elites. Introduction of the vague concept of a "military-bureaucratic dictatorship" in China—inherently temporary and wracked by contradiction—lent a semblance of theoretical grounding of public Soviet discourse on the tumultuous developments in Beijing.[3]

3. The concept of a Chinese "military-bureaucratic dictatorship" was first introduced over the authoritative signature of "I. Aleksandrov" at the height of the Cultural Revolution. See "Vopreki interesam kitaiskogo naroda," *Pravda*, August 16, 1967. See also the three-part series of unsigned articles in *Kommunist* in early 1968: "Korni nyneshnikh sobytii v Kitae," no. 6, pp. 102–13; "O kharaktere 'kul'turnoi revoliutsii' v Kitae," no. 7, pp. 103–14; and "O politicheskom kurse Mao Tsze-duna na mezhdunarodnoi arene," no. 8, pp. 95–108. The

Clearly, however, this approach could not answer Soviet questions about what to expect next in China. From the early 1970s on, such developments as the end of large-scale public disorder in China, the rise of acute tension on the Sino-Soviet border, and the advent of improved Sino-American relations challenged Soviet analysts to reassure their multiple audiences that Moscow adequately grasped the past, present, and likely future of the confrontation with China.

Soviet Sinologists apparently approached this problem with a mixture of confidence and anxiety. From the mid-1960s, they had been given a clear mandate by the party leadership to renovate and expand their own profession, to identify the key questions both solved and unsolved, and in general to resume the lively debates that have surfaced from time to time in Soviet writings on China, particularly in the late 1920s.

The convening of the extraordinary national conference of Soviet specialists on China in Moscow at the end of November 1971 was a major milestone in this effort to grapple with urgent and sensitive questions.[4] Even before Mao's death in 1976, it was becoming evident that the effort had not been fruitless, at least in the eyes of Soviet leaders. A tentative but well-defined assessment of probable Chinese domestic and foreign policies in the years ahead was emerging, best conveyed in an elaborate unsigned essay on China that appeared in the authoritative Communist Party journal *Kommunist* in the late summer of 1975.[5]

According to this article, the main motif of Chinese domestic politics was now becoming stability rather than ever-increasing disorder. Earlier assertions about the pivotal role of Mao himself and the flourishing of improvised political organizations such as the Red Guard gave way to emphasis on the interplay of institutional interests among the professional military, the enduring administrative organs of the state, and the remaining elements of a modernizing elite. In short, Soviet analysis at this juncture held out the prospect that not only could an institutional oligarchy arise to supplant the Cultural Revolution even before Mao's demise, but such a development might be self-stabilizing for an indefinite period. In light of this argument about the new focus of Chinese politics, the status and prospect of every

---

essays in *Kommunist* were preceded by V. G. Gel'bras, "K voprosu o stanovlenii voenno-biurokraticheskoi diktatury v Kitae," *Narody Azii i Afriki*, no. 1, 1968, pp. 21–34.

4. Proceedings of the conference were published in an edition of one thousand copies through the Institute of the Far East. See *Problemy sovetskogo kitaevedeniia: Sbornik dokladov Vsesoiuznoi nauchnoi konferentsii kitaevedov, sostoiavsheisia v noiabre 1971 goda* (Moscow: Akademiia nauk SSSR, Institut Dal'nego Vostoka, 1973).

5. "Maoistskii rezhim na novom etape," *Kommunist*, no. 12, 1975, pp. 103–23.

previously noted organization and social force could be charted by Soviet observers. The Chinese Communist Party, for example, was deemed inoperative as a Marxist-Leninist body, with the earlier perceived struggle between "internationalist" and "Maoist" tendencies at an unhappy end. The entity now calling itself the party was deemed simply another tool at the disposal of the emergent oligarchy, just as the still-living Mao and the cult surrounding his personality had become similar tools. Though conflict was continuous within the new ruling stratum, it involved only the choice of means toward an already given end. References to "healthy internationalist forces" at work at the lower levels of the Chinese system persisted, but involved few specific claims, let alone forecasts of favorable events.

Another main feature of the Soviet image of China that emerged in the mid-1970s was the coming reformation and resurgence of the Chinese industrial economy. It is easy to underestimate the seriousness with which Soviet analysts and commentators approach the overall question of where and under what conditions real industrial growth can take place. This is especially so when the country under study is portrayed (credibly enough) as a backward, exploited, massively overpopulated nation which, after a decade of supposedly close cooperation with the USSR, was barely prepared to introduce elemental socialist practices in basic economic sectors.[6] On top of this, Soviet analysts of the 1970s customarily looked back on Chinese economic life since the end of the 1950s, again credibly enough, as a succession of gross irrationalities, sweeping catastrophes, and negative overall growth.

How much more significant it is then that Soviet analysis of China looking beyond the 1970s should hold out the prospect that not only might the whole endeavor survive these shocks, but it might in fact display real growth.[7] To justify this analysis, Soviet observers increasingly cited the existence of a remarkable two-tiered economy in China, apparently without historical precedent. Floating atop a still backward, awesomely labor-intensive agricultural sector—itself organized nationwide into a vast cellular network of "self-sufficient" local production units—was said to be a burgeoning sector of modern industry. This modern industrial sector, Soviet Sinologists argued, was optimized solely around the creation of expanded

---

6. For examples of Soviet analysis of the political setting of Chinese industrialization, see V. I. Vanin, *Gosudarstvennyi kapitalizm v KNR* (Moscow: "Nauka," 1974); *Problemy i protivorechiia industrial'nogo razvitiia KNR* (Moscow: "Mysl,'" 1974); and especially the reports on economic subjects to the 1971 China studies conference in Moscow, in *Problemy sovetskogo kitaevedeniia*, pp. 185–240.

7. "Maoistskii rezhim na novom etape" (see note 5 above).

military capabilities that in turn required vast amounts of capital, as well as technology available only from abroad. Chinese leaders—here again apparently acting in oligarchic concert—had allegedly fostered this dual economy in order to realize their platform of traditional national expansion and collective historical vengeance. Their main domestic strategy toward this end involved systematic extraction of a social surplus from the vast rural economy.[8] This coercive developmental approach was to be maintained through a combination of outright repression and a steady flow of hysterical antiforeign, antisocialist propaganda.

Accompanying this was a tendentious historical argument too elaborate to summarize easily. Suffice it to say that this Soviet critique of Chinese development emphasized the supposed perpetuation of just about every imaginable negative feature to be found in China both before and after 1911. With a few words of regret over the birth defects of the Chinese Communist Party, this argument linked such phenomena as the Confucian world view, the legalist tradition in Chinese public life, the experience of foreign subjugation in the nineteenth century, the existence of ancient tribute relationships with the nations bordering China, and the negative impact of "petit bourgeois" Western philosophies such as social Darwinism on the nascent Chinese revolutionary movement.[9] Perhaps to echo Soviet reckonings of the 1920s, a major role is ascribed to the "Kuomintang Right" as a potent historical embodiment of these negative features.[10] In this analytic milieu, the political biography of Mao Zedong merges relatively smoothly with the history of Chinese social and economic development from the early 1920s, defining a downward trend relieved only by the brief interval of Sino-Soviet cooperation after 1949.[11]

8. See E. A. Konovalov and M. M. Nikol'skii, "Sotsial'no-ekonomicheskie problemy sovremennogo Kitaia," *Problemy Dal'nego Vostoka*, no. 4, 1974, pp. 39–52.

9. See V. F. Feoktistov, "Ob etapakh ideologicheskoi evoliutsii maoizma," *Problemy Dal'nego Vostoka*, no. 4, 1974, pp. 85–94.

10. On this point, see V. N. Nikiforov, "Nereshennye problemy noveishi istorii Kitaia," in *Problemy sovetskogo kitaevedeniia*, pp. 121–22. See also L. A. Bereznyi, "O bor'be demokraticheskikh i antinarodnikh tendentsii v kitaiskoi revoliutsii, 1925–27 gg.," *Sed'maia nauchnaia konferentsiia "Obshchestvo i gosudarstvo v Kitae,"* vol. 2 (Moscow: "Nauka," 1976), pp. 344–51.

11. No full-scale biography of Mao has yet been published in the USSR, nor is one likely to appear pending completion of a comprehensive history of the Chinese Communist Party, a work supposedly under preparation for more than a decade. Various aspects of Mao's political career have been treated separately in journal articles, with frequent references to Western works by such scholars as Stuart Schram and Benjamin Schwartz. A pamphlet entitled *Mao Tsze-dun: Stranitsy politicheskoi biografii* has been widely circulated in the Soviet Union

The key component of this ostensibly unified image is quite clearly psychological. It appears as though such "scholarly" reinterpretations of events and phenomena not previously linked were fostered primarily to bolster and legitimize Moscow's political judgments about the causes and possible consequences of the collapse of Sino-Soviet relations during the 1960s. The migration of such analyses into authoritative political writings during the mid-1970s may well mark the point at which Soviet leaders reached a consensus that an authentic Chinese threat to the USSR was likely to endure and worsen in the coming years, regardless of such approaching milestones as Mao's death.

Surely it must strike some observers that a Soviet perception of a threat from China is preposterous, however severe Moscow's historical sense of insecurity may be. The concluding portion of this essay will attempt to show that preposterous or not, this perception could profoundly affect future Soviet conduct. Here it might be noted only that Soviet arguments that Maoism had reached a "new stage" in 1975 broke new ground in the following ways: these arguments identified Indochina clearly as the main focus of intended Chinese expansionism; they invoked the powerful metaphor of Munich, accusing the West of appeasement toward China now as toward Nazi Germany in the late 1930s; and they clearly signaled that Maoism—a term that increasingly was synonymous with assertive Chinese nationalism in any of its varieties—was to be regarded as the main threat to world peace confronting every other country "regardless of social system."[12]

The most striking, perhaps most volatile aspect of the Soviet image of China is one that is never stated outright: the Chinese (or if preferred, the Maoists) are quite simply the Nazis of our era. The elements of a full-blown argument that China has been transformed into a fascist state are all present, yet remain unassembled. These elements include assertions that the political consciousness of the entire Chinese populace has been altered through terror and mass brainwashing, that social ownership of the means of production has degenerated into a bizarre, antipopular form of state ownership, and even broad hints that internal demographic pressure dictates that China must acquire arable land and "living space" outside its borders. The closest public brush with this argument came in the final 1975 issue of *Problemy Dal'nego Vostoka*. There an unsigned editorial devoted

---

but is of little analytic value; one or both of its pseudonymous authors "Vladimirov" and "Riazantsev" apparently served as Soviet advisers in China during the Yenan period.

12. See "Maoistskii rezhim na novom etape" (note 5 above), as well as "Novyi etap evoliutsii maoizma," *Problemy Dal'nego Vostoka*, no. 4, 1975, pp. 184–89.

to the themes taken up in *Kommunist* several months earlier declared: "China's further development can be either toward a return to scientific socialism—if healthy elements within Chinese society can organize the working class and the conscious strata of the peasantry in the struggle against Maoist distortions—or toward the establishment of a militaristic dictatorship of a fascist or semifascist type."[13]

The process by which such a judgment, here expressed in one prominent but isolated instance, would come to suffuse the entirety of Soviet conduct toward China would no doubt be lengthy and complex. The existence in the USSR of a growing cadre of professional Sinologists who must at least intermittently put facts ahead of prejudice is only one of many factors that might inhibit a retreat into gross misperception. But any conjecture about Soviet thinking on China must leave vast room for assimilated biases and working simplifications, especially if attention is primarily to be devoted to key political rather than academic figures. Adversary perception in general remains a little-explored political and psychological phenomenon, always open to the effects of stress and frustration.

SOVIET DIPLOMACY IN THE FAR EAST: PATIENCE OR PARALYSIS?

Soviet policy toward China during the latter half of the 1970s appears to have failed. Soviet leaders might not share that assessment, of course. They can point to success in forming an anti-Chinese alliance with Vietnam, as well as to an apparently uninterrupted military build-up by Soviet forces in the Far East. They may deem the outcome of the Sino-Vietnamese conflict of 1979 as proof that Soviet policy is successfully "containing" China. The Soviet move into Afghanistan, though its ultimate success is yet to be demonstrated, might also be justified by Moscow as turning back the Chinese threat.

But if the aim of Soviet policy has been to exert influence over Chinese actions—or to strike major diplomatic bargains with key third parties, such as the United States, that would effectively isolate China and discredit Beijing's anti-Soviet appeal—then it is difficult to see how the last five years of the 1970s can be called successful for the USSR.

The full story of Moscow's attempts to establish a working dialogue with Beijing is likely to remain unknown. At its most public level, however, it resembles a succession of dogged yet perhaps never sincere efforts to involve Beijing in protracted talks over vague "principles of relations" while awaiting China's capitulation on the concrete political issues.

The logic of a Soviet bid to China following Mao's passing and especially following the ouster of the Gang of Four is clear enough, even still assuming

13. "O nekotorykh aktual'nykh voprosakh marksistskogo kitaevedeniia," *Problemy Dal'nego Vostoka*, no. 4, 1975, p. 11.

that the earlier analysis of Maoism's "new stage" was a genuine reflection of minimal Soviet expectations of the post-Mao era.[14] Surely Moscow had little to lose by its February 1978 proposal that Sino-Soviet talks be convened at the highest level, with the nominal aim of formulating merely a joint statement of basic principles of relations that might concede that the two states actually have "differing social systems."

Yet the Soviets may well have been jarred by the vehemence of the Chinese public rejection of this bid, delivered personally by Hua Guofeng from the rostrum of the National People's Congress. Not only did the Chinese side reiterate its claim that the USSR reneged on Kosygin's supposed promises to Zhou Enlai in September 1969, but Beijing now insisted that Soviet forces withdraw from Mongolia. The public Soviet rejoinder was swift and harsh. Another possible reflection of this diplomatic short circuit was the long train ride taken by President Brezhnev, accompanied by Defense Minister Ustinov, through Siberia in the early spring.

The remainder of 1978 was full of major diplomatic events, adding up to a Chinese tour de force at Soviet expense. Hua Guofeng's trip through Moscow's East European front yard was perhaps only symbolic, but irritating all the same. The conclusion of the Sino-Japanese friendship treaty, on the other hand, did lasting damage to Soviet policy in the Far East; Soviet allegations that the green light for the treaty came from the United States following Zbigniew Brzezinski's visit to Beijing in May 1978 were loud and probably sincere.

The most significant development of the year, however, was the final normalization of U.S.-China relations—well in advance of successful conclusion (not to say ratification) of a SALT II pact between Moscow and Washington. This, too, the Soviets credit to Dr. Brzezinski's productive travels.

Leaving aside U.S.-Soviet relations for a moment, a prime illustration of Moscow's failure to acquire leverage over China through diplomatic victories with key third parties is Soviet-Japanese relations during the late 1970s.[15] During the first half of the decade, the belief had grown that Japan

14. On Sino-Soviet relations after 1976, see "Kitai posle Mao Tsze-duna," in *Kommunist*, no. 12, 1977, pp. 110–21; and "Kitai posle Mao Tsze-duna," *Problemy Dal'nego Vostoka*, no. 4, 1977, pp. 45–72. The same period is most usefully analyzed from a Western scholarly perspective by Harry Gelman, "Outlook for Sino-Soviet Relations," *Problems of Communism*, 28, no. 5–6 (September–December 1979): 50–66; and by Steven I. Levine, "Some Thoughts on Sino-Soviet Relations in the 1980s," *International Journal* (Canadian Institute of International Affairs), 34, no. 4 (Autumn 1979): 649–67.

15. On Soviet-Japanese relations, see Rodger Swearingen, *The Soviet Union and Postwar Japan: Escalating Challenge and Response* (Stanford: Hoover Institution Press, 1978). Added perspectives are provided by William H. Mac-

and the USSR would soon score major achievements in diplomatic as well as economic cooperation; when the Soviets endorsed a reference to "unsolved questions" remaining from the Second World War in the communiqué that marked Prime Minister Tanaka's visit to Moscow in 1973, it surely seemed that Moscow had decided on a forward diplomatic strategy on such issues as joint development of Siberian resources as well as the Soviet-Japanese territorial dispute.[16]

But the anticipated elevation of Soviet-Japanese ties never came, for reasons that go to the heart of Soviet policy in East Asia and worldwide. The failure of Foreign Minister Gromyko's visit to Tokyo at the start of 1976 apparently closed the chapter opened in 1973, though it took several years for the prospect of large-scale cooperation to recede.[17]

Why did the USSR recoil from the needed initiative toward Japan? Some individual threads can be unraveled: the precedent that a territorial reversion would set, the greatly altered domestic economic policies that might be required to sustain heavy Japanese investment, perhaps just the unseemliness of the petitioner's role. At a more fundamental level, however, we encounter Moscow's refusal to signal by its actions that its basic security policies can be altered by circumstance—or worse, actively manipulated. Soviet concerns must indeed have been deep-seated; at the time, relations with the United States seemed well on their way toward long-term regulation, perhaps putting a lasting ceiling on U.S. resort to the "China card," and perhaps even on any pursuit of expanded U.S.-Japanese military cooperation against an evaporating Soviet threat.

The remarkable ruin of Soviet-American relations during the last half of the 1970s is too broad a topic to be discussed fully here; besides, the tale is hardly complete. By now, in an atmosphere of rising tension with the United States, Moscow has seemingly abandoned the task of offering a painstaking

---

Kenzie, "Japan-USSR Negotiations on Safe Fishing and the Reversion of Disputed Islands in the North Pacific," *Marine Affairs Journal* (University of Rhode Island), no. 5, January 1978, pp. 1–31; Chae-jin Lee, "The Making of the Sino-Japanese Peace and Friendship Treaty," *Pacific Affairs*, 52, no. 1 (Spring 1979): 64–77. Though it averts the current period, the most interesting Soviet treatment of relations with Japan is found in an anthology published by the Institute of the Far East, *SSSR-Iaponiia: K 50-letiiu ustanovleniia sovetsko-iaponskikh diplomaticheskikh otnoshenii (1925–1975)* (Moscow: Akademiia nauk SSSR, Institut Dal'nego Vostoka, 1978).

16. See Swearingen, *The Soviet Union and Postwar Japan*, pp. 121–42, 152–55, 196.

17. The failure of Gromyko's visit was immediately visible; see the account in the *New York Times*, January 13, 1976. The first public warning by the USSR to Japan not to sell military technology to China came shortly afterward; see the commentary by A. Arov in *Pravda*, February 21, 1976.

public analysis of each new step forward in U.S.-China relations, as was the custom early in the decade.[18] Soviet leaders may simply feel that too much has happened too fast in establishing a real security link between Washington and Beijing to be assimilated into one article in *Kommunist*, or even into one essay by a reliable "commentator."

The fact that the United States—under the administration of a president ostensibly loyal to the aims of improved relations with Moscow and expanded arms control agreements—had now endorsed the military modernization of China through deed as well as word must surely have perplexed Soviet analysts. Some Soviet observers are even ready to suggest that China is well on the way to reintegration into the world capitalist system.[19]

For Soviet leaders not to regard this trend as evidence of a massive diplomatic failure on their part, they must surely be convinced of the cynical malevolence of an entire spectrum of Chinese political figures. But this assessment on Moscow's part might not be too far off the mark: in Soviet eyes, Beijing's apparent resolve to keep anti-Sovietism as the anchor of its post-Mao foreign policy is only the clearest of many illustrations that Moscow has in this case inherited the worst of both worlds. Looking to the 1980s, the USSR confronts an oligarchy in Beijing that displays a unity of anti-Soviet purpose that would flatter the Gang of Four, yet shows precious little of the radicals' apparent desire to run China's economy and society into the ground—a tendency on which the Soviets may have been counting heavily. Perhaps it is little wonder that Soviet Sinologists look to the Kuomintang Right or the nineteenth-century "self-strengthening" imperial reformers in China in search of relevant parallels.

In sum, at the start of the 1980s, the USSR seemingly has fewer options against the emerging entente among its prime adversaries in East Asia than it did during the mid-1970s. Perhaps Soviet policy makers are already learning to regard a working security relationship between Washington and Bei-

---

18. For fairly recent examples of efforts by Soviet analysts to pin down the status and prospects for U.S.-Chinese relations, see I. A. Alekseev, "SShA–Kitai: Raschety, manevry, problemy," in *SShA: Ekonomika, Politika, Ideologiia*, no. 2, 1978, pp. 26–39; V. P. Lukin, "Vashington-Pekin: 'Kvazisoiuzniki'?" in *SShA*, no. 12, 1979, pp. 50–55; and A. B. Parkanskii and A. A. Nagornyi, "Aktivizatsiia amerikano-kitaiskikh ekonomicheskikh sviazei," in *SShA*, no. 12, 1979, pp. 65–70. The last two articles, appearing in the same issue of the journal of the Institute of the United States of America and Canada, nonetheless present markedly differing viewpoints on whether the main initiative for ongoing improvement in U.S.-Chinese relations lies in Washington or Beijing.

19. See, for example, Parkanskii and Nagornyi, "Aktivizatsiia," and D. A. Smirnov, "Maoistskaia kontseptsiia 'novoi demokratii'—pravorevizionistskaia versiia 'natsional'nogo' sotsializma," *Problemy Dal'nego Vostoka*, no. 4, 1979, pp. 92–105.

jing as a simple reality, to be parried, channeled, subverted, or confronted on tactical issues. In geopolitical terms, however, this would be an awkward challenge even if our mythical "Soviet policy maker" were habitually calm and detached. If the actual psychological underpinnings of Soviet policy are closer to those sketched above, then the burden of stress under which Moscow will labor in the years to come could be severe indeed.

Obviously this is not inevitable. Real Soviet successes such as the recruitment of Vietnam or the seeming evaporation of major arms deals between China and various West European states should not be overlooked, nor should Moscow's continuing ability to make the most of its opponents' problems be underestimated. In short, we might well stop to ask whether Soviet policy toward China is in such a fix after all. Perhaps Moscow's approach to its China-related security problems should be characterized not as paralyzed but as rightly patient.

The optimism that Moscow continually professes might indeed be justified. China's desire to "modernize" every aspect of its national life while persisting in confrontation with the USSR may be unattainable; the "neo-Maoist" program could be crushed by the country's sheer backwardness, its bureaucratic fear of uncontrolled change, and its inability to risk a major war. On the other hand, the United States—even under a new president—might consciously adopt renewed efforts to set U.S.-Soviet relations on a new and stable footing, with every other international question coming afterward. Or the United States might, for whatever internal reason, become a lesser participant in the politics of conflict in Asia over the next decade—hardly a key security partner for China.

According to another "optimistic" scenario, Soviet leaders would find surprisingly little difficulty in leaving East and Southeast Asia to the Chinese under the proper circumstances. After all, it is nowhere chiseled in stone that the Soviet Union must not only be an Asian power but the primary such power. With a new appreciation of their domestic needs as well as of the complexities of international involvement, Soviet leaders might conceivably offer concessions to China unheard of today—perhaps even a willingness to acknowledge dominant Chinese interests in Southeast Asia.

Such conjecture, though thought provoking and therefore necessary, still seems thoroughly improbable. Beneath the veneer of intermittent diplomacy and unending propaganda about China's internal miseries and internecine conflicts, Soviet policy makers still perceive no means of influencing Chinese behavior. In 1980, with the symbolic watershed of Mao's passing well in the past and Brezhnev's prospective demise unlikely to matter much, the USSR's policy toward China indeed seems paralyzed. Moscow's threats lack credibility, or at least immediacy; its blandishments about the future benefits of renewed relations are even less believed. In either case, the Soviet Union has no leverage over a hostile China. But China, through its enduring malevolence toward the USSR, together with its advance toward domestic economic "great expectations," projects a growing ability to command Soviet attention.

THE UNCERTAIN STATE OF SINO-SOVIET DETERRENCE

Deterrence between rival states is not a static condition. It is instead a process of mutual influence between reckoning adversaries. Expressed as a constantly evolving set of inhibitions, confidences, and enduring ambitions, the concept of mutual deterrence for all practical purposes defines the "rules of the game" in any protracted conflict between states, including nuclear-armed states.[20]

It is not yet clear to analysts why relationships of deterrence endure or fail. In the nuclear era, successful deterrence is not yet an established phenomenon, let alone a recurrent one. Indeed, one of the main reasons the Sino-Soviet conflict should be of interest in this regard is that the nuclear interaction to be scrutinized does not directly involve the United States. Useful analysis of the maintenance or failure of deterrence between the USSR and China might yield insights on the deterrence process that are free of the conceptual burden of critical self-regard.

Yet there is some difficulty even in establishing that the problem of Sino-Soviet deterrence exists. War between the USSR and China is widely regarded as simply too implausible a prospect. It presumably follows that the participants themselves grasp this folly as well, and will govern their actions accordingly despite their belligerent rhetoric.

It seems doubtful to me that a U.S.-Soviet apocalypse is the only one worth contemplating. In order to overlook the real hostility that now prevails between Moscow and Beijing, it is necessary to argue that politics as usual between states with centuries of foreign experience will not be practiced in this instance. If only the simplest assumptions about the real utility of military strength are introduced—assumptions that are routinely assimilated into discussions of U.S.-Soviet rivalry—it becomes difficult to argue persuasively that a clash of interests over issues of common concern in Indochina, Korea, or Japan could not lead to direct confrontation between the USSR and China.

The key concept here is not violence but crisis. Only the advent of an actual crisis, involving mutual contemplation of the possibility of war, can

20. A multitude of studies on the maintenance or failure of deterrence could be cited here, but three come to mind at once: Alexander L. George and Richard Smoke, *Deterrence in American Foreign Policy: Theory and Practice* (New York: Columbia University Press, 1974); John Steinbruner, "Beyond Rational Deterrence: The Struggle for New Conceptions," *World Politics*, 28, no. 2 (January 1976): 223–45; Robert Jervis, "Deterrence Theory Revisited," *World Politics*, 31, no. 2 (January 1979): 289–324.

ever test definitively the real intentions of the antagonists. Such a crisis takes on a life of its own, as the two sides realize that immense values may be at stake over a single outcome. In such a political and psychological environment, all previous oaths against war or surrender will surely be reviewed.

This is not to say that such a crisis is inevitable between the USSR and China. The choices to be made by the leaders of both states over the next decade may indeed bring about further perpetuation of the state of "no war, no peace" that gives Sino-Soviet relations their present appearance of equilibrium. The question to be considered here is whether there exists a condition of accurate mutual perception—perhaps better referred to as "analytic empathy"—that can provide the psychological foundation for stable expectations of mutual, self-imposed restraint. Though perhaps awkwardly phrased, this refers to the process by which any two competitors who will never in fact be subject to a common authority begin acting on their own volition to regulate their conflict.

I would argue here that Sino-Soviet deterrence, while it may have been successfully tested over Indochina during 1979, rests at the start of the 1980s on a very fragile psychological foundation, especially with reference to Soviet perceptions of China. My sense is not that war will break out one fine day, or even that it will come about as a prepared response to an anticipated contingency. My preoccupation is with the effects of crisis-induced stress in the Soviet Union in light of the preexisting, possibly quite defective image of the Chinese adversary that seems to me to have been fully assimilated by a significant segment of the Soviet political elite.

What are some of the effects of crisis-induced stress? Summarized much too briefly, these can include such collective as well as individual reactions as increased frustration, increased misperception of received information, increased intolerance of ambiguity, increased propensity to take risks, altered bargaining behavior, and marked decay in the performance of routine tasks.[21] Such manifestations of stress in a crisis may lead to decisions that essentially represent the "repetition of prior responses regarded as successful and to a reduction in alternatives perceived as available to self and allies," while the enemy enjoys complete freedom of action.[22]

Without going further along this avenue, it is clear that a vital concern for the maintenance of Sino-Soviet deterrence is not that war itself be averted but that advent of crisis be avoided. Once a direct confrontation between the USSR and China has opened the psychological chamber in

21. See Raymond Tanter, "Crisis Management: A Critical Review of Academic Literature," in *Jerusalem Journal of International Relations*, 1, no. 1 (Fall 1975): 71–101.
22. Ibid., p. 95.

which these signs of stress are usually secluded, the restoration of the previous atmosphere can become the most difficult task of all; the resort to violence, sustained by the conviction that what choices remain are to be made by others, becomes correspondingly "logical."

It may be important here to emphasize some of the qualities that might significantly condition Soviet or Chinese actions in crisis. Neither shares with the United States a willingness to make competing versions of the opponent's motives and capabilities routinely available, to the extent that such alternative views become a standard feature of communications within the political elite. Whatever their differences, the Soviet Union and China are both closed systems, in which such speculation is not even a typical political ritual, let alone a public process of real cognition. Exchanges of signals between the USSR and China do occur, but not via multiple, unrestricted channels. An extremely thin and uninsulated wire apparently carries all political messages between these two closed systems, each of whose ability to handle adverse information under stress is yet to be proved.

The Sino-Soviet conflict is not only genuine but rooted deeply in geographic, political, and cultural bedrock. This conflict is likely to become more intense during the coming decade, even as both antagonists desire to avoid the large-scale violence that neither can afford. If the psychological ground is not too barren, then Sino-Soviet deterrence can become a working system of mutual influence, eventually enabling the two sides to compete for status in Asia without feeling compelled to take immense risks.

But I would contend that the ground is indeed barren. The Soviet Union has little grasp of Chinese motives and interests, at least insofar as these can be separated from possible Soviet losses. So long as "zero sum" axioms apply in Moscow, it can be argued that brittle Sino-Soviet deterrence will have difficulty surviving many more tests that do not somehow bring about new learning. Sino-Soviet warfare may be far from inevitable, but Sino-Soviet crisis—the only test of reality vivid enough to compel the adversaries to make real decisions—may be truly difficult to avoid.

Rather than the Soviet image of China, the focus of this paper might better have been the USSR's image of itself. The key variable in the foregoing analysis might well be the self-regard of Soviet leaders. During the 1980s, it seems all the more likely that the self-perceived legitimacy of Soviet actions will be vital to sustaining the momentum of specific policies. For the USSR today faces massive internal challenges. The solution of the problems facing a constricting economy and society will require both great changes and great continuity. To preserve its claim to full authority, the Communist Party may choose to place massive reliance on the mobilizing power of values such as national solidarity and willingness to sacrifice for goals such as security against the external threat, however defined.

Yet it may prove difficult to employ these values internally without markedly affecting foreign policy. Carried too far, this approach can have a serious impact on both Soviet-Chinese and Soviet-American relations, leading the Soviets to merge their consideration of the two problems. Should this come about, Soviet leaders will have failed a crucial test of their ability to conduct a poised, responsible foreign policy in a world of multiple power centers rather than "two camps." Such a failure might be costly indeed—to many nations as well as the Soviet Union.

Economic Problems and Policies

The Economic Background and Implications for China

DWIGHT PERKINS

Economics was never at the heart of the Sino-Soviet dispute, even if economics was the lever sometimes used by one side, mainly the USSR, to influence the other. Politics has been in command among the leadership of both countries. Yet underlying economic trends in the two countries have had an important role in determining the resources available to the two sides that could be used to implement policies connected with the dispute.

In analyzing the economics of relations between two nations the usual pattern is to concentrate on trade and capital flow. The issues then are whether the terms of trade are turning for or against one country or the other, and whether there are clear trends in the commodity composition of that trade. These subjects in the case of Sino-Soviet economic relations were of real interest in the 1950s when those relations were close and China's development program was dependent in important ways on the Soviet Union. But such issues were of little interest in the 1970s when Sino-Soviet trade had slowed to a trickle, and, for reasons that will become apparent, are not likely to be of great interest in the 1980s either.

The important economic element in Sino-Soviet relations is how underlying trends in the economic development of the two countries affect the capacity of those countries to influence each other through methods other than direct trade relations. First of all, there is the question of the relation between economic development and military power. Hostile relations between two countries can be of major concern to more than just the parties involved if both sides can bring enormous power to bear, or such relations can be of little interest if neither party can do much to translate hostility into action. If great powers did not stand behind the participants, for example, there would be little interest beyond the Ogaden desert in whether Ethiopia or Somalia was winning the war there. A war over the deserts of Xinjiang, on the other hand, would be a very different matter.

Second, even if direct trade relations between two countries are insignificant and likely to remain so, developing trade between one or both countries with other nations may give the country whose trade is growing greater influence with those trading partners and thus indirectly affect the nation with which it has a dispute. Japan has considerable influence throughout Southeast Asia not because of military power or a history of friendly relations, but because the nations of the area depend on Japanese markets for their raw materials and because Japan is an important source of technology and consumer goods. The Soviet Union's influence in the region, in contrast, is limited to what power it can bring to bear through its Pacific fleet or through its close ties with the Vietnamese army.

In the discussion that follows, questions of Sino-Soviet trade in the 1970s and into the 1980s will be the initial focus. In the latter part of the essay we shall return to the issue of the relation between economic development and military power. That discussion will look beyond the 1980s, because the full implications of what is happening in the 1980s will be clearer in this longer term perspective.

SINO-SOVIET TRADE

The history of Sino-Soviet trade relations is so well known that only a brief summary is needed here. When the victory of the Chinese Communist Party in the Chinese revolution was followed a year later by Chinese entry into the Korean War, the United States imposed an embargo on all trade with China and America's allies and most of the rest of the noncommunist world followed suit. China undoubtedly would have developed closer economic ties with the Soviet Union in any case, because the Soviet Union was seen not only by China but by India and many other nations as a successful model for pulling a nation out of poverty and dependency on the industrial capitalist nations. The embargo reinforced this move with a vengeance, however, and China became dependent on the Soviet Union and its East European allies for three-quarters of its trade.

Given that China's development program had as its core the rapid growth of heavy industry, the Soviet Union had what China needed. The USSR, having concentrated on the production of steel and machinery for two decades, had developed a considerable capacity to build plants to produce these products and to help others do so. It was not important if the plants were not particularly sophisticated, because China, in the early stages of developing its heavy industry, needed quantity more than quality. If costs were not necessarily competitive with the West, that was not important either, because China had no Western supplier.

TABLE 1
Sino-Soviet Trade
(in million U.S. dollars)

Year	China's Trade with All Communist Countries (including the USSR)			China's Trade with the USSR		
	Exports	Imports	Balance	Exports	Imports	Balance
1950	210	140	70	190	135	55
1955	950	1,300	−350	645	1,055	−410
1960	1,335	1,285	50	850	815	35
1965	650	515	135	225	191	34
1970	480	380	100	20	25	−5
1975	1,380	1,010	370	150	129	21
1979	1,685	1,914	−229	166	190	−24

SOURCES: CIA, *China: A Statistical Compendium*, July 1979, p. 13, *China: International Trade Quarterly Review, Fourth Quarter, 1979*, May 1980, and various other CIA reports; Feng-hwa Mah, *The Foreign Trade of Mainland China* (Chicago and New York: Aldine-Atherton, 1971), pp. 197–98; and A. H. Usack and R. E. Batsavage, "The International Trade of the People's Republic of China," in Joint Economic Committee, Congress of the United States, *People's Republic of China: An Economic Assessment* (Washington, D.C.: U.S. Government Printing Office, 1972), pp. 345–47. The Soviet trade data and the trade data for the communist countries were taken from separate sources, and the methodologies used to estimate these two sets of figures are not entirely comparable. The figures, therefore, should be used as rough estimates of the Soviet contribution to total communist country trade with China.

TABLE 2
Soviet Trade as a Share of Total Chinese Foreign Trade
(in million U.S. Dollars)

Year	Total Trade with All Countries, Communist and Others (exports plus imports)	Trade with the USSR (exports plus imports)	Percentage
1950	1,210	325	26.9
1955	3,035	1,700	56.0
1960	3,990	1,665	41.7
1965	3,880	416	10.7
1970	4,340	45	1.0
1975	14,575	279	1.9
1979	28,245	356	1.3

SOURCES: See Table 1.

The figures on Chinese trade with the Soviet Union are presented in Tables 1 and 2. The totals rose in real terms throughout the 1950s right up to the break in 1960. China's balance of trade with the USSR turned negative for a time in the early and mid-1950s, but then came back into balance in the late 1950s, when the Soviet Union stopped granting China further long-term credits well before there was any consideration of a break. The USSR extended China credits totaling 5.3 billion rubles, or about U.S. $1.3 billion, but roughly a quarter of this sum appears to have been used to pay off the Soviet Union for its shares in joint stock companies located in China.[1] The net transfer of real resources from the USSR to China came to only U.S. $1 billion, or less than 5 percent of China's foreign exchange earnings in the 1950–60 period. Furthermore, this net resource flow came to an end not in 1960 but in 1955.

The main value to China of Sino-Soviet economic relations came not from aid but from trade. Throughout the 1950s Chinese imports from the USSR were dominated by machinery and equipment used in the core enterprises of China's drive to build a base in heavy industry. In 1957, for example, of all Chinese imports from the Soviet Union 49.9 percent were machinery and equipment (38.4 percent were complete plants) and another 16.6 percent was Soviet petroleum, because China at that time had negligible amounts of its own petroleum.

The other contribution of the Soviet Union to China's development program was technical assistance. Over ten thousand Soviet specialists spent protracted periods in China helping to set up not only steel and machinery plants but the planning and management systems to run these enterprises, scientific research institutes, and much else.[2]

The Chinese side of the polemics that followed the break in 1960 might lead one to conclude that what the Soviet Union provided to China was small in amount and overpriced. In a sense both charges have an element of truth,[3] but it is also true that China could not possibly have pursued an industrialization drive centered on steel and machinery in the absence of this trade and technical assistance. The other side of the coin, of course, is that the Chinese paid in full for what they received.

1. Alexander Eckstein, *Communist China's Economic Growth and Foreign Trade* (New York: McGraw Hill, 1966), p. 157.

2. For different perspectives on Soviet technical assistance, see M. Gardner Clark, *Development of China's Steel Industry and Soviet Technical Aid* (Ithaca: New York State School of Industrial and Labor Relations, Cornell University, 1973), and Mikhail Antonovich Klochko, *Soviet Scientist in Red China*, trans. Andrew MacAndrew (New York: Praeger, 1964).

3. See Feng-hwa Mah's study of the prices the Chinese paid for Soviet goods, *The Foreign Trade of Mainland China* (Chicago and New York: Aldine-Atherton, 1971).

The reason for this brief recitation of history is to underline how different the situation is today (1980). The question for the future then is whether Sino-Soviet economic relations in the 1980s and beyond will or could be more like those of the 1950s, or whether the pattern prevailing in the 1970s will continue. Put differently, the issue is whether there is any incentive for close economic ties between China and the USSR or whether renewed closeness in relations would have to depend on something other than economics.

Data on Chinese and Soviet trade patterns in the late 1970s are presented in Table 3. Chinese imports should be compared with Soviet exports and vice versa, because the issue is whether the trading patterns of the two countries are complementary or competitive. If they are complementary, there is at least some basis for speaking of the possibility of renewed trade relations on a scale considerably greater than the current trickle of goods between the two countries. Even with complementary patterns, it still may make more sense for China and the Soviet Union to turn elsewhere for goods available from the other country. In China's case, for example, the same items might be available by shorter transport from Japan. If the patterns are competitive, however, there is no basis for substantial trade unless the pattern can be expected to change.

A glance at Table 3 suggests that the trade patterns of China and the Soviet Union in the late 1970s were more competitive than complementary. The Soviet Union's single largest export, for example, is petroleum, and China is also an exporter of petroleum and hopes to become a larger exporter if enough oil is found offshore. If the Soviet Union develops the full potential of its Siberian petroleum and gas resources, China and the USSR will be competitors in a very direct way in the Japanese market. But Japan's large domestic energy requirements suggest that the country can easily absorb as much petroleum as both China and the Soviet Union will ever supply and still have plenty of excess demand to be supplied by the Middle East. The point here is that there is no potential now or in the 1980s for either China or the Soviet Union to export petroleum to the other.

One of the major items in the import bill of both countries is foodstuffs in general and grain in particular. The Soviet Union, with a half-century history of agricultural difficulties, has increasingly turned abroad for supplies to improve the standard of food consumption of its people. China attempted to do without grain imports in the 1950s after having been a net importer in previous decades. In the 1960s, however, China once again became a net importer and by the late 1970s was averaging 10 million tons of wheat and corn purchases abroad each year. There is little prospect that China will become an exporter of grain in the 1980s or later. China's land endowment, or more accurately its land with adequate supplies of water, is comparable to that of Korea and Japan, and both Korea and Japan have

TABLE 3
Chinese and Soviet Trade Patterns in the Late 1970s
(in million U.S. dollars)

Item	Chinese Imports (1977)	Chinese Exports (1977)
Manufactures	3,555	3,415
Machinery and equipment	1,200	—
Iron and steel	1,570	110
Nonferrous metals	265	65
Textile yarn and fabric	175	1,300
Clothing	—	560
Crude materials, fuels, edible oils	1,445	2,045
Rubber	225	—
Textile fibers	55	290
Petroleum	—	1,015
Chemicals	885	380
Fertilizer	345	—
Foodstuffs	1,115	2,025
Grain	745	455
Other	100	95
Total	7,100	7,955

	Soviet Exports (1978)	Soviet Imports (1978)
Machinery and equipment	10,277	21,354
Base metals and manufactures	2,987	3,414
Ferrous metals	2,987	3,400
Nonferrous metals	—	14
Textile raw materials and semimanufactures	1,313	1,025
Cotton fiber	1,229	93
Wool fiber	—	420
Fuels, lubricants, related materials	18,695	—
Petroleum	14,776	—
Ores and concentrates	887	—
Chemicals	1,284	2,188
Wood and wood products	2,339	747
Consumer goods	2,288	14,692
Foodstuffs	1,149	8,794
Other	12,362	7,378
Total	52,432	50,798

SOURCE: CIA, *Handbook of Economic Statistics, 1979* (ER 79-10274, August 1979), pp. 100, 101, 103, 104.

The Economic Background and Implications for China 97

increasingly turned abroad to feed their people. China had very good harvests in 1978 and 1979, and the growth rate of the Chinese population has begun to fall, thus reducing one source of increased food demand. As incomes in China begin to rise under the new wage and incentive policies, however, demand for food will also rise, and China's communes will be hard pressed to keep up with demand. China can sell tea to the Russians, and the Russians no doubt can find a few of their food items to export to China, but the quantities involved will not be large.

One can quickly pass through many of the other items traded by the two countries. Neither country is a major rubber producer and both countries tend to be rich in nonferrous metals, but not always the same ones, so there may be a small trade potential there. The Soviet Union exports steel and China is a major importer, but it is not likely that the Chinese will want to import much steel thousands of miles by rail from the mills of European Russia when they have some of the world's most efficient steel mills almost next door in Japan. The Soviet Union does export cotton, and China imports large quantities and is following the lead of other Asian nations in promoting textile exports. A more detailed analysis of these items, therefore, would reveal some trade potential, but not enough to have more than a marginal influence on the totals.

What about machinery and equipment? As indicated above, items within this broad category made up much of China's imports from the Soviet Union in the 1950s. The Soviet Union still exports over U.S. $10 billion worth of machinery and equipment to nations other than China. Could the pattern of the 1950s be recreated? There are at least two reasons for thinking such a result would be unlikely. First, Chinese machinery and equipment imports are no longer centered on the kinds of items in which the Soviet Union is strong in the sense that it has substantial surpluses for export. In recent years China's complete-plant imports have concentrated on such sectors as petrochemicals, in which the USSR is also weak. The Chinese also import vehicles (trucks and mining and construction equipment), but only another Western embargo could force China back to Soviet suppliers for these items.

Needless to say, there would be even fewer items in the machinery and equipment category that China could export to the Soviet Union. The Chinese industrial system as late as the 1970s could still be seen as patterned on that of Russia, and there would be little reason for the Soviet Union to begin buying back items that it already has in surplus.

This item-by-item look at the trading patterns of the two countries, therefore, suggests that the Soviet Union will not soon rival Japan or even the United States and West Germany as major Chinese trading partners. This conclusion does not mean that trade will fail to increase in the 1980s and beyond. It is easy to imagine trade in real terms doubling or tripling if political relations between China and the Soviet Union improve over the next few years. What is for all practical purposes impossible to imagine is trade with the USSR rising again to nearly half of China's total trade. In fact, it is difficult to imagine Soviet trade rising much above 5 percent of China's foreign trade any time soon. As a share of Soviet trade, the percentage would be even lower, although the day may come when the size of China's foreign trade passes that of the USSR, for reasons that will be discussed below. A figure of 5 percent is not trivial. With dozens of industrial countries in the world it is unusual for any one country to dominate the trade of another, even when that one country is the United States or Japan. Still, a figure of 2 or 3 percent or even 5 percent of a nation's foreign trade is not likely to be large enough to influence China's political leadership to alter its overall attitude toward the Soviet Union unless there were other good reasons to do so. For now and for the foreseeable future China and the Soviet Union could establish a total embargo on their mutual trade without any serious danger of that embargo having much effect on either's development programs.

TRADE WITH THE REST OF THE WORLD

Before going on to the relation between economic development and military power, it is useful to take a brief look at China and the Soviet Union's trading relations with other nations. The question is whether developing trade relations with these other countries could materially affect direct Sino-Soviet relations.

If this were a study of history, the subject raised here would not be of great interest. Both Soviet and Chinese foreign trade have been minuscule fractions of total world trade over the past three decades (3.7 percent and 0.9 percent respectively in 1973, for example). Only in the case of Eastern Europe has Soviet trade been important enough to be a major factor in the economic development of the region. It is the Soviet army, however, that is the real source of Russia's influence in Eastern Europe and a major factor in the development of close trading relations. Thus it is not worth spending much time on how the Soviet Union's economic influence in Eastern Europe affects its relations, or on East European relations with China. Most of the rest of Soviet trade is with Western Europe and only $12.3 billion was with less developed noncommunist countries in 1978, or 12 percent of total Soviet trade.

Chinese trade has also been a minor element in the trade bills of most of China's trading partners. China's largest trading partner by far is Japan, with whom exports plus imports in 1979 reached U.S. 6.47 billion, or 23 percent of all Chinese foreign trade. As a share of Japanese trade, however, this figure constituted less than 4 percent of total trade. China's next largest trading partners in 1979 were Hong Kong (U.S. $3.36 billion, or 12 percent of total Chinese trade), the United States (U.S. $2.32 billion, or 8 percent), and West Germany (U.S. $1.96 billion, or 7 percent). But Chinese purchases abroad have been a major element in the world markets for a few commodities. China, like the Soviet Union, has played a significant role in the world grain market. And China is also an important purchaser of chemical fertilizer and steel. Still, when one talks of the way China has used foreign trade to achieve other foreign policy goals, it is more often the myth of the China market rather than the reality that is the source of Chinese influence. For centuries foreign businessmen and governments have been lured by the prospects of 400 million and then 600 million and now 970 million customers. The fact that expectations have seldom been realized has little to do with hopes for the future.

If the patterns of the past were to be continued, this discussion could end here, but in the late 1970s China's leadership made a fundamental break with the nation's autarchic past, and the implications of that break need to be explored. The issue is, if policies instituted after 1976 continue for a decade or two into the future, could China become another Japan in international markets, the Japan of 1960 or 1970, needless to say, not the Japan of 1980 or 1990? China, after all, has taken a conscious look at the export-led growth performance of its East Asian neighbors, and some planners at least have liked what they saw. China's new joint venture laws, the decision to increase imports of cotton so that exports of textiles can be expanded, and increasingly close ties with Hong Kong businessmen all reflect a concerted effort by China to accelerate export growth. Restoration of China's membership in the World Bank and the International Monetary Fund is further evidence of a fundamental change in policy.

If China by these measures did become a major trading nation in a decade or two, countries around the world would have to take notice of China as a potential trading partner or competitor. China's influence on world developments could be based on something other than a large army and nuclear missiles. China, like Japan in the 1970s, could force its way into the highest economic councils of Western Europe and North America, because those countries could not afford to keep China out. Less developed nations could turn to China as an alternative supplier of needed machinery and equipment. In short, China could become a major player in the construction of the international economic order of the 1990s and beyond. The contrast with a Soviet Union that continued to pursue autarchic policies within the Comecon bloc is stark. The Russians could make propaganda about a new international economic order, but only Soviet military power would give the Russians any say in how that new order was constructed. And military power is a very crude instrument for such purposes.

Simply to state these propositions, however, is to make clear that fundamental changes in the international economic positions of China and the USSR of this magnitude are not going to occur in the 1980s. Chinese foreign trade by the end of the 1980s might well catch up in total size with that of the Soviet Union, but will be nowhere near the totals of Japan of the 1970s, let alone the Japan of 1990.

Still, if China's outward-looking policies continue throughout the 1980s, leaders of the industrial nations will increasingly have to pay attention to Chinese developments. Japan, for example, might buy large amounts of oil and gas from Siberia, but Japanese industrialists and planners with an eye to the future will be more concerned with building bridges to China than with the Soviet Union. Economic trends, therefore, could reinforce Japan's preference on other grounds for building close ties with China rather than the Soviet Union.

Much of the political rhetoric of the past decade or two has argued that only by reducing dependence on foreign trade and investment can a less developed nation achieve true independence and sustained economic development. The Soviet Union's systematic pursuit of autarchic growth, however, demonstrates that achieving independence in this way also means that one opts out of any meaningful influence on how the rest of the world orders its economic relations. For nearly three decades China also opted out in this way, and it remains to be seen how long the current policies will last. Certainly this outward turn is the most vulnerable to change of all the policies instituted since 1976. The Gang of Four may be gone, but there are numerous skeptics within the current leadership when it comes to the value of having hundreds of thousands of tourists and building joint ventures with foreign capitalists. If China does hold to this course, however, the long-term effects will be profound.

GROWTH OF THE NATIONAL ECONOMIES

The size of a country's foreign trade is determined by many elements, of which the attitude of the government toward foreign involvement is only one—and often not the most important one. In general, trade grows along with a rise in a nation's gross national product (GNP). National product growth determines not only trade, of course, but also the ability of a nation to raise the standard of living of its people and its ability to fund a large military establishment.

One way to understand how Sino-Soviet relations are evolving, therefore, is to compare Chinese and Soviet economic growth over the past decade or two and attempt to forecast that relative performance into the 1980s. Forecasts of this sort cannot tell one much about what to expect in Soviet and Chinese intentions toward each other, but such forecasts tell a great deal about the capacity of each side to act on those intentions. Having the capacity does not mean that a country will use it, but the absence of a capacity to act, whether through military or other means, will certainly preclude taking action to carry out a nation's goals.

Analysis of comparative GNP performance is of direct relevance to an understanding of Sino-Soviet relations, most of all because military power is closely related to economic growth, although, as will be pointed out in the next section, economic and military power are not one and the same. It is worth a digression into what has been happening to the growth of the domestic economy of each country, therefore, and what is likely to happen over the next decade.

Western estimates of past growth of the Soviet GNP come up with a rate that is a little above 5 per cent for both the 1960s and 1970s. Because population growth has averaged only 0.9 percent a year in recent years, per capita GNP grew at over 4 percent a year, a fairly high rate in international comparative terms. Different estimates give slightly different results, but Soviet GNP at 1978 market prices passed the U.S. $1,000 billion market in either the middle or late 1970s, and per capita GNP was over U.S. $3,000. In aggregate terms the USSR, by the late 1970s, had the largest GNP in Europe, a GNP only slightly smaller than that of France and West Germany combined. In per capita terms, however, Russia was at a level comparable to that of Spain, or only about 40 percent of the level of West Germany.

Still, if the USSR were able to maintain a 4 plus percentage rate of growth year in and year out into the future, the gap between Soviet per capita incomes and those of Western Europe would continue to close, and the gap in the absolute size of GNP between the USSR and any single European nation would continue to widen. At 5 percent a year, a nation's economy doubles in fourteen years, which means that Soviet GNP by the mid-1990s would be well above U.S. $2,000 billion in 1978 prices.

But the Soviet economy by the mid-1970s had begun to run into difficulties. Growth after the early years of the decade was closer to 3 than 5 percent a year. It is the job for someone with long experience in analyzing the Soviet economy to explain why this slowdown has been occurring. Here it will simply be pointed out that most explanations of this slowdown involve fundamental long-term problems with the Soviet economic system, not short-term cyclical factors that could be expected to disappear soon. If the Soviet slowdown has to do with the inefficiencies of highly centralized planning and control of the economy and with the closed nature of the economy, then this slowdown is likely to be around for a long time. In the short run the effects of a slowdown from 5 to 3 percent per year will not be dramatic, but by the year 2000 the difference would be between a GNP of U.S. $3,000 billion and U.S. 2,000 billion. If growth falls even farther, the difference, of course would be even greater.

What makes this subject of particular interest at this time is that the growth rate of the Chinese GNP accelerated during the latter half of the 1970s, and there is reason to believe that this accelerated growth will continue through the 1980s.

There is still some debate over estimates of China's economic growth rate in the 1960s and 1970s. The Chinese recently published a figure of 337 billion yuan for national income (net material product) for 1979 in 1979 prices, and the 1976 figure in 1976 prices is 243.5 billion yuan. The only reliable earlier figures we have are for the 1950s, ending in 1957. Even in current prices the average annual growth rate of national income between 1957 and 1976 was 4.9 percent. Since there was some rise in prices—albeit an extremely modest one—over this period, mainly in the early 1960s, it is likely that the growth of national income in real terms was more like 4.5 percent or even lower. Since 1976 the growth rate in real terms has averaged 9.0 percent.

Western economists, in estimating China's GNP growth over the 1960s and 1970s before the Chinese published their own estimates, have typically come up with growth rates of around 5 percent for the 1957–76 period. Given the difficulties of estimating Chinese GNP from inadequate data, this 5 percent figure can be seen as confirming that China's recently published estimates are broadly consistent with the series for gross value of industrial output, grain output, and other similar data that were used to construct the Western estimates. There are, of course, differences between the Chinese concept of national income, or net material product, and the Western GNP concept, but it is unlikely that these differences account for much if any of the differences in growth rate estimates.

Thus if one compares Chinese and Soviet growth rates in the 1960s and 1970s, the Soviet Union appears to have grown marginally faster than China. In per capita terms the gap would be even wider, because China's population growth rate at 2 percent per annum was double that of the USSR. But one cannot make meaningful precise comparisons of this sort. The price structures of China and the USSR are quite different, and price structure has a major influence on estimates of growth rates. Still, while index number problems of various kinds exist, the conclusion that Soviet GNP in the 1960s and 1970s grew at least as fast as that of China is not likely to be changed by more systematic comparisons, using the prices of one country to measure the GNP of both.

Comparing the levels of Chinese and Soviet GNP and GNP per capita in comparable U.S. dollars is more difficult than comparing growth rates. Major efforts have been made to convert Soviet GNP into U.S. dollars, but efforts to convert Chinese GNP have been very crude. Official exchange-rate conversions of Chinese estimates of national income in 1979 of U.S.

$224 billion would convert to a GNP figure per capita of perhaps U.S. $270, but there are reasons to believe that the Chinese yuan is even more undervalued in purchasing power parity terms than are the currencies of other developing countries such as India. Until more work is done, it is impossible to do more than suggest that if China were to be placed in the typical World Bank table, a figure of $400 per capita would be more appropriate than $270. If one were to go all the way to a Kravis type of commodity-by-commodity recalculation of Chinese GNP in international prices, Chinese per capita GNP would be about 0.2 percent of that of the United States, or more than $1,000. A figure comparable to the above U.S. $1,000 billion and $3,700 per capita for the USSR, however, in China's case, would be around U.S. $400 billion total and U.S. $400 per capita.

Clearly it would be a long time before China could close the gap between Chinese and Soviet per capita incomes. Even if Soviet per capita income remained completely stagnant over time, a highly unlikely occurrence, Chinese per capita GNP would have to grow at 4.5 percent a year for fifty years to catch up. At Korean or Japanese per capita growth rates of 9 percent per annum it would still take twenty-five years to close the gap, and China has yet to achieve anything like a 9 percent per capita growth in GNP for any sustained period. It will be well into the twenty-first century, therefore, before the Chinese standard of living approaches the lower end of the European spectrum even if rapid growth is maintained.

From the standpoint of Sino-Soviet relations, however, the most interesting trend is not in standard of living but in what is happening to the aggregate size of the GNP of the two nations. It is the absolute size of an economy, not whether individuals in that economy are rich or poor, that determines the amount of resources that can be diverted to build up military power.

In terms of absolute size, China's GNP is already nearly one-third as large as that of the Soviet Union. If Soviet GNP were to grow at only 3 percent a year for the next twenty years, a Chinese growth rate of 8 percent per annum would raise the size of China's GNP to over 70 percent of that of Russia. In short, in a relatively brief period China would have a national economy almost as large as that of the USSR. In 1978 dollar terms, Chinese GNP would be around U.S. $1,800 billion, a considerable figure and larger than Soviet GNP today.

But how realistic it is to expect the growth rate of the Chinese GNP to accelerate to 6 or 7, let alone 8 percent a year? Certainly one cannot use the 1977–79 three-year growth rate of 9 percent as a guide, because growth in 1977 and 1978 was in part simply recovery from the disruptions of the Cultural Revolution, and recovery rates tend to be high. Since 1978 the Chinese growth rate has fallen to around 6 percent a year, but this 6 percent rate is also not a very good guide to the future. The slowdown in 1979 and 1980 has been part of a three-year "readjustment" in plan priorities to make way for accelerated development in the future. In the case of petroleum, for example, the 1979–81 period is a period of renewed exploration and only modest increases in production, because existing oil fields have already reached their maximum potential. If the large-scale exploration effort now going on offshore pays off, China can expect renewed substantial growth in petroleum output by the mid-1980s.

There is no completely reliable way of forecasting China's economic growth rate over the next decade or two, even if one had access to the same data available to China's leadership. It is possible, however, to set some limits on what is likely to occur.

To begin with, it is difficult to see how China could grow at much less than 5 percent a year if present policies or ones motivated by the same spirit are maintained. From 1957 through 1976 China managed to grow at 4.5 percent a year despite the massive mistakes of the Great Leap Forward, the Soviet withdrawal of technical support, and the disruption of the Cultural Revolution, which was most virulent in 1967–68 but continued to interfere with economic development off and on through 1976. Of course, if the kind of political infighting that characterized these earlier periods were renewed, economic performance would once again be disrupted. But without Mao most analysts feel that a return to the extreme forms of political disruption that characterized the pre-1976 period is unlikely.

The upper limit on China's growth possibilities should be set somewhat below the 9-10 percent per annum rates achieved by Japan, South Korea, and Taiwan throughout the 1960s and early 1970s, prior to the OPEC-induced rise in petroleum prices. There are several reasons for thinking that China will not be able to match these extraordinary performances on a sustained basis. To begin with, an export-led growth strategy is not quite as easy to carry out in the 1980s as it was in the 1950s and 1960s, because of increased barriers to entry into the markets of the United States, particularly for textiles. Furthermore, it is unlikely that China's Soviet type system of central planning will be as effective in promoting Chinese exports as Japanese and other Asian trading companies have been.

An even more important drag on Chinese future growth is agriculture. There has been much talk about the agricultural successes of Japan, Korea, and Taiwan over the past several decades, but the fact is that these nations have increasingly met their food requirements with imports rather than domestic production. Something like one-third of all Japanese food consumption in 1980 was purchased abroad. The reasons for this reliance on imports are not difficult to understand. These Asian nations have very little arable land per capita, and it is cheaper to buy from nations such as the

United States, Canada, and Australia, with their huge per capita endowments of good farm land.

China, however, is not in a position to follow the lead of its Asian neighbors when it comes to agricultural imports. One-third of China's grain imports alone (excluding other food imports) would involve purchase abroad of 110 million tons of grain, which at current world prices would cost nearly $15 billion or an amount equal to China's total foreign exchange earnings in 1979. Of course, if China imported anything like 110 million tons of grain, world grain prices would skyrocket, raising the foreign exchange cost to China to even more prohibitive levels.

The point of this hypothetical calculation is simply to underline why China cannot meet rising demand for food through imports, but must instead meet most of its needs from its own farms. Given China's poor land resources, however, it will take large investments to achieve even modest increases in per capita production. The reasons this is so have been developed elsewhere and will not be repeated here. As long as China has to divert substantial resources to a slow-growing agricultural sector, overall economic growth will be reduced.

There are other bottlenecks to rapid Chinese economic development, but most are the kind that any nation faces. China's port facilities are clogged and its railroads are overburdened. Industrial enterprises in China face electricity shortages that hold utilization rates well below capacity, and the energy resources used to fuel electrical power plants are in short supply. But these problems can be overcome by further investment in the appropriate sectors. China's energy shortage, after all, is much less serious than that faced by Japan or Korea, which must import virtually all of their requirements. For China the issue is whether a surplus of energy resources will be left over for export.

It is difficult to translate the above considerations into precise numbers, but a plausible figure for the upper limit on China's growth potential would be 8 percent a year in the 1980s. Thus we have a range of 5 to 8 percent a year as a forecast of sorts. If China can maintain the kinds of policies introduced in the late 1970s, and if unforeseen problems of particular severity do not arise, a growth rate at the upper end of the range is likely, say 7 or even 8 percent a year. If Deng Xiaoping's successors cannot agree on a coherent strategy and careen from one extreme to another, then a 5 percent rate is more likely.

The main point of going through this exercise is to emphasize that a closing of the gap between the Chinese and Soviet GNPs over the next decade or two is not merely a possibility, it is probable. Given a 3 percent rate for the Soviet Union, Chinese GNP in 1990 would be nearly 60 percent of that of the USSR if growth is 7 percent, and nearly 50 percent if growth is 5 percent. By the year 2000, only two decades off, the percentages would be 86 and 59 percent respectively. In the next section we shall explore the implications of these changing ratios for the balance of power in Asia and beyond Asia.

ECONOMICS OF THE SINO-SOVIET MILITARY BALANCE

There is more to national military power than the size of a country's gross national product, but the relationship is a close one. The availability of a large manpower pool, for example, enhances military strength even when average per capita income is low. Geographic location and the size of a nation's territory can also make a military difference. Israel is an example of a nation that suffers on both counts. Israel's population is small relative to its neighbors, and in time of war an unusually high percentage of that population must be mobilized, thereby severely disrupting other economic activities if mobilization were to continue for any prolonged period. The small size of Israel's territory similarly gives the nation almost no room within which to make a strategic withdrawal.

But neither China nor the Soviet Union suffers from limited population or territory within which to maneuver. Both could field an army of ten million men if necessary and still have well over one hundred million people (in the case of the USSR) or over five hundred million (in the case of China) to run the domestic economy. Russian history is replete with examples from Napoleon to Hitler of how Russian generals have traded territory for time to wear out the enemy and to regroup and rebuild the nation's armed forces. Chinese policies of this sort are less well known but have often been similar in nature. The Nationalist government of Chiang Kaishek bought four years of valuable time between 1937 and 1941 by slowly giving up territory to a superior Japanese invasion force. When the Japanese turned their attention elsewhere in 1942, much of China's population was still under Chinese government control. Mao Zedong's ideas about using a "people's war" to defend China were based in part on the notion that the nation's territory was too vast ever to be conquered by any likely invasion force. Invading armies would instead be swallowed up in a sea of armed guerrilla defenders. The invading force might control one or another piece of territory for a time, but it could never control all or most of the land and people for long.

Chinese and Soviet geography is similar in one other important respect. Both China and the USSR are large continental nations bordered by many smaller nations. Most important, these two continental nations share a common border of several thousand miles. Soviet and Chinese forces do not have to cross a sea to come into contact. They are in more or less constant direct contact on this common border.

How then does the size of these two economies fit into this discussion of the Sino-Soviet military balance? One must begin by distinguishing between the ability to pay for weapons systems and personnel and the technological capacity to produce sophisticated modern arms. If a nation lacks the technological sophistication to produce smaller weapons, and such weapons are not available for purchase from abroad, a large GNP will be of only limited value. That GNP can be used to pay the salaries of a very large army, but an army equipped with limited firepower.

The technical capacity to produce sophisticated weapons is not systematically related to the size of a country's national product. The ability to pour more dollars (or yuan) into a project does not guarantee success. The capacity to build an ICBM, for example, involves several thousand highly skilled scientists and technicians and various kinds of support equipment. The total cost of the effort will come to several billion dollars, a substantial sum but one well within the reach of most of the world's larger nations and many smaller ones. China, for example, could finance an annual nuclear and missile research and development effort of several billion dollars a year with only 1 percent of its gross national product.

China had to wait until 1980 to test its first intercontinental missile not because of any unwillingness to spend more money on research and development in this area, but because it takes time for the limited number of scientists with the requisite skills to perfect the necessary techniques. Political disruption undoubtedly helps to account for some of the delay between China's first medium-range missiles and the recent intercontinental tests, but budgetary restraints probably had much less if anything to do with the delay. Paying scientists higher salaries does not speed up their thinking processes nor can one accelerate research much by tripling the number of scientists involved once some critical minimum has been achieved.

This point is relevant to conventional weaponry as well. China in 1980 lacks the technical capacity to produce fighter aircraft that are a match for the Soviet MIG-23 or MIG-25. China in particular lacks the know-how to produce the electronic systems that make the modern fighter and many other defense systems so formidable. To obtain this capacity, China must train a cadre of sophisticated scientists and engineers who can build these systems. There is little question about China's ability to identify such people and provide them with the necessary training either at home or abroad, but it will take time.

It is possible, of course, that as China trains the personnel to staff its military research and development effort, potential adversaries such as the Soviet Union will maintain their technological lead, and China's relative technological position in 1990 or the year 2000 will be the same as in 1980. It is possible but not likely. Follower nations generally do not have to copy the precise steps taken by the technological leaders, but can learn to avoid the inevitable mistakes and dead ends that go with leadership. If China continues to make a major effort to develop a skilled cadre of scientists and engineers, therefore, there is every reason to think that China's technological sophistication will catch up with that of the USSR and eventually even the United States.

How long this catch-up process will take will vary from one system to another, and I, at least, am not qualified to put a precise number on the years needed to close the gap. If the Chinese concentrate their efforts on weapons, however, the time needed to catch up will be measured in terms of a decade or two, not a half century or more, as some commentators would have one believe. If China fails to close the gap, it will be because of China's own political inability to concentrate its efforts on this goal, not because of the inherent superiority of Soviet or Western science or because China is too poor to spend the resources required.

The point when the size of China's gross national product will make a difference is when China moves beyond the research and development stage to the production and deployment of particular weapon systems. China, of course, could skip the research and development stage entirely if it could purchase required weapon systems abroad, but going abroad could prove to be expensive in a way that China can least afford. As indicated in the discussion of China's trade, the Chinese ability to earn foreign exchange through exports in the 1970s was quite limited. The purchase in the early 1980s of one thousand fighter aircraft at U.S. $20 million each, even if the purchase were spread out over five years, would use up roughly one-fifth of all foreign exchange earned in those years. Such a large sum would cut significantly into the foreign exchange available to China's economic development program. Furthermore, these fighter aircraft would be only a fraction of the weapon systems that China would require in order to match Soviet power.

If China's trade expands rapidly over the next decade or two, the nation could conceivably afford to spend several billion dollars a year of foreign exchange for weapon purchases abroad, but there are reasons unrelated to cost why China is unlikely to go a long way down this path. Armament purchases from foreign countries make one dependent on those countries, and even such nations as Britain and France have been reluctant to become overly dependent on as good an ally as the United States. Except as a short-term expedient, China is not going to put itself in the position of having to depend on any outside power for replacements and spare parts.

Given that China is going to rely mainly on itself for arms, how large a military budget can China afford? As indicated in the previous section, the Chinese GNP in 1980 is about U.S. $400 billion. By 1990, at a 7 percent growth rate, it would be U.S. $800 billion, and in the year 2000 it would be U.S. $1,600 billion. The published military budget for 1979 was 22.3

billion yuan or about U.S. $15 billion, but the published budget, like that of the USSR, does not include all defense expenditures. Western estimates place China's total defense expenditures at around 7 to 8 percent of GNP, which translates into a dollar figure approaching U.S. $30 billion. If the same percentage were maintained in the future, Chinese expenditures on the military would rise to around U.S. $50 billion in 1990 and U.S. $100 billion in the year 2000.

Sums this large clearly can pay for a very large defense establishment. At present, only the United States and the USSR spend more on defense. A dollar in each country, of course, does not buy the same thing. Personnel costs in the United States eat up a large fraction of the U.S. defense budget, but in China average wages for skilled workers come to only 1,000 yuan per year (a bit over U.S. $1,000 per year at the purchasing power parity exchange rate being used in this essay). A 4.4 million man military in China therefore, involves the expenditure of only U.S. $5–6 billion, or about 1 percent of GNP.

The real costs of sophisticated weapons in China, on the other hand, are probably much higher than in the United States (or the USSR). While advanced industrial nations have large numbers of the kinds of people and equipment needed to produce such weapons, China has few, and using them to produce weapons means they are not available to other important sectors. Even if the salaries of highly skilled personnel are low, the opportunity cost on loss incurred when they are removed from these other priority activities is high. For the purposes of discussion here, I shall assume that these higher costs are balanced off by lower military salaries and that a dollar of the Chinese defense budget is equal to a dollar of the USSR defense budget.

A rough calculation would suggest that China's military budget in 1980 was about one-sixth the size of the military budget of the Soviet Union. If war were imminent, both China and the USSR could greatly increase the resources devoted to the military. A doubling of China's budget, for example, would bring total Chinese expenditure to U.S. $50–60 billion, a formidable figure by any standard, and about 12 percent of Chinese GNP.

Since Chinese consumption has been held down so long, a further reduction of personal consumption in order to raise military expenditures would hurt already weakened material incentives. Thus most of the increased expenditure would probably have to come out of investment. Since gross domestic capital formation (GDCF) in China in the late 1970s was averaging 30 percent or a bit more of gross domestic product, diversion of 6 percent of GDP or 20 percent of GDCF would reduce the capital formation rate to 24 percent, still high by international standards. In fact, if China learned how to use its investment funds more efficiently, a 24 percent rate could support a GNP growth rate of as much as 7–8 percent. Given current levels of efficiency, however, the GNP growth rate would fall from say 7–8 to 5.5–6 percent as the investment level fell.

The point of these calculations is to show that even very large increases in Chinese defense expenditures would not bring Chinese economic growth to a halt. China's GNP is sufficiently large to pay for both guns and butter. Only if China raised defense expenditures to something like a quarter of GNP or U.S. $100 billion, could one talk of growth being brought to a standstill. Lesser increases in military expenditures would reduce growth and thus lower future GNP (and potential future military expenditures).

Although China could increase defense expenditures without ending growth, there is little incentive for Chinese planners to do so. The reason is not that the perceived threat from the Soviet Union or its ally in Vietnam is minimal. The more likely reason is that increased expenditures at this time would buy little in the way of enhanced security. China could produce more MIG-19s or more obsolete tanks, air defense weapons, but for what purpose? The number of active-duty military personnel could be doubled or tripled and equipped with infantry weapons, but China's ability to stop an armored assault on Xinjiang would not be improved. China already has many millions of trained and equipped militia that could be mobilized quickly anyway.

Once China has overcome the technological barriers to production of modern fighter aircraft, air defense, and antitank weapons, there will be a real test of the relative priorities that China's leadership gives to defense versus economic development. Until those barriers are overcome it makes more sense, even on narrow military grounds, to concentrate on economic development.

Many Americans talk as if China's current military shortcomings will persist well into the twenty-first century. It is unlikely that Soviet military planners perceive the future in such a light. The Soviet Union itself has demonstrated how rapidly a determined nation can catch up with the world's greatest power, and it would be natural for Soviet planners to think that others could do so as well.

For the Soviet Union, therefore, the realistic forecast for the 1980s is of a China that is gradually closing the technological gap and whose economy is approaching in absolute size that of the Soviet Union itself. The only question is when China will be in a position to achieve military parity with the USSR, if it chooses to do so. Parity will not exist within a decade, but it is a real possibility by the year 2000, only two decades off.

CONCLUSION

What is happening to the economies of China and the Soviet Union is a part of similar events occurring on a worldwide basis. Some of the world's poor are becoming poorer, but many are beginning to catch up with those nations that began their industrialization drive in the late nineteenth and early twentieth centuries. The term being coined for such nations is "NICs" or "newly industrialized countries." Their emergence on the world economic stage has been less dramatic than that of the OPEC nations, but their long-term impact is likely to be more profound.

Although China is not usually included in lists of these newly industrialized countries, it ought to be, because its industrial sector is bigger than that of all the others combined. China's emergence as an industrial nation has been less noted, in part because China is not yet a major trading nation, nor has it followed an export-led growth strategy like that of South Korea. China also has not gone deeply into debt to international banks to finance its industrialization drive, as Brazil has.

The country that is probably most aware of China's emergence as an industrial power is the Soviet Union. Unlike many in Japan and the West, Soviet planners do not see this emergence as an opportunity for trade and profit. As pointed out earlier in this essay, the Soviet and Chinese economies are not very complementary, and Soviet, and until recently Chinese, devotion to autarky further reduced trade potential.

For the Soviet Union and for China the real significance of the economic trends described in this essay is for the shift in the balance of power. In the 1950s and 1960s China was at best a regional power capable of defending itself against an all-out attack and of playing a role in the defense of its immediate neighbors who share a common border. China is still basically a regional power, although its small arsenal of nuclear weapons gives it the capacity to inflict substantial damage on at least one of the superpowers.

The real impact of economic change on Sino-Soviet relations lies not in the immediate present but in the implications of current trends for the not very distant future. The Communist revolution of 1949 brought to power a government that by unifying China politically ended the nation's semi-colonial status. Economic development since 1949 has given China the economic base from which to transform itself back into a nation with power commensurate with the size of its territory and population.

The Economic Background and Implications for the USSR*

HENRY W. SCHAEFER

Sino-Soviet economic relations are difficult to analyze with the economist's concepts and tools. The erratic and unpredictable course of economic ties between the Soviet Union and the People's Republic of China has been essentially the result of political developments. As a consequence, familiar economic criteria such as comparative advantage, terms of trade, or debt ratios do not readily come to mind when one thinks about the trends and prospects for Sino-Soviet economic relations.

There is also the data problem. With Sino-Soviet economic relations at such a low level, the data problem primarily involves questions of potential, particularly the resource potential of regions where mutual development might be feasible. Yet in many cases the countries themselves have only recently begun to uncover this potential. The prospects of Siberia and the Far East, even—or particularly—where development is well under way, are still debated in the Soviet Union; and, as reflected by the exaggerated Western expectations of China's oil potential a few years ago, many uncertainties remain about what China will have to offer prospective trade or development partners in the future. Even the composition of existing Sino-Soviet trade has become more of a question during the 1970s, as the unaccounted residual in Soviet statistics has risen sharply for both imports and exports (tables 5 and 6).[1]

But even though economic considerations do not appear to have significantly influenced the level or nature of economic ties in the past, it does not follow that the opportunities forgone have been unappreciable or that these opportunities may not now be rising to a point where they could intrude more forcefully into leadership calculations. Historically Sino-Soviet economic relations have not been extensive, and it is not easy to divine the basis for a natural division of labor on a significant scale in the classic

---

* Mr. Schaefer is employed by the Arms Control and Disarmament Agency. The views expressed in this chapter are his own and are not necessarily those of the Arms Control and Disarmament Agency or of any other agency of the U.S. government.

1. The CIA now assumes that this residual reflects manufactured goods not otherwise classified (see CIA, *China: International Trade Quarterly Review, Second Quarter, 1979*, ERCIT 80–001, January 1980, note 4, p. 21).

The Economic Background and Implications for the USSR 113

comparative advantage sense. Nonetheless, it will be argued in this paper that Soviet developmental needs are such that the economic costs of confrontation have been rising appreciably, and that the potential Soviet gains from an easing of the burden of maintaining large military forces facing China and from long-term economic cooperation with China will rise in the 1980s.

In addressing the potential for Sino-Soviet economic relations, the basic assumptions made about the rest of the world are also very important. Just as it is difficult to address the prospects for trade creation or trade diversion without making assumptions about the political-economic opportunities both countries face on the world market, it is difficult to project the potential for economic cooperation without making assumptions about the feasibility of involving complementary Western capital and technology.

SINO-SOVIET TRADE RELATIONS

In both theory and practice foreign trade dominates Western approaches to international economic relations. Yet in the Sino-Soviet context, trade turns out to be of limited interest and potential, except in conjunction with economic cooperation and joint investment. Given the structure of the two economies, their technological positions, and the transportation costs involved, the impetus for trade has been limited, and appears likely to remain so if left to the mercies of comparative advantage.

The rapid expansion of Sino-Soviet economic relations in the 1950s, and particularly their collapse at the end of the decade, left an important legacy. From the Soviet perspective, the Chinese never really repaid them, either economically or politically, for the massive economic and military deliveries during China's first five-year plan (1953–57). In 1958 China accounted for one-quarter of Soviet trade with communist countries. Yet Sino-Soviet trade was quite unstable, both in volume and, especially, in commodity composition; and China's imports of Soviet machinery and equipment had already dropped as a result of China's efforts to become self-sufficient.

For economic as well as political reasons, the Soviets were pressing China to sign a long-term trade agreement and to accede to a "socialist division of labor" under the Council for Economic Mutual Assistance (CEMA). Despite some initial tentative moves toward acquiescence, with the Great Leap Forward China refused to do either at a crucial time for Soviet efforts to bring other Asian communist countries and, especially, Eastern Europe into closer economic integration.[2] Thus, even though the economic impact of the break may have been much greater on China than

---

2. For a more detailed discussion of these developments, see Oleg Hoeffding, *Sino-Soviet Economic Relations in Recent Years* (Santa Monica: Rand P-2087, 1960).

on the USSR, the Soviets have continued to view their "withdrawal" as fully justified on the grounds of China's perfidy for never having accepted its designated political and economic role as the newest member of the socialist community. The Soviet antipathy, more than two decades later, must reflect a strong sense of how much easier life would have been economically and especially politically if China had only accepted its role model back in the 1950s. Not only could socialist economic integration have proceeded more expeditiously with even a modicum of Chinese acquiescence, but the costs of Soviet economic competition in the Third World and for the allegiance of nonbloc socialist countries, such as Cuba and Vietnam, could have been appreciably reduced.

Sino-Soviet trade during the 1970s was not particularly exciting to watch. It is primarily of interest for its continuity with past patterns and apparent reaffirmation of the lessons of the 1950s. While trade remained very modest, at less than half of 1 percent of total Soviet foreign trade in 1979, it jumped sharply when political conditions warranted, as in 1971–72, 1976, and 1978 (see Table 4). In each case, Soviet deliveries of capital equipment

TABLE 4
Soviet Trade with China
(in million rubles)[a]

Year	Soviet Exports	Soviet Imports	Total Trade
1970	22.4	19.5	41.9
1971	70.1	68.6	138.7
1972	100.2	110.4	210.6
1973	100.5	100.8	201.3
1974	108.4	105.5	213.9
1975	93.1	107.8	200.9
1976	179.8	134.6	314.4
1977	118.4	130.1	248.5
1978	163.8	174.9	338.7
1979	175.2	157.3	332.5

SOURCE: *Vneshniaia torgovlia SSSR*, various editions.

[a] In current dollar terms trade would have grown considerably faster, the foreign trade ruble having "strengthened" against the dollar during the 1970s from a (fixed) $1.11/ruble in 1970–71 to about $1.50/ruble by 1979, because it was tied to stronger Western currencies.

were the most important factor in the trade increase, and they were also the main reason for the abrupt drop in trade in 1977 (see Table 5).

It should be noted that only in 1976 was the jump in Soviet capital equipment exports to China not accompanied by a roughly equivalent surge in Chinese exports to the Soviet Union (see Table 6); this suggests that

TABLE 5
Soviet Exports to China
(in million rubles)

Year	Machinery, Equipment, and Transportation	Raw Materials	Residual	Total[a]
1970	14.7	3.3	2.6	22.4
1971	49.2	6.9	9.7	70.1
1972	75.8	11.5	7.5	100.2
1973	74.9	12.7	9.6	100.5
1974	80.5	16.9	10.0	108.4
1975	69.9	12.4	9.1	93.1
1976	122.8	27.5	26.8	179.8
1977	64.2	20.6	32.2	118.4
1978	95.9	26.9	38.3	163.8
1979	100.6	16.9	53.4	175.2

SOURCE: *Vneshniaia torgovlia SSSR*, various editions.

[a] Preceding columns may not add up to the total because small amounts of exports are listed in other categories.

TABLE 6
Soviet Imports from China
(in million rubles)

Year	Raw Materials	Food	Industrial Consumer Goods	Residual	Total[a]
1970	2.7	4.9	11.9	—	19.5
1971	21.5	17.1	28.2	1.6	68.6
1972	24.1	19.6	55.8	13.1	110.4
1973	17.1	28.0	45.4	10.3	100.8
1974	19.6	23.0	55.7	7.1	105.5
1975	20.3	29.4	51.9	6.2	107.8
1976	12.6	25.2	54.7	42.2	134.6
1977	18.9	23.7	42.7	44.9	130.1
1978	16.5	34.4	64.0	60.0	174.9
1979	18.0	36.3	53.8	49.2	157.3

SOURCE: *Vneshniaia torgovlia SSSR*, various editions.

[a] Preceding columns may not add up to the total because small amounts of imports are listed in other categories.

Soviet incentive and hopes were greatest with the passing of Mao. It should also be noted that virtually all the recorded gain on the Soviet import side over the decade was in Chinese deliveries of food and industrial consumer goods.

This growth is an indicator of where trade opportunities may lie in the

1980s. But, given the distances involved and the transportation costs, aside from border trade there is probably little that either country could not get more easily and on as good or better terms elsewhere. The Third World and Eastern Europe can offer the kinds of soft goods to the Soviet Union that have dominated the growth in Chinese deliveries. Thus, although trade manipulation is a policy tool readily available to planned economies when political gains are anticipated, the economic case for a major expansion of Sino-Soviet trade appears unpersuasive.

SINO-SOVIET ECONOMIC COOPERATION

After the communist takeover of China, the Soviets were apparently quick to recognize that the conditions for rapidly expanding trade ties simply did not exist, and that Soviet political objectives would not be served adequately by a gradual development of such ties on the basis of existing economic conditions. Chinese developmental needs and ambitions were such, however, that massive infusions of capital, technology, and skilled manpower were required, and Chinese relations with the rest of the world were such that the best potential source for meeting these requirements was the Soviet Union. The Soviets evidently saw the initial sacrifices involved in underwriting the PRC's first five-year plan as worthwhile if the payoff were to be sufficient on economic and, especially, political grounds. It was probably hoped that the Chinese economy could be developed to the point that it could repay credit and provide a long-term source of goods of sufficient hardness and of reasonably high quality, but the real payoff was certainly to be political. China, as noted, was to be brought into the socialist division of labor through CEMA and a long-term trade agreement. In the event, when neither of these expectations was fulfilled, the Chinese paid off their debts largely in consumer goods and did not become a reliable long-term supplier of hard goods to the Soviet Union.

With the split, economic cooperation disappeared. It would be a mistake, however, to conclude from this record that Sino-Soviet economic cooperation had no economic rationale or that the potential economic gains from Sino-Soviet economic cooperation today are necessarily insignificant. Depending on endowments of production factors and development policies, the possibilities for economic cooperation may be appreciable, even if present production patterns and development levels offer few apparent trade opportunities and current cooperation is minimal. Economic cooperation with China may now offer growing potential because of the Soviet Union's deteriorating economic prospects.

The Soviet economy grew at a rate of less than 1 percent in 1979 and probably did not fare much better in 1980. Although those years were particularly difficult ones because of agricultural failures, adverse long-term trends—such as energy shortfalls, rapidly rising costs of raw materials, and declining investment resources and productivity—make the economic outlook for the 1980s bleak.³ At the same time, the natural resources, including energy resources, necessary for future Soviet development almost all lie well to the east of the European industrialized region, as does much of the potential labor force. Labor, resources, and infrastructure are, of course, at present not all together in the right places, but after the Baikal-Amur Mainline (BAM) is completed, the case will be strengthened for pressing ahead with costly development of the region along the Chinese border and with industrialization of Central Asia on the basis of indigenous labor and the new resources opened up.⁴

Indeed, the building of BAM would appear to indicate a prior commitment to such a course, as well as to the development of resources for export that will require Western participation.⁵ But the deferrals and delays, both in BAM itself and in other major development projects, have suggested equivocation, despite ostensible strong leadership commitment to development of the region and to individual projects. As John Hardt has argued, the traditional Soviet overcommitment of resources is one underlying explanation for this wasteful approach, and the recruitment and retention of manpower has been a major problem—one that China could alleviate under different circumstances. But of more interest here is the ratchet effect that Hardt observes, through which Soviet development policy in the east appears to be whipsawed by conflicting internal and external pressures—the former for economic development and modernization and the latter to meet more immediate perceived military needs.⁶

Soviet plans to industrialize Siberia—in addition to developing its resources—appear to be the subject of considerable uncertainty and disagreement, and the differences over this question may well be a significant factor in the apparent difficulties in drawing up the Eleventh Five-Year Plan (1981–85) and in the perennial problem of establishing long-range plans. As recently as 1979, Soviet planners did not seem to anticipate that development along the BAM would involve any significant population influx

3. CIA, *The Soviet Economy in 1978–79 and Prospects for 1980*, ER 80-10328, June 1980.
4. See G. Kurbatova, "Problemy razvitiia mashinostroeniia v Sibiri," *Planovoe khoziaistvo*, March 1980, pp. 32–39.
5. For a discussion of Soviet motives in building BAM, see Theodore Shabad, "The BAM, Project of the Century," in *Soviet Economy in a Time of Change: A Compendium of Papers Submitted to the Joint Economic Committee, Congress of the United States*, 96th Cong., 1st sess., vol. 1, October 10, 1979 (Washington, D.C.: U.S. Government Printing Office, 1979), pp. 164–76.
6. John Hardt, "Military-Economic Implications of Soviet Regional Policy," presented at the Colloquium on Regional Development in the USSR, NATO Economic Directorate, Brussels, Belgium, April 25–27, 1979.

beyond that necessary for resource exploitation.[7] But, in 1980, as preparations for the Twenty-sixth Party Congress and for the Eleventh Five-Year Plan progressed, a number of references were made to the need for major energy-industrial complexes in Siberia "in order to utilize the cheap energy and raw material wealth on the spot."[8] The need for machine-building enterprises in Siberia to serve local needs has also been argued.[9] In the latter part of 1980, it was stated that "several new territorial production complexes" will be built along the BAM,[10] and that the "question has been raised of creating a new metallurgical base in the USSR's east."[11] In his report to the October 1980 session of the Supreme Soviet on the 1981 plan, Gosplan Chairman Baybakov reported that East Siberia would have "considerable increases in the production of electricity, plastics, chemical fibers, caustic soda, pulp, electrical equipment industry products and cement."[12]

The form and location of development in the east have generated considerable debate, particularly in the energy sphere. One commentator argued that even though the "whole country's attention is now riveted on Siberia," there has been a lack of exploratory oil drilling because of "subjective reasons . . . , a loss of perspective and of strategic thinking," and disregard for "the acuteness of the present moment."[13] While it is often not clear just what parts of Siberia commentators have in mind, the question of how to develop regions vulnerable to Chinese incursion or to disruption in time of border conflict is clearly much more complicated than is suggested by comparatively anodyne debates over the extent of local raw-material processing or the allocation of scarce oil-drilling equipment. Whatever decisions are finally made about the degree of industrialization to pursue in regions proximate to China, the state of Sino-Soviet and East-West relations will be a major consideration, both in the decisions themselves and in the economic gains anticipated.

Many of the potential projects would rely heavily on Western technology for their cost effectiveness if not their feasibility, and Western hesitancy to plunge into more ambitious joint undertakings has reflected concern over Sino-Soviet tensions as well as over the staying power of East-West détente. Western attitudes toward investment in Soviet resources have also been affected by emerging rival opportunities to invest in China. For prospective

7. Shabad, "The BAM," p. 170.
8. A. Illarionov, *Izvestiia*, June 29, 1980.
9. Kurbatova, "Problemy."
10. E. Rusanov, *Pravda*, September 19, 1980.
11. TASS, October 15, 1980.
12. Report to the October 22, 1980, session of the USSR Supreme Soviet, *Pravda*, October 23, 1980.
13. A. Trofimuk, *Sotsialisticheskaia industriia*, July 1, 1980.

Western investors, as for the Soviets, the very large and long-term commitment of resources required to develop the eastern part of the Soviet Union, and the growing vulnerability of the region to threat by improved Chinese military forces, would appear to make relaxation of political/military confrontation the necessary if not the sufficient condition for moving ahead. One factor which may provide an incentive for the Soviets to reassess the costs of continued confrontation is the markedly changed energy situation in which the Soviets now find themselves.

The Soviet and Chinese positions on oil production have changed dramatically since the 1950s. In the latter part of the 1970s, the growth in Soviet oil production slowed and production may have nearly peaked.[14] Shortages have begun to hit the domestic economy and are now expected to depress GNP growth in the next few years. Yet Soviet oil exports are still the main source of hard currency earnings and vital to the hard-pressed East European economies.

As Soviet oil production has slowed and the search for more has moved eastward, China has discovered and developed major new oil fields in the north—and may have significant offshore potential. By contrast, in 1957, when the Soviet Union had a growing oil surplus, China's oil production was under 1.5 million tons—less than what was imported from the Soviet Union.[15] By 1979 China was producing over 100 million tons of oil, of which about 17 million tons were exported.[16] Given their location and potential, China's oil resources may appear increasingly tempting to the Soviet Union, particularly when BAM relieves transportation problems.

But China's oil growth slowed sharply in 1979,[17] evidently for much the same reasons that Soviet oil production has run into trouble,[18] and cutbacks in oil exports to Japan—its major buyer—are now expected. Both China and the Soviet Union lack modern exploration and production equipment, particularly for deep drilling and offshore development. Both countries also face a scarcity of investment capital. Joint development of oil, like

14. CIA, "The Soviet Economy," p. 4.
15. Bobby A. Williams, "The Chinese Petroleum Industry: Growth and Prospects," in *China: A Reassessment of the Economy: A Compendium of Papers Submitted to the Joint Economic Committee, Congress of the United States, July 10, 1975* (Washington, D.C.: U.S. Government Printing Office, 1975), pp. 225–63.
16. CIA, *International Energy Statistical Review*, ERIESR 80-011, July 29, 1980.
17. Ibid.
18. Vaclav Smil, "China's Energetics: A System Analysis," in *Chinese Economy Post-Mao: A Compendium of Papers Submitted to the Joint Economic Committee, Congress of the United States, November 9, 1978*, vol. 1 (Washington, D.C.: U.S. Government Printing Office, 1978), p. 342.

most other resource development projects, thus appears to hold much more potential if Western technology and investment are involved. In view of the vulnerability of oil production to disruption and the exposed location of the border and offshore areas of greatest cooperative potential, a much improved political climate, not only in Sino-Soviet relations but in East-West relations, would appear to be a prerequisite to serious consideration of cooperative oil ventures.

For coal and gas development, cooperation with Japan to develop Soviet and particularly China's reserves would appear to hold the most promise. Japan is stepping up its reliance on coal and has financed coal development in both the Soviet Union and China. China is a major coal producer, with large reserves, and may have considerably greater gas potential.[19] Japan's reluctance to become dependent on either Soviet or Chinese energy deliveries, and consequent unwillingness to invest as heavily as her economic needs and the development potential of China and the eastern regions of the Soviet Union would appear to dictate, again are essentially due to political, not economic, factors.

THE MILITARY BURDEN

The economic costs to the Soviets of their rift with the PRC are ultimately estimates of what level mutually beneficial trade and economic cooperation might reach under improved political relations. The military burden should, in principle, be more readily calculated, since a finite amount of Soviet resources is involved. There is unfortunately little agreement among Western observers about the burden imposed by Soviet military expenditures and about how to gauge the impact of hypothetical reductions.

From CIA estimates it can be calculated that about 2 percent of Soviet GNP is devoted to military forces facing the PRC: it is now estimated that some 13 percent of Soviet GNP goes to the military, and that the cost of the forces disposed against China make up about 15 percent of Soviet military expenditures.[20] Although both of these shares may be rising, even if this burden were completely eliminated, available econometric models show that the projected boost to GNP growth would be minimal.[21] These models,

19. Ibid., p. 344, and K. P. Wang, "China's Mineral Economy," in *Chinese Economy Post-Mao*, vol. 1, p. 392.

20. *The Soviet Economy in 1978–79* (see note 3 above) and *Allocation of Resources in the Soviet Union and China—1978: Hearings before the Subcommittee on Priorities and Economy in Government, Joint Economic Committee, Congress of the United States, Part 4—Soviet Union* (Washington, D.C.: U.S. Government Printing Office, 1978), p. 89.

21. The defense slowdown option tested in the CIA's model, which assumed a reduction in military manpower by a half million men between 1980 and 1985 and in the growth of other defense expenditures to 2 percent (half the projected

however, do not allow for what a number of observers view as potentially the most important impact of Soviet military restraint: the boost to productivity throughout the economy.[22] Evidence from a variety of sources suggests that the economic burden of Soviet military spending in opportunity-cost or growth-forgone terms may be considerably higher than is suggested by models that do not allow for such factors as productivity changes or resource constraints that require new approaches to economic growth. There has, in fact, been increasing recognition in both East and West that the military burden on the Soviet economy has become significant, that this burden appears destined to grow in the 1980s, and that declining economic growth and changing growth requirements appear to have increased the competition between the military and civilian sectors of the Soviet economy for resources.

Because the Soviet military sector preempts large shares of growth-generating resources (such as research and development, and machine building), the opportunity costs of the Soviet military sector must be gauged in terms of efficiency forgone throughout the economy, not merely the military's share of GNP. It has been persuasively argued that military spending imposes its main burden on the Soviet economy through its restraint on productivity growth, and that the burden on growth of devoting so much of Soviet research and development effort to the military is high.[23]

---

base-line rate), yielded a GNP gain of only one billion rubles (from 627 to 628 billion rubles) by 1985. (CIA, *Simulations of Soviet Growth Options to 1985*, ER 79-10131, March 1979).

22. The CIA model assumes constant returns to scale. It is argued that this reflects the Soviet extensive growth pattern adequately: "the constant-returns-to-scale assumption, made in order to obtain statistically acceptable results, picks up some of the technological change effect because actual returns-to-scale are probably below unity in most sectors. The absence of a disembodied technology term on the sector level is consistent with Soviet development, which has been characterized more by extensive rather than intensive application of technology. This would be reflected in the general rise of the capital stock in each sector, not in a separate trend of improvement in total factor productivity" (ibid., note 2, p. 26).

23. A recent analysis argues that the Soviet military industry is inefficient, operates at a relatively low scientific and technological level, has an "organic" relationship with the rest of the economy, and should be viewed as "a form of parasite or malignant growth, seriously affecting the well-being of the whole economy" (Mikhail Agursky and Hannes Adomeit, "The Soviet Military-Industrial Complex," *Survey*, Spring 1979, pp. 106–24). See also Stanley H. Cohn, "The Economic Burden of Soviet Defense Outlays," in *Economic Performance and the Military Burden in the Soviet Union: A Compendium of Papers, Joint Economic Committee, Congress of the United States* (Washington, D.C.: U.S. Government Printing Office, 1970), pp. 166–88; and Gur Ofer, *The*

Refocusing Soviet development priorities and transference of such growth-generating resources to civilian uses could, in the long run, have a major impact on Soviet development, particularly if accompanied by amelioration of the overcommitment of resources and the institutional rigidities that have developed in considerable part to enforce the priority accorded military growth.

If, however, one examines the resources devoted to the Chinese military theater, a rather different picture of the burden to Soviet economic growth is indicated than is suggested by overall assessments. By 1978 it was estimated that 650,000 to 700,000 men were facing China, up from about 400,000 in 1969.[24] These troops constitute some 25 percent of Soviet ground and air forces, and are certainly more costly to maintain than those facing NATO or stationed in other areas closer to sources of supply. The Soviets also hold an estimated 700,000 military men in their central reserve of ground and tactical air force personnel, and because some one million men are in the Western USSR with wartime missions against NATO (in addition to about 600,000 in Eastern Europe),[25] a considerable share of these central reserves is undoubtedly maintained primarily with reinforcement of the Chinese border forces in mind.

The ground forces and tactical air forces facing China are major consumers of three basic resources most often cited as in increasingly short supply and most likely to produce production bottlenecks in the 1980s—steel, oil, and manpower. The already high opportunity costs of tying up so many resources, including transportation, in support of this military effort would thus appear to be rising. As reflected by the frequent complaints in the Soviet media over transportation delays and bottlenecks in Siberia and the Far East, release of resources from the military, especially transportation, could facilitate a jump in trade and an expansion of investment in infrastructure and production facilities. It could also facilitate the expansion of the transportation network required once development begins and energy resources and raw materials need to be moved westward.

This is not to suggest that conversion of the resources now devoted to the eastern front would be cheap or that sunk investment is of the right kind or in the right place for economic development, but only that given the Soviet Union's present developmental needs, the short-run opportunity costs of continuing to maintain such large military forces facing China are probably rising faster than average costs suggested by the military's GNP share, and that these opportunity costs are likely to become higher as the

---

Opportunity Cost of the Nonmonetary Advantages of the Soviet R&D Effort (Santa Monica: Rand R-1741-DDRE, 1975).

24. *Allocation of Resources,* pp. 87 and 89.
25. Ibid., p. 88.

economy slows further, especially if oil production turns down and crash programs to overcome shortages become necessary.

The military burden of maintaining forces opposing the PRC thus differs in a significant way from the costs of forgoing economic relations with China and from maintaining the large Soviet military sector as a whole. Release of the manpower, fuel, industrial capacity, and support and transportation facilities preempted by the eastern front to the civilian economy, and release of the military equipment and spare parts to other commands, would provide a fairly rapid boost to the Soviet economy. By contrast, the release of long-term growth-generating resources, especially in research and development, to be anticipated from a reduction in military competition with the West, would require considerably longer to generate economic returns. Thus, given the immediacy of Soviet economic problems and the pressures to come to grips with them in the Eleventh Five-Year Plan, it would appear that the military burden on economic performance associated with the split with China must have become increasingly apparent. But the significance of this for Soviet leaders and policy will be conditioned by perceptions of a quite different economic nature.

SOVIET ECONOMIC POLICY

The economic contribution to the Soviet Union of improved relations with China through reduced military expenditures and economic cooperation has been found to be primarily "extensive." That is, the gains would come largely by prolonging the traditional "Stalinist" growth model, under which growth results from incremental additions to productive factors rather than from more efficient use of those factors. Particularly in the short run, reduced tension could free scarce resources—manpower, energy, steel, transportation—for economic uses.

Yet extensive economic growth is not what Soviet leaders have been seeking in recent years. Instead, productivity gains have been seen as the key to economic growth, even though—as many Western observers anticipated—results to date have proved Soviet expectations wrong. According to the deputy chairman of Gosplan, "for a number of reasons, and to a significant extent because of the shortage of raw material resources, production growth rates have fallen, and labor productivity growth rates in their wake. . . . a more substantial, preferential growth of labor productivity compared with production growth has not been achieved."[26] The failure to achieve intensive growth ought to make extensive economic growth opportunities more attractive, but the Soviet leadership has equivocated in addressing the problem domestically. This situation, along with

26. Ia. Riabov, "Rezervy povysheniia effektivnosti ekonomiki," *Planovoe khoziaistvo*, no. 9, September 1980, pp. 3–12.

foreign policy vicissitudes, has hampered formulation of a consistent policy for seeking relief through international cooperation.

When the Soviets turned to the West for advanced technology and equipment in the first stages of détente in the late 1960s, the argument became popular that the Soviets, having recognized the necessity of intensive development (and having shied away from internal economic reform), saw Western economic relations as helping to maintain their economic growth through productivity gains. Yet in 1975, just as they were making productivity gains the key to their Tenth Five-Year Plan, productivity began to drop more sharply, and the prospects for help from the West, especially through investments in Siberia and the Far East, were changing from dubious to poor. With marginal cost curves now generally rising even more steeply than they were five years ago, and prospects of extensive Western help even worse, it is no wonder that the Eleventh Five-Year Plan appears to be in trouble.

Much of the problem is that the paradoxes of economic policy encountered in the late 1960s and in 1975 have been compounded in the interim. Western technology and investment in industry are still needed to meet intensive development goals, but on a much greater scale and much more effectively integrated into the domestic economy than anticipated or allowed in the past. A growing realization in the Soviet Union of its own economic plight and of the military-economic burden imposed by the prolonged split with China may help to account for the equivocal, even hopeful, treatment of Chinese economic questions in some Soviet media.

It is of course difficult to fathom Soviet views on future economic relations with China. The level of vituperation has been such in recent years that economic relations do not generally appear to be addressed seriously, but only in a polemical political-military context. Yet, as usual in Soviet interpretations of international affairs, the escape hatches are there. For one thing, despite Chinese "hegemonist" aspirations and "feverish" preparations for war, the threat is not necessarily imminent. In *Krasnaia zvezda* it was recently argued that "Beijing strategists regard world war as the 'shortest way' to attain their hegemonist goals," and that the 1979 plan changes did "not mean that Beijing has renounced its militarist designs." But it was also found that China was "graciously agreeing to defer world war until the end of the twentieth century," despite massive military preparations.[27] In *Izvestiia* certain Western circles were chided for seeing a softening in Mao Zedong's militarism under the new leadership, and it was argued that China is conducting a propaganda maneuver to "gain time to increase its military and industrial potential, [because] the essence of

27. B. Gorbachev, "Under the Slogan of Modernization: Militarist Preparations in China," *Krasnaia zvezda* (*Red Star*), July 11, 1980.

China's foreign policy remains unchanged," even though at present it is "experiencing a lack of the material potential for imposing its will on other peoples."[28]

The respite granted by China's lack of preparation to carry out its warlike aims apparently may provide an opportunity for them to be thwarted. At present, Soviet audiences are told, the Chinese economy is in serious trouble and is an "unstable organism" that has had difficulty absorbing even limited amounts of Western technology and equipment because "there are no cadres who can make use of the modern technology or master the modern technological processes."[29] There is hope also in the long run, for the "main objective obstacle" to alliance between China and the West is the "radical divergence between the Chinese people's interests and the expansionist aspirations" of the imperialists and the present Chinese rulers.[30] According to an article in *Kommunist*, because "imperialists remain imperialists," economic ties with the West will lead to exploitation of the Chinese working people through credit repayment and maximum profits, which will "inevitably" lead to growing resistance to the present leadership's policies.[31] The Soviet people are also told, "if we soberly assess the potential for scientific and technical contacts between the United States and China, we can expect these conflicts to be considerably exacerbated in the near future."[32]

As a consequence of all this, the Chinese people are found to be "on the verge of losing faith" in the present regime's ability to solve the nation's problems.[33] In fact, the "anti-Maoist movement is running high in China," and it will inevitably grow, for the economic situation is very grave and the Chinese people are not surrendering: "scientific socialism ... will ultimately prevail and will lead the Chinese people onto the path of victorious socialist building, and friendship and cooperation with the USSR and the other socialist countries."[34] While the economic determinism of these arguments may appeal more to an economist or a propagandist than to political analysts, the interpretation of China's economic future presented and the patience seemingly advocated suggest that the Soviet Union's own economic

28. G. Mosko, *Izvestiia*, July 30, 1980.
29. Moscow Domestic Service, 1140 GMT, July 15, 1980.
30. Mosko, *Izvestiia*, July 30, 1980.
31. V. Lazarev, "Antimaoistskoe dvizhenie v KNR," *Kommunist*, no. 8, May 1980, pp. 101–12.
32. A. A. Nagornyi and A. B. Parkanskii, "Nauchno-tekhnicheskie kontakty SShA s Kitaem," *SShA: Ekonomika, Politika, Ideologiia*, no. 8, August 1980, pp. 29–37.
33. Y. Semyonov, "China: The Crisis Continues," *International Affairs*, July 1980, p. 31.
34. Lazarev, "Antimaoistskoe dvizhenie v KNR," p. 101; for a similar argument, see Semyonov, "China," p. 31.

realities may already be having some impact on Soviet thinking about future relations with China.

PROSPECTS

This paper has dealt with the economic costs of the Sino-Soviet split, including the question of potential Soviet economic gains from expanded economic cooperation and a reduction in military forces deployed against China. It is concluded that the costs are higher than is often appreciated and are rising as the Soviet Union's economic growth slows, but that quite heroic assumptions about improvement in both Sino-Soviet and East-West relations are necessary before the potential gains can be anticipated. What the Soviets decide to do about this will depend in considerable part on how they assess their competitive prospects in the West and in the Third World in relation to China.

On this score, recent events have undoubtedly made the Soviets less sanguine about their near-term outlook than they appear to be about the immediate Chinese military threat. China's rush to develop economic ties with the West and to seek military-related technology has been the most noted and criticized factor, but no matter how unsettling such developments may be to the Soviets, in doing this China has only been catching up with Soviet and East European practice after years of self-denial. In fact, as with some of its flirtation with domestic economic reform, China's apparent commitment—or obliviousness—to institutional change in reordering its international affairs is much more remarkable. China's steps to expand foreign trade and economic cooperation have moved rapidly by communist standards. Although negotiations over joint ventures requiring significant Western investment have progressed slowly, Chinese efforts to obtain equity financing from abroad resulted in the first such agreements in early 1980, by which time over 2,400 contracts with foreign firms had also been signed, at the provincial level, which provide for processing or assembly for export.[35] In 1980, China joined the International Monetary Fund and the World Bank, something the Soviet Union has always been unwilling to do, despite pressures from Eastern Europe and the obvious opportunities forgone by remaining on the outside. The Soviet opportunity costs from continued abstention from such commitments to long-term economic ties with the West will rise with China's participation, as China's claim to offer an alternative to economic relations with the Soviet Union is strengthened.

This situation exacerbates the Soviet dilemma over how to contain China, particularly in Southeast Asia. The Soviet military and economic build-up in the eastern regions obviously serves power-projection purposes that exist independently of the Soviet economic needs addressed in this

35. CIA, *China: International Trade Quarterly Review, First Quarter, 1980*, ERCIT 80-004, September 1980.

chapter. The prospect of an economically resurgent China successfully competing for Western economic and technological cooperation would appear to up the ante well beyond what the Soviets anticipated with the passing of Mao.

As seen, part of the Soviet response has been to attack the present Chinese regime as "militarist." On their face, such accusations appear ridiculous. Although China has deployed a minimum nuclear deterrent force, Chinese military spending is estimated to have remained almost constant during the 1970s,[36] despite the massive Soviet build-up on the border. The Soviet Union's posture probably reflects several factors—mirror imaging, paranoia, an ex post facto justification for its own build-up, and propaganda designed to persuade the West not to contribute to China's military capability or related economic and technological development. But there is a sense in which the Soviets' accusations may also have substance, at least to them. The Soviets are acutely aware that today's economic and technological development provides the basis for tomorrow's military potential. Underlying the Soviets' militarism charge there may be serious apprehension that while the Soviet Union appears destined to engage in a revived and very taxing arms race with the West in the early 1980s, the Chinese will be building economic capacity more rapidly than if military production were a greater current drain: hence China may offer a more formidable future challenge in both economic and military terms. Soviet arguments that China will be the ultimate winner of an East-West confrontation may thus be based on real (and perhaps realistic) projections of potential long-term shifts in the "correlation of forces."

Given the failure of the intensive growth strategy originally built into the Soviet Tenth Five-Year Plan in 1975, and in view of the darkening Soviet economic picture since the original plan was effectively abandoned in 1977, it was clear that the Soviets were overextended even before the economically costly events of the past two years—notably the very bad 1979 and 1980 harvests, the invasion of Afghanistan, and recent developments in Poland. The struggles over investment allocations in preparation for the Eleventh Five-Year Plan reflect these developments and also the consequence that détente somewhere with someone has become an even greater economic and technological requirement for the Soviet Union than it was in the latter part of the 1960s when it first got under way in Europe. Given their economic prospects in the 1980s, present and particularly prospective Soviet leaders ought to be contemplating with trepidation the possibility of moving from a one-front to a two-front arms race toward the end of the decade—a race likely to be bolstered by closer economic and technological links among their main adversaries.

36. CIA, *Chinese Defense Spending, 1965–79*, SR 80-10091, July 1980.

PART 2

International Repercussions of the Dispute

PART 2

Institutional Repression of the Deviate

The Global Impact

International Politics and the Sino-Soviet Dispute

WILLIAM E. GRIFFITH

We see the past—*pace* the false consciousness of prideful claims to "objectivity"—through the glasses of how we see the present and expect the future. First, therefore, my view, through my glasses, of the present.

1980: A PERSONAL VIEW

By the end of 1980 seven principal developments dominated international politics. The most dynamic one was the continued military build-up of the Soviet Union toward global power and influence at least equal to that of all its potential enemies put together. Two motives interacted and reinforced each other. One was expansionist: Russia's "grasp for global power."[1] The other was, at least initially, defensive: for example, the Soviet preemptive breakout,[2] in the "arc of crisis" in the Middle East and Southwest Asia, to counter in advance the looming danger, as Moscow sees it, of its encirclement by China, America, Japan, and West Germany. By this preemptive breakout, Moscow is bringing about, like Imperial Germany

---

1. The term is Fritz Fischer's, in his *Germany's Aims in the First World War* (New York: W. W. Norton, 1967).
2. See William G. Hyland, "The Sino-Soviet Conflict: A Search for New Security Strategies," in Richard H. Solomon, ed., *Asian Security in the 1980s: Problems and Policies for a Time of Transition* (Santa Monica: Rand R-2492-ISA, 1979).

before it, the encirclement it so fears. For since the Red Army marched into Kabul, the United States has become a reluctant, limited partner in a quasi alliance with Beijing, with the beginning of a military dimension to it. Conversely, Moscow has long been trying to encircle Beijing, thus intensifying the Chinese drive to encircle the Soviet Union.

Second, the Afghan and Iranian crises deepened policy differences toward the Soviet Union between the United States and France and West Germany, who dominate Western Europe. Third, after the post-Vietnam withdrawal syndrome, the American build-up of military capabilities, along with the revival of the political will be to use them to defend its interests abroad, has begun. Fourth, rising instability in the Middle East, and the stagnation of the Camp David process, have resulted in the first signs of another Arab attempt to use the "oil weapon" to intervene, via Washington, in Jerusalem on the Palestinian issue, and, last but perhaps most important, in the September 1980 Iraqi-Iranian hostilities. Fifth, in America, the Soviet Union, and China conservatism is on the rise.

The sixth development is the leap forward of increasingly unverifiable military technology. The Soviet nuclear build-up, which will soon make American land-based ICBMs theoretically vulnerable to a Soviet first strike, combines with the American deployment of MaRVed mobile ICBMs (MX), cruise missiles (CMs), which theoretically could also give the United States a nuclear first-strike capability, and the Soviet and American deployment of precision-guided munitions (PGMs) to create the perception in Moscow and Washington that each is trying to gain nuclear superiority over the other. The seventh point is that all these developments have so eroded Soviet-American détente that its survival is seriously in doubt.[3]

The Soviet leadership also fears nuclear encirclement. It believes that because of the central, vulnerable Soviet geographical position and the opposition to Soviet policies of all other actual (the United States, Britain, France, and China) or potential (West Germany and Japan) major nuclear powers, Moscow must have nuclear parity with all of them together. But the United States will never accept its consequent nuclear inferiority. Thus Moscow's geographical centrality and political isolation are obstacles to arms control.

An important example of this situation is the Soviet deployment of SS-20s and the proposed NATO deployment, in reply, of modernized long-

3. See Dimitri K. Simes, "The Death of Détente?" *International Security*, 5, no. 1 (Summer 1980): 3–25; Robert Legvold, "Containment without Confrontation," *Foreign Policy*, no. 40 (Fall 1980): 74–98; and Paul H. Nitze, "Strategy in the Decade of the 1980s," *Foreign Affairs*, 59, no. 1. (Fall 1980): 82–101.

range theater nuclear forces—LRTNF: Pershing II and ground-launched cruise missiles (GLCMs).⁴ Perhaps two-thirds of Soviet SS-20s are targeted on Western Europe and one-third on China. But perhaps one-half of both are retargetable, from Western Europe to China and vice versa. The Soviet Union, for whom any nuclear weapon targeted on it is by definition "strategic," therefore rejects the NATO definition of SS-20 and LRTNF as "Eurostrategic" and the Western desire for "Eurostrategic" nuclear parity. On the contrary, Moscow wants to have enough ICBMs to have at least nuclear parity with the United States and enough SS-20s, BACKFIREs, and other shorter-range nuclear weapons to equal U.S., U.K., and French "Eurostrategic" weapons plus Chinese ICBMs and IRBMs.

The Soviet expulsion from Egypt, and later invasion of Afghanistan,[5]

---

4. Excellent treatments of the TNF issue can be found in Gregory F. Treverton, "Nuclear Weapons and the 'Gray Area,'" *Foreign Affairs*, 57, no. 5 (Summer 1979): 1075–89, and Roger Metzger and Paul Doty, "Arms Control Enters the Gray Area," *International Security*, 3, no. 3 (Winter 1978–1979): 17–52. The best running commentary on the TNF has been by Kurt Becker and Lothar Ruehl in *Die Zeit*, and Richard Burt in the *New York Times*.

5. William E. Griffith, "Super-power Relations after Afghanistan," *Survival*, 22, no. 4 (July–August 1980): 146–51; Zalmay Khalilzad, "Afghanistan and the Crisis in American Foreign Policy," ibid., pp. 151–60. See also Hannah Negaran, "The Afghan Coup of April 1978: Revolution and International Security," *Orbis*, 23, no. 1 (Spring 1979): 93–113; Louis Dupree, "Afghanistan under the Khalq," *Problems of Communism*, 28, no. 4 (July–August 1979): 34–50; Richard S. Newell, "Revolution and Revolt in Afghanistan," *World Today*, 35, no. 11 (November 1979): 432–42; Zalmay Khalilzad, "The Superpowers and the Northern Tier," *International Security*, 4, no. 3 (Winter 1979–1980); Cheryl Benard and Zalmay Khalilzad, "Secularization, Industrialization and Khomeini's Islamic Republic," *Political Science Quarterly*, 94, no. 2 (Summer 1979): 229–41; William E. Griffith, "The Revival of Islamic Fundamentalism: The Case of Iran," *International Security*, 4, no. 1 (Summer 1979); Firuz Kazemzadeh, "Afghanistan: The Imperial Dream," *New York Review of Books*, February 21, 1980; the series by Louis Dupree, "Red Flag over the Hindu Kush," in *American Universities Field Staff Reports*, part 1, "Leftist Movements in Afghanistan" (LD-2-'79, no. 44); part 2, "The Accidental Coup, or Taraki in Blunderland" (LD-3-'79, no. 45); part 3, "Rhetoric and Reform, or Promises! Promises!" (LD-2-'80, no. 23); part 4, "Foreign Policy and the Economy" (LD-3-'80, no. 27); part 5, "Repressions or Security through Terror, Purges 1–4" (LD-4-'80, no. 28); part 6, "Repressions or Security through Terror, Purges 4–7" (LD-5-'80, no. 29); part 7, "Afghanistan: 1980, The World Turned Upside Down" (LD-6-'80, no. 37). See also Dupree's "The Democratic Republic of Afghanistan, 1979" (LD-1-'79, no. 32) (Hanover, N.H.: American Universities Field Service, 1979).

highlighted, even more than the Soviet victories in Angola and Ethiopia,[6] the increasing political instability in much of the Third World, and the Soviet (and American) desire to profit from it. This instability centers in what I think we should call the "extended Middle East," from Kabul to Casablanca, because of its geographical nearness to the Soviet Union, decisive Western and Japanese dependence on Middle Eastern oil, the American commitment to Israel and Saudi Arabia, and the probable Soviet need in the late 1980s to import oil from the Middle East.

The efforts of China and the Soviet Union to encircle each other have recently been intensified by the Soviet alliance with Vietnam, which has resulted in the new Soviet air and naval bases in Vietnam, aimed both at China and the United States. This also brought China and the United States closer together and became a further obstacle (if any were needed!) to Brezhnev's aim since 1964 of a partial Sino-Soviet rapprochement at the state level, intended initially to block a Sino-American alliance against him. Finally, probably prolonged racial violence in South Africa will cause more Soviet support to black urban guerrillas and increased American concern about these Soviet activities.

Is to say that conservatism is rising in the United States, the Soviet Union, and China the view of one of Burckhardt's predicted "terrible simplifiers"?[7] More accurately, America and China are in the grip of the "conservatism of revulsion" while the Soviet Union is characterized by the "conservatism of stagnation."

In the United States, endemic, high domestic inflation, the cultural counterrevolution against the bohemianism of the 1960s,[8] and disillusionment with "big government" have produced more Americans who say they are conservative than those who say they are liberal—just the opposite of what they said thirty years ago. The United States also has deeper problems: the decline in industrial productivity, the tilt in the global military balance in favor of the Soviet Union, rising Third World instability and its threat to OECD energy supplies, and, some analysts maintain, a crisis in the American political system: the declining effectiveness of Congress and its lack of cooperation with a presidency that has not recently had an impressive in-

6. John A. Marcum, *The Angolan Revolution*, 2 vols. (Cambridge, Mass.: M.I.T. Press, 1969 and 1978). See the forthcoming article by Paul B. Henze in *Problems of Communism*; Tom J. Farer, *War Clouds on the Horn of Africa: The Widening Storm*, 2d rev. ed. (New York: Carnegie Endowment for International Peace, 1979).

7. Jakob Burckhardt, *Weltgeschichtliche Betrachtungen* (Stuttgart: Deutsche Verlags-Anstalt, 1929).

8. Daniel Bell, *The Cultural Contradictions of Capitalism* (New York: Basic Books, 1976), and *The Winding Passage: Essays and Sociological Journeys, 1960–1980* (Cambridge, Mass.: ABT Books, 1980).

cumbent.⁹ Whether or not there is such a crisis, or only a cyclical downturn which better leadership can reverse, only time will tell. Finally, unique in the Western world, a major religious revival is under way in the United States, centering among Protestant fundamentalists. It has many causes, among them the alienation arising from rapid urbanization and technological change, and it arises, as does Reagan's appeal politically, from a desire to reject cultural modernism—abortion, gay liberation, the Equal Rights Amendment for women—and return to simpler, unquestioned religious beliefs and moral standards. Politically, and even more culturally, it strengthens conservatism.

Most post-1917 American conservatives have always deeply distrusted the Soviet Union. They now fear the Soviet military build-up, Moscow's use of it and of Cuban troops to increase its influence in the Third World, and Soviet attempts to divide the United States from its allies and to hold as hostage its and their energy supplies. Moreover, just as after the 1939 Soviet-Nazi pact and the 1948 Prague coup, many present (and past) American leftists are becoming more anti-Soviet, for other reasons in addition to those of the conservatives: Soviet authoritarianism, bureaucracy, and repression of intellectual dissidents. These leftists are led ideologically by a small, brilliant group of "neoconservative" intellectuals, many of them former Marxists. This switch from left to right, particularly marked, and politically important, among some leading Jewish intellectuals, has deprived the American left of one of its traditional sources of inspiration and support, and has helped move the traditionally Democratic American Jewish community toward conservatism. The November 1980 landslide election of Ronald Reagan to the presidency, and even more the Republican capture of the Senate and by May 1981 the de facto conservative majority in the House of Representatives, showed that conservatism has become the dominant force in American politics today.

In the 1970s the Soviet Union also faced increasing domestic problems: declining economic growth; rising male and infant mortality; massive, endemic alcoholism; eroding ideological commitment at home and abroad; the probable rising percentage of Soviet Muslims in the Soviet work force and military; the looming greater demand for petroleum over supply in the Soviet Union, and therefore the need, by the late 1980s, of oil from the Middle East; and the rising resource demands of the steadily expanding Soviet military machine.¹⁰ The victorious Polish sit-down strike in 1980 and the resultant Polish political pluralism highlighted the instability of Mos-

---

9. Walter Dean Burnham, "Reflections on the American Political Crisis," *The Washington Review*, Special Supplement, Autumn 1980.

10. Seweryn Bialer, *Stalin's Successors: Leadership, Stability, and Change in the Soviet Union* (New York: Cambridge University Press, 1980).

cow's East European empire. Yet Soviet military power, and the resultant Soviet influence, continued to rise. Despite the current economic difficulties, the Soviet elite and masses remain basically satisfied with the status quo and with rising Soviet power. The dissident movement among the Great Russians was largely crushed.

Western Europe and Japan, weak and fearful of American indecision and weakness, gave Moscow opportunities to exploit them. French and West German disillusionment with the America that had twice saved the French from the Germans and, many Germans thought, the Germans from themselves reminds one of Tacitus's lapidary epitaph for the Emperor Galba: *Omnium consensu capax imperii nisi imperasset.* (During the Vietnam War, many Americans, most ruefully but some with *Schadenfreude*, came to agree.) Brezhnev believed that it would remain true for Russia, as it had for Rome, that *arma loquuntur*. Expansionism, fear of encirclement, and domestic problems made the Soviet Union also become more conservative. The result was the rise of Great Russian chauvinism, anti-Semitism, an almost paranoic obsession with the Chinese "yellow peril," and extreme hostility toward the West and toward the dissidents in the Soviet Union.

Moscow had concluded by 1979 that it had nothing to lose and nothing to fear from Washington by invading Afghanistan. By late 1980 Soviet-American détente was not dead but it was seriously—perhaps incurably—ill. Conservatives in the United States, the Soviet Union, and China had at least one conviction in common: détente was, as it should be, on the ropes.

China's problems were immense: poverty, overpopulation, lack of natural frontiers, slow economic growth, the disastrous legacy of the Cultural Revolution, the massive Soviet army and air force on its northern border, the Soviet Far Eastern fleet on its eastern border, and by 1980 the Soviet navy and air force on its southern flank, at Danang and Camranh Bay. This situation drove Beijing toward conservatism and toward Washington. By 1980 China had some reason to hope that the United States was at last listening—as Confucian tradition maintained the foreign barbarians should —to China's superior wisdom, and was therefore beginning to join China's grand design: the encirclement of the Soviet Union. China has completely subordinated its previous revolutionary aims to this, and therefore supports the status quo throughout the world, with two exceptions: the Soviet Union and its sphere of influence, notably Indochina.

After Mao's death, in alliance with his successor Hua Guofeng, Deng Xiaoping helped purge the radical Gang of Four. Thereafter Deng whittled down Hua's power. By late 1980 Deng was clearly on top. Reformist at home and anti-Soviet abroad, he was preparing something very rare under communist rule: a peaceful succession.[11] China had embraced what Deng

11. Lucian W. Pye, *The Dynamics of Factions and Consensus in Chinese*

and his patron Zhou Enlai had wanted since 1971: Washington's post-Afghanistan quasi alliance with Beijing.[12]

Deng's reforms seem popular, for the Cultural Revolution—an extremist, revolutionary convulsion—had been hated by the great majority of educated Chinese, because its fanatical hot gospelers had deeply humiliated so many of them. They therefore now prefer social stratification, private initiative, and nationalism to the Cultural Revolution's fanatical, poverty-stricken egalitarianism. China is thus also going conservative: meritocratic, not egalitarian; nationalist, not internationalist; and pragmatic, not ideologically fervent.

THE INTERNATIONALIZATION OF THE DISPUTE

Little systematic research on Sino-Soviet relations has been published,[13] largely, I suspect, because of their increasing interconnection with the overall foreign policies of the two communist giants and with international politics *toute entière*. Moreover, communist foreign policy is the product of the interaction between interstate and interparty foreign relations. For example, for the Soviet Union, good relations with large nonruling communist parties

---

Politics: A Model and Some Propositions, (Santa Monica: Rand R-2566-AF, 1980). See also Lowell Dittmer, "The Legacy of Mao Zedong," *Asian Survey*, 20, no. 5 (May 1980): 552–73; Joyce K. Kallgren, "China in 1979: On Turning Thirty," *Asian Survey*, 20, no. 1 (January 1980): 1–18; Kenneth Lieberthal, "The Politics of Modernization in the PRC," *Problems of Communism*, 27, no. 3 (May–June 1978): 1–17; and Victor C. Falkenheim, "Political Participation in China," ibid., pp. 18–32. For the factional struggle in Beijing, see Thomas M. Gottlieb, *Chinese Foreign Policy Factionalism and the Origins of the Strategic Triangle* (Santa Monica: Rand R-1902-NA, 1977), and Kenneth Lieberthal, *Sino-Soviet Conflict in the 1970's: Its Evolution and Implications for the Strategic Triangle* (Santa Monica: Rand R-2343-NA, 1978).

12. See the most authoritative account in Henry Kissinger, *White House Years* (Boston: Little, Brown, 1979).

13. Donald S. Zagoria, *The Sino-Soviet Conflict, 1956–1961* (Princeton: Princeton University Press, 1962); William E. Griffith, *Albania and the Sino-Soviet Rift* (Cambridge, Mass.: M.I.T. Press, 1963), *The Sino-Soviet Rift* (Cambridge, Mass.: M.I.T. Press, 1964), and *Sino-Soviet Relations, 1964–65* (Cambridge, Mass.: M.I.T. Press, 1967); Harold C. Hinton, *The Bear at the Gate: Chinese Policymakers under Soviet Pressure* (Washington, D.C.: American Enterprise Institute for Public Policy Research, and the Hoover Institution, Stanford, 1971); Zbigniew Brzezinski, *The Soviet Bloc*, 3d rev. ed. (Cambridge, Mass.: Harvard University Press, 1971), pp. 397–432; Hugh Seton-Watson, *The Imperialist Revolutionaries: Trends in World Communism in the 1960s and 1970s* (Stanford: Hoover Institution Press, 1978); Harry Gelman, "Outlook for Sino-Soviet Relations," *Problems of Communism*, 28, no. 5–6 (September–December 1979): 50–66.

are major assets in Moscow's relations with the states in which these parties exist, because interparty relations can be used either to cultivate or to obstruct these states' ruling political elites. China would also like to cultivate or obstruct them but has rarely had the opportunity.

Another obstacle to research is the vast amount of material that must be acquired, processed, and retrieved, and the lack of linguistic ability and familiarity with international politics and with the key regions of Sino-Soviet competition. Because the Soviet Union *in esse* and China *in spe* are global powers, their policies in America, Europe, Asia, and the Middle East interact with each other more than Russian and Chinese imperial policies did.

Some new factors on the international scene must also be taken into account. The three most important are the revival of Western Europe (particularly West Germany) and of Japan; the energy vulnerability of all OECD countries and the economic destabilization of most of the West, and even more of most of the Third World, as a result of high OPEC petroleum prices and the resultant massive resource transfers to the OPEC countries; and the existence of nuclear weapons and the present thrust forward in nuclear and conventional weapons technology, caused by (almost entirely American) breakthroughs in information acquisition, processing, and retrieval and consequently in the accuracy of delivery systems.[14]

Although the 1970s were the key decade to date in the internationalization of the Sino-Soviet dispute, the process began earlier. Indeed, the internationalization of Soviet foreign policy in part caused the dispute. Khrushchev's priority for détente with the United States through nuclear arms control, rather than for alliance with China, was a major cause of the Sino-Soviet split in 1959. But its main cause was different: Mao's determination that China should eventually become a superpower and Khrushchev's determination to prevent it. The Sino-Soviet split could therefore probably

---

14. Regarding military technology, see, with extensive bibliographies, Johan J. Holst and Uwe Nerlich, eds., *Beyond Nuclear Deterrence* (New York: Crane, Russak, 1977), Richard Burt, *New Weapons Technologies*, Adelphi Papers, no. 126 (London: International Institute for Strategic Studies, 1976), and especially his "Reassessing the Strategic Balance," *International Security*, 5, no. 1 (Summer 1980): 37–52; and "Technology and East-West Arms Control," *International Affairs*, 53, no. 1 (January 1977): 51–72; Kosta Tsipis, "Cruise Missiles," *Scientific American*, February 1977, pp. 20–29; and James Digby, *Precision-Guided Weapons*, Adelphi Papers, no. 118 (London: IISS, 1975), and "New Technology and Superpower Actions in Remote Contingencies," *Survival*, March–April 1979. See also John H. Mearsheimer, "Precision-guided Munitions and Conventional Deterrence," ibid., and Christopher J. Makins, "Western Europe's Security: Fog over the 'Grey Areas,'" *World Today*, 35, no. 2 (February 1979): 55–62.

not have been avoided. After 1957 at the latest, the more Sino-Soviet relations deteriorated, the more Moscow and Beijing searched for allies against the other, and the less each was willing to risk support from such allies to aid the other's vital interests rather than its own.

In the process of such a *bouleversement des alliances*, one's own motives are usually complex but are rarely so viewed by one's opponent. This was particularly true in China, so weak compared with Moscow or Washington and so fearful of General de Gaulle's bête noire: double hégémonie disguised as détente. As they say in Vienna, Moscow and Beijing have fallen prey to *das Gesetz der Gegengrenzlichkeit*: each saw the enemy of its enemy as its friend.

Three examples before 1970 will suffice. When Adenauer went to Moscow in 1955 after the Geneva summit conference to take up diplomatic relations with the Soviet Union, in order to compensate for what he saw as Eisenhower's reciprocation there of Khrushchev's policy of Soviet-American *double hégémonie*, Khrushchev asked him to help the Soviet Union against China. (Adenauer wrote later that he said nothing but thought to himself that he could well afford to wait, for Khrushchev would need him more later!) In 1957–58, when Mao tried to bluff the United States into abandoning Quemoy and Matsu, Khrushchev's aid was too verbal and too late, Mao thought, also because of his preference for the same *double hégémonie*.[15] In 1961, one year before the signing of the partial test ban treaty, Khrushchev told Mao that he was going to sign it,[16] thus confirming to him that Moscow had chosen Soviet-American *double hégémonie* over alliance with China.

These were choices of priorities on the global chessboard. Other examples occurred in the Third World. What many in the West have so long not understood, or not wanted to, is that Soviet détente policy was always intended to appear to stabilize the global status quo but in fact sought to help destabilize it. As Moscow sees it, the Western-dominated capitalist status quo is destabilizing itself. Revolution will therefore slowly but surely destroy it. Moscow must speed this process along, and build the military capability to do so. Khrushchev and Brezhnev have genuinely wanted détente in order to limit the risk of nuclear war by accident or miscalculation. But they also anticipated that détente would politically and therefore militarily demobilize the West, and thus block Western response to Soviet expansionism in the Third World. Nor did Moscow wholly miscalculate. Most Western arms control advocates have given priority to arms control

---

15. See my *Ostpolitik of the Federal Republic of Germany* (Cambridge, Mass.: M.I.T. Press, 1978), and *Sino-Soviet Relations, 1964–65*.
16. Walter C. Clemens, Jr., *The Arms Race and Sino-Soviet Relations* (Stanford: Hoover Institution, 1968).

agreements with the Soviet Union over blocking or reversing Soviet Third World expansionism, because attempts to alter what they have seen as far away, unimportant, reversible Soviet gains (as Goethe put it, *hinten, weit in der Türkei*) would endanger the salvation of the world from nuclear holocaust through arms control.

Thus when opportunities presented themselves for expanding Soviet influence in the Third World—and, a fortiori, when it could encircle China and push back America—the Soviet Union exploited them. The more military power it acquired, the faster it moved.

The earliest, best example was India. Khrushchev's forward policy in the Third World, begun by his foreign minister's visit to Cairo in 1955, soon after the Geneva summit meeting, saw India as one of the most important Third World areas wherein Moscow could push back the West. Khrushchev therefore began massive economic and military aid programs to India. When the first Sino-Indian border skirmishes broke out in mid-1959, the Soviet declaration of neutrality they sparked was one of the main causes of the Sino-Soviet break in that year.[17]

Another such example has been Vietnam. Chiang Kai-shek's China was weak and anticommunist. The Chinese Communist Party was weak and dependent on the Soviet Union. Moscow was hostile to France and America, who were for Vietnamese communists the principal colonialist and neocolonialist obstacles to Vietnam's independence and revolution. Moscow was so powerful and so predominant in the international communist movement that in the 1920s the Vietnamese revolutionary nationalist leader Ho Chi Minh became a Comintern agent, while maintaining good relations with Mao. In the 1950s Khrushchev sent arms aid to Ho's communist guerrillas. At that time major combat operations were begun in South Vietnam against the Viet Cong, a branch of Ho's forces. Ho needed Moscow much more for massive modern arms supply and to help deter the United States from invading North Vietnam. He profited from Lyndon Johnson's two naïve and incorrect assumptions: that Hanoi's main ally, and therefore Washington's main enemy, was China, not the Soviet Union; and that Brezhnev would get Ho to compromise with him. They were naïve because Moscow always intended to help Ho defeat the United States.

Ho and his successors also tilted toward Moscow for several other reasons. By 1965 Sino-Soviet hostility was intense and Mao was harassing and sometimes interrupting Soviet overland arms shipments to Hanoi. Brezhnev cut back Khrushchev's policy of collective mobilization against the Chinese but only apparently. Moscow proposed a partial détente with Beijing at the state, not the party, level, probably not because it thought Mao would agree but in order to improve the Soviet image with other communist states

---

17. See my *Sino-Soviet Rift*.

and parties. Moscow also proposed a new general line for the "international communist and workers movement": "united action to aid Vietnam."

Ho's predictable tilt toward Moscow had significant consequences for forward planning in Hanoi, Beijing, and Moscow. Ho believed that he would defeat the United States, as he did; thereafter conquer not only South Vietnam but also Laos and Cambodia; and therefore need a firm alliance with Moscow to keep out of China's sphere of influence, a fortiori because of his determination to dominate Indochina. Moscow was very powerful, strongly anti-Chinese, and far away—therefore the best ally Hanoi could have to preserve its conquests and keep as independent as possible.

Beijing shared the desire of Moscow and Hanoi to defeat America. A violent factional struggle was raging in Beijing over the policy to follow regarding the United States. The radicals (Lin Biao and the Gang of Four) wanted hostility toward both Washington and Moscow, and the moderates (led by Zhou Enlai and Deng Xiaoping) wanted to improve relations with the former and thereby more effectively oppose the latter. All probably foresaw the danger to China of a Moscow-Hanoi alliance after a defeat of the United States.

Moscow drew the opposite conclusions from those Beijing finally reached. Calculating that Sino-Soviet tension would probably continue high indefinitely, Brezhnev wanted to keep it within some limits and therefore proposed a partial détente at the state level. But because he also sought to further the Soviet encirclement of China and to counter American power, he wanted to get naval and air bases in Indochina.

It may be that some Americans in authority were thinking along these lines at that time, but I know of none. Nor were they likely to have been, for—unlike Moscow, Beijing, and Hanoi—they did not then contemplate the possibility that America could lose the war. In any case, the American decision to intervene in Indochina was in my view an important example of the influence of actions by noncommunist powers on the Sino-Soviet dispute.

By 1980 the Soviet Union had encircled China to the south as well as to the north and east. The new Soviet bases in Vietnam lie athwart American sea and air communications from Yokosuka and Subic Bay to Diego Garcia and thence to the Arabian Sea and the Gulf. Vietnam must remain bound to Moscow as long as it is determined to dominate Indochina, which probably means a long time indeed. China thus has one more reason to remain hostile to the Soviet Union and cultivate the United States. The United States, along with such ASEAN states as Thailand and Singapore, who fear Soviet and Vietnamese more than Chinese policy in Southeast Asia, is moving closer to China.[18]

18. On Indochina, see Stephen R. Heder, *Kampuchean Occupation and Re-*

Soviet policy in West Germany also has an anti-Chinese component. Khrushchev's remark to Adenauer in 1955 was obviously in part intended to lead him down the garden path—which Adenauer never trod, outside his Rhöndorf rose garden—of the revival of traditional German *Schaukelpolitik* (between West and East), thus splitting Bonn from Washington.[19] Since World War II, Soviet policy toward Western Europe has been designed slowly to erode the American military and political presence there, thereby gradually "self-Finlandizing" Western Europe and thus giving Moscow what it has believed to be its natural right since 1945 (as Tsar Alexander I did after 1815): hegemony over all of Europe.[20]

But Soviet-American détente both stabilizes peace in Europe and destabilizes it—the latter, so far, more in Eastern than in Western Europe.[21] The 1980 Polish events[22] would hardly have occurred in a period of intense

---

sistance (Bangkok: Institute of Asian Studies, Chulalongkorn University, Asian Studies Monographs, no. 027, January 1980), and "From Pol Pot to Pen Soran in the Villages," paper presented at the International Conference on Indochina and Problems of Security and Stability in Southeast Asia, Chulalongkorn University, Bangkok, January 19–21, 1980; Dieter Heinzig, "The Role and Interests of the USSR in Indochina," ibid.; Nguyen Manh Hung, "The Sino-Vietnamese Conflict: Power Play among Communist Neighbors," *Asian Survey*, 19, no. 11 (November 1979): 1037–52; Douglas Pike, "The USSR and Vietnam: Into the Swamp," *Asian Survey*, 19, no. 12 (December 1979): 1159–70; and the regular coverage by Nayan Chanda in the *Far Eastern Economic Review*.

19. For the German factor in Sino-Soviet relations, see my *Ostpolitik of the Federal Republic of Germany*, and "Ostpolitik Revisited," MIT/CIS C/80-3, mimeographed, April 1980. See also in general Wolfram F. Hanrieder, ed., *West German Foreign Policy, 1949–79* (Boulder, Colo.: Westview, 1980), and Josef Füllenbach and Eberhard Schulz, eds., *Entspannung am Ende?* (Munich: Oldenbourg, 1980).

20. John Van Oudenaren, "The Soviet Conception of Europe and Arms Control," and Robert Legvold, "The Soviet Union and the Political Significance of Military Power," papers prepared for a conference at the Stiftung Wissenschaft und Politik, Ebenhausen/Obb., June 10–12, 1980. See also Van Oudenaren, "The 'Leninist Peace Policy' and Western Europe," MIT/CIS C/89–1, mimeographed, January 1980, and Legvold, "The Soviet Union and Western Europe," in William E. Griffith, ed., *The Soviet Empire: Expansion and Detente* (Lexington, Mass.: Lexington Books, 1976).

21. Pierre Hassner, "Europe: Old Conflicts, New Rules," *Orbis*, 17, no. 3 (Fall 1973): 895–911.

22. The best recent analysis is Christoph Royen, "Der polnische Sommer 1980—Zwischenbilanz und Ausblick," *Stiftung Wissenschaft und Politik*, SWP-LN 2271, October 1980. See also John Darnton (from Warsaw), "Sixty Days that Shook Poland," *New York Times Magazine*, November 9, 1980. For earlier, from Warsaw, see Erik-Michael Bader, "Die Hoffnung liegt im Schock," *Frank-*

cold war.[23] Bonn's Ostpolitik, which aimed at bringing about "change through rapprochement" (*Wandel durch Annäherung*) in East Germany, brought millions of West German visitors there each year and much greater West German trade with the East. But Moscow has two advantages over Bonn. Bonn's Ostpolitik helps keep the Soviet western flank quiet. Fearful that Moscow might wreck Ostpolitik in retaliation, Bonn has not tried, as Washington has, to improve relations with Beijing in order to counterbalance Moscow's military superiority on the Elbe. Because of Moscow's hostility to Bonn and support of East Berlin, the Federal Republic's non-nuclear status, the overwhelming Soviet military superiority over the Bundeswehr, and the extreme vulnerability of West Berlin, Bonn has maintained its principal alliance with Washington. Even so, relations between Bonn and Washington have deteriorated, primarily because of their different responses to the Soviet invasion of Afghanistan.[24] After the invasion, Schmidt and Giscard, like Brezhnev (although with very different motives), tried to keep Europe an island of détente in a second cold war—centered in the Middle East and Southwest Asia—between Moscow and Washington. Carter and Deng, on the contrary, gave priority to countering Moscow's

---

furter Allgemeine Zeitung, September 2, 1980, and "Das 'neue Bewusstsein' und die alte Partei," ibid., September 15, 1980, Bernard Margueritte, "Une fissure dans l'ordre socialiste," *Le Figaro*, September 1, 1980; from Katowice, Thomas Wybraniec, "Weiss-rote Fähnchen im polnischen Revier," *Frankfurter Allgemeine Zeitung*, September 13, 1980; and from Gdańsk, Kazimierz Zborowski, "Das Eisenkreuz des Schweissers Petruszka: Arbeiterschaft und Kirche in Polen," ibid., September 15, 1980; Bernard Guetta, "Le P.C. polonais désemparé," *Le Monde*, October 7, 1980; and two more general ones, Viktor Meier, "Die Krise des Sozialismus," *Frankfurter Allgemeine Zeitung*, September 3, 1980, and Adam B. Ulam, "How Long Will Polish Victory Last?" *Boston Globe*, September 4, 1980. The best running coverage is from Warsaw by Margueritte, Bader, and Guetta, and from Munich by Jan de Weydenthal in *Radio Free Europe Research*. For documentation and initial analyses, see William F. Robinson, ed., *August 1980: The Strikes in Poland* (Munich: Radio Free Europe Research, October 1980), and for background the special issues on Poland of *Survey*, part 1, Autumn 1979, and part 2, Autumn 1980, and Jan B. de Weydenthal, *Poland: Communism Adrift*, Washington Papers, no. 72 (Beverly Hills and London: Sage, 1979). I also profited greatly from conversations in Warsaw in June 1980 and with Professor Seweryn Bialer. See also my "1980: A Year of Crises," MIT/CIS C/80–9, mimeographed, November 1980, chap. 5, "Poland Is Not Yet Lost."

23. See the penetrating essay by Arrigo Levi in *The Times* (London), September 10, 1980.

24. William E. Griffith, "The West German–American Relationship: The Threat of Deterioration," *The Washington Quarterly*, 2, no. 3 (Summer 1979): 83–89.

strategic gains from the invasion. Brezhnev's offer to Schmidt—after refusing to offer it to Carter—to begin Soviet-U.S. negotiations on nuclear weapons in Europe (LRTNF, SS-20, and also, Brezhnev insisted, FBS) showed again how Moscow was trying to erode the alliance between Bonn and Washington, *inter alia* to prevent Bonn from playing the Beijing card, and gradually to maneuver Bonn toward the first stage of its own ("self-Finlandization": becoming a "mediator" between Moscow and Washington.[25] Moscow will be disappointed, and American and Chinese fears not fulfilled, for Schmidt has no such intention.

The Eurocommunists have also helped to internationalize the Sino-Soviet dispute,[26] for they have moved, for electoral reasons, toward the foreign policy consensus of their countries and therefore away from Soviet foreign policy, state and party. The Italian Communist Party (PCI) has long had an autonomous and reformist ideology, going back to one of its founders, the political philosopher Antonio Gramsci. Togliatti, his successor, chose exile in Moscow over jail in Italy (while Gramsci wrote in a Fascist jail his *Lettere dal carcere*) but under the surface continued to hold Gramsci's views. Togliatti returned to Italy in 1944 to try to carry out a peaceful, parliamentary, Italian road to socialism—by winning, as Gramsci had advocated, first cultural and only thereafter political *egemonia* (Gramsci's term). In 1948 Togliatti felt it tactically desirable to follow Stalin in condemning Tito, especially because the United States so strongly supported the Christian Democratic leader De Gasperi, who had thrown the PCI out of the cabinet, but he did so *à contre-coeur*.

Togliatti first publicly differed with Moscow, and made clear his true aims, in June 1956, just before the Polish October and the Hungarian Revolution, in his slogan of "unity in diversity": full autonomy from, accompanied by continued party relations with, the CPSU. After the Revolution he again executed a tactical retreat. But he had already made clear, after the first Soviet-Yugoslav rapprochement in 1955, that he and Tito were moving toward each other. By the late 1950s a PCI-Yugoslav axis had developed, joined, after its 1964 ideological declaration of autonomy,

25. Uwe Nerlich, "Change in Europe: A Secular Trend?" *Daedalus*, Winter 1981, pp. 71–104; my "1980: A Year of Crises," chapter 4.

26. Rudolf L. Tökés, ed., *Eurocommunism and Detente* (New York: New York University Press, 1978); David E. Albright, ed., *Communism and Political Systems in Western Europe* (Boulder, Colo.: Westview Press, 1978); William E. Griffith, ed., *The West European Left* (Lexington, Mass.: Lexington Books, 1979); and the regular coverage by Kevin Devlin in *Radio Free Europe Research* and by Heinz Timmermann in the *Berichte des Bundesinstituts für ostwissenschaftliche und internationale Studien*. The most recent analysis is Timmermann, "Neue Tendenzen in europäischen Kommunismus," *Europa Archiv*, July 25, 1980.

by the Romanian Communist Party. At the 81-party meeting in Moscow in 1960 the PCI made its sympathies for the Yugoslavs clear. Thereafter it began to try to slow down, and if possible reverse, Khrushchev's escalating hostility to the Chinese and his determination to bring about communist "collective mobilization" against them. This PCI position, shared by the Romanian, Australian, and—after Dubček came to power in Prague in January 1968—Czechoslovak communists, along with Moscow's invasion of Czechoslovakia in August 1968, delayed the last international communist conference to date, held in Moscow, until 1969. The PCI, the Spanish Communist Party (PCE), which thereupon joined the PCI-Yugoslav-Romanian axis, and even the French Communist Party (PCF) publicly condemned the invasion. Since 1969 PCI and PCE relations with the CPSU have gradually, and with interruptions, deteriorated. Only the PCF, as one result of its decision to lose the 1968 French elections rather than be the junior partner of the socialists in a ruling left coalition, has largely returned to the Soviet fold. PCI and PCE relations with the CPSU have deteriorated further as a result of their condemnation of Moscow's invasion of Afghanistan and of their reestablishment of party relations with Beijing.

The PCI and PCE moved toward a position critical of Moscow for domestic electoral reasons. But to avoid discord in their own parties, they did not break off party relations with Moscow. Conversely, in order not to split still further what is left of the "international communist movement," Moscow has not broken with them. Thus the Eurocommunists became little more than nominal allies, and more often active opponents, of the Soviet Union. This further eroded not only CPSU prestige but Soviet influence in Italy and Spain. Much the same occurred in Japan and North Korea.[27]

The interaction between international politics and the Sino-Soviet dispute continues. Nationalism, not internationalism, in states and parties, communist or other, is the principal driving force in international politics in our times. Rising political and social mobilization, the global shortage of resources, and the growing gap between rich and poor countries make it even more so. The Sino-Soviet dispute has decisively contributed to making

27. For a detailed exploration of CPSU-PCI relations during the 1970s, see Joan Barth Urban, "Moscow and the PCI in the 1970s: Kto Kovo?" *Studies in Comparative Communism*, 13, nos. 2–3 (Summer–Autumn 1980): 99–167. For Soviet attitudes toward the West European CPs, see Urban, "Contemporary Soviet Perspectives on Revolution in the West," *Orbis*, 19, no. 4 (Winter 1976): 1359–1402; Robert Legvold, "The Soviet Union and West European Communism," in Tökés, *Eurocommunism and Detente*, pp. 14–384; Richard Lowenthal, "Moscow and the 'Eurocommunists,'" *Problems of Communism*, 27, no. 4 (July–August 1978): 38–49; Claudio Terzio, "L'URSS e l'eurocommunismo," *Il Mulino*, May–June 1978.

Soviet and Chinese foreign policy and national interests more differentiated and pluralized and each less centered on relations with the other and more a part of international politics as a whole.

The Challenge of the "New Internationalism"

KEVIN DEVLIN

The decade of decisive change in the post-Stalinist transformation of the international communist movement was the 1960s. When the decade opened, the movement was still in outward appearance—with the sole exception of deviant Yugoslavia—what it had been since Lenin's day: a disciplined international movement, with its national components acknowledging the unquestioned leadership of the CPSU, and when required sacrificing to it their own political interests. When the decade ended, that monolithic tradition—the product of Leninist myth and Stalinist discipline in a world of "socialism in one country"—had ended with it.

That oversimplified picture was deceptive, of course: this was a prolonged, complex, and subtle historical process that defies facile formulation; and its origins can be traced much farther back. Thus it could be said that Tito's decision to defy Stalin in 1948 marked the beginning of the end of the monolithic world movement as surely as the Irish struggle for independence in 1920–22 marked the beginning of the breakup of the British Empire. What began with Tito's rebellion continued with surges of popular unrest in the client regimes of Eastern Europe (East Germany in 1953, Poland and Hungary in 1956) and with "revisionist" tendencies among some West European communist parties. But it was the outbreak of the Sino-Soviet dispute in the early 1960s that made the process of post-

Stalinist transformation irreversible by providing another "pole" in the communist world. After that some communist parties, and many factions within communist parties, could give substance and significance to their rejection of Soviet authority by turning to the Chinese pole. At the same time some other parties, perhaps acting more subtly and boldly, could exploit the "no man's land" opened up by the Sino-Soviet conflict to increase their own freedom of maneuver and strengthen their claim to independence.

In understandable preoccupation with the two giants, students of communist affairs have generally tended to neglect these minor protagonists; yet some of them have played important if secondary roles in the complex drama. Of no communist party—certainly of no nonruling party—is this more true than of the Italian PCI. An examination of its role will shed valuable light on the post-Stalinist evolution of the international communist movement as a whole. Broadly speaking, our concern is with two periods. The first is the time during the 1960s (say, 1964 to 1969) when the PCI played a leading part in resisting Soviet pressures for a "showdown conference" which would produce something like a collective denunciation of Chinese positions and policies. The second is the recent, largely post-Mao period, during which the PCI and some other independent communist parties (notably the Yugoslav, Romanian, and Spanish) have established new relations with a Chinese leadership that is itself on a new course—this in the name of a "new internationalism" which in practice means the repudiation of "proletarian internationalism," Moscow style.

During the early years of the Sino-Soviet dispute—that is, between the scandalous though private revelation of the split to the communist party leadership of the world at the 81-party conference in November 1960 and what can be called the point of no return in July 1963 (the breakdown of the secret Sino-Soviet talks in Moscow and the publication of the CPSU's "Open Letter")—the PCI seemed to have settled down, however uneasily at times, in its expected place on the Soviet side. The Chinese certainly had no doubt about that, as evidenced by their implacable denunciation of Comrade Togliatti's modern revisionist errors (they could not, perhaps, have been expected to appreciate the extent to which that subtle spirit was revising "modern revisionism").[1]

"UNITY IN DIVERSITY AND AUTONOMY"

The Italian communists had already manifested concern about possible Soviet moves to meet the Chinese challenge by what Togliatti was to call

1. See in particular the polemical Chinese articles, "The Differences Between Comrade Togliatti and Us," December 31, 1961 (English text in *Peking Review*, no. 1, January 4, 1963), and "More on the Differences Between Comrade Togliatti and Us," March 4, 1963 (English text in *Peking Review*, no. 10–11, March 15, 1963).

the "method of excommunications."[2] It was, in fact, in answer to such moves in the fall of 1963—by pro-Soviet parties,[3] but clearly at the behest of the Kremlin—that the PCI was led to declare its antishowdown colors, and to do so in historically significant terms. It was in late October, a few weeks after the French Communist Party's Central Committee had issued a detailed denunciation of Chinese positions and called for the convocation as soon as possible of a new world conference "to reaffirm the general line,"[4] that the PCI adopted a seminal manifesto of what was to become known, more than a decade later, as the "new internationalism." The key phrase in the long resolution adopted at this Central Committee plenum was a new formula that was to become the PCI's watchword: "Unity in diversity and autonomy." Coolly reasoned criticism of Chinese positions was combined with sophisticated exposition of the PCI's own views on the international situation, the struggle for socialism in capitalist countries, relations with noncommunist revolutionary or progressive forces, the shortcomings of existing socialist regimes (and the PCI's right to criticize them), and, above all, the need to establish new norms of interparty relations. The PCI stood for open debate and confrontation of opinions in the international movement; but the debate should "always be carried on in such a way as to avoid exacerbations and splits." In particular, the PCI would reject any attempt to reimpose neo-Stalinist discipline on the world movement ("It is not even conceivable that there can be a return to organizational forms of the type that existed in the past"). Finally, the Italian party flatly opposed the calls for a conference: "At the present time such a conference could find itself faced, in effect, with a choice between two solutions, both of them detrimental to the communist movement: either a further worsening of the present divergencies, even to the extent of a rift, or else a completely formal and unsatisfactory compromise."[5]

The Soviets had been able to distort or ignore "antishowdown" initia-

2. In an interview in early 1963 Luigi Longo, Togliatti's deputy, said that a new world conference to deal with interparty differences should be held "only if one can see concrete possibilities of agreements and unity on fundamental questions" (*l'Unità*, February 24, 1963).

3. The first calls for a conference, coupled with denunciations of the Chinese and particularly their factionalist activities, came in early September 1963 from the Portuguese and Paraguayan communist parties, and were duly publicized by *Pravda*, as was the stand taken by the French PCF in early October.

4. *L'Humanité*, October 8, 1963. During this plenum Secretary-General Thorez vented his personal animus against Togliatti by rebuking "certain persons [who] say they deplore the Chinese position, but do not want to condemn it."

5. *L'Unità*, October 26, 1963.

tives by smaller parties, such as the British.⁶ But this open opposition to a Soviet-inspired project by the most important nonruling communist party was a very different matter. The hesitant Soviets made a tactical retreat. The day before the publication of the Italian resolution, the substance of which must have been communicated to him, Khrushchev called for an end to open Sino-Soviet polemics, and implicitly dissociated himself from the calls for an early conference by remarking that time would show which side was in the right. The conference project was shelved—for a time.

Before it was taken off the shelf again in February 1964 (with the Suslov Report) an important interparty development occurred. This was Togliatti's visit to Belgrade in January 1964 for a week of talks with Tito. At the Moscow Conference in 1960 Luigi Longo had vainly sought to get the conference statement's condemnation of Yugoslav revisionism (on which the Chinese, aiming at one target to hit another, had insisted) at least toned down; and in January 1963 Togliatti had flatly declared that the condemnation was "mistaken." But this rapprochement went beyond such ideological affinities: it made the Rome-Belgrade axis an important and enduring factor in international communism.

The joint communiqué of Tito and Togliatti spoke of the need to achieve a "new unity" in the international communist movement which would "remove the danger of a deep rift or even a split," while stressing that on such issues as peaceful coexistence "compromises with dogmatic and sectarian positions are not possible."⁷ It made no mention of the conference project, but in his Belgrade press conference Togliatti remedied this. The agreement reached on all fundamental questions did indeed apply to the Sino-Soviet dispute, he said:

> [There is] no divergence. Both we and the Yugoslav comrades hold that the Chinese positions are mistaken and harmful to the struggle for peace and coexistence. Equally, we condemn the Chinese party's attempt to split, through factionalist positions, the unity of the international communist movement. Finally, we agree that the divisions cannot be overcome through

6. In mid-September 1963 the British Communist Party leadership issued a statement saying that British communists "refuse to accept that a [Sino-Soviet] split . . . is inevitable"; the CPGB therefore urged that bilateral Sino-Soviet talks be resumed; it asked all communist parties to "consider the necessity to start preparations for a world conference some time next year," and it suggested that in the meantime public polemics should be stopped. *Pravda* (September 17, 1963) reprinted the British Communist Party's criticism of the Chinese but omitted the rejection of a split and the call for new Sino-Soviet talks; it cited the British Communist Party as suggesting discussions to prepare for a conference, but dropped the procrastinatory phrase "some time next year."

7. *Borba* (Belgrade), January 23, 1964.

verbal proclamations or anathemas, but [only] by examining the conditions in various countries, discovering in concrete terms how the differences arise, and overcoming them in . . . a debate founded on reality. . . .

Our party (and the Yugoslav comrades are in agreement) has many reservations regarding the project for a world conference of communist parties, which would run the risk of limiting itself to the repetition of general condemnations, aggravating them.[8]

It is worth pausing at this point to note the qualitative difference between the Italian-Yugoslav attitude to interparty disputes and that of both the Soviets and the Chinese. Both the Soviet claim to exemplary leadership in the international communist movement and the Chinese charge that the Soviets had forfeited that position were expressed in terms of a universally valid ideology. This was what made a settlement of their differences so difficult, even when, in the later 1960s, it became predominantly a matter of a conflict of state interests between the two regimes. While the Italian and Yugoslav communists spoke of the "mistakes" of the Chinese and of their "disagreements" with the Soviets, both of the latter used the language of anathema: the Soviet regime had taken the road of "capitalist restoration"; the Chinese were guilty of "betrayal of Marxism-Leninism"; and so on. Attack and counterattack took place on the dogma-laden level of "proletarian internationalism." Thus while the Soviets made repeated efforts to obtain a collective criticism of the Chinese at a world conference of communist parties, the Chinese and their Albanian allies spent much of their energy from 1963 on in promoting the growth of a sort of rival international of "Marxist-Leninist" parties, splinter parties, and factions. In his impressive book *L'Héritage de Lénine*, François Fejtö says of the Sino-Soviet conflict in the mid-1960s: "The fact is that in their way of thinking, of governing, of manipulating the masses, of posing as the guardians of the sole revolutionary truth, the two regimes were alike as two brothers."[9]

TOWARD A SHOWDOWN

The PCI and the Yugoslav LCY were not, of course, alone in their opposition to Soviet plans for a conference that would deal a "collective rebuff" to the Chinese splitters (in Suslov's terms), although attitudes and motivations varied widely within the antishowdown spectrum. By this time, in fact, only half of the fourteen existing communist regimes remained fully loyal: the other seven were either directly anti-Soviet (China and Albania) or independent/neutralist (Yugoslavia, Romania, Cuba, North Vietnam, and North Korea).

Of these, Romania was of particular importance, precisely because it

8. *L'Unità*, January 22, 1964.
9. Paris: Le Livre de Poche, 1977, p. 366.

was able to exploit the Sino-Soviet dispute to gain increased freedom of maneuver and a measure of independence *within* the Soviet bloc. It was the Romanians who obtained postponement of the publication of the Suslov Report for nearly two months, so that they could undertake successive missions of mediation which had really no chance of success, and used the interval to prepare their own "declaration of independence" stressing the full autonomy of each socialist regime and communist party.[10] This reflected the concern of the independent parties that the "collective rebuff" to the Chinese would also mean a reaffirmation of Soviet authority. Togliatti told a PCI Central Committee plenum in late April that a final split would leave the international movement divided in two around opposing centers, so that its energies would henceforth be exhausted "in an organized struggle between these two centers, with little splinter parties of a Chinese stamp merging almost inevitably in every country, and with a tightening-up, on both sides of the struggle, of forms of organization and discipline not suitable for present situations and necessities."[11]

One important effect of the independent parties' resistance was that the whole process of convening the conference was subject to delays, which were to prove decisive. In their letter of March 7, 1964, to the Chinese, the Soviets had "proposed" that a 26-party preparatory meeting (on the basis of the 1960 precedent) be held in June–July 1964, and that the actual conference be held "in the autumn of 1964."[12] In May they were still pressing, in secret interparty negotiations, for a preparatory meeting in July.[13] But when the Soviet leader finally convened the meeting at the end of July, his first schedule having perforce been abandoned, he had to put it off until December 15, 1964—a crucial delay which was to ensure that "Khrushchev's showdown" would not, in fact, show up.

One development which strengthened the position of the PCI and of the independent parties in general was the dramatic episode of the Yalta Memorandum: the challenging exposition of Italian communist positions (and critique of Soviet positions) that Togliatti composed in preparation for a

10. *Scinteia*, April 23, 1964.
11. Palmiro Togliatti, "For the Unity of the International Workers' and Communist Movement," in *Il Partito Comunista Italiano e il Movimento Operaio Internazionale* (Rome: Riuniti, 1968), p. 232.
12. Letter of the CPSU Central Committee to the CCP Central Committee, July 30, 1964; *Peking Review*, no. 36, September 4, 1964, pp. 8–9.
13. See Alessandro Natta, *Le Ore di Yalta* (Rome: Reunita, 1970), p. 31. In this account of the background to Togliatti's Yalta Memorandum, Natta tells how in early May 1964 a PCI delegation (Berlinguer, Ingrao, and Colombi) went to Moscow to try to persuade the Soviets to drop their plan for an early conference. They found Khrushchev "insisting on the necessity of the conference," and proposing to convene the preparatory committee in July.

meeting with Khrushchev a few hours before he suffered a fatal stroke in the Crimea in August 1964. The interparty impact came less from Togliatti's arguments than from the bold and skillful use that his party made of the memorandum. The decision to publish this private, unwontedly outspoken document, and to declare it "a precise expression of the position of the party on the problems of the international workers' and communist movement and its unity,"[14] was apparently taken by Togliatti's successor, Luigi Longo, as the veteran leader still lay in his terminal coma in Yalta.[15] With that, the Yalta Memorandum became the Yalta Testament; and the PCI had committed itself to a radical critique of the Soviet response to the Chinese challenge. The right way to meet that challenge, the memorandum argued, was to avoid being drawn into dogmatist polemics, but rather to "combat the Chinese with deeds, not just with words." Debate (not invective) over differences was necessary, but it should be based on and linked with a pattern of practical initiatives, promoting the better adaptation of the international movement and its constituent parts to environmental realities, and paying particular attention to the need for anti-imperialist unity of action: "The unity of all socialist forces in a common action, going beyond ideological divergences, against the most reactionary imperialist groups is an indispensable necessity. It is inconceivable that China and the Chinese Communists could be excluded from this unity. From now on we should therefore act in such a way as not to create obstacles to the achievement of this unity.... our whole struggle against the Chinese position must be conducted as a struggle for unity."

The publication of the full text of the memorandum without commentary in *Pravda* of September 10 amounted to an admission that the Soviets had been outmaneuvered on that sector of the interparty front. But they made clear their determination to press on with the main offensive. The next issue of *Pravda* carried "Theses on the 100th Anniversary of the First Interna-

14. Secretary-General Longo's preface to the published text of the Yalta Memorandum, *l'Unità* and *Rinascita*, September 4, 1964.

15. According to Alessandro Natta, Longo told him that if Togliatti died, they would have to publish the memorandum immediately: "And he explained why: that it would be unthinkable and, moreover, mistaken to say nothing about a document like this, or keep it hidden; that its importance and political impact were such that we were obliged to make it known; that no other act or stand by our party could at this point do more to make our line and orientations, in the communist movement and in Italy, persuasive, incisive, and penetrating; and that, finally, we could not hesitate about this if we were convinced that our positions—the ideas expressed by Togliatti in the memorandum—were correct and valid, not just for our party but more generally for the whole workers' movement" (*Le Ore di Yalta*, p. 48).

tional," issued by the CPSU Central Committee's Institute of Marxism-Leninism. Among the "most important organizational principles of proletarian internationalism" still valid for the present were the "duty to observe the decisions adopted within the framework of the International on the part of all parties entering into it" and the "banning of factionalist, schismatic activity."[16] There was to be a tightening of discipline among reduced ranks. Accepting the boycott of the meeting by independent-neutralist parties like the Japanese,[17] Khrushchev had evidently resolved, against the opposition of the Italians and others, to rally the loyalist majority of communist parties for a world conference at which Chinese ideological positions and their factionalist activities would be subjected to collective criticism. There would be no "excommunication," but the Chinese could henceforth be presented as having, regrettably, cut themselves off from the world communist community.

But at this point—one might put it flippantly—a funny thing happened to Nikita Khrushchev on his way to the showdown. His sudden ouster in mid-October 1964 left the new Soviet leadership in a defensive, uncertain mood and not inclined to seek unnecessary trouble. The shift from showdown to climbdown began—with the help of the PCI. Two weeks after Khrushchev's fall Luigi Longo announced almost casually that the Italian communists "reject the convocation of the international conference."[18] Struck with Khrushchev's commitment to hold the preparatory meeting of the "editorial commission" for the international conference in mid-December 1964, the new Soviet leadership first postponed it until March 1965, and then accepted the PCI's demand that it be "of a predominantly consultative character, thus avoiding giving to the presence or absence of a [particular] party any politically discriminating significance."[19] Even so, the Romanians joined the pro-Chinese and neutralist parties—seven out of the twenty-six invited—in boycotting the meeting. To save some face, the resulting communiqué still put forward an international conference as an eventual goal, but stated that consultations would now be necessary "to solve the question of calling . . . a preliminary [81-party] meeting," which

16. *Pravda*, September 11, 1964.
17. In the summer of 1964 the CPSU publicized its rift with the Japanese Communist Party and began giving open support to the antiparty faction of Yoshio Shiga.
18. Interview in *l'Express* (Paris), November 2, 1964. Longo added that the PCI believed that the interparty debate should be continued and deepened "on a basis of reciprocal respect and tolerance, with the aim above all of seeking new forms of articulation and unity for the international communist movement."
19. Giuliano Pajetta's report to the PCI Central Committee, *l'Unità*, December 14, 1964.

in turn might (or might not) convene a conference of "all the fraternal parties."[20] In fact, the project had been shelved.

While the implacable Chinese exulted contemptuously over the outcome of this "schismatic" meeting, the Italian and British party leaderships emphasized their victory by publishing separate communiqués of their own on the meeting. The Italian statement stressed that an eventual conference must be viewed "not as the condition for, but as the end-point of, a gradual unitary process," and warned against "any future initiative which, because of its untimeliness or its character, may be based on different considerations."[21]

NEW CONFERENCE PROJECT

A year and a half later, however, the pro-Soviet parties took to the conference trail again, encouraged by two developments in particular. The first was the Maoist refusal to accept "anti-imperialist unity of action" in support of North Vietnam, even after the "escalation" of the war through the bombing of the North in February 1965 and the subsequent massive build-up of the U.S. military effort in the South had made this a rallying slogan to communist parties all over the world. The second was the outbreak of the Cultural Revolution in August 1966, bringing years of social chaos and Maoist excesses. In the circumstances it was understandable that the calls for a new international conference, which came first from East European leaders in the fall of 1967, soon swelled into a chorus that included the overwhelming majority of the world's communist parties.

But one voice that had made itself important was missing from the chorus. The PCI was ready enough to criticize the excesses of the Cultural Revolution, and to condemn the Chinese rejection of unity of action on Vietnam; but it maintained its "reservations about making the 'Chinese question' the subject of a new world conference, which would function as a sort of tribunal charged with passing judgment on the errors of the CPC."[22]

It may seem incredible, but the evidence imposes the conclusion: the Italian Communist Party was able to hold up the new conference project, backed by the CPSU and the great majority of fraternal parties, for a full

20. *Pravda*, March 10, 1965.
21. Communiqué of PCI Directorate, March 10, 1965, *Documenti politici dal X all'XI Congresso del PCI* (Rome, 1966), p. 557. In violation of tradition the PCI also published Enrico Berlinguer's address at the Moscow meeting, in which he criticized "other comrades" who wanted to set a date for an international conference—evidence that the proshowdown forces gave way only at the meeting itself.
22. Luigi Longo, *Opinione sulla Cina* (Milan: La Pietra, 1977), p. 124.

year, until it finally gave the "green light" on its own terms. This came in October–November 1967, through a series of four articles in the party weekly *Rinascita*, which in effect laid down the PCI's conditions for participation in a new international conference. The main conditions, set forth in Longo's last article,[23] were that the conference must be of an "informative, consultative, and coordinative" character, with no binding programmatic content; the principle of the autonomy of each party must be strictly respected; nonattendance must not affect any party's status as part of the international movement; any party must have the right "not to accept, or to accept only partly or with reservations any eventual [collective] decision"; and a basic purpose of the meeting should be to establish "new forms of unity and collaboration, which must exclude any return to "leading centers and forms of monolithism."

That these conditions were substantially observed when the conference eventually took place in June 1969 may not of itself prove that the PCI was able to block the project until it was prepared to "give the green light." What does seem to prove it is that after Longo's final article had appeared, the announcement that the first preparatory meeting for the new international conference would be held in Budapest in February 1968 was made simultaneously, in Moscow and in Rome, by the CPSU and the PCI. Moreover, the Romanians were also getting into this act: they agreed to take part in the Budapest meeting only after the Hungarian hosts had assured them that there would be no moves to "excommunicate" any party, and further specified that "the Chinese Communist Party's internal situation cannot be the theme of either the Budapest consultative meeting or the international conference."[24]

What followed over the next year and a half might be described as the institutionalization of diversity and dissent in the international communist movement. From the Soviet viewpoint, one woeful precedent followed another (and we must keep reminding ourselves how important precedent is for communist party bureaucracies). This time around, for instance, the conventions of unanimity and secrecy were abandoned, so that any party could publicize its often dissident contributions or use "leaks" to promote its interests; all parties that wished to do so could take part in editorial sessions to draft conference documents; in the later stages particularly there was genuine debate, with hundreds of amendments being tabled. The Soviets did not help their own cause by invading Czechoslovakia in August 1968: one result was that the conference already fixed for November 1968

23. Luigi Longo, "New Forms of Unity and of International Collaboration," *Rinascita*, November 10, 1967.
24. *Partelet* (Bucharest), December 1967.

had to be postponed until May (later June) 1969, on the insistence of a dozen Western communist parties (following the lead of the PCI), and the draft document already prepared by June 1968 was scrapped, so that the drafting process had to start all over again on terms more favorable to the independent parties. The Sino-Soviet military clashes on the Ussuri River in March 1969 did not help the Soviet cause either: it reinforced the determination of the independent/neutralist parties not to take sides in the conflict.

It was fairly certain in advance that the conference would not produce any "collective rebuff" to the Chinese. Part of the price for getting the project launched in the first place had been the agreement at the Budapest consultative meeting that no communist party, absent or present, would be condemned in the conference documents. Failing that, the best the Soviets could hope for was to have the Chinese criticized as vigorously as possible by the maximum number of delegations: the conference could then be presented as a sort of majority consensus of the world movement, from which the Maoists had excluded themselves by their errors, extremism, and splitting activities.

As it turned out, it was not a very impressive consensus. Brezhnev's massive attack on the Chinese on the second day[25] was duly followed by similar polemics from the East European regimes (except Romania) and Mongolia, from a small number of conservative or client West European communist parties, and finally from a parade of Latin American and Middle Eastern parties which made up the numerical majority of the loyalist contingent. But the independent/neutralist parties did not join in at all; another group criticized Maoism in terms so mild that they could be regarded as having failed to respond to the Soviet lead; and several other delegations expressed such criticism in terms that could be read as an implicit rebuke to the Soviets.

There was certainly no doubt that the days of monolithic unity were over. In the end, fourteen parties out of seventy-five—with thirteen absentees—expressed opposition to or reservations about a document that already contained important Soviet concessions: for example, the failure to assign any special status to the CPSU, the new interparty principle of noninterference in the affairs of others, and the crowning fact that the document was not in any case binding on anyone. Five did not sign the final document at all; four (including the PCI) signed only the section on anti-

---

25. Brezhnev felt constrained to claim defensively that "until a short time ago we did not have the intention of raising this question at the conference," but that "recent events . . . oblige us to dwell on it." See *International Meeting of Communist and Workers' Parties, Moscow, 1969* (Prague: Peace and Socialism Publishers, 1969), p. 157.

imperialist unity; and five signed only after having expressed reservations of various kinds.[26]

One could hardly dig through the layers of contemporary Maoist propaganda with any hope of discovering to what extent the Chinese leaders appreciated the important changes in interparty relations and procedures that had taken place during the few years preceding the 1969 conference on the "Soviet side" of the great rift. Did they, for example, ponder the significance of two statements that Enrico Berlinguer of the PCI made in February 1969? There was this firm commitment: "In all circumstances we shall oppose any form of excommunication with regard to the Chinese Communist Party."[27] And this, a few days earlier, to complement it: "[The PCI wishes] to intensify its relations with all components [of the international communist movement], without any exception whatsoever."[28]

During the 1960s the Italian Communist Party led other independent communist parties in resisting Soviet efforts to obtain from the great majority of the parties in the international movement something like a collective condemnation of Chinese positions and policies. During the 1970s, and particularly during the closing years of the decade, the PCI, joined notably by the Spanish Communist Party, sought gradually and cautiously to reestablish a certain relationship with the Chinese party, as the expression of, and an aid to, the maintenance of an independent attitude toward the CPSU—a process pioneered and promoted by the independent regimes of Romania and, later, Yugoslavia.

As long as Mao Zedong lived, occasional approaches or gestures of rapprochement by independent Western communist parties received little or no encouragement from Beijing. The "deideologization" of Chinese foreign policy—to use an ugly but useful neologism—was already under way when the decade opened, and found its most dramatic expression in Henry Kissinger's visit to China in July 1971. The visit of President Ceausescu of Romania to China a month earlier had shown a corresponding sense of Realpolitik on the interparty level. But perhaps this decline in ideological commitment would itself have led the Maoists to maintain a critical distrust of Western communist "revisionists," as a help toward preserving their own revolutionary credentials.

26. The five that did not sign were the Cuban and Swedish observers and the British, Norwegian, and Dominican communist parties; the four which signed only the anti-imperialist section were the communist parties of Italy, Australia, San Marino, and Reunion; the five that signed after expressing reservations were those of Romania, Spain, Switzerland, Morocco, and the Sudan.
27. *L'Unità*, February 20, 1969.
28. Ibid., February 16, 1969.

ITALIAN SIGNALS

In the years following the Moscow conference of 1969 the Italian Communist Party distinguished itself by paying a good deal of often sympathetic if not uncritical attention to developments in China. On the twentieth anniversary of the proclamation of the People's Republic of China the PCI went beyond sympathetic interest to a direct though cautious approach—which, however, met with no response. In a message of greetings from one central committee to the other, the Italian party said that anti-imperialist unity of action was more than ever necessary, "despite the existing conflicts and divergences." It went on:

> In accordance with a conception of internationalist unity founded on the recognition of the autonomy and independence of every [communist] party and state, the Italian Communists renew their commitment and their appeal for a new real unity of the international communist and workers' movement. They hope that the great Chinese People's Republic will to a progressively greater extent carry out its historical task, and they will continue their struggle for the recognition of China on the part of the Italian government, and for the restoration of the legitimate rights of the Chinese People's Republic in the United Nations Organization and in all international institutions.[29]

The Chinese ignored this message, but a year later they began to respond, to a certain extent and on a different level, to Italian communist overtures. They did so by granting entry visas to individual Italian communists—not as representatives of the party but as journalists. This began in late 1970 with a six-week visit to China by two Sinophile members of the PCI: Alberto Jacoviello, foreign editor of *l'Unità*, and his wife, Maria Antonietta Macciocchi, a member of the Foreign Affairs Commission of the Italian Chamber of Deputies. The long series of articles that Jacoviello contributed to *l'Unità* on his return (January 1971) gave such an enthusiastic description of China during the Cultural Revolution that an Italian communist senator was moved to complain of a total lack of "Marxist criticism" in the articles, and to warn that the PCI would be "taking the worst possible course if, after giving up one set of myths" (the Soviet ones about China), it should now "embrace another," based on Maoist propaganda.[30] But the PCI itself made a more important point through an editorial preface to the series, which said that differences in the positions of the Italian and

---

29. Ibid., October 1, 1969. A few days later the PCI's weekly *Rinascita* (October 3, 1969) celebrated the twentieth anniversary with several articles, including one in which Editor in Chief Luca Pavolini described the PRC as "an inalienable component of [the anti-imperialist] alignment."

30. Senator Giovanni Brambilla, letter in *l'Unità*, January 17, 1971.

Chinese communist parties, even on "essential" questions, "have not kept, and do not keep our party from reaffirming—as it has done—its readiness to resume relations with the Chinese Communist Party."[31]

In his uncritical enthusiasm for the Chinese experience, Jacoviello was on a course which was not that of his party; while his pro-Chinese sentiments came to involve increasing distrust and criticism of the Soviet regime, the important thing for the PCI, then and later, was to restore relations with the Chinese Communist Party without endangering its relationship of "critical solidarity" with the CPSU. When Jacoviello published a book, *Capire la Cina* (*Understanding China*), on his first visit to China, the views expressed in it were "disowned" by the then editor in chief of *l'Unità*, Aldo Tortorella, and Jacoviello was later demoted from foreign editor of the party daily to special correspondent on foreign affairs. In December 1972 this book was the target of a polemical attack by the Soviet journal, *Literaturnaia gazeta*, which charged that Jacoviello was "more Maoist than Mao"; he replied that some Soviet journalists were "more Stalinist than Stalin." After another visit to China in 1972, Jacoviello published a second book, *In Cina due anni dopo* (*In China Two Years Later*)—with a mocking dedication "to the comrades of the *Literary Gazette* of Moscow, so that they may also make use of this further, humble contribution to the understanding of China and its environs." When it came out, in April 1973, *l'Unità* refused to accept paid advertisements by the publishers.

The episode was significant because it demonstrated the concern of the PCI leadership to keep the whole delicate matter of the movement toward (possible) relations with the Chinese Communist Party under control, because of both the effect on PCI-CPSU relations and the effect on the ranks of the party, to mention two obvious factors. Six months after Jacoviello's trip, a more fitting envoy (from the party's viewpoint) went to China for two weeks: among a party of Italian journalists was Luca Pavolini, who not only held a high position on the staff of *l'Unità* but also was a member of the PCI Central Committee. The four articles that Pavolini wrote on his return were informed, sympathetic studies of "a model of development profoundly different overall from that adopted in other socialist societies, starting with the Soviet model," and which was in itself "confirmation of the luminous historical superiority of [the socialist] system."[32] They amounted to a clear, if implicit signal, of a kind repeated many times during succeeding years by party spokesmen such as Guiseppe Boffa. While Mao Zedong lived, these interparty signals were ignored, although the Chinese continued to make some response by granting entry visas to Italian communists in their capacity as journalists or members of parliament—while pointedly

31. Ibid., January 3, 1971.
32. Luca Pavolini, "The Choices of China," *l'Unità*, June 6, 1971.

and repeatedly refusing visas to French communist journalists and parliamentarians. Five years later Gian Carlo Pajetta commented dryly on Pavolini's visit: "The Chinese Communists were courteous enough to treat him like any other Italian journalist; I must also say, more with regret than with irony, that among the courtesies extended to Comrade Pavolini was that of ignoring the fact that he is a member of our party's Central Committee."[33]

It is perhaps characteristic that the PCI's first direct approach, as distinct from such "signals," was made in secret, using the more outspoken Spanish communists as intermediaries. In late October 1971, Secretary-General Santiago Carrillo led a strong five-man delegation to Beijing in an effort to reestablish interparty relations—the Romanians having apparently helped to arrange the four-week visit.[34] On his return to Europe, Carrillo spoke as if normal interparty relations had been restored, and did so in significant terms. Reporting on an interview that Carrillo gave to his own clandestine weekly, *Mundo Obrero*, the PCI's *l'Unità* gave this as his answer to a question on "the significance which this reestablishment of relations can have for the international communist movement":

> Carrillo affirms that this is to be regarded as a positive experience, insofar as, having frankly and sincerely noted the divergences which still exist, as well as the convergences to be found between the two parties, it was decided, in mutual agreement, "to leave aside the divergences, since time and experience will show who is right, and to collaborate on that which unites us," in a spirit of perfect equality, recognizing the right of each party to use the forms and methods of action appropriate to it, and excluding all interference and every attempt by one party to impose its viewpoint on the other. We consider that these general principles are fundamental for arriving at a new unity—a unity in diversity—of the communist movement and of the anti-imperialist forces.
>
> The reestablishment of relations between our party and the Chinese Communist Party—Comrade Carrillo concludes—will contribute to this unity and to clarification of the bases on which it can be realized. Anyone who imagines that unity can be reached through the simple return of the Chinese Communist Party to the international communist movement, in the state in which it finds itself today, is mistaken. To clarify and make concrete the new bases on which unity can one day be achieved is one of the noblest tasks that a communist party can undertake. . . . This is the

33. Interview in *l'Expresso* (Rome), August 15, 1976.

34. In August 1971, Carrillo visited Bucharest for talks with President Ceausescu, who had been given a red-carpet reception in Beijing two months earlier. In September 1970, after expelling Enrique Líster and his pro-Soviet followers from the party, the PCI Central Committee had announced that it was "making the necessary efforts to normalize its relations with the Chinese Communist Party."

The Challenge of the "New Internationalism" 161

substance of the position and the initiative that the Communist Party of Spain has taken.[35]

This is valuable as a statement of what Carrillo wanted to achieve; for it was not what he did achieve. It transpired that the Spanish delegates were not received by any top-ranking Chinese leaders, and there was no joint communiqué. In March 1973 the Spanish Communist Party (PCE) issued a strong protest on principle when China established diplomatic relations with the Franco regime (as it did when East Germany took the same step); but the protest ended with a reaffirmation of the PCE's "internationalist position, its determination to strengthen ties of unity, even when there are differences of opinion, and despite the negative consequences of actions such as the one meeting with our disapproval here."[36] Later, PCE spokesmen were ready to admit that their initiative had, in effect, failed, and that lack of response on the Chinese side had caused a continued "suspension of relations" (as Manuel Azcárate put it).[37]

Five years after Carrillo's ultimately vain initiative, it was revealed that the PCI had also been involved. In an interview one month before Mao Zedong's death, Gian Carlo Pajetta disclosed that before leaving for Beijing, Carrillo was asked by the PCI "to make our position known to the Chinese comrades, and to let them know that we desired meetings with the leaders of the Chinese Communist Party, in Italy, or in China"—which Carrillo duly did. The result was disappointing: "On the Chinese side, there has been no sign of interest in the positions of the PCI." Why not? Pajetta suggested that it might be "because they are not yet ready to meet people who ask questions and are not content to listen." When asked if this interview could be considered a "message" to the Chinese, Pajetta reaffirmed that the PCI was ready to reestablish relations with the Chinese Communist Party—whenever the Chinese were ready: "We have no intention at present of sending any signal toward Beijing. It is known, and we can confirm it, that we are interested, today as yesterday, in clarifying the respective positions on the basis of full autonomy and complete parity of rights and duties. However bitter the phrase may seem, I repeat that we believe in peaceful coexistence among Communists."[38]

35. *L'Unità*, December 9, 1971. Earlier in the interview Carillo said: "The reestablishment of normal relations with the Chinese Communist Party certainly does not mean exchanging one 'guiding party' for another—that is, passing from being under the guidance of the CPSU to the guidance of the Chinese Communist Party. . . . On the other hand, in the course of the talks which took place in Beijing between the two parties, the Chinese comrades affirmed that they do not want to assume this role, and will not dictate policy to other parties."
36. Radio España Independiente broadcast, March 28, 1973.
37. Private discussion in Cologne, October 1975.
38. Interview in *l'Expresso*, as cited in *l'Unità*, August 11, 1976.

ALLIANCE OF INDEPENDENTS

Despite Pajetta's disclaimer, this was, of course, a "signal," a message; and it was significant, not only for its content but also for its timing. With the Maoist era in China obviously coming to an end, this was also a period of important changes in European communism, particularly with regard to interparty relations. For nearly two years, within the framework of the pan-European conference project, a prolonged struggle had been going on between an independent minority and the conservative majority of the twenty-eight parties concerned.[39] The independent alliance consisted of the two independent Eastern regimes, Yugoslavia and Romania, and the nonruling communist parties of Italy, Spain, Great Britain, Sweden, and San Marino —to be unexpectedly joined in the closing stages, at least on some issues, by the French party.

In retrospect, it appears that the Soviets and their followers made a decisive mistake at the outset: at the preliminary consultative meeting held in Warsaw in October 1974, they yielded to the demand of the independent parties that a new procedural rule of "decision-making by consensus" be adopted (the Yugoslav party evidently made this a condition for its participation). In at least fifteen "editorial" sessions over twenty months—a full year beyond the original schedule—the independent parties exploited the new principle to resist successive attempts to impose on the European communist parties something like an ideological and political "general line."[40] If a collective document was to be based on genuine consensus, they argued, it must, on their insistence, emphasize the principles of autonomy, equality, and noninterference in interparty relations (one corollary being that no special status would be accorded to the CPSU); it must contain no criticism of any party, present or absent (for example, the Chinese); and, in any case, it was not to be binding on any party. In the end, they had their way on almost all important points. The text adopted by consensus at the East Berlin conference of June 1976 (no one signed it) even dropped the hallowed pro-Soviet formula of "proletarian internationalism," replacing it with a bland reference to "voluntary cooperation" between equal and autonomous parties.

During this process, the independent West European communist parties developed a greater sense of their identity as what came to be called Eurocommunist parties—their proclaimed commitment to pluralistic, constitu-

39. The independent Dutch Communist Party turned up for the conference itself, held in East Berlin at the end of June 1976, having boycotted the entire preparatory process. This made a total of twenty-nine parties.

40. For an account of the protracted struggle over the character and content of the conference document, see Kevin Devlin, "The Challenge of Eurocommunism," *Problems of Communism*, 26, no. 1 (January–February 1977): 1–20.

tional democracy, and civil rights; their explicit rejection of the East European "model"; their interest in dialogue or collaboration with "progressive" noncommunist forces; finally, their stress on independence, particularly in relation to the CPSU.

During the last quarter of 1975, the traditionally pro-Soviet French Communist Party (PCF), in a major shift of policy, joined the ranks of the independent parties, and signaled the fact through some sharp criticism of the Soviet regime and its failings in respect to socialist democracy and human rights—as when the Politburo expressed its "most formal reprobation" of Soviet labor camps,[41] or Secretary-General Georges Marchais, in his report to the Twenty-second Congress of the PCF in February 1976, charged that in the Soviet Union the communist ideal had been "stained by unjust and unjustifiable acts."[42] The PCF also adopted the Eurocommunist label, which it had earlier derided, and in mid-November 1975, Marchais and Berlinguer signed what amounted to a Eurocommunist manifesto in Rome.[43] But when the "Eurocommunist summit" brought Berlinger, Marchais, and Carrillo together in Madrid in March 1977, the PCF was within months of the swing back to "neo-Leninist" positions that would bring about the unexpected defeat of the Left in the French elections of March 1978, and culminate in Marchais's approval of the Soviet invasion of Afghanistan on his visit to Moscow in January 1980.

Meanwhile, however, the death of Mao Zedong in September 1976 gave all three parties a chance to demonstrate independence of Moscow by turning in homage toward Beijing. Both *l'Unità* and *l'Humanité* devoted four pages to the career of the man Georges Marchais called "one of the greatest figures of history." The element of opportunism in the PCF's reaction was the more obvious in that it was only seven months since this same Marchais, at the party's Twenty-second Congress, had denounced the "profoundly reactionary . . . senseless, and dangerous" policies of a Chinese regime that was "playing the game of imperialism."[44] Now, the long history of mutual hostility was played down, and the PCF Central Committee's

---

41. *L'Humanité*, December 13, 1975. The Politburo statement was issued in connection with a television documentary on Soviet labor camps, and noted that "there have, in fact, been trials of citizens in the Soviet Union prosecuted for their political stands."

42. *L'Humanité*, February 6, 1980. A few weeks later, he reaffirmed independence from Moscow by declining to attend the Twenty-fifth CPSU Congress. One notes the contrast in style with the Italian communists, who tend to act *suaviter in modo, fortiter in re*.

43. Berlinguer had earlier signed a similar communiqué/manifesto with Carrillo, with whom Marchais later signed one. The network of bilateral Eurocommunist statements spread to include the British and Japanese communist parties.

44. *L'Humanité*, February 6, 1976.

message of condolence to its Chinese counterpart said disarmingly: "Certainly, grave divergences subsequently arose between our two parties regarding both international problems and the very conception of socialism. We profoundly regretted that these divergences changed our relations. This was not our doing, and it is not our desire."[45]

When the Chinese rejected the condolence messages of the PCF and the PCI (as they did those of all East European parties, except the Romanians and Yugoslavs), Jean Kanapa, of the PCF Politburo, said that his party regretted this, but it would not change its "deep-rooted conviction that, no matter how grave our divergences are, they should not result in a deterioration of relations between the French and Chinese Communists . . . [and] that, in future, another form of relations between our parties can be established—relaxed, understanding, and friendly relations." Paradoxically, the mild reaction strengthened the impression that the French communists, at least, were concerned less with seeking a true rapprochement with the Chinese than with emphasizing their independence in relation to the CPSU.

The Italian Communist Party (like the Spanish) contented itself with letting it be known that it was interested in resuming relations, whenever the Chinese were ready. But one discordant Italian communist voice went far beyond that. In an article written for *Le Monde*, Alberto Jacoviello, foreign affairs correspondent of *l'Unità*, provocatively declared that Mao's death provided an occasion for "a new rift between the Soviet Communist Party and the great communist parties of Western Europe." What did China and the Eurocommunist parties have in common? The answer, he suggested, lay in "the Chinese rejection of Soviet hegemony, both within what was then called the communist world, and within what is still called the international communist movement." Jacoviello added: "History . . . poses again the same problem to the great [West] European communist parties . . . which at the time of the Chinese schism took the side of the USSR. What lies behind the search for autonomy, for the 'Italian way' as for 'socialism in French colors,' if not the awareness that, on the level of theory as on that of practical action, nothing is possible until Soviet hegemony over the lives of the parties of Eurocommunism has been shaken off?"[46]

An editorial note in *l'Unità* next day dissociated the PCI from the "one-sided judgments" of Jacoviello. In the circumstances, it was a remarkably

45. Ibid., September 10, 1976. The *Unità* editorial on Mao's death (also September 10) expressed, with more restraint and dignity, a readiness to resume relations with the CPC: "[The PCI] hopes, as it has always done, that between the two parties . . . there may be established relations of reciprocal knowledge, collaboration, and friendship."

46. Alberto Jacoviello, "Eurocommunism Facing Moscow and Beijing," *Le Monde*, September 12–13, 1976.

mild rebuke, because what Jacoviello was advocating was one thing that the PCI was determined to avoid. If a rapprochement with the Chinese was to take place some day, it was not to be at the cost of a break with the Soviets.

THE PCI'S "NEW INTERNATIONALISM"

This was not just because the PCI was against rifts on principle, or because the link with the CPSU was important for its communist identity, or because of pro-Soviet sentiment in the ranks of the party. It was also because the PCI was developing, in theory and in practice, a "new internationalism" which would, in effect, negate, and for the Italian Communist Party replace, the old internationalism of either the Soviet or the Maoist brand. In a sense, it might be said that the new internationalism represented the transference onto other levels of the PCI's domestic strategy of the *compromesso storico*: the shift away from ideology and toward practical political activity in a pluralistic world.

Perhaps the most striking characteristic of the new internationalism was its emphasis on *noncommunist* political forces, with particular reference (for the PCI) to social-democratic and Catholic forces in Western Europe. This, in turn, may be linked with the party's efforts in recent years to "contribute to the construction of an Italian foreign policy which would be a factor of national unity and no longer, as in the lacerating years of the Cold War, a factor of vertical division between the political forces of our country,"[47] and also with its commitment to West European integration, as expressed in its support for the extension of the European Economic Community (EEC) to Greece, Spain, and Portugal, and for the granting of supranational powers to the European Parliament.

This pluralistic perspective was cogently expressed by Antonio Rubbi of the PCI Central Committee in an article in the January 1977 issue of *World Marxist Review*,[48] as if in answer to one in the previous issue, in which the Bulgarian leader Todor Zhivkov criticized "the ideological principles and objectives of 'Eurocommunism,'" and warned that "all tolerance or neutrality in regard to anti-Sovietism is, in effect, a departure from proletarian internationalism."[49] Rubbi argued that this was an age of "deep

47. Sergio Segre, "Outlines for a History of 'Eurocommunism,'" in *A chi fa paura l'Eurocomunismo?* (*Who's Afraid of Eurocommunism?*) (Rimini-Firenze: Guaraldi, 1977), pp. 13–40, at p. 17.

48. Antonio Rubbi, "The New Internationalism," *World Marxist Review*, 20, no. 1 (January 1977): 123–29. Rubbi's article was preceded by one in which the Bulgarian Asen Kozharov criticized pluralism as a "bourgeois theory and methodology incompatible with Marxism-Leninism."

49. Todor Zhivkov, "Year of Peace, Year of Struggle," *World Marxist Review*, 19, no. 12 (December 1976): 3–15, at p. 11.

changes in the socioclass structure of society," which found expression in "the variegated and pluralistic systems of representative trends, different political and social forces." Under the circumstances, the Italian communists believed that "the definition of internationalism as 'proletarian' has become restrictive and does not accord with the new social reality." The PCI was calling on forces of various ideological inspirations to join in a great "project of renewal and transformation" for Western Europe; but for this what was required, above all, was "unity of the communist, socialist, and social-democratic forces by overcoming the historical split, which for over half a century now has kept the West European working class divided."[50]

It was hardly a coincidence that the rapprochement between the Italian and Chinese communist parties came at the same time as a marked intensification of the PCI's efforts to establish friendly relations with the social-democratic parties of Western Europe, as expressed in Enrico Berlinguer's meetings with Willy Brandt, Mário Soares, Felipe González, and François Mitterand in early 1980, and the dispatch of envoys to Britain for talks with Labour Party representatives and to Scandinavia for talks with Socialist leaders.[51] These were complementary aspects of the PCI's grand strategy on the international and interparty levels; and both implied rejection of Soviet authority.

THE ROAD TO BEIJING

Ironically, the normalization of relations between communists was a much slower and more difficult process than the improvement of relations between communists and socialists (although the "Euroleft" that Georges

---

50. This opening up to noncommunist forces has remained one of the principal Soviet grievances against the Italian and Spanish communist parties. A recent Soviet review of Konstantin Zarodov's new book, *Economics and Politics in Revolution*, welcomes the author's emphasis on "the international community of the proletariat in the class struggle," since "the advocates of the 'new internationalism' are now proposing to replace that international community with a 'wider consolidation of various social and political forces in the struggle against imperialism. In fact, the rejection of proletarian internationalism disunites the international working class vis-à-vis the world bourgeoisie" (*Pravda*, September 18, 1980, as summarized by TASS of the same date).

51. One perceptive observer has suggested that Berlinguer's meetings with Socialist leaders were "intended to indicate . . . that, henceforth, the criterion for internationalism was not membership of a particular camp, but loyalty to certain principles and that, in this respect, the PCI felt closer to certain noncommunist parties and states than to certain communist ones." See Pierre Hassner, "Eurocommunism in the Aftermath of Kabul," *NATO Review*, 28, no. 4 (August 1980): 13.

Marchais denounces so vehemently has still a long way to go before it becomes politically relevant in practice). The normalization of relations between the Italian Communist Party and the Chinese—as between the Spanish Communist Party and the CCP—came as the final fruit of a long and cautious process on both sides, particularly on the Chinese side. As far as the Chinese were concerned, the measured steps in this direction came mainly in the year preceding Berlinguer's visit to Beijing in April 1980, as part of a wider pattern of domestic "modernization" and selective international dynamism. For the Italian communists, on the other hand, normalization of relations would fit into the protracted and gradual evolution, over a decade and a half, of the "new internationalism."

A turning point in the post-Mao development of Chinese diplomacy came in August 1978 with Chairman Hua Guofeng's visit to Romania and Yugoslavia, which could be viewed as one arm of a strategic design to be completed, over a year later, by his visit to major West European countries. Hua had hardly left Belgrade when Gian Carlo Pajetta, the PCI's "foreign minister," again issued "an invitation [to the Chinese] to reconsider the problem and reexamine the possibility of restoring relations, which could be useful to both parties and, we believe, to the workers' movement as a whole."[52] This would be "a natural development within the framework of a workers' movement within which there should be no guiding party and no guiding state—and neither should there be anyone who is the enemy of others." At another point in the interview, Pajetta touched on the thorny question of the effect that a PCI-CCP rapprochement might have on his party's relations with the CPSU. "We have nothing to hide from any communist party," he said, "hence no one should think that a restoration of relations with the Chinese Communist Party can be [regarded as] a sort of plot against Moscow. That said, the reply is clear and brief: it is our business, and we certainly shall not go and ask permission of anyone."[53]

After that, signs of changes to come became more frequent. One significant signal came from Beijing, where, on October 1, 1978, Deputy Foreign Minister Yu Zhan became the first Chinese spokesman to speak warmly of Eurocommunism in general. Addressing an audience of French provincial

52. Interview in *Epoca*, extensively reported in *l'Unità*, September 1, 1978.
53. It is worth noting that the PCE drew similar conclusions from Hua's Balkan visit: Antonio Muller commented, in *Mundo Obrero* (August 17–23, 1978), that this could "also be the beginning of a new stage in relations between the [West] European parties and the Chinese Communist Party." In contrast, the PCF's *Humanité* reported Hua's stay in Bucharest and Belgrade dispassionately, but then when he had moved on to Tehran, attacked the Chinese for having caused "so much harm to the struggle of the peoples against imperialism, dictatorships, and capitalist exploitation through a foreign policy based primarily on anti-Sovietism" (Jean-Emile Vidal in *l'Humanité*, August 30, 1978).

journalists—including one who seems to have been the first French communist to get a visa in nearly two decades—Yu said that, in general, the Eurocommunist parties showed a "certain independence" from the CPSU and opposed its hegemonic aspirations, but that "our views differ in the ideological field."[54] One "could not yet speak of a normalization [of Chinese-Eurocommunist relations]; it is too early for this." But the Chinese were making efforts "to pursue the development of the situation."

The gradual process of rapprochement was temporarily interrupted in the early months of 1979 by events in Indochina—the Vietnamese intervention in Kampuchea to overthrow the Pol Pot regime and the subsequent punitive incursion of Chinese forces into Vietnam. After an initially uncertain reaction to the Vietnamese invasion of Kampuchea, which the Spanish Communist Party had condemned from the start,[55] the PCI returned to an evenhanded position: at the party's Fifteenth Congress at the end of March, Berlinguer criticized both the Vietnamese invasion of Kampuchea and the Chinese attack on Vietnam as violations of the same principles of noninterference and respect of sovereignty. By that time, the gradual process of rapprochement had been resumed, as evidenced by the benign presence of the Chinese ambassador at the congress. Straws in the wind varied from the Chinese trade union delegation that visited Italy in April–May 1979 to the Chinese cyclists who, rather absurdly, came halfway across the world to take part in a local race sponsored by *l'Unità*.

During the latter half of 1979, a series of exchange visits by Chinese and Italian journalists, labor union leaders, and parliamentarians amounted to something like an informal normalization of relations.[56] And, indeed, the visit of the leader of the Italian communist youth federation to Beijing in January 1980 could perhaps be considered normalization on a lower level. During the same period, the Spanish Communist Party and the Chinese were engaged in a similar process of gradual rapprochement. In November 1979 the PCE's "foreign minister," Manuel Azcárate, visited China formally as a journalist, in his capacity as director of the party's theoretical journal, *Nuestra Bandera*, accompanied by the editor in chief of the daily/weekly *Mundo Obrero*, Angel Mullor. But Azcárate apparently put on his

54. AFP report from Beijing, October 2, 1978.

55. It may be noted that Italy's communist-dominated CGIL labor federation broke with the party on this issue: on January 12, 1979, its Secretariat condemned the Vietnamese invasion of Kampuchea.

56. One important visitor was Sergio Segre, member of the PCI Central Committee and of the European Parliament, who went to China in August 1979 with a delegation from the Italian Institute of International Affairs. He has special responsibility for EEC affairs, and said that during talks he "noted the interest with which Beijing is following the process of European integration" (*l'Unità*, September 7, 1979).

"party hat" before the visit ended. The PCE weekly reported: "A broad exchange of opinions took place, after which both sides emphasized their desire to step up contacts with a view to reaching a full reestablishment of relations"—a final step which it would, however, take exactly a year to reach.

A decisive turning point was the Soviet invasion of Afghanistan, which the Italian and Spanish communist parties strongly condemned, while Marchais of the PCF chose to announce his endorsement of it on a "normalization" visit to Moscow. For the PCI, the shock of the invasion, which it has continued to denounce on every occasion, reinforced its stand against what it calls the "logic of blocs," and showed it that both superpowers can threaten the climate of détente, on which its long-term hopes depend.[57] Yet, while this firm stand on Afghanistan facilitated the rapprochement with the Chinese, it did not obviate the need to avert anything like a rift with the CPSU.

Announcing Berlinguer's pending visit to China at a Central Committee meeting, Gian Carlo Pajetta said: "We would like to emphasize strongly that this step is certainly not directed against any other communist and workers' party or parties or in any way inimical to any other socialist country or countries, or liberation movements."[58] But he also stressed that this resumption of relations was taking place on a basis long advocated by his party:

> On many occasions, we have expressed our concern for the expansion of relations among all the forces of the workers' movement in various and flexible forms; we have held that diversity, full autonomy, and even conflicts and polemics should not impede relations, exchanges of experiences, and the search for convergence. . . .
>
> Frankness in relations, the rejection of impossible forms of monolithism, and the affirmation that the era of organizational relations has passed, and with it the attribution of a leadership or central role to one party or state—these are principles for which we have worked, and which, for that matter, were formally accepted by all the communist parties present at the [1976] Berlin conference.

In line with this perspective, differences between the Italian and Chinese parties emerged repeatedly in public during the nine-day visit of the PCI delegation in April 1980, and must have played an important part in the four sessions of "frank" talks. The Italians, indeed, seemed to be at pains

---

57. During a round-table discussion on Afghanistan published in the Rome daily *La Repubblica* (February 13, 1980), the PCI's outstanding journalist, Guiseppe Boffa, did not hesitate to say that "the invasion of Afghanistan is obviously imperialistic."

58. *L'Unità*, March 16, 1980.

to draw attention to the differences, whereas the Chinese hosts were more concerned to play them down. In his closing press conference in Beijing, Berlinguer actually listed these differences on important issues. "We do not agree that one must regard the Soviet Union as an enemy," he said firmly. "We also do not agree with regarding China as an enemy."[59] The PCI had also clearly stated its disapproval of the (Chinese) concept of a united front against the Soviet Union linking the United States, Japan, China, and Western Europe (and he might have added that the Chinese, for their part, had no time for the Italian communist dream of a "neutralist" Western Europe on good terms with both superpowers—though that dream has faded in recent years). Again, the PCI disagreed with the Chinese view that a world war is inevitable. He repeated the PCI's "disapproval" of the Chinese "interference" in Vietnam, but more than balanced this with another remark: "Our position on the Soviet Union's intervention in Afghanistan is one of criticism and condemnation."[60]

But the significance of this normalization of relations lay precisely in the fact that it was between equal partners who agreed to differ on important issues. Gian Carlo Pajetta summed it up:

> Now we can understand each other, but that doesn't mean that we reach the same conclusions. We are against all monolithism; we are [both] jealous of our autonomy, and respect the autonomy of others. This must apply to all, and in all directions....
>
> Neither side tried to exploit the other.... No one asked for or offered concessions, and I believe that we have spoken in Beijing as we speak in Rome or in Moscow. We can allow ourselves to be straightforward and to be friends in Beijing, because we are straightforward and do not launch anathemas when we go to Moscow.[61]

Berlinguer's historic visit to China gained even more importance from the fact that it coincided with yet another Soviet attempt to turn the interparty clock back. This time, it was through the pan-European communist conference on peace and disarmament, convened by the French and Polish parties, but clearly at the behest of the CPSU, and held in Paris at the end of April 1980. After the PCI, the Yugoslavs, and other parties had resisted or rejected the Franco-Soviet proposal when it was first circulated in December 1979—and Marchais had personally assured Berlinguer at their meeting in early January that the PCI's participation was a precondition for the meeting—the pro-Soviet organizers resorted to a unilateral abandonment of the interparty principle of consensus established at the Berlin conference of 1976. As a PCI spokesman tells it, the project seemed to have

59. Reuter dispatch from Beijing, April 22, 1980.
60. Xinhua report, April 22, 1980.
61. *L'Unità*, April 20, 1980.

The Challenge of the "New Internationalism" 171

been dropped—until the invitations were unexpectedly sent out in mid-March, "with times, procedures, and contents already fixed by the organizers, without any consultation or consensus."[62]

The outcome was instructive. An unprecedented one-third of the communist parties concerned rebelled against this attempt to rally communist ranks around the Soviet standard. Of the thirty-one parties in question, twenty arrived in Paris as full participants,[63] as against eleven rebel parties. Of these, nine boycotted the meeting—the parties of Yugoslavia, Romania, Spain, Italy, Great Britain, the Netherlands, San Marino, Sweden, and Iceland—while the Belgian and Swiss parties sent only observers.[64] The meeting's appeal to peace-loving European forces, criticizing Western policies and ignoring Afghanistan, found no echo at all; and it was hard to see what satisfaction the Kremlin could draw from this empty exercise in anachronism.

Meanwhile, some other communist parties—with significantly selective encouragement from the Chinese—have also been taking the road to Beijing. Santiago Carrillo of the PCE returned there in November 1980—exactly nine years after his first fruitless effort to breach the Maoist wall. Shortly before that, the Eurocommunist "Interior" Greek Communist Party announced that its head, Babis Dracopoulos, had been invited to lead a delegation to Beijing "within the framework of the restoration of relations."[65] The Chinese have already made a preliminary contact with the Belgian Communist Party.[66] Among other parties that may take the same path some time are the British, Swedish, Australian, and Mexican communist parties.

The "new internationalism" may not be the wave of the future, although it seems likely to continue to make headway among those communist parties sufficiently aware of their own political interests to emphasize independence. But the old internationalism can surely be described as the wave of the past.

62. Antonio Rubbi, "The International Initiative of the PCI," *Rinascita*, April 11, 1980.
63. The number would have been only nineteen if the minuscule Maltese Communist Party, founded in 1970, had not been invited to take part for the first time in an international communist gathering.
64. The Belgian observer did, however, participate to the extent of reading out a statement which included criticism of the Soviet intervention in Afghanistan.
65. *Avghi* (Athens), September 2, 1980.
66. See Kevin Devlin, "Belgian CP's Rapprochement with the Chinese," RAD Background Report/162 (World Communist Movement), *Radio Free Europe Research*, July 1, 1980.

The Regional Impact: Northeast and Southeast Asia

The Impact of the Sino-Soviet Dispute on Northeast Asia

DONALD C. HELLMANN

International affairs in Northeast Asia during the decade of the 1970s were conducted in the shadow of the Sino-Soviet dispute. This shadow not only changed shape and was differently perceived by those it touched, but it brought into being unanticipated results often contrary to the policy aims of the Soviet Union and China. For Japan and the two Koreas, the main effect was to define the regional configuration of power and accordingly the basic parameters of their national security policies. American policy constituted a critical independent variable, but because U.S. policy shifts were in large part responses to the Sino-Soviet rivalry, the dispute can be seen as the filter through which global strategic maneuvers passed to reach Northeast Asia. Economic issues were also affected, and for Japan matters such as Siberian development and investment in China actually dominated the diplomatic landscape for much of the last decade. Nevertheless, the critical impact of the Sino-Soviet dispute for Japan and the Koreas was to define the basic nature of the strategic and geopolitical realities they faced.

By focusing on the pattern of change over a decade and on a few benchmark events, we can gain a perspective absent in most of the detailed case-study analyses that are common fare regarding this question. In addition to suggesting the shape of the forest through the trees, the broader perspective poses questions about conventional wisdom regarding the role of the Soviet Union and China in Northeast Asian international affairs. Implicit in most analyses is an assumption that the critical factors shaping international events are the explicit policy choices made in Moscow and Beijing to counterbalance one another, to influence other nations, and to gain advantage in the regional and global strategic situations. To be sure, the policies of China and the Soviet Union were important, but other considerations beyond the control of the policy makers are at least equally significant in the long term. The Soviet needs and frustrations in developing Siberia and the maritime provinces, the economic and military weaknesses of China, the extraordinary economic strength of Japan, the capacities of small powers such as North and South Korea to operate with notable independence from their great-power protectors, and the intrusion of domestic politics (and nationalism) into the foreign policies of Japan and the Koreas—all of these shaped and constrained the capacities of Beijing and Moscow to project their power effectively. However fundamental, the Sino-Soviet rivalry was but one feature of the Northeast Asian international landscape.

The mutually obsessive concern of China and the Soviet Union with each other's policies itself contributed to the limitations of each party in conducting foreign policy effectively and often made the Sino-Soviet dispute a shadow without substance in terms of basic international realities. For example, from the viewpoint commonly taken in the United States, the massive Soviet arms build-up in Asia and the Pacific is evidence of Soviet power and predatory designs, and in an important sense this is correct. But seen in terms of its impact on Japan and Korea, the vastly expanded deployment of Soviet arms has a different meaning. There is little evidence to suggest that this has enhanced Soviet influence in Pyongyang or on the Korean peninsula generally, and it became the main incentive for expanded Japanese defense expenditures and further soured bilateral relations with Tokyo. Whatever the global implications, within the region it is questionable whether the costs and benefits of an expanded military presence were balanced. The complex and unanticipated ways in which the Sino-Soviet dispute became entangled with specific issues involving Japan and Korea over the past decade provides a glimpse of Northeast Asian international relations from a unique and illuminating vantage point.

RELATIONS WITH JAPAN

For both the Soviet Union and China, Japan was the key to strategic stability and economic development in the region, and during the 1970s there were three basic considerations for these countries giving priority to Japan. First, Japan became a principal source for meeting the pressing needs of both nations for capital, technology, and trade. Second, because Japan was closely allied with the United States, it was integrally involved in the Asian dimension of great-power politics. Third, the failure of the Japanese to play an independent and activist political-strategic role commensurate with their economic might made the future direction of Japanese foreign policy a matter of intense concern in Beijing and Moscow—particularly as the global system became increasingly indeterminate in the wake of repeated economic and military crises. The importance of Japan was magnified during the past decade as the geographical focus of the Sino-Soviet dispute shifted to Asia. This Asian emphasis found its initial impetus in the Sino-Soviet border war in 1969, which led Moscow to shift its military priorities to the immediate containment of China. The focus on Asia was further encouraged as China vastly expanded relations with the United States, Japan, and other Western nations to counterbalance the military superiority and perceived threat of the Soviet Union. In short, the importance of Japan for each of the communist powers was augmented by the drift of international events during these years.

Although China and the Soviet Union share common interests in and perceptions of Japan, there are also profound differences, historical and psychological as well as geopolitical, which distinguish the way in which each of these countries approaches Japan. Even more important is an appreciation of the contrasting way in which Japan perceives China and the Soviet Union, and this is a useful preface to discussion of specific bilateral issues and their link to the Sino-Soviet dispute.

During the 1970s, as in the greater part of this century, China has been central in Japan's relations with the world. To a degree exceeded only by relations with the United States, China has been critical to the Japanese foreign policy debate. Extraordinary emotional and symbolic importance surrounds this matter for all politically articulate groups in ways that supersede party lines and ideological divisions. This is owing partly to cultural-historical connections so profound as to cast an aura over things Chinese that transcends immediate political and economic considerations. It is also partly owing to the links between and competition of the nationalist movements in each country which accompanied the entry of these two Asian societies into the industrialized and Western dominated modern world. The Japanese move to normalize diplomatic relations with Beijing in the early 1970s was on the back of a broad popular movement led by a motley coalition of nostalgic, conservative Sinophiles from the prewar era, opportunistic businessmen in search of the legendary China market, and left-wing Maoist revolutionaries. The salience of the China issue within Japan and the reservoir of political good will on this issue provided a backdrop sharply different from Japanese attitudes toward the Soviet Union.

Throughout Japan's modern history Russia has had a highly negative image, and little has happened in the years since World War II to alter this picture. Just five days before the surrender of Japan, the Soviet Union broke a nonaggression treaty with Tokyo and entered the war. This led to Soviet occupation of Japanese territory (some still under dispute) and to the incarceration for several years of hundreds of thousands of Japanese military and civilians captured in Manchuria and North Korea. Moscow refused to sign the San Francisco Peace Treaty of 1952, and only in 1956 was a separate "peace agreement" reached restoring diplomatic and trade ties but leaving the territorial issue unresolved. Despite substantial expansion of trade and some broadening of diplomatic and cultural contacts in subsequent years, little has been done to mitigate the image of the Soviet Union as a menacing Asian neighbor, a challenge to the nation's security if not an enemy in war. This picture has been deeply impressed on the Japanese populace in history books, films, and the mass media. In annual opinion polls the Soviet Union has competed only with Korea as the "most disliked" nation. These widespread and intense negative attitudes have colored all efforts to improve bilateral relations and stand in sharp contrast to both popular and elite opinions of China.

Three issues were prominent in bilateral Japanese-Soviet relations during the 1970s: (1) the territorial dispute over four islands north of Hokkaido; (2) economic questions (notably investment in Siberia and fishing in the northern seas); and (3) Sino-Japanese ties (and derivatively the American alliance). All of them were affected by the Sino-Soviet dispute in ways that tied these issues to the broader strategic considerations on which Japan's foreign policy rests.

The Territorial Issue. The most important and divisive issue in bilateral Soviet-Japanese relations concerns the ownership of four northern islands that were occupied by the Soviet Union at the end of World War II. These islands (Etorofu and Kunashiri in the Southern Kuriles and Shikotan and the Habomais off northern Hokkaido) have taken on exaggerated importance with the passage of time. The Japanese claim has become a rallying point for nationalist and anti-Soviet sentiment in Japan, and as a result of Soviet maneuvers and the Chinese policies, the islands have become something of a political football eluding the grasp of any player on the international field.

The history of the dispute is rather straightforward. Japanese historical claims to the Southern Kuriles date to the nineteenth century, while Shikotan and the Habomais were administered as part of Hokkaido Prefecture until the end of World War II. The Japanese historical claim to the former and legal and historical claim to the latter are clear and strong. But under the terms of the San Francisco Peace Treaty (which the Soviet Union did not sign) Japan renounced claim to the Kurile Islands, and subsequently Prime Minister Shigeru Yoshida indicated in Diet interpellation that this included the Southern Kuriles.[1] During the negotiation of the Peace Agreement of 1956, Tokyo suddenly made claim to the Southern Kuriles, Etorofu, and Kunashiri (as well as the other islands), and this position has been maintained ever since. Under the terms of the Peace Agreement the Russians agreed to transfer the Habomais and Shikotan to Japan once a peace

1. "Shugiin, Heiwa Jayaku oyobi Nichi-Bei Anzen Hosho Joyaku Tokubetsu Iinkai Giroku" ("Proceedings of the Special Committee on the Peace Treaty and the Japan–United States Security Treaty"), no. 4, Twelfth Diet, pp. 18–19.

treaty was signed, but in 1960 the Soviets hardened their position, making return conditional on the removal of all foreign troops from Japanese soil (abrogation of the U.S.-Japan Security Treaty). Moscow has remained relatively unchanged in its position, but the policy has fluctuated slightly in terms of broader strategic maneuvers, particularly those related to Sino-Japanese relations.

In the wake of Japan's normalization of diplomatic relations with Beijing in the fall of 1971, the Soviet Union adopted an unusually conciliatory position on the issue, in the hope of restraining Tokyo and Washington from rapidly developing relations with Beijing (for example, in a visit to Tokyo in January 1972, Andrei Gromyko indicated that the territorial issue was "not settled").[2] Shortly thereafter, Chinese Premier Zhou Enlai publicly proclaimed that China supported the Japanese position on the northern territories and if necessary would "send troops" in support of Tokyo.[3] This prompted reversion to a rigid posture by the Soviets, tempered only by a strong drive to induce Japanese investment in Siberia during the first part of the 1970s. By 1976 the Russians were asserting de facto sovereignty over the two islands they promised to return in 1956, and on the eve of the signing of the Sino-Japanese Peace and Friendship Treaty, Moscow informed a visiting Japanese politician that there was no obligation to return any territory.

From 1975 on, the pattern of policies regarding the disputed territories was linked to Sino-Japanese relations. The Japanese policy of seeking "equidistance" from the two Asian powers (a policy that was progressively abandoned in the late 1970s as Tokyo "tilted" toward Beijing) led one foreign minister to state openly that China's support for Japan in the northern territories dispute was "counterproductive." Perhaps the most serious and important move by the Soviet Union on this matter was the deployment of several thousand new troops in the disputed islands in 1978, a policy of marginal military significance but of truly substantial political impact.[4]

Three aspects of this territorial dispute as it evolved in the last decade are of note. First, the improvement of Sino-Japanese relations added a China dimension as a result of anti-Chinese Soviet policy actions and because of the intrusion of Chinese policy into this matter. Second, by the end of the decade the bilateral impasse had become frozen in ways indicative of the deterioration of Soviet-Japanese bilateral relations. Questions

2. *Asahi Shimbun*, January 20, 1972.

3. It should be noted that there was intense Chinese interest in this issue and Soviet intransigence in part because China had similar territorial claims against Russia.

4. For a review of bilateral relations in the mid-1970s, see Peggy L. Falkenheim, "Some Determining Factors in Soviet-Japanese Relations," *Pacific Affairs*, 50, no. 4 (Winter 1977–78): 604–23.

TABLE 7
Japanese Trade with China and the Soviet Union, 1970–79
(in million U.S. dollars)

	China			Soviet Union		
Year	Exports	Imports	Total	Exports	Imports	Total
1970	569	254	823	341	481	822
1971	579	322	901	378	497	875
1972	619	499	1,118	512	604	1,116
1973	1,042	973	2,015	488	1,078	1,566
1974	1,983	1,304	3,287	1,095	1,417	2,512
1975	2,258	1,529	3,787	1,626	1,169	2,795
1976	1,666	1,373	3,039	2,254	1,169	3,423
1977	1,955	1,560	3,515	1,951	1,433	3,384
1978	3,381	1,859	5,240	2,782	1,321	4,103
1979	4,048	2,664	6,712	2,689	1,722	4,411

SOURCE: International Monetary Fund, *Direction of Trade, 1969–75* and *1970–77* (April 1979 and April 1980).

of security and the nature of alliance relations with the United States (and possibly China) were now inextricably entwined with the territorial dispute. Further rigidity was added by the intensity of anti-Soviet feeling among the public at large (for example, the Diet passed a resolution demanding the withdrawal of Soviet troops from the disputed islands). Third, this issue had clearly become a major bargaining chip in the strategic maneuvers in Northeast Asia, and its resolution would ultimately depend on the balance of power in that part of the world.

Economic Issues: Trade and Siberian Investments. Trade between Japan and the Soviet Union has proceeded virtually independent of any influence of the Sino-Soviet dispute. As seen in Table 7 there has been a steady growth in bilateral exchanges, which expanded more than fivefold during the decade. This substantial increase closely paralleled the overall growth of Japan's trade, so that while Soviet trade was 2.2 percent of total Japanese trade in 1970, in 1979 it was 2.1 percent. Reflecting Tokyo's tilt toward China, the last few years have seen a sharp increase in Sino-Japanese trade, which now is half again as large as that with the Soviet Union. An examination of the composition of trade with the USSR shows that the vast proportion of both imports and exports involved the economy of Siberia and the maritime provinces.[5] During the past decade roughly two-thirds of all Japanese exports to the Soviet Union were iron and steel products (primarily pipes and joints for oil development) and machinery (mainly min-

---

5. These figures are regularly available in the annual "white paper" of the Japanese Ministry of International Trade and Industry.

ing equipment, railway cars, and special construction vehicles directly related to Siberian development). Roughly 80 to 90 percent of Soviet exports to Japan were products from Siberia—lumber, coking coal, oil, and nonferrous metals. To a very substantial degree the sizable Soviet-Japanese trade can be seen as Siberian-Japanese trade and in this way is directly connected with the participation of Japan in Siberian development, an area entangled in the Sino-Soviet dispute.

Since 1965 there have been continuous, albeit sporadic, efforts to involve Japan in the development of Siberia, and Japan is the only nation to have a substantial stake in this endeavor.[6] The main vehicle for these efforts has been the Joint Japanese-Soviet Economic Cooperation Committee which meets at one- or two-year intervals. Japanese companies deal directly with the Soviet government on many of the specific projects, but the Japanese government exercises final control not only over the nature of the loans involved but over the political and strategic considerations central to most of these activities.

In strictly economic terms, there are truly compelling incentives for extensive Japanese participation in Siberian development. Gaining access to resources critical to maintaining her economy has been an important aim of Japan's foreign policy—an aim that has taken on greater urgency in light of OPEC's success and the prospect that other commodity cartels may follow suit. This is the obvious and main reason for the interest of Japanese business in Siberian development. At the same time, Moscow clearly recognizes that Japanese capital and technology will accelerate the development of this remote region and (among other things) provide assistance in the area of activity that holds the greatest prospect for the Soviet Union to earn foreign credits—the export of natural resources.

All but a fraction of the more than $1.5 billion in credits and technical assistance that has been provided to the Soviet Union over the past decade has been for projects dealing with the development and export of natural resources. The major projects that were subject to extensive negotiation or actually initiated during the 1970s include the production of coking coal and natural gas at Yakutsk, a massive project for the development of crude oil at Tyumen, the successful efforts to develop oil and natural gas on the continental shelf of Sakhalin, and sporadic efforts to involve Japan in the

6. Of the many articles dealing with this subject three of note in English are Boris N. Slavinsky, "Siberia and the Soviet Far East within the Framework of International Trade and Economic Relations," *Asian Survey*, 17, no. 4 (April 1977): 311–29; chapter 13 in Violet Conolly, *Siberia Today and Tomorrow* (London: Collins, 1975); and Gerald L. Curtis, "The Tyumen Oil Development Project and Japanese Foreign Policy Decision-Making," in Robert A. Scalapino, ed., *The Foreign Policy of Modern Japan* (Berkeley: University of California Press, 1977), pp. 147–73.

Baikal-Amur Mainline Railroad. What is notable about these projects is that most have been postponed or only partly completed and all have critical strategic as well as economic implications. Some of the projects (such as Tyumen) have foundered for technical as well as political reasons. Others have proceeded slowly, because the size of the credits involved (at least several billion dollars) is so great that the Japanese have been wary of undertaking the risks without American participation, and the United States has for various reasons (for example, the Jackson amendment, détente with Beijing) refused to take part. Both the scope and strategic nature of these projects have raised questions about their long-term political implications—concerns that the Chinese have occasionally raised with Tokyo. Moreover, in the latter part of the 1970s, as the Chinese began to seek international credits and technical aid for their internal economic development, they became competitors with the Soviets for the favors of the world of Japanese business and banking, thereby adding an economic dimension to the Sino-Soviet rivalry. In aggregate, however, the major impediments to fulfillment of joint Siberian development projects have not been simply economic issues but the political-strategic considerations of improved transportation facilities and the development of critical resources in Soviet Asia *as they have been assessed by China and the United States* and the resultant pressure brought to bear on Tokyo. The substantial and growing economic relations between the Soviet Union and Japan are likely to proceed as in the 1970s because of clear reciprocal advantages, but they will move within limits established by the strategic maneuvering of the two superpowers and China.

To deal with their passive and difficult role in the power politics of the region during the 1970s the Japanese adopted a policy of "equidistance" from China and the Soviet Union. In effect it was a euphemism that allowed Tokyo to separate politics and economics and proceed incrementally through the tangle of international developments. The decade had hardly begun when Japan moved to full diplomatic recognition of China, the first in a chain of events that led to a decided tilt in the direction of Beijing by the end of the decade. As will be discussed, two of the striking features of the tilt toward China are the extent to which it was shaped by Japanese domestic politics and the degree to which the timing and content of Sino-Japanese rapprochement was shaped by external (international) pressures. The Soviet Union showed a notable capacity for dealing ineffectively with this development and for encouraging through clumsy diplomacy precisely those trends most disadvantageous to Soviet interests—an increase in armaments in Japan and an international climate in which strategic entente between the United States, Japan, and China was openly considered.

Sino-Japanese Relations and Soviet Policy. The decision by Japan to normalize relations with China in 1972 came in the wake of international developments that left Tokyo little choice. Not only was China in the United

Nations and recognized by all other major nations except the United States, but the American president had visited Beijing and was in the process of making the "opening to China" a cornerstone of American global strategy. In this context continued refusal by Japan to recognize China was likely to involve far greater costs than recognition. Political pressures in Japan also assured that normalization of relations would occur soon. These pressures allowed China to dictate the basic conditions under which ties would be established and made any Soviet attempt to block recognition all but impossible. In this case, Moscow made few efforts to impede a decision which had serious potential for adversely affecting the Sino-Soviet balance in Asia.

When in 1975 the Chinese and Japanese began in earnest three-year negotiations for a peace and friendship treaty, the Soviet Union actively tried to obstruct their successful conclusion.[7] The principal cause for concern was the Chinese insistence that the proposed treaty include a clause that would bind Japan to oppose efforts by any nation (that is, the Soviet Union) to establish "hegemony" in the region. This treaty was also seen by Moscow as part of a broader effort by China to contain and isolate the Soviet Union in Asia and the world. By raising this matter in specific contexts such as talks on bilateral fishing rights, by publishing the text of a draft Soviet-Japanese peace treaty, by threatening unspecified "retaliation" if a Sino-Japanese agreement was signed, and by greatly augmenting the deployment of naval (and later land) forces in Soviet Asia, the Soviets sought to deflect the Japanese from tilting any farther toward Beijing. Not only did these efforts prove abortive, but they served to focus Japanese attention on the Soviet Union as a threatening adversary and provided the United States with additional leverage to urge Sino-Japanese rapprochement.

The conclusion of the Sino-Japanese Treaty of Friendship and Amity in August 1978 was not only condemned by Moscow as an "anti-Soviet alliance," but it was a precipitating factor in the conclusion three months later of the Soviet-Vietnamese Treaty of Friendship and Cooperation, and which was in effect a quasi-military alliance. Beijing in turn broadened its contacts and, in a surprise move, normalized relations with the United States on December 15. Shortly thereafter Vietnam invaded and quickly controlled most of Cambodia. Slightly over a month later (and immediately after Deng Xiaoping had visited the United States and Japan), China invaded Vietnam in a "punitive action." Although the war ended inconclusively, the Soviet presence in Vietnam remained a new reality in the tangle

---

7. For a summary of these events in English, see Shinkichi Eto, "Recent Developments in Sino-Japanese Relations," *Asian Survey*, 20, no. 7 (July 1980): 726–43, and Peggy L. Falkenheim, "The Impact of the Peace and Friendship Treaty on Soviet-Japanese Relations," *Asian Survey* 19, no. 12 (December 1979): 1209–23.

of great-power politics in East Asia. In this case, the diplomatic move by Japan toward China was integrally involved in projecting Soviet power further into the region.

The expansion of the Soviet military presence in Asia and the Pacific for the main purpose of containing China and checking American influence has led to fundamental changes in the Japanese approach to defense. In a series of defense "white papers" published annually in Japan since 1977, the Soviet Union is noted as constituting the major military threat to the country—the first time that a specific judgment of this sort has appeared in an official document since the end of World War II. The enhanced military presence of the Soviets, together with the reduced military capabilities of the United States in the Pacific and unclear commitments regarding American strategic intent toward the region, has raised doubts in Japan about the meaning of strategic alliance with the United States. Although any thought of even informal military cooperation between China, the United States, and Japan (a vague and rather extraordinary concept promoted by the Carter administration) is rejected by Tokyo, the defense debate and the accompanying protonationalist political developments are one of the most significant additions to the Japanese foreign policy agenda in the last three decades. Soviet policies toward Japan, particularly strategic policies, have been shaped by the Sino-Soviet dispute in ways that not only have resulted in diplomatic frustration for Moscow but have sown seeds that could sprout into the one development that would benefit neither China nor the Soviet Union—a more politically independent and significantly better armed Japan.

Sino-Japanese Relations and Japanese Policy. During the 1970s, Sino-Japanese contacts expanded in a positive way on both the economic and political levels, and there developed in Japan a mood that encouraged and romanticized these changes. Although the Soviet Union persisted as one of the "most disliked" nations, China briefly replaced the United States as the most admired country, and the craze for everything Chinese (especially pandas) created a salubrious atmosphere in which political and economic relations could flourish. China's invasion of Vietnam in 1979 and the subsequent drastic curtailment of economic development plans did take some gloss off the relationship, but the reaction of Japanese domestic politics to the Sino-Soviet dispute was much like a glass through which things Chinese are seen favorably and things Russian are grotesquely refracted.

A feature of Japanese politics that bears directly on the pattern of growth of Sino-Japanese relations during the past decade is the essentially immobilist nature of the Japanese foreign policy-making process. It is difficult for any government in Japan to undertake bold policy initiatives. With the popular mood so favorably disposed to China, and the strong actions of the United States to bring the Chinese into the international system closely associated with the Western world in an anti-Soviet posture, the opportunities for Chinese influence on Japanese diplomacy were virtually limitless. The results of the last decade are stunning triumphs from the Chinese viewpoint. Normalization occurred on terms dictated by Beijing, the Japanese rushed to bestow billions of dollars of credits and offer technical assistance to Chinese modernization plans, the ostensible compromise on the "antihegemony" clause in the Sino-Japanese Treaty of Friendship and Amity was essentially a triumph for Beijing, and Tokyo never strongly condemned China's invasion of Vietnam. Only in the area of overt military cooperation, including the sale of weapons, has Japan not fallen into step with Chinese diplomatic desires, and here its American ally is seemingly moving to fill the breech.

Japanese business was attracted to China in the 1970s in part because of a desire to establish a major claim on the China market and Chinese resources before other industrialized nations arrived—an incentive that was almost completely lacking regarding Siberian development. Another consideration behind this drive to become involved in China was a recognition of the limitations of the markets in developed societies and the increasing encroachment of the newly industrialized countries (such as South Korea and Taiwan) in areas previously dominated by Japanese products. China offered a new economic challenge to Japan at a moment when it was needed. To be sure, these attractions seriously dimmed as the 1970s drew to a close and Chinese economic plans were tempered by reality, but the lure of opportunities in China are likely to outweigh the appeal of Siberian resources in the years immediately ahead. Although the various actions enhancing Sino-Japanese trade and economic ties did elicit Soviet efforts to discourage them, and Japanese responses linked to the territorial issue, this matter remained on the periphery of the strategic maneuvers surrounding the Sino-Soviet dispute and Japan. Despite the rather dramatic upsurge in trade between China and Japan in the late 1970s as shown in Table 7 (to 3.2 percent of Japan's total trade), there are clear limits to the magnitude of economic intercourse, except in the unlikely event that a mutual political decision is made to have Japan assume the major responsibility for underwriting Chinese modernization.

The security implications of Sino-Japanese entente have been given exaggerated attention by both the Soviet Union and the United States, but the fears of Moscow and the hopes of the United States about participation by Japan in a "quasi alliance" to contain the Soviet Union have been and are likely to remain badly wide of the mark. Because Japan remains vulnerable to Soviet military pressure in ways that China and the United States are not, there are few strategic benefits and enormous risks for Japan to take an overtly anti-Soviet position. Moreover, the issue of rearmament in Japan is so politically explosive that it must proceed on its own course and find legitimacy in some new form of Japanese nationalism—not in a collective security arrangement imposed from abroad. But China's open encouragement to Japan to increase its defense budget (now strongly supported by the United States), together with the perceived threat from the Soviets, may well serve as the catalyst to push Tokyo toward an expanded and more activist security policy.

RELATIONS WITH KOREA

The Sino-Soviet dispute is integrally involved in the Korean question in ways that hold enormous risks for the preservation of peace but also opportunities for creative diplomacy by the great powers. Involved are the peculiarly influential roles that small powers have in relation to their superpower patrons, the persistence of nationalism as the critical force in international affairs, and the tension between regional conflicts and global strategic confrontation. The cliché that Korea is the place where the interests of the four major powers in Asia (the United States, the Soviet Union, China, and Japan) are most intently focused deserves restatement. China and the Soviet Union are so deeply involved, both militarily and in political-symbolic ways, that they are both vulnerable to the maneuvers of the North Korean government, the military tensions between the North and the South, and the capacity of the United States (and its allies) to affect the delicate balance on the Korean peninsula. The history not only of the 1970s but of the past three decades illustrates how sensitive the Soviets and the Chinese are to changes in the strategic situation there and the limitations on the capacities of Moscow or Beijing to control these events to the extent they desire.[8]

More important than the details of the twists and turns of policy, in which Pyongyang tilts first toward Beijing and then toward Moscow, is the nature of the links between the two communist superpowers and their small client. Both China and the Soviet Union supply North Korea with the hardware for its substantial military establishment—with the Soviets supplying the critical element. Despite this, Moscow has been frustrated since the early 1960s by its inability to control Kim Il Sung, especially his policies toward China, but also his initiatives against the South. China, toward which Kim seems to have tilted since the early 1970s, also has been concerned about possible military actions by Kim, especially since Beijing has been courting

8. For an elaboration of these events see William J. Barnds, ed., *The Two Koreas in East Asian Affairs* (New York: New York University Press, 1976); Franklin B. Weinstein and Fuji Kamiga, eds., *The Security of Korea* (Boulder, Colo.: Westview Press, 1980); *The Triangular Relations of Mainland China, the Soviet Union and North Korea* (Seoul: Asiatic Research Center, Korea University, 1977); and Wayne S. Kiyosaki, *North Korea's Foreign Relations: The Politics of Accommodation, 1945–75* (New York: Praeger, 1976).

the United States as a counter to the Soviet Union. Any move by Kim to unite the Korean peninsula would place both the Soviet Union and China in extremely awkward positions in relation to each other and to the United States. In large part because of the inability of China and the Soviet Union to control events in Korea, both tend to give it low priority in their competition with each other and in their foreign policy more generally. Both—particularly China—are obliged to give public support to Pyongyang's policies, but both prefer the status quo. Neither can compel the North to accept a divided Korea. Hence there is the paradox of deep involvement by China and the Soviet Union leading both countries to downgrade Korean policy because of the risks and intractability of the situation.

American support of South Korea poses many of the dilemmas that face the Soviet Union and China in their relations with the North. A continued presence of American forces is necessary to secure the military balance and to provide symbolic strategic balance, but the capacity of the United States to control Seoul's policies is also limited. Because of the substantial economic ties between the South and the global capitalist economy, and because of the impressive economic gains of the South in recent years, the Seoul government has constraints on it that the North lacks. Thus Seoul will accept a divided Korea because the momentum of economic growth is seen as providing a long-term advantage.

What is striking about the Korean problem is that all the major powers have a direct stake in the situation, none can realistically disengage, all now favor the status quo, and all are concerned that a local problem could escalate into a strategic confrontation. Hence a second paradox: although the situation is risky and fluid, it does provide an opportunity for policy initiatives by the great powers. It is an instance in which the Sino-Soviet rivalry could serve to reduce, not exacerbate, tension in Northeast Asia if the United States were to employ the appropriate diplomatic initiatives. These were not evident during the 1970s.

A review of the impact of the Sino-Soviet dispute on international affairs in Northeast Asia in the decade of the 1970s demonstrates the growing complexity of international relations in this region and the limitations on the ability of any state—no matter how powerful—to project its power into the region. Unless the dispute between China and the Soviet Union disintegrates into a full-scale war, it will remain an important but not preeminent variable in the Asian balance of power and continue to be hostage to regional developments not easily managed by leaders in Beijing and Moscow.

The Impact of the Sino-Soviet Dispute on Southeast Asia

DOUGLAS PIKE

This chapter examines the Sino-Soviet dispute in that vast eight-nation arc stretching from Burma to China known as Southeast Asia. The focus is Indochina, which in practical terms means Vietnam.[1] The chapter is divided into three parts. First, there is an overview of the subject which fixes the dispute in the region's affairs and establishes its basic meaning. Second, there is a brief history of the dispute chiefly in terms of the Indochinese communists, most dynamic of the region's actors at the moment. Third, there is a discussion of the dispute in recent years—its contemporary condition—along with an assessment of the impact it is likely to have on the region in the future.

OVERVIEW

We begin by attempting to establish clear context—that is, to fix Southeast Asia in global affairs—and then to place the Sino-Soviet dispute within this scheme of things. We ask three questions: Where exactly is Southeast Asia today, in relation to the rest of the world? To what extent, and in what way, is the Sino-Soviet dispute a factor in the region's current affairs? What role is the dispute likely to play in the region's future?

Because of its many permutations, and now because of its long duration, the Sino-Soviet dispute has had various meanings over time and from capital to capital, often turning on the vagaries of domestic and local politics. Generalizations are few and not very durable. One fact seems clear, that the dispute's chief meaning for Southeast Asia is in intraregional and interregional power arangements. The dispute has little ideological impact on Association of Southeast Asian Nations (ASEAN) peoples. Eventually it

---

1. Source material for this paper includes documentation from the author's forthcoming nine-volume *Documentary History of the Vietnam War on Microfilm*, as well as the standard works on the Sino-Soviet dispute by Alan Cameron, William Griffith, Edward Crankshaw, Robert Rupen, and Donald Zagoria, to name a few. I am particularly indebted to William Richard Smyser's exhaustively detailed dissertation on Hanoi and the Sino-Soviet dispute in the early period, circa 1965. See W. R. Smyser, *The Independent Vietnamese: Vietnamese Communism between Russia and China, 1956–69* (Athens, Ohio: Ohio University Center for International Studies, 1980); this is a condensed version of Smyser's dissertation, done at Georgetown University, 1978.

may assume great geopolitical significance, but this has yet to happen. It is profoundly important, however, in that it has turned the region into an arena for the global power struggle. In fact, the Sino-Soviet dispute can be regarded as one facet of history's ongoing, never-ending orthodox balance-of-power struggle among Pacific nations.

For Southeast Asian governments, of all the external factors with which they must deal on a day-to-day basis none is more perplexing than the Sino-Soviet dispute and its apparent irreconcilability. The dispute in a hundred ways intrudes into their world, shaping attitudes, influencing behavior, and affecting decisions. It is a mix of countervailing forces that pull and haul at the region. The dispute is a threat, for it could drag Southeast Asia into war. Or, if the response to the threat of war causes increased mutual self-defense efforts, the dispute would be a force for regionalism. The dispute is divisive, automatically, both among the countries and within each country. Moscow and Beijing constantly vilify each other. Each seeks to entrap Southeast Asians in alliances. Each muddies local political waters, often upsetting delicate local socioethnic arrangements.

For years the dispute has narrowed the region's foreign policy options. Realization of its more or less permanent nature effectively obliterated that great golden vision of a nonaligned Southeast Asia. This is discussed in detail below. Suffice it to say here that if the idea of neutralization of the region ever was feasible, it was only under monolithic world communism.

All of this was true at the start of the dispute and remains true today. In many ways it can be said that the impact of the rift on Southeast Asia is about what it always has been, extended and deepened somewhat by Vietnam's recent decision to weigh in on the side of the USSR. The trend of the dispute is toward complexity as it evolves from a bilateral to a three-way power struggle in which each contender—Moscow, Beijing, and Hanoi —seeks to serve its own national interests. This means that if the original dispute eases or disappears, a struggle for power in the region will continue. Fundamental differences on policy among the three communist states will always exist. The stakes in the game will increase. Vietnam does not wish to see excessive influence exerted by either of the two communist superpowers, and in this respect is simply another Southeast Asian country. Thus it seems that Southeast Asia is destined to remain an arena of contention for the three communist states, whether or not locked in fratricide.

Because of the struggle among communist nations in Asia, and for other reasons, it is unlikely that any nation will come to dominate Southeast Asia during the next decade or so. Nor is it likely that ASEAN will develop sufficient unity and sinew to be able to control events in the region. Rather the prospect is for a fluid and contingent Southeast Asia.

In the longer run, it appears that history is pushing the region, almost inexorably, toward some new, still undevised, regional system. Of course there is nothing irreversible about this trend, and there will be periodic setbacks and temporary reversals of direction. But a powerful historical force is at work. Future historians may some day record that the major contributor to this historical process, albeit unintentionally, was the Sino-Soviet dispute.

BRIEF HISTORY

In general historical terms during the past two decades, the Sino-Soviet dispute largely dictated what sort of relationship both China and the USSR had with each of the Southeast Asian states. The respective moves of each, in various capitals and especially in Hanoi, were the result of each seeking to outmaneuver the other and gain a position of dominant influence. To the extent that the region loomed large in the calculation of either Beijing or Moscow (perhaps often exaggerated by outsiders) it was in terms of what the other was up to. Throughout the years the struggle seesawed, with neither able to secure permanent dominance.

For Southeast Asians, well aware of the nature of the game, this struggle meant that relations with each of the two communist superpowers had to be measured in terms of the dispute—its product, its benefits, and its inherent encumbrances. Most of the time, for most of the nations, this was a rather nominal business; only for Hanoi was it serious and at times a life and death matter. This was particularly true earlier when the dispute was hidden, but even after it broke into the open and heated up, it still only marginally affected those nations that came to be the ASEAN countries. There was widespread awareness and discussion of the dispute, but it was generally viewed parochially, not in strategic terms. Its importance seemed to diminish with the distance from its epicenter: most significant for Vietnam, Laos, and Cambodia, for instance, and least important say for the Philippines or Malaysia.

The USSR, in the early days (late 1950s), had only minimal local presence, martial or otherwise, hence was at best regarded as an abstract threat. No country exhibited much warmth for it, but neither was much hostility demonstrated. Only Indonesia experienced what might be called a serious flirtation with the USSR, and that turned out badly.

China evoked stronger feelings, especially in Indonesia and Malaysia. But in strict security terms China did not have the air and naval power necessary to present a credible threat. The ninety million overseas Chinese in the region did always represent something of a fifth-column threat when tied to local revolutionary groups. Feelings for China were more deeply ingrained than those for the USSR, since they were based on long-standing historical fears of Chinese claims of hegemony. But even here antipathy for things Chinese was low-grade, and the periodic expressions of hostility were directed against local ethnic Chinese rather than China itself.

Southeast Asian nations were never able to capitalize on the dispute or to turn it to their advantage. Hanoi was the exception to this, as Hanoi always seems to be the exception to regional trends and developments.

To the extent that nations of the region felt obliged to address themselves to the dispute, it was to attempt not to take a position. Nonalignment, it was hoped, would become the foundation on which the region built its external relations. Southeast Asia then could stand neutral in all power struggles, whether communist-capitalist or among communists. This almost desperate hope stemmed from a sense of impotency. Leaders throughout Southeast Asia knew the international facts of life.[2] They understood the roots of the dispute: Moscow's traditional fear of a two-front challenge (NATO plus China), as well as China's never-ending impulse toward suzerainty over rimland barbarians. They had noted the transformation of Soviet policy under Khrushchev, with its broadened definition of what constituted Soviet external interests (then further broadened by the Brezhnev Doctrine). They had watched the growth of Moscow's ability to project its power into the waters of the region. And they had experienced firsthand Chinese efforts to aid and abet revolutionaries and other indigenous challengers in their midst. But about these things they could do little, even if so inclined, since they simply had no leverage in Beijing or Moscow. Hence the forlorn hope that somehow the nations of the region could opt out of the growing power struggle. It can even be said that North Vietnam in its own way attempted to remain nonaligned in the power struggle, although the dispute for it was far more complicated than for the rest of Southeast Asia.

Probably nonalignment always was no more than a chimera. Certainly its feasibility was undermined by injection of this outside power struggle. In fact, as events proved, nonalignment of Southeast Asia became the first major casualty of the Sino-Soviet dispute.

Hanoi and the Dispute. For the Vietnamese communists, the Sino-Soviet dispute throughout the years always represented an inextricable mix of danger and gain, alarm and opportunity. Seen from Hanoi, the dispute can be divided into three periods: (1) from its start until February 1965,[3] when the United States announced full involvement in the war, (2) from February 1965 until communist victory in April 1975, and (3) from April 1975 to date.

In the early period the dispute was chiefly embarrassment and nuisance.

2. Some of these leaders, Lee Kuan Yew in Singapore for instance, have possessed a remarkable clarity of view for the past several decades, as an inspection of their old speeches and interviews demonstrates.

3. The date for the start of the Sino-Soviet dispute can be fixed at almost any point one wishes. Most writers establish it in the late 1950s or at the latest 1960, when Moscow called home its corps of military and economic aid advisers in China.

The Vietnamese communists did not at first fully appreciate either the seriousness of the split or its significance for them. They viewed it largely as a spirited ideological tiff laced by certain nationalistic rivalries.[4] In both the first and second periods Hanoi demonstrated remarkable consistency in dealing with the dispute, by evaluating it and basing responses to each unfolding development on a single, undeviating objective: unification. Control of all Vietnam was the regime's sole *raison d'être*, and all was put to its service.

Three guiding principles can be discerned in Hanoi's handling of the dispute during the first two periods. First, it sought to minimize its importance while working behind the scenes to heal the breach. Hanoi officials said little publicly about the rift, at international conferences of communists for instance, and what was said was either cryptic or bland. Open references to it were forbidden in the North Vietnamese mass media, although not within the party.[5] Speeches, final communiqués, and so on, emanating from high-ranking visits could not be censored, of course, thus the North Vietnamese public was aware of the dispute, but was not constantly reminded of it.

The Vietnam War soon pushed itself into the maw, as far as Hanoi was concerned, and the dispute became central to all of its plans and estimates. The war, which can be said to have started in mid-1959, was not a significant issue in the dispute until the arrival of U.S. ground troops in 1965, although from the earliest days there were sharp differences between China and the USSR on assessment of the Vietnam scene and on the strategy to be employed.[6] But there is no evidence, as some have suggested, that the

4. It is clear from early Hanoi pronouncements that DRV officials believed the dispute would be of relatively short duration and would probably end as a result of leadership change in Moscow or Beijing. At some point Hanoi concluded that the dispute was not transitory but for practical purposes was permanent. This realization may have been gradual, but we need to fix it more precisely. I am inclined to think it came in the months following Khrushchev's fall, when his successors brushed aside renewed mediation efforts by Ho Chi Minh; possibly, however, it did not come until after the death of Mao, when it became clear that Mao's successors were of the same mind as Mao and had no intention of ending the rift.

5. At Xuan Mai, the big infiltration training camp outside Hanoi where People's Army of Vietnam (PAVN) troops earmarked for duty in the south were indoctrinated, a lecture course was taught called "Contradictions of Communism" which dealt specifically with the Sino-Soviet dispute. An examination of the texts used in the course indicates an effort to maintain balance between the two disputants. But those who took the course said the cadre instructors blamed China more than the USSR for causing the dispute but blamed both equally for allowing it to continue.

6. This turned on the proper balance between armed struggle and political struggle, on the allocation of resources within the war effort, and on other issues

Vietnam War *caused* the Sino-Soviet dispute. Nor does it appear that the war was ever *the* commanding issue in the dispute as far as Moscow and Beijing were concerned.

The Democratic Republic of Vietnam (DRV) sought a worldwide united front to support its war effort. This would not have required ending the dispute, but it did mean that the USSR and China should agree on supportive action and specifically on a single integrated logistics system. Hanoi put the blame for failure here on both sides, but chiefly on the Chinese. A single supply system was proposed by Kosygin during a visit to Hanoi in February 1965, and rejected outright by Mao Zedong a few weeks later. Moscow renewed the proposal periodically in the next few years—chiefly, it seems, to irritate the Chinese.

Ho Chi Minh's efforts to mediate the dispute began in the late 1950s and continued sporadically until his death a decade later. (Even his last will and testament prominently pleaded for an end to the rift.) Essentially he proposed an international conference of interested communist parties at which the whole matter would be thrashed out and resolved. Ho apparently had great faith in this process of bringing the two sides together in face-to-face dialogue and under great pressure from friends and allies so that the breach could be healed, or at least made manageable. Ho's offer of good offices was made in the name of socialist unity. He and other leading Vietnamese communists wanted communist world unity not only to facilitate their war in South Vietnam but because of their basic philosophy. To a man they were ideological fundamentalists who hated and feared schisms and even regarded developmental doctrinal change as heretical. For instance, each year they still enthusiastically celebrate Joseph Stalin's birthday. They were—and are—the world's most anachronistic communists.

The second principal guiding Hanoi in handling the Sino-Soviet dispute was never to allow itself to be co-opted by either disputant. The technique here was to maintain a bristly, almost aggressive, independence. Hanoi rep-

---

involving priorities and primacy of emphasis. The two basic options always were (1) emphasis on armed struggle, either guerrilla war or regular force (big unit) war, or (2) emphasis on political struggle—that is, protracted conflict or "politics with guns," use of diplomatic or proffered "political settlement" gestures, and so on. The USSR initially stressed political struggle, then switched to support of armed struggle after the 1968 Tet offensive. China's strategic advice was more complex. Its base was to assert that the Vietnamese were fighting a Maoist style people's war which properly fought meant fought by the people themselves, never by outsiders. Frequently China asserted that the DRV was misinterpreting Maoist strategy. China had the best of both worlds. It avoided being drawn into the quicksand of war and maintained maximum freedom of action. It could involve itself to whatever degree it wished, or it could hold back, citing its definition of people's war as justification.

resentatives lectured the parties frequently at international gatherings, then took a standoffish position when called on to align the DRV. This independent posture was seen by many outsiders as the product of a never-ending doctrinal dispute within the Hanoi Politburo, between pro-Chinese and pro-Soviet elements. Possibly this notion was encouraged by the Vietnamese themselves. In retrospect this view, which was extraordinarily influential in U.S. government circles, does not appear valid. In truth, the Politburo members were neither pro-Soviet nor pro-Chinese, only pro-Vietnamese, first and last.

We have little reliable information on how hard it was for Hanoi not to be co-opted during the Vietnam War years. Its best protection against excessive pressure from either side, of course, was the fact of the dispute itself, which allowed China and the USSR to nudge but never shove. Neither apparently ever issued any ultimata; no demands, only "suggestions," emanated from Moscow and Beijing.

Hanoi's third operating principle in dealing with the Sino-Soviet dispute was always to maintain symmetry by employing what might be called the alternating tilt gambit. From the Bucharest Conference of 1960 on through the Paris Agreements of 1973, the DRV treated each contentious issue with judicious balance. This was not neutralism, for Hanoi could never hide behind the nonalignment façade as could the rest of Southeast Asia. Nor was it simply evenhanded treatment, as outside observers frequently wrote—that is, the DRV carefully walking the narrow line between the USSR and China. In truth there was often no line to walk. On some questions, for example whether to sign the nuclear test ban treaty, there was no intermediate position possible.

Instead the DRV employed a more dynamic device, of tilting first toward Moscow then toward Beijing, to maintain a balance. Alternately and simultaneously it alienated and placated. No sooner did it tilt toward Moscow on a particular issue than it sought out some issue on which it could take a pro-Beijing position. Public treatment of the two countries—as evidenced, for example, in *Nhan Dan* editorials on anniversary greetings—was scrupulously balanced, down to the exact column inch. Politburo members traveling to one of the two capitals would always stop at the other, no matter how roundabout this made the journey.

Maintaining this balance was no easy task, because various issues had greater or lesser saliency, hence it was not simply a matter of tilt for tilt. Furthermore, the disputants sometimes shifted *their* positions, and sometimes even reversed them—for example, the position taken on a political settlement of the Vietnam War.[7]

7. Early in the war China stood for clear-cut victory for the Vietnamese communists, with no partial solutions or anything that smacked of *status quo ante*. Only a doctrinally pure resolution of the struggle would reassert the valid-

Outside observers tended to regard the Sino-Soviet dispute as pure opportunity for Hanoi. Neither party could ever pressure the DRV because of the dispute, and joint pressure was out of the question. Thus the DRV was free to play one side against the other, turning the dispute to its own advantage. There is validity in this view, but generally it has been overstated. Hanoi never approached the dispute exploitively. It apparently felt wisdom lay in healing the breach, because the DRV had more to gain from bloc unity than from exploiting the rift. This explains why the DRV was able to do what no one else was ever able to do, and that is make the Sino-Soviet dispute redound to its benefit. Paradoxically it profited from the split by not exploiting it. Had it tried to do so, both Moscow and Beijing would have been instantly alerted and would have acted negatively. The DRV always took a helpfully positive attitude toward both disputants. Apparently it convinced both that its attitude was sincere and its call for mediation genuine.

The Ideological Dimension. The Sino-Soviet dispute neatly if painfully encapsulated two Vietnamese communist dogmas, important ones for the Hanoi Politburo, for it always viewed the dispute in two dimensions—material or supportive and ideological.

The first doctrinal issue was philosophic, the decline of the spirit of transnational communism. It involved the erosion, under the force of nationalism, of transcendental proletarian solidarity, usually under the guise of polycentric communism, or "many roads to socialism." The code word here was "revisionism," and a revisionist was one who betrayed the ideals of world revolution by placing his country's national interests above the interests of the world communist movement. The second doctrinal issue

---

ity of the people's war principles as set down by Mao Zedong. Moscow, on the other hand, seemed agreeable to any outcome that would leave the USSR in a preeminent position in Vietnam. By the end of the war China almost desperately hoped that Hanoi would not win decisively, while the USSR, smelling the blood of total victory, urged the Vietnamese forward. Initially China wanted no political settlement of any sort, while the USSR indicated such an arrangement could become a useful way station en route to the ultimate goal of communization of Indochina. By the end of the war these two positions had been reversed. But at no time were the arguments of either very persuasive in Hanoi. At the start of the war China hoped that the United States would be driven from the region, its credibility as a dependable and effective ally totally destroyed. By the end of the war the Chinese fervently hoped for continued U.S. presence in the region. Initially the USSR hoped to see the United States discredited in Indochina but not driven out completely, since that would leave the field for the Chinese; this view changed after the 1968 Tet offensive. Throughout, neither the USSR nor China was averse to the idea of the other going to war with the United States over Vietnam, and apparently there was some scheming to this end by both of them.

was tactical and concerned the proper communist attack on capitalism, whether it should (would) employ the device called peaceful coexistence (later détente), or whether total (nuclear) war between communism and capitalism was inevitable and necessary. Its code word was "dogmatism" or—the Vietnamese preference—"right-wing opportunism." A dogmatist was one who timidly or hesitantly approached battle with the capitalists.[8] Within the worldwide communist movement, revisionism was equated with fundamentalism, although Lenin (particularly in the pre-1918 days) tended to apply the term chiefly to those who advanced any interpretation of Marx to which he did not subscribe. Dogmatism was originally equated with experimentalism, but Lenin used it against those who argued with him in the early days about the course of the Revolution; later under Stalin and Khrushchev it came to mean failure to adapt to changing reality, the mere parroting of Marxist text. Essentially, revisionism had to do with theory while dogmatism had to do with policy.[9]

Fundamental to revisionism was the matter of the correctness and inevitability of the use of violence in finally ridding the world of capitalism, specifically the proper degree of risk to take with respect to nuclear war. There can be no question that orthodox communist dogma—that is, original Leninism—held both that war was inevitable, as long as capitalism remained anywhere on earth, and that violent revolutions were mandatory. It is clear in reading Lenin that he believed that economic competition drove capitalist nations into warfare, and this was desirable because it engendered discontent and revolution; that the more revolutions the better; and that the more violent a revolution was, the better it was. In the Soviet view (that is, Khrushchev's) all this was changed by the atomic bomb. The Soviet position became that the world should be transformed through the "application

8. These terms did not have the same usage in Hanoi as in Moscow, nor in Beijing for that matter. In Moscow and Beijing, revisionism within the Sino-Soviet dispute had to do with communist unity, while dogmatism had to do with communist strategy. In Moscow, a dogmatist was a fanatic; in Beijing, a revisionist was a capitulationist. In Hanoi, each term had to do with both unity *and* strategy, but with somewhat changed meaning, as is seen below. To complicate matters further, in the early years all of this was coded: Moscow attacked the Albanians as dogmatists but actually meant the Chinese, while the Chinese condemned the Yugoslavs as revisionists but were referring to the men of the Kremlin. Hanoi accepted this indirect targeting device and made Tito the archrevisionist and Hoxha of Albania the archdogmatist.

9. The reverse or opposite of a pejorative term must, of course, be some term equally pejorative. In this case the opposite of "revisionism" would be "rigid mindlessness," while the opposite of "dogmatism" would be "appeasement." Revisionism to its advocate (although he would never accept the term) is merely advocating flexible international relations, while dogmatism to its defender (who also would not use the term) is fearlessly advancing the cause of communism.

of nonviolence" in which "defensive violence" would be used only in cases of "acute struggle." There is much latitude here, but it does not extend to risking nuclear war. The Chinese—and DRV—position favored unlimited revolution and unrestricted violence, creating an offensive state of mind, one willing to chance nuclear war.

The central meaning of both these dogmas, to the Vietnamese true believer, has to do with doctrinal change. The two sins of revisionism and dogmatism are worse than deviationism, which is sort of a mental lapse in discerning the true path and thus is correctable. They are even worse than hegemonism, which is imposing one's notions on others, thus is merely aggression. Both are immoral in that they alter the holy writ and gloss over certain fundamental differences between socialism and communism, and thus are *corruptive*. Both are equated with change: revisionism deliberately and openly calls for changed relationships among communists, and dogmatism—with its confrontational divisiveness—engenders it. Change is disruptive for the Vietnamese communists and encourages disunity. Disunity, or factionalism in communist parlance, is Vietnamese communism's great bête noire. The history of the movement in Vietnam is one long account of the campaign to blot out divisiveness, splinterism, geographic regionalism, and parochial challenge of the center. Ho Chi Minh spent a lifetime trying to weld the Vietnamese communists into monolithic unity and keep them there. It is, as has been expressed, the great Sinic disease of factionalism. In Vietnamese politics the daily game seems to be *bung di*, or "bash the faction." Revisionism and dogmatism then are venial sins that combine into the mortal sin of doctrinal change.

Hanoi's position thus was extraordinarily fundamentalist. Nor was it one designed to win easy support either within or outside the socialist world. It challenged one of the great forces of this era, nationalism. And it exhibited a kind of bravado contempt for the natural universal fear of nuclear devastation. But Hanoi stood doctrinally fast. And it remains fast. To this day Vietnamese communism's leaders would like to revert to that primitive communism that pits all the workers of the world against everyone else. And they say that they are ever ready, eager even, to march to Armageddon against the capitalists.

The War Years. The general trend of the DRV's two bilateral relationships during the Vietnam War was from good to bad with China, and from very poor to very good with the USSR. Just as we now know that the Sino-Soviet dispute began earlier and went deeper than the world realized at the time, so was the case with the Sino-Vietnamese split. In the 1950s there were difficulties, but they were well papered over. By the mid-1960s the divisions had become serious. Near the end of the war, in the early 1970s, it was clear that China did not want a decisive Hanoi victory. But it was never able to bring itself to do those things that might have prevented victory. It was inhibited by the fact of the Sino-Soviet dispute, of course, and it counted on greater American tenacity.[10]

Relations with the USSR took the opposite course. They hit rock bottom in the last years of Khrushchev, bumped along a rough road for several years, then began an upturn in the mid-1960s and had a sharp upturn in 1968. It still is not clear exactly how supportive the USSR was in the middle years of the war. Most observers believe that up to 1968 the USSR dragged its feet in backing Hanoi's war. Moscow apparently responded to Hanoi's supply requests according to their intended use. It was quite generous in supplying defensive war materials used in the north, such as antiaircraft weapons, but niggardly with arms for use in the south, such as infantry weapons. This policy was apparently meant to discourage the war in the south on the grounds that Hanoi could never win there. This changed after the 1968 Tet offensive, when Moscow realized for the first time that Vietnamese communist victory was a possibility.

As the war dragged on, Hanoi leaders increasingly came to regard the Sino-Soviet dispute as a major impediment to victory.[11] A visceral reaction began to develop—first ill-concealed irritation, then muted outrage. Eventually it reached the proportions of scarcely contained rage, a fact never appreciated by outsiders. This sour view of the disputants is implied in some of the writings at the time and by the personal behavior of the DRV leaders at Hanoi diplomatic functions. It is most clearly found in the testimony of prisoners and defectors held in South Vietnam. The author spent much of

10. Mao told the West German ambassador to Beijing that Americans had never been "serious" about Vietnam, since they had departed after suffering "only 50,000 casualties." This was interpreted as a sardonic remark. Actually Mao meant it quite literally. Such is the difference in magnitude in Asia.

11. If we are to believe Hanoi's retrospective view (1980) of the Vietnam War, Chinese behavior throughout amounted to little more than collusion with the United States to defeat the Vietnamese communists. For instance, General Vo Nguyen Giap told a Cuban journalist: "The Chinese government told the U.S. that if the latter did not threaten or touch China, then China would do nothing to prevent the attacks [on Vietnam]. It was really like telling the United States that it could bomb Vietnam at will, as long as there was no threat to the Chinese border.... We Vietnamese leaders felt that we had been stabbed in the back.... When we recount all these events and link them to the war in the southwest [i.e., Kampuchea], we can see the treachery of the Chinese leaders." This was said to Miguel Rivero of the *Verde Olivo* (Havana) in an interview published February 10, 1980. Giap's references to Kampuchea, as well as Vietnam's present dependency on the USSR, are self-evident motives for his remarks, and good reason why we should not take the general's rewriting of history very seriously.

the summer of 1967 in POW and Chieu Hoi camps in South Vietnam interviewing North Vietnamese cadres about the Sino-Soviet dispute.[12] Opinions held by the hundred or so individuals interviewed were uniformly consistent: neither China nor the USSR was supporting the "revolution" to the extent they should; such support as was made available was for the wrong reason; vital weaponry was withheld; the overriding point to make was not how much the two had done for Vietnam but how much they had not done, which was much more. This view—of inadequate commitment by both Moscow and Beijing—was expressed by all without significant deviation. It led to the inescapable conclusion that the same perception, perhaps in somewhat more sophisticated form, extended upward in the Hanoi command all the way to the Politburo.

What would these men of the Politburo say today, in retrospect, about the dispute, if we could persuade them to speak candidly? Probably they would make these points: (1) Throughout the Vietnam War, North Vietnam wanted—and felt it had the right to—total commitment from both the USSR and China, which it never got. Their policy on the war was a mixture of ideological identification and selfish pursuit of their own national interests, the latter consistently dominating the former. (2) Despite the great material aid provided, it was never adequate—not all of the right weapons or troops were supplied,[13] nor were they sent in sufficient large numbers. In critical moments, when the DRV needed material or psychic support, both Moscow and Beijing would temporize or hedge their responses. Both, at various times, were "soft" on the idea of a negotiated settlement, which the DRV always opposed, unless the alternative was annihilation.[14] (3)

12. Chieu Hoi, literally "open arms," was the Government of Vietnam returnee or defector program.

13. A captured PAVN general complained to the author that while the Soviets had given antiship missiles "to Nasser and Ben Bella, they never gave them to us to use against Yankee Station and Dixie Station [the two U.S. naval task forces] off Vietnam."

I have never found any evidence for the frequently encountered assertion that the DRV did not want Chinese troops in the war because once in they might refuse to leave. A contrary case can be made that the DRV in the 1965–66 period schemed to entrap the Chinese into the war but the Chinese understood the game and refused to play it. Mao made it clear in mid-1965 that troops would not be forthcoming. After the Cultural Revolution developed, the matter became academic as far as the Vietnamese were concerned. In retrospect it is clear that China saw Vietnam as a trap and had no intention of repeating the mistake of the Korean War. To this day the opposite perception—what might be called the Fulbright Red Hoard intervention myth—persists among many Americans.

14. Although political settlement was a legitimate form of political struggle strategy, the DRV's heritage of betrayal by comrades at the conference table

Neither the USSR nor China truly *cared* about the Vietnamese communist cause. Such support as was provided was for the wrong reason, not to advance the great golden revolutionary dream of unification, but to injure the other. (4) Both Moscow and Beijing, if truth be known, were paper tigers. Both had a sense of limitation of their own power and both excessively feared that DRV military offensives might somehow draw them into war with the United States. The DRV felt its cause justified high risks, while Moscow and Beijing always treated the Vietnam War as a potential trap. In sum, each disputant considered his victory in the Sino-Soviet dispute far more important than Hanoi's victory in war. When forced, as they sometimes were, to choose between serving the war or serving themselves in the dispute, each unhesitatingly chose the latter. Neither was staunchly in the forefront of the Vietnamese Revolution, and that is their final, unforgivable sin.

THE DISPUTE TODAY AND TOMORROW

Southeast Asia this past half decade has witnessed one astounding unexpected development after another. Looming largest was the North Vietnamese army's crushing military sweep down through South Vietnam. The expectation had been that the Vietnam War, in a stalemate, would continue to seesaw back and forth for at least several years. On the heels of that disaster came a long string of startling events. The chief ones, in no particular order of importance, were the arrival on the Indochinese peninsula for the first time of USSR air and naval power; the advent of a full-scale cold war between two erstwhile allies, China and Vietnam, marked finally in 1979 by a bloody seventeen-day border war; the breakup of such unity as did exist within Indochinese communism followed by a Vietnamese military invasion of Kampuchea; the holocaust in Kampuchea which quickly took on the character of a proxy war of China versus Vietnam and the USSR; extraordinary internal strife in Vietnam involving racist persecution, Gulag style reeducation camps and New Economic Zones, and the mass expulsion of ethnic Chinese and the exodus of middle-class Vietnamese—a social trauma that came to be symbolized by the boat people; the improved socioeconomic condition, resilience, and plain good luck of the ASEAN nations (in stark contrast with communist Indochina); and finally, the U.S.-Chinese rapprochement. To some extent all these developments were both caused by and had an effect on the Sino-Soviet dispute.

Hanoi's victory probably had more of a profound meaning for China

---

was so strong that the leadership never again wanted to run that risk. Initially China shared this opposition to negotiations but gradually changed its attitude, so that by the 1970s it favored a negotiated end to the war. The USSR to some extent advocated it before 1968 but gave only lip service to it after that.

than for the USSR. Shock waves are still being felt in Beijing. Quite simply put, the Chinese, during the last years of the war, badly miscalculated the direction events would take. They had expected an indeterminate condition in which neither side could develop the strength to defeat the other. They had expected the continued existence of two Vietnams, probably with South Vietnam moving to the left or turning neutralist. They had anticipated a reasonably stable working relationship among Indochinese communists. They had expected that Hanoi would continue to rely on China for economic assistance. When these expectations proved wrong, Beijing was struck with a nearly untenable position, having entrenched itself through actions taken on the basis of false assumptions.

Within the broader geopolitical region, China was alarmed by the quantum jump in Vietnamese strength and influence, and by the new power balance it faced as Hanoi began to tilt toward Moscow. All of China's calculations for Southeast Asia were upset by this, and it was presented with a host of old problems in new guise. It badly needed to redress the balance. China began moving toward the United States.

Most important of all, perhaps, the Hanoi victory destroyed a centuries old Sino-Vietnamese relationship, one based on a *sensei*-pupil association and rooted in fundamental deference by the Vietnamese. Victory required, the Vietnamese believed, that a new relationship be established, one more fixed in egalitarianism, Asian style. There began the peculiarly Asian manifestation of transition from one psychological state to another. What is important in this process—and the reason it is so singularly Asian—is that it involves not the substance of the association so much as the *act* of delineation. The 1979 Sino-Vietnamese border war was part of this process of redefinition, a process that has not yet run its course.

For Moscow, on the other hand, the DRV military success in South Vietnam was an occasion for unalloyed elation. The USSR had been on the right track, and early, anticipating final Hanoi victory months earlier than the Chinese, and pouring in support and making lavish promises for the future. The result was that victory found the USSR in as favorable a position in Hanoi as China's position was unfavorable. This trend—up for the USSR, down for China—continues to the present. Today the USSR is Vietnam's most supportive friend, while a full-scale cold war rages with China.

With respect to the dispute itself, the Hanoi victory both intensified and complicated the existing rivalry. Also, stakes in the game were raised throughout the region. Both Moscow and Beijing threw themselves with renewed energy into new bloc-building schemes for the region. This drew the ASEAN nations deeper into a complex struggle.

Southeast Asia, immediately after the fall of South Vietnam, was in a state of near panic. The relative stability and security which the ASEAN nations had enjoyed for more than a decade vanished overnight, and they found themselves, particularly Thailand, facing the guns of Vietnam and in danger of stark confrontation. Most of this anxiety wore off in the next half decade. It was not, as it turned out, entirely a negative phenomenon, for it gave impetus to regional development that turned ASEAN into the first Southeast Asian organization that was not a mere diplomatic joke.

The emergence of an all-communist Indochina, however, ruined prospects for neutralization of Southeast Asia. Indeed, even the term came to take on new meaning. Today, neutralization or nonalignment of Southeast Asia can mean "matching" the Chinese, Soviet, and Vietnamese presence, which, in practice, usually means reducing Chinese presence to match the more modest presence of the other two, and thus is covertly anti-Chinese. Or it can now mean an anticommunist posture in that the influence of each of the three communist nations of Asia is reduced to a minimum so as to avoid being forced to choose from among them. Gone almost totally now is the original meaning of neutralization—that is, Southeast Asia as a region that has opted out of the international power struggle.

The final result of these various developments in the past five years was to destroy forever the symmetry that had previously been the isosceles triangle of the USSR, China, and Vietnam relationship (with Vietnam being the narrow side). No longer is Vietnam the object of the game, the shuttlecock of the dispute. Vietnam now is the third largest communist country, possessor of the world's fifth largest standing army. It is a major geopolitical force in its own right, and henceforth must be viewed, by Moscow and Beijing, in terms of its potential as an ally or as a rival. The triangle now is equilateral within the region.

Vietnam's new position of enhanced power and prestige has forced the Hanoi Politburo to think anew about its former allies and the Sino-Soviet dispute; about the future political configuration of the Indochinese peninsula; and about Vietnam's strategic position in Southeast Asia and beyond. In short, victory forced Vietnam to redefine all its external relations. The men of the Politburo were singularly unprepared and ill-equipped for the role suddenly thrust on them. All their lives they had been turned inward, single-mindedly concentrating on the drive to achieve unification. Nothing else had mattered; foreign relations hardly were attended to, unless they were related to victory. The result was a leadership unskilled in the conduct of affairs in time of peace. It proved to be a fateful weakness.

The men of the Politburo plunged into the post–Vietnam War world. Operating in woeful ignorance, employing a host of questionable assumptions, they made a series of vital decisions that launched their country on enterprises that almost without exception proved to be ghastly mistakes. Trouble developed and Politburo members fell back on their wartime device for solving problems, the total and prolonged application of force. Their mental attitude—implacable tenacity—was exactly the kind needed to fight a long war, but the worst kind for a time of peace, when what is required is amicable relations with one's neighbors, and flexible and decentralized internal policies to promote economic development. China, irked over Vietnam's "high posture" and its intimacy with the USSR, could have been mollified by a more diplomatic Vietnamese leadership. The Pol Pot "problem" in Kampuchea could have been handled by outmaneuvering and shunting off what was only one of three major Khmer Rouge factions, had the skill to do this existed in the Hanoi Politburo. Good relations could have been achieved with the ASEAN nations, and diplomatic relations established with the United States.

The worst mistake, or at the least the central mistake, was handling the Sino-Soviet dispute. Victory meant an end to Hanoi's absolute dependence on the USSR and China for the tools of war—that is, assuming peace had arrived and would stay. The men of the Politburo saw this as liberation from the chafing control (or restraint) that both China and the USSR—never with much success—had tried to exercise throughout the war years. No longer did survival turn on the whims of the two allies. Of course the leaders recognized that the economic development now to begin would impose continued economic reliance on China and the USSR. But aid no longer was a life-or-death matter. Furthermore, it could be diversified—obtained from Japan, the United States, and other noncommunist countries. And Hanoi had just inherited a $12 billion windfall, the economic plant in South Vietnam, which was only a few years away from economic takeoff. The future was bright in 1975 as Party Secretary Le Duan announced the new emulation slogan: "Economics is in Command." Economic development would proceed with or without the aid of socialist countries.

But economic development of a country imposes certain behavior, and "economics in command" is a stern task master. Swords must be turned into plowshares. Reasonably amicable relations with one's neighbors are required. The psychological wounds of war in the country must be healed. External economic aid must be solicited by genuine deference to the sensitivities of potential donors. Needed economic institutions must be created in the country to facilitate the assistance from abroad.

None of this happened in Vietnam. It did not happen even though it was intended. Instead, the Politburo made a series of disparate decisions, about internal and external matters, which had the unintended result of bracketing Vietnam between two implacable enemies, ruining its relations in Southeast Asia, wrecking its economy, and tearing its society apart, north and south. The short-run way out of some of these troubles, it seemed, was by moving closer to Moscow. There was security and money in doing so. Hence Vietnam began drifting toward the USSR, less as a reasoned plan than as a desperate effort to rectify earlier mistakes. Decisions on collectivization of agriculture, creation of the vastly ambitious New Economic Zones, and governmental take-over of the domestic trade sector (chiefly in the hands of ethnic Chinese) created an economic chaos that made Vietnam dependent on the USSR for some 20 percent of the grain consumed and for all of its oil and industrial raw materials. Attempting to pacify Kampuchea and defend itself from China threw Vietnam into total dependence on the USSR for weaponry and other war materials. Eventually Hanoi found itself bound to Moscow, relying on Soviet food shipments to prevent rice riots and locked together with the USSR in what was a military alliance in all but name. Yet all the while the leaders of Vietnam were telling the world that economics was "in command," that Vietnam had but one interest, which was postwar reconstruction, and that it was determined to remain "independent" in the Sino-Soviet dispute. These professions were probably sincere. Hanoi leaders simply could not translate their intentions into relevant policy.

Most Southeast Asia watchers, including this author, assume that the Sino-Soviet dispute is permanent—as permanent as any condition in international relations.[15] It seems reasonably clear that Southeast Asia in the next decade or so is destined to be an arena of contention and one of the several battlefields of the Sino-Soviet dispute. This will increasingly involve Vietnam, as Soviet ally, but also as a contender in its own right. Since it is unlikely that either Beijing, Moscow, or Hanoi can decisively win this contest, the prospect for the region is a contentious ideological, security, and economic struggle.

Not too many years ago it seemed that the unified communist movement had a bright fuutre. It was seen as a dynamic monolithic machine driven by an incredibly powerful ideological engine. (Not too many years ago serious attention was paid the thesis that the "apparent" division among communists was a great communist plot designed to lull capitalists' fears.) The issue of communist monolithism appears settled: it is not to be. This is no small matter, and we should give thanks for an enormous advantage from history. It means we can think less about the menace of communism and think more about balance of power.

The communist states' essential choice in fixing on tactics against the ASEAN states is whether to woo them as they are now constituted—that is, as corporate capitalist societies—and deal with their existing governments, or whether to back local communist elements in the expectation that eventu-

15. There are dissenters, however, who question its durability. They cite, as one possibility, a Chinese decision to end the matter, possibly as the result of a leadership change, and add as evidence the general changeability of China on policy matters. Many of the Beijing watchers in Southeast Asia note that the Chinese communists have changed basic policy every five years since coming to power. It is more likely, however, that the dispute will remain.

ally they will seize power. Past efforts to compartmentalize state-to-state and party-to-party relations have never succeeded well, and will be even less successful in the future. Probably Moscow and Beijing will work through the center and not the insurgent, hoping to nudge the ASEAN ruling systems to the left, but not clubbing them in that direction.[16] Vietnam may also follow this moderate approach, but on this we have less assurance.

The Sino-Soviet dispute's regional impact during the years ahead, in terms of day-to-day activity, will stem from the area's pressing concerns of the moment. As of this writing, there are three major concerns: the war in Kampuchea, Hanoi's intimate relationship with Moscow, and Vietnam's self-generated social pathology, which has created the phenomenon known as the boat people. All three of these relate to, and are affected by, the Sino-Soviet dispute.

Kampuchea and the holocaust there is the region's central problem. As long as it continues—and the war gives every indication of being a protracted conflict—Kampuchea will be a chief destabilizing factor in regional affairs. ASEAN nations and others believe the only satisfactory outcome in Kampuchea is some new governing structure that incorporates all of the power contenders.[17] The operative question here is whether the Vietnamese will be able both to pacify Kampuchea and to transform the People's Republic of Kampuchea into a viable government. Opinions on this vary, but it seems agreed that even if it can be done it will take at least five years. If Kampuchea was not a proxy war when it began, it now has become one, because both China and the USSR have deliberately made the conflict there part of their dispute.

USSR military prowess in Vietnam—symbolized by Soviet submarines lying at anchor in Camranh Bay—cuts to the core of the Sino-Soviet dispute. China now sees itself flanked on the south with the enemy force augmented by a large battle-trained army. Moscow's move into Vietnam, if truth be known, probably was not part of a calculated effort to encircle China but a seductive opportunity that Soviet generals simply could not resist, although no one will ever be able to convince Beijing generals of this. The Soviet military presence in Vietnam concerns ASEAN nations, but

16. This probably means that the era of insurgency has ended in Asia. It does not mean there will be no guerrilla war, but it is unlikely there will be systematic organization and lavish funding by outsiders as a means of bringing down the existing government. The possible exception to this is Laos.

17. These are the Democratic Kampuchea (DK) under Pol Pot, the Peoples Republic of Kampuchea (PRK) under Heng Samrin, and the so-called Kampuchean third force represented by the Khmer Serai, Son Sann forces, Prince Sihanouk supporters, and remnants of the Lon Nol government. Any new governing structure must be acceptable to all three of these forces, since any one is strong enough to sabotage such an effort.

probably not as much as it concerns Tokyo and Washington. In part this reflects the reality of ASEAN's inability to cope with the USSR in any serious way, for instance in a power showdown. ASEAN's best hope is that the United States will act as a blocking force against USSR intimidation, in effect becoming ASEAN's surrogate in Moscow.

The USSR and SRV (Socialist Republic of Vietnam) military link-up will continue to be one of the dominating facts of life for Southeast Asia in the next several years. But it is a mistake to conclude that Vietnam is permanently in the USSR camp, or is prepared to sacrifice very much for the USSR. The present relationship is neither as durable nor as intimate as appears from the outside. But it is rooted in Vietnamese dependency and therefore will remain, regardless of Hanoi's wishes, at least until Vietnam can feed itself and until the threat from China subsides.

China's view of Vietnam is as a regional challenger, not simply a provocateur acting as Moscow's agent, and these "expansionist and hegemonistic" tendencies can be counted on to endure regardless of the future of SRV-Soviet relations. PRC-SRV rapprochement would require that Hanoi distance itself somewhat from Moscow, that it ease its efforts to dominate Kampuchea and Laos, and that it stop mistreatment of ethnic Chinese in Vietnam. All of these would be within the realm of possibility as far as Hanoi is concerned. The essential fact is that the Vietnamese leaders blundered into cold war with China. Studies based on interviews with Vietnamese on the general subject of the Sino-Soviet dispute, noted earlier, strongly indicate that most Vietnamese—including future policy makers—believe that in the long run Vietnam simply must get along with China. Its neighbor is too immense and too close ever to permit permanent confrontation. Sooner or later a workable relationship will be established. The trick in inaugurating this is to find a face-saving formula for rapprochement. Hanoi's present leaders probably will not be able to find one, but the next generation of leaders can, and will.

Even if there is a marked change in Hanoi's position with respect to the Sino-Soviet dispute, nothing much will change for Southeast Asia. It will merely mean Vietnam will go its own way, serving its own national interest, not that suddenly ASEAN-SRV interests coincide. Whatever the configuration of this rivalry, Vietnam in the future can be counted on to be particularly active. Its long-range goal (or dream) appears to be control of Southeast Asia in a hegemonistic sense, but achieved without recourse to war. This theme—dominance without war—explains most past Hanoi actions and will explain most of its future behavior.

The cutting edge of the Vietnamese sword will be ideological. All of Hanoi's external relations have the same cast. Present Vietnamese leaders passionately believe it is Vietnam's great historic mission to contribute to the transformation of the Southeast Asian social structure. They see ASEAN societies as neither legitimate nor durable. They expect all of them eventually to be swept away, replaced by people's republics. Vietnam is prepared to make sacrifices to this end.

This commitment to fundamental change in Southeast Asia is reinforced by a second ideological conviction—faith in the eventual emergence of a monolithic world system. The present Hanoi Politburo does not see international affairs, even bilateral relations, as the working out of competitive national interests under agreed ground rules with the outcome acceptable to both parties. Rather they see only a great historical confrontation between two world social systems, with only one survivor. Thus changing a neighbor's social system is what Vietnamese foreign relations is all about. This transcends ordinary Marxism. It is rather a singular Vietnamese brand, to be distinguished from the deviationist Marxism practiced in China, the USSR, and almost everywhere else. It can be fairly labeled, as Pol Pot has done, as ideological aggression.

Refugees, the worldwide symbol of this century's inhumanity, plague Southeast Asia by creating economic burdens, destabilizing existing political arrangements, exacerbating regional relations, and troubling consciences. More than a million Indochinese have left or been expelled from their homelands since the end of the Vietnam War, and the hemorrhage continues. China is a victim of this flow, having received some 250,000 ethnic Chinese from Vietnam. And it contributed to the problem by forcing a face-off with Vietnam. The USSR cynically supports Vietnam's refugee policies. Thus the refugees became pawns in the Sino-Soviet dispute and the broader power struggle. The twin problems here are to halt the exodus and to arrange eventual repatriation for the majority. The situation appears to defy short-run solution. There is every prospect at this writing that it will worsen. This seemingly never-ending exodus of people from Indochina is, of course, not merely an ASEAN problem, but a world problem that should be dealt with by the world.

THE PACIFIC COMMUNITY

Predictions of Asia's future are risky, as an inspection of past efforts at prognostication indicates. But one reasonably certain prediction for the area has to do with the rise of regionalism. The great danger of Asia in the next years is anarchy, a particular kind that is here labelled "engendered anarchy." China's Cultural Revolution was a classic example of this. Kampuchea under Pol Pot is a second. The fact is there is no certain means by which outsiders can cope with engendered anarchy, but the most fruitful approach clearly seems through the mechanism of regionalism.

Probably regionalism is destined to become a major force in international affairs throughout the world. It is simply a historical force at work that is on the ascendency and has not yet peaked. The regionalism of Asia—in

ASEAN and the likely Federation of Indochina (and possibly a Northeast Asia regional grouping)—suffers the normal threats. There is the danger of competing interests and there is the animosity of history. The process has far to go, but also it has in recent years come a good distance. ASEAN, for example, counts for more today than any previous regional grouping, including SEATO, and its importance grows daily. It appears that in the years ahead the region will become increasingly interdependent. Certainly this is a sound assumption on which to proceed. Ultimately this may result in the creation of a Pacific economic community, possibly one so broad as someday to include communist nations as well.

For the Sino-Soviet dispute, regionalism promises to be the chief force with which it must contend, but it also may prove to be the best mechanism for outsiders to use in dealing with the dispute. Indeed the history of the next few years in Asia may be an account of the forces of regionalism versus the Sino-Soviet dispute.

The Regional Impact: South Asia and the Middle East

The Impact of the Sino-Soviet Dispute on South Asia

WILLIAM J. BARNDS

Contrasting Soviet and Chinese policies toward the Indian subcontinent have been both a cause and a consequence of the Sino-Soviet dispute over the past two decades. Conflicting Soviet and Chinese policies toward India in the late 1950s and early 1960s were important, though not central, in the development of the Sino-Soviet dispute, and were one of the earlier indications of the growing antagonism between Moscow and Beijing. The Soviet Union supported bourgeois India against its Chinese ally after Sino-Indian friendship changed to animosity and led to the Sino-Indian border war in 1962. China gave similar support to Pakistan throughout the 1960s in an effort to counter the Soviet Union and India. These decisions established the basic pattern of great-power relations involving South Asia that continued throughout the 1960s.

The decade of the 1970s began and ended with the USSR and China sharply at odds over South Asian affairs. The impact of the Sino-Soviet dispute on South Asia during the 1970s can best be appraised by examining Soviet and Chinese actions in three situations. The first occurred when Soviet support of India enabled New Delhi to prevail over Pakistan in the 1971 crisis in South Asia, while Chinese policy revealed the limitations as well as the consistency of Beijing's backing of Pakistan. Second, in the mid-1970s the trend of events within the subcontinent, as well as Soviet and Chinese preoccupation with other areas, reduced the intensity of their competition. Third, the communist coup in Afghanistan in April 1978, and the Soviet invasion of that country in December 1979, confirmed China's convictions of the need to counter the expansionist activities of the USSR, both in the subcontinent and elsewhere. Since a continuation, or even an intensification, of Sino-Soviet competition is at least as likely as diminished tensions between these two intractable communist powers, South Asia is likely to remain a focal point in their struggle.

The policies of the Soviet Union, and, to a lesser extent, of China, toward South Asia have been characterized by a large measure of continuity over the past two decades. The same is true of the policies of India and, again to a lesser extent, of Pakistan, the two South Asian countries most deeply involved in world affairs during the 1960s and 1970s. Such continuity is particularly striking in view of the shifts between democracy and authoritarianism in both India and Pakistan, the division of Pakistan and the birth of Bangladesh, and the changes that have characterized world politics as well as Chinese and Soviet foreign policies in recent years. The persistence of close Indo-Soviet links, and of Sino-Pakistani cooperation, suggests that certain enduring elements in their policies are involved, although there is no assurance that such continuity will characterize the future. In fact, each of the four countries has from time to time explored possible shifts in their relationships. No basic changes have resulted so far, but the considerations of Realpolitik that underlie the policies of all four powers indicate that none of them would hesitate to shift course if their leaders came to believe that different policies would advance their interests. Moreover, the Soviet invasion of Afghanistan, as well as other changes in world affairs, will force all four countries periodically to reexamine the premises of their policies and the options available to them. Bangladesh, the other sizable South Asian country, has played a much less active role than India or Pakistan since its birth in 1971 amidst the upheaval of the Pakistani civil war. The smaller South Asian countries, such as Nepal, Bhutan, and Sri Lanka, have only been peripherally involved in the maneuverings of the USSR and of the People's Republic of China (PRC). Afghanistan, currently a focal point of Sino-Soviet hostility, assumed its present central role after a series of dramatic upheavals altered its widely accepted position as an independent country closely linked to the Soviet Union.

When appraising the relations between the USSR, the PRC, and the South Asian countries, it is important to keep in mind that the countries of the subcontinent have seldom been mere passive objects manipulated by Moscow and Beijing. India and Pakistan, and to a certain extent the smaller countries, have also taken the initiative in their dealings with the Soviet Union and China. Just as the USSR and China have made use of differences within South Asia for their own ends, the South Asian countries have attempted to play Moscow and Beijing off against each other. Such maneuvers have rarely been completely successful, but even partial success has often provided important gains to the South Asian powers. These gains have consisted of such tangible benefits as large-scale economic and military assistance, as well as diplomatic and political backing, which have strengthened the recipients' positions in their dealings with their neighbors and the West. Thus although the impact of the Soviet Union and China on the countries of the subcontinent has been greater than the South Asian impact on the USSR or China, it is only part of the record.

It is also important to keep in mind the inherent limitations of any attempt to evaluate the impact of the Sino-Soviet dispute on a particular region.[1] A move by the Soviet Union or China is often only one of a number of influences in South Asia, which are usually a combination of domestic pressures, intraregional maneuvers, and the actions of external powers other than the USSR or China. The role of the United States has often been as important as that of the Soviet Union or the PRC, but that is largely outside the scope of this essay. Moreover, while many Soviet and Chinese actions probably were taken as a consequence of their rivalry, others would have occurred in any event. These limitations need not paralyze one's judgment, but they should temper it.

THE VIEW FROM SOUTH ASIA

Neither the development and course of the Sino-Soviet dispute nor the origins and consequences of the Indo-Pakistani quarrel are the topic of this chapter. The importance of the first topic is self-evident, and it is the subject of other chapters. But it is impossible to analyze the policies of either the Soviet Union or China toward the subcontinent in any meaningful way outside the context of the Indo-Pakistani conflict.[2] This conflict has been the central feature of the international politics of South Asia that has confronted—and often bedeviled—external powers. Indo-Pakistani hostility has made it relatively easy for external powers to gain a foothold in the region by supporting one or the other local power. The same hostility has so far placed limits on the influence of any external power, for none has found the secret—if there is one—of establishing close relations with both India and Pakistan on an enduring basis. The United Kingdom, the United States, the Soviet Union, and China have all learned this through bitter experience.

It would be too simplistic to assert that Indo-Pakistani antagonism involved nothing more than the centuries old Hindu-Muslim conflict, which

1. The problems of evaluating the *impact* of the policies and actions of one country on another are similar to an effort to appraise the influence of one country on another. For a consideration of this matter, see Alvin Z. Rubinstein, ed., *Soviet and Chinese Influence in the Third World* (New York: Praeger, 1975).

2. For some typical Indian views of this relationship, see the special issue "Indian Relations with Pakistan," *International Studies*, 8, nos. 1–2 (July–October 1966); and for typical Pakistani views, see "Pakistan's Relations with India—The Recent Phase," by the editorial staff of *Pakistan Horizon*, 12, no. 3 (September 1959): 263–75.

caused the partition of British India in 1947. Yet this underlying antipathy between the Hindu and Muslim communities, which became institutionalized with partition in the form of Indo-Pakistani hostility, retains its position as the central determinant of Indo-Pakistani relations. (In certain respects this quarrel is similar to the one between Greece and Turkey.) Widespread communal violence still breaks out periodically in India, as it did when hundreds were killed in August and September 1980.[3] The virtual absence of Hindus prevents such horrors from occurring in Pakistan. Moreover, both India and Pakistan have suffered at the hand of the other in numerous ways—including three wars—since 1947, and this has left bitter memories in both countries. While these wars have created a conviction among many Indians and Pakistanis that their two countries must learn to live together, they have only begun the task of finding a mutually satisfactory way of doing so. Thus the Indo-Pakistani dispute probably has played as important a role as has the Sino-Soviet dispute in the evolving pattern of relations between China, the Soviet Union, India, and Pakistan.

Before examining the evolution of this pattern, however, it is important to set forth the basic perceptions of each of the four powers that have shaped their policies toward each other during the 1970s. The views of each of the countries as they entered the decade of the 1970s were influenced by the legacy of the recent past—the 1950s and 1960s—as well as by earlier experiences, and by their geographic proximity.

It is no exaggeration to say that Pakistan was born in a state of insecurity, and has lived in such a condition throughout its existence. If the dangers it has faced have not appeared as great to outside observers as to Pakistanis, the apprehensions of the latter have been the motivating force behind the country's foreign policy. With Pakistan's two disparate parts separated by a thousand miles of Indian territory, its search for security and status in relation to its much larger and stronger neighbor became the consuming goal of its foreign policy. Most Pakistanis were convinced that India was determined to dominate, if not destroy, Pakistan. India's refusal to allow the Muslim majority province of Kashmir to become part of Pakistan, and its military role in bringing about the bifurcation of Pakistan and the birth of Bangladesh in 1971, only served to convince Pakistanis that their suspicions were well founded.

Pakistan felt it had little choice but to seek external support to offset India's greater strength. Nearly all Pakistanis were convinced that accommodation was possible only at the price of subordination to India, and they felt that there would have been no purpose in struggling for partition if subordination were acceptable. They were also aware that as the smaller

3. *New York Times*, August 15, 1980; *Far Eastern Economic Review*, August 29, 1980.

country they would have to concede more for external support than India would, and their signing of an alliance with the United States in 1954 demonstrated that they were willing to pay the necessary price.

Although willing to ally themselves with the United States, Pakistanis tried to do so without unduly offending the Soviet Union and China. They felt themselves in no immediate danger from either the Soviet Union or China, but they saw no reason to offend their large neighbors. The exploits of the USSR and China against foreign invaders during World War II were admired, as was their determination to become strong modern nations, although Pakistan's Western-educated leaders and Muslim populace felt little attraction for either Soviet or Chinese communism. Pakistan failed, and for a time abandoned, its attempts to placate the USSR, but from the beginning was able to convince Chinese leaders that its alliance with the United States was not directed against the PRC.

Pakistan was basically satisfied with its alliance with the United States during the 1950s. It provided economic aid, arms, and a sense of security, even though it proved no help to Pakistan in gaining control of Kashmir. Pakistani leaders hoped that the development of the Sino-Indian dispute in the late 1950s and early 1960s would lead India to be more accommodating to Pakistan. They were dismayed when New Delhi managed to secure both Soviet and American support against China, and resentment of U.S. actions severely strained U.S.-Pakistani ties.

Pakistani President Ayub Khan gradually moved to expand his country's links with China without cutting Pakistan's ties to the United States. Ayub, fearful that Soviet and American support for India was leading to a decisive shift of power in South Asia, began to press India in ways that eventually led to the 1965 Indo-Pakistani war. The United States, unable to prevent the conflict between two friendly powers, abandoned its military role in the subcontinent. The USSR, which was seeking to broaden its role in the region—partly in order to try to keep Pakistan from moving from the Western to the Chinese orbit—adopted a relatively neutral stance during the war. It was able to use its good offices to bring about a limited agreement when Premier Kosygin met with Ayub and Indian Prime Minister Lal Bahadur Shastri at Tashkent in January 1966. Pakistan then tried to expand its relations with Moscow, again without cutting its ties to the United States or China. For a time Ayub was able to walk this "triple tightrope" successfully, but it left Pakistan in a vulnerable position when the 1970s began, particularly since its links with Moscow were tenuous ones.

India's position, aspirations, and perceptions of the world were quite different from those of its neighbor. Its preoccupation with Pakistan—while intense and enduring—had not been as all-consuming as had the latter's concern with India. Indians regard their country as a potential great power in view of its size, population, resources, and cultural and political traditions. Just as Pakistan has sought a status equal to that of India, the latter has regarded itself as the equal of China. India has resented policies by outside powers that equated it with Pakistan, or failed to regard it as the equal of China. The drive to become a major world power has been as important an element in Indian policy as its effort to reduce and eventually eliminate the poverty of many of its citizens. Soviet awareness of this fact, combined with the failure of the United States to appreciate its full significance, has had a major effect on the relations each country has enjoyed with New Delhi.

Equal to India's aspiration to be accepted as a major world power was its determination to play a dominant role in South Asia.[4] In view of their disparities in size and strength, India needed no external backer to deal with Pakistan. India's major concern, and one that still exists, is that Pakistan's ability to secure external support will cause it to try to undermine the "natural" order of things in the subcontinent by challenging India's dominant position. India's concerns on this score, which grew out of its suspicion that external powers would follow a variant of the divide-and-rule strategy that Indians believed characterized British rule in colonial times, were confirmed by the U.S. decision in 1954 to provide military assistance to Pakistan.[5] Indians also feared that external military support for Pakistan would strengthen the position of the military relative to the civilians in Pakistan, which in turn would intensify the Pakistani inclination to pursue a policy of confrontation rather than conciliation toward India. Some Indians go even further, and argue that U.S. support for Pakistan has been designed to counter India and keep it from assuming its rightful position in world affairs.[6]

Faced with American (and later Chinese) support of Pakistan, India has been receptive to the Soviet desire for closer relations, which enabled

---

4. For an appraisal of India's attitude toward South Asian security affairs, see William J. Barnds, "Indian Conceptions of Asian Security," *Asian Forum*, 8, no. 4 (Autumn 1976): 85–96.

5. Indians are partly correct in their judgment that Britain followed a divide-and-rule strategy in South Asia during the late nineteenth and early twentieth century. But they overlook the fact that the British could only have followed such a strategy because there were indigenous divisions in the subcontinent. They also minimize Britain's later efforts to create all-India institutions, such as the Indian Civil Service and the Indian Army, in an effort to transcend these divisions, and pass on what many British regarded as their major contribution to the subcontinent—a united India—to their local successors.

6. See K. Subrahmanyam, "U.S. Policy Towards India," *China Report*, 8, nos. 1 and 2 (January–February and March–April 1972): 36–53, and Baldev Raj Nayar, "Treat India Seriously," *Foreign Policy*, no. 18 (Spring 1975), pp. 133–54.

New Delhi to obtain Soviet economic aid and military equipment as well as Soviet diplomatic support at key junctures. Prime Minister Nehru also recognized that Indian nonalignment would be more solidly grounded if he were able to balance India's early links with the West with good relations with Moscow. Nehru had been impressed with the material progress of the Soviet Union in the 1930s, although his awareness of the human costs involved limited the attraction of the USSR.[7] Finally, good relations with Moscow would reduce the local appeal of the Indian communists.

In the early 1950s Indians were even more impressed with achievements and the promise of the new communist government of China, although there was concern over Beijing's insistence on establishing direct control over Tibet. Yet India felt it had no choice but to accept this, and moved closer to China as well as the USSR in response to the U.S. alliance with Pakistan. The Chinese suppression of the Tibetan revolt in 1959 brought Chinese troops to the Sino-Indian frontier, ending Indian hopes that Tibet would remain a de facto buffer area. The development of the Sino-Indian border dispute the same year outraged Indian public opinion, which felt that India had gone out of its way to befriend the newly established People's Republic of China.[8] New Delhi, its confidence bolstered by Soviet and American support, moved to reassert its control over the disputed Himalayan border areas. Step-by-step events led to the Sino-Indian border war of 1962, in which India suffered a humiliating defeat. Indian suspicion, bitterness, and hostility toward China became key elements affecting its foreign policy. Henceforth any friend of China was regarded with suspicion by New Delhi, while those at odds with Beijing were regarded as potential supporters.

SOVIET AND CHINESE PERCEPTIONS AND OBJECTIVES

South Asia has been an important focus of both Soviet and Chinese foreign policies. The subcontinent's strategic location would have made it important under any circumstances. The USSR's pre-World War II interest in the region was demonstrated during the Soviet-Nazi negotiations concerning spheres of influence, which took place following the signing of the

---

7. The general idea of state-controlled economic development, and state-owned heavy industries, has long appealed to most of the Indian elite. But specific Soviet policies and writings on economic development have had a limited impact on Indian thinking and policies. See Stephen Clarkson, "The Low Impact of Soviet Writing and Aid on Indian Thinking and Policy," *Survey* (London), 20, no. 1 (Winter 1974): 1–23.

8. For excellent analyses of these matters see W. F. Van Eckelen, *Indian Foreign Policy and the Border Dispute with China* (The Hague: Martinus Nijhoff, 1964), and Alastair Lamb, *The China-India Border: The Origins of the Disputed Boundaries* (London: Oxford University Press, 1964).

Soviet-Nazi pact in 1939.[9] When the United States formed its alliance with Pakistan in 1954, both Moscow and Beijing moved to counter the U.S. action by establishing closer relations with New Delhi. Once the USSR and China came into conflict it was inevitable that their rivalry would spill over into the subcontinent. Had the USSR and China remained partners, their main goal would have been to keep the United States from having an influential position in South Asia, although the specific concerns of each of them would have prevented them from achieving complete harmony in outlook or policy.

No absolute measure of South Asia's importance to the USSR and China can be devised, but a comparison of how it ranks relative to other areas of the world yields some useful insights. The subcontinent is not a region of top priority for either the Soviet Union or China. Moscow's main concerns are relations with Western Europe and the United States and its relations with East Asia—especially China and Japan. Threats to security of the Soviet state have come from the west or from the east—not from the south.[10] The Middle East, with its vast oil reserves, also occupies a higher priority in Moscow than South Asia does. In Beijing's eyes, relations—whether good or bad—with the USSR, Japan, and the United States take precedence over South Asia. On the other hand, South Asia is more important than Latin America or Africa to both communist powers, and is at least as important as Southeast Asia to Moscow—if not to Beijing. Such relative priorities do not determine specific Soviet and Chinese policies toward South Asia, but they provide the context that shapes their conceptions of their national interests and influences their broad policies.

The importance of the subcontinent to the USSR and China, it should be noted, is largely political and strategic, although both have used economic instruments to advance their broader aims. Nonetheless, the PRC's economic relations with the area are minimal. Those of the Soviet Union, while more significant, are still modest in terms of the totality of the USSR's external economic relations. For example, Soviet trade with all the South Asian countries in the late 1970s amounted to only about 5 percent of total Soviet trade.[11]

Two broad geopolitical considerations have influenced Soviet policy toward the region. First, if the Soviet Union was to succeed in its quest for

9. U.S. Department of State, *Nazi-Soviet Relations, 1939–1941: Documents from the Archives of the German Foreign Office* (Washington, D.C.: U.S. Government Printing Office, 1948).

10. For an excellent discussion of Soviet views of different regions, see Thomas P. Thornton, "The U.S.S.R. in Asia," in Wayne Wilcox et al., eds., *Asia and the International System* (Cambridge, Mass.: Winthrop, 1972).

11. International Monetary Fund, *Direction of International Trade Yearbook, 1980*, p. 385.

the status of a global power it needed to play a prominent role in the Afro-Asian world, and specifically in the lands to the south of Soviet territory from the eastern Mediterranean through the Indian subcontinent. This is not to suggest that an abstract interest in status was the principal concern motivating Khrushchev and the other post-Stalin leaders during the mid-1950s. They were worried about the practical consequences of the efforts of the United States to forge a set of alliances and establish its military presence in the region. Moscow sought to counter the United States by offering Soviet support to the nonaligned states in order to increase their capability and willingness to stand outside the U.S.-led security system. Soviet leaders have always been aware that no South Asian country had the indigenous strength to threaten the Soviet Union—unless allied to a major power hostile to the USSR.[12] This has remained a central concern of the USSR throughout the postwar period, although as the Soviet Union was successful in expanding its role in the subcontinent, positive goals assumed greater importance in its defensive concerns.

The second Soviet motivation has to do with the Asian balance of power. In view of China's hostility, Japan's suspicions and security ties to the United States, and—except for Vietnam—Southeast Asia's wariness or indifference to the USSR, the latter's ability to play a central role in the Asian balance of power requires Moscow to have a strong position in South Asia. The Soviet Union acquired this through the establishment of its broad-based links with India, the key country in the subcontinent. Neither the expansion of its own military power in East Asia and the Western Pacific nor Hanoi's assumption of a dominant role throughout Indochina has lessened the value Soviet leaders place on the USSR's relations with India.

Moscow has periodically tried to expand its relations with Pakistan, principally to try to reduce the latter's links with the United States and the PRC. (Moscow's efforts along these lines after the mid-1960s were also part of a broader Soviet effort to improve relations with Iran and Turkey by taking advantage of their disappointments with the West during a time the cold war was declining in intensity.) Such overtures to Pakistan have strained Indo-Soviet ties, but New Delhi's need for Soviet support tempered its reactions. Perhaps Soviet leaders thought an occasional demonstration that the USSR's position was not entirely dependent on India would even increase their leverage with New Delhi.

12. This could change over time if India, which has already demonstrated its ability to build nuclear weapons, succeeds in its efforts to develop a ballistic missile capability. Such a development probably would create some unease in Moscow—despite Soviet assistance to India's missile program—but would only increase the benefits the Soviets see in maintaining good relations with New Delhi.

China is in the unenviable position of having a greater direct security interest in the subcontinent than the USSR while having less national power to use to protect its interests there. This has given Chinese policy a more consistently defensive character than that of the USSR, despite South Asia's greater direct importance to Beijing than to Moscow.[13] China's changing interests depend on the PRC's foreign policy orientation during a specific time, as well as the state of its relations with other countries involved in South Asia. China's enduring interests grow out of the subcontinent's location on China's southwest border adjacent to the minority—at times unstable—Tibetan and Xinjiang regions.

An unfriendly power in South Asia could threaten Chinese control of these areas. A belief of China's that India was attempting to undermine the PRC's position in Tibet in the late 1950s was a major reason behind the deterioration of Sino-Indian relations then. This Chinese concern about Tibet and Xinjiang was intensified by the existence of a dispute between the two countries over the sovereignty of about 50,000 square miles of territory along their Himalayan frontier. China's success in defeating India in their 1962 border war probably diminished Beijing's apprehensions over these matters. But the PRC cannot be indifferent to the danger India could pose to these areas, particularly if it were cooperating with a major power hostile to China. The development of an Indian nuclear weapons and ballistic missile capability could pose a threat of a completely different order of magnitude to China's security.

One way China could deal with these problems would be to develop good relations with India, which would reduce or even eliminate any danger from that direction. The PRC tried this policy in the 1950s, but it foundered because of differences over Tibet, inability to settle the border dispute, and a general attitude of rivalry in Asian politics. But recent developments suggest that the PRC still regards this as an option over the long term. China could also seek to be on good terms with those major powers that might involve themselves in South Asia, in order to reduce the chances of their supporting India against China. The problem with this approach is that China's relations with the superpowers depend on considerations more central to Chinese concerns—and those of the United States and the USSR—than South Asian affairs. If neither of these approaches succeeds, Beijing has little choice but to seek a close working relationship with Pakistan in order to keep New Delhi as preoccupied as possible within the subcontinent and thus less able to threaten China. China's ability to frustrate Soviet designs

13. For an interesting perspective on the relative importance of South Asia to the Soviet Union and China (and the United States), see Robert Jackson, "The Strategic Outlook for the Indian Sub-continent," *Asian Affairs*, 59, part 3 (October 1972): 259–69.

is also furthered by keeping Pakistan outside anything resembling a Soviet sphere of influence.[14]

During the late 1960s the Soviet Union continued to seek to supplement its ties with India by improving its relations with Pakistan. But progress was slow and uncertain, for Moscow was unwilling to abandon India, and Pakistan was not willing to break off with China or the United States, despite China's absorption in its cultural revolution and America's preoccupation with Vietnam. One reason for Soviet persistence in pursuing its opening to Pakistan during these years was its concern over disarray within India, as well as what Moscow perceived as a drift to the right there. Moreover, New Delhi rebuffed Soviet appeals that it sign the Nuclear Nonproliferation Treaty, and turned aside Brezhnev's call for an Asian collective security system.[15] In 1968 Indira Gandhi even suggested that India and China try to normalize relations, indicating that she wanted Moscow to be aware that India had other options. For a time it appeared that a looser pattern of relations was emerging, but this pattern was soon to be tested by the most dramatic upheaval South Asia had experienced since the departure of the British.

THE BANGLADESH CRISIS

The 1971 crisis in South Asia, which gave rise to the bifurcation of Pakistan and the birth of Bangladesh, is a classic example of the interrelation between domestic, regional, and great-power politics in terms of their impact on the affairs of the subcontinent. The policies of the Soviet Union and China played a major role in the eventual outcome of the crisis, and thus in the new constellation of power in South Asia. At the same time, both the USSR and the PRC were responding to developments originating in the subcontinent rather than undertaking moves on their own initiative.

The overriding political division within Pakistan since its inception had been the one between its two disparate wings, whose attachment to Islam

---

14. For a perceptive analysis of Sino-Pakistani relations up to the mid-1960s, see Khalid Bin Sayeed, "Pakistan and China: The Scope and Limitations of Convergent Policies," in A. M. Halpern, ed., *Policies Toward China: Views from Six Continents* (New York: McGraw-Hill for the Council on Foreign Relations, 1965).

15. The vagueness of the proposal, and its implicit anti-Chinese focus, led Asian governments to ignore or reject it. For respective different appraisals, see Ian Clark, "Collective Security in Asia: Towards a Framework for Soviet Diplomacy," *The Round Table*, October 1973, pp. 473–81; V. Pavlovsky, "Collective Security: The Way to Peace in Asia," *International Affairs* (Moscow), no. 7, July 1972, pp. 23–27; and Bhabani Sen Gupta, "Soviet Thinking on Asian Collective Security," *Institute for Defence Studies and Analyses Journal*, 5, no. 2 (October 1972): 173–95.

and fear of India were their only elements in common. Historical circumstances resulted in a military establishment and civil service which were overwhelmingly West Pakistani in origin. Since Pakistan was an authoritarian state for most of its existence, the government was effectively dominated by these groups, even though East Pakistan contained a majority of the population. Two decades of West Pakistani domination had convinced the Bengalis of the eastern wing that the only way they could gain control of their own destiny was to secure complete provincial autonomy, with the central government controlling little more than foreign affairs and defense. In the eyes of West Pakistanis, however, such extensive autonomy would have spelled the end of Pakistan. The outcome of Pakistan's first national elections, held in December 1970, exacerbated rather than resolved this dilemma. The country's newly elected political leaders were unable to resolve this issue in the negotiations with Ayub's successor, President Yahya Khan. Emotions rose rapidly in East Pakistan, and by March supporters of Bengali leader Sheikh Mujibar Rahman and his Awami League had taken almost complete control of the province. Yahya responded by suspending negotiations and trying to suppress the Bengalis by resorting to what amounted to a virtual campaign of terror. Within a few months hundreds of thousands of Bengalis were dead, and several million East Pakistani Hindus had fled to India.

These developments not only dashed Indian hopes that an East Pakistani-led government would be friendly toward India but created fears that the presence of so many refugees would undermine the already precarious stability of much of eastern India. New Delhi condemned the Pakistani resort to arms, and pressed Yahya to free Sheikh Mujib and to negotiate a political settlement with the Awami League which would make it possible for the refugees to return. India also urged foreign governments to press Yahya to negotiate, while New Delhi simultaneously began to provide assistance to the Bengali guerrilla forces that were struggling against the Pakistani army.

The upheaval forced difficult choices on the Soviet Union, China, and the United States.[16] Both the USSR and China were in the process of moving toward détente with the United States, a factor that was to influence developments involving South Asia. Moscow had continued its efforts to expand relations with Pakistan after Ayub was overthrown in 1969. Yahya had been invited to Moscow in 1970, and the USSR had agreed to build a one-million-ton steel mill in Pakistan. But once fighting began in East Pakistan, Soviet leaders decided that their effort to foster good relations with both India and Pakistan was not viable in view of their rapidly increasing hostility toward each other. President Podgorny's letter of April 3 to Yahya

16. For an appraisal of U.S. policy during the crisis, see William J. Barnds, "India, Pakistan and American Realpolitik," *Christianity and Crisis*, 32, no. 10 (June 12, 1972): 143–49.

(published in *Pravda* the next day) called on the Pakistani government to halt the "bloodshed and repression." Although the letter avoided taking a formal position on Pakistan's internal crisis, it did refer to the Awami League leaders as having "received . . . convincing support by the overwhelming majority" in the December 1970 elections.[17] Pakistani leaders were angered and dismayed about such blunt criticism, but apparently decided that any public rebuttal would lead Moscow to harden rather than to moderate its position.

Moscow, having taken what was essentially a pro-Indian position, became rather restrained in its public statements over the next few months. This probably was less a response to Pakistani restraint than to two broader considerations. Most Muslim nations opposed the division of what was then the world's most populous Muslim country. Other Afro-Asian nations were likely to be concerned if they concluded that the USSR favored secessionist movements. The Soviet desire to avoid alienating these countries, as well as some hopes of limiting its losses in West Pakistan, led the USSR to issue ambiguous statements about the need for a settlement acceptable to the "entire people" of Pakistan.

A more direct, and perhaps more important reason, behind the Soviet Union's public caution was its concern about the Chinese role, particularly if the upheaval led to another Indo-Pakistani war with the consequent danger of Chinese involvement. China hesitated only briefly before passing up the chance to support the Bengalis in the hopes of turning what was essentially an ethnic and cultural struggle—although with important economic aspects—into a more radical movement or a war of national liberation. On April 11 Zhou Enlai sent a note to Yahya supporting Pakistan's efforts to preserve its national integrity.[18] The note also attacked India, the Soviet Union, and the United States for interfering in Pakistani affairs. This suggests that the Chinese leaders not only continued to see India as an expansionist power but also saw the Soviet Union and the United States as colluding to support New Delhi. But once it had stated its position, Beijing —like Moscow—adopted a low profile for several months, although the PRC and the USSR continued to provide economic and military aid to Pakistan and India respectively.

Events in the wider international environment soon dramatically changed the context of the South Asian upheaval. India had been concerned over the unwillingness of the United States to break completely with Pakistan, and its apprehension on this score was sharply intensified by the announcement in July that Henry Kissinger had made a secret visit to China—via

---

17. *Pravda*, April 4, 1971, in the *Current Digest of the Soviet Press*, hereafter *CDSP* (Columbus, Ohio), 23, no. 14 (May 4, 1971): 35–36.

18. *Peking Review*, April 16, 1971.

Pakistan—and had opened the way for a Sino-American rapprochement. Even if the United States had not been friendly to Pakistan, India would have feared that Sino-American détente would rule out the possibility of the United States supporting India in the event China intervened in a new war on the subcontinent. Now New Delhi had visions—or nightmares—of a Sino-Pakistani-American axis in Asian affairs, and the Indian foreign minister spoke about the danger of the "domination of the two countries over this region."[19] New Delhi believed that it had strengthened its military position in relation to China since 1962, but it wanted to reduce the risks of any Chinese military moves. Thus Soviet support became more important than ever to New Delhi.

Moscow was as stunned as New Delhi by the Sino-American rapprochement, and exhibited considerable uncertainty as to how to respond. Yet a Soviet riposte in the subcontinent was both necessary and possible, and Soviet leaders quickly moved to demonstrate that they recognized the increased value of closer Indo-Soviet ties. The two countries signed a twenty-year Treaty of Friendship and Cooperation on August 9, and Moscow sharply increased the flow of Soviet arms to India. While not a formal military alliance—and while explicitly recognizing India's policy on nonalignment—the agreement in effect committed the two countries to closer cooperation.[20]

In November 1971, after growing Indian military pressure along the borders of East Bengal prompted the desperate Pakistanis to launch attacks on western India, the USSR stood firmly in India's corner. Soviet vetoes prevented the United Nations Security Council from approving any resolution critical of India, while the military build-up undertaken by India in the east enabled it rapidly to defeat the beleaguered Pakistani forces in East Bengal. China had shown little concern over the Indo-Soviet treaty when it was signed, but once the Indian military moved into East Pakistan it reacted strongly. China's fear of implications of Indo-Soviet collaboration for the PRC's position in Tibet is illustrated by remarks of China's United Nations representative, Huang Hua, before the Security Council. On December 4 he said:

> The Indian Government asserts that the purpose of its sending troops to invade East Pakistan is to help the refugees of East Pakistan to return to their homeland. This is utterly untenable. At present, there are in India large numbers of so-called "refugees" from Tibet, China; the Indian Government is also grooming Dalai Lama, the chieftain of the Tibetan counterrevolutionary rebellion. According to the Indian Government's assertion, are you going to use this also as a basis for aggression against China?[21]

19. *Radio Delhi Domestic Service*, July 20, 1971.
20. The text of the agreement is in the *Hindustan Times*, August 10, 1971.
21. *Peking Review*, December 10, 1971.

On December 6 Huang Hua revealed more about China's apprehensions. He referred to a TASS statement that explained Soviet concern over the war on the ground that fighting was "occurring in direct proximity to the borders of the USSR and, hence, involved its security interests," and said:

> The "secure boundaries" of the Soviet Union have all of a sudden been extended to the Indo-Pakistan subcontinent and the Indian Ocean. The aim of the Soviet leaders is to gain control over the subcontinent, encircle China, and strengthen its position in contending with the other superpower for world hegemony. What the Soviet leaders of today are frantically seeking is the establishment of a great empire which the old tsars craved after but were unable to realize, a great empire controlling the whole Eurasian nation.[22]

Beijing also charged India with trying to establish a puppet state in East Bengal like the one the Japanese had set up in "Manchukuo."[23] It issued equally scathing denunciations of attempts by Soviet "social imperialism" to start a war pitting "Asians against Asians."[24] But Moscow and New Delhi were not deterred by such charges. The Chinese made no serious military threats until the war was all but over, perhaps because of their concern about the large Soviet army on China's northern border. The assertions by the United States that India was principally to blame for the conflict, and Washington's dispatch of a carrier task force into the Bay of Bengal, infuriated India without deterring it—or helping Pakistan. Prime Minister Indira Ghandi had waited until winter to launch her attack (when movement in the Himalayas is extremely difficult) and quickly declared a ceasefire once the fighting ended in East Pakistan, thus making clear that India had no intention of trying to seize West Pakistan. Bangladesh was soon an independent country, West Pakistan was defeated and demoralized, India was dominant on the subcontinent, and the Soviet Union had achieved its greatest triumph.

COMPETITION IN A NEW CONTEXT

Both the Soviet Union and China were faced with an altered environment in South Asia after the 1971 upheaval, and an appraisal of their respective responses provides insights into the role of South Asia in their foreign policy considerations during the 1970s. But before turning to the situation in the subcontinent and Soviet and Chinese policies toward it, it is important to

22. Ibid., December 17, 1971. The TASS statement is in the *CDSP*, 23, no. 49 (January 4, 1972): 1–2.
23. *Peking Review*, December 10, 1971.
24. NCNA (Peking), December 23, 1971, reported in *Foreign Broadcast Information Service Daily Report—People's Republic of China*, December 23, 1971.

note several features of the broader international environment which prevailed during most, if not all, of the decade. The Sino-Soviet conflict continued unabated despite the death of Mao Zedong and the dramatic shifts in Chinese policy inaugurated by his successors. In addition to its continuing efforts to contain and isolate China, the Soviet Union's principal foreign policy initiatives were directed toward fostering détente with the United States and Western Europe, both to reduce the dangers of war and to secure Western credits and technology in order to spur its lagging economic growth. China was also moving toward a more cooperative relationship with the United States, Japan, and Western Europe. This was partly because of increased concern over its security following the Soviet invasion of Czechoslovakia and the enunciation of the Brezhnev Doctrine in 1968, the fighting on the Sino-Soviet border early in 1969, and—later after the mid-1970s—because of its need for expanded economic relations with the industrial world to speed up its economic development. Although such considerations did not by themselves require either country to pursue a particular course of action, they limited the need to give priority to South Asia in the absence of a major crisis or opportunity there. Neither occurred until late in the decade, but Soviet and Chinese policies during "normal" periods may be as illuminating as their behavior in a crisis.

In the years immediately after 1971, India, Pakistan, and Bangladesh were attempting to establish new relations within the region. India was in a stronger position than ever, but was not so strong that Pakistan had to accept whatever terms New Delhi offered. Pakistani President Zulfikar Ali Bhutto and Prime Minister Gandhi reached an agreement at Simla on July 2, 1972, which represented a genuine compromise on some of the issues left over from the 1971 war and earlier disputes, although several key issues (such as Kashmir, and Pakistani recognition of Bangladesh's independence) proved intractable and were set aside.[25] The agreement was an important first step designed to set the two countries on the path of reconciliation. Hard bargaining over the next few years finally brought about the settlement of other issues necessary for a normalization of relations within the subcontinent.[26] While India achieved its minimum goals, Bhutto had done better for Pakistan than seemed possible at the end of 1971.

Pakistan's "success" was due partly to the country's relatively quick recovery from the war and the loss of East Pakistan, and partly to Bhutto's

25. The text of the Simla Accord is in *Pakistan Horizon*, 25, no. 3 (3d quarter, 1972): 117–18.
26. For detailed appraisals of these developments, see William J. Barnds, "Pakistan's Foreign Policy: Shifting Opportunities and Constraints," in Lawrence Ziring, Ralph Braibanti, and W. Howard Wriggins, eds., *Pakistan: The Long View* (Durham, N.C.: Duke University Press, 1977); K. P. Misra, "Trilateralism in South Asia," *Asian Survey*, 14, no. 7 (July 1974): 627–36.

political skills. Another important reason, however, was continued Chinese support, and the PRC's actions demonstrate why Pakistan holds China in high regard. This is not to suggest that Beijing ever gave Pakistan a blank check. In fact, China proceeded cautiously both during and after the 1971 upheaval. The PRC never approved the Pakistani government's actions in East Pakistan, and after the conflict was over, a *People's Daily* editorial indicated China's attitude by quoting an unnamed Pakistani who said that "the Pakistani government had made mistakes and very serious mistakes indeed in the past in handling the question of East Pakistan."[27] In February 1972 Bhutto revealed that China had refused Pakistan's request for a defense pact.[28] China's central concern was not that Pakistan remain united, but that West Pakistan remain independent and not come under Indian or Soviet domination.

Yet if China's support was limited during the conflict, its actions in the post-1971 period demonstrated its consistency. Beijing could, it should be noted, have attempted to weaken New Delhi's ties to Moscow by actively working for a rapprochement with India. Many observers of Asian politics thought such a shift would be a logical response on Beijing's part to Prime Minister Gandhi's cautious 1968 overture, especially in view of the PRC's more flexible post-Cultural Revolution foreign policy. Yet the very modest easing of Sino-Indian tensions that took place in the late 1960s was reversed by the 1971 upheaval. China's leaders probably believed that New Delhi's need for Soviet support would prevent the Indian government from making any substantial policy changes. New Delhi's stake in its links to Moscow was underscored by a move made by the USSR. Moscow had issued maps in the 1960s supporting Chinese border claims along the Himalayas even after the eruption of the Sino-Soviet dispute, but in 1972 it hinted that it might be shifting its position when it allowed publication of an article openly backing India's claims.[29]

China demonstrated its steadfastness by continued provision of military and economic assistance to Pakistan.[30] Even though a smaller Pakistan was

27. *Peking Review*, February 4, 1972.
28. *New York Times*, February 13, 1972.
29. G. V. Matveyen, "Peking's Political Machinations on the Hindustan Peninsula," *Problemy Dal'nego Vostoka* (Moscow), no. 4, 1972, pp. 39–45, excerpted in *CDSP*, April 11, 1973, p. 4. India had earlier endorsed the Soviet position in the Sino-Soviet border dispute, which probably strengthened China's conviction that India was a tool of Moscow (Reuters dispatch from New Delhi, April 8, 1969).
30. The U.S. government has stated that Chinese arms for Pakistan amounted to $133 million between 1965 and 1972. See *U.S. Foreign Policy for the 1970s: The Emerging Structure of Peace: A Report to Congress by Richard Nixon, February 9, 1972* (Washington, D.C.), p. 147. In February 1972 China agreed to

less useful as a counter to India, Chinese leaders recognized that West Pakistan was the source of most of the country's military strength, and of its most deep-seated anti-Indian sentiments. Given China's antagonism toward India, and its limited prospects in a Bangladesh oriented toward India, Beijing had little choice but to make a virtue out of its consistency. Nor did Pakistan have so many friends that it could demand complete support from the PRC.

The PRC's diplomatic support in the United Nations proved particularly important to Pakistan, for China was willing to veto Bangladesh's application for membership, and to withhold diplomatic recognition of Bangladesh until Pakistan normalized its relations with Dacca. This greatly strengthened Bhutto's bargaining power in his negotiations with Prime Minister Gandhi and Sheikh Mujib, who was now the leader of Bangladesh.

China remained suspicious of any moves that might lead to Indian domination of the subcontinent. Nonetheless, in 1973 and 1974 Chinese leaders voiced their approval of the agreements reached between the South Asian governments which created "favorable conditions . . . for a detente in the South Asian region,"[31] and which would facilitate the "normalization of relations among the countries of the subcontinent."[32] After Pakistan recognized Bangladesh in 1974, the PRC reversed its 1972 veto and supported Bangladesh's application for United Nations membership, and extended diplomatic recognition to Dacca in August 1975.[33]

If China's choices in South Asia were limited in the early 1970s, the Soviet Union had a wider range of options. One possible course was to take advantage of its recent achievements by committing its prestige and resources to a major effort to expand its influence in the subcontinent. (The Soviets were willing, as later events were to demonstrate, to undermine détente in pursuit of specific advantages, but only if the prospects for gain were favorable.) Another, and less ambitious policy, would have been to do only what was necessary to consolidate the position it had already won, unless the United States and China made major efforts to rebuild their positions.

The USSR moved rapidly to build up a comprehensive relationship with Bangladesh. Prime Minister Mujib strongly praised the USSR when he

---

convert four earlier loans of $110 million for economic aid to grants, and to defer the repayment period on a $200 million loan made in 1970 for twenty years. See *Peking Review*, February 4, 1972.

31. *Survey of the China Mainland Press*, nos. 5452–55 (September 10, 1973), p. 90.

32. *Peking Review*, May 17, 1974.

33. For a detailed analysis of Chinese policy toward Pakistan, see William J. Barnds, "China's Relations with Pakistan: Durability Amidst Discontinuity," *China Quarterly*, no. 63 (September 1975), pp. 463–89.

visited Moscow in March 1972, and he agreed that the two countries would conduct regular political consultations.[34] The Soviet Union also provided some civilian aircraft, as well as a squadron of MIG fighter planes, and cleared two important ports of sunken ships at no cost to Bangladesh. It also extended economic aid of $121 million between 1972 and 1975, which was more a demonstration of Moscow's determination to limit its activities than an indication of Soviet largess in view of Bangladesh's hugh needs.[35] In moving cautiously regarding Bangladesh, Soviet leaders may have been influenced by India's determination to be the key external influence in Dacca.

The USSR also continued its policy of providing economic credits to the smaller South Asian countries, such as Sri Lanka and Afghanistan. The former received a loan of $57 million in 1975, and the latter was promised $437 million for its Fifth Five-Year Plan.[36] Such moves broke no new ground, however, and were a sign of continuity rather than an expanded Soviet effort.

The USSR's caution may have represented a Soviet decision that the costs of a more ambitious course would have made sense only if Moscow could achieve tangible gains, such as guaranteed use of Indian and Bangladesh naval facilities, or adherence to Brezhnev's Asian collective security system. Since both the United States and China were at odds with New Delhi and Dacca, the USSR may have had hopes for progress on such matters. India's military forces were heavily dependent on Soviet equipment, the Soviet Union was India's second largest trading partner, and economic and scientific cooperation between the two countries was expanding in many areas. But neither New Delhi nor Dacca wanted an expanded Soviet naval role in the Indian Ocean. Moscow was also unsuccessful in obtaining their endorsement of its Asian collective security proposal.

Such developments led Soviet leaders to conclude that there were substantial obstacles to a more ambitious course. India's determination to be in control of its own destiny led it to resist any Soviet effort to expand its influence further. India's enhanced position in the subcontinent, while achieved partly as a result of Soviet support, limited New Delhi's need for further Soviet backing. Prime Minister Gandhi's comment to an American correspondent in 1972, "we are unable to display gratitude in any tangible sense for anything," was clear warning to Moscow not to press for a greater

34. *Izvestiia* (Moscow), March 26, 1972, in *CDSP*, April 19, 1972, p. 18.
35. For an analysis of Soviet-Bangladesh relations, see Bhabani Sen Gupta, "Moscow and Bangladesh," *Problems of Communism*, 24, no. 2 (March–April 1975): 56–68.
36. Central Intelligence Agency, *Communist Aid to Less Developed Countries of the Free World, 1975*, ER 76-10372U, July 1976.

role in the area.³⁷ The possibility that the Soviets would become the "mediator" of the security affairs of the subcontinent, as they had done at Tashkent in 1966, was eliminated by Prime Minister Gandhi's insistence that Indo-Pakistani differences be adjusted on a bilateral basis. Finally, India's development of a heavy industrial sector reduced its need for major Soviet aid projects. Soviet technology no longer appeared as attractive to India once Moscow began to seek Western and Japanese technology. Raw materials and (periodically) foodstuffs were India's major import requirements. Moscow would provide such products in barter for Indian goods only in limited amounts or during emergencies, such as it did with its two-million-ton wheat loan in 1973.

Moscow also tried once again to establish a better position in Pakistan, whose location made it more important to the USSR than distant Bangladesh. While arms aid would alienate India, trade and economic aid would not. Thus the Soviet leaders renewed their offer to finance a one-million-ton steel mill near Karachi, and agreed to provide $435 million in credits for the project.

Moscow also urged the South Asian countries to seek compromise settlements to their disputes. The USSR supported the agreements dealing with the consequences of the 1971 upheaval reached between India, Pakistan, and Bangladesh beginning in July 1972.³⁸ Pakistanis feared that Moscow would urge the Afghans to support dissident ethnic groups. But these fears were eased by communiqués issued at the end of the Moscow visits of Pakistani Prime Minister Bhutto in October 1974 and Afghan Prime Minister Muhammad Daoud in April 1977, which urged that disagreements between the two countries over the status of the border people in Pakistan be settled by peaceful means.³⁹ Prime Minister Bhutto also stressed that although Pakistan would not reduce its connections with China, these were not directed against the USSR.

Developments in the subcontinent during the mid-1970s probably confirmed the judgment of Soviet leaders that limiting their involvement had been a wise decision. Such satisfaction was temporary, however, for events in the major countries of South Asia threatened to weaken or even undermine their position in the region. Corruption, poor economic conditions, and the continued absence of public order in Bangladesh weakened Sheikh Mujib's government. Public anger focused on India in view of its close ties with Mujib. Both India and the Soviet Union were alarmed when more

37. *New York Times*, February 19, 1972.
38. See P. Kutsobin and V. Shurygin, "South Asia: Tendencies Toward Stability," *International Affairs* (Moscow), no. 4, April 1973, pp. 43–48.
39. *Pravda*, October 27, 1974, in *CDSP*, November 20, 1974, p. 15; and *Pravda*, April 19, 1977, in *CDSP*, May 11, 1977, pp. 17–18.

conservative forces overthrew Mujib in August 1975 and pulled away from New Delhi. The opportunity these developments might provide for China and the United States was not lost on the USSR.

Another cause for Soviet anxiety was the trend of events in Pakistan. Popular opposition to the blatantly rigged national elections of March 1977 led to such turmoil that a conservative, Islamic-oriented military coup took place a few months later. Bhutto had always been regarded with suspicion and distrust by Soviet leaders, but his moves toward accommodation with India, and his social and economic reforms, had been praised by the Soviet Union.[40] Soviet distaste for unpredictability gave Moscow's reaction to the coup a cautious quality.

Developments in India were of even greater concern to Moscow. Prime Minister Gandhi was unable to capitalize on her 1971–72 election victories. Ill-conceived policies, poor management of government affairs, and bad monsoons led to widespread popular agitation by 1974. The Soviet government backed Mrs. Gandhi's declaration of an emergency in June 1975 as necessary to counter right-wing forces.[41] (The Soviet Union has not, of course, hesitated to work with reactionary forces when that suited its leaders, although it is easier to do this in countries that have no significant communist movement.) *Izvestiia* insisted that "everything India has achieved during its thirty years of independence has been directly connected with the Indian National Congress."[42] Moscow was stunned by the defeat of the Congress Party by the newly formed Janata (People's) Party in the March 1977 elections, installing the conservative and anticommunist Morarji Desai as prime minister.

One reason for Soviet concern was that China had been moving carefully to improve its relations with India and Bangladesh without weakening its ties with Pakistan. A Sino-Bangladesh trade agreement was signed in 1976. General Ziaur Rahman, who had emerged as Mujib's successor, was given a lavish welcome when he visited China in January 1977, and several new economic agreements were signed. He denounced "expansionism and hegemonism," and that probably worried the USSR as much as it satisfied China.

China and India also showed renewed interest in improved relations, but progress was slow and uneven. Beijing did not criticize India's nuclear explosion in 1974, but it attempted to reassure Pakistan by reiterating its support for the latter's efforts to protect its independence from foreign aggression and interference in general, and specifically from "nuclear threat and

40. *Pravda*, March 11, 1977, in *CDSP*, April 6, 1977, p. 20.
41. *Pravda*, July 2, 1975, in *CDSP*, July 23, 1975, p. 12; *Izvestiia*, July 4, 1975, in *CDSP*, July 30, 1975, p. 17; and *Pravda*, in *CDSP*, August 6, 1975, pp. 17–18.
42. *Izvestiia*, March 13, 1977, in *CDSP*, April 13, 1977, pp. 15–16.

nuclear blackmail."[43] Stronger Chinese criticism followed India's annexation of its Himalayan protectorate of Sikkim the same year. Soviet support for this move, and continued Indo-Soviet cooperation, made it hard for China to see New Delhi as anything but a willing accomplice of Moscow. China's condemnation of the annexation illustrated its general view of India:

> The Indian Government's shameless act of annexing Sikkim has been strongly condemned by all countries and people that uphold justice. The Soviet Union alone, however, has blatantly cheered India and expressed support for Indira Gandhi's government. This is another proof that Soviet revisionist social-imperialism is the boss behind the scenes as well as the abettor of Indian expansionism.[44]

China apparently was not willing to move toward an accommodation until New Delhi demonstrated that it was its own master, but Indian leaders felt no obligation to prove that they made their own decisions.

Despite many obstacles, India and China gradually did move toward a less hostile relationship. In 1976 the two countries exchanged ambassadors for the first time since the early 1960s. But major obstacles remained to any substantial improvement in Sino-Indian relations. New Delhi was convinced that China had provided arms and training to dissident tribal groups in northeastern India and could easily continue to do so. China felt it had every right to develop cooperative relations with the smaller countries of South Asia, but India was suspicious of such ties. China's relations with Pakistan continued to be regarded as a danger by New Delhi. The Sino-Indian border dispute remained unsettled, although neither country was disposed to challenge the status quo. Beijing's suspicions of India's intentions toward Tibet continued, abetted by such moves as Prime Minister Desai's meeting with the Dalai Lama in July 1977. Finally, Moscow could be expected to do whatever it could to keep the two countries apart, and New Delhi would move cautiously lest any improvement in Sino-Indian relations would antagonize Moscow and weaken rather than strengthen India's international position. But a start toward better relations had been made, and this opened up new options for both India and China.

The advent of the Carter administration, which was more favorably inclined toward India than its predecessor, was another cause for Soviet concern. Moscow feared that the Desai government and the Carter administration would see their interests as overlapping, and that could weaken the position of the USSR. Soviet apprehension was increased when Prime Minister Desai stated that his government would follow a policy of "genuine"

43. *Peking Review*, July 15, 1974.
44. *Peking Review*, September 20, 1974.

nonalignment and insisted that the Indo-Soviet treaty of 1971 would not be permitted to constrain India's friendship with other countries.

But the problems facing the USSR in South Asia turned out to be manageable. One reason for this was Moscow's flexibility in dealing with the Janata government. This government also gave priority to continuity in foreign policy, as Foreign Minister Gromyko discovered during his visit to New Delhi in April. The Janata government was determined to work for improved relations with China and the United States, but it wanted to preserve India's links with its only great-power supporter. Gromyko offered new credits of $252 million for heavy industrial projects, a move that was largely symbolic in view of past unused Soviet credits. Indian Foreign Minister Atal Bihari Vajpayee commented that "Indo-Soviet friendship had been a stable factor and was of mutual benefit."[45] Indian reaffirmation of the validity of the Indo-Soviet treaty of 1971 during Desai's visit to Moscow in October 1977 further pleased the USSR. If the rhetoric of Indo-Soviet communiqués was much more restrained than in the past, the reality of mutual dependence remained.

Soviet anxiety regarding Chinese ability to take advantage of developments in the subcontinent also declined during the 1970s. The Janata government approached China warily. The PRC's attack on Vietnam in February 1979, and Chinese comparisons of its action against Vietnam with its military moves against India in 1962, touched raw nerves in New Delhi. Foreign Minister Vajpayee, who was in China, cut short his visit in protest.

The USSR's worry about an expansion of American influence in the subcontinent also gradually declined. South Asia, it developed, did not rank high in U.S. priorities, the Carter administration's nonproliferation policies created problems in America's relations with both India and Pakistan, and all U.S. aid to Pakistan—except foodstuffs—was cut off in April 1979 when that country was discovered to be developing a nuclear weapons capability. The Carter administration's human rights policies also posed problems for U.S. relations with Pakistan.

AFGHANISTAN: UPHEAVAL AND INVASION

The USSR encountered a new opportunity with the communist coup in Afghanistan in April 1978. A brief appraisal of the evolution of that country's internal affairs and its international position is necessary before turning to the Soviet and Chinese responses to developments in Afghanistan, and to the significance of what has transpired for world affairs.

Afghanistan began a modernization effort after World War II, an effort stressed by the government of Prime Minister Daoud (a cousin of King Zahir Shah) between 1953 and 1963. Daoud, conscious of the deeply re-

---

45. *Hindustan Times*, April 25, 1977.

ligious and tribal loyalties of the society, moved carefully regarding internal social changes. He was more adventuresome in foreign affairs, and was able to take advantage of the cold war to secure significant amounts of aid from both the Soviet and Western blocs. The United States refused Afghan requests for military support. U.S. security interests in Afghanistan apparently were seen as minimal, and the United States regarded Pakistan as a more important country. The Soviet Union became the principal supplier of arms to Afghanistan, which followed a nonaligned stance with a decided tilt toward the USSR.

Afghanistan's efforts to develop its economy and build up its military forces created a need for trained manpower. Educational opportunities expanded rapidly, but so did the frustrations inherent in the development process. This led some of the newly educated people—including some military officers—to turn to Marxism. More open political activity during the mid-1960s gave Marxist elements an opportunity to organize. They set up the People's Democratic Party (PDP) in 1965. But it suffered from factional disputes growing out of personal rivalries, cultural and ethnic differences, and conflicts over how to cope with alternating periods of governmental repression and co-optation. The party soon split because of such divisions, and again had to contend with the bitter antagonism which had characterized relations between the Khalq (Masses) faction, led by Nur Muhammad Tariki and Hafizullah Amin, and the Parcham (Banner) faction, led by Babrak Karmal.

Prime Minister Daoud returned to power in a coup that overthrew the monarchy as well as the government in 1973. His gradual shift away from reform cost him the backing of younger civilian and military elements. He also moved to ameliorate Afghanistan's troubled relations with Iran and Pakistan. These moves alarmed the Soviets, and led the Khalq and Parcham factions to reunite in July 1977. This laid the basis for the April 1978 coup.

The origins of the coup, and the extent of Moscow's knowledge and encouragement, remain subjects of controversy.[46] The Soviet Union strongly backed the new regime, which in October 1978 signed a twenty-year treaty of cooperation with the Soviet Union which linked the two countries closely. But the identification of Marxism with atheism, and the regime's subser-

---

46. Articles that describe the evolution of the Afghan scene and the development of the Marxist movement there before and after the April 1978 coup include Robert G. Neumann, "Afghanistan," *Review of Strategic and International Affairs*, July 1978, pp. 115–18; Louis Dupree, "Red Flag over the Hindu Kush—Parts I and II," *American Universities Field Staff Reports*, nos. 44 and 45, 1979; Richard S. Newell, "Revolution and Revolt in Afghanistan," *World Today*, 35, no. 11 (November 1979): 432–42; and Louis Dupree, Afghanistan under the Khalq," *Problems of Communism*, 28, no. 4 (July–August 1979): 34–50.

vience to the traditionally hated Russians, severely restricted its popular appeal among a deeply religious people with a history of violent resistance to the attempts of external powers to control the country.

Moscow was also hampered by the divisions within the PDP. These intensified after the coup, and led to a series of purges, including one against the Parcham leaders in July 1978, and another in September 1979 within the dominant Khalq faction, in which forces led by Prime Minister Amin ousted President Tariki. The narrowly based regime attempted to push through a drastic reform of Afghan society, which alienated both the religiously oriented rural, conservative forces and the moderate, urban-based reformers as well. The Soviets recognized the problems created by the regime's brutality, by its internal divisions, and its determination to remake Afghan society, but were unable to persuade their local clients to proceed more cautiously.

The localized resistance that began in 1978 turned into an insurgency that spread throughout the country in 1979. Governmental authority was confined to the major cities and provincial centers, and even in some of them it vanished with nightfall. The strength of the security forces declined steadily because of desertions, sometimes involving entire units which joined the insurgents. The Soviets sent large quantities of arms and several thousand military advisers, which were enough to slow but not halt the disorganized insurgency's growth.

This confronted the Soviet leaders with a difficult choice late in 1979. Should they leave a communist regime to its fate, even if this meant its overthrow, or should they intervene with whatever forces were necessary to save their client? They chose the latter course, and during December they rapidly expanded their troop strength in Afghanistan. On December 27 they carried out a coup that resulted in the execution of President Amin and the installation of the strongly pro-Soviet Babrak Karmal as the new president. Tens of thousands of Soviet troops poured across the border—the first time that Soviet armies had moved beyond the line between the communist and noncommunist worlds that grew out of the defeat of Germany and Japan in World War II. (The Soviets claimed that they were invited to enter the country by Amin, but soon were justifying his removal by claiming he was a CIA agent.)

Why did the USSR invade Afghanistan, when Soviet leaders were aware it would involve significant costs as well as benefits? Several reasons probably influenced the Soviet decision, beginning with Moscow's fear that a *neighboring* communist regime would be destroyed unless it intervened. The polarization of forces within Afghanistan meant that the communist regime probably would have been replaced by militantly Islamic and anti-Soviet forces. This would have been a matter of great concern to a leadership and people traditionally sensitive to the security of their borders, particularly in view of the upsurge of Islamic fervor and disorder in Iran.

Soviet leaders may also have feared that an upsurge of Islamic militancy would have created problems for them among the rapidly growing Muslim population of Soviet Central Asia. Outside observers have found little hard evidence of a religious revival among Soviet Muslims. But the absence of such evidence would not mean that Soviet leaders (who are largely Russian) had no fears of such a possibility.

A major question facing Western governments was whether the Soviet invasion was essentially a defensive move or whether it was but a first step toward further expansion in South Asia and the Persian Gulf. George Kennan argued the first case when he said:

> In the official American interpretation of what occurred in Afghanistan, no serious account appears to have been taken of such specific factors as geographic proximity, ethnic affinity of peoples on both sides of the border, and political instability in what is, after all, a border country of the Soviet Union. Now specific factors of this nature, all suggesting defensive rather than offensive impulses, may not have been all there was to Soviet motivation, nor would they have sufficed to justify the action; but they were relevant to it and should have been given their due in any realistic appraisal of it.[47]

Helmut Sonnenfeldt, former counselor of the State Department, took a different view, and one which put the Soviet move in the context of broader Soviet policies:

> For many years, the Soviet Union has used its growing military capabilities to assert its influence and establish its presence around the world. But apart from suppressing popular uprisings and pressures for liberalization in Eastern Europe by the actual use of military force, the Soviets have generally avoided injecting their own organized combat units into regional conflicts or domestic upheavals. . . .
>
> The events in Afghanistan in one sense represent the culmination of these trends in that the Soviets are now unabashedly and directly using their own forces. They also represent a new departure because Soviet military power is being used for the first time since the 1940s in an effort to extend Soviet dominance beyond its previous perimeter on the Eurasian landmass by preserving a new addition to the "Socialist camp." . . .
>
> Whatever the "defensive" rationale for the Soviet action . . . a "defensive" set of motives may serve as a more powerful stimulus to action than the desire for pure aggrandizement. And, of course, once having invested blood, military power and prestige to maintain Afghanistan's orientation and to suppress resistance to its regime, it is not so far-fetched a step for

47. *New York Times*, February 1, 1980.

the Soviets to push beyond that country's borders in order to secure them against external incursions, real or imagined.[48]

The Soviet invasion of Afghanistan, and the future course of Soviet policy, cannot be considered apart from the general state of Soviet relations with the outside world, especially the United States. Soviet leaders probably were influenced by a combination of fears and hopes. American military power relative to that of the Soviet Union had declined during the 1970s. The United States had not saved the shah's pro-Western regime in Iran, or prevented the new Iranian regime from seizing and holding U.S. embassy officials in Tehran. The United States had not reacted strongly to Soviet support for Marxist regimes in Angola, Ethiopia, and South Yemen. Yet the USSR was clearly worried that the United States, Japan, and Western Europe were moving toward closer cooperation with China. U.S. defense spending was increasing after a period of decline. Prospects for Senate ratification of the SALT II treaty were uncertain. Moscow may have felt it had little to fear from the United States if it invaded Afghanistan, and little to gain if it did not invade.

At this writing, nine months after the Soviet invasion, it is clear that the Afghan insurgency presents far more difficult problems for Moscow than did its military actions against Hungary and Czechoslovakia. The Soviets have so far achieved none of their goals in Afghanistan. Their 85,000 man force has failed to subdue the disorganized and lightly armed insurgents. The Soviets have failed to strengthen the Afghan security forces, which have disintegrated to about one-fourth of their former size. They have failed to create a government loyal to Moscow and acceptable to the Afghan people —probably an impossible task. Assertions that Afghanistan is the Soviet "Vietnam" are too facile, and ignore important differences between the two situations, but the insurgency shows no signs of diminishing.

Soviet leaders have justified their military intervention on the grounds of their duty to support "revolutionary" regimes.[49] They also charged that the United States, China, and Pakistan were supporting the insurgents, but their charges have not been backed up by any significant evidence. One of the most striking aspects of the Afghan developments is the marginal role the PRC has played, a situation that is likely to continue in view of China's extremely limited capabilities for influencing the USSR's southern neighbor.

The Soviet invasion was condemned by most of the world, and the strong reaction of nearly all Islamic countries probably was a matter of particular

---

48. Helmut Sonnenfeldt, "Implications of the Soviet Invasion of Afghanistan for East-West Relations," *NATO Review*, 28, no. 2 (April 1980): 1–5, quotation pp. 1–2.

49. For what some observers see as an enlarged version of the "Brezhnev Doctrine," see *New Times* (Moscow), January 18, 1980.

concern to Moscow. Yet public criticism has only a marginal impact on the USSR's actions if its leaders conclude that high stakes are involved. They probably believe that in time the world will accept their control of Afghanistan as it has accepted their dominance of Eastern Europe. The reactions of the United States and of Pakistan and India were more central to Soviet concerns than anything as vague as "world public opinion." The two South Asian countries have reacted quite differently.

Pakistan, although it did not accept the offers of the United States for a renewed military relationship, has strongly opposed the presence of Soviet troops in what had been a buffer state. Most Pakistanis see a Soviet-controlled Afghanistan as a direct threat to their country's security. (Neither Afghanistan nor the USSR has accepted the validity of the Durand Line as Pakistan's western boundary.) Pakistan's leaders condemned the Soviet invasion, but felt that their country needed external support to meet the Soviet challenge over the long term. Some Pakistanis probably wondered if they should not explore the possibility of reaching an accommodation with Moscow, even though they feared that such an accommodation could encourage further Soviet pressures rather than satisfy the USSR. Soviet leaders have attacked Pakistan harshly throughout 1980 for its alleged aid to the insurgents. One suspects that private Soviet threats have been even more explicit than their public ones, since Moscow appears to be following a course involving 90 percent threat and 10 percent inducement to secure Pakistani acceptance of the new order in Afghanistan. Pakistan is particularly concerned that the Soviet Union will attempt to destabilize the country by supporting dissident ethnic groups, or will conduct large-scale military raids across the border. Underlying these specific anxieties is the fear that the USSR and India will move together to destroy and divide what remains of Pakistan.

The Soviet approach to India has been quite different. Moscow has tried to persuade New Delhi that its move into Afghanistan is a temporary one that poses no threat to India. Early in 1980 the USSR agreed to provide $1.6 billion in arms for India on extremely favorable terms. After some initial wavering, New Delhi has on several occasions called for the withdrawal of Soviet troops from Afghanistan. But India has also suggested that Moscow has legitimate security interests there, and New Delhi believes that those must be accepted and accommodated. Prime Minister Gandhi's reluctance to be at odds with Moscow has led her to give some credence to Soviet charges of external support for the insurgents. New Delhi's ambivalent stance reflects its difficulty in developing a policy that balances its fears of an expanded Soviet military role in South Asia, its dependence on the USSR for arms and diplomatic support, and its fear of a rearmed Pakistan backed by China and the United States.

India's main fear is that a Sino-American-Pakistani-Islamic alliance will be formed to counter the Soviet move into Afghanistan. Most Indians believe that arms sent to Pakistan will be used to threaten India in the long run. Indians are extremely reluctant to admit that Soviet troops in Afghanistan create a serious security problem for Pakistan. To the extent that they acknowledge this problem they simply suggest that Pakistan move troops from the Indian to the Afghan border to deal with the problem. Indian public statements stressing the dangers being created by U.S. actions designed to build countervailing military strength in the region indicate that Indian foreign policy will continue to tilt toward Moscow. Underlying these views is India's concern that increased great-power involvement in South Asia—and in the Indian Ocean—will prevent India from being the dominant power in the region.

While China has had little ability directly to affect the course of events inside Afghanistan, it has tried to support Pakistan while simultaneously moving to improve relations with India. The former course essentially represents a continuation of its previous policy. Pakistan was grateful for such backing, but realistic enough to recognize that the PRC could offer nothing comparable to the funds of the Saudis or the modern arms of the West. Beijing's attempt to improve relations with New Delhi, despite the latter's tilt toward Moscow, probably represents an awareness by Chinese leaders that a hard line toward India would only drive it closer to the USSR. Deng Xiaoping's public suggestion in June 1980 that the two countries try to settle their long-standing border dispute probably was an attempt to set the stage for a major breakthrough. So was his acknowledgment that Kashmir was a problem to be settled bilaterally between India and Pakistan—a marked shift from China's earlier support for self-determination in Kashmir.[50] Nonetheless, the legacy of mistrust, as well as important differences in perspective and policy, make any rapid improvement in relations doubtful in the absence of a major shift in the Indian perspective on world affairs.

THE SOVIET AND CHINESE IMPACT ON SOUTH ASIA

An appraisal of the consequences of Soviet and Chinese policies toward South Asia must answer three broad questions. First, what had been the impact of Soviet and Chinese actions on the principal countries of the subcontinent before the Soviet invasion of Afghanistan? Second, to what extent have these Soviet and Chinese policies, and their impact, grown out of the Sino-Soviet dispute? Third, what can be said—even tentatively—about the likely impact of the Soviet move into Afghanistan on the Soviet and Chinese positions in the region? In assessing these matters, we should keep in mind that Moscow has until recently faced an international environment more

---

50. *Peking Review,* June 30, 1980; *Far Eastern Economic Review,* July 4, 1980.

responsive to American power and influence than to Soviet activities. This has placed constraints on the efforts of the USSR to expand its role. If Soviet power were to surpass American power—or American determination—the Soviets would find it much easier to exploit new opportunities. Some observers believe such conditions have already come to pass, and that Moscow's behavior in the past few years is an indication that it is moving to take advantage of what it sees as a new and more favorable "correlation of forces."

Moscow has achieved its present role in South Asia by giving top priority to its relations with India and Afghanistan, which it has backed with arms, economic aid, trade, and diplomatic support. India has felt confident enough of Soviet support to make close relations with the USSR a key element in its foreign policy. Moscow's periodic criticism of India, and its occasional overtures to Pakistan, have led New Delhi to conclude that it must be sensitive to Moscow's concerns rather than take its support for granted. Moscow's approach has made it impossible to develop a significant position in Pakistan, or to keep that country from developing close relations with the PRC. Soviet leaders probably regret this constraint, but show no signs of thinking they made the wrong choices.

The Soviet Union has long been the largest supplier of arms to the subcontinent. The Soviet bloc has made arms commitments to India and Afghanistan of some $4 billion and $700 million respectively since the mid-1950s and this support has been essential to Indian and Afghan efforts to develop their military forces. But India's expanding defense industry and its purchases of some arms from the West in recent years have enabled it to avoid complete dependence on Moscow. No accurate figures are available concerning the volume of Chinese arms to Pakistan. Yet even if they amount to no more than $500 million, China's consistency of support, and its willingness to help Pakistan to establish its own defense industry, have caused Pakistani leaders to give considerable weight to Chinese views.

Soviet and Chinese economic assistance has also played a major role in their policies toward South Asia in recent decades, as shown in Table 8. Soviet aid has been no match for the approximately $25 billion extended by Western nations—except in Afghanistan. But its political impact in India has been increased many-fold, because it has supported the construction of large-scale state-owned industrial establishments, which successive Indian governments have regarded as important to the country's drive for economic independence. Soviet and Chinese technicians and training have increased local capabilities, although Western training apparently still is preferred when it is available. China, it should be noted, has supplied more aid to Nepal and Sri Lanka than has the USSR, and nearly two-thirds as much as Moscow to Pakistan.

The change in the volume of Soviet and Chinese trade with the South

TABLE 8
Communist Economic Assistance to South Asia, 1954–78
(in million U.S. dollars)

Recipient Country	USSR	Eastern Europe	China	Total
Afghanistan	1,263	39	76	1,378
Bangladesh	304	159	74	537
India	2,282	455	—	2,737
Nepal	30	—	183	213
Pakistan	921	126	598	1,645
Sri Lanka	158	93	222	473
Total	4,956	872	1,153	6,981

SOURCE: CIA, *Communist Aid Activities in Non-Communist Less Developed Countries, 1978* (ER 79-10421U, September 1979), p. 12.

Asian countries since 1955 is shown in Table 9. Two points should be made. First, despite the substantial increases in Soviet trade with all the countries except Nepal, the trade of all the South Asian countries was overwhelmingly with the noncommunist countries as late as 1975. Except for Afghanistan, this pattern apparently has continued. Soviet purchases and sales of particular products have on occasion been important to India, especially since Moscow did not demand hard currency for its exports. Even if the Soviet Union is still a secondary trading partner, it is no longer an insignificant one. Second, Chinese trade is a marginal factor in the total trade of all the countries except Sri Lanka. If Moscow's ability to use trade as a political instrument is limited, Beijing's is nonexistent outside of Sri Lanka.

Soviet support has substantially enhanced Indian military strength and international stature, and enabled India to maintain a firm position in its disputes with Pakistan and China. The PRC's support of Pakistan has improved Pakistan's bargaining position in relation to India. Neither Soviet nor Chinese policy was primarily responsible for Pakistan's division in 1971, which was mainly a result of the shortsightedness of the country's West Pakistani rulers. Yet Soviet support of India—and to a lesser extent the limitations the PRC placed on its support of Pakistan—contributed to the ultimate loss of East Pakistan.

Both Moscow and Beijing have supported—or at least accepted—Indian and Pakistani efforts during the 1970s to shift from confrontation to accommodation. Yet each of the communist powers has continued to support its respective South Asian partner. No one can reprogram history in a computerized politicomilitary war game and prove that Soviet and Chinese neutrality—or noninvolvement—would have led to a settlement of Indo-Pakistani disputes. What one can say with some confidence is that the inclination of either of the South Asian countries to search for an accommo-

TABLE 9

South Asian Foreign Trade (Imports plus Exports), 1955 and 1979

| Country | 1955 ||||| 1979 |||||
| | USSR and Eastern Europe || China || Rest of World || USSR and Eastern Europe || China || Rest of World ||
	Million U.S. $	%	Million U.S. $	%	Million U.S. $	%	Million U.S. $	%	Million U.S. $	%	Million U.S. $	%
India	25.9	1.0	19.7	0.7	2,645.1	98.3	2,210.0	11.0	4.0	0.0	17,955.0	89.0
Pakistan[a]	5.7	0.8	31.9	4.4	684.1	94.8	176.7	2.8	122.2	1.9	6,019.6	95.3
Bangladesh	N.A.	N.A.	N.A.	N.A.	N.A.	N.A.	152.2	5.7	93.9	3.5	2,421.8	90.8
Afghanistan[b]	33.4	20.0	N.A.	N.A.	81.6	71.0	212.9	22.8	5.5	0.5	701.6	76.7
Sri Lanka	1.9	0.3	42.3	5.9	669.7	93.8	69.7	2.9	121.8	5.0	2,238.5	92.1
Nepal	N.A.	N.A.	N.A.	N.A.	N.A.	N.A.	11.5	6.0	12.8	6.6	168.2	87.4

SOURCES: UN, IMF, IBED, *Direction of International Trade*, Statistical Papers, Series T, vol. 10, no. 8 (New York, 1959), annual data for the years 1955–63; IMF, *Direction of International Trade Yearbook, 1980*; Bureau of Intelligence and Research, U.S. Department of State, *Communist States and Developing Countries: Trade and Aid in 1971*, RECS-3, May 15, 1972, p. 27.

[a] 1955 data include trade of area not comprising Bangladesh.
[b] 1955 data not available; 1956 figures used.

N.A.: Not available.

dation has been—and will be—less if they are convinced that they have external sources of support whether they are intransigent or not.

The role of the Sino-Soviet dispute as a motivating force behind the moves of these two countries is something that can hardly be appraised with any precision. Yet a few observations are warranted. If there has been no Sino-Soviet dispute *and* no Sino-Indian dispute, it seems likely that the broad features of Soviet policy that have characterized recent decades would be much the same. The magnitude of the Soviet effort to support India in order to check the United States probably would have been more modest. Chinese support of Pakistan would hardly have been as substantial as it has been. Yet each country would have wanted to play a role in South Asian affairs, and each might have on occasion emphasized support for a different South Asian country. Given the existence of both disputes, the size of the Soviet military assistance program—and particularly its continuation during the 1970s—can be attributed as much or more to the Soviet concern about China as to its apprehension about the United States. This probably is less true of the Soviet economic aid and trade programs, for in these areas Moscow seldom had to fear Chinese competition if Soviet leaders wanted to enter the race.

Finally, the continued existence of the Sino-Soviet dispute makes it more difficult for India and China to reach an accommodation. Moscow hardly controls New Delhi's policy on this issue, but no Indian government can afford to alienate Moscow in the search for a settlement with China. If Moscow were not at odds with Beijing, it would be seeking to foster improved Sino-Indian relations instead of regarding such moves as likely to weaken its position in the subcontinent.

The ultimate impact of the Soviet invasion of Afghanistan on South Asia, and on the Soviet and Chinese positions there, will obviously depend on events that are still unfolding. The reactions of all the countries involved will be affected by developments in the Iraqi-Iranian conflict, and by the outcome of the Polish upheaval. The direct gains that the Soviets would realize by dominating as poor an area as Pakistan would be modest. Moreover, the costs would be substantial if such a move alienated India, although New Delhi might decide it should accommodate Moscow in such circumstances. A Soviet advance to the Persian Gulf would represent a great gain, however, in view of the critical dependence of the West and Japan on oil from the area.

It is useful to appraise the Afghan crisis in terms of the following three possible outcomes. First, the Soviets could fail in their effort to control Afghanistan. Moscow could encounter such heavy costs in Afghanistan, or in its relations with other nations, that it would withdraw its troops and allow its client regime to fall. The costs of such a defeat to the USSR, and its ability and willingness to pay a heavy price over a period of years, make such a development unlikely, though not impossible.

Even if such an outcome occurred, it would not destroy the Soviet position in South Asia. India would still want good relations with Moscow, and Pakistan would see little reason to pursue an active anti-Soviet course. But the impression of inevitable Soviet gains that Moscow has sought to project would have been badly damaged, and the countries of the region would be less influenced by the views of a "superpower" that had failed to conquer the poorly armed Afghans. China would clearly benefit from such an outcome, although perhaps more in a general sense than in terms of specific gains.

Second, the conflict could develop into a stalemate. Moscow would not be defeated, but would find its occupation costly enough over a prolonged period so as to be willing to seek a compromise solution. The terms of such a compromise can hardly be specified at this point, but probably would include some kind of guaranteed neutralization or nonalignment internationally, and a coalition of diverse forces domestically.

The international aspects of such an outcome appear theoretically feasible, but in the absence of a balance of power in the region Moscow probably would move slowly to accept such a solution. The domestic component of such a settlement is difficult to envisage, however, for the Afghan people are bitterly polarized between a few thousand Marxists and millions of militantly anti-Marxists tribesmen and townsmen in a country where blood feuds and revenge are matters of honor. Moderates acceptable to both sides—if they have not already been decimated—have little if any political base. Yet wars do not always end with clear victors and vanquished, and a prolonged stalemate could eventually lead to at least some temporary accommodations.

Before the USSR would agree to such a setback, it probably would strike at Pakistan in the belief that outside support was the source of insurgency's durability. Moscow probably would also attempt to subvert dissatisfied groups, such as the Baluchis in Pakistan, in order to weaken Pakistan and cause it to accept the new order in Afghanistan. Thus the risks of an expanded conflict would increase, and the countries of the area—and the West—would have to be prepared to meet such challenges for there to be much likelihood of a compromise solution.

The need to accept such an outcome probably would harm the Soviet—and help the Chinese—positions in South Asia. The Soviet need to find a compromise solution would reduce but not destroy Moscow's influence. Nonetheless, India would still seek good relations with the USSR, while perhaps breathing easier that the limits of Soviet power had been demonstrated.

Third, the Soviets could succeed in their Afghan venture and eventually create local political and military forces that were loyal to Moscow and able to control most of the country. This might lead to closer cooperation between India and Pakistan—the West and China—and between them, in an effort to contain Soviet power. But the deep-seated differences between India and Pakistan, combined with Soviet success in Afghanistan, suggest that accommodation rather than confrontation would characterize Indian, and probably Pakistani, policy. Yet this could also require Pakistan to subordinate itself to India. This could in time so demoralize the key groups in Pakistan, who have yet to create a viable political system, that it would lead to national disintegration. Even if such dramatic developments did not occur, Moscow would have become the predominant external power in South Asia, and the positions of China and the West would have been sharply curtailed. The temptation of Middle Eastern countries to reach their own accommodations with Moscow would increase, thus eroding the Western position in the lands from the eastern Mediterranean through the Indian subcontinent.

The Sino-Soviet Interaction in the Middle East

BETTIE M. *and* OLES M. SMOLANSKY

In the 1970s, which were marked by a continuing deterioration of relations between the Soviet Union and the People's Republic of China and by a gradual rapprochement between Beijing and Washington, the Middle East emerged as one of the regions of an occasionally intense rivalry between the two communist powers.[1] This competition reflected their bitter struggle

1. As used in this chapter, the term "Middle East" encompasses four sub-

for political supremacy in Asia, a conflict that centered, in part, on the Kremlin's proposal of 1969 to establish a continental collective security system. Beijing resolutely opposed this initiative on the ground that it represented a regional "power grab," an effort by Moscow to spread its influence at the expense of the other Asian states, especially China.[2] Since Afghanistan and Iran were among the countries approached by the USSR to join the proposed collective security pact, the Sino-Soviet dispute spilled over into the Middle East as well. Moreover, Moscow and Beijing have allowed their conflict to extend into some of the regional issues of the Middle East, among them the Arab-Israeli dispute and the problems of security in the Persian Gulf and the Red Sea areas. Nevertheless, it is imperative to remember that in the context of the Sino-Soviet conflict the Middle East, in contrast to East, Southeast, and South Asia, has been but an ancillary area: the central issue in the international politics of the region has been the rivalry between the Soviet Union and the United States.

Foreign policy, like most human endeavors, involves a balancing of ends and means, a trading off of the "desired" and the "possible." To understand the foreign policy of a given state in a specific region one should first examine the likely interests that determine the goals of that nation and then the factors that condition and constrain efforts to achieve the "desired" and thus create the "possible."

For purposes of analysis, the interests of a nation-state may be categorized under a number of discrete headings, even though in actual content those interests may be sufficiently complex and interlarded as to make the categorical distinction solely analytical. One possible schema incorporates four such categories: military-strategic, political, economic, and ideological.

DEFINITIONS

Military-Strategic Interests. Military-strategic interests primarily involve countering perceived threats to one's national security (sometimes offensively, sometimes defensively) as well as creating and maintaining a favorable military balance for one's self and one's allies in relation to one's adversaries (this means acquiring bases, denying them to adversaries, and the like). The Soviet leaders apparently see themselves as having both an "intrinsic" and "relational" interest in the Middle East, a region that lies on the southern border of the USSR.[3] To put the matter bluntly, they want

---

regions: the Persian Gulf, the Fertile Crescent, North Africa, and the Red Sea.

2. For details, see the chapter in this volume by William J. Barnds (note 15).

3. *Intrinsic* refers to those direct interests that emanate from some aspect of the very nature of a given region (its geographic position, natural resources, and the like), while *relational* interests are those that stem from the importance of the region to other nations with which the government in question has a signifi-

the Americans out. Barring that, they at least want relative military equality with the United States. After twenty-five years of involvement, the Kremlin has also acquired a considerable "vested" interest in the area. The Chinese, on the other hand, have no comparable intrinsic or vested interests. Their interests in the region appear to be completely relational and are part of Beijing's overall determination to weaken the Soviet Union whenever and wherever possible. In the specific case of the Middle East, applying pressure on the USSR has the net effect of establishing a kind of "second front" that serves to relieve the pressure along China's long common border with the Soviet Union.

Political Interests. This category is divisible into two subcategories: international and domestic. The typical international political interests of a nation entail, among other things, establishing influence among other states in order to gain support in any peacetime confrontations with one's adversaries (manifested by diplomatic support of one's views and actions, favorable United Nations votes, etc.). Eliciting a willingness to act in concert on economic issues in order to gain noneconomic ends can be an important component of such policies (for example, support for an economic boycott designed to gain political ends). Moscow's behavior in the Middle East during the past twenty-five years presents in some ways a virtual merger of military-strategic and political objectives: it is difficult to know where one begins and the other ends. Thus the Soviets have typically tried to use whatever leverage their political and economic practices have been able to generate to acquire tangible military gains (such as bases and port facilities). These practices have often resulted in short-range successes and long-range disasters: the Kremlin has frequently overplayed its hand and discovered that it had less leverage than its leaders thought (witness the Soviets' ouster from Egypt in 1972 and Somalia in 1977). In any case, Moscow's major dual objectives appear to be to undermine American positions and to gain its own rightful place in the sun. Of lesser significance is the USSR's competition with the PRC. The Chinese have not in recent years had nearly so forward a posture as the Russians, partly because of the upheavals attendant to the Cultural Revolution of the late 1960s, when China essentially cut itself off from many nations it considered ideologically hostile or suspect. During the 1970s, however, Beijing has made a major effort to normalize relations with Middle Eastern states; its policy appears to be aimed primarily at undermining Soviet positions in ways that generate as little cost to itself as possible.

---

cant relationship (either amicable or antagonistic). Such interests are differentiated from the *vested* ones that have arisen historically as one of the first categories, but which have come to have a life of their own even though the original circumstances that generated them have changed or disappeared.

In the domestic sphere, the major political interest of any regime is in promoting policies that find support among key domestic constituencies: leaders must have some "successes" to show for their efforts in the international arena, and they must avoid major embarrassments. The extensiveness and range of Soviet activities in the Middle East have come to be a kind of vested interest also for domestic political purposes. The regime simply cannot afford too great a political defeat, given the massive influence-building effort expended during the last twenty-five years. To withdraw or even curtail its efforts in the region would be a tacit admission of failure. When the unexpected happens, attempts are made to score new political "victories": after the loss of Egypt, an effort was made to build up the Soviet position in Syria and Iraq; after Somalia, in Ethiopia. (International motivations obviously play a part in such maneuvers, but the domestic considerations should not be underrated.) For the Chinese, the current domestic political situation is a great deal more flexible and supportive of the kind of pragmatic approach they are now taking toward diverse political regimes than was the case during the Cultural Revolution. This is fortunate from Beijing's point of view, since the resources available to expend on adventurism in scattered parts of the world are severely limited. Indeed, those limitations appear to make China's current "low profile" and "correct" diplomatic-political activities about the only reasonable option open to it.

Economic Interests. Subsumable under the heading of economic interests, are among other things, such objectives as acquiring needed resources, securing adequate markets for one's products, gaining needed currency, and effecting a favorable balance of trade in order to undergird one's national economic stability and development. In this regard, the Soviet Union has a significant economic interest in the Middle East as a source of petroleum (for itself and especially its East European allies) and as a market—one that pays for goods and services in hard currency. This interest is likely to grow in the years ahead, considering the difficulties encountered in efforts to expand the USSR's own oil and natural gas production. In contrast, the Chinese appear to have little need for Middle Eastern resources, and the area has little potential as a market for China's limited exports. Although there has been a modest surge of interest in Beijing recently in the exportation of "contract laborers" as a way of securing hard currency, the Middle East simply appears to have no significant role in Chinese economic plans.

Ideological-Cultural Interests. The major ideological-cultural emphasis is on winning converts to one's system, partly out of a sincere belief in its superiority but more because of the pragmatic purposes implied in the earlier discussions (that is, gaining allies in the pursuit of the other three interests). That the Soviet Union assigns low priority to winning ideological converts is demonstrated by its almost cavalier attitude toward indigenous communist parties. Moscow's record in this regard has been one of *ceteris paribus* (other things being equal, the Soviets push support for indigenous parties; if that policy proves costly, they back off). Since the end of the Cultural Revolution, Beijing's admission to the United Nations, and the establishment in power of Vice-Chairman Deng Xiaoping, ideology has played almost no role in Chinese Middle Eastern policy other than on a lip-service basis. Indeed, one can observe that the closest the PRC has come to an "ideological" commitment in recent years was in the elevation of the dictum "the enemy of my enemy is my friend" to a tenent of the faith.

In sum, while the Kremlin apparently sees itself as having a full range of interests in the Middle East, most of all it seeks full recognition as a superpower coequal in status with the United States. The Chinese have more modest aspirations, principally the thwarting of Soviet objectives. In order to assess their relative chances for success in these aims, we will survey their current positions in the various regional subsystems of the Middle East.

REGIONAL SUBSYSTEMS

While in the public mind the term "Middle East" conjures a vision of petroleum beneath burning sands or conflict between Arab and Jew, or both, the Middle East is actually a complex system of subregions, each with its own relational networks, major problems, and regional agenda. At least four major subdivisions are recognizable: the Red Sea states, North Africa, the Fertile Crescent, and the Persian Gulf area. Since regions are not isolated entities, analysis of Middle Eastern affairs must also touch on some of the South Asian states that border the Gulf region.

The Persian Gulf. Since December 1979, in Afghanistan, the world has witnessed a new initiative in Soviet policy that still reverberates not only in South Asia but throughout the Persian Gulf area. The direct use of Russian troops in a non-East European context represents a significant departure from previous Soviet postwar practice, and, as such, has sent nervous tremors throughout the West and parts of the less-developed world as well. Coming as it did hard on the heels of the recent upheavals in neighboring Iran, the Soviet occupation raised new questions about Moscow's intentions in the Middle East. Amid renewed cries of "hegemonism" from Beijing, many Western analysts even interpreted the move as the first step in some grand design for the conquest of the Persian Gulf. Their scenario suggested that the Kremlin was laying the groundwork for an invasion of Iran across its border with Afghanistan and also wished to gain access to the Indian Ocean by establishing a satellite state in Baluchistan. What this plot analysis ignores is that the Soviet Union already has its own lengthy common border with Iran and that the creation of a pro-Soviet Baluchistan is likely to lead to a major U.S. involvement in that situation. (It might also be noted that Chinese anxiety about Soviet policy toward Afghanistan, or, to be more precise, about Moscow's willingness to use force beyond its borders, may have some justification, but *not* on the basis of its ramifications for the Sino-Soviet dispute in the Middle East.)

The revolution in Iran and the continuing domestic turmoil that it has generated has put all of Tehran's international relations in a state of flux. While the regime seems intent on venting most of its spleen on the "satanic U.S. regime," it also has less than friendly relations with most of the other great powers. Many of the economic agreements with the Soviet Union and the PRC effected under the shah are now in abeyance, although both states continue to maintain diplomatic relations with Iran. Both Moscow and Beijing had taken some pains in recent years to establish cordial relations with the shah's regime. Thus the Kremlin had extended approximately $1.8 billion in aid to Iran during the past twenty-five years and the shah had even purchased some military equipment from the USSR.[4] The Chinese had confined their cordiality to the symbolic variety, topped by the visit to Tehran of Chairman Hua Guofeng in August 1978.

The Kremlin leaders are now confronting an interesting dilemma: even though Khomeini is supporting the Afghan rebels with arms and money, they apparently hate to see all their earlier efforts to cultivate friendly relations with Iran and the beneficial trade arrangements that resulted go down the drain. Thus, as recently as August 1980, the Russians made Tehran a formal offer of assistance, including military aid. When the revolutionary regime rejected the offer promptly and unceremoniously, spokesmen for the PRC applauded from the sidelines.[5] Much of the rest of the world has prudently adopted a wait-and-see attitude toward Iran until such time as the internal situation stabilizes. Given their more passive regional policy, this course is easier for the Chinese to follow than for the Soviets.

On the western side of the Gulf, the Soviets have fared little better in the past decade. The dominant regional power on the Arabian peninsula, Saudi Arabia, will have nothing to do with either communist power as a matter of religious commitment. (Riyadh is reinforced in this commitment by a strongly pro-Western tilt in its foreign policy.) As in most other interna-

4. Throughout this discussion the summary comments on economic aid and arms purchases are based on data found in U.S. Arms Control and Disarmament Agency (Washington, D.C.), *World Military Expenditures and Arms Trade, 1963–1973; 1965–1974; 1966–1975; 1967–1976;* and *1968–1977;* and in Central Intelligence Agency (Washington, D.C.), *Communist Aid to Less Developed Countries of the Free World, 1975; 1976; 1977;* and *Communist Aid Activities in Non-Communist Less Developed Countries, 1978.*

5. *Beijing Review*, no. 36, September 8, 1980, pp. 14–15.

tional issues, Bahrein, Qatar, and the United Arab Amirates have simply followed the Saudi lead. Thus none of these states have diplomatic relations or any substantial economic ties with either the Soviet Union or the PRC. As long as their current regimes remain in power, this state of affairs is likely to continue.

The foreign policy of Oman, which lies on the southeastern tip of the peninsula, is also heavily influenced by that of the Saudis. The only significant difference from the other smaller Gulf powers is that Oman does have diplomatic relations with the PRC. They were established in 1978 at the behest of the shah. (The latter's influence in Omani policy will be touched on below in the case analysis of the Sino-Soviet rivalry in the context of the Dhufar rebellion.)

Kuwait, of all the Gulf states, has the most balanced foreign policy. It has strong ties with the West, especially the British, but at the same time has diplomatic relations as well as some economic links with both the Soviet Union and the PRC. But neither of the communist powers has any influence in Kuwait.

The most striking theme to emerge from an analysis of the impact of recent international events on Kuwait and the other littoral states to the west and south of the Gulf is the recurrence of expressions of anxiety over the fruits of Khomeini's Islamic revival (the November 1979 seizure of the Great Mosque in Mecca by armed religious extremists was to many a confirmation of their worst fears about the broader impact of Iran's Islamic revolution) and the meaning of the Soviet invasion of Afghanistan. The result has been a growing awareness of the need to reinforce regional stability and to strengthen the area's autonomy in relation to the rest of the world. Given that the main Chinese objective in the region is the "relational" one of "countering Soviet hegemonism," the resulting state of affairs is probably much more to Beijing's liking than it is to Moscow's.

The Fertile Crescent. Turkey lies along the northern periphery of the Crescent, and until recently, as a member of NATO, has been thought of more as the southeastern outpost of the North Atlantic alliance than as a member of the Middle Eastern community of nations. But in the wake of domestic upheavals and the strain on Turkey's ties with the Western alliance that followed the Turkish invasion of Cyprus in 1974, the Kremlin has made some overtures to the government in Ankara. What will become of the growing economic ties between Turkey and the USSR now that a military junta has displaced the civilian regime of Prime Minister Süleyman Demirel remains to be seen, but the officers heading the ruling group are clearly pro-Western. These recent developments have not been viewed favorably in the Kremlin, and that cannot but delight Beijing, given its own relative lack of stature in Turkey.

The situation in Iraq is one of the most complex and least understood in all of the Middle East. The country has been historically important in Middle Eastern affairs, serving as it does as a link between the states of the Gulf and those of the Fertile Crescent. The historic role assigned Iraq by geography has been augmented in recent times by its economic importance and, of late, by Baghdad's political venturesomeness. Thus, after its ascent to power in 1968, the Iraqi Ba'th, as part of its rejection of everything reminiscent of the "yoke of Western colonialism," pursued the path of nominal nonalignment while establishing close economic and military ties with the Soviet Union and other Eastern bloc nations. (The result was more than $1 billion in economic aid between 1958 and 1976 and over $3.5 billion in arms transfers between 1964 and 1977.) These ties culminated, in 1972, in the signing of a treaty of friendship and cooperation with the USSR, an event that led many Western analysts to write off Iraq as essentially a Soviet satellite. But under their new strongman, Saddam Husayn, the Iraqis have begun to broaden their economic arrangements and, in 1979, contracted with the French for a significant arms purchase involving Mirage fighters as well as other military equipment. A part of that diversification program has been the establishment of some modest commercial arrangements with Beijing. While the Soviets have struggled to maintain a restrained attitude, Baghdad has from time to time seemed intent on "pulling the Bear's tail" and asserting its independence. Thus, Saddam Husayn's support of the anti-Soviet Eritrean rebels in Ethiopia, his intermittent suppression of Iraqi communists, and, most recently, his outspoken denunciation of the Soviet invasion of Afghanistan have all sorely tested the Kremlin's forbearance. Iraq's military action against Iran in September 1980 has done little to alleviate Moscow's misgivings. At the time of this writing, both the USSR and the PRC have officially adopted a neutral position on the war and have urged an early termination of hostilities. Privately, as noted, the Kremlin appears to have offered assistance to Iran.

Another leader noted for his independent thinking, Hafiz al-Asad of Syria, is supposedly numbered among those in the region on whom the Soviets can count for support. Unlike Saddam Husayn, Asad did, in fact, offer verbal sanction of the Russian occupation of Afghanistan. This ostensible backing may well have been the price of Syria's retention of its place as the single largest Soviet arms recipient in the Middle East. (The paucity of interaction with China is probably also a tacit part of the bargain.) Even so, the USSR has experienced ups and downs in its relations with Syria during recent years, and the current positive tone may simply reflect Asad's need for stability in one of his key relationships amid a climate of domestic and regional turmoil in which he has not been doing all that well.

Neither communist power appears to have made much of an effort to win influence with the regime of King Husayn of Jordan. Both have nominal diplomatic relations with Amman, and modest economic ties with the PRC and with some Eastern bloc nations have been initiated. But despite his refusal to support the Washington-orchestrated peace negotiations between Egypt and Israel, Husayn has remained pro-Western in both his outlook and policies.

For quite different reasons, neither Moscow nor Beijing has tried of late to involve itself directly in Lebanese affairs. Lebanon is currently so fragmented that to speak of "seeking influence," given that the idea implies a relationship with those who systematically exercise internal power and authority, is to ignore the reality of the chaos in that country. In short, Lebanon has traditionally been pro-Western but is now essentially a factional battleground, one from which the prudent international actor with no direct stake in its survival must simply stand aloof.

One of the most important elements in the political life of Lebanon is the Palestine Liberation Organization. In 1970 the PLO was ousted from Jordan by King Husayn. Since that time the Palestinians have used Lebanon as their main base of operations for raids on Israel. Their efforts to establish and maintain that operational base have inevitably involved them in Lebanese politics. By 1975 the central government in Beirut had essentially disintegrated, and a civil war had erupted between PLO-supported left-wing Muslim factions and right-wing Christian groups. In one of those ironies that make Middle Eastern politics simultaneously appalling and fascinating to outside observers, Syria intervened in the conflict on the side of the Christians. Asad was not prepared to tolerate a militant Lebanon that could have driven Damascus into an unwanted conflict with Israel. As a result of the Syrian intervention, the PLO suffered its most serious defeat since the "Black September" 1970 days in Jordan. Asad, of course, could not afford politically to crush the PLO completely, and, in the end, the conflict was resolved in a way that allowed the Palestinians some autonomy in a portion of southern Lebanon. Even here, however, it is assumed that Asad's watchful eye is on the situation.

Their relations with the Palestine Liberation Organization exemplify some of the relative advantages and disadvantages of the Soviet Union and the PRC in Middle Eastern affairs. The Chinese, who saw the PLO as a "national liberation movement," extended recognition to the group in the 1960s, long before most other outside powers, including the USSR, took the organization seriously. In the 1970s, as Beijing began to shore up its relations with the legitimate governments in the area, Chinese support of the PLO began to weaken. Concurrently, Soviet interest in the Palestinian cause began to rise. It was stimulated, above all, by the realization that the PLO was a potentially useful wedge to ensure that a peaceful resolution of the Arab-Israeli conflict would not be completed without direct Soviet participation. It was not until 1978, coincidental with the beginning of the Camp David process, that Moscow finally recognized the PLO as "the sole legitimate representative of the Palestinian people" (the Chinese had beaten them to the punch on this point far back in the 1960s), thus supplementing its earlier insistence that no comprehensive settlement in the Arab-Israeli conflict could be achieved without direct participation by the PLO in the negotiation process. In light of the known Israeli inflexibility on this point, such an insistence has effectively blocked a comprehensive peace settlement.

While there have been some temporal discrepancies in Soviet and Chinese policy in relation to the PLO, they are in essential agreement on their position regarding Israel. Although both communist powers claim adherence to the United Nations resolutions that recognize Israel's right to exist within its pre-1967 borders, Beijing never established and Moscow severed diplomatic relations in the wake of the 1967 war. In practice, Israel not only has the "right" to exist, but its existence is a *necessity* for the operation of the current policy of both powers in the region: Israel is a convenient "whipping boy" for both in their dealings with the Arabs.

In summary, the political issue that vivifies most of the politics of the Crescent is the Arab-Israeli conflict; thus whatever eventually happens in the region will depend on the peace process. Although the Kremlin has some opportunity for mischief making, the Americans are still the dominant power in this area.

North Africa. Iraq has been characterized above as belonging to two regions. Even more complex is the situation of Egypt, for it is the bridge from the Fertile Crescent to both North Africa and the Red Sea states. As such, Egypt, both historically and currently, is regarded by many analysts as the most pivotal of all the Middle Eastern nations.

Those interested in playing the game of Middle Eastern politics should read the story of Moscow-Cairo relations as a cautionary tale. The vagaries and vicissitudes of Soviet policy in Egypt have been widely chronicled in the West but deserve a brief recapitulation here. As a result of Egypt's defeats at the hands of the Israelis in 1948, 1956, and 1967, it has had a chronic need for large-scale military aid. Beginning in 1955, and for almost twenty years thereafter, the Kremlin acted as Cairo's major arms supplier. (Between 1964 and 1977 alone, the USSR and its East European allies provided almost $3.7 billion in arms to Egypt.) The result was the development of a "special relationship" between the two countries, which culminated in the late 1960s and early 1970s in the establishment of Soviet air and naval bases on Egyptian territory and the signing (in 1971) of a treaty of friendship and cooperation. But Cairo's disenchantment with Moscow's failure to supply Egypt with large quantities of offensive weapons in preparation for the next round of hostilities with Israel led Anwar al-Sadat to kick out his Russian advisers and close the air bases in 1972. Relations were maintained between the two states but were punctuated by mutual sniping and bickering. When the crunch came, in the October 1973 war, the Soviets supported the Arabs, including the Egyptians. Shortly after the cease-fire, however, relations began to cool again as a result of Moscow's refusal to rebuild the Egyptian arsenal on a scale and at a pace satisfactory to Cairo. Finally, in 1976, Sadat delivered the *coup de grâce* by closing the naval facilities at Alexandria and abrogating the treaty of friendship and cooperation. From that time on, Sadat looked to the conservative Arabs, chiefly the Saudis, and ultimately to the West for needed aid and arms. In November 1977 he made his historic trip to Jerusalem, thus opening up the negotiation process that continues to this day.

The Chinese were essentially out of the picture as long as the "special relationship" with Moscow remained intact. Sino-Egyptian relations improved significantly in 1976 with the final expulsion of the Russians from Egypt. Although the absolute monetary value of the aid that has subsequently been forthcoming from the PRC has been modest, it has been important to the Egyptians, because Beijing has been able to supply some replacement aircraft engines for MIG fighters as well as other spare parts needed to keep the Soviet-built equipment operational. The Chinese have also been openly supportive of Sadat's role in the peace negotiations. In short, the chief beneficiaries of the precipitious decline of the Soviet position in Egypt after 1972 have been primarily the Western powers and secondarily China; however, given the volatility of the situation, one would hesitate to make any long-term predictions on the stability of the existing arrangement.

The potential explosiveness of Middle Eastern politics is nowhere more evident than in the case of Egypt's neighbor, Libya. Newly oil rich and vociferously anti-Western, Libya, under Colonel Muammar al-Qaddafi, is currently contemplating a union with Syria. Given the record of such merger attempts (between Egypt and Syria, Egypt and Libya, Libya and Tunisia, and Syria and Iraq), many observers regard the prospects with some irreverence. In any case, such a union, if implemented, would only serve to cement already strong ties with the USSR. For example, in 1978 Libya was second only to Ethiopia in terms of a Soviet technical presence and was the fourth largest Soviet arms recipient in the region. One cannot but wonder whether Moscow regards its relations with Tripoli as an unmixed blessing. The great virtue of its current situation is Libya's ability to pay for what it orders, while the great liability is Qaddafi's unpredictability. As has become their pattern, the Chinese, in 1978, established diplomatic relations and modest economic and technical ties with Libya.

The Kremlin, in a bow to reality, has not made a particularly concerted effort to win over the strongly pro-Western regime in Tunisia. The Soviets have offered only modest economic and technical aid and no arms to Tunis since their post-1955 entry into the region. The Chinese, on the other hand, seem bent on cementing their Third World credentials in states like Tunisia;

thus they have extended, by their standards, considerable aid ($57 million in 1977 alone) and have contracted recently for a $10 million arms transfer.

The USSR has made much more of an effort in Algeria, especially in the aftermath of the successful revolt against French colonial rule. But although the Algerians have received considerable economic aid and arms shipments, especially before the oil boom of recent years, Algiers has maintained extensive ties with the French and, like Iraq, has begun to show a distinct preference for Western, rather than Soviet, technology.

Despite the 1978 signing of one of the single largest economic deals ever contracted by the Soviet Union with a Third World nation (a $2 billion phosphate industry construction loan to be repaid by barter with the resulting product), Morocco must still be counted as a pro-Western nation. In other words, the arrangement appears to be a strict economic *quid pro quo* one, in which the Moroccans will receive development aid and the Russians will get needed phosphates. In both Algeria and Morocco, one finds evidence of only a token Chinese presence.

Thus in North Africa, once again the pattern is that of a modest level of commitment by Beijing and a considerable effort by Moscow. How much they have gained as a result is an arguable matter. But since the eviction of the Soviets from Egypt, Libya has become the cornerstone of Moscow's strength in the area, and any policy based on interdependence with so mercurial a character as Colonel Qaddafi rests on shaky ground, indeed.

The Red Sea. In the late 1960s and early 1970s, the Kremlin appears to have made a decision to pursue what some have described as a "Red Sea strategy"—a component of its more general movement into the Arabian Sea and the Indian Ocean. This arena had been dominated by the British before their decision in 1968 to withdraw from the area "east of Suez." In response to the power vacuum which that withdrawal would presumably produce, both American and Soviet policy makers adopted a much more active position regarding the region. This superpower competition has, of course, spilled over into the states surrounding the strategic waterway known as the Red Sea. Thus although the Sino-Soviet dispute appears to have had no direct role in the Kremlin's decision to establish its presence in this region, Beijing's anxiety about superpower politics in the Indian Ocean, and especially the outflanking maneuver which a Soviet presence there represents to the PRC, guaranteed Chinese interest in events in that part of the world.

While some Soviet activity in the Sudan predates the past decade, the 1970s have brought numerous disappointments to the Kremlin. There have been two attempted coups in which local communists were implicated and for which President Jaafar al-Numayri has held the Russians at least partly responsible. After the dust of the abortive coup in 1971 had settled, Moscow reestablished diplomatic ties and once again gradually improved its relations with Khartoum. But in 1976, after putting down the Libyan-supported coup, Numayri kicked the Soviets out again. Although diplomatic relations and some economic links have been restored, the current Sudanese regime is basically pro-Western; moreover, in the most significant local regional dispute it has, until recently, supported the Somalis against the Soviet-backed Ethiopians. As Soviet prestige in Sudan diminished, the Chinese emerged as an important communist aid donor.

Ethiopia currently represents the major Soviet stronghold among the African Red Sea states. As such, it is a linchpin—with Aden—of Moscow's Red Sea strategy. Beginning in 1977 the Kremlin launched an extensive military aid program to the regime of Colonel Mengistu Haile Mariam, although economic aid has proceeded so slowly that the Ethiopians are still drawing on credits originally extended to Emperor Haile Selassie in 1959. The Chinese maintain only a token presence in the country. Thus although the Soviets seem firmly entrenched militarily (according to Western analysts, as many as twenty thousand Cuban troops and numerous Soviet advisers are stationed in the country), the internal situation is rife with economic disarray and sectional strife, most notably with the secessionist guerrilla movements in the provinces of Eritrea, Tigre, and Ogaden.

The Soviet position of strength in Ethiopia has by now probably begun to seem a considerable vested interest to the Kremlin, for it has been established at substantial cost, namely the disintegration of Moscow's earlier position in Somalia. Indeed, the recounting of Soviet relations with these two countries is yet another exemplar of the limits of nonmilitary power in the game of nations. When President Siyad Barre came to power in 1969 through a military coup and announced his devotion to "scientific socialism," many Western observers assumed that yet another Soviet puppet had been implanted. Indeed, in the early years of Barre's regime the Kremlin seemed to need only to be there to pick up the chips: Somalia followed Moscow's line in international affairs; the Russians were granted several military bases, including a large naval and air facility at Berbera; and the two states signed a treaty of friendship and cooperation in 1974. But once again the Soviets overplayed their hand. After the overthrow of Emperor Haile Selassie, they began to court the Ethiopians with whom the Somalis had long been bitterly engaged over the rightful status of the Ogaden Province. Eventually Barre had had enough. In 1977 he closed the Soviet bases, kicked out the Russian advisers, and abrogated the friendship treaty. Numerous nations, both Western and Arab, as well as the PRC, have stepped in to fill the economic gap left by the departing Russians, while the United States has recently replaced the USSR as a military supplier to the regime. The Somalis did reestablish diplomatic relations with the Soviet Union in 1979, but, in late December, following the Soviet occupation of Afghanistan, they formally offered the United States the Berbera naval and air facilities earlier built and occupied by the Soviets.

The ultimate fate of the small but strategically important nation of Djibouti, which gained its independence from France in 1977, is far from certain. (Djibouti lies on the western side of the Bab al-Mandab, the narrow passage connecting the Red Sea and the Gulf of Aden.) The viability of a small territory with only about a quarter of a million citizens split by two tribal factions is highly questionable. Djibouti walks a thin neutral line of evenhanded, correct relations with both Somalia and Ethiopia, and depends for financial backing on the wealthy Arab states and for military support on France. Earlier fears that it would simply be gobbled up by Somalia, since much of its population has ethnic origins similar to those of the Somalis, have abated for the time being, principally because of the presence of five thousand French troops in the country. As befits a nation whose existence is so precarious, Djibouti has formal diplomatic relations with most of the great powers, including China and the Soviet Union.

On the opposite shores of the Red Sea are a vast reach of Saudi territory and, at the southern end, the Yemen Arab Republic. For many years, the YAR has been a prototype of the poor, struggling Arab nation dependent on its oil-rich neighbors for economic and military support. In the case of San'a, its main benefactor throughout the 1970s has been neighboring Saudi Arabia, which, deeply suspicious of the avowedly Marxist regime to the south (People's Democratic Republic of Yemen), has felt it important to support San'a in its intermittent quarrels with the PDRY. The lack of indigenous material resources has, however, apparently bred in the North Yemenis considerable diplomatic resourcefulness. One of the recent manifestations of this trait was San'a's announcement of a significant arms deal with the Soviet Union. (Although this development undoubtedly annoyed the Saudis, it was but another of the twists and turns of Yemeni policy designed to preserve the nation's fragile independence.) The Chinese have made a modest contribution to economic development in the YAR, but simply cannot compete as an arms supplier with either the West or the USSR.

As will become clear in the case study below, the People's Democratic Republic of Yemen is a critical component of Soviet policy in the Middle East, one in which the Kremlin has invested heavily. In the early days of the Marxist regime, both Moscow and Beijing were supportive. But in recent years the Chinese have essentially bowed out of the picture, and the PDRY has become one of the Soviet Union's most reliable area clients. Thus in 1979 the PDRY was granted observer status in Comecon (Iraq is the only other Arab state accorded this privilege) and later in the year signed a treaty of friendship and cooperation with the USSR. But recent internal shifts may signal some loosening of ties with the Kremlin. Some restiveness in regard to their patron was perhaps predictable in light of the timing of the aforementioned arms deal with the YAR. The sporadic hostilities along the border between the two Yemens flared, in February 1979, into serious fighting, which included an invasion into the North by South Yemeni forces. In March, representatives of the Arab League managed to negotiate a peace agreement that provided for the withdrawal of the PDRY troops. One can surmise, however, that the South Yemenis were less than thrilled with the Kremlin's decision to supply arms to San'a so soon after the two states had been engaged in open combat.

Thus for all its material investment and diplomatic maneuvering among the states of the Red Sea area, Moscow's record for the decade is decidedly unimpressive. Only in Ethiopia and the PDRY are the Soviets firmly entrenched, and both of the states have little to offer save fortuitous geographic location. As events in Egypt and Somalia should illustrate, what appears to be a firm position can, in short order, simply disappear.

Space limitations have necessitated a relatively superficial review of Soviet and Chinese activities in the Middle East during the 1970s. But an intensive case analysis of their involvement in a little-known and now closed chapter in the regional politics of the Persian Gulf is very instructive of some of the dilemmas they have faced and continue to confront in a number of other instances in the Middle East.

CASE ANALYSIS: THE DHUFAR REBELLION

The Sultanate of Oman is located in the southeastern part of the Arabian peninsula. Over the past twenty-five years there have been a number of attempts to bring down the conservative regimes of Sultan Sa'id ibn Taymur and, subsequently, his Sandhurst-educated son Qabus, who ascended the throne in 1970.

One such challenge was mounted in the Jabal Akhdar region in June 1970 by the newly formed National Democratic Front for the Liberation of Oman and the Arab Gulf (NDFLOAG). Founded by members of the educated urban intelligentsia, the organization drew its inspiration from the Syrian branch of the Ba'th party and soon established cells among immigrant Arab workers throughout eastern Arabia. In time, NDFLOAG switched its allegiance to the Iraqi Ba'th, more willing and able to extend material assistance than its Syrian counterpart. Because of the threat that the subversive activities of NDFLOAG constituted to the security of Oman and of the other oil-rich Gulf principalities, the organization was singled out for special attention by the British-led Omani security forces. As a result, NDFLOAG suffered serious reverses, paving the way for its December 1971 merger with the Popular Front for the Liberation of the Occupied Arab Gulf (PFLOAG). The new organization was named the Popular

Front for the Liberation of Oman and the Arab Gulf (still PFLOAG). At the time of the union, the two Fronts had little in common except their determination to overthrow the regime of Sultan Qabus. Unlike the urban-oriented and Ba'th-inspired NDFLOAG, the original PFLOAG was, by that time, a "Marxist-led guerrilla movement."[6]

The other major recent threat to the authority of the central government was mounted in the Sultanate's southwestern province of Dhufar by an organization called the Dhufar Liberation Front (DLF). It was founded in 1964 by a group of pragmatic middle-class nationalists who were exasperated with Sultan Sa'id's neglect of the province's many problems. In 1965 the rebellion spread to the countryside, for the mountain tribesmen—the "Jabalis"—resented the sultan's refusal to offer them employment in the newly established oil fields. In a few years' time, however, the original leadership of the Front was replaced by a group of hard-core Marxists whose ideology had been shaped by that of some of the radical Palestinian organizations operating among the workers of the Gulf's oil fields and of the Marxist activists of the National Front of South Yemen, whose Hadramout region is adjacent to Dhufar. It should be noted that Aden's support was crucial to the success of the Dhufari rebels. Not only did its territory serve as a site for DLF supply bases and sanctuaries, but after its independence in late 1967, the Democratic Republic of South Yemen (later renamed the People's Democratic Republic of Yemen, or PDRY) also channeled Chinese supplies to the Dhufari guerrillas.[7]

The switch from the moderate to radical leadership was formalized at the DLF's congress, held in the village of Hamrin in September 1968, when the organization altered its name to the Popular Front for the Liberation of the Occupied Arab Gulf (PFLOAG).[8] This change reflected both the arrival of the Marxist leaders and the adoption of a revolutionary strategy in Oman, as well as elsewhere in the Gulf. As noted by *International Affairs* (Moscow), the goals of PFLOAG were "to overthrow the existing regimes before the withdrawal of British troops from the Persian Gulf region in 1971 and to establish its power from the frontier of South Yemen to the Trucial Oman principalities [now the United Arab Amirates (UAA)], and later to Qatar and Bahrein, excluding only Kuwait."[9]

6. Mordechai Abir, *Oil, Power and Politics* (London: Frank Cass, 1974), p. 13. The above paragraph is based on Abir, pp. 12–13, and D. L. Price, "Oman: Insurgency and Development," *Conflict Studies*, no. 53 (January 1975), p. 5.

7. Abir, *Oil, Power and Politics*, p. 103. See also Yitzhak Shichor, *The Middle East in China's Foreign Policy, 1949–1977* (Cambridge and New York: Cambridge University Press, 1979), p. 153.

8. Price, "Oman," p. 5, and Shichor, *The Middle East*, p. 153.

9. "New Stage in the Liberation Struggle," *International Affairs*, no. 4, April 1969, p. 89.

The Hamrin decisions—a milestone in the history of the Dhufari rebellion—had important consequences for the future of the Front. On the one hand, they changed its international status to that of a "national liberation movement" and, in so doing, facilitated recognition and support from states and groups that theretofore had felt no obligation to extend themselves on the Front's behalf. On the other hand, however, the adoption of "scientific socialism" as the official ideology of the organization could not but seriously restrict its popular base. As noted by John Duke Anthony, the mountain tribesmen of Dhufar who formed the backbone of the rebellion had no conception of ideologies, including communism, and therefore could not identify with "scientific socialism."[10]

The espousal of Marxism-Leninism also cost the Front heavily in terms of Arab support. Whereas, before Hamrin, the organization had enjoyed the backing of such Arab states as Saudi Arabia and Egypt, after 1968 it received assistance only from the ideologically akin PDRY and, on occasion, from Iraq, Algeria, and Libya.[11] In the early 1970s, PFLOAG encountered other problems as well. The most serious was probably the ascent to the throne in Muscat of Sultan Qabus and his subsequent campaign to win the "hearts and minds" of the rebellious Dhufaris. Because the Front's rank-and-file members, unlike its leadership, were not committed to communist ideology, the all-out effort by the central government to improve the well-being of the province and its inhabitants began to produce the desired results. The provision of health care, educational facilities, and various kinds of development programs resulted in a dramatic improvement in the standard of living of ordinary Dhufaris. These efforts were supplemented by a general amnesty to all rebels and by a gradually increasing military pressure on loyal PFLOAG formations. In late 1973 the units of the Omani army, led by British officers, were joined by Iranian detachments, and the pacification program got under way in earnest.[12]

As the military pressure continued to build and as battlefield reverses were accompanied by mounting political problems, the Front's leadership held another congress in August 1974. Among other things, the name of the organization was altered once again, from PFLOAG to Popular Front for the Liberation of Oman (PFLO). The change indicated not only the Front's decision to confine its operations to the Sultanate but also, and equally significant, to drop its ideological commitment to Marxism-Leninism in

10. John Duke Anthony, "Insurrection and Intervention: The War in Dhofar," in Abbas Amirie, ed., *The Persian Gulf and Indian Ocean in International Politics* (Tehran: Institute for International Political and Economic Studies, 1975), p. 288.
11. For details, see abid., pp. 293–94.
12. For details, see ibid., pp. 288–90.

order to identify, once again, with Omani nationalism.[13] These efforts proved ineffectual, and by 1976-77 the Front ceased to be a military or political factor in Dhufar, the Sultanate of Oman, or elsewhere in the Gulf.

In retrospect, it appears that the initial successes scored by PFLOAG as well as NDFLOAG before their merger in 1971 demonstrated to Great Britain—the then dominant Western power in the Gulf—both the extent of popular dissatisfaction in Oman and the inability of Sultan Sa'id to cope with the rapidly deteriorating situation. The result was his replacement by Sultan Qabus and the mounting of a major effort to modernize the country and defeat the insurgents. In addition to concern over the fate of Oman, the Western powers felt that the fall of the monarchy there could set off a reaction in the other, highly vulnerable Gulf principalities whose conservative governments controlled access to some of the region's major oil reserves—oil held vital to the economic survival of the Western world.

With this background, it is possible to examine the attitudes of Beijing and Moscow to the rebellion in Dhufar. During the Cultural Revolution (1966-69), the PRC's foreign policy was marked by a distinct lack of interest in cooperation with the governments of the developing nations and a corresponding rise in the level of support of the Third World revolutionary movements. For this reason, despite reported "initial doubts" about the DLF, Beijing emerged as its main non-Arab backer. In 1967 an elite group of Front members was brought to China for training, and after the British withdrawal from South Yemen, the PRC (as will be seen below) initiated a modest military supply program to the Dhufari rebels.[14]

Even after the end of the Cultural Revolution in 1969, when the PRC, in a drive for recognition as a world power, once again attempted to normalize relations with many Asian and African states, Beijing, for another two years, continued to exhibit some concern for the revolutionary movements. This was particularly true of PFLOAG. Thus the New China News Agency (NCNA) regularly reported on the Front's successes, and a number of PFLOAG delegations came to Beijing and were received by Chinese dignitaries, including Zhou Enlai.[15] Although moral backing was extended

---

13. Ibid., p. 291.
14. Stephen Page, *The USSR and Arabia* (London: Central Asian Research Centre, 1971), p. 115, and Abir, *Oil, Power and Politics*, p. 102. As noted by Abir, support of the revolutionaries also had the advantage of being cheaper than the technical or military aid programs to selected Third World countries which preceded the Cultural Revolution. In addition to the DLF, Beijing, at that time, also supported the Eritrean Liberation Front and, in cooperation with Somalia, the Fronts for the Liberation of Western Somalia (Ogaden) and of the Somali Coast (see Abir, p. 131).
15. On one such occasion, the PRC expressed its full support of the Front:

freely, the same was not true of material support. To be sure, some assistance was, in fact, given—in the form of training, instruction, and a limited supply of arms channeled through Aden—causing PFLOAG spokesmen to express their gratitude to the PRC.[16] Nevertheless, even at the height of their cooperation, the Front was never "overwhelmed" with Chinese largess, for restraint had been the cardinal feature of Beijing's relations with the revolutionary movements in the Third World.

This PRC attitude was one of the reasons prompting PFLOAG not to take a pro-Chinese stand in the Sino-Soviet dispute. The other contributing factor reflected the Front's pragmatism: it made no sense to antagonize the USSR, whose support the rebels were openly seeking. PFLOAG's position was stated in a letter from the Front's political office in Aden to the Arab nationalist newspaper *al-Hurriyah* (Beirut), published on September 22, 1969. It noted with gratitude the support extended to PFLOAG by the People's Republic but added, "the Soviet Union has [not] totally discarded us. We are still hopefully trying in this direction."[17] Doctrinal considerations reinforced the Front's decision to remain aloof from the Moscow-Beijing dispute, for PFLOAG's own ideology appears to have been fashioned after neither the Soviet nor the Chinese model. Rather it reflected the influence of the Cuban example and the thought of its chief ideologue, Ché Guevara.[18]

China's attitude toward PFLOAG and, for that matter, all the "liberation movements" in the developing areas changed dramatically in 1971 as a result of yet another reorientation of Beijing's foreign policy. Having terminated the Cultural Revolution with its attendant disruptions, the PRC leaders once again endeavored to reestablish normal working relations with the governments of the Third World. In the particular case of the Persian Gulf, it was decided that the most effective approach to halting Soviet advances into that region—one of the main Chinese foreign policy objectives in the Middle East—lay in cooperation with the established governments rather than revolutionary movements such as PFLOAG. Put differently, the earlier policy of fomenting political instability was found to be counterproductive,

---

"The excellent situation of the victoriously developing armed struggle of the Dhufar people is bound to promote and inspire the development of the national liberation struggle of the people of the entire Gulf region." NCNA, March 21, 1970, as quoted by Shichor, *The Middle East*, pp. 153–54.

16. Thus Hasan Ghasani, director of the Front's office in Aden, in June 1970 conveyed the organization's "heart-felt thanks to socialist countries, particularly the People's Republic of China, for their moral and material support and aid to our revolution." NCNA, June 10, 1970, as quoted ibid., p. 154.

17. As quoted by Page, *The USSR and Arabia*, p. 116.

18. *Al-Hawadith* (Beirut), February 20, 1970, as quoted by Shichor, *The Middle East*, p. 153.

because the conservative regimes of the Gulf appeared to offer a far better chance of stopping Soviet penetration than did the region's revolutionaries who were openly interested in securing Moscow's support for their aspirations.

This new Chinese policy manifested itself in the establishment of diplomatic relations with Kuwait and Iran (1971) and in the discontinuation, in 1972, of PRC backing of the Dhufar rebellion. Beijing ceased all "encouragement and coverage of PFLOAG operations," withdrew its instructors, and stopped the flow of supplies.[19] During his June 1973 visit to Iran, Foreign Minister Ji Pengfei stated that the PRC was no longer involved in guerrilla activities in the Gulf region and supported the shah's determination "to combat subversive activity" there.[20]

This rapprochement between the People's Republic of China and some of the area's conservative governments inevitably resulted in strained relations with such radical regimes as those of Iraq and especially the PDRY. As Aden and Baghdad moved closer to the Kremlin, and as the latter endeavored to exploit this opening to advance its own interests in the Gulf, the cooperation between the USSR and the PDRY and Iraq increased to the point that the Soviets became the dominant outside power in these two countries. Under these circumstances, it was only logical for Moscow to espouse PFLOAG's cause as well. As will be shown below, it did in fact do so, even though this meant the adoption and pursuit of what, in essence, was an internally contradictory policy in the Gulf. On the one hand, the Soviets, too, were attempting to normalize relations with the conservative states of the region, among them Kuwait and, above all, Iran. On the other hand, they established close cooperation with the radical regimes as well as PFLOAG, which, according to Moscow's own publications, was bent on overthrowing the very governments with which the Soviets were attempting to establish "normal" relations.

It may well be, as Yodfat and Abir have argued, that the Kremlin's support for the Dhufari rebels was conditioned by the "erroneous belief that what had happened in the PDRY would recur in the Gulf area, with PFLOAG following the pattern created by the N[ational] L[iberation] F[ront] in the PDRY."[21] It is much more likely, however, that the decisive factors prompting a change in Moscow's policy were its political rivalry with China and, more important, its military and political competition with the United States. In the former connection, the important element, as the Kremlin saw it, was not PFLOAG but the PDRY. Thus, presented with an opportunity to displace Beijing in Aden, the Soviets took it. In the latter

19. Ibid., pp. 173 and 182, respectively.
20. As quoted ibid., p. 182.
21. A. Yodfat and M. Abir, *In the Direction of the Persian Gulf: The Soviet Union and the Persian Gulf* (London: Cass, 1977), p. 75.

instance, strategically located South Yemen offered the USSR enormous advantages in its growing Indian Ocean competition with the United States. Since the Soviet press was expressing concern about the U.S. and British military presence in the Persian Gulf–Indian Ocean area, including the American decision to proceed with the development of a major naval and air base at the island of Diego Garcia,[22] a chance to acquire its own naval and air facilities in the northwestern part of the Indian Ocean must have seemed to Moscow an opportunity that could not be ignored. Since the PDRY was committed to backing PFLOAG, the USSR, which had been courting Aden's favor, could not have done less.

Be that as it may, the Kremlin's concern for the fate of PFLOAG, which became evident in the early 1970s, signified a marked shift in the Soviet position toward the Dhufar rebellion. As noted by Yodfat and Abir, "the USSR was at first critical of this movement because of its belief that the region was not yet ripe for 'scientific socialism' and because of the strong ties between PFLOAG and the PRC."[23] Even if the Soviets had had their doubts about the DLF, however, they could not but voice public approval of the establishment of PFLOAG. Thus *International Affairs* welcomed this new "national liberation front" dedicated to uniting "in its ranks all the [region's] revolutionary forces fighting against imperialism, feudalism and reaction." The adoption of Marxism-Leninism as the organization's official ideology, it was noted, reflected the leaders' awareness that communism was "the only instrument capable of solving existing contradictions and achieving genuine independence in the Persian Gulf principalities."[24]

Nevertheless, before 1971 the Kremlin refrained from extending to PFLOAG anything but verbal support. Its caution was occasioned by a desire not to antagonize such conservative regimes as that of the shah, by wariness about the Front's Chinese connection, and by some uneasiness about the nature of its "scientific socialism," which the Soviet media, significantly, had never subjected to public elaboration. As noted by Stephen Page, the "only other gesture of support was to allow the Soviet Afro-Asian Solidarity Committee to invite a PFLOAG delegation to the Soviet Union; they were not said to have had talks with any members of the government."[25]

In any event, in 1971 the USSR emerged as the chief patron of the PDRY and, through it, of PFLOAG as well. One of the early manifestations of

22. See, for example, Iu. Tomilin, "Indiiskii okean v agressivnykh planakh imperializma," *Mirovaia ekonomika i mezhdunarodnye otnosheniia*, no. 8, August 1971, pp. 19–29.

23. Yodfat and Abir, *In the Direction of the Persian Gulf*, p. 74.

24. "New Stage in the Liberation Struggle," p. 89. See also "A New Liberation Front," *New Times*, no. 1, January 1, 1969, p. 25.

25. Page, *The USSR and Arabia*, p. 116.

this change in the Soviet attitude was the visit to Moscow of a group of PFLOAG functionaries in September 1971. It was headed by Ahmad 'Abd al-Samad, member of the Executive Committee of the Front's General Leadership, and, unlike the 1969 mission, was received by Secretary of the CPSU Central Committee K. F. Katushev. This time the Soviet media publicized the event. According to *Pravda*, the delegation shared with its hosts information about the "struggle of the Dhufari patriots and of the other oppressed peoples of the Arabian peninsula against Great Britain's colonial rule" and thanked the "Soviet people for the support of the people's liberation struggle, headed by the Front." Upon his return to Aden, 'Abd al-Samad declared that the Soviet government had expressed its "readiness to double" its "varied assistance" to PFLOAG.[26]

By 1972, as Beijing lost all interest in PFLOAG, the Soviet press increased significantly its coverage of the Front's activities. Thus, commenting on the military operations in Dhufar, G. Drambyants wrote that they had been stepped up and, in a pointed jab at China, concluded that "the liberation struggle in this important province . . . enjoys the sympathy and support of progressives everywhere."[27]

In another indication of improving relations between Moscow and PFLOAG, a delegation of the Front's Central Executive Committee visited the USSR in September 1973. Hosted by the Soviet Afro-Asian Solidarity Committee, the visit, according to *Pravda*, provided an opportunity for discussions on "further development of bilateral cooperation." The PFLOAG delegation thanked the "Soviet people for consistent support of the Arab peoples in their just war for the liquidation of the consequences of the Israeli aggression [and] for aid to the anti-imperialist struggle of the peoples of the Arabian peninsula and the Persian Gulf region." For their part, the Russians expressed the "invariable solidarity of the Soviet people with the just struggle of PFLOAG for liberty, national independence, and social progress."[28] One of the manifestations of such "solidarity" was a January 1974 statement by the Soviet Afro-Asian Solidarity Committee condemning the "efforts of imperialism and reaction to strike a blow at the liberation movement in Dhufar" and expressing "firm conviction that the patriotic forces of the southern Arabian peninsula will be able to . . . repel the forces of imperialism and reaction."[29]

In addition to moral backing, the USSR also extended to PFLOAG a

26. *Pravda*, September 14, 1971, and *Arab Report and Record*, 1971, p. 516, respectively.
27. G. Drambyants, "Persian Gulf States," *International Affairs*, no. 1, January 1972, p. 102. For a typical Soviet comment on the successes scored by the PFLOAG guerrillas, see A. Vasil'ev, *Pravda*, April 26, 1973.
28. *Pravda*, September 19, 1973.
29. *Pravda*, January 17, 1974.

measure of material support. Modest in volume, it consisted of channeling through the PDRY limited quantities of arms and ammunition and, after 1973, of providing military training administered by Cuban advisers stationed in South Yemen. According to David Lynn Price, training camps for the PFLOAG guerrillas had been established at Huaf, Mukallah, and al-Ghaydah, on the Gulf of Aden. Furthermore, Cuban pilots flew MIG aircraft along the Oman-PDRY border, and Cuban personnel manned artillery positions on the South Yemeni side of the frontier.[30] Concurrently, Moscow used its support of PFLOAG to attack Beijing for what was described as the latter's duplicity in dealing with the Arabs. Thus, commenting on Foreign Minister Ji Pengfei's visit to Iran in June 1973, *Pravda* cited *al-Hawadith* (Beirut) to the effect that China's position was "anti-Arab" because it was "directed against the national-liberation movements in the Arab East, [and] particularly against PFLOAG." In contrast, according to *al-Jumhur al-Jadid* (also of Beirut), such movements enjoyed the full support of the USSR.[31]

As the fighting in Dhufar intensified in 1973–75, and as PFLOAG was forced on the defensive by the sultan's armed forces, which in late 1973 were joined by an Iranian contingent, the Soviet media continued their coverage by praising the "patriots" for "successes" in repelling the enemy's superior forces. The reports of the fighting contained occasional references to the presence of Iranian units but, in contrast to the British involvement, no condemnation of Tehran's intervention. The closest the Soviet press came to protesting the Iranian military presence in Oman was to reproduce PFLOAG's own call on "all progressive forces" to fight the Iranian "invaders."[32]

The reasons for Moscow's relative reticence were not too difficult to discern. An examination of Soviet commentaries appearing in middle and late 1974 leaves the analyst with a distinct impression that the Kremlin was hard pressed to reconcile its growing interest in broadening relations with the conservative regimes of the Gulf, especially Iran, with its continuing support of revolutionary groups, such as PFLOAG. It was almost with a sigh of relief that the Soviet press reported on PFLOAG's congress held in the summer of 1974. Noting that the organization had decided to change its

30. David Lynn Price, "Moscow and the Persian Gulf," *Problems of Communism*, 28, no. 2 (March–April 1979): 9.

31. As quoted by *Pravda*, June 29, 1973. See also a statement by Fuad Nasser, first secretary of the Jordanian Communist Party, ibid., May 23, 1975. For a later comment, see L. Dadiani, "Peking's Middle East Policy," *International Affairs*, no. 5, May 1978, p. 52.

32. *Pravda*, February 11, 1974. In the ensuing months, in the Dhufari context, Soviet publications would refer only to "foreign mercenaries." See *Pravda*, December 17, 1974.

name to PFLO, *Pravda* stated that its main tasks were the "liberation of Oman from all forms of colonial oppression . . . , the establishment of a unified, democratic, [and] sovereign state [in Oman], and the implementation of broad socioeconomic reforms."[33]

As PFLO's position continued to deteriorate, the Soviet press made occasional brief references to its "successes." The only time Moscow displayed concern over the situation was in late 1975, when a major offensive by the Omani forces carried them to the vicinity of the PDRY border. Vasil'ev wrote that the "renewed interventionist activity in Dhufar" had "created a dangerous source of tension" and warned that in their struggle to prevent the "establishment in Arabia [of] colonialism of a new type . . . , the patriots of Arabia are not alone."[34] The last reference to the activities of PFLO was published in *Pravda*, April 6, 1976. Nothing else has been said on that subject (before or after) until a short reference to Sultan Qabus's efforts "to put down the national-liberation movement" in Oman appeared in January 1979 in connection with his appeal to President Sadat for Egyptian military assistance.[35]

In summing up, an examination of the respective policies of the People's Republic of China and of the Soviet Union in the general Persian Gulf area over the past fifteen years reveals certain tactical differences, influenced by their intensifying rivalry, but also a number of parallels, caused, in part, by the necessity of operating in the same geographic and political environment. From the mid-1960s, Beijing centered its attention on assisting the liberation movements rather than on maintaining normal diplomatic relations with the established state governments. In the case of the Persian Gulf and the northwestern Indian Ocean, this approach entailed support for such groups as DLF-PFLOAG, the NLF of South Yemen (before and after independence), and the Eritrean and Somali liberation fronts.

A change in China's policy occurred in the late 1960s and early 1970s, when the end of the Cultural Revolution signaled the abandonment of guerrilla movements and led to the normalization of relations with many Third World nations. In the Persian Gulf–Indian Ocean region, an added impetus to this new approach was provided by Great Britain's 1968 decision to withdraw from areas "east of Suez" and the subsequent activization of Soviet policy designed to establish a Soviet presence in a few strategically important locations, such as the PDRY and Iraq. Since the maritime link between the European and Far Eastern sections of the USSR —the "southern route"—has been of great strategic importance to Moscow,

33. *Pravda*, August 10, 1974. See also L. Medvedko, *Pravda*, June 11, 1975.
34. *Pravda*, October 23, 1975. See also A. Vasil'ev and V. Peresada, *Pravda*, November 4, 1975, and January 24, 1976.
35. *Pravda*, January 20, 1979.

the PRC, in the early 1970s, decided to do what it could to stop Soviet advances in the Gulf and elsewhere in the Indian Ocean. Beijing was quick to recognize that the best chance of blocking the USSR lay in cooperating with the mostly conservative, pro-Western governments of the region, because they constituted the front line of defense against Soviet expansionism. It should be noted in passing that the implementation of this new policy brought the PRC into harmony with U.S. interests. For this reason, it was not surprising that imperial Iran, which after the promulgation of the Nixon Doctrine emerged as the mainstay of Washington's quest for regional stability, was also one of China's earliest friends in the Persian Gulf. This harmony of U.S.-PRC interests was temporarily obscured by the Vietnam War but blossomed openly in the late 1970s after the termination of the American involvement in the Southeast Asian conflict.

In contrast to the People's Republic of China, the USSR has pursued a more ambivalent policy. Moscow's competition and rivalry with both Washington and Beijing dictated, in the late 1960s and early 1970s, rapprochement with those Persian Gulf–Indian Ocean states which, for whatever reason, were interested in cultivating the Soviet connection. These included Iraq and, in the western part of the Indian Ocean, the PDRY, Somalia, and, finally, Ethiopia. At the same time, the Kremlin, as the self-appointed leader of "world communism," could not entirely turn its back on a regional revolutionary organization such as PFLOAG, which had openly proclaimed its adherence to "scientific socialism." As shown above, however, the Soviets were never entirely at ease with this arrangement and assumed a degree of responsibility for the Dhufari rebels only as part of the price for befriending the strategically vital PDRY. (The extent of Moscow's interest in South Yemen was demonstrated in 1973 by the dispatch to Aden of Cuban military advisers, and they have been stationed there ever since.)

Since 1973, the policies of the USSR and China in the Gulf have been marked by a clear desire to normalize relations with the established governments of that region. But they have had different motives. Whereas Beijing has been primarily concerned with blocking Soviet advances, Moscow, besides establishing positions of strength and competing with the PRC, has been especially guided by the desire to weaken the political and economic power of the West. This Soviet attitude, which eventually led to the loss of whatever interest Moscow may have had in PFLOAG, did not escape the attention of its regional clients. Subsequently, the PDRY, as well as Iraq, diminished their support of PFLOAG/PFLO. Thus in the face of stepped-up military operations by the Omani and Iranian forces, the Front was forced on the defensive and, by 1977, was driven out of Dhufar.

As a result of the interplay of the various political, economic, and military factors, Moscow, like Beijing before it, by the mid-1970s had bowed out of openly subversive activities in the Persian Gulf. Instead, and in direct competition with the People's Republic of China, the Soviets have been trying to court the favor of the region's conservative regimes. In the political tug of war between the two communist rivals that has ensued and in which U.S. sympathies have been clearly on the side of Beijing, neither party has been able to secure a clear advantage over the other. Their relative lack of success rests primarily on the fact that the conservative rulers of the Gulf are among the world's leading anticommunists. At the same time, however, some of these rulers have not been averse to manipulating outsiders (even Marxist-Leninists) for their own advantage, and their attitude has provided both the USSR and the PRC with some room for political maneuvering. As for the so-called radicals, Iraq has long since developed an independent foreign policy, while maintaining political and economic contacts with Moscow and Beijing (the economic ties, for obvious reasons, are weighted heavily in the USSR's favor), and only the PDRY remains outwardly committed to the USSR. But even in Aden, with the removal from power of former strongman 'Abd al-Fattah Isma'il and his replacement with the more pragmatic 'Ali Nasir Muhammad in early 1980, the Kremlin's position may be shakier than is generally assumed.

CONCLUSION

In terms of the analytical framework suggested at the beginning of this chapter, the USSR may be said to have a wide array of perceived national interests in the Middle East. In military-strategic terms, the Soviets have an intrinsic and relational interest in being able to exercise some control over activities of states situated near their southern border. They would like to deny the United States access to an obvious staging area in the event of hostilities between the two nations. The Kremlin leaders are exceedingly sensitive about recognition of their status as one of the two preeminent world powers. Thus they feel it their *right* to match American involvement in all the key political issues of our age, and the problems of the Middle East rank high on Moscow's list of priorities. The region has also grown steadily in economic importance to the USSR. First, the Kremlin has been handsomely reimbursed, in hard currency, for weapons supplied to a number of Arab states. Second, the enormous OPEC petroleum price hikes since 1973 have made the Soviet Union's own oil exports its main hard currency earner. Third, the USSR has now entered a number of highly profitable barter arrangements with various area states (among them Turkey, prerevolutionary Iran, Iraq, Syria, and Morocco). As the self-designated guardian of "Marxism-Leninism," Moscow cannot afford to be shown up ideologically by its fellow socialists in Beijing, even though, in recent years, neither appears to have been willing to engage concretely in spreading communism in the Middle East. In sum, although the Middle East has loomed large in the thinking of the Kremlin leaders, this has not been primarily because of their dispute with the People's Republic of China. Rather, Moscow's "adversarial" efforts have been aimed mainly at the United States, its rival superpower. In this respect, the Soviet record is one of mixed results: the USSR has often found itself thwarted in its attempts to be treated as a primary actor on the Middle Eastern scene.

The Chinese, for their part, in the 1970s, have pursued mainly "relational" political interests in the Middle East. This is not to say that Beijing has been unaware of the strategic importance of the area or of the possible long-term negative impact on China's security that a Soviet entrenchment in that region would represent. But, for a number of reasons, among them political upheavals, major economic problems, and the lack of ability to project military power into a geographically noncontiguous area, the PRC has found it impossible to compete with the superpowers (of late this means, above all, the USSR) on other than the political plane. Put differently, compared with the Soviets, the Chinese leaders have pursued much more modest objectives in the Middle East and thus have been *relatively* more successful of late than their Kremlin counterparts. After their flirtation, in the late 1960s, with supporting a number of guerrilla organizations, the Chinese have come, since the end of the Cultural Revolution, to seek normal and correct relations with most of the area's governments. In the process, the PRC has rarely missed the opportunity to goad the Russians about what is invariably depicted as overbearing superpower intrusiveness in the affairs of smaller nations. At the same time, China never fails to portray itself as a fraternal Third World state struggling with its own massive problems of modernization.

In short, the Sino-Soviet dispute has manifested itself in the Middle East mainly on the political plane. The USSR is determined to gain official recognition as a major participant in the region's affairs and to pursue its interests in accordance with such a status. The People's Republic of China, in contrast, objects to any great-power intervention but, given a choice between Moscow and Washington, clearly prefers the United States. Beijing's position is that Soviet "hegemonism" has replaced Western imperialism as the number one enemy of the PRC. As a result of the activities of the USSR and China, there has been a great deal of Sino-Soviet interaction in the Middle East. Nevertheless, their conflict per se has had no major, direct impact on the international and regional politics of that area. This state of affairs, characteristic of the previous two decades, is not likely to change in the 1980s.

A final point needs to be made as one reviews this survey of the Soviet and Chinese interaction in the Middle East: with few current exceptions (specifically, Afghanistan, Syria, Ethiopia, the PDRY, and, militarily, Iraq and Libya), Western influence and activities are still much more pervasive than those of all the communist states. It is as if some of the anti-Western reaction endemic to the end of the colonial era has begun to play itself out. The result is that a mere claim to being the "enemy of imperialism" no longer ensures automatic friendship with most of the nations of the region. The motives of the Soviets and the Chinese will more and more be subject to separate scrutiny on their own account.

The winds of change are blowing in the Middle East, and, as recent events in Iran have demonstrated once again, the influence of outside powers can be notably ineffective in controlling local events. For their own, separate reasons, the United States, the USSR, and the PRC had all cultivated good relations with the shah. Yet the combined support of all three was insufficient to save him. Therefore, although the Soviet Union and the People's Republic of China, as well as the United States, may be expected to continue their competition in the Middle East in the 1980s, opportunities for stable, tangible successes are likely to remain rather limited.

The Regional Impact: Europe

The Impact of the Sino-Soviet Dispute on Eastern Europe

TROND GILBERG

Much has been written on the Sino-Soviet conflict and its impact on the major participants; some scholars have also addressed the influence of this ongoing controversy on third parties, notably the other communist systems in the world.[1] Much of this literature is highly perceptive and analyzes the problem in skillful fashion, but some of these contributions were made several years ago, and the time has come for an update of the analysis. Furthermore, recent events and developments concerning the international communist movement, the major participants in the conflict, and several of the third parties involved necessitate another look at this long-standing controversy.

MAJOR DIMENSIONS OF THE CONFLICT

As discussed by William Griffith and others,[2] there are many dimensions to the Sino-Soviet conflict; one of the most important is ideology. The Chinese Communist Party (CCP) has accused the Communist Party of the Soviet Union (CPSU) and the leadership of the Soviet state of serious deviations from correct Marxism-Leninism, and this deviation in theoretical matters manifests itself in policy as well to such an extent that the Soviet leadership no longer functions as a Marxist group but rather as the most developed representative of "state capitalism" and "bureaucratism." The Soviets, then, have become the main enemy of "progressive" forces everywhere and repre-

---

1. One of the classics in this field is still William E. Griffith, *Albania and the Sino-Soviet Rift* (Cambridge, Mass.: M.I.T. Press, 1963).

2. For example. Donald Zagoria, *The Sino-Soviet Conflict, 1956–1961* (Princeton: Princeton University Press, 1962).

sent the most dangerous form of imperialism, against which true Marxist-Leninists must guard with fierce determination. Furthermore, the CCP has issued a clear-cut challenge to the Soviet goal of leadership in the international communist movement, and has worked assiduously to wean entire communist parties or factions thereof away from the Soviet fold. This blanket attack on Soviet aspirations for leadership in the international movement has been pressed with a great deal of vigor in the Third and Fourth Worlds of developing countries,[3] but the offensive has also been carried to Eastern Europe, as will be discussed below.

The Chinese challenge is not limited to ideological matters. The Beijing leadership has made it clear that the Soviet model of socioeconomic and political development is inappropriate for other countries, especially less developed systems; furthermore, the debasement of ideological purity allegedly rampant in the USSR and the CPSU makes the Soviet model inappropriate for *any* country, including the socialist systems of Eastern Europe. The Chinese have argued that the Soviet way, "neocapitalist" as it is, represents a path leading to personal alienation and societal problems, including all the manifestations of social decay found in the capitalist West, whereas the Chinese approach paves the way for the liberation of all individuals and socioeconomic strata according to the principles of true Marxism-Leninism.[4]

One of the most highly publicized aspects of the Sino-Soviet conflict has been the ongoing dispute between the two systems in the field of *state* relations, notably over certain territories in present-day Siberia which have been claimed, directly or indirectly, by the Chinese with reference to certain "unequal and unfair" treaties imposed on the Chinese by the tsars and maintained by the "so-called communist" rulers in the Kremlin. This conflict led to the famous border clashes on the Ussuri River and subsequent tension along much of the extended frontiers of the two states. Both parties to the conflict have maintained large troop concentrations in these areas for years, in a high state of military readiness.

The territorial conflicts mentioned above represent only the most dramatic manifestations of the simmering hostility between the USSR and the People's Republic of China (PRC) acting as states. Other dimensions of this state conflict include constant disputes in the United Nations, competition in Africa, Asia, and elsewhere in economic and military aid, and vari-

3. See, for example, Bruce D. Larkin, *China and Africa, 1949–1970: The Foreign Policy of the People's Republic of China* (Berkeley: University of California Press, 1971).

4. Considerable has been written on this subject. See, for example, Al Imfeld, *China as a Model of Development* (Maryknoll, N.Y.: Orbis Books, 1976); Alexander Eckstein et al., eds., *Economic Trends in Communist China* (Chicago: Aldine, 1968); Alexander Eckstein, *China's Economic Revolution* (New York: Cambridge University Press, 1977) .

ous efforts designed to establish friendly relations with the West and block similar efforts by the other party. Since the death of Mao Zedong, these state conflicts between the USSR and the PRC have overshadowed the ideological conflicts between the CPSU and the CCP.[5]

One of the most important elements of the state conflict discussed above has been the competition for increased influence in East and Southeast Asia. In this troubled region the USSR has backed certain powers in international disputes (such as Vietnam and India) while the PRC has lined up on the other side (Kampuchea and Pakistan). In this competition the USSR, as a global power, has become involved in a region where the *regional* power PRC also has major interests; in the case of the Vietnamese invasion of Kampuchea, this state conflict also involved the Soviets and the Chinese as self-proclaimed leaders of the international communist movement, and this development in turn produced repercussions in areas geographically remote but ideologically *close* to the problems of Southeast Asia, notably Eastern Europe. The influence of state and ideological conflicts in the Vietnam-Kampuchea war exceeded the PRC's caution and led to the Chinese invasion of parts of Vietnam, with subsequent escalation of verbal hostilities between the two communist giants.[6]

RECENT DEVELOPMENTS IN THE CONFLICT

During the last five or six years, further developments have taken place affecting the two principal protagonists, the international communist movement, and international politics generally, to produce a situation even more complex than the one outlined above. Furthermore, the socialist states of Eastern Europe have developed in ways that have had a profound, if indirect, effect on the Sino-Soviet conflict and on Soviet foreign policy in general. And changing relations between the United States and the USSR, as well as the emergence of a more moderate and pragmatic leadership in the PRC, have produced a different constellation of forces in the world, with resultant ramifications for the main protagonists of the Sino-Soviet conflict and third parties to that controversy, notably Eastern Europe.

---

5. On territorial disputes, see Dennis L. Doolin, *Territorial Claims in the Sino-Soviet Conflict: Documents and Analysis* (Stanford: Hoover Institution, 1965). Chinese relations with various areas of the world have been discussed in Jay Taylor, *China and Southeast Asia: Peking's Relations with Revolutionary Movements* (New York: Praeger, 1974); Edwin W. Martin, *Southeast Asia and China: The End of Containment* (Boulder, Colo.: Westview Press, 1977); and Larkin, *China and Africa, 1949–1970.*

6. As usual, Czechoslovakia spearheaded the "loyalist" criticism of the Chinese and of the "autonomists" (especially Romania); see *Radio Free Europe Research*, Romania/3, February 23, 1979, for an analysis.

The CPSU leadership has been confronted with a fundamental dilemma resulting from its own relative successes in the field of socioeconomic modernization and the quest for global power status. After forty years of accelerated development of heavy industry, weapons procurement, and an educational offensive designed to produce a highly qualified citizenry equal to the task of running a modern society and a sophisticated economy, the Soviet leadership has reached part of its goal. The USSR is now recognized as a global power on a par with the United States, and in some fields of military power the Soviets appear to be ahead. At the same time, the educational efforts of the regime have produced a citizenry no longer content to obey and produce without question; the technical and managerial intelligentsia, indispensable to the functioning of the system itself, is beginning to demand payoffs, be they economic, political, or in terms of social prestige. Soviet society is therefore undergoing a process of pluralization, and this process is threatening to spill over into the political realm as well, thereby threatening the monopoly of power hitherto enjoyed and exercised by the party *apparat*. The USSR is therefore vulnerable to charges that the modernization process has led to *embourgeoisement*—a charge that the Chinese were making even fifteen years earlier. The problems of informal societal pluralization and increasingly meaningful Chinese charges of betrayal of Marxism-Leninism in this context have led to greater truculence toward Soviet foreign policy. On the one hand, the USSR now has the capability of competing with the United States as a global power, and this opportunity has been joined with great gusto in many areas of the world; on the other hand, the trend toward domestic *embourgeoisement* in segments of the Soviet population has forced the CPSU into an aggressive ideological stance, demanding domestic ideological orthodoxy and acceptance of the Soviet claim to "first among equals" status in the international communist movement.[7]

Thus both in state policy and in interparty relations the USSR and the CPSU have produced policies that run directly counter to the interests of the PRC and the CCP. The Sino-Soviet conflict has therefore been deepened and broadened at the same time.

Developments in the USSR have been rather dramatic in recent years, as discussed above, but the Chinese political landscape has been altered even

7. On the Soviet economy, see Alec Nove, *The Soviet Economic System* (London: George Allen and Unwin, 1977); on changes in Soviet society, see, for example, Mervyn Matthews, *Privilege in the Soviet Union: A Study of Elite Life-Styles under Communism* (London: George Allen and Unwin, 1978); on Soviet global capabilities, the best recent treatment is Vernon V. Aspaturian, "Soviet Global Power and the Correlation of Forces," *Problems of Communism*, 29, no. 3 (May–June 1980): 1–18.

more fundamentally in the same period. The PRC has experienced the death of Mao and the rise of a new pragmatic leadership within the CCP, with concomitant repercussions for Chinese foreign policy and the Sino-Soviet conflict. This leadership is determined to lead China away from the Maoist preoccupation with politics and ideology to focus instead on the need for socioeconomic modernization and education. But this very emphasis on pragmatic policies at home has made the PRC a more credible actor in foreign policy and international relations, and China's greater stature abroad has in turn resulted in increased rivalry with the USSR in state relations. At the same time, the CCP leadership is taking great pains to emphasize its orthodoxy in ideological terms and its strict adherence to Marxism-Leninism (if not vintage Maoism), thus increasing the ideological polemic with the CPSU and its allies. Into this equation has been added the U.S. policy of formal recognition of the PRC and expanded economic and technical cooperation with Beijing. The oft-repeated hint of U.S. use of the "China card" has produced new rounds of mutual recriminations and accusations between the two communist giants.[8]

During the last decade or so, the process of pluralization in the international communist movement has accelerated. This is not an entirely new phenomenon. As early as the mid-1950s the famed leader of Italian communism, Palmiro Togliatti, advanced the thesis of polycentrism, and the decade of the 1960s saw several manifestations of "national roads" to socialism and communism, in terms of both policy and economics. It was during the 1970s, however, that some of the West European communist parties—notably the Italian (PCI), Spanish (PCE), and for a time the French (PCF)—openly challenged any notion of a leading center in the movement and also openly criticized many aspects of Soviet state policy as well as the CPSU's relations with other parties. This trend, which is well and thoroughly documented elsewhere,[9] will not be discussed here; suffice it to say that this challenge to the USSR and the CPSU "from the right," in conjunction with the Chinese challenge "from the left," further unsettled the Kremlin both in its functions of state leadership and as the center of ideological orthodoxy. While the Chinese had debunked the idea of *one* center, and postulated an alternative one, the Eurocommunists rejected the idea of *any* center, and instead advocated the need for *national* communism. These contending claims and analyses provided an extremely fluid ideologi-

8. For an analysis of recent trends in the relationship between Moscow and Beijing and prospects for the future, see Harry Gelman, "Outlook for Sino-Soviet Relations," *Problems of Communism*, 28, no. 5–6 (September–December 1979): 50–66.

9. For example, Vernon V. Aspaturian et al., eds., *Eurocommunism Between East and West* (Bloomington: Indiana University Press, 1980).

cal situation in which the USSR and CPSU were forced to take additional measures to ensure continued political and ideological control over their most prized allies, the socialist states and communist parties of Eastern Europe.

THE IMPACT OF THE SINO-SOVIET CONFLICT IN EASTERN EUROPE: 1959–60 TO 1968

The outbreak of open polemics between the Soviet state and the CPSU, on the one hand, and the PRC and the CCP, on the other, produced almost immediate reactions in Eastern Europe. The effects varied from country to country, and in each country over time, but no state or communist party in the region escaped some measure of this impact. In some cases, the effect was "merely" ideological; in others, state policies were fundamentally affected as well. In only a few areas did *all* these elements combine to produce party and state policies fundamentally different from the established pattern in Eastern Europe.

Although the effects of the Sino-Soviet dispute were substantial in Eastern Europe, they did not materially alter the balance of power in the region. Only Yugoslavia and Albania remained outside predominant Soviet influence at the end of the 1960s. Of the two, Yugoslavia had been forced out of the Soviet camp by Stalin in 1948. Albania, whose membership in the bloc had been an uneasy balancing act between Yugoslav control and Soviet domination, joined the Chinese ideological sphere and stayed there until the mid-1970s, when Tirana also broke away from the tutelage of Beijing and established itself in splendid isolation as the sole bastion of Marxist orthodoxy. For the rest of the states and communist parties of the region, the reality of Soviet predominance at the state and party levels remained an inescapable fact, and any political or socioeconomic "autonomy" that might result from the Sino-Soviet conflict must be seen against this backdrop of continued hegemony for the Kremlin in the region. But even within these carefully monitored parameters there was plenty of room for individual country differentiation. The effects of the Sino-Soviet conflict can best be examined in the fields of ideology, the postulation of a development model, state conflicts, and the relation between the Chinese challenge and the increasing fragmentation of international communism in general.

The open ideological dispute between Beijing and Moscow came hard on the heels of serious setbacks for the Soviet claim to ideological supremacy that had prevailed during the 1950s. There was, first of all, the shock of Stalin's death in 1953, which removed the linchpin of ideological orthodoxy from the communist movement. This traumatic development was followed in quick succession by the East Berlin uprising of the summer of 1953, the "events" in Poland and Hungary in the fall of 1956, and the Khrushchev mission to Belgrade in 1955 and the first secretary's speech at the Twentieth Congress of the CPSU in early 1956—a speech that tore the veil of Stalin's infallibility and dramatically exposed the internal contradictions and power struggles in the Soviet party. Soviet efforts to reestablish the supremacy of Moscow in ideological matters were never quite successful after the traumatic events of 1956, and manifestations of "domesticism" and even "nationalism" began to appear in some countries of Eastern Europe.[10]

It was in this clouded atmosphere that the Sino-Soviet dispute broke, immediately establishing an area of ideological dispute that allowed the various states and parties of the region to begin the process of formulating responses to the new challenges in the ideological field. For one country, Albania, the response to the Sino-Soviet conflict soon became enthusiastic endorsement of the Chinese side. After lengthy and acrimonious debates with Moscow, Tirana wholeheartedly adopted the position of the CCP in ideological matters and even outpaced its mentor in the ferocity of its anti-Sovietism. As shown by William Griffith, Peter Prifti, and others, this dispute was not merely over ideology, but revolved around the larger question of national autonomy in the international communist movement. In Tirana's view, the dispute with Moscow served to enhance the position of Enver Hoxha personally, and this improved position furthermore ensured that no pro-Yugoslav faction could interfere with the Albanian party's emerging quest for autonomy and sovereignty.[11]

Other parties in Eastern Europe seized on the ferocious war of words either to enhance their autonomy in relation to the CPSU or to demonstrate their loyalty to the Kremlin. Yugoslavia, which had been unceremoniously ousted from the Cominform in 1948, used the dispute to emphasize the need for national autonomy and sovereignty, and for ideological independence within the general confines of Marxism-Leninism. Throughout the lengthy Yugoslav commentaries on the dispute there emerged also an occasional hint that the "Yugoslav way" was a possible alternative to the ideological versions of Marxism-Leninism that had been established in Moscow and Beijing. But at the same time Belgrade exhibited great caution, lest its position be interpreted as simply "counterimperialism" in the ideological realm.[12]

10. See Zbigniew K. Brzezinski, *The Soviet Bloc* (Cambridge, Mass.: Harvard University Press, 1960), esp. chap. 12.

11. For a good overview of Albanian politics, see Nicholas C. Pano, "The Albanian Cultural Revolution," *Problems of Communism*, 23, No. 4 (July–August 1974): 44–57; see also Griffith, *Albania and the Sino-Soviet Rift*, and Peter R. Prifti, *Socialist Albania since 1944* (Cambridge, Mass.: M.I.T. Press, 1978).

12. See, for example, Trond Gilberg, "Yugoslavia, Albania, and Eastern Europe," in Charles Gati, ed., *The International Politics of Eastern Europe* (New York: Praeger, 1976), chap. 6.

There emerged also a third "autonomist" party in Eastern Europe as a result of the Sino-Soviet conflict. Scholars differ on the sources of the Romanian quest for autonomy, and also on the starting point of it, but there is general agreement that the Sino-Soviet dispute helped to trigger more open assertions of the "Romanian way" in ideological matters. The most forceful statement of this attitude was confirmed in the so-called Romanian declaration of independence in early 1964, in which Gheorghe Gheorghiu-Dej claimed the right to formulate the ideological program of the Romanian Communist Party (RCP) in the context of the national environment within the general parameters of Marxism-Leninism. After the death of Gheorghiu-Dej in 1965, his successor, Nicolae Ceausescu, made ideological autonomy an integral part of his political program.[13]

In all three cases of "autonomism," the Sino-Soviet dispute over ideology afforded the local party leaders an opportunity to enhance their legitimacy in the eyes of both other societal elites and the general population. For the latter, ideology mattered little, but some measure of independence from Soviet control mattered a great deal, and any increment in such "independence" became a source of mass support for regimes that could claim little of that precious commodity on the basis of economic performance and political acceptance in their own right.

While Albania, Yugoslavia, and Romania used the Sino-Soviet conflict to enhance their foreign policy autonomy and the legitimacy of their own leaderships, the other socialist states and the communist parties of the region opted for continued close relations with the Kremlin and acceptance of the CPSU stand in the dispute. During much of this early period in the conflict, the German Democratic Republic, Poland, Czechoslovakia, Hungary, and Bulgaria carefully lined up with Moscow and indeed frequently provided the most searing criticism of Beijing's alleged "deviation" from true Marxism-Leninism. Once again, motivations may have varied, as did the opportunities for foreign policy maneuvering. Bulgaria leaned close to the CPSU position out of political loyalty to Moscow and because of the personal relations between Todor Zhivkov and Soviet leaders. János Kádár in Hungary needed continual demonstrations of loyalty to the Soviet leadership in ideological matters in order to safeguard the ambitious (and unconventional) economic reform that became known as the New Economic Mechanism (NEM). The East German leadership, still perceived as a temporary phenomenon in an unnatural state by elements of the GDR's population as well as most of the world community, clearly needed strong Soviet support for the maintenance of its own power as well as the crucial *Abgrenzung* against the strong influences from the Federal Republic. In Poland,

13. See, for example, Trond Gilberg, "Ceausescu's Romania," *Problems of Communism*, 23, no. 4 (July–August 1974): 29–43.

the personal propensities of Wladyslaw Gomulka and the continuing quest of the Polish leadership for political consolidation in a population that had experienced the heady days of October 1956 once again required strong external support that could only be supplied by Moscow; the price for such support was ideological loyalty to the CPSU and the Soviet Union. In Czechoslovakia, ideological conformity in the dispute prior to 1968 was ensured by the fact that the "Stalinist" elements of the leadership naturally supported the Kremlin because of their own outlook, while the "liberal" elements vied with their conservative colleagues for position in order to safeguard their quest for *domestic* political and economic reform. After August 1968, ideological conformity was ensured by the "normalization" process and the presence on Czech and Slovak soil of a large Soviet occupation army.[14]

As discussed above, the Chinese challenge to Soviet supremacy in ideological matters was amplified by Beijing's claims that the Soviet socioeconomic developmental model was also defective. Unlike the ideological challenge, the CCP's claim to have the correct developmental model met with little interest in Eastern Europe. The reason for this is fairly clear. Beijing's model of development, both as postulated theoretically and as practiced in China itself, may have had some validity in underdeveloped countries, but there was no economic rationale for regime leaders or the general population in Eastern Europe to adopt such a model. The level of existing socioeconomic development throughout the region was simply too advanced for the possible application of the Chinese model. The only coun-

14. Throughout the 1970s *Problems of Communism* ran a series of insightful articles on the countries of Eastern Europe and their domestic and foreign policies. Examples are Vernon V. Aspaturian, "Soviet Global Power and the Correlation of Forces," 29, no. 3 (May–June 1980): 1–18; Walter D. Connor, "Dissent in Eastern Europe: A New Coalition?" 29, no. 1 (January–February 1980): 1–17; Ernst Kux, "Growing Tensions in Eastern Europe," 29, no. 2 (March–April 1980): 21–37; Jiri Valenta, "Eurocommunism and Eastern Europe," 27, no. 2 (March–April 1978): 41–54; Lawrence T. Caldwell, "The Warsaw Pact: Directions of Change," 24, no. 5 (September–October 1975): 1–19; Hartmut Zimmermann, "The GDR in the 1970's," 27, no. 2 (March–April 1978): 1–40; Adam Bromke, "A New Juncture in Poland," 25, no. 5 (September–October 1976): 1–17; Jan F. Triska, "Messages from Czechoslovakia," 24, no. 6 (November–December 1976): 26–42; Charlis Gati, "The Kádár Mystique," 23, no. 3 (May–June 1974): 23–35; Trond Gilberg, "Ceausescu's Romania," 23, no. 4 (July–August 1974): 29–43; F. Stephen Larrabee, "Bulgaria's Politics of Conformity," 21, no. 4 (July–August 1972): 42–52; Nicholas C. Pano, "The Albanian Cultural Revolution," 23, no. 4 (July–August 1974): 44–57; and William Zimmerman, "The Tito Legacy and Yugoslavia's Future," 26, no. 3 (May–June 1977): 33–49.

try in which the Chinese model had some impact was Albania, where the Hoxha regime adopted certain aspects of the Chinese approach such as an expansion of the "communal" life in the countryside and the militarization of labor. But for the rest of Eastern Europe, the Chinese model was largely irrelevant.[15]

The irrelevance of the Chinese development model as a possible blueprint for East European economic policy did not invalidate its importance in symbolic terms, but rather enhanced it. What the Chinese were demonstrating was that socioeconomic models developed in one national context could not be transferred to other entities. By extension, this also meant that other models were equally nontransferable, and this discovery, in turn, emphasized the need for national models of socioeconomic and political development. Thus the irrelevant Chinese model could be used to justify the trend toward national communism that became evident in Eastern Europe during the 1960s.

The combination of the ideological challenge and the existence of a separate (if economically irrelevant) development model, both produced in China, had profound effects in Eastern Europe, but the patterns of this impact were unpredictable and can only be analyzed on a country-by-country basis. In the case of Yugoslavia, the Chinese challenge simply highlighted the need for national approaches to politicoideological matters and socioeconomic development. Belgrade deviated from both the Soviet and the Chinese models "to the right." Hungary used the opportunity for ideological conformity to strengthen a socioeconomic development model that deviated from Soviet ("orthodox") practice in several crucial aspects. To some extent, a similar pattern was followed by the German Democratic Republic in the form of economic experimentation. In Bulgaria, ideological conformity produced heavy infusions of economic assistance from the Soviet Union. Czechoslovakia, in the period 1963–68, experienced a steady trend toward "liberalization" in political and socioeconomic terms while maintaining foreign policy orthodoxy and ideological conformity with the Kremlin. In Romania, the existence of the Chinese challenge produced the opportunity for Ceausescu to emphasize foreign policy autonomy and a national economic development plan of heavy industrialization at the same time. Romania became more and more "Stalinist" economically and politically as she increased her foreign policy autonomy. In Poland, Gomulka strengthened his personal position in the Polish United Workers' Party

15. Other aspects of Albanian politics include sweeping purges which resemble the Chinese Cultural Revolution; see, for example, Louis Zanga, "The Congress of The Great Purge," *Radio Free Europe Research*, RAD Background Report/230 (Albania), November 9, 1976.

(PUWP) at least in part by referring to the need for continued trust in Moscow.[16]

This astonishing variety in responses to the opportunities produced by the Sino-Soviet conflict illustrates better than any other element the extent to which ideological and practical political solidarity had worn thin even as early as the 1960s. Each state and communist party acted primarily in its own self-interest in response to the Sino-Soviet conflict, and this propensity boded ill for the following decade, which was fraught with dangers of a more profoundly centrifugal nature, both in party and state matters.

Given the predominance of Soviet power in the region, the Chinese challenge in the fields of ideology and developmental models could not effectively and directly spill over into interstate relations in Eastern Europe. On the other hand, the challenge from Beijing pointed to a general weakening of the Kremlin's control over international communism, and this decline of power and influence allowed greater autonomy for the states of the region in their bilateral relations, as long as the fundamentals of political and socioeconomic power (monopoly of power in the hands of each communist party and public ownership of the means of production) remained intact. Thus old animosities, which in some cases predated the communist era by centuries, reappeared during this period of declining Soviet influence in the region: the old quarrel between Yugoslavia and Bulgaria over Macedonia flared up; the rivalry between Romanians and Hungarians in Transylvania resurfaced with a vengeance; and elements in the Romanian party leadership and in other strata of the population began to murmur about the Soviet annexation of most of Bessarabia in 1940.[17] The Chinese, although only indirectly involved in fomenting these controversies, helped fuel the flames by judicious comments about them at selected times. These comments, which invariably referred to the need for national sovereignty and the destruction of big-power control, were clearly designed to help reduce Moscow's influence in the region. This effort was to become considerably more pronounced during the following decade.

While the Sino-Soviet conflict directly affected the states and parties of Eastern Europe in ideology and in the choice of developmental models for

16. The policies of the East European parties and states in the 1970s have been thoroughly analyzed in Stephen Fischer-Galati, ed., *The Communist Parties of Eastern Europe* (New York: Columbia University Press, 1979).

17. A thorough analysis of the controversy over Macedonia is found in Robert R. King, *Minorities under Communism* (Cambridge, Mass.: Harvard University Press, 1973). On the Romanian-Hungarian controversy over Transylvania, see *Scinteia* (Bucharest), July 9, 1971. The polemics over the Bessarabian question have been thoroughly discussed by King in *Radio Free Europe Research*, RAD Background Report/38 (Rumania), February 12, 1976.

The Impact of the Sino-Soviet Dispute on Eastern Europe 279

the modernizing elites of the region, it also helped reinforce other trends in the international communist movement; the feedback effects of these trends in turn produced direct effects in Eastern Europe. Of primary importance in this context was the trend toward pluralization of the movement, which had begun to accelerate after the death of Stalin. This tendency, which has always existed in international communism, has produced a perennial dilemma between the need of local communist parties to function in their national environment and the need to remain loyal to the movement, which transcends any boundary. Temporarily subdued by the overwhelming presence of Stalin, this conflict broke upon communist parties everywhere after the dictator's death. The movement has not been the same since 1953, and it is highly unlikely that the "synchronization" of the movement achieved during the Stalinist era could ever be reproduced. The multifaceted Chinese challenge, emerging toward the end of the 1950s, virtually ensured that unity in the movement would be lost forever.

During the 1960s, the impact of the Sino-Soviet conflict on nonruling communist parties helped influence events and trends in Eastern Europe during the same period. In the following decade, political developments in West European communism *directly* influenced every state and communist party in the Eastern part of the continent.

The Sino-Soviet conflict had an immediate impact on most communist parties in Western Europe. Factional splits developed in almost all of them, and typically a Maoist faction would break away from the mother party and form a competing unit. The harsh criticism by the Maoists of the CPSU and the USSR encouraged those who had remained in the main party to examine the policies of the former international center. Thus the many searching questions that had been raised in the West European communist parties after the Twentieth Congress of the CPSU and the events of 1956 were reinforced in the general atmosphere of questioning that the Chinese challenge had posited. Several parties—notably the Italian, Swedish, British, and Norwegian—began to examine the policies of the CPSU and the Soviet state in light of Western concepts of human rights, the road to power and the nature of the political system after a presumed communist victory, and the kind of economic system that would prevail under such circumstances.[18] This buffeting of the ideological center from both the left and the right was bound to have an effect on the parties and states existing in the Soviet shadow.

18. An excellent discussion of the policies of West European communist parties in this period is found in David E. Albright, ed., *Communism and Political Systems in Western Europe* (Boulder, Colo.: Westview Press, 1979). Chapters on the Italian, Swedish and Norwegian, and British parties are written by Giacomo Sani, Trond Gilberg, and David Lynn Price, respectively.

CZECHOSLOVAKIA AND BEYOND: 1968–80

The multiple centrifugal forces represented by the Chinese challenge in ideological matters, the growing differentiation in international communism, and the increasing assertiveness of the West European communist parties in the 1960s combined with domestic tendencies in the East European states themselves to produce a volatile political situation in the region in the second half of the 1960s. Modernization, as exemplified by industrialization, urbanization, social stratification, functional specialization, and the achievement of higher levels of education both among the masses and the societal elites, increased the difficulties of political leaders in maintaining societal control. When the assertion of political monopoly and the right to define ideological orthodoxy came under increasing attack from a growing number of sources in the 1960s, regime stability was brought under great strain in several countries.

The regimes of the area responded differently to this development. In some, the local communist parties tightened the ideological reins and refused to make concessions to the pluralistic tendencies of their modernizing societies. This was the case in Poland, Romania, and Bulgaria. In Hungary, economic reform was marked by careful "decompression" in the political realm, which allowed more individual autonomy and a somewhat greater role for technical experts and managers, without endangering the party's essential control. In the German Democratic Republic, tight political controls remained while economic reform proceeded cautiously. But in Czechoslovakia, the pressures for economic reform and political liberalization coincided in a powerful drive which resulted in the leadership change of early 1968 and the subsequent Prague Spring. The tragedy of the invasion and the subsequent "normalization" ensued.[19]

Although the Czechoslovak crisis and its aftermath were not directly caused by the Sino-Soviet conflict, that dispute had an indirect impact on events in Czechoslovakia. By the same token, the Soviet-sponsored invasion of that ill-fated country produced clear repercussions for Sino-Soviet relations and among all of the East European states and communist parties. Soviet actions during the invasion and the flood of statements about it emanating from Moscow (including the so-called Brezhnev Doctrine) firmly established the limits of "autonomism" in Eastern Europe and consequently provided benchmarks for East European responses to the Chinese challenge, especially in ideological matters. The Soviet leadership made it clear that at least three conditions must be met in any East European *state* (violation of any of the conditions would result in such "actions as might

19. For a good overview of East European policy in the postinvasion period, see Fischer-Galati, ed., *Communist Parties of Eastern Europe*.

be deemed necessary" by the Kremlin leadership): (1) The local communist parties must maintain political monopoly in their respective states. Real political decentralization and pluralization would not be tolerated. (2) The socioeconomic system must remain one of public ownership, predominantly central planning, and political control. (3) Each state must support the Soviet Union when it acts as a state in international forums, in relations with the West, and in bilateral relations. The principal control mechanisms of Soviet foreign policy—the Warsaw Pact and Comecon—would remain essential to political and military relations in the region, and no state would be allowed to leave these organizations. The communist parties of the region were required to maintain the proper ideological stance in international communism, in relations with the nonruling parties of the West, and in the Sino-Soviet conflict. Furthermore, each party was admonished to maintain its internal vigilance against "deviationism" of any kind, including the tendencies toward societal pluralization resulting from the modernization process.[20]

The postulation of ideological and political parameters for the states and parties of Eastern Europe in the wake of the Czechoslovak invasion could not defuse the political storm engendered by the Warsaw Pact move into a member state. The Chinese reaction was predictable: Beijing charged that the Soviet Union had acted in conformity with its imperialistic tendencies, and that this act had violated all rules of socialist and proletarian internationalism (relations among socialist states and communist parties, respectively). The Chinese leadership now voiced vociferous support of national sovereignty and the right of each state to decide its own path to socialism and communism; the CCP also expressed the absolute need for rejection of any center of international communism as envisaged by Moscow.[21] These themes were also argued by several West European communist parties, notably the Italians and the Spanish party in exile; the French Communist Party also voiced grave concern over the Soviet action in Czechoslovakia and the subsequent postulation of parameters for "autonomism." A similar storm was building in many other West European parties, especially the Swedish, British, Norwegian, and Icelandic parties.[22]

Disturbing as the West European reaction was, three parties and states in Eastern Europe produced statements that further aggravated the diffi-

20. Vernon V. Aspaturian, "Has Eastern Europe Become a Liability to the Soviet Union?: The Political-Ideological Aspects," in Gati, ed., *International Politics of Eastern Europe*, pp. 17–37; A. Ross Johnson, "Has Eastern Europe Become a Liability to the Soviet Union?: The Military Aspect," ibid., pp. 37–59.

21. Richard F. Staar, ed., *Yearbook on International Communist Affairs, 1969* (Stanford: Hoover Institution Press, 1969), pp. 161–63.

22. See Albright, ed., *Communism and Political Systems in Western Europe*, esp. chaps. 1, 2, 3, 7, and 8.

culties experienced by the CPSU in its effort to control the international movement in the wake of August 1968. The Yugoslavs, Romanians, and Albanians condemned the invasion and used arguments that sharply resembled the accusations voiced by Beijing. Both Marshal Tito and Nicolae Ceausescu made trips to Prague during the political crisis that preceded the invasion; subsequently, Belgrade and Bucharest instituted increased military alertness and agreed to coordinate their defense plans. In both countries, these measures were highly popular among the general population, and helped strengthen such legitimacy as the regimes possessed at the time. Albania predictably denounced the Soviet action as a logical outcome of the imperialistic policies of the "renegades" in Moscow.[23]

Of the three reactions, the Romanian attitude was clearly the most disturbing to the Kremlin leadership. Albania had long ago rejected Moscow on ideological and foreign policy grounds, and Yugoslavia had never shown any willingness to reintegrate itself with the Soviet sphere after the 1948 Cominform expulsion. Romania, on the other hand, was a full-fledged member of the Warsaw Pact and Comecon, and the open defiance shown by Bucharest, coupled with the evident popular support for such a policy, was a clear danger signal to those who wanted to define strict parameters of "autonomism," at least in the Balkans.[24]

From the vantage point of the Kremlin, developments in the international communist movement now took on ominous aspects. Ideological criticism, emanating from the Chinese state and party, coincided with protests from the West; the "Eurocommunists" (the term was coined somewhat later, in the 1970s, but the manifestations were clear in the 1960s) and the Maoists were no longer attacking Moscow from the right and the left respectively, but converged in a forceful emphasis on the need for national sovereignty and national communism. The third element in this new and reinforced challenge to the CPSU and the Soviet Union was the nationalistic emphasis of leaders such as Tito and Ceausescu, who saw in the new situation an opportunity for strengthening their own legitimacy by "being tough" on Moscow. How long, and by what means, could the Soviet state and party curtail this three-pronged attack?[25]

The Soviet-sponsored invasion of Czechslovakia had contradictory effects in Eastern Europe. On the one hand, it achieved the immediate objec-

23. Gilberg, "Yugoslavia, Albania, and Eastern Europe," in Gati, ed., *International Politics of Eastern Europe*, chap. 6.

24. Romania has continued its "deviant" position on this and other questions; see the *Scinteia* editorial on "Hegemonism," October 7, 1979, and another editorial, ibid., February 20, 1979, reconfirming the basic principles of Romanian foreign policy.

25. For a discussion of the tensions developing in Eastern Europe and Soviet worries about them, see Kux, "Growing Tensions in Eastern Europe," pp. 21–37.

tive, the restoration of "orthodox" elements in the Prague leadership and the destruction of the Czechoslovak reform movement; on the other hand, this action helped to channel a variety of challenges from several sources into a powerful mainstream challenge against Soviet control and supremacy in socialist and proletarian internationalism. The CPSU and the Soviet state have been attempting to regain firm control over the regimes and parties of Eastern Europe ever since.

During the twelve years since the August invasion, the Kremlin has used a variety of political means to strengthen its control in Eastern Europe and thereby blunt the triple challenges of domestic East European nationalism, the Chinese ideological offensive, and Eurocommunism. In this period, too, Moscow had to contend with drastic changes in the policies of the Chinese state, namely the partial opening to the West, which culminated in the establishment of diplomatic relations with the United States in 1979.

Several rather specific policies were instituted to combat these multiple challenges. First, the CPSU took on the CCP in the ideological debate by periodically hammering home *its* version of Marxism-Leninism while denouncing Maoism as destructive, misguided, and directly helpful to "imperialism," insofar as the Chinese were instrumental in splitting the "progressive" forces of the world, thus aiding and abetting the "imperialists." This theme, which was reiterated with great bitterness during the entire postinvasion period, was only occasionally toned down in response to some specific event, such as the death of Mao Zedong.[26]

Second, the CPSU sponsored international meetings of communist parties for the purpose of isolating the CCP, and perhaps even excluding the Chinese party from the movement. Much of the sponsorship of such meetings was in fact promulgated by other parties, occasionally even parties outside of Eastern Europe. In most cases, however, there was little doubt about the real sponsor. The most important achievement in this field was the conference of communist parties in East Berlin in 1976.[27]

Third, the CPSU sponsored numerous meetings of the ideological *apparat* of the East European parties, in which the challenges of Chinese "dogma-

26. The Soviet view was expressed both directly and indirectly; in the latter case, it was often the Czechoslovaks themselves who carried the "loyalist" point to the Chinese; for example, see *Rudé Právo* (Prague), February 9, 1973, and *Pravda* (Bratislava), February 26, 1973. See also *Rudé Právo*, January 9, 1974, and July 2, 1976 (in the wake of the East Berlin Conference of Communist Parties), and *Tribuna* (Prague), July 27, 1977, on proletarian internationalism.

27. The proceedings of the 1976 conference are discussed in Richard F. Staar, ed., *Yearbook on International Communist Affairs, 1977* (Stanford: Hoover Institution Press, 1977), pp. 571–83. The Soviet leaders also used the negotiations for the European Security Conference as a means of enforcing control; see *Yearbook, 1974*, pp. 80–82, and *Yearbook, 1975*, pp. 97–100.

tism" were debated and countermeasures were established. Such meetings have become annual (occasionally semiannual) occurrences. Further opportunities have developed in the annual meetings of East European communist leaders with the Soviet leadership ("all on vacation") in the Crimea, usually in August of every year.[28]

The Chinese challenge increasingly was combined with criticism of the Eurocommunists during the various ideological meetings held during the 1970s. At the East Berlin Conference in 1976, open clashes took place between the most outspoken Eurocommunists, such as representatives of the Italian, French, and Spanish communist parties, on the one hand, and the "loyalists" grouped around Moscow's version, notably the East Germans, Poles, Czechoslovaks, and Bulgarians, on the other. The challenge of Eurocommunism was also met directly in various journal articles in the Soviet Union and in the "loyalist" states.[29]

Fourth, the CPSU leadership attempted to meet the problems of ideological erosion by frequent visits to each East European party, and return visits to Moscow by the leaders of those parties. A steady stream of such consultations took place during the postinvasion era. Favorite occasions included local party congresses, the congresses of the CPSU, and official state and party meetings at the bilateral level.[30]

While the ideological threat from Beijing, Rome, Paris, and Madrid was

28. Participation in these meetings has been routine for all party leaders in Eastern Europe with the exception of the Yugoslav and Albanian leaders; Nicolae Ceausescu of Romania participated intermittently during the 1970s.

29. See, for example, Andrei A. Rodionov in *Pravda* (Moscow), March 12, 1976, on the need to recognize Soviet leadership in the world revolutionary movement.

30. During the 1970s, the following party congresses were held in Eastern Europe, with strong Soviet representation: Hungarian Socialist Workers' Party, Tenth Congress, November 23–27, 1970 (*Yearbook, 1971*, p. 46); Bulgarian Communist Party, Tenth Congress, April 20–25, 1971 (*Yearbook, 1972*, p. 10); Communist Party of Czechoslovakia, Fourteenth Congress, May 1971 (ibid., p. 20); Socialist Unity Party of Germany, Eighth Congress, June 15–19, 1971 (ibid., p. 27); Polish United Workers' Party, Sixth Congress, December 1971 (ibid., p. 47); Romanian Communist Party, Eleventh Congress, November 1974 (*Yearbook, 1975*, p. 68); Hungarian Socialist Workers' Party, Eleventh Congress, March 1975 (*Yearbook, 1976*, p. 40); Polish United Workers' Party, Seventh Congress, December 1975 (ibid., p. 51); League of Communists of Yugoslavia, Tenth Congress, May 1974 (ibid., p. 91); Bulgarian Communist Party, Eleventh Congress, March 29–April 2, 1976 (*Yearbook, 1977*, p. 11); Communist Party of Czechoslovakia, Fifteenth Congress, April 12–16, 1976 (ibid., p. 17); Socialist Unity Party of Germany, Ninth Congress, May 1976 (ibid., p. 27); Romanian Communist Party, November 1979 (*Scinteia*, November 20, 21, 24, 1979).

combated in several ways, the Soviet state employed its military control over the Warsaw Pact to ensure the continued loyalty of the East European regimes and armed forces. Joint maneuvers were held regularly, and a network of joint command structures and consultative meetings was used. Soviet control over the command structure of the Warsaw Pact, the USSR's virtual monopoly on the production of weapons and the supply of spare parts, and the physical presence of Soviet troops in several countries—along with the vivid memory of the rapid invasion of Czechoslovakia—all illustrated the extent to which the Soviet Union exercised military hegemony in the region. This was indeed a forceful reminder to the Chinese and the East Europeans alike that "autonomism" had definite limits.[31]

As the 1970s progressed, the Soviet Union increasingly used economic means to enforce politicoideological control over the East European states and parties. The Yom Kippur War of 1973 and the formation of an effective oil cartel in OPEC quickly brought about a worldwide energy crisis and enormous increases in the price of energy. The East European economies, heavily dependent on Soviet energy and raw materials for their continued rapid economic development through extensive industrialization,[32] found themselves in a position whereby their subsidized oil prices, held low by administrative fiat in Moscow, were seriously out of line with world market prices; this development in turn led to a gradual, but substantial, increase in the price of Soviet oil as well, thus sharpening the pressures on already strained economic systems in Eastern Europe. The East Europeans, unable to compete in hard-currency export markets because of the low quality of their products, could not earn the funds to acquire oil from OPEC; the temporary remedy of indebtedness in the West and importation of Western technology through investments in the socialist economies and joint ventures in the Eastern part of the continent foundered on the discrepancy between capital and technological needs and East European ability to absorb such technology, on the one hand, and the very size of the resulting indebtedness, on the other. The East Europeans found themselves forced to rely more heavily than ever on the Soviet Union for energy and raw materials, and they also had to rely on the Soviet market as the main outlet for their finished products. This advantageous position was fully exploited by the Kremlin to tie the East European economics more closely to the Soviet system.[33] Typically, the following policies were pursued in this area:

31. See, for example, Caldwell, "The Warsaw Pact: Directions of Change," pp. 1–19.

32. "Extensive" in this context means industrial expansion by increasing the work force rather than improving output per worker.

33. Some of the "autonomists" balked at this kind of policy; see, for example, *Scinteia*, June 9, 1979, on the forthcoming Comecon Council meeting, which was to debate integration and more economic coordination.

1. *Pressure for increased East European investments in economic ventures sponsored by Comecon.* The Soviets have clearly and forcefully pressured their allies in Eastern Europe into an accelerated investment program under the auspices of Comecon. The most important of these projects is the plant at Ust-Ilimsk, which produces paper and pulp products, but there are other ventures under study, such as prospecting for oil and natural gas and the construction of pipelines.

2. *Bilateral economic agreements that tie the East European economies to the Soviet system.* These kinds of agreements increasingly establish the Soviet Union as the chief supplier of raw materials and energy to the respective East European systems, while also acting as the main customer for the finished product. In most cases, these agreements also call for East European import of Soviet machinery and technology, thus reducing East European ability to purchase such equipment and know-how in the West. These relationships become a vicious circle for the Soviet allies: since the prices of raw materials and energy continually rise, the East Europeans must export more to the Soviet Union just to stay even; at the same time, the enforced importation of Soviet machinery and technology, which frequently lag behind Western products in quality, ensures perpetuation of the present inferior level of quality and productivity in East European industry. Both trends reinforce the symbiotic ties with the Soviet Union.[34]

Military and economic control mechanisms are not directly related to the Sino-Soviet conflict and the Chinese challenge, but they help tie the East European states intimately to the Soviet Union. Under such circumstances, outright ideological deviation on the part of East European states and parties is increasingly unlikely, thus blunting the effects of the Chinese challenge and the attacks from the Eurocommunists.

THE EFFECTS OF THE SINO-SOVIET CONFLICT
AND EUROCOMMUNISM IN EASTERN EUROPE IN THE 1970s:
NATIONAL COMMUNISM IN PRACTICE

The three-pronged problem of domestic development trends the Chinese challenge, and the criticisms of the Eurocommunists affected the various states and communist parties of Eastern Europe differently, and the powerful control mechanisms used by the Soviet Union and the CPSU could not reimpose ideological and political uniformity in the region. Several kinds of response to the three challenges and the Soviet countermoves emerged during the 1970s. They are discussed in five categories below.

34. A typical trade agreement of this kind was the 1977 agreement; see *Népszabadság* (Budapest), November 19, 1976. See also the terms of the 1979 agreement, in *Világgazdaság* (Budapest), December 22, 1978 (discussed in *Radio Free Europe Research*, Hungary, January 11, 1979).

1. "*Loyalists.*" This group is made up of states and parties staunchly supportive of the CPSU in the Sino-Soviet conflict and in the struggle with the Eurocommunists, and closely follows the edicts of Soviet foreign policy generally. In this group can be found the German Democratic Republic, Czechoslovakia, and Bulgaria. Among these "loyalists," the Czechoslovak leadership has taken the lead in castigating the Chinese and the Eurocommunists and has conducted frequent and sweeping purges of domestic dissidents.[35] Bulgaria's attachment to Soviet and CPSU policies has never been questioned,[36] and this relationship now extends to close cooperation and coordination in all matters of ideology, foreign policy, major economic planning, and military coordination. The GDR, which is dependent on the Soviet Union for its policy of national building and *Abgrenzung* in relation to the Federal Republic, has closely followed the Soviet line in socialist and proletarian internationalism and has often acted as the "junior partner" of the USSR in ideological matters and in economic coordination in Comecon, as well as in foreign affairs, notably in the Soviet penetration of Africa.[37]

2. *Poland.* Edward Gierek and his leadership forcefully castigated the CCP and the PRC for its serious deviationism in ideological matters and in foreign policy generally; this criticism was sharp and uncompromising. Eurocommunism, on the other hand, has been handled with more finesse in Poland, and the criticisms of the PCE, PCI, and, for a time, the PCF, have been less stringent and more germane to substantive debate than the comments emanating from the strictly "loyalist" group. At the same time, the domestic political situation in Poland since the mid-1970s has allowed a considerable amount of internal pluralization and dissent, reflecting a system considerably different from the highly managed polities of the GDR, Czechoslovakia, and Bulgaria.[38]

The events in Poland during the fall of 1980 further set this country apart from the Soviet Union and the loyalists in the bloc. The Polish crisis is multifaceted and fundamental, because it includes social, economic, and political elements all mixed together; and it involves broad segments of the population, not just the dissident intelligentsia or elements of the industrial

35. On the Czechoslovak view of Eurocommunism, see *Nová Mysl* (Prague) (theoretical organ of the Czechoslovak Party) October 1976; the party's purge of the Charter 77 movement was extensively documented in the Czech and Slovak press during the period January–June 1977.

36. This stand was forcefully reiterated in a speech by Todor Zhivkov to the National Council of the Fatherland Front, in *Rabotnichesko Delo* (Sofia), February 15, 1980.

37. Zimmermann, "The GDR in the 1970's," pp. 1–40.

38. On the domestic situation in Poland, see Bromke, "A New Juncture in Poland," pp. 1–17.

working class. The Polish crisis, therefore, is an important juncture in Eastern Europe and in the Kremlin's policy in that area. Once again, the Soviet leadership must establish the parameters of autonomism. Once again, Moscow must somehow intervene, possibly militarily, to reestablish its authority. And once again, Soviet policies will merely succeed in buying time. The crisis this time is engendered by the very development process under way in Eastern Europe in general and Poland in particular. It is ironic that the Marxists, claiming to have history by the tail, now must watch as history catches up with them.

3. *Hungary*. Hungary represents yet another nuance in response to the multiple challenges to Soviet supremacy and the policies undertaken in Moscow to deal with them. Hungarian criticism of the CCP and the PRC, while loyal to the Soviet line, has been less frequent and less intense than that of most of the loyalists. Kádár has on occasion seemed willing to accept the right of the Eurocommunists to maintain their positions and even to criticize certain aspects of political life in Eastern Europe. During the last year and a half, however, there has been a notable hardening of Budapest's attitude in this matter, and it is probably no accident (to quote the famous Marxist phrase) that this change followed rather intensive consultations between the Hungarian and Soviet leaderships. At the present time, the Hungarian approach is more analogous to the stand taken by the Polish leadership on the issues of China and Eurocommunism.[39]

4. *"Autonomists."* A distinct group of states and parties can best be described as "autonomist" in the questions of Sino-Soviet relations, national sovereignty and national communism, and Eurocommunism. Included here are Romania and Yugoslavia. The two parties have refused to accept the idea that the CCP represents a fundamental deviation in international communism and therefore should be excluded from the movement; instead, both Belgrade and Bucharest have argued that no party can claim leadership in the movement, hence no party can dictate specific positions to another party, and thus no party can exclude another. Tito and Ceausescu have staunchly maintained the need for "mutual respect, noninterference in internal affairs, and relations based on mutual advantage" in both state and party matters. Romania and Yugoslavia have maintained relations with the CCP and PRC; Ceausescu has been especially active in this regard. In 1978, Chairman Hua Guofeng of the CCP paid a visit to Romania and Yugoslavia. despite vociferous Soviet criticism of the trip. And a multitude of economic, political, and even military ties flourish between Beijing and Romania, with Yugoslavia lagging somewhat behind in these areas. Both Belgrade and

39. The Hungarian Party press debated Eurocommunism in great detail after the visit of PCF Head Georges Marchais to Budapest in November 1977; see, for example, *Népszabadság*, November 27, 1977.

Bucharest have in fact gone so far as to take a neutral stand in conflicts that directly involved either the PRC or the USSR or their proxies; thus both Romania and Yugoslavia condemned the Vietnamese invasion of Kampuchea, and Romania remained neutral in the subsequent Chinese military action against Vietnamese border areas (Yugoslavia, somewhat reluctantly, supported the Romanian position). Both of these states and party leaderships have lamented the Soviet invasion of Afghanistan, albeit in veiled terms, indicating the profound and understandable uneasiness of the "autonomists" in the face of Soviet willingness to resort to forceful action to maintain the status quo. Despite the potential dangers to countries such as Romania and Yugoslavia reflected in recent Soviet assertiveness and aggressiveness throughout the world, the basic positions on national sovereignty and national communism have not been abandoned in Belgrade and Bucharest.[40]

5. *The Maverick.* Alone among the states of Eastern Europe, Albania has categorically rejected the Soviet attempt to define the parameters of East European deviationism and at the same time has castigated Eurocommunism and, in the mid-1970s, also criticized the Chinese for ideological and socioeconomic mistakes. Albania has become increasingly isolated from other socialist states and communist parties, and the present regime in Tirana, preparing for the elite turnover which must come within the next few years, shows no inclination to reassess its Olympian stand of Marxist-Leninist rectitude, calling down a plague on all sides in the Sino-Soviet dispute and the verbal struggles of international communism.[41]

CONCLUSION: INTO THE 1980s

This discussion, which has admittedly touched only the "commanding heights" of the Sino-Soviet conflict and the pluralization in the international communist movement, has shown that the impact of the Sino-Soviet conflict and its many ramifications cannot be separated from the other challenges that have buffeted the local regimes and Soviet control in the area, but must rather be considered a logical and integral part of the multifaceted trends that are now straining to the utmost the political and socioeconomic capabilities of the imperial power in the region. These problems will not "go away." Rather, they will develop further and take on altered

---

40. Romania asserted its position on several occasions; see, for example, *Scinteia*, January 10, 1979, and March 8, 1979. The Yugoslav position was confirmed in meetings between high Yugoslav and Romanian officials; see *Tanjug*, March 14, 1979.

41. For a summary of the Albanian position, see Louis Zanga, "Albanian Leader Reiterates His Foreign Policy Stand," *Radio Free Europe Research*, RAD Background Report/233 (Albania), October 24, 1979.

forms, and they will always represent a major challenge to Soviet hegemony in the area.

The problems of the 1980s, then, have several dimensions, of which the Sino-Soviet conflict at the state and party levels is an important part. The Kremlin will face problems arising from domestic developments in the Soviet Union and Eastern Europe; new challenges in international communism; increased assertiveness by important West European communist parties and the development of new forms of leftism, both in Western and Eastern Europe; a continuation of the Chinese challenge in interstate and interparty relations, especially the former; a new strategic constellation, involving a modernizing China under a more pragmatic leadership, actively wooing the United States and other noncommunist industrialized systems; a likely upsurge in American strategic capabilities, hence a more assertive U.S. foreign policy, including an expanding relationship between Washington and Beijing; and, finally, the worsening of the global energy balance (coupled with increasing Soviet shortages of oil), which will force further strains on *all* alliance systems, including the Warsaw Pact and Comecon.[42] Given all these complexities, the analyst may establish several scenarios, all with a fair amount of plausibility. All these scenarios, however, must reckon with certain tendencies and trends that are likely to continue and perhaps strengthen during the 1980s.

The processes of modernization, social stratification, and functional specialization will continue to evolve in the systems of Eastern Europe and the Soviet Union during the 1980s. These processes have been set in motion by the regimes themselves, and they cannot be reversed or even significantly slowed. The very survival of the regimes of the region depends on economic and social development. There is not adequate *political* legitimacy to weather a period of serious economic retrenchment. But this need for continued development and modernization carries with it undesirable side effects for the autocratic regimes of the region; a modern society with modern individuals in it can no longer be ruled by the kind of mobilization regime that started the development process in the area at the onset of communist rule. East European and Soviet societies have become too modern for the anachronistic polities supervising them. There will be increasing demands for political change, for a "loosening up" of these political systems, for political pluralization. Such pluralization will not of itself lend greater credence to the revolutionary messages of the CCP and the PRC, but a more "modern," semipluralistic political system is likely to accept the idea that men may differ, even about ideology. Hence the "modern" communist in

42. An excellent overview on these and other problems is furnished by William E. Griffith in *The Soviet Empire: Expansion and Detente* (Lexington, Mass.: Lexington Books, 1976), pp. 1–25.

Eastern Europe may demand that the Chinese should be heard, even if the message of the latter is largely irrelevant.

The ruling elites of Eastern Europe and the Soviet Union will also have to face the problem of a populace increasingly concerned with material well-being, with the right to think and to question (presumably a natural outgrowth of the higher educational levels which represent the most tangible and impressive achievement of the communist regimes of the area to date), and with civil rights per se—as rights of the individual qua individual, not merely as a part of the larger collective, society itself. These demands cannot be met without fundamental changes in the economy, in the political systems themselves, and in the relation between polity and society. Such fundamental changes would destroy the political monopoly currently claimed by the communist leaders of Eastern Europe and the Soviet Union. It is hard to imagine that such fundamental changes will be accepted by the ruling elites. There will be instability and repression; policies will zig and zag between accommodation and crackdowns. But such policies will produce weakness, with no real possibility of lasting solutions, given the regimes' commitment to certain socioeconomic and political fundamentals. The result will be continual social challenge and corresponding regime counterattacks. Out of such dynamics develop the chance for increased external pressures and influence, whether from the right (Eurocommunism) or the left (the Chinese challenge), but probably much less from the latter than from the former.

It is even conceivable that the message of the CCP may be more palatable to certain groups and individuals in modernized communist systems than was the case in earlier periods of development. As the shabbiness of the race after the "almighty ruble" becomes even more apparent, and the widespread cynicism of the general population about the ruling elite becomes more intense, there may be room for the true believer, who hearkens back to a simpler, leaner, more revolutionary, and more dedicated system, "before the fall" from ideological purity. The propensity for extreme left-wing commitment among certain elements in the developed West may provide clues to this possibility. The general population probably cares little about such developments, since the process of depolitization has already made deep inroads among the masses of the entire region. As for the societal elites, their demands for increased participation in the existing system, coupled with the growing alienation in such circles from the closed-thought systems of modern autocracies, will produce a great deal of trouble for the *apparatchiki* of the region. Once again, outside challenges, including the persistent one from Beijing, will have a great chance of partial success. But in the 1980s it is the impact of Western ideas and practices that will predominate in Eastern Europe.

The very nature of the Chinese challenge will change to some degree during the coming decade. As China begins the arduous process of rapid modernization, the ideological purism of the Maoist era will recede, at least in part, and the PRC will edge closer to becoming a superpower that can hold its own in a new, triangular relationship between Moscow, Washington, and Beijing, with Japan and Western Europe competitive in economic power but lagging behind in military might. The most important of the OPEC countries, notably Saudi Arabia, will have achieved greater ability to influence matters around the world, not just in the Persian Gulf region. This pluralization of influence and power in the world will tend to reduce the power distance between the real global powers—the United States and the Soviet Union—and the other major powers. An increase in real capabilities (economic, political, and military) on the part of the PRC will reduce this distance even further. The relationship between Washington and Beijing is likely to become somewhat closer during this decade, as each uses the other to help offset the military capabilities of the Soviet Union. Thus the Chinese challenge in the 1980s will be more visible at the state level, less prevalent at the party level. But this is no real consolation for the leaders in the Kremlin, who must deal with both challenges.

The forces of nonruling, "unorthodox" communism, especially in Western Europe, will continue to play a part in the complicated equation of power in the Soviet Union's "front yard"—an equation in which the Sino-Soviet dispute plays an important role. The West European communist parties will be forced to continue on the path to "democratic communism," whether their commitment to it is genuine or not. It is a matter of political survival. Only a major socioeconomic catastrophe, such as widespread and devastating societal dislocation as a result of massive energy crises or war, would relieve the West Europeans of this requirement (and should such a catastrophe occur, most of the other elements in this complicated equation would also change). The arguments of Eurocommunism will coincide with some of the pluralizing tendencies in Eastern Europe discussed above. It should become a powerful combination.

As the challenges to Soviet political hegemony in Eastern Europe grow, the abilities of the Kremlin to meet them shrink. The Soviet Union is no longer able to control the processes of economic development and their side effects in the region. Political legitimacy in Eastern Europe, if it exists at all, does not stem from a close alliance with Moscow (with the possible exception of Bulgaria), but from domestic economic development, political nationalism (occasionally even chauvinism), and anti-Sovietism. The Soviet Union represents no palatable model for socioeconomic, political, and cultural development; the young generation prefers Western music and blue jeans, not the proletarian blouse from the East. Only in the military realm does the Soviet Union maintain monopoly. The relationship between Moscow and the capitals and lands of Eastern Europe will increasingly become that of imperial master and unwilling subject, whose principal bond is partial military occupation or the threat of coercion. The imperial relationship is very costly. It is going to strain Soviet resources to the utmost.

Soviet appetites are not limited to the maintenance of the status quo in Eastern Europe. The leaders in the Kremlin achieved strategic parity with the United States in the 1970s, and they now represent a global power, presumably with interests everywhere in the world, and with corresponding military capabilities. This is indeed a heavy burden in a society beset by serious economic difficulties, low political legitimacy, and widespread depoliticization and cynicism. The vastly increased commitments of globalism can only be met by continued heavy investments in armaments, standing armed forces, and a corresponding low level of consumption. Sooner or later, the discrepancy between the economic aspirations of the population and the regime's ability to meet them will produce the need for readjustments in goals or an even heavier commitment to the use or threat of coercion in the domestic realm. This crisis point is in the future; the regimes' awareness of it approaching will produce the opportunity for greater autonomy in Eastern Europe.

The East European reaction to these opportunities is bound to be ambivalent, and vary from state to state and party to party. The regimes of the area must be aware of the increasing challenges to their power. In this context it is also clear that the Soviet leadership is the only force that can help maintain their positions. At the same time, anti-Sovietism may provide an element of badly needed legitimacy. In either case, the Sino-Soviet conflict and the Chinese challenge can only provide limited opportunities for "autonomism" in Eastern Europe; they cannot provide a real solution to the fundamental conflict between communist polities and modern societies.

Lest this fundamental dilemma of the Soviet Union and other communist systems lull us into complacency, it should be pointed out that the liabilities of the Kremlin are partly matched by the rapid increase in Soviet military capabilities. This fact provides a scenario in Eastern Europe (and perhaps elsewhere) that is far from comforting. A state that has newly acquired the status of global power in the military realm with no matching capability in the economic or political fields is likely to rely on its only success to achieve ambitious goals. Given the Kremlin's commitment to the "irreversibility of the Marxist advance," it is likely that the Soviet Union will resort to military force in Eastern Europe if the centrifugal forces now battering the regimes and societies of the region appear to get out of control. Under such circumstances, the Sino-Soviet conflict will become a sideshow, albeit an important one. Neither we nor the East European leaders need such a fierce reminder that "distant waters cannot quench fires."

Soviet military intervention is not inevitable, of course. The leaders in the Kremlin are willing to accept considerable change and innovation in economic practices; such developments indeed appear necessary if the systems of the region are going to survive. Limited social pluralism, some dissent, and greater intellectual freedom may also be considered acceptable. But there is always in the Kremlin the perceived need to draw the line at the question of political power. If the innovations in the economy and the limited societal pluralization of the East European states are seen as detrimental to the maintenance of communist power locally and the predominance of the Soviet Union in the region, the Kremlin leadership will take any step, including military intervention, that it deems necessary to reestablish political power. For the leaders in Moscow, the fundamental question in the 1980s will be this: can desperately needed changes in the economy be compartmentalized, or will they of necessity spill over into the political realm? To what extent can the influence of a changing Eastern Europe be incorporated into Soviet society without changing the position of communist power in the latter system? These are questions stemming from historical processes that transcend the Sino-Soviet dispute. That conflict will remain important in some ways, but it is no longer a central problem for the Soviet leadership. The central problem is simply this: how does a communist elite control the developmental forces it has released? The supreme irony of this problem is surely not lost on any proclaimed Marxist, or anyone who seriously studies communist systems.

The Impact of the Sino-Soviet Dispute on Western Europe*

JOAN BARTH URBAN

For Western Europe, as for the United States, the impact of the Sino-Soviet dispute in the 1970s was to "triangulate" international relations. Neither the West European powers—France, West Germany, the United Kingdom, and Italy for the purposes of this essay—nor the European Community (EC) as a whole could undertake any policy toward Beijing without an eye to its effect on relations with Moscow. The same was true, if to a lesser degree, with regard to European policy toward the Soviet Union. And, of course, a similar triangular perspective influenced Soviet and Chinese conduct toward Europe, with the important difference that each communist regime was concerned not so much with the impact of its European policy on Sino-Soviet relations as with the impact of that policy on European ties with its communist archrival.

Specific West European initiatives to the PRC were in some cases prompted by varying degrees of hostility toward the USSR or at least by the wish to gain some extra leverage over the Soviet regime—to play the "China card." In this context domestic partisan cleavages over the advisability of détente with the Soviet Union often shaped the attitudes of contending parties or coalitions toward the PRC. Particularly during the later 1970s conservative forces tended to use the Chinese connection, both at the national and regional (EC) level, to promote their opposition to détente with Moscow (Thatcher). Center-left groupings, in contrast, favored détente with both communist giants with a clear priority given to relations with the Soviet Union (Schmidt). Yet another set of views evolved among third-force elements, who had long seen the simultaneous development of ties with both Moscow and Beijing as a means of asserting independence from U.S. influence without becoming too entangled with one or the other communist power. During the 1960s this attitude had led to unprecedented overtures toward China as well as Russia (de Gaulle). By the late 1970s on the other hand, third-force tendencies had multiplied and diversified to the point where some tilted toward one communist power rather than the other in order to enhance their maneuverability not simply in relation to

---

* The author would like to express her gratitude to Daniel F. Sarp for his meticulous survey of the West European press preparatory to the writing of this paper.

the United States (Giscard d'Estaing) but in relation to the Soviet Union as well (the Italian Communists and the European Community).

It is clear in retrospect that the eruption of the Sino-Soviet conflict in the early 1960s provided one of the psychological preconditions for the relaxation of tensions between Western Europe and the Soviet Union that gathered momentum during the second half of that decade. During the years of Nikita Khrushchev's ascendancy in Moscow, the specter of the communist world a billion strong was as instrumental as sputnik in fostering West European fear and suspicion of Soviet prowess. Khrushchev's bellicose posturing over West Berlin from 1958 through 1961 was unduly heeded—and his overtures for an East-West rapprochement often discounted—in large part because of the widespread Western assumption of communist-bloc cohesion. To grasp the enormity of the change in the Western perception of international alignments, one need only recall Zbigniew Brzezinski's comment regarding the nature of Sino-Soviet relations in the first edition of *The Soviet Bloc*, completed in late 1959: "It would probably be idle to expect an open break between the two states in the foreseeable future, given their common ideological aspirations, the Soviet commitment to an expanding Communist world and the Chinese commitment to rapid industrialization, and their mutual hostility to the external world. At this stage much more binds them together than divides them. In some respects, one could draw an analogy to Anglo-American relations, which have survived repeated strains and disagreements."[1]

By 1963, however, most observers on both sides of the Atlantic were coming to understand that the Soviet Union had "lost" China as a reliable ally. By 1966 even the most hidebound skeptics had to admit that a China wracked by the excesses of the Cultural Revolution had lost its practical value to the USSR. The Sino-Soviet border clashes in 1969 finally forced them, too, to concede the depth of hostility between Moscow and Beijing. Such perceptions facilitated subsequent Western efforts to reach an accommodation with the Soviet leaders.

This chapter will begin with a brief discussion of the connection between the emergence of the Sino-Soviet dispute in the 1960s, on the one hand, and the initiation of a policy of East-West détente by Charles de Gaulle and the Bonn government on the other. It will continue with an examination of how the USSR and the PRC, in the 1970s, depicted one another's intentions with regard to Western Europe. In a nutshell, each portrayed the other as entertaining a "grand design." The Chinese accused the Soviets of aiming to encircle and subjugate Western Europe. The Soviets accused the Chinese of colluding with Western reactionaries to encircle the USSR and disrupt

---

1. Zbigniew K. Brzezinski, *The Soviet Bloc* (Cambridge, Mass.: Harvard University Press, 1960), p. 369.

détente. The policies pursued in conjunction with this rhetoric as well as the possible motives underlying both the words and the actions of the two communist powers will also be analyzed. The final section will consider how the major Western European political groupings on foreign policy issues— ranging from the center-left through the third-force elements to the conservatives—reacted to the respective Soviet and Chinese appeals for bilateral cooperation and détente. By way of conclusion some conjectures will be ventured on the overall impact of the Sino-Soviet dispute on the Atlantic Alliance.

THE SINO-SOVIET DISPUTE, GAULLISM, AND OSTPOLITIK

From the American perspective of 1980 it is all too easy to forget that the pathbreakers on the road to East-West détente were not Richard Nixon and Henry Kissinger but Charles de Gaulle and Willy Brandt. While de Gaulle's purpose in seeking détente was to weaken the sway of *both* superpowers over Europe and thereby to enhance French independence and clout, the means that he chose to achieve this goal were notably similar to Nixon's. In a word, France's announcement on January 27, 1964, of its diplomatic recognition of the PRC had the effect (whether intended or not) of prodding Moscow into a more expeditious relaxation of tensions with Paris.

France's dramatic normalization of relations with Peking, to the surprise of the Western world and in defiance of the United States government, was undertaken in tandem with overtures to the USSR. That very same month Valéry Giscard d'Estaing, then minister of finance, traveled to Moscow to explore the prospects for greater Franco-Soviet trade,[2] a prelude to the conclusion of the first five-year trade agreement between Paris and Moscow the following October. Shortly thereafter, former Premier Edgar Faure, whom de Gaulle had entrusted with laying the groundwork for the Franco-Chinese rapprochement,[3] made a visit to the Soviet Union (where he confirmed that France would vote for the admission of the PRC to the United Nations).[4] Moscow responded to these French initiatives with a flurry of expressions of official interest in improving Franco-Soviet relations. In February 1964 Politburo member Nikolai Podgorny, in his capacity as head of a parliamentary delegation to France, stated that he was "convinced that in the future friendship between France and USSR will be strengthened."

2. François Fejtö, "France and China: The Intersection of Two Grand Designs," in A. M. Halpern, ed., *Policies toward China: Views from Six Continents* (New York: McGraw-Hill, 1965), pp. 42–76, at p. 67.

3. De Gaulle press conference of January 31, 1964, in Charles de Gaulle, *Discours et messages*, vol. 4 (Paris: Plon, 1970), pp. 162–82, at p. 180; see also Fejtö, "France and China," pp. 61–62.

4. Ibid., p. 76, n. 80.

In March Brezhnev, then Soviet chief of state, informed the new French ambassador to Moscow, "the USSR attributes great significance to [the] continuation and strengthening of its ties of friendship and collaboration with France, a great power which plays an important role in international affairs." The very next month Aleksei Adzhubei, Khrushchev's son-in-law and at that time editor of *Izvestiia*, declared on the eve of a good-will mission to Paris, "the USSR in no way seeks to suppress France's aspirations to grandeur."[5] If the eventual Franco-Soviet détente of 1966–67 reflected Moscow's desire to exploit French discord with the United States, these earlier steps signaled the Soviet leadership's intention of countering the PRC's incipient international activism, in Europe and elsewhere, during the brief interlude between Beijing's recovery from the Great Leap Forward and her immersion in the Cultural Revolution.

De Gaulle's early playing of the "China card" did not represent an anti-Soviet maneuver, as would often be the case with the use of this tactic in the 1970s, but an attempt to offset French dependence on American power with multiple sources of diplomatic leverage.[6] There were, of course, more specific reasons for the Paris-Beijing rapprochement. The opposition of both Maoist China and Gaullist France to the partial nuclear test ban treaty signed by the United States, the United Kingdom, and the USSR in July 1963 underscored their mutual antipathy toward the existing global distribution of power and parallel quest for nuclear weapons as the symbol of strategic independence. Some observers have maintained that Sino-French cultural affinities, rooted in the French intelligentsia's fascination with things Chinese, both Confucian and communist, as well as in the influx of radical Chinese students to France during the first decades of this century, also encouraged the rapid normalization of relations.[7] More to the point, one might argue, the French and Chinese elites shared a preoccupation with sovereign equality and a self-perception of historical grandeur. All the same, the chief impetus for de Gaulle's cultivation of ties with the PRC as with the USSR was his desire to enhance French stature in a projected multipolar international environment.

At the same time, Gaullist overtures for détente with Moscow were predicated on the assumption that the USSR was both weakened and threat-

---

5. Ibid., p. 70.

6. For de Gaulle's view on the international system and France's place therein, see Stanley Hoffmann, "De Gaulle's Foreign Policy: The Stage and the Play, the Power and the Glory," in his *Decline or Renewal: France since the 1930's* (New York: Viking, 1974), pp. 283–331; and Edward A. Kolodziej, *French International Policy under De Gaulle and Pompidou: The Politics of Grandeur* (Ithaca: Cornell University Press, 1974).

7. Fejtö, "France and China," pp. 46–51.

ened by the PRC's defection from the Soviet bloc. The French president reasoned that fear of China would induce the USSR to take its place as a partner within a European system of free and independent states stretching "from the Atlantic to the Urals."[8] This rather sanguine view of Soviet policy toward Europe was echoed during the mid-1960s by many French publicists. As a case in point, the noted journalist François Fejtö, writing in 1965 of a Soviet-American urge for a "sort of global condominium," argued that neither the USSR nor the United States "appear to the Europeans . . . to possess the political or ideological means which would permit them, in the existing framework, *to impose their will on the malcontents in their own camp.*"[9] The Soviet-led Warsaw Pact invasion of Czechoslovakia revealed instead that the USSR still had the will to dominate its allies and thus shattered the Gaullist vision of pan-European solidarity. Thereafter, Franco-Soviet détente, more notable for the formal consultative mechanisms to which it gave rise than for the actual harmonizing of policy that resulted, endured primarily as a symbol of French aspirations to greatpower status.

Still, negligible though the substantive achievements of French détente with the USSR and China in the 1960s may have been, the Sino-Soviet dispute unquestionably opened up dormant and uncharted avenues for de Gaulle's pursuit of an independent global role for France.

The connection between the Sino-Soviet dispute and the development of West Germany's Ostpolitik during the 1960s is less easy to establish. Bonn's partial overtures to Eastern Europe for the establishment of trade missions in the early 1960s, when Konrad Adenauer was still at the helm, can be more clearly linked to Sino-Soviet tensions than the full-blown Ostpolitik of Willy Brandt. Adenauer disclosed in his memoirs that when he visited Moscow in September 1955 to establish West German–Soviet diplomatic relations, Khrushchev expressed serious concern about the PRC. In Adenauer's words: "He declared that Red China was the great problem. 'Just think, Red China already has a population of over six hundred million. Its yearly increase is twelve million. They all live from a handful of rice. What,' and he clapped his hands together, 'what will come of all this?' "[10] The Soviet party leader then asked of the West German chancellor, "Help us. Help us to deal with Red China." Adenauer—influenced by the predictions of a German analyst, Wilhelm Starlinger, regarding the eventuality of Sino-Soviet enmity—concluded from this incident that a future split between Moscow and Beijing would enhance Bonn's opportunities for lever-

8. Kolodziej, *French International Policy*, p. 90.
9. Fejtö, "France and China," p. 44, emphasis added.
10. Quoted in William F. Griffith, *The Ostpolitik of the Federal Republic of Germany* (Cambridge, Mass.: M.I.T. Press, 1978), pp. 71–72.

age in the Soviet bloc.[11] It is in this light that the initial FRG opening to Eastern Europe in 1961–63—so soon after the shock of the Berlin Wall and in spite of Adenauer's long-standing intransigence on the issue—becomes comprehensible. For these were precisely the years that the Sino-Soviet conflict was coming into public view.

As for West Germany's relations with the PRC, after de Gaulle's recognition of Beijing in January 1964 Bonn responded favorably to Chinese approaches (begun in 1962) for steps toward a normalization of relations. Low-level negotiations on a formal trade treaty were initiated in Switzerland, only to be broken off the following autumn as a result of the PRC's refusal to accept the Berlin clause (that is, Bonn's right to represent West Berlin in trade and other matters).[12] In the meantime, however, in July 1964 Khrushchev had dispatched Adzhubei to the Federal Republic—as he had to Paris several months earlier—to speak of the Chinese threat and to convey his father-in-law's interest in visiting Bonn.[13] One may surmise that this initiative, which puzzled observers at the time and was foiled by Khrushchev's fall from power three months later, was intended in part to counter a possible Bonn-Beijing rapprochement.

By the time Willy Brandt became FRG foreign minister in late 1966, the PRC had withdrawn into the self-imposed isolation of the Cultural Revolution, thereby making the question of a normalization of relations moot and the specter of a Chinese threat to anyone scarcely credible (except in Washington). At the same time, Brandt publicly resolved not to play the "China card" in his pursuit of Ostpolitik. As he wrote in late 1968: "We are going a long way in order ... not to give [the Soviet Union] the impression that we are speculating on differences of opinion in the Communist camp. Thus we have rejected taking any initiative as far as the relations with the People's Republic of China are concerned ... A possible later settlement of our relations with the People's Republic of China will ... have to ... avoid arousing Moscow's suspicion that we might wish to exploit the Soviet's difficulties with China."[14] Despite his silence on the subject, Brandt—like Adenauer and de Gaulle—doubtless believed that the Sino-Soviet dispute had weakened the Soviet Union and strengthened the hand of those forces working for détente in Moscow. The speed with which the USSR moved toward rapprochement with Bonn and a resolution of the Berlin problem in the aftermath of the Sino-Soviet armed clashes on the Ussuri River gave credence to this assumption.[15]

11. Cf. ibid., p. 72.
12. I am grateful to Dr. Dieter Heinzig for clarification on this point.
13. Griffith, *Ostpolitik*, p. 129.
14. Willy Brandt, *A Peace Policy for Europe* (New York: Holt, Rinehart and Winston, 1969), pp. 94–95.
15. Cf. Griffith, *Ostpolitik*, pp. 165–66.

CHINESE PERCEPTIONS OF THE SOVIET "GRAND DESIGN" AND POLICIES TOWARD EUROPE

The PRC's strategic line in foreign policy for the 1970s was spelled out in the theory of the three worlds.[16] Its articulation first in 1974 and then more elaborately in 1977 closely paralleled Deng Xiaoping's rising political fortunes and Beijing's expanding ties with the advanced industrial states of Western Europe—in terms of diplomatic visits, commercial transactions, and overall political contacts. After several West European–Chinese exchanges at the foreign ministerial level in the first years of the 1970s, French President Georges Pompidou made a state visit to the PRC in September 1973, the first ever by a Western head of state; during 1974–75 FRG opposition leaders Helmut Kohl and Franz Josef Strauss as well as former British Prime Minister Edward Heath were warmly received in Beijing; and Sino-European trade experienced a simultaneous surge.[17] All these developments reflected, in turn, the normalization of Sino–West European diplomatic relations that accompanied the Sino–American rapprochement of 1971–72. An even more intense pattern of exchanges and trade began with the post-Mao transition and continues to this day. Beijing's practice was thus consistent with its theory. For the thrust of the three-worlds formula was the call for a united front between the Third World (with the PRC as the standard-bearer) and the Second World (above all Western Europe and Japan) against the more dangerous of the two imperialist superpowers, the Soviet Union.

While according to the three-worlds concept imperialism remained inherently aggressive, the United States was said to be on the decline and hence less expansionist and virulent than the Soviet Union, whose power was on the ascendancy. The prime target of Soviet hegemony, so the theory went, was Western Europe, the economy and technology of which would provide the wherewithal for the USSR to advance its ultimate goal of world domination. Moscow's praise of détente, push for the Helsinki accords, and participation in arms control negotiations were simply tactical maneuvers, a "smokescreen" to help cloak the Soviet Union's preparations to encircle and overrun Western Europe. PRC publicists argued, therefore, that those

---

16. The three worlds theory is spelled out in Deng Xiaoping's speech to the Sixth Special Session of the United Nations General Assembly, *Peking Review*, no. 16, April 19, 1974, pp. 6–11; also the *People's Daily* editorial, "Chairman Mao's Theory of the Differentiation of the Three Worlds Is a Major Contribution to Marxism-Leninism," *Peking Review*, no. 45, November 4, 1977, pp. 10–41.

17. For the surge in PRC-EC trade during 1973–74, see Commission of the European Communities, "The People's Republic of China and the European Community," *European Information* (Brussels), no. 17, February 1979, p. 9.

Western statesmen who responded favorably to Soviet blandishments on these accounts and who, to boot, extended aid to the Soviet economy were as guilty of appeasement as the signatories of the Munich agreement had been in 1938.[18] In the words of one of Beijing's chief commentators on this subject: "The attempt to use 'detente' to keep Soviet expansionism in check, the belief that the Soviet Union, as the 'Sonnenfeldt Doctrine' makes out, would be satisfied with its so-called 'organic relationship' with Eastern Europe and would not attack Western Europe, are policies of appeasement."[19]

All this rhetoric was but the mirror image of Chinese polemics on the threshold of the 1960s. Then, as in the 1970s, Beijing opposed détente (qua "peaceful coexistence") and steps toward arms control (the partial ban on nuclear testing); but in those days the Maoists maintained that the threat to peace came from the United States and its West European lackeys, while the Soviet leaders were seen as capitulationist but not yet imperialist. The evolution of the Beijing regime's theoretical outlook is beyond the scope of this essay.[20] As for the role of ideological conviction in the Chinese communists' world view, my assumption is that the PRC leaders, largely veterans of the civil war and true believers in a profound if inchoate (and often conflicting) vision of socialism, were compelled for the sake of their own self-respect and integrity to explain their shifting policy toward the West in an ideologically coherent manner. Pat references to Realpolitik would hardly have sufficed for either them or their followers. What is important here, however, is the utter constancy of Beijing's opposition to détente between Moscow and Washington. And the root of that opposition is to be found in national interest. Only under conditions of Soviet-American polarization and open hostility could the PRC hope to gain, from one bloc or the other, the political leverage to compensate for its military weakness and the economic and technological aid to satisfy its developmental needs. Hence its perennial role as international spoiler.

Beijing's portrayal of Soviet aggressive intentions toward Western Europe developed in tandem with its increasingly active support for West European economic integration and military strength. At the same time, the PRC justified such steps with reference not just to the hegemonic am-

---

18. See, for example, Ren Guping, "What Does the Situation Show One Year after the European Security Conference?" *Peking Review*, nos. 32–33, August 9, 1976, pp. 11–13; and by the same author, "The Munich Tragedy and Contemporary Appeasement," ibid., no. 50, December 9, 1977, pp. 6–11.

19. Ren Guping, "What Does the Situation Show One Year After," p. 12.

20. For an excellent overview see John Gittings, "New Light on Mao: His View of the World," *China Quarterly*, no. 60 (October–December 1974), pp. 750–66.

bitions of the Soviet Union but to its *vulnerability* as well. Chinese ideologues stigmatized Soviet "social-imperialism," like the U.S. brand two decades earlier, as in fact a "paper tiger," tough outside but brittle inside.[21] If only the Second World with Western Europe in the lead would rally behind the antihegemonist united front, they argued, the Soviet regime's aggressive aims could be curbed and war postponed into the indefinite future.

Beijing's Ties with the European Community. Chinese policy toward the European Community was far more favorable than that of the USSR. Throughout the 1970s Beijing welcomed the addition of new members, both actual and anticipated. In May 1975 it formally recognized the EC, and this resulted in the accreditation of a permanent PRC mission to the EC Commission in Brussels and in an increase in the number of official delegations traveling between EC headquarters and China. On April 3, 1978, the growing contacts culminated in the signing of an EC-PRC five-year trade framework agreement which included the most-favored-nation clause, provided for the creation of a joint committee to promote the growth and oversee the balance of trade, and held out the promise of the EC granting China the preferential treatment on tariffs enjoyed by the developing countries. In early 1979 a vice-chairman of the PRC National People's Congress expressed satisfaction at the coming direct elections to the European Parliament, which he called an event of great significance for the promotion of West European unity, and in June 1980 a Chinese delegation sat in as observers on a session of the—by then—directly elected body.[22]

By way of contrast, the USSR refused to recognize the EC or to enter into trade agreements with it, stipulating that the EC Commission instead enter into negotiations with Comecon.[23] Moscow thereby hoped not only to increase its leverage over East European trade with the EC member states but also to see its dependent trade bloc accorded the same international standing as the European Community. The Soviets also denounced the enlargement of the Community and the direct elections to the European Parliament, the latter on the ostensible grounds that the enhancement of the

---

21. "Soviet Social-Imperialism—Most Dangerous Source of War," *Peking Review*, no. 29, July 15, 1977, pp. 4–10, at pp. 9–10; cf. Ren Guping, "The Munich Tragedy," p. 11.

22. European Parliament, "Report on Economic and Trade Relations between the European Economic Community and the People's Republic of China," in *Working Documents, 1977–1978*, no. 76 (May 5, 1977), and "Report on the Trade Agreement between the European Economic Community and the People's Republic of China," in *Working Documents, 1978–1979*, no. 198 (July 3, 1978); see also Commission of the EC, "The People's Republic of China and the European Community."

23. See note 64 below.

supranational character of the EC would benefit big capital while the supposed democratization of its institutions would deflect the attention of the masses from their worsening economic plight.[24] Doubtless more to the point was Moscow's fear that a strengthened European Parliament might assume an even more pro-Chinese posture than it had in the past. As rather accurately reported in a spring 1979 *New Times* piece with regard to that body's conduct in the late 1970s:

> Some deputies, especially those from the conservative wing, take an active part in anti-Soviet campaigns. Noteworthy in this connection is the fact that EEC leaders, among them prominent M.P.'s, actively advocate promotion of economic and political ties with China, which the Peking leadership hopes to make use of to realize its hegemonistic and militarist plans. Visits to Peking were made early this year by CEC President Roy Jenkins and European Parliament's President Emilio Colombo, both of whom sought to establish closer relations between the Common Market and China.[25]

The divergent Sino-Soviet attitudes toward the European Community reflected, of course, the Chinese wish to strengthen West European unity and the Soviet hope of weakening it. In the words of then PRC Foreign Minister Qiao Guanhua before the United Nations General Assembly in October 1976, "We support the union of Western Europe, and we want to create a powerful Western Europe."[26] As early as 1971, in the aftermath of the Warsaw Pact invasion of Czechoslovakia and the Sino-Soviet skirmishes on their Manchurian border, PRC spokesman clearly signaled this intent. To be sure, the Chinese overtures to the EC during the early years of the decade were rife with appeals for West European defiance of U.S. hegemony as well as vigilance against the USSR's similar designs.[27] As Zhou Enlai said of France and China during President Pompidou's state visit in September 1973, "We both treasure our independence and sovereignty; we both brook no control, interference or aggression by any superpower in the world; and we both are against the monopoly of world affairs by the one or two superpowers."[28] At the time the EC-PRC trade treaty

---

24. I. Aleksandrov, "Evropeiskii parliament i aktualnye voprosy evropeiskoi politiki," *Pravda*, May 24, 1979; and Anatoly Savin, "Direct Elections to the European Parliament," *New Times* (Moscow), no. 21, May 1979, pp. 18–20.

25. Savin, "Direct Elections," p. 18.

26. European Parliament, "Report on Economic and Trade Relations," p. 9.

27. Dick Wilson, "China and the European Community," *China Quarterly*, no. 56 (October–December 1973), pp. 645–66, at pp. 649–52.

28. Text of banquet speech in *Peking Review*, no. 37, September 14, 1973, pp. 10–11.

was signed in 1978, however, the Chinese Foreign Trade Minister Li Qiang stressed the need for Western Europe to withstand above all the threat from Soviet hegemony.

The Call for German Reunification. The 1970s witnessed the normalization across the board of the PRC's relations with the individual states of Western Europe as well as with the European Community. Diplomatic relations were established where they had not hitherto existed (the FRG in October 1972, Italy in November 1970). Ambassadors were exchanged where representation had formerly been confined to political attachés (Great Britain in March 1972). The Sino–West German rapprochement, however, may be said to have even exceeded the normal: in ever more explicit terms, Beijing endorsed the goal of German reunification. On the occasion of the formal establishment of diplomatic ties, the Chinese foreign minister—at a banquet honoring his West German counterpart, Walter Scheel—spoke of the "abnormal situation" still prevailing as a result of the postwar division of Germany.[29] Two years later Chinese officials reportedly told visiting Christian Democratic Union leader Helmut Kohl that Beijing did not accept the notion of two Germanies, and they publicly toasted the "one German nation." On October 29, 1975, the day of Chancellor Helmut Schmidt's arrival in Beijing for a state visit, a *People's Daily* editorial affirmed that "the Chinese people deeply sympathize with and support the German people's firm opposition to a permanent splitting up of the German nation and their just desire for national unification." Thereafter, Schmidt met with Deng Xiaoping and Mao, and, according to German press reports, the two sides reached unanimity in support of the reunification of Germany.[30] When Hua Guofeng visited the FRG in October 1979, he reiterated the Chinese position on this issue in language almost identical to that used in 1975.[31]

As can be seen from the above references, Beijing refrained from explicitly calling for German reunification under West German auspices. On the other hand, the East German authorities had formally abandoned the goal of unification in the early 1970s, in the process of reaching an accommodation with Bonn over Berlin and the basic character of GDR-FRG relations. Thenceforth, for them as for their Soviet patrons, there existed two sovereign and separate Germanies, with one of them "forever and irrevocably allied with the USSR." All references to a united German nation

29. Text in *Peking Review*, no. 42, October 20, 1972, pp. 8–9.
30. U.S. Library of Congress, Congressional Research Service, Foreign Affairs and National Defense Division, *Recognizing the People's Republic of China* (Washington, D.C.: U.S. Government Printing Office, 1979), pp. 29–30.
31. Michael Getler, "Hua Calls for Reunification of Germany during Visit to Bonn," *Washington Post*, October 23, 1979.

or state were expunged from the revised GDR constitution and Soviet–East German treaty of alliance.[32] In contrast, the underlying premise of Willy Brandt's Ostpolitik had been to maintain a sense of German nationhood while moving incrementally toward a resolution of East-West differences and eventual reunification of Germany (and of Europe). His successor, Helmut Schmidt, remained no less committed to this vision. As he said in an interview with the London *Economist* shortly before Hua's state visit to Bonn: "I do not foresee under what auspices and conditions the Germans will get together again, but they will. . . . Maybe only in the 21st century. . . . But it would obviously be wrong for any European nation to believe that the nation-state is normal for any nation but not for the Germans."[33] In other words, since the FRG alone supported reunification, there was no need for the PRC to compromise itself ideologically by taking an explicit position for Bonn and against East Berlin on the sociopolitical character of a future unified Germany. All the more so since a reunified Germany would, in the Chinese perspective, belong to the Second World, hence could be expected to oppose the Soviet Union—a stand that would rule out any role for the current GDR political elite.

Beijing's expressions of support for German reunification represented an easy way of currying favor with the FRG public and thereby encouraging greater amity between Bonn and Beijing as well as, possibly, more beneficial trade terms. By raising the specter of a united Germany oriented toward the West, the PRC regime may have also hoped to alleviate Soviet pressure against China. Beyond such political considerations the Chinese leaders—themselves so intransigently opposed to the notion of "two Chinas"—may have felt a certain empathy for the Germans as a result of their mutual experience of truncated nationhood.

Sino–West European Strategic Independence. A logical corollary of the three-worlds theory was that Western Europe should beef up its military defenses against the Soviet threat and thus strengthen NATO as well. By the same token, it should contribute to the military modernization of China. As a *People's Daily* editorial pontificated when Hua Guofeng returned from his good-will tour of Western Europe in the fall of 1979, "It is imperative that the people of China and Western Europe work together *to defend world peace and security in both the Eastern and Western sides of the globe —the Asian and European continents.*"[34] Throughout his European travels

32. Foreign Broadcast Information Service, "USSR Counters West German Speculation on Reunification Issue," *Trends in Communist Media,* April 11, 1979, pp. 16–18.

33. "Schmidt's Calculabilities," *Economist,* October 6, 1979, pp. 47–54, at p. 54.

34. "Premier Hua's Historic Visit," *Peking Review,* no. 46, November 16, 1979, p. 8, emphasis added.

Hua had stressed, in modulated tones, the two regions' common strategic interests in containing Soviet expansionism.

In the early 1970s Beijing's appeals for NATO solidarity and strength were made *sotto voce*, in private conversations with visiting Western dignitaries. The PRC's public position was one of support for an independent West European defense force.[35] By the end of the decade, however, Chinese media and officials spoke in a matter-of-fact way about the Warsaw Pact's edge over NATO in regional weapons systems and force deployment, and about the need to rectify that imbalance. A spring 1979 editorial in *Peking Review* thus warmly endorsed the decision of the NATO countries to increase their military expenditures by 3 percent a year as well as the projected deployment of a U.S. "intermediate-range missile system" in Europe, observing approvingly that "Western Europe and the United States have improved cooperation to cope with the Soviet threat."[36] Feelers regarding the PRC's purchase of West European arms likewise intensified with the exchange of visits by Western and Chinese chiefs of staff and other ranking military officials. The first such delegation came from France in June 1976 —that is, after its leader, French Chief of Staff Guy Mery, as well as President Giscard d'Estaing, had signaled an interest in cooperating more closely with the NATO command.[37] Then in May 1978 British Chief of Staff Sir Neil Cameron traveled to Beijing, where he was heard to remark that Great Britain and China had "a common enemy with its capital in Moscow."[38] Meanwhile, the exchange of military delegations proliferated not only with France and Britain but also with West Germany, Italy, and other European states.

During the late 1970s, the most significant arms deal in sight was the anticipated British sale to the PRC of some eighty to one hundred Harrier jump jets, a vertical-takeoff defensive fighter particularly well suited to the vast undeveloped Sino-Soviet border areas. Discussed off and on since mid-1972, official talks on the subject were initiated during a ten-day visit to London by Chinese Vice-Premier Wang Zhen in November 1978 and continued during Hua's visit to London in November of the following year.[39]

35. Wilson, "China and the European Community," p. 650.
36. "Soviet Military Menace to West Europe," *Peking Review*, no. 15, April 13, 1979, pp. 22–24, especially p. 24.
37. "Quarterly Chronicle and Documentation," *China Quarterly*, no. 67 (September 1976), p. 681.
38. Reinhard Rummel, "China's Fixation on Western Europe," *Aussenpolitik* (English edition), 29, no. 3 (1978): 275–88, at p. 285.
39. Bih-jaw Lin, "British Relations with Communist China: An Evaluation," *Issues and Studies*, 15, no. 3 (March 1979): 65–76, at pp. 72–73; cf. Paul H. B. Godwin, "China and the Second World: The Search for Defense Technology," *Contemporary China*, 2, no. 3 (Fall 1978): 3–9, at p. 4.

At that time, press reports indicated that Prime Minister Margaret Thatcher was prepared to proceed with the sale, pending the outcome of interallied talks on the strategic implications of such a step.[40] In the end the deal did not go through, reportedly because of Beijing's reluctance to use scarce hard currency reserves or even credits for the purchase of outright—as opposed to "borderline"—military equipment. On the other hand, the expansion of Sino–West European trade, facilitated by China's signing of long-term trade agreements with France, Great Britain, and the FRG (December 1978, March 1979, and October 1979, respectively),[41] may in some cases have military ramifications.

SOVIET PERCEPTIONS OF THE CHINESE "GRAND DESIGN" AND POLICIES TOWARD EUROPE

Soviet ideologues have long accused the PRC of seeking to provoke a military collision between Moscow and Washington on the premise that China alone among the great powers would survive a nuclear holocaust to rule the world. But whereas in the 1960s the Soviet media portrayed the Maoists as pseudo-leftist chauvinists undermining "peaceful coexistence" from the sidelines, so to speak, in the 1970s the Soviets depicted the Chinese as virulent militarists who were actively colluding with the most reactionary imperialist forces, in Western Europe and elsewhere, to encircle the Soviet Union with a ring of hostile states. After a brief moratorium on anti-PRC attacks following Mao's death and a period of restrained polemics thereafter, the Brezhnev regime launched in the spring of 1978 an anti-Chinese campaign that rivaled the worst of the earlier periods of Sino-Soviet hostility.[42] Presumably a reaction to the intensified PRC overtures to Western Europe and Japan for trade, technology, and (in the case of Europe) arms, the renewed polemics coupled denunciations of Beijing's collaboration with imperialism with warnings against Western attempts to play the "China card." Beijing sought to torpedo détente, cautioned the Soviets, merely to further its own great-power ambitions and, to this end, to secure material and military advantages from the West. As a prominent Soviet publicist remarked in a commentary on Hua's autumn 1979 European tour, "they have decided to get everything they can from West Europe in

---

40. London Press Association in English, November 1, 1979, *Foreign Broadcast Information Service Daily Report—Western Europe*, November 2, 1979, pp. Q3–Q4.

41. See U.S. Department of Commerce, *China's Economy and Foreign Trade, 1978–1979* (Washington, D.C.: U.S. Government Printing Office, 1979), p. 11.

42. Morris Rothenberg, "The Kremlin Looks at China," *Contemporary China*, 3, no. 2 (Summer 1979): 25–35, at pp. 26–27; cf. the same author's *Whither China: The View from the Kremlin* (Washington, D.C.: Center for Advanced International Studies, University of Miami, 1977), passim.

order to strengthen China,"[43] an interpretation that was probably not far off the mark as far as it went. In a manner reminiscent of the 1960s, the USSR's charges against China thus focused more on power political arguments than on fitting Beijing's conduct into a global theory of international relations.

The Soviet media's frequent perorations on the PRC's instigation of an anti-Soviet axis of imperialism, reaction, and militarism (read China) were characteristic of Moscow's bent for hyperbole and conspiratorial explanations. All the same, there was a ring of truth to the Soviet rhetoric, if only because it so closely mirrored Beijing's admitted goals: namely, the creation of a united front between China and Western Europe against Soviet hegemony. On balance, however, it would appear that the Soviet leadership's anxiety over the PRC's intensification of contacts with Western Europe stemmed not from fear of any immediate threat to the USSR but from concern lest Chinese anti-Sovietism reinforce the views of Western conservatives and thereby abet the emerging West European hard-line opposition to Soviet military preeminence on the European continent.

From mid-1978 onward the Brezhnev regime resorted to a blend of blandishments and threats to counter rising Chinese influence in Western Europe (much as it had done during the preceding months with regard to the movement toward a peace and friendship treaty between Beijing and Tokyo, finally signed in August 1978). Two sequences of events stand out in particular. First, in the autumn of 1978 the projected British sale to China of Harrier jump jets prompted, on the one hand, a wide-ranging, concilitory interview on Soviet foreign policy by the Kremlin's "house liberal" Georgii Arbatov and, on the other, a volley of personal letters from Brezhnev to the leaders of Great Britain, France, West Germany, and Italy warning of dire consequences in the event of West European sales of military equipment to the PRC. Second, in the autumn of 1979, Hua's unprecedented visit to the major West European capitals may well have contributed to Moscow's decision to reduce unilaterally Soviet troops and tanks stationed in the GDR and to propose a conditional cutback in Soviet-based SS-20 missiles as well, a move quite obviously useful in offsetting Hua's anticipated philippics against Soviet expansionist designs. At the same time, Brezhnev threatened the European members of NATO, again in personal messages to their leaders, with stern countermeasures should they proceed with the deployment of U.S. Cruise and Pershing II missiles, a step that the Chinese publicly favored.

Since the early 1970s Beijing had been buying "dual purpose" technology—that is, civilian equipment that has some military utility—from the West. In December 1975 Beijing signed a "turnkey" contract with

43. A. Bovin, "Beijing's European Flirtation," *Izvestiia*, November 11, 1979.

Rolls-Royce for the purchase and licensed production of the Spey 202 engine. During 1977–78 the Chinese leaders began exploring opportunities for the procurement of a wide range of actual weapons, albeit largely defensive in character. The potential shopping list reportedly included French antitank and antiaircraft missiles, Italian helicopters, and West German Leopard tanks and armored vehicles.[44] But the initiation of formal negotiations for the British sale of the Harrier jump jets in early November 1978 represented a significant new threshold in Sino–West European relations.[45] Moscow clearly perceived it in this light. Earlier Soviet press warnings against unspecified military cooperation between China and the West were now spelled out in personal letters from Brezhnev to the leaders of the major West European powers. The specific contents of the notes were not publicly divulged, but informed sources indicated that the Soviet leader threatened an end to any semblance of arms control and détente and also forecast the eventual betrayal of the West by Beijing.[46]

At the same time, Arbatov's interview was published in the *Observer* and the *International Herald Tribune*. Some sense of its impact on informed British opinion may be gleaned from the reaction of Edward Crankshaw, the *Observer*'s seasoned expert on communist affairs, who called it "the most interesting thing to have come out of official Moscow since the fall of Khrushchev 14 years ago."[47] The interview did in fact represent a marked change of tone from official Soviet commentaries of the previous spring and summer. Among other things, the USSR's leading specialist on American affairs attributed President Carter's mid-1978 "tough" talk on U.S.-Soviet relations to the need to compensate for the "post-Vietnam syndrome" and downplayed the political influence in the White House of National Security Adviser Zbigniew Brzezinski. He thus conveyed an impression of Soviet reasonableness and receptivity to Soviet-American conciliation and movement toward arms control. On one point alone Arbatov was inflexible and alarmist: the prospect of China becoming "some sort of military ally to the West, even an informal ally . . . on an anti-Soviet basis." Such an eventuality, he warned, would put an end to détente, "even in a narrow sense," and lead to a surge "of chain reactions in the arms race." When queried specifically about the contemplated sale of the Harrier jets, he replied that "to begin arms sale to a country with a very hostile posture toward us and

44. David L. Shambaugh, "Military Modernization and the Politics of Technology Transfer," *Contemporary China*, 3, no. 3 (Fall 1979): 3–13, at pp. 6–9.

45. See note 39 above.

46. Dusko Doder, "Brezhnev Warns Britain on Sale of Jets to China," *Washington Post*, November 24, 1978.

47. Edward Crankshaw, "From Russia, with Reason," *Observer*, November 12, 1978.

many other countries cannot be considered a step that can be reconciled with good intentions."[48]

Moscow's none too subtle use of intimidation and cajolery provoked indignation at first, but in the end it seemed to have some impact. The four recipients of Brezhnev's letter refrained from a reply until the Guadeloupe summit meeting of Carter, Schmidt, Giscard, and the British Prime Minister, James Callaghan, in early January 1979. At that time Callaghan announced that his government would go ahead with the Harrier agreement anyway, a decision that dominated the first day of the summit talks. President Carter's press secretary said that the United States "would neither encourage nor discourage defensive weapon sales" to China, adding, "we understand from the British that the Harrier is defensive."[49] But the issue remained far from settled. Callaghan took pains to reassure Moscow that the arms deal with Beijing was in no way aimed at the USSR. British relations with the Soviet Union were as important as relations with China, he insisted; indeed, ties to Moscow were central to the efforts to reduce tension in Europe.[50] Schmidt, however, was by far the most eager to soothe Soviet sensitivity on the subject. He assured journalists that the FRG would stay away from the "explosive theme" of arms sales altogether, and reportedly warned the allies not to "poke a stick into the cage of the bear."[51] Giscard apparently remained wholly aloof from the controversy, presumably to project the image of France as a mediator among the contending European and Atlantic powers. All four heads of government publicly affirmed their support for SALT II and their conviction that U.S. normalization of relations with Beijing would not endanger détente with Moscow.[52]

Moscow's use of the carrot and the stick in the autumn of 1979 was even more dramatic. On October 6, in a speech delivered in East Berlin on the GDR's thirtieth anniversary, Brezhnev unexpectedly announced the withdrawal of twenty thousand Soviet troops and one thousand tanks from East Germany and also proposed to reduce the number of medium-range nuclear

48. Georgii Arbatov interviewed by Jonathan Power, "The New Voice of the Kremlin," ibid., pp. 15–17; see especially p. 17 on the Harrier jets.

49. Flora Lewis, "Britain Will Sell Fighters to China, Callaghan Says at Summit Meeting," *New York Times*, January 6, 1979.

50. Laurence Marks, "West Fears for Arms Pact," *Observer*, January 7, 1979; cf. Thomas Kielinger, "China darf niemals Hindernis für Entspannung mit Moskau sein," *Die Welt*, January 8, 1979.

51. Diethart Goos and Thomas Kielinger, "In der sonnigen Karibik Suche nach dem Gleichgewicht der Welt," *Die Welt*, January 6, 1979; Terence Smith, "At Summit Talks, Britain, France and West Germany Join in Vow that Relations Won't Harm Détente," *New York Times*, January 7, 1979.

52. See notes 49–51 above.

missiles deployed in the western USSR, with the latter offer contingent on a U.S.-NATO freeze on theater nuclear weapons. The Russian leader pledged, furthermore, that countries refusing to accept nuclear arms on their soil would never become the target of Soviet nuclear retaliation.[53]

These overtures, uncharacteristic of the Brezhnev leadership in that it had in the past opposed in principle the idea of unilateral force reductions,[54] were above all aimed at forestalling the contemplated NATO decision to deploy U.S. Pershing II and Tomahawk Cruise missiles. All the same, the Chinese connection here—as in so many other Soviet–West European interactions—was not far below the surface. Any doubts regarding a linkage between Brezhnev's speech and Hua Guofeng's European tour were laid to rest when, on the eve of Hua's arrival in Europe in mid-October, the Soviet chief dispatched to all the NATO leaders a four-page personal letter reiterating his October 6 offers as well as the threat of an open-ended arms race should his proposal regarding a missile freeze not be heeded.[55]

Moscow's reaction to Hua's European trip was otherwise relatively low-key if contrasted with the autumn 1978 warnings against a Sino–West European military entente or the Soviet media's August 1978 outburst against Hua's East European tour. With regard to coverage of the latter event in the central Soviet press, the PRC premier's trip to Romania and Yugoslavia provoked a barrage of hostile commentaries while his activities in Western Europe a year later elicited only a few critical articles. The explanation for this discrepancy is not entirely clear. It was doubtless related in part to the fact that the East European trip involved ties between communist party-states, with one of them a Soviet ally at that, while the West European trip could be construed as harmonizing, at least formally, with the USSR's much touted policy of peaceful coexistence. The Soviet reserve in 1979 may also have been induced by the concurrent if ultimately unsuccessful Sino-Soviet reconciliation talks as well as by a reluctance to inform the Soviet public of the details of Hua's Western tour.

Still, the coincidence *in timing* between Brezhnev's force-reduction offer and Hua's visit to Paris, Bonn, London, and Rome underscored the Soviet leadership's worry that Chinese agitation regarding a Soviet military build-up and expansionist threat in Europe might stiffen the will of those European leaders prepared to accept the new U.S. missiles. In short, the unconditional force-pullback announcement—if not the more provisory offer of a reduction in missiles—was partly intended to blunt the impact of Beijing's anti-Soviet rhetoric.

53. Text in *Pravda*, October 7, 1979.
54. Foreign Broadcast Information Service, *Trends in Communist Media*, October 11, 1979, p. 4.
55. Leonard Downie, Jr., "Brezhnev Appeals to U.S. Allies," *Washington Post*, October 17, 1979.

The Soviet gambit had an appreciable if limited effect. The Western press generally depicted Hua's hosts, with the exception of Prime Minister Thatcher, as bending over backward to avoid provoking Moscow. They reportedly urged Hua's public restraint on the subject of the USSR.[56] Indeed, Herbert Wehner, chairman of the parliamentary faction of the German Social Democratic Party (SPD), was quoted as saying before Hua's arrival in the FRG: "We will not let ourselves be prodded into taking a position against the Soviet Union,"[57] a view that was echoed by some government spokesmen. Official circles in Bonn and elsewhere were agitated even by the Chinese leader's rather circumspect allusions to the threat from "aggression and hegemonism." As a result of this pervasive fear of appearing to be "anti-Soviet," one perceptive Italian commentator, Piero Ostellino, wrote of the "psychological hegemonization" of Europe.[58] In the end, however, Moscow's campaign against the modernization of the Atlantic Alliance's theater nuclear forces was itself foiled when the NATO defense ministers decided in principle the following December to proceed with the deployment of the controversial U.S. missiles (conditional upon the failure of regional arms control talks).

PARTISAN CLEAVAGES AND WEST EUROPEAN POLICY TOWARD MOSCOW AND BEIJING

West European cleavages over how to deal with the Sino-Soviet dispute may be said for analytical purposes to have developed along three major lines, which, for want of more felicitous terms, shall be called center-left, conservative, and third-force. Let me point out that I use these terms solely with reference to foreign policy positions. The center-left favored good relations with both the USSR and the PRC but accorded priority to détente with the USSR. Conservatives were suspicious of détente from its inception and ever more prone to improve their ties with Beijing as a means of exerting pressure on Moscow. Third-force elements sought to maneuver within the Moscow-Washington-Beijing triangle in order to enhance their own and, incidentally, West European independence and influence. It should be emphasized that both the conservatives and the center-left remained committed to NATO and Atlanticism: hence the initial Soviet and Chinese preference for the third-force groups, or Europeanists. During the course of the decade, however, as Soviet-American ties soured and Sino-American friendship blossomed, the rapport between Beijing and the West European

56. John Vinocur, "Chairman Hua in the West," *New York Times*, October 29, 1979; cf. note 31 above.
57. "Heute erste Gespräche Hua Kuo-fengs mit Schmidt," *Frankfurter Allgemeine Zeitung*, October 22, 1979.
58. "Che cosa propone all'Italia l'uomo che viene da Pechino," *Corriere della sera*, November 3, 1979.

conservatives intensified while the center-leftists strove to preserve an atmosphere of détente with Moscow. The third-force groups meanwhile tilted either toward Moscow or Beijing, depending on which orientation appeared to them most likely to enhance their own power position within Europe.

The third-force elements, albeit highly heterogeneous in their *domestic* political profiles, shared in common a preference for West European unity of action in relation to both superpowers. Their ranks thus included *inter alia* the successive French "regimes" of Presidents Pompidou and Giscard d'Estaing, the European Community Commissioners, and even to some extent the Europeanist wing of the British Conservative Party led by Edward Heath and the increasingly revisionist Italian Communist Party (the French Communist Party remained on the far left in terms of its largely pro-Soviet foreign policy alignment). These diverse groups will be discussed in reverse order.

The Italian Communist Party (PCI) from the early 1970s proclaimed its support for a Europe "neither anti-Soviet nor anti-American," and, as its divergence with the CPSU deepened, it assumed a conciliatory position toward Washington and made discreet overtures for a reconciliation with Beijing. This gradual realignment was temporarily halted during 1977–78, owing to complications arising from the PCI's quasi-governmental role at the Italian national level. Paradoxically, the Italian communist leadership's policy of political accommodation at home obliged it to mend its bridges with Moscow in order to reassure its rank-and-file militants of its ongoing revolutionary credentials. With its return to the parliamentary opposition in 1979 and the shock of Afghanistan soon thereafter, however, the PCI proceeded once again to distance itself from Moscow, to seal its rapprochement with Beijing, and to intensify its search for political space and influence among West European centrist and moderate leftist forces in general as well as within the European Parliament.[59]

Less attention need be devoted to the third-force tendency of Edward Heath, because he represented on this issue a minority current within his party's ranks and remained, to boot, supportive of the Atlantic Alliance. Still, on his trip to Beijing in mid-1974 Heath was given an "unprecedented" and "rapturous" welcome, apparently because of his pro-EC policies and support for greater West European autonomy in relation to Washington and Moscow. As NCNA reported, the former prime minister maintained

---

59. For a study of PCI foreign policy and relations with the USSR in the 1970s, see Joan Barth Urban, "Moscow and the PCI in the 1970s: Kto Kovo?" *Studies in Comparative Communism*, 13, nos. 2–3 (Summer–Autumn 1980): 9–167.

that "it is right that you in China and we in Europe and many other countries should have our say and that when we speak the superpowers should listen."[60] Heath was received by Mao both then and during a second trip to Beijing some fifteen months later.[61] Yet soon his authority within his own party was to diminish as Margaret Thatcher became the Conservative Party leader and shadow prime minister.

As for the EC Commission, its third-force character could be discerned in its urge to increase its powers and to implement those that the member states had already granted it. With this goal in mind it welcomed the PRC's recognition of the EC in 1975, and Eurocrats in Brussels took care to expedite agreement on the PRC-EC trade framework treaty signed in April 1978. On the one hand, this move helped to concretize the authority accorded by the EC members to the Commission since January 1975 to conduct trade negotiations with the state-trading countries of Eastern Europe and Asia.[62] On the other hand, the Commission hoped thereby to exert pressure on the USSR (and its Comecon associates) to recognize the EC and to deal with it directly on matters of East-West trade.[63] In this sense the Commission may be said to have played the "China card" but with the ultimate goal of enhancing its own stature rather than, as in the case of the conservatives, of containing Soviet power.

It was, of course, official France under Pompidou and, to a lesser extent, Giscard that played the third-force role to the hilt. As already noted, President Pompidou was, in September 1973, the first West European head of state to visit Beijing. On that occasion he spoke eloquently of the cultural affinities and mutuality of views shared by China and France, stressing their "right of not allowing themselves to be disarmed" and their joint recognition of the need to build, "by the side of the very big powers, strong, coherent and united communities that are necessary for the equilibrium and peace of the world."[64] In May 1975 Deng Xiaoping paid a return visit to France—his first ever to the West—during which similar sentiments were

60. "Quarterly Chronicle and Documentation," *China Quarterly*, no. 59 (July–September 1974), p. 649.
61. Ibid., no. 64 (December 1975), pp. 812–13.
62. John Robinson, "Europe's Links with China," *European Community*, no. 7, July 1975, pp. 9–10.
63. Leo Ryan, "China, Comecon Tense Rivalry for European Community Tie," *Journal of Commerce*, October 17, 1977; John Robinson, "EEC Quickly Approves Trade Talks with China" and "EC Interest Growing in Economic Links with China" in *Washington Post*, November 23, 1977, and November 9, 1978.
64. Text of banquet speech in *Peking Review*, no. 37, September 14, 1973, pp. 11–12.

voiced, with then Premier Jacques Chirac extolling the French and Chinese appreciation "that they should not give way to anyone, however strong, to decide their affairs."[65] Throughout the rest of the decade President Giscard reiterated these same themes of sovereign independence and the right to nuclear self-defense, notwithstanding the growing tacit cooperation between the French military establishment and NATO.

All the while, of course, both Pompidou and Giscard continued to encourage the periodic Franco-Soviet consultations at the highest level that de Gaulle had initiated. Moscow responded in kind, even as the *union de la gauche* mounted its electoral challenge in France. Brezhnev went hunting with Pompidou in the western USSR just weeks before the March 1973 election to the French National Assembly. The Soviet ambassador to France chose the week between the two rounds of the May 1974 French presidential contest to consult with then candidate Giscard in his capacity as finance minister. In March 1975 Premier Chirac visited the USSR, to be followed by President Giscard in October 1975. And in June 1977 Brezhnev paid a return visit to Paris. This unabated display of Franco-Soviet amity at the governmental level angered the French Communist Party to the point that it publicly accused the CPSU of preferring the status quo to social transformation in France and launched a two-year flirtation with Eurocommunism beginning in late 1975.[66]

Official Franco-Soviet harmony during the 1970s was clearly related to Moscow's pursuit of East-West détente and France's preoccupation with its third-force role. Yet the relationship between the USSR and France cannot be fully understood without reference to the PRC. Had Beijing not been so eager to court the French, Moscow probably would have shown more restraint in its relations with the Élysée at such a delicate time in domestic French politics. On the other hand, as the 1970s drew to a close and Sino-American ties began to flourish, Paris evidently started to worry that its public image (if not its public philosophy of global balance-of-power politics) might suffer from too close an association with China. The French government thus tilted perceptibly toward Moscow. Paris, for example, blocked for several months during the spring of 1979 the start of PRC-EC negotiations on a projected textile trade agreement, reportedly in order that Giscard might make a favorable impression on the Soviet Union during his

65. "Vice-Premier Teng Hsiao-ping Visits France," *Peking Review*, no. 20, May 16, 1975, pp. 3–5, at p. 3; cf. "Vice-Premier Teng Concludes Visit to France," ibid., no. 21, May 13, 1975, pp. 3–4.

66. For details see Joan Barth Urban, "The Ties that Bind: West European Communism and the Communist States of East Europe," *The European Left: Italy, France, and Spain*, ed. William E. Griffith (Lexington, Mass.: Lexington Books, 1979), pp. 203–37.

trip to Moscow in late April.⁶⁷ Similarly, Giscard's controversial talks with Brezhnev in May 1980, the first by a Western leader after the Soviet invasion of Afghanistan, seemed intended above all to distance France from the mounting Sino-American entente,⁶⁸ a relationship that was publicly highlighted by the steady stream of official delegations between Washington and Beijing, including a visit by the U.S. secretary of defense to the PRC in January 1980.⁶⁹

In contrast to most third-force groups, the center-leftists and conservatives actively supported the Atlantic Alliance, including military coordination within NATO. Their principal foreign-policy differences for our purposes centered on their attitudes toward Moscow and Beijing (which obviously reflected, in turn, their assessment of the Soviet threat to Europe). The center-leftists called for an evenhanded approach to both communist powers; hence they were reluctant to countenance any ties with the PRC that might destabilize relations with the USSR. Their ranks included among others the SPD government in Bonn, the left wing of the British Labour Party, and the mainstream French Socialists. The conservatives for their part were openly pro-Chinese. They included Prime Minister Thatcher's government in London and the West German opposition, the Christian Democratic Union/Christian Socialist Union alliance (CDU/CSU). The divergent views of these two broad political constellations may be briefly illustrated by detailing their reactions to Hua Guofeng's European tour, on the one hand, and their position on EC relations with China, as articulated in the debates of the European Parliament, on the other.

The domestic West German differences over the proper policy to follow toward China emerged from the carefully choreographed reactions of government and opposition spokesmen to Hua's visit in October 1979. The ruling SPD's worry about possible anti-Soviet polemics, publicly voiced on the eve of the PRC leader's arrival, has already been noted. As it turned out, Hua respected his hosts' sensitivities—and demonstrated his own political acumen—by emphasizing the PRC's support for German reunification rather than dwelling on China's perception of the Soviet military

67. See the analyses by Guy de Jonquieres, "China Seeking to Treble Sales of Textiles to EEC" and "Paris Block on Textiles Negotiations with China" in the *Financial Times*, March 15, 1979, and April 4, 1979.

68. Cf. Ronald Koven, "French-Soviet Meeting Puzzles Europe," *Washington Post*, May 27, 1980; Koven argues, unconvincingly, that Giscard met with Brezhnev in order to win French communist support in the French presidential contest in 1981.

69. For a rosy official assessment of Sino-American friendship as of mid-1980, see Richard C. Holbrooke, "China and the United States: Into the 1980s," *Department of State Bulletin*, 80, no. 2041 (August 1980): 49–51.

threat.[70] Both positions were, of course, anathema to the USSR. Consequently, despite the Soviet media's generally restrained response to Hua's tour, Radio Moscow reacted virulently to the talk of reunification in a broadcast to Germany. After alluding to "revanchist politicians on the Rhine," the commentator added: "With their thesis on the continuing existence of a unified German nation Hua Guofeng and his Federal German admirers and worshipers are far away from all historical reality."[71] All the same, the SPD leaders had little choice but to welcome Hua's public stance on this issue, since it so closely coincided with their own. At the same time, Bonn clung to its evenhanded policy by concluding during Hua's visit a trade framework agreement with Beijing which treated the latter no differently from Moscow—despite the PRC's pressing need for low-interest state credits if bilateral trade was to grow.[72] Moreover, the FRG Foreign Ministry announced a forthcoming visit to Bonn by Soviet Foreign Minister Andrei Gromyko on October 26, the day of Hua's arrival in Munich for extended talks with the CDU/CSU candidate for the FRG chancellorship, Franz Josef Strauss.[73]

Strauss, in his capacity as Bavarian premier as well as federal candidate, made the most of Hua's visit to Munich and to the FRG in general by challenging the hypersensitive federal government on foreign policy and strategic matters at every turn. As a start, he received Hua at the Munich railway station with much pomp and circumstance, a step which was greatly played up by his campaign strategists, since Schmidt did not greet the Chinese visitors in an airport ceremony upon their arrival in Bonn. More important, in his public encounters with Hua the Bavarian leader spoke of the Soviet Union's "unreasonably high" arms expenditures, Europe's military weakness, and the danger of détente becoming a "smokescreen" behind which one side might alter the military balance in its favor.[74] On all three accounts he was expressing views known to be held by Beijing as well. And in doing so he was in effect appealing for countermeasures on the part of Europe and NATO. Strauss made a point of thanking Schmidt for calling for a "strong China." No public mention was made of possible future FRG

70. Cf. "Wirtschafts- und Kulturabkommen mit China unterzeichnet," *Frankfurter Allgemeine Zeitung*, October 25, 1979.

71. Valentin Zakharov, "By the Federal German-Chinese Fireside," Moscow in German to Germany, October 30, 1979, in *Foreign Broadcast Information Service Daily Report—Soviet Union*, November 1, 1979, p. F2.

72. Hans-J. Mahnke, "Chinas Forderungen," *Die Welt*, October 25, 1979.

73. Hamburg DPA in German, October 26, 1979, in *Foreign Broadcast Information Service Daily Report—Western Europe*, October 29, 1979, p. J3.

74. "Gut, wenn Schmidt mir folgt," *Die Welt*, October 27, 1979; see also the commentaries by Herbert Kremp and Peter Schmalz in *Die Welt*, October 29, 1979.

arms sales to Beijing, a step allegedly favored by elements within the CDU/ CSU but opposed by official Bonn. One may only speculate on the extent to which these themes were elaborated during the two-hour private luncheon in Strauss's home that formally concluded Hua's visit to West Germany.

During the Chinese premier's visit to London the internal British differences over relations with Russia and China did not surface as markedly as they had in the FRG, partly because the right wing of the Labour Party was not all that far apart from Prime Minister Thatcher on this issue. It was, after all, former Prime Minister Callaghan who had first approved the sale to China of the Harrier jump jet, his professed interest in good relations with the Soviet Union notwithstanding. There were, to be sure, remonstrances against the zeal with which Hua and Thatcher expressed their mutual agreement on the "enormity" of the Soviet threat and their aversion to any kind of "yielding" to it.[75] As the *Manchester Guardian* protested, editorially, "We are beginning to get the measure of the Soviet problem. . . . It complicates this process if Chairman Hua . . . tries to force us into anti-Russian postures which we do not want to adopt."[76] But a better understanding of the British version of the conservative and center-left split on how to deal with the Sino-Soviet-European triangle can be had, in capsule form, by looking at the EC parliamentary debates on this question.

British delegates to the European Parliament were among the most outspoken supporters or opponents, as the case might be, of developing an EC-PRC political entente directed against the USSR. Immediately after the conclusion of the April 1978 trade framework agreement between the European Community and Beijing, Lord Bessborough of the European Conservative Group launched a campaign to broaden the scope of EC-PRC ties to include political and even military issues. He hailed the agreement as an opportunity to seal the "increasingly close relations" between the Community and China—"two regions which, I fear I must say, must seek to contain the expansionary aims of a region inbetween"—and included in the potential list of items to be sold to Beijing "aircraft and defense equipment."[77] His suggestion of giving a political cast to the trade agreement was

75. Clare Hollingworth, "Hua Has Talks at No. 10" and "Thatcher Praised by Chairman Hua," *Daily Telegraph*, October 30 and 31, 1979.

76. "Tweedledee and Chairman Hua," *Manchester Guardian*, November 1, 1979.

77. *Official Journal of the European Communities: Debates of the European Parliament*, no. 229 (April 1978), Sitting of April 11, 1978, pp. 73–74. Illustration of the British viewpoint through references to debates in the European Parliament shows the prominence of the Sino-Soviet-European triangle in EC thinking. Moreover, in the 1970s British Members of the European Parliament were (after their belated entry) among the most active in that body's deliberations, and Conservative MEPs placed particular emphasis on the discussion of foreign

promptly rebuffed by his compatriot Lord Kennet, speaking on behalf of the Socialist Group. The latter argued that the April 1978 agreement was merely a trade treaty and should remain just that.[78] In February 1979 when Lord Bessborough again raised the issue of broader Community ties with China, Lord Kennet replied that the Socialist Group would welcome a "high level of *mutually* beneficial trade with China" but insisted that this desire was "not a function of anything we may feel about the Soviet Union."[79] The following month Mr. Dalyell of Scotland took the political bull by the horns, flatly conceding that some of the delegates had "very grave difficulties about the export of arms to China." The PRC should understand, he warned, "that it really would be reckless to provoke the Russians by exporting great amounts of arms to the Chinese."[80] Subsequent discussions became more technical, often focusing on the question of how Beijing might make repayments in kind for its purchases of capital equipment from the EC without unduly disrupting West European markets, a subject on which the Labourites displayed keen sensitivity. As one M.P. commented soon after the mid-1979 initialing of the much debated EC-PRC textile agreement, "It would appear to my constituents in Yorkshire West that every decision that the Commission takes in the field of textiles results in a loss of jobs to them."[81] Foreign policy differences thus reflected —or acquired—a domestic economic rationale.

A few more words should suffice on the question of the West European partisan differences on how best to pursue relations with Moscow and Beijing. In the European Parliament as elsewhere the French Socialist delegates frequently echoed the views of their British associates in the Labour Party. The Italian Christian Democrats (DC) sided with Lord Bessborough in the EC but were more restrained at home, a reflection of the fragility of the successive coalition governments presided over by the DC in Rome. At the root of all the differences, of course, lay divergent assessments of the meaning and feasibility of genuine détente between Western Europe and the USSR.

Briefly to tie together the central themes of this chapter, the Sino-Soviet dispute facilitated the emergence of East-West détente. At the same time,

---

policy issues; see Geoffrey Pridham and Pippa Pridham, "Transnational Parties in the European Community I," *Political Parties in the European Community*, ed. Stanley Henig (London: George Allen and Unwin, 1979), pp. 245–77, at pp. 264–68.

78. *Official Journal . . . : Debates*, no. 229 (April 1978), p. 76.

79. Ibid., no. 239 (February 1979), Sitting of February 15, 1979, p. 207; emphasis added.

80. Ibid., no. 241 (March 1979), Sitting of March 14, 1979, p. 127.

81. Ibid., no. 245 (September 1979), Sitting of September 27, 1979, p. 233.

as long as there was a real relaxation of tensions between Moscow and Western Europe, on the one hand, and Moscow and Washington on the other, little political space remained in which Beijing could effectively maneuver. Conversely, it was perhaps natural that in the later 1970s those West Europeans who perceived the global correlation of forces to be shifting in the USSR's favor—in terms of political will as well as military power—would urge support across the board for Beijing as a means of putting pressure on the Soviet Union's Eastern flank. These observations are by now commonplace. What is not so often spelled out is the extent to which China was a *player* rather than a "card" in the international politics of the 1970s. The PRC's eagerness to cultivate close ties with Western Europe was apparent at the outset of the decade, and it was plainly as instrumental as the calculations of Western policy makers in effecting the international realignments that occurred.

There is yet another conclusion that may be drawn with regard to the overall impact of the Sino-Soviet dispute in Western Europe. It may be argued that the PRC's assertion of sovereign independence in relation to the USSR served as an example and prod to West European rejection of the postwar pattern of U.S. patronage. Although the American–West European relationship was not fraught with the official and popular antagonism that characterized the Sino-Soviet experience, West Europeans nevertheless often exhibited the same sense of cultural superiority toward the United States that the Chinese so readily flaunted with regard to the USSR. To be sure, specific differences between Washington and its European allies over Middle East policy, the geopolitical purview of NATO, and the very definition of détente increasingly weakened Atlantic solidarity. Still, one may surmise that the sight of Beijing "standing up" to Moscow elicited a sympathetic response among West European policy makers and encouraged them, for reasons other than sheer Realpolitik, to do the same with regard to their own erstwhile patrons. As a British writer commented in 1973, "It may seem increasingly attractive to Europeans to call in the old world of China to redress the balance of the brash new worlds of America and the Soviet Union."[82]

The real novelty on the threshold of the 1980s, however, was that as Soviet-American tensions revived fears of a new cold war, U.S.–West European disagreements over détente multiplied while the urge of the continental Europeans to distance themselves from the United States intensified. The definition of détente by center-left and third-force European statesmen had long embraced political and economic considerations as well as the military balance. It was now extended to include the character of relations with China: in their view, Western normalization of ties with the PRC was not to be undertaken in such a way as to reinforce international bipolarity.

82. Wilson, "China and the European Community," p. 664.

Thus as Washington turned toward Beijing, Paris and Bonn turned toward one another. During early July 1980 President Carter made his most explicit allusion to date of Sino-American cooperation aimed against the Soviet Union. Shortly before talks with Hua Guofeng in Tokyo, Carter called the U.S.-PRC normalization of relations "a means by which we can share our long-range strategic concerns to minimize the threat of the Soviet military buildup."[83] At that very time President Giscard d'Estaing was in West Germany on the first state visit by a French chief of state in eighteen years. The end result of the ceremonial Giscard-Schmidt summit was to bring into the international limelight the community of interests and complementarity of power that undergirded the mounting Franco–West German initiatives in foreign policy. It seems entirely too facile to ascribe this development simply to malaise over the Carter administration's vacillation in foreign policy or, worse yet, to a kind of "self-Finlandization" in relation to the Soviet Union. A broader purview would see France and the FRG assuming the role accorded them by virtue of their geopolitical attributes and postwar political culture. Sooner or later this trend toward a more politically self-sufficient, coalescing Europe led by Paris and Bonn was bound to develop. But it seems probable that Washington's precipitous tilt toward Beijing hastened its emergence.

83. William Chapman, "Carter, Hua Meet for Wide-Ranging Talks," *Washington Post*, July 10, 1980.

PART 3

Overview and Assessment

Perspectives

Alternative Western Views of the Sino-Soviet Conflict*

DONALD W. TREADGOLD

"Heaven is high and the emperor is far away," says both a Russian and a Chinese proverb. It was no doubt true for thousands or millions of ordinary subjects of the Russian and Chinese emperors. For the Russians, this would apply to the period from 1721 to 1917, when the term "Empire" was the official one, and to the era of the tsars of Muscovy during the previous quarter millennium; for the Chinese, the period stretches from 221 B.C. to 1911. The worm's eye view of the Russian and Chinese peasant may not have changed much during the centuries concerned; in the opinion of many scholars there were also important elements of continuity in both countries to be found in the way the state was operated and society was organized. But foreign relations were a different matter. The identity of the neighbors of both Russia and China changed many times. For a time both Russia and China were ruled by the same power, the Mongols; direct relations between the two states date only from 1689 and more or less close contact only from the mid-nineteenth century. Many of the books and articles that will be examined below have little to say concerning the past, and the summary statements about it they contain are often inaccurate in the sweeping form in which they are presented. What they do say about the subjects they explore in detail is apt to be factual, detached, and objective.[1] Their authors, feeling

---

* I acknowledge with thanks the assistance of Lawrence Lerner and Bert Patenaude in bibliographical and research assistance rendered in the preparation of this essay, as well as support from the School of International Studies of the University of Washington.

1. Contrast, for example, the quality of the spate of books published during the last decade or two on the so-called cold war, or those dealing with the con-

no particular obligation to defend the polemical positions taken up by either Moscow's or Beijing's spokesmen at a given moment, strive to study the topic in a scholarly manner. Nevertheless, like any other works of scholarship, they may legitimately be subjected to critical evaluation.

THE ZAGORIA BOOK

Donald S. Zagoria's *Sino-Soviet Conflict, 1956–1961*, was the pathfinding study.[2] In its account of events and its analysis it has stood up very well. (Zagoria in the introduction to the 1964 reprint wisely disclaimed any intention to keep revising and updating the book, p. xii.) Its predictions were less successful: not only is there no possibility, he wrote, of a Soviet-U.S. alliance, but there is even less prospect of "wooing China away from the USSR" (p. 22). Granted, "wooing away" does not well describe Nixon's policy in 1971–72, but there was certainly no expectation on the author's part of any kind of Chinese-U.S. rapprochement. Moreover, there was no hint that a post-Mao leadership might pursue such a relationship; the author cites a joke current in Moscow in 1964 (p. xi) that no improvement in relations with Beijing could be looked for until there was a "Maosoleum." There now exists a Mao tomb in Lenin style, and relations are worse than ever.

Zagoria declares that there are—continuing now to use 1961 as basis for the present tense—three schools of thought on the dispute. The first holds the conflict to be of little consequence, as the PRC and the USSR share a single overriding aim. The second declares a break between the two inevitable. The third believes that a common commitment to the revolutionary process on a worldwide scale will set limits to the dispute. The first school, asserts the author, ignores the evidence; few will quarrel with his statement, and little is heard from such quarters nowadays. The second, he says, fails to understand international communism, for the conflict "in large measure derives from the fact that although both partners are committed to worldwide revolution under Communist leadership, they often disagree on the strategy and tactics for pursuing that goal" (p. 5). Zagoria places himself in the third school. In his preface of 1964, he admits that he underestimated the extent of rationality on the part of both Moscow and Beijing and thought that the ideology would set limits, whereas it has in fact sharpened the conflict. From the foregoing it is clear that Zagoria takes the communism of

---

flict in Vietnam, quite irrespective of the bias or partisanship of the authors. There are, of course, honorable exceptions, as there exist far from objective discussions of the Sino-Soviet dispute.

2. Donald S. Zagoria, *The Sino-Soviet Conflict, 1956–1961*, with a new preface (New York: Atheneum, 1964). Reprinted from Princeton University Press ed., 1962.

Alternative Western Views of the Sino-Soviet Conflict 327

both Moscow and Beijing seriously and in fact sets his whole analysis in the framework of the story of the international movement and its ideological commitments.

He dates the dispute to the Twentieth Congress of the CPSU and Khrushchev's secret speech. In so identifying the beginning of the conflict, he has been followed by most of those who came after him. The reasons for doing so he gives as Khrushchev's definition of Soviet policy on the way to building socialism in communist-ruled states, the fact that the Chinese communists themselves trace the dispute to that time, and China's subsequent entrance into East European affairs. Those who would explain the dispute as basically prompted by different responses to the death of Stalin (1953) on the part of Moscow and Beijing may still be willing to accept the Twentieth Congress as the best date for its inception, for the intervening three years were ones of hesitation and uncertainty in each capital about how to proceed, and of caution about reaction in the other capital.[3]

Zagoria then lists six factors underlying the dispute (pp. 13–20):

1. Claims made for Mao as one of the Fathers (my term) of Marxism
2. Differences in revolutionary experience: the Russians came to power all at once, the Chinese by degrees
3. Existence of a competing claimant to legitimacy in China (Taiwan) and not in Russia, a fact that impelled China to take considerable risks to "liberate" Taiwan
4. The connection between China's foreign militancy and economic weakness
5. China's military weakness, compelling reliance on the USSR
6. "Separate revolutionary interests" of the two, China concentrating on Asia and Africa, Russia on Europe

As of 1961, the list had much to commend it, perhaps with one noteworthy exception: there was no such neat division of labor as is implied by the sixth point. The USSR, not China, was the sponsor of the series of communist uprisings in South and East Asia beginning in 1948, ranging from India through Burma, Malaya, Indochina, Indonesia, and the Philippines, and to which the Korean War of 1950 may be related. If the author had written, "different kinds of appeal to different parts of the world" (some would say, to intellectuals in different parts of the world), he would have been on firmer ground. The appeal of the USSR was scarcely strong in Europe, Eastern or Western (as the development of Eurocommunism was to show); it was to grow mightily for those everywhere outside Europe who admired power. The appeal of China was for a time to the poor and weak; longer to Westerners determined to pay homage to the exotic, the less understood the bet-

---

3. On the period 1953–56, see the discussion of David Floyd's book below.

ter; all along to some influential nonwhites. My own addition to Zagoria's list would be "different stages of communist development," a point to which we shall return.

As "immediate causes" of the conflict Zagoria mentions disillusionment with Khrushchev (the apparent "leftist" who overthrew Malenkov turned into a "rightist" urging domestic restraint and détente with the United States) but mainly Chinese response to Soviet technical breakthroughs in 1957—that is, Sputnik I and the ICBM. Beijing was impatient with Soviet unwillingness to brandish new weapons and support its own readiness to take risks. But in the secret letter to the Soviet party dated September 10, 1960, the Central Committee of the Chinese Communist Party went to the heart of the matter in tracing the "real differences" to Khrushchev's secret speech of February 1956, when Khrushchev "denied Stalin's positive role" (Zagoria's phrase, and an erroneous one: Khrushchev partly exposed Stalin's negative role—indeed, his crimes) without consultation with other communist parties. The consequences of de-Stalinization, says Zagoria, are what the Chinese feared. It seems to have been quite true. There were consequences Beijing disapproved of for Soviet domestic policy, Soviet relations with the West, and internal relations of the communist international movement; above all, the legitimacy of the "second revolution," at the threshold of which the Chinese stood, was thrown into question. Only one authority could replace the partly repudiated Stalin for that purpose: Mao Zedong.

The Chinese response was not unequivocal or instantaneous, and began to take shape only in 1957. Zhou Enlai visited the USSR, Poland, and Hungary, not to stir up anti-Soviet feeling but to patch up interbloc relations. Nevertheless, enough encouragement was given the Poles so that in summer the abrupt cancellation of Mao's projected visit to Warsaw had its effect and signaled the change occurring in Beijing. In mid-June the six-week-long Hundred Flowers policy of encouraging criticism was reversed; by September the Left was in control, revisionism was the main announced enemy, and plans were under way for the Chinese campaign of 1958 usually termed in the West the Great Leap Forward, whose domestic centerpiece was creation of the "people's communes," accompanied by the threatening actions taken in the Taiwan Strait. Overall claims were implied, rather than advanced outright, that China was moving to the achievement of the final stage of "communism" (as distinguished from the "socialism" Moscow said it had been first to attain) ahead of the USSR. The campaign failed in all its major aims. Mao had to back down and resign his chairmanship of the government—not the party. Khrushchev countered the Chinese claims with the publication in 1959 of *Osnovy marksizma-leninizma*. The conflict erupted into the open with the World Federation of Trade Unions meeting in Beijing in June 1960 and the Bucharest conference a few weeks later.

The split was papered over by the Moscow conference of 81 communist parties in November, whose communiqué acknowledged that the USSR was the "universally recognized vanguard" of the world communist movement. At the Twenty-second Congress of the CPSU in 1961 Khrushchev returned to the attack—on Stalin and on Albania (the picturesque surrogate for China in Muscovite polemics at this juncture). Here Zagoria's account ends.

His final pages examine some implications of his study for the West. The Sino-Soviet conflict does not necessarily benefit the West; the word "necessarily" makes it difficult to fault the assertion, and may serve to remind us, as Zagoria does elsewhere, that the dispute is between two communist centers neither one of which has any basic values in common with the West. But in 1980 the benefits loom fairly large, as in 1961 they did not. The West, continues Zagoria, is not dealing with "another Hitler" in Khrushchev or Mao (p. 400): they are both professional revolutionaries mixing bluster and bluff with caution and circumspection. One is not sure what their being professional revolutionaries has to do with it. They certainly mixed bluff with caution; so did Hitler. It is uncertain whether Zagoria is seeking to reassure his readers or warn them, or both. Of course, Khrushchev and Mao were not Hitler. A wise man has said that what history teaches above all is to avoid fixation on false historical analogies. There might, however, be a similarity or two that the author could have mentioned. Lastly, Zagoria asserts, without expanding the point: "In all Communist states, the ally of the West is nationalism" (p. 401). I would agree. Other writers on the subject would not, as will be seen below.

THE GRIFFITH VOLUMES

I count thirteen books since 1963 that William E. Griffith has written or edited that include some reference to the Sino-Soviet dispute, six of which mention Russia and China together, as nouns or adjectives, in the title. The first was *Albania and the Sino-Soviet Rift* (1963).[4] It may be the only book ever to have studied a major international issue by focusing on the tiny country of Albania, and the author quite clearly enjoys the task of trying to persuade the reader that it makes sense to do so. Only four pages are devoted to Albanian history up to World War II, so that it is left unexplained why Wilhelm of Wied, first ruler of independent Albania, fled the country after only half a year (p. 6), or indeed how he became ruler. But the treatment of Albania's role in the dispute is thorough, and we are helped to understand that for some Albanians the claim that "we and the Chinese make up 901 million people" (the figure may be revised to reflect census estimates for any given year) may have been more than a hilarious witticism.

---

4. William E. Griffith, *Albania and the Sino-Soviet Rift* (Cambridge, Mass.: M.I.T. Press, 1963).

One point in the book deserves note in connection with Griffith's interpretation of problems of world communism generally and its Russian and Chinese varieties specifically. The author writes that the Albanian "affair" shows again that "ours is indeed an age of nationalism—and not least so in the Communist camp." Albania's "extreme nationalism" was the "major cause" of Hoxha's and Shehu's defiance of Moscow, "quixotic as it first seemed to a postnationalist West, and for the popular support without which they could hardly have brought it off" (p. 174). Contrast Zagoria's assertion that "the ally of the West is nationalism" in all communist states. Here is no place to pursue the issue of Albanian nationalism; that the West is "postnationalist," however, might come as a surprise to those striving to hold together Walloons and Flemings in Belgium; Scots, Welsh, and Englishmen in Britain (to say nothing of Ireland); Canadians of French and English descent; and perhaps even to those wrestling with bilingualism and the claims of ethnic minorities in the United States.

Griffith's basic book on the issue before us is *The Sino-Soviet Rift* (1964)[5]. An initial "Date Summary" gives a useful brief chronicle of events, beginning with Khrushchev's secret speech at the Twentieth Congress in 1956— Zagoria's starting point. Griffith addresses himself directly to the question whether "the previously generally accepted history of the Sino-Soviet dispute," which a footnote identifies as Zagoria's book, needs revision (p. 16), and his answer is that "some, though not fundamental, revision" is needed. A somewhat puzzling passage follows. Three areas are said to be affected by new documents: the 1956–57 period, the atomic issue, and the issue of the Sino-Soviet border. New material is said to indicate that Sino-Soviet differences first became serious in the spring of 1956 just after the Twentieth Congress. How that differs from Zagoria's view is not explained; a footnote deals not with that question but with the Chinese attitude to the Yugoslavs in 1954, on which there *is* new material. Next, the atomic issue: the Chinese "have now stated" that on October 15, 1957, the Soviets promised to aid them in obtaining atomic capability, a promise that was probably a prerequisite to Chinese concessions at the November 1957 meeting of communist parties in Moscow. On the Sino-Soviet border, Beijing "has clearly implied that Moscow unjustly holds the territory annexed by the Tsars from the Chinese Empire" and accused the Soviets of enticing thousands of Chinese (Kazakhs) over the border for subversive purposes. (Not long afterward the "clearly implied" criticism became overt.) All of this and more adds to what Zagoria knew or could know, but how it "revises" his book remains cloudy.

The issue of the "point of no return" is raised in *The Sino-Soviet Rift*, an

---

5. William E. Griffith, *The Sino-Soviet Rift* (Cambridge, Mass.: M.I.T. Press, 1964).

issue that may be of relevance to the broader problems of analysis. It is a way of testing general statements about the causes and course of the dispute if it can be plausibly demonstrated that there was such a "point," and can be established what led to it. Griffith's choice is the Lushan plenum of July–August 1959, when Marshal Peng Dehuai was purged after a sharp confrontation in which the foreground was occupied by both Soviet sympathy for the Chinese Right and the latter's opposition to the lengths to which the Left had gone in the Great Leap Forward.[6] Next came the article "Long Live Leninism" published in *Hongqi* in April 1960, then the "first overt Chinese attempt to detach other Communist parties from Soviet control" at the WFTU meeting in Beijing in June, and then Khrushchev's verbal counterattack the same month in Bucharest, after which he recalled Soviet specialists and reduced trade. In November 1960 came the 81-party meeting in Moscow, which Griffith calls "the first major attempt to contain, if not to reconcile, the differences." Well and good. But was not the attempt impossible, if the "point of no return" was over a year in the past? We know from other sources that the dispute was revealed to Chinese other than the privileged leaders only in 1961,[7] after the Twenty-second Congress of the CPSU. No doubt the "point of no return" will remain controversial, and not even Khrushchev or Mao, if either could communicate from wherever he is, could claim to know for certain. But it is a detail closely linked with deeper problems of interpretation.

Griffith then advances to summarize the main causes of the dispute. One area is rooted in history: the interest of "any strong Chinese state and any strong Russian state must and do conflict." The "common boundaries are too long, their historic hostility has been too ancient and too great, and the Chinese have over the last three hundred years lost too much territory to Russia" (p. 28). What is one to make of such remarks, which appear in the writings of Western journalists today as regularly as assertions of an exactly opposite kind used to appear in Soviet and Chinese communist publications? Three hundred years ago, by the Treaty of Nerchinsk (1689), the Russians were shut out of the Amur region, instead of annexing it. No doubt the Chinese remember and resent annexation by the Russian Empire of the Amur-Ussuri 120 (not 300) years ago, as they do the nick of Ili territory in the same period. But historic hostility? Not any more than to other European powers, arguably less than to Japan; and the focus of Chinese concern was, during the past century, much less on the bleak and thinly populated

---

6. The importance he attaches to the statement that the summer of 1959 was the "point of no return" is shown by the fact that it occurs in the first sentence of his *Sino-Soviet Relations, 1964–1965* (Cambridge, Mass.: M.I.T. Press, 1967).

7. Bao Ruo-wang and Rudolph Chelminski, *Prisoner of Mao* (New York: Coward, McCann and Geoghegan, 1973), pp. 255–56.

Amur-Ussuri region than on the coastal ports and areas where England, France, and Germany were influential. The most important area of the Chinese Empire where Russia did have ascendency was Manchuria with the Liaotung Peninsula, from which Russians are gone; the largest area where it retains paramount influence is Outer Mongolia, where annexation is not the issue. As for long common boundaries, that they do not determine hostility is suggested by the Canadian-U.S. and, for many centuries, the Sino-Indian borders, and perhaps others.

In this context Griffith does not invoke nationalism, an interesting fact given the emphasis in his book on Albania and the rift. In the very last paragraph of *The Sino-Soviet Rift*, however, he returns briefly to the theme: "Stalin replaced ["proletarian internationalism"] by Soviet nationalism, and China has now forced its abandonment. This was not surprising, since ours is an age of nationalism." But that fleeting reference is all. One is not sure what is meant by "China forced its [presumably "proletarian internationalism's"] abandonment." By the USSR? By the world communist movement? It evidently is not an important point for the author, or he would explain it.

When Griffith moves to the causes of the dispute that relate directly to the development of the PRC and USSR, he is more convincing. In a few decades the USSR became a nuclear superpower; within fifteen years China, for a century prostrate, became as in the past the most powerful state in Asia. The power relationships had certainly altered. Specifically, in the 1964 context, Soviet attitudes toward the United States and India were unacceptable to China: the United States was protecting from conquest Taiwan and the rest of Asia; the Soviets feared Chinese predominance, and their strategy toward "underdeveloped" (how fast the terminology changes!) areas impelled them to good relations with India; Khrushchev's policy of economic aid to underdeveloped areas lessened what could be given to China. All these things were true in 1964, though the passage of a decade and a half has altered or made obsolete every one of them. Where, then, is one to look for an explanation of the continuing factors underlying the dispute? Not in this book.

In his own essay that introduces *The World and the Great-Power Triangles* (1975),[8] which he edited, Griffith does offer an enumeration of "major causes" of the dispute (pp. 3–8).[9] First, as historical causes, he repeats in slightly different form what was quoted above from *The Sino-*

8. William E. Griffith, ed., *The World and the Great-Power Triangles* (Cambridge, Mass.: M.I.T. Press, 1975).

9. The passage differs little from that given in Griffith's booklet *Peking, Moscow, and Beyond: The Sino-Soviet-American Triangle* (Washington, D.C.: Center for Strategic and International Studies, Georgetown University, 1973), and

Soviet Rift, and adds "the multinational character of both states, the artificiality of the border between them, and the presence of both sides of it of the same ethnic groups (Kazakhs, Uighurs, and Mongols)." No doubt such circumstances need to be considered. The author declares, "In the 1950s, the first decade in history in which a simultaneously strong Russia and China faced each other across common borders, these factors alone would probably sooner or later have eroded the Sino-Soviet alliance." One doubts that the fate of Turks and Mongols was of sufficient concern to either Moscow or Beijing to determine its relation to the other; that it was an issue that could be exploited by either side if it wished to make trouble is clear. One thinks of the Kazakhs who, after hearing Chinese charges of the "restoration of capitalism" by the Soviets and finding that prospect attractive, were reported to have escaped across the frontier, only to be disappointed and on returning to Chinese territory announcing ambiguously that the reports that capitalism had been restored in the USSR were "untrue." But the opportunities for each side to foment discontent across the border were manifold and probably extensively explored by both.

Griffith continues: "Its collapse [the alliance's] was made more certain by what is usually but, in my view, incorrectly termed the 'ideological' factor in Sino-Soviet relations, which I prefer to call the organizational factor: the Sino-Soviet struggle for supremacy within the international communist and radical world. The history and ideology of Marxism-Leninism, like that of Roman Catholicism, require one center of power. Moreover, the orthodox of any faith always hate heretics more than heathens. Finally, the Soviet Communist party's domestic legitimacy rests in part on its claim to be the recognized leader of the international communist movement" (p. 3).

This is an interesting passage. The author has in earlier books compared Moscow to Leo X (Luther's contemporary) and communists in their view of the link between theory and practice to Augustine or Calvin, and has cited Edward Gibbon's explanation of the schism between Rome and Constantinople as relevant to the split between Moscow and Beijing. I have no quarrel with the religious comparison, and in fact find it more likely to illuminate the internal dynamics of communism than any other; I simply wish it were often handled more carefully. It is tempting to make precisely the opposite case from Griffith's: in the words of a prominent Indian diplo-

---

with respect to the minor differences the 1975 volume presumably is intended to supersede the treatment of 1973.

10. Some evidence may be found in Donald W. Treadgold, *A History of Christianity* (Belmont, Mass.: Nordland, 1979). The quotation from the Indian is briefly discussed on p. 45.

mat who happened to be a Muslim, "the more orthodox, the more tolerant" are the adherents of several world religions.[10] But the case need not be made here. More important, even Roman Catholicism may not have had for centuries and may not today have in the Vatican a center in which all power is concentrated, "required" or not. Certainly Christianity as such does not and has never had a single power center of any kind, from the very beginning of the church. To the extent that the history of religion is relevant, the existence of a powerful faith does not compel a single power center at all; if significant disagreements over proper understanding of the faith correspond with different political and geographical units, dual or multiple power centers are certain, not prohibited by history. No dissident group ever called itself heretical, and often such a group proclaims its orthodoxy loudly. These points have been applicable, at least hitherto, to relations between Moscow and Beijing.

The first sentence in Griffith's quoted passage probably represents excessive conciseness. Within the international communist movement both ideological and organizational imperatives and forces are at work. There is no reason why they ought not to be examined separately when they can be separated. Sometimes they are closely intertwined, and need to be studied together. It is certainly true that the Soviet leaders today lay great stress on the claim to be something between the center of all world communism and *primus inter pares* of communist countries, and that is significant for both their domestic and foreign policies. It is also true that the Sino-Soviet split affected the whole international communist movement: Moscow feared and China hoped it would, in both cases probably to a much greater extent than is true in 1980. In the 1960s several parties seemed to be lining up with or leaning toward Beijing: Albania was an apparently staunch ally, Cambodia became a client state of China, North Vietnam and North Korea seemed to waver between Chinese and Soviets. Now Albania has deserted Beijing; Cambodia has been largely conquered by the firmly pro-Soviet regime in united Vietnam and given a pro-Soviet regime of its own; North Korea, like Romania, perhaps, has good relations with the PRC without being subservient to it. Other ruling and nonruling parties may be seeking to distance themselves from Moscow to a greater or lesser extent but refrain from acknowledging Beijing as the seat of the new and true faith. But Moscow knows that the potential for a credible counterorthodoxy remains, and that both ideology and organization are aspects of the danger.

Griffith then passes to a third area of causation, one of "asymmetries." The Soviet Union was far more developed economically than the PRC; Stalin had liquidated the old party and installed a "postrevolutionary technocratic[?] elite," while the Chinese leaders remained the veterans of Yenan trusting in political compulsion. Since the Great Proletarian Cultural Revolution, it may be argued, represented Mao's attempt to do the same as Stalin had done in the Great Purges, but the post-Mao leadership headed by Deng Xiaoping emerges as considerably more technocratic—or at least more committed to removing ideological obstacles to efficiency—than the Brezhnev regime (let alone Mao's favored Gang of Four who carried out the GPCR), that asymmetry requires revision, even as of 1975 when Mao was still alive but when the sharpest phases of the Cultural Revolution were several years in the past. Nevertheless, "asymmetries" there certainly were. Even if one believes both regimes to have gone through remarkably similar stages (except that China had no NEP, but neither did the post–World War II East European, North Korean, and North Vietnamese regimes), it is surely true that the Soviets' substantial head start, or the PRC's lateness, in going through those stages led to sharp differences in the needs of the two regimes at any given moment. Often the Soviets offered warnings to the Chinese, or certain Chinese more or less inclined to the Moscow connection warned their colleagues, based on earlier Soviet experience. Thus in 1959 Peng Dehuai seems to have invoked Stalin's "dizziness from success" statement of 1930; *Pravda* in lampooning and expressing alarm at the GPCR in China constantly evoked, intentionally or not, the images of the Purges in the minds of Soviet readers.

Finally, states Griffith, the conflict was intensified by certain issues of foreign policy: Chinese and Soviet attitudes differed about the United States—as Beijing first attacked Khrushchev for seeking détente and then sought it itself—and about India (these two points repeat and update *The Sino-Soviet Rift*); the Soviets preferred nonproliferation to continuing nuclear aid to China; the Vietnam War increased tensions between Moscow and Beijing; the 1969 climax of border incidents brought the two to the "brink of limited war." The Soviet threat to invoke the Brezhnev Doctrine ended the crisis, but the consequent build-up of forty-five divisions near the frontier "drove the Chinese toward the Americans. Moscow thus made real its own worst nightmare: a potential Sino-American coalition against the Soviet Union" (p. 4). A telling point. Griffith's conclusion: "In sum, the fundamental cause of the Sino-Soviet split was the determination of China to become a superpower and thus to be equal to the Soviet Union, and the Soviet determination to prevent it." It may well be so. It is not so clear that his conclusion follows from his own discussion of causation. But sometimes it is best to put down what one thinks, and let the next book refine the logic and the components of the argument.

HINTON, LOW, AND THORNTON

Harold C. Hinton has produced a number of articles, unbound monographs, and books dealing with the Sino-Soviet dispute in one way or another. The first substantial effort was the monograph *The Bear at the Gate: Chinese Policymaking under Soviet Pressure* (1971),[11] written between the announcement that Kissinger had visited Beijing and Nixon's visit of February 1972. In this work Hinton is largely concerned with the 1959 border crisis, its origins and aftermath, but he begins by summarizing the causes of the overall Sino-Soviet dispute. They are, he writes, Mao's feelings of ideological and political superiority to Stalin's successors after Stalin died, coupled with antipathy to Khrushchev's policies, notably the secret speech of 1956. In the debate of 1956–60, the main issue was how to deal with the United States and promote revolution in the Third World, but there were also disagreements about how to proceed with the "liberation" of Taiwan, if at all, and how to handle India. There were also increasing hints of Chinese territorial claims on the USSR, but they were effects rather than causes: they "would probably not have been raised by Peking if the general political relationship between China and the Soviet Union had not been deteriorating" (p. 8). From 1960 to 1964 the dispute increased in sharpness, culminating in a "tense atmosphere" in which Khrushchev was overthrown (partly as a result of the tension?). Hinton turns next to examine the basis of Chinese foreign policy generally, declaring that "usually in combination rather than separately" both Chinese national and communist traits may be found in it. He declares that security comes first for Beijing as for "every other national leadership" but exaggeration of threats may be partly explained by Chinese victimization by foreign powers, especially Japan, during the past century. But China also seeks expansion, to reclaim Taiwan, take options on the Amur-Ussuri and Mongolia without advancing clear claims, increase its influence in Asia, and support communist and noncommunist revolutionary movements everywhere.

Hinton's full-length study, *Three and a Half Powers: The New Balance in Asia* (1975),[12] similarly contrasts two periods, "the accumulation of issues (1953–59)" and "the surfacing of the dispute (1960–64)" (pp. 70–71). The book deals with international relations in Asia (other than the Middle East) as a whole rather than the Sino-Soviet dispute or Sino-Soviet relations, and thus the discussion is again brief. Khrushchev's secret speech is regarded as the beginning of the dispute, chiefly because he suggested Soviet unwillingness to risk military confrontation with the United States. Moreover, by his attack on Stalin, whom Mao "respected," he gave

11. Harold C. Hinton, *The Bear at the Gate: Chinese Policymaking under Soviet Pressure* (Washington, D.C.: American Enterprise Institute for Public Policy and Research, and the Hoover Institution, Stanford, 1971).

12. Harold C. Hinton, *Three and a Half Powers: The New Balance in Asia* (Bloomington: Indiana University Press, 1975).

Mao's colleagues "a lever with which to reduce his political position to a more modest scale," as they soon proceeded to do. Khrushchev's pursuit of détente with the United States "after the death of John Foster Dulles in the spring of 1959" is interpreted as the trigger for Mao's adding Soviet "revisionism" to U.S. "imperialism" as a major target of propaganda, and the Chinese denunciation of Khrushchev (apparently "Long Live Leninism," referred to above) in April 1960 opened the new stage. There followed the Soviet quarrel with Albania, the Chinese criticism of Khrushchev over the withdrawal of missiles and bombers from Cuba followed by Soviet support for India in the Sino-Indian border clashes of October–November 1962, and the nuclear test ban treaty of summer 1963. The level of tension with China in the fall of 1964 "was very probably a major although unannounced count against him" for the cabal that overthrew Khrushchev.

Subsequently Kosygin's visit to Beijing in February 1965 brought a Soviet offer to patch things up and undertake "united action" in Vietnam. It was rejected. Though the Chinese decided to refrain from direct intervention in Vietnam, the militancy they sought to foster elsewhere backfired with the failure of the coup in Indonesia in September 1965 and the humiliation about the same time of Pakistan in the fighting with India (helping to set the framework of Sino-Pakistani and Soviet-Indian alliances which split Pakistan and made Bangladesh independent in the 1971 war). That did not deter Mao from pursuing the Cultural Revolution, which was coupled with cessation of normal diplomatic relations with almost all foreign countries. The Soviet invasion of Czechoslovakia, the enunciation of the Brezhnev Doctrine justifying the move, and the Ussuri border incidents of March 1969, accompanied by Soviet threats to apply the Brezhnev Doctrine to China, helped to precipitate (though there were also reasons internal to China) the end of the chaotic phase of the Cultural Revolution in 1969.

Implied rather than made explicit in Hinton's narrative is that 1969 began a fundamental change in conditions attending the Sino-Soviet dispute: the United States had hitherto been the unambiguous enemy, and from 1956 to 1969 Chinese suspicions that the Soviets were "soft" on the American threat were profound, the red thread running through the whole of the polemics. But in 1968 Chinese response to what was regarded as signals by the United States of lessened hostility to Beijing was positive—specifically, says Hinton, with Zhou Enlai's invitation of November 25 to the Nixon administration to resume Sino-American ambassadorial talks in Warsaw in February 1969. From then on the change moved slowly up to July 1971, when it was announced that Kissinger had visited China and that Nixon would do likewise, and September 1971, when the fall in unclear circumstances of Lin Biao, the spokesman of intransigence in Beijing, became known. Nixon's visit and the Shanghai Communiqué put the seal on a shift to "equidistance" between Moscow and Beijing as the focus of U.S. policy and on identification of the USSR as the main enemy for the PRC. But although Hinton explains all this clearly, he does not attempt to provide periodization for the dispute beyond 1964. It is scarcely his problem alone that if hostility to the United States accounts for much of the Sino-Soviet conflict, the conflict has persisted and even intensified after that hostility was muted or relegated to the background of Beijing's immediate concerns.

In the pamphlet *The Sino-Soviet Confrontation: Implications for the Future* (1976)[13] Hinton gives a different and fuller explanation of the "origins and issues" of the dispute under two headings, past and (the communist) present. From the past come a "racial dislike" of Chinese by Russians, coupled with the fearful memory of medieval Asian invaders (that is, the Mongols and many hordes before them), and Chinese resentment at tsarist and Soviet encroachment and exploitation. From the present may be found Soviet suspicions of "unorthodox" (with respect to the organization and methods of the Soviet system rather than in ideology) Chinese policy and practice; Mao's personal claims after 1953 to be the senior communist leader; the PRC's dissatisfaction with Khrushchev's policies, leading to labeling the Soviets "revisionist"; the mounting of Chinese pretensions to independent authority in the communist movement up through the GPCR. Then follows a periodization of the sort that appears in the earlier works; again the events after 1969 are traced, without extensive inquiry into the meaning of the alteration of Chinese hostility to the United States. One point deserves mention, to Hinton's credit: he refers to the internal political forces at work in the USSR that may have influenced Sino-Soviet relations (p. 40). His examples are Alexander Shelepin's "less anti-Chinese" position than that of most of his colleagues, though Shelepin was probably dropped from the Politburo "not primarily" for that reason, and the allegedly "more anti-Western than anti-Chinese" character of the post-Twenty-fifth Congress Politburo. He also mentions Moscow's assessment of the internal Chinese situation: Zhou Enlai wished a milder stand in relation to Moscow than his colleagues, the assertion being buttressed by a probably faked "testament" of Zhou's; there are "healthy [i.e., pro-Soviet] forces" in the Chinese party, especially the army. It is striking how little attention is paid by most of the works here examined to Moscow's side of the dispute.

Hinton does not directly address himself to either Zagoria's or Griffith's analysis. Alfred D. Low does so in *The Sino-Soviet Dispute: An Analysis*

---

13. Harold C. Hinton, *The Sino-Soviet Confrontation: Implications for the Future* (New York: Crane, Russak, for the National Strategy Information Center, 1976).

of the Polemics (1976).[14] He acknowledges his debt to Zagoria, Griffith, Hinton, and Gittings (see below) in his introduction. (There seems to be some tendency for authors of this literature to ignore works other than their own. Low is an exception.) But Low finds only one point on which he thinks revision is needed: Griffith's identification of the "point of no return" as 1959. Low argues that the Cuban missile crisis and "the bursting of the schism into the open in 1962–63 presented the crucial divide in the dispute." It then grew in depth and breadth up to the border clashes of 1969, which "represented the final climax" (p. 32). It is difficult to understand what could be meant by such a statement in a book published in 1976, unless the author seriously believed that a movement toward resolution of the dispute began after that "climax"; but he did not, for he declares that there has been "no let-up" in the dispute. With regard to 1962–63, however, he has a plausible case.

When assessing the issues, Low declares that the dispute puzzles "those who are inclined to overestimate the role of ideology in international affairs" (p. 16). That may be so. If one uses the comparison with religion, as Griffith has tried to do, however, one may avoid being misled. In religion one may distinguish the areas of doctrine (the basic discipline for which is theology), ritual, ecclesiastical organization, and local, regional, national, ethnic, linguistic, and other secular forces which exert pressure on the faith and the church. Each may have its own importance, certainly including religious doctrine. A tendency among modern social scientists (even some of them who hold a religious belief), however, is to assume a rigoristic, quasi-moralistic stance in regard to ideology, and communist ideology in particular; if ideology can be shown to be affected by secular and especially power forces, there is a readiness to explain it away and reduce it to something quite different, on the grounds that those professing it must be hypocrites only masking their contemptible self-serving motives by high-flown rhetoric. If more than a handful of specialists can be identified as those who "overestimate the role of ideology" in this area, that would be a feat; much the more common is the contrary phenomenon. Thus Low himself, after plausibly asserting that not only ideology but also tactics and strategy of international communism are involved in the dispute, adds with emphasis, "The dispute is also a continuation of the centuries-old hostility between Russia and China. It is a clash of two great powers whose adoption of the language of internationalism scarcely hides their selfish nationalist drives. Their ideological supranationalism is only a poor camouflage for a most extravagant nationalism nurtured by both sides" (p. 16). No definition or explanation of the term "nationalism" is given, and no instance is cited

---

14. Alfred D. Low, *The Sino-Soviet Dispute: An Analysis of the Polemics* (Rutherford, Madison, Teaneck, [N.J.]: Dickinson University Press, 1976).

except Beijing's raising of the issue of tsarist annexations of Chinese territory. In the conclusion Low adds a bit to his argument, but complicates it by contending that in some ways the episode is comparable to medieval and Reformation-era "religious disputes of hostile sects . . . , though it has, of course, both global and secular aspects" (p. 341). (So did the Reformation.) Low continues, "It is also a clash of rival states and power centers with far-reaching territorial and ideological aspirations." True. Then comes the reductionist charge: "The dispute, whatever its modern, Marxist-Leninist, external appearance, has excessive nationalism, imperialism, and power struggle as its old-fashioned core." It is curious, not only or even especially in Low's book, that the most significant analytical statements of all are made almost in passing, without effort to explain the comparisons (religion in the Middle Ages and Reformation) or concepts (nationalism or imperialism) employed. One might argue that such statements often have little or nothing to do with the actual narrative anyway and that since the authors do not seem to take them seriously, the readers should not either. If so, then the state of Western study of international relations is worse than one thought.

Richard C. Thornton has not sought, in *China: The Struggle for Power, 1917–1972* (1973),[15] to focus on the Sino-Soviet dispute, or even on one of Griffith's "triangles." His study of the "struggle for power" is not an exercise in domestic power politics or "Beijinology" but an attempt to examine the contest for influence in China that involved the United States, USSR, and other European and Asian states. As for the Sino-Soviet dispute, it receives not even a heading or subheading, but is viewed from the Chinese side in connection with Chinese needs. Beijing's most significant response to Khrushchev's secret speech was the Great Leap Forward. After a decade in which "various groups contended," the GLF polarized Chinese politics into two factions, which are said to have persisted and have culminated in the GPCR. The subsequent account offers no radically different interpretations, but does treat briefly an issue that none of the other books discussed in this chapter even mention: the revival of "the long-buried concept of the 'Asiatic mode of production' " in 1962–64.[16] Perhaps some of the authors were too busy reducing ideology to something else that they overlooked certain of the actual ideological issues in the debate. What was the significance of this apparently esoteric discussion? Thornton contends that the implication was that the Chinese were not only not socialist but actually

15. Richard C. Thornton, *China: The Struggle for Power, 1917–1972* (Bloomington: Indiana University Press, 1973).

16. Thornton treated the issue at some length in an article in *Problems of Communism*, 17, no. 2 (March–April 1968): 71–75, entitled "Soviet Historians and China's Past."

were "heading into a blind alley of societal development," and that the groundwork was being laid for an argument that under Mao China "had regressed into a more primitive stage of development rather than progressing toward socialism" (p. 248). Since the fall of Khrushchev apparently terminated such discussion, the ideological hand grenade was never thrown. But its explosive power was doubtless great.

The book ends with 1972, and a cogent observation: the Chinese communist leaders were shaped by their training and experience in the international movement. "They were obliged to determine policy in terms of the relationship with the Soviet Union. Even when they subsequently made the decision to develop independently of the Soviet Union, the new alternatives were also shaped to a great extent by that relationship" (p. 340). The remark might have deserved a few more words of explanation and embellishment.

THE JOURNALISTS[17]

David Floyd, correspondent for the London *Daily Telegraph*, has written a scholarly study, coupled with ample documents, in *Mao Against Khrushchev: A Short History of the Sino-Soviet Conflict* (1963).[18] He acknowledges his debt to Griffith in particular for *Albania and the Sino-Soviet Rift*, but otherwise does not address himself to revising his predecessors. One useful point he makes relates to the period immediately following the death of Stalin: his successors exerted themselves to "appease Mao Tse-tung's wounded pride" (p. 17) by showing Zhou Enlai special favor at Stalin's funeral, which Mao did not attend; by doctoring a 1950 photograph to show Mao as flanked by Stalin and Malenkov; by replacing the secret policeman Panyushkin by Kuznetsov—"of less sinister reputation"—as ambassador to Beijing; by raising the Chinese party (ranked after the Polish party in 1952) to the second place in public ranking within the communist movement; and by increasing aid to the PRC. Thus Khrushchev's secret speech, which began the "trouble" (Floyd's term), came as a more than ordinary shock, even though the initial reaction in Beijing was ostensibly favorable. The rest of the narrative covers familiar ground. In his conclusion, "Two Romes?"—an evocation of the religious comparison which is not, however, even mentioned in the text—the author sums up the "factors" behind the dispute: the personalities of Khrushchev and Mao; different economic needs; Chinese

17. The term is intended to be descriptive of the kind of writing in question and not to denigrate the writers. Perhaps it is well to remember that the best overall study of the Russian Revolution to this day was written by one journalist (W. H. Chamberlin) and that the whole subject of Chinese communism was introduced to the West by another (Edgar Snow).

18. David Floyd, *Mao Against Khrushchev: A Short History of the Sino-Soviet Conflict* (New York: Praeger, 1963).

resentment at the failure of the Soviets to assist their nuclear development; the alleged fact that the USSR is a "satisfied" power while the PRC is not, in regard to Taiwan and other areas; the differing ages of the two communist revolutions; ideological issues, though they are said to be "secondary"; and the upset of international communist organization. Doubtless all these issues are real; but they have all been presented before.

John Gittings produced a Chatham House Memorandum, *The Sino-Soviet Dispute, 1956–63: Extracts from Recent Documents* (1964), a book entitled *Survey of the Sino-Soviet Dispute: A Commentary and Extracts from the Recent Polemics, 1963–1967* (1968), and a volume called *The World and China, 1922–1972* (1974).[19] The *Survey* is a book of documents prefaced by a twenty-six-page introduction, which begins by noting that both Chinese and Soviet leaders say February 1956 began the dispute, and then questions the assertion in a brief narrative starting with 1911 and 1917. Gittings ends by forecasting continuing conflict.

The World and China allots the Sino-Soviet dispute not even a chapter heading, and stresses the continuity of Chinese communist views and policies. The purpose of the book, Gittings writes, is "to show that China's discussion and analysis of international affairs, both in the revolutionary past and since 1949, is neither the product of dogma, nor a justification of policies undertaken for reasons of narrow national interest, nor liable to change automatically in response to domestic political changes" (p. 12); he regards Mao as the "inspirational source of these ideas" (p. 9). The treatment is chronological. The chapter on 1954–59 is remarkable for not even mentioning Khrushchev's secret speech of 1956. His chapter on "Mao and the Soviet Union" points out that of the known speeches and writings of Mao since 1949, well over two-thirds deal with "the Comintern, Stalin, Khrushchev, and the successes and failures of the Soviet experience in building socialism" (p. 236). Gittings, unlike most other authors examined here, clearly identifies with Mao as against Moscow: "just as the seeds of Khrushchev's revisionism lay in Stalin's deformation of socialism in the Soviet Union, so the various strands in the Sino-Soviet dispute as it burst forth in the 1960s could be traced back through the 1950s and further (as I hope to have shown during [sic] this book)" (p. 255). The Khrushchev secret speech is mentioned in this chapter, but only briefly and without emphasis. In his conclusion Gittings declares that all along the Chinese viewed "national interest" as "that of a country making its revolution—at first national-democratic and now socialist—in the teeth of imperialist opposition" (p.

19. John Gittings, *The Sino-Soviet Dispute, 1956–63: Extracts from Recent Documents* (London: Royal Institute of International Affairs, 1964); *Survey of the Sino-Soviet Dispute: A Commentary and Extracts from the Recent Polemics, 1963–1967* (London: Oxford University Press, 1968); *The World and China, 1922–1972* (New York: Harper and Row, 1974).

265). In 1946, he writes, the Chinese accepted the needs of the "socialist national interest" of the Soviet Union, and now place their own first. "They are and always have been national revolutionaries, not internationalist conspirators." But he obviously disagrees with the Western "school of thought" that believes Chinese foreign policy to be "predominantly" motivated by national interest, "reducing theory and ideology behind it to no more than the vehicle for expedient rationalization." So does he contest the "school" that sees Chinese foreign policy as the consequence of shifts between the domestic Left and Right; he declares, "I hope to have shown that the sequence of cause and effect is the reverse" (p. 267)—that is, foreign relations determine shifts in the domestic political scene.

Klaus Mehnert, born in Moscow of German parents, spent five years in the USSR and five years in China aside from numerous additional visits to both. Thus he was in a position to write a broad-gauged work, *Peking and Moscow* (1963), on the basis of experience that few could match.[20] In his introduction he declares that there are two schools of interpretation of the Sino-Soviet relationship: the first, including the communist leaders of the two countries and some Western observers, asserts that communism is the logical outcome of the history of both Russia and China; the second holds communism to be the "complete antithesis" of the true nature of the two—the position held by Chiang Kai-shek, many Russian émigrés, and many foreign friends and admirers of both countries. But reality, declares Mehnert, "corresponds to neither of these two theses; it is more complicated and thus more interesting" (p. 8). Perhaps so. But the point is not raised again at the end of the book, and thus we might feel left in doubt regarding to what thesis, precisely, reality corresponds. Out of 454 pages of text, the first 132 are devoted to the precommunist past of both countries, and in the final subsection, entitled "Communism Was Not Inevitable," the notion of a "logical development toward Communism" is rejected. Thus Chiang Kai-shek and the émigrés apparently prove to be right; or if not, we are not told exactly why. As in the case of other works here examined, the predictions have not worn well: the closer China comes to obtaining nuclear weapons, "the more frequent might be the instances of joint interests" between the Soviet Union and the West, especially the United States (p. 453). As it has turned out, the Soviet approach to nuclear superiority has driven the PRC and the United States closer together. China's modest nuclear capability may alarm Moscow but not notably Washington, D.C.

The bulk of Mehnert's volume, however, has many and great merits. It is not a history of Russia and China in any ordinary sense; it is not mainly a history of the Sino-Soviet dispute, though the last 129 pages are just that; it seeks to explore the dispute with sufficient consideration of its back-

20. Klaus Mehnert, *Peking and Moscow*, trans. of 1962 German ed. (New York: G. P. Putnam's Sons, 1963).

ground to make possible a full understanding of all aspects. As such it is unique, and the fact that there is nothing remotely like it puts American scholars to shame. It is laden with useful observations: in China no places or institutions were named after Mao; a "temperature chart of diplomatic relations" (p. 294), based on the number of lines in greetings telegrams, is instructive (rather than conclusive); Beijing's attitude toward the Polish and Hungarian events of 1956, despite much Western misunderstanding of the facts, was the same as Moscow's, and China was the only country to term the killing of Imre Nagy, in violation of the safe-conduct given him on leaving the Yugoslav embassy, "welcome news" (p. 339); China "never expressed" a claim to skip "socialism" on the road to "communism," though to be sure Chinese statements "amounted to" raising the issue (p. 357). Not every observation will meet with agreement, to be sure. Invoking Ruth Benedict's distinction between the "shame culture" of Japan but also China and the "guilt culture" of Christian Europe may be titillating and even partly illuminating, but will not persuade everyone that the contrast goes very deep. Mehnert declares that "as a European I felt closer to the old Russia than to the old China, and even the establishment of [communist governments in both] could not alter these natural ties"; perhaps "one day even the men in the Kremlin will realize that they are more closely linked to the West by their European origin than to China by Communism" (pp. 453–54). Mehnert's feelings of kinship are his own and not for a critic to challenge; what kinship the Soviet leaders feel may be difficult to establish, for Moscow continues to maintain that nascent Chinese socialism has been betrayed but not destroyed. Perhaps Americans, with their intimate involvement for well over a century with China, start with different feelings than Europeans, and fascination with China continues strong as fascination with Russia is now rare in this country. But I am inclined to doubt that common features or contrasts in cultural background provide any safe guide to the future of the Sino-Soviet relationship or its implications for relations with other powers. However, Mehnert never talks nonsense, and is unfailingly interesting.

He subsequently wrote a sort of travelogue called *China Returns* (1972), after his first visit since 1957.[21] Only one passage need be cited here. "Unlike many Western observers," he writes, "I do not have the impression that the roots of the Sino-Soviet conflict are to be found in the border dispute." Chinese are uncomfortable with Soviet encirclement of Manchuria by land and resent the name Vladivostok ("ruler of the East"), "but nobody ever spoke with fondness or enthusiasm for the Soviet Far East or Siberia, and I do not believe there is any sense of affinity with these re-

---

21. Klaus Mehnert, *China Returns*, trans. of 1971 German ed. (New York: E. P. Dutton, 1972).

gions" (p. 229). I know of no evidence to the contrary. There may be a danger that the outsider, baffled by the complexities of international communism and constantly tempted to reduce them to simple issues he is familiar with from other areas, will exaggerate the importance of the border dispute. Against this, one must recognize that the 1969 incidents seemed to carry both powers close to the brink of war—how close, to be sure, we do not know. But since then, and before then, evidence that the border was of first importance to Beijing is lacking, and of course Moscow does not regard the question as open.

A Hungarian-born French journalist, François Fejtö, has written an interesting account entitled *Chine–USSR: La fin d'une hégémonie*, Volume 1: *Les origines du grand schisme communiste, 1950–1957* (1964).[22] He begins with October 17, 1961, which he calls "commencement du schisme"—when Khrushchev attacked Albania at the Twenty-second Congress. He then moves to a background discussion beginning with Lenin, quickly reaching 1950 (February's treaty of alliance between the USSR and PRC), and ending with 1957 (the November 1957 conferences of twelve and then sixty-eight parties in Moscow). Nearly half of the book is documents; the rest is elegant narrative, but without attempt at full analysis of causes or issues of the split. (Neither a second volume, *Le conflit: Le développement du grand schisme communiste, 1956–1966*, same publisher, 1966, nor an abridged and updated version of both, *Chine–URSS, de l'alliance au conflit, 1950–1972*, Editions du Seuil, 1973, was available to me at the time of writing.)

Two American journalists may be chosen for discussion who have written books on the dispute, Drew Middleton and Harrison E. Salisbury. Middleton's *Duel of the Giants: China and Russia in Asia* (1978) is frankly based on a three-week visit to China.[23] He declares that worsening relations from 1949 to the break a "decade later" were provoked by three factors: Soviet recognition of the resources of Eastern Siberia, PRC dependence on Russian economic aid, and "development, in both countries, of national interests—some new, some revived from the past" (p. 34). But the very chapter heading, "Four Centuries of Rivalry [?] and a Decade of Amity," indicates that the decade was not one of worsening relations. One supposes that a journalist is apt to be tempted to write sentences like "the guns firing on Damanski Island on March 2, 1969, echoed those of Yermak centuries before" (p. 51), but Yermak's attack on the Turkic khanate of Sibir, just across the Urals, in the 1580s does not seem to have anything clearly to do with Soviet-Chinese skirmishes. His summary of issues (chapter 11) is a

22. François Fejtö, *Chine–URSS: La fin d'une hégémonie*, vol. 1: *Les origines du grand schisme communiste, 1950–1957* (Paris: Plon, 1964).
23. Drew Middleton, *The Duel of the Giants: China and Russia in Asia* (New York: Charles Scribner's Sons, 1978).

reasonable one, but cannot be said to advance beyond works already examined.

Salisbury rather prematurely entitles his book *War Between Russia and China* (1969).[24] It is written "out of concern over the tension" between them and "the proliferation of signs that the two superstates are headed toward a collision course and war," and believes that "the United States can profoundly influence this struggle" and should do so in order to preserve peace. (Compare Middleton: "American capability to control military events in East Asia is negligible," p. 231.) The book begins with a chapter recounting a visit to Karakorum in May 1969, and ends by stating that however war between Russia and China might start, "Mongolia will hold the center role in the unfolding conflict" (p. 28). One is left uncertain why, though despite not having been in Mongolia I can imagine the spell of the ghost of Chingis Khan. The approach is one of arguing that the roots of the Sino-Soviet dispute, "in many ways, go deeper than those of any Great Power rivalry in the modern era" (p. 63), and that the past of Russia and China determines present hostility. Communism is brushed aside in an ingenious manner. In the chapter "Is Mao a Communist?" the answer is given that Moscow says he isn't, and Beijing says "the Kremlin" is not communist: "neither side sees the other as Communist. Therefore there is no ideological barrier to hostility, conflict, war" (p. 82). *Quod erat demonstrandum.* Comment would be superfluous. It deserves mention that Salisbury writes very well.

Of course journalistic treatments of the dispute often appear in the form of magazine articles and newspaper stories, much of the material consciously "fugitive" but all of it indispensable to the scholar. The journalists of every country write on the subject. By way of sampling the immense volume of this literature, one example may be given: Antonie C. A. Dake, *In the Spirit of the Red Banteng: Indonesian Communists Between Moscow and Peking, 1959–1965* (1973),[25] takes his curious title from a statement by the Indonesian communist leader D. N. Aidit in 1964, used as epigraph to the book. The word "banteng" (lower case) might refer to the Afro-Asian conference in Bandung (1955), but that conference is scarcely mentioned in the book and the title is nowhere explained or used. The "three main issues" of the Sino-Soviet dispute (p. 70) are said to be cold war or peaceful coexistence, the question of inevitability of war, and the "chances of a non-violent communist take-over." The main value of the book is to show in detail how the PKI (Indonesian Communist Party) was Soviet-dominated

---

24. Harrison E. Salisbury, *War Between Russia and China* (New York: W. W. Norton, 1969).

25. Antonie C. A. Dake, *In the Spirit of the Red Banteng: Indonesian Communists Between Moscow and Peking, 1959–1965* (The Hague: Mouton, 1973).

up to 1948, shifted toward the Chinese side especially after 1960, and marched with Beijing up to the doom that befell it with the abortive coup of 1965. The book is execrably edited.

O. Edmund Clubb's book *China and Russia: The "Great Game"* (1971) may conclude this section, though Clubb's main career was in diplomacy.[26] Beginning with the Mongols—the first map is of Eurasia in 1290—he surveys Sino-Russian relations to 1969. There are 521 pages of text; the Russian Revolution comes at page 161, the Chinese communist victory of 1949 at page 377, the Khrushchev secret speech at page 413. Clubb's study of the relations between Russia and China may be contrasted with Mehnert's *Peking and Moscow*, which studies both countries and compares the two, rather than focusing on diplomacy. The narrative is judicious, the analysis somewhat dated. Beijing's policy, Clubb writes, "has from the beginning been molded in good part by the urge to *li yung* (profitably utilize) Soviet strength to achieve the expulsion of American power from [the Asian periphery]," as Soviet policy toward China has been strongly influenced by American strategic aims (p. 512). Chinese objectives (said to be "hypothetical," but he evidently means it) seem to be (1) gaining new territory for its population surplus and (2) redistributing the world's wealth to relieve its poverty; to achieve them China would need to maneuver the United States and USSR into fighting each other or to mobilize the "rising anger of the poor nations." As of 1971 his forecast was that though the "old-style imperialists" who ruled China and Russia in the seventeenth century were "probably better able to understand each other" than China, the USSR, and the United States today, China and the USSR would probably "sustain a measure of collaboration in Asia" (p. 520), and there is danger that world war might eventuate from the "triangle." It is true that China's preoccupation with Soviet help in opposing the United States was an apparently crucial element from the outset of the dispute—until 1971, though the signs of a shift appeared, as is clear in retrospect, as early as late 1968 (see discussion of Hinton above). The timing of Clubb's book was unfortunate, but the bulk of it remains useful independently of his conclusions.

SOME ADDITIONAL OBSERVERS

Zbigniew K. Brzezinski published in 1960 a study of *The Soviet Bloc* (actually a history since 1945), which dealt mainly with the USSR and Eastern Europe; a revised edition of 1967, since "in recent years the Sino-Soviet relationship has loomed large on the *East European* horizons" (my emphasis), included new material on the dispute.[27] He finds the split to have

26. O. Edmund Clubb, *China and Russia: The "Great Game"* (New York: Columbia University Press, 1971).
27. Zbigniew K. Brzezinski, *The Soviet Bloc: Unity and Conflict*, rev. and enl. ed. (Cambridge, Mass.: Harvard University Press, 1967).

been "a tragic disaster, comparable in some respects to the split in Christianity several centuries ago" (p. 397). Khrushchev tried to replace Stalin's crude "supranational autocracy" with a new international communist system, with the USSR recognized voluntarily by the other communist states as head and arbiter; the Chinese also wanted that but also "militant unity, actively directed against the enemy." Brzezinski then summarizes the issues under three headings: party, foreign policy, and state. Party issues include the role of the CPSU, "revisionism" or "dogmatism," whether the era was dominated by the conflict between now-winning "socialism" and "imperialism" (PRC) or its decisive event was the appearance of the "world socialist system" (USSR), the possibility or desirability of avoiding war, the possibility of peaceful transition to socialism, the position of the dictatorship of the proletariat and class struggle especially in the USSR, the prospective affluent or nonaffluent nature of communist society, Stalin's role, the CPSU's right to expel any country (Albania) from the bloc, and the propriety of interparty polemics. Foreign policy issues, partly applying certain items from the "party" list, are these: should strategy concentrate on fomenting immediate world revolution, should support for "national liberation" struggles be pressed to the limit, was détente with the United States thinkable, was the Test Ban Agreement a step toward Soviet-U.S. *alliance*, and what should be the attitude toward India? Finally, the state issues: Soviet military and economic assistance to the PRC and territorial claims. The enumeration and discussion of these issues, eighteen in number, go beyond any work thus far discussed, and Brzezinski indicates full recognition that with such a lengthy list there is bound to be overlapping and a close relation between certain items.

He deals well with several causes that have been advanced to explain the dispute. First comes the contention that ideology is merely a screen for nationalism in the dispute, the example in his footnote being Harry Schwartz's *Tsars, Mandarins, and Commissars* (1964),[28] but the view has already been encountered above. Of course Russian and Chinese "national styles and ambitions" have an influence, but Brzezinski concludes that "nationalism may be seen as a constant source of strain but not as the cause of specific sources of conflict, especially in the case of states led by nationalists who subscribe overtly to a common ideological doctrine that ostensibly overrides their nationalism" (p. 404), and gives reasons why this is so. Second, there is the "stages of growth" argument: the USSR has passed through an industrial revolution and become bureaucratized, the PRC has not; this explanation makes the Chinese "dedicated revolutionaries," the Soviets de-

---

28. Harry Schwartz, *Tsars, Mandarins, and Commissars: A History of Chinese-Russian Relations* (Philadelphia: Lippincott, 1964).

viants. There may be merit in the argument, but he asks how it explains moderate Chinese behavior before 1957. (He recalls how widespread the view was then that the Chinese, their communism restrained by Confucianism, were the true moderates within the movement.) Or how does it explain Khrushchev's recklessness in 1962? A variant (or third) explanation deals with generations: the Old Bolsheviks are gone in Russia, the veterans of the Long March in China are still in power. Again, yes, but—. In these respects Tito is like Mao but Soviet-Yugoslav relations "have been steadily improving." A fourth argument is that there was (chiefly) an ideological and organizational struggle for supremacy in the international communist movement. Yes, he says, but the other factors played some part as well.

His conclusion is that a series of specific moves had much to do with the dispute. His term is "dynamic escalation," and he follows the process in a very good though brief account (pp. 406–27) of the period 1960–65 only. For example, Khrushchev was specifically provoked in certain ways to his outburst in Bucharest in 1960, which in turn had to be acted on, thus withdrawal of aid to China. And so forth. He then examines six alternatives for the future, ranging from (military) confrontation to either Moscow or Beijing's yielding to the other. What seems most likely to him is continuing quite bitter hostility.[29] It is noteworthy that this political scientist moves in the direction of considering as important—even decisive in given situations—personal feelings, impulses, concern for appearing logically consistent, strong, and conscious of the proper obligations, and other qualities that make up the human being. Disputes, like other events, develop a momentum of their own, but individuals do much to shape them. If a political scientist wishes to call all this "dynamic escalation," well and good. Others might simply call it "history."

Geoffrey Jukes, in *The Soviet Union in Asia* (1973),[30] stresses Soviet exclusion from the Bandung meeting of 1955, and consequent concern about possible Chinese assumption of regional communist leadership in Asia, as a significant part of the background of the Khrushchev secret speech and the whole dispute (pp. 218–19). He concludes by emphasizing that the Soviet Union cannot "pack up and go" (p. 252) from Asia, as the United States and Australia can, reminding us that well over half of Soviet land borders are with Asian countries, that its Asian population is large and growing faster than the European portion, that Soviet Asian development has been so extensive as to be equaled only by Japan (pp. 291–92)

---

29. This is approximately the perspective of Richard Lowenthal in "Russia and China: Controlled Conflict," *Foreign Affairs*, 49, no. 3 (April 1971): 507–18.

30. Geoffrey Jukes, *The Soviet Union in Asia* (Berkeley: University of California Press, 1973).

(though what of Taiwan, Korea, Singapore?). The book *Sino-Soviet Military Relations* (1966), edited by Raymond L. Garthoff,[31] usefully traces at several points the role of military and in particular nuclear assistance from the USSR, extended or denied, in shaping the growth of Chinese resentment and antipathy. Peter Van Ness, in *Revolution and Chinese Foreign Policy: Peking's Support for Wars of National Liberation* (1970),[32] argues that "almost invariably" the issues raised by Chinese in the dispute through 1965 "related to foreign policy" (p. 191). W. A. Douglas Jackson, in *The Russo-Chinese Borderlands* (2d ed., 1968),[33] helpfully studies the frontier areas sector by sector as background to the geographical aspect of the dispute.

The literature is enormous, the space available limited. Many books and articles of merit must be slighted or omitted. Many more books and articles on the topic will doubtless be written. Everyone will judge for himself whether the point of diminishing returns has come somewhere earlier in this chapter, or has as yet not been reached.

SOME CRITICAL REMARKS

From Zagoria's laudable pioneer effort to Brzezinski's analysis, both precise and concise, scholarly examination of the issues, causes, and origins of the Sino-Soviet dispute has made notable advances. Remarks made above about the efforts of authors to be objective and detached are not weakened by specific disagreements or correctives presented about the works that have been discussed.

Nevertheless, some general observations may be added. It is familiar to teachers of history that most textbooks on Europe assume a knowledge, and even a common interpretation, of what Christianity is and never try to characterize it, but when it comes to challenges to Christianity, especially in the eighteenth century and later, those are explained in detail. Most of the works on the dispute do something similar: they take for granted that readers know, or even agree, on what communism is, and then proceed to study questions raised within the communist framework—not only of ideology in the strict sense but also of organizational, strategic, tactical, and even ritual matters. To be sure, most of the works considered are not "textbooks," and some assumptions must be made regarding what readers know or think already, or authors may never get to the narrative at all.

31. Raymond L. Garthoff, ed., *Sino-Soviet Military Relations* (New York: Praeger, 1966).

32. Peter Van Ness, *Revolution and Chinese Foreign Policy: Peking's Support for Wars of National Liberation* (Berkeley: University of California Press, 1970).

33. W. A. Douglas Jackson, *The Russo-Chinese Borderlands*, 2d ed. (Princeton, N.J.: D. Van Nostrand, 1968).

Especially the Americans concerned have assembled several impressive, accurate, and well-documented narratives accompanied by at least some detailed analysis. In certain other cases the narratives are simply prefaced by short sections, on causes or issues, which are not clearly related by the authors to what follows, or are supplemented by brief conclusions that predict the future, chart courses for U.S. policy to follow, and sometimes make sweeping statements about the world past and present, but do not appear to emerge from the evidence presented.

A few of the authors read both Russian and Chinese with some fluency. Others clearly do not, but read one or the other. In some cases the scholarly apparatus leaves the question in doubt. It might be worthwhile to urge writers on the subject (and not only on the Sino-Soviet dispute) to make clear what sources they have used in the original. American scholarship is often thought to err, if anywhere, in the direction of overdocumentation, but however that may be readers deserve to see readily which languages an author has actually used, whatever the "research density" of the work.

Aside from language, authors of books on the dispute can be fully confident of their preparation only when they have had some immersion in the history and culture of both countries and the character and development of the communist movement from Marx to Mao, from the First International to the communist parties of 1980. If they are to differentiate Russia and China from each other and from other countries, and the communist movement from its own direct European antecedents, intellectual and organizational, well before the mid-nineteenth century, still other work is needed. No scholar will be equally a master of all the foregoing, but greater consciousness of the perils of venturing into the borderlands of *terra incognita* cannot but help us all. Scholars frequently complain about journalists in such respects, but they are not entirely immune to the same failings. In dealing with the contemporary scene, whatever the professional training of the writer, it is tempting to try to sum up earlier Russo-Chinese relations in a few lines or pages, and the past is all too likely to be casually and inaccurately handled in background sections.

One feature of most of the literature seems to be that the Chinese side of the dispute is more fully studied than the Soviet side—indeed, sometimes the imbalance is severe indeed. There may be reasons for some imbalance. But the question of what if any internal pressures and considerations motivated Khrushchev, Brezhnev, and other leaders to act as they did is often not even raised. Gittings seems to have internalized the view of the PRC leaders to a point where he can make the case plausibly and coherently for them; no one seems to have tried to do the same for the Soviets, let alone for both separately. Few of the authors seem to challenge the close relation between domestic and foreign policy in Beijing, whether the former is believed to govern the latter, vice versa, or neither is thought to dominate.

For the Soviet side, foreign policy on the part of state or party is usually studied broadly in relation to powers other than China, especially the United States, but is seldom related to domestic policy in any way. Perhaps the relation is much less close in the USSR. If so, the case needs to be made rather than simply assumed.

There seems no doubt that Americans even more than others are ready to discount ideology and to stress power, and skirt the edge of reductionism —or simply adopt it outright—where ideology is concerned. It is widely conceded that neither Khrushchev nor Brezhnev is to be considered a brilliant theorist and that Mao's sophistication and delicacy in the field were, in the most favorable interpretation, well concealed in order to reach an enormous, ill-educated, and earthy audience. (Example: "Every fart has some kind of smell, and we cannot say that all the Soviet farts smell sweet. Everyone is now saying that they stink, and we can say so too." Mao speech to the Politburo, 1956, cited in Gittings, *The World and China*, p. 236.) It seems just as widely forgotten that the entire educational system of both countries is based on Marxism-Leninism as currently interpreted by the leaders concerned. (One sometimes suspects this or that writer on communism of never having met any garden-variety communist of whatever nationality, and therefore not knowing in what terms they habitually think and talk, in many cases even after "choosing freedom." But that cannot be, of course.)

On this issue several writers examined above have written well, pointing out in different ways that ideology and power intertwine with each other in subtle fashion. Brzezinski is a good example of a writer determined not to settle for abstractions in this area, as shown above. But even Brzezinski uses the term "nationalism," though rarely in this connection, without explanation.

The evidence is mountainous that in neither country are the communist leaders nationalist, if that term is properly used to refer to the movement that took shape in Europe in the nineteenth century, placing the category of the nation ahead of all other categories (Herder was one of the main fathers, though he believed each nation had its own rights) and, finally, one's own nation ahead of all other nations (Treitschke, Tisza, Katkov). Moreover, they have amply demonstrated that their commitments are opposed to the national feeling and the national heritage of Russians and Chinese, leaving aside the discrimination or oppression felt by the ethnic minorities in both states. In Russia the whole heritage of Orthodox Christianity, the liberal aspirations of the nineteenth and early twentieth century, the entire precommunist corpus of village tradition, ceremony, and the arts, and other elements have been subjected to prohibition of scholarly study, direct attack, or grotesque and deliberate distortion by state fiat. In China the various strands of Confucianism, Buddhism, and Taoism, the part

Christianity played at various stages of Chinese development, the monuments and written reminders of the past that were sprinkled through the whole of China, traditional music, painting, poetry, and novels, and folk and family behavior of various kinds, have suffered similarly. A GPCR slogan called for war on the "old culture," but with or without slogans the struggle has been waged for decades—now fiercely, now in muted form. "Modernizing" regimes in this century have often been uncomfortable with what they inherited and have sought to alter it; only the communists have steadily fought battles against it all. National feeling, not to mention nationalism, has often had as an ingredient concern for the mass of the people, and communists have expressed such a concern loudly; but it was not any regard for what the peasants and workers were actually like that constituted the basis of that concern but rather a determination to change their lives and attitudes drastically. When he wrote that in communist states nationalism was the ally of the West, Zagoria was much nearer the truth than all those authors who identify nationalism with communism but do not discuss the specific ingredients of national feeling and heritage in relation to the nation concerned.

Both Soviet and Chinese forms of communism have proceeded through distinct stages of development: seizure of power, consolidation of power, use of power to nationalize industry and collectivize agriculture, the purging of opposition, and the attempt to find a communist "normalcy" under which the system can operate with some semblance of regularity and tranquillity. The "stages of growth" argument has been annexed by economists, but it appears that the politically determined stages may be the crucial ones. Few have tried to discuss such stages in detail, or have sought to explain why China has time and again duplicated what the Soviets have done, or have attempted to account for the similarities between Mao and Stalin and their respective policies, other than in terms of Chinese imitation of Soviet policy. But plainly much of the duplication occurred *after* Beijing repudiated Moscow's leadership and, at least in part, rejected the USSR as a model. Does the communist system have some sort of internal dynamics that leads it through certain steps, and if so, why? To be sure, the duplication is not complete: in Karl A. Wittfogel's terminology, "just as no colony is an exact replica of the mother country (cf. Australia and Britain), no *derivative revolution* is an exact replica of the *root revolution*."[34] Given the enormous differences in the historical background of Russia and China, one may observe with amazement the extent of the similarity of stages through which their communist systems have passed.

To use Griffith's term, "asymmetries" of great significance result precisely

34. "The Russian and Chinese Revolutions: A Socio-Historical Comparison," *Yearbook of World Affairs, 1961*, p. 43.

because the two countries passed through similar stages at different times. China's "second revolution" impended at the very moment that Khrushchev was striving to repair the damage Stalin had done in Russia's second revolution, and was talking in terms radically unsuitable for the tasks Mao confronted. To Brezhnev, Mao's purges in the GPCR were embarrassingly reminiscent of Stalin's purges, which he was seeking to forget and yet was unable to avoid recalling every time Moscow attacked the GPCR. And so forth.

These and other considerations may still need to be dealt with by future writers. But one aspect quite different from communist dynamics and the relation to domestic national feeling involves the dramatic switch (1969–72) of Chinese foreign orientation from merely squabbling with the USSR to actively organizing opposition to it, especially by closer relations with the United States. Griffith wrote that Moscow made real its own worst nightmare, and the turn of phrase is brilliant; but the causes probably go beyond the quip. Anyone familiar with Chinese diplomacy in the 1970s cannot but believe that Beijing was in earnest in seeking to buttress what it perceived as the weak U.S. resolve to deter Soviet aggression, to rally the relaxed and sated West Europeans to meet the danger, to bring Japan into the actively anti-Soviet camp. All of that can be explained by fear for the safety of the citadel of true communism, Beijing, or it may go beyond that and, coupled with Deng Xiaoping's apparent wish for genuine domestic modernization, portend an abandonment of parts of the communist doctrine and system. It would be a paradox indeed if any tendencies of that kind were thwarted and stifled through Beijing's perception of the West's lethargy, sclerotic defense systems, and mediocrity of leadership. But study of why the shift occurred is necessary in any event, and is far from adequately represented in the literature that has been examined.

Finally, one might hope eventually to find scholarly attention devoted to what the Sino-Soviet dispute has meant to the ordinary people of the PRC and the USSR; in particular, how the dispute may have affected the domestic policies of the leaders of both countries, and more broadly the differences between Soviet and Chinese communism—recognizing that there were bound to be many differences independently of the dispute. The question of the human casualties of Mao's real or ostensible rule has scarcely been opened, though the assessment of how many died under Stalin's heel is advancing. But for those who did not die, what has it been like to live under such regimes in the various periods concerned, with respect to their standard of living, family life, education, and culture? We seem to have passed beyond the era of assuming that no one was starving in China and no flies were left there, but much remains to be done in understanding the real complexities of the situation. What is the credibility of the regime in both countries? Is what is said about China more readily accepted in the

USSR than other assertions and claims of the official press, and are statements about the Soviets more apt to persuade the Chinese public?

Certainly for most citizens of both countries, Heaven has been abolished, and the "emperor," no longer far away, is close to their lives in a way never true in the imperial past. Better understanding of what that means to the hundreds of millions of human beings concerned must still be sought. The admirable work of the writers examined above has not exhausted the topics still open to those who follow them.

The Sino-Soviet Dispute in the 1970s: An Overview

HARRY GELMAN

Fifteen years ago last summer, the two old men who now dominate the Soviet and Chinese communist parties met in Bucharest to argue face to face for the last time—the last time, indeed, that any Soviet and Chinese leaders have met in their party capacity.[1] Since that episode, Leonid Brezhnev and the Soviet Union, on the one hand, and Deng Xiaoping and China, on the other, have moved along paths and through experiences that could hardly stand in greater contrast. Partly because of this, the intervening years have drastically conditioned and transformed the attitudes each power now

1. Soviet and Chinese Politburo members did meet on one other occasion, but in their governmental rather than party capacities. This was the encounter between Premiers Zhou and Kosygin at Beijing airport in September 1969 which negotiated a halt to the border incidents of that year and the start of border negotiations. There is no evidence of any other meeting of any kind between Soviet and Chinese Politburo-level figures since the Deng-Brezhnev encounter at the Romanian party congress in 1965, despite repeated Soviet efforts to obtain such a meeting.

brings to the Sino-Soviet conflict. In the process, certain of the old grounds of contention that preoccupied Brezhnev and Deng at their final encounter have vanished. But the most fundamental issue—the incompatible geopolitical interests of the two states—has emerged in much sharper relief.

THE TWO RIVALS

In contrast to the situation with regard to China, the two most important aspects of Soviet experience over the last decade and a half show an extraordinary continuity. Soviet internal politics since Khrushchev's fall have been dominated by Brezhnev's slow and methodical consolidation of personal power within an immobile oligarchy representative of all major bureaucratic interests. Soviet external politics have meanwhile been conditioned, more than anything else, by the Soviet Union's equally methodical and continuous pursuit of ever-greater military power. This multiplication of all categories of military strength has in turn furnished one of the essential prerequisites for the growth of a more assertive Soviet foreign policy over the last decade,[2] and for a spectacular expansion of Soviet presence and influence abroad at the expense of the interests of both the United States and China.

At the same time, however, just as the years have increasingly enfeebled Brezhnev in the physical use of the personal power he has won, they have imposed a hardening of the bureaucratic arteries on the increasingly powerful state he leads. Side by side with their single-minded enlargement of the Soviet military machine and Soviet geopolitical weight, the Soviet leaders over the last decade have witnessed a dramatic secular decline in the rate of growth of the Soviet economic base that nourishes that machine.

By the beginning of the 1980s, faced with these worsening economic rigidities and resource constraints at home, engaged in one war of conquest in Afghanistan and supporting another in Cambodia, striving to hold down a restive population in Poland, the Soviet leadership remained determined to defend and expand the new areas of influence achieved over the last decade through the military operations of the Soviet Union and its clients in Africa and Asia. It seemed equally determined to make no significant concession to either the United States or China to reduce the hostile reaction of either to the broad thrust of these Soviet policies. And it showed no sign of readiness to modify the military investment policies that have supported this Soviet posture.

In contrast to the Soviet process of continuous internal political and

2. There have obviously been others, such as a confluence of favorable opportunities in the Third World and a widespread impression of declining U.S. influence, presence, capability, and inclination to act.

economic calcification and continuously growing assertion of geopolitical claims as a world actor, China has experienced extraordinary swings between extremes in both internal and external policy. Not long after Deng's last talk with Brezhnev in 1965 he vanished into the maelstrom of the Cultural Revolution. This great "calamity," as the Chinese now call it,[3] was, among many other things, Mao's prolonged effort both to purge the Chinese party as led by Liu Shaoqi and Deng and to scourge from the party, and from Chinese society as a whole, that taint of "revisionism," or decay of ideological purpose, which Mao saw lurking in weak human nature and whose supreme example was said to be the Soviet Union. In the process, Mao and various of his protégés caused what the Chinese now acknowledge to have been immense human suffering and injustice, occasioned great setbacks for Chinese economic and technological development and education, and for some time enforced an almost total political isolation of China from the capitalist and communist worlds alike.[4]

Shortly before the beginning of the 1970s, China began to emerge from this condition, above all because of the shock administered by the events of 1968 (Czechoslovakia) and 1969 (Zhenbao) in dramatizing the extent of the Soviet military threat to the Chinese state. The Chinese recognition of this danger transformed toleration of external isolation and internal chaos into an excessive luxury. It therefore helped to influence Mao to allow Zhou Enlai to begin a decade-long process of reaching out into the world—above all, the capitalist industrialized world—for support against this Soviet threat. At the same time, Mao's perception of this heightened Soviet danger probably contributed to his decision to place somewhat greater limits on the power of the ideologues and to initiate a succession of purges of certain of his erstwhile "ultra-left" lieutenants.[5] Because of Mao's enduring ideo-

---

3. "The havoc which the counterrevolutionary gang wrought for ten long years spelt calamity for our people . . ." (Ye Jianying speech on the thirtieth anniversary of the PRC, *Xinhua*, September 29, 1979).

4. "Yet to promote their ultraleft-wing foreign policy line, Lin Biao and the 'gang of four' righteously shouted: We are not afraid of severance of relations, we are not afraid of isolation." See Zhang Mingyang, "An Analysis of Lin Biao and the 'Gang of Four's' Ultraleft-wing Foreign Policy," in *Fudan Xuebao* (Shanghai), no. 2, March 1980, translated in JPRS *Translations on Chinese Political, Social and Military Affairs*, no. 103, July 30, 1980. This viewpoint was enforced essentially from late 1965 until late 1968, but, as the article cited shows, was revived later, after Lin's death in 1971, and took the form of periodic behind-the-scenes attacks by Jiang Qing and her three colleagues against the foreign policies of Zhou Enlai and Deng Xiaoping.

5. Notably, his former secretary and ghost-writer, former Cultural Revolution Group head Chen Boda, in 1970, and his heir Lin Biao, in 1971.

logical prejudices, however, it was only after his death in 1976 that either process—external or internal—could be carried to completion.

By the close of the decade, a sharply transformed Chinese leadership dominated by a resurrected Deng Xiaoping faced the Soviet Union. A consensus in this leadership was more than ever convinced, by what seemed fresh and rapidly accumulating evidence, that the broad thrust of Soviet policy, both worldwide and around China's periphery, was incompatible with China's vital interests. At the same time, however, the Deng leadership had achieved a new and more realistic awareness of the extent of China's economic and military weakness, both in absolute terms and in relation to the scope of the perceived Soviet threat. The men now in charge in Beijing retained a strong desire to continue to expand China's association with the capitalist world—particularly the United States—to counterbalance Soviet geopolitical pressure. But they were also convinced, after the traumatic experiences of the Maoist past, of China's need for major pragmatic changes in her economic choices and practices, and they realized that these changes would make it difficult indeed to devote those resources to improvement of the Chinese military position that seemed to be commensurate with the anticipated dangers. An inner tension has thus come to exist between post-Mao China's perception of its immediate domestic policy needs and its foreign policy imperatives. We shall return to the implications of this "contradiction."

THE TRANSFORMED SCOPE OF THE CONFLICT

Both sides are thus now well aware that the events of the Brezhnev era have introduced radically new features into their relationship, which have transformed the nature of the Sino-Soviet conflict. Of these new features, five are particularly important.

The Military Confrontation. First, and most significant, is the fact that the conflict has been militarized. This phenomenon has by now been a prominent feature of Sino-Soviet relations for so many years that it is worth recalling that the military confrontation is essentially a post-Khrushchev addition to the quarrel. Viewed in historical perspective, the long-term Soviet military build-up against China, initiated early in the Brezhnev regime, has proceeded methodically alongside the accelerated development of Soviet strategic capabilities in relation to the United States. It thus reflects, and is part of, that broad, continuous, and heightened allocation of resources by Khrushchev's heirs to the wide variety of Soviet military purposes alluded to earlier. It is also worth stressing that the adoption of this policy toward China does not appear to have been a response to any specific event. Rather, the build-up against China has reflected a generalized perception of intense Chinese hostility, as well as an estimate evidently made at the outset of the Brezhnev regime, and reinforced thereafter, that this hostility was likely to endure.[6] Although the series of clashes along the Sino-Soviet border in 1969 undoubtedly strengthened the Soviet conclusions about China that have prompted this build-up, they did not precipitate it. By the same token, the evident dampening of such fire fights and the initiation of border negotiations since 1969 have not brought an end to the build-up.[7]

In sum, the shift of a substantial portion of Soviet military weight to Asia to confront the Chinese has been a considered national policy throughout the Brezhnev era, and almost certainly remains a matter of long-term planning and investment intended to be carried on incrementally into a distant future. The Soviets apparently intend in this way to maintain a continuously updated decisive advantage in firepower facing China at every step up the potential ladder of escalation, with the criterion for sufficiency heavily influenced by the need to compensate for dependence on a long rail line for reinforcement. The evidence of the past decade suggests that the momentum of this process is little affected by tactical shifts in Chinese behavior toward the Soviet Union, and would require revolutionary changes in the Soviet perception of China to halt, let alone to reverse. In this respect, as well, the build-up against China resembles the Soviet build-up of its strategic forces against the United States, which proceeded throughout the decade with undiminished intensity regardless of the changing U.S. political posture toward the Soviet Union or the pace of U.S. weapons programs.

The powerful forces the Soviets continue gradually to assemble in Siberia and Mongolia, however, seem to the Chinese—and indeed to many Western observers—greatly to exceed Soviet defensive needs, particularly since the Soviet advantage over China in military technology continues to widen.[8] This does not mean that this build-up reflects any concrete decision, already taken, eventually to attack China, nor is it probable that the Chinese

6. To the extent that any one event did make a particularly important contribution to the Soviet assumptions that produced the build-up, this is likely to have been Mao's detailed accusations, made in 1964, that Russia and the Soviet Union had seized enormous amounts of Chinese territory, and his comment, "We have not as yet settled these matters with the Soviet Union." These statements were made to a Japanese delegation while Sino-Soviet border discussions were being held, and were initially published in *Shekai Shoho* (Tokyo), August 11, 1964.

7. In his 1980 interview with the Italian journalist Oriana Fallaci, Deng alluded to information demonstrating that "the Soviets go on concentrating in the areas near China." See the *Washington Post*, August 31, 1980.

8. "Even as the PLA seeks, for example, current anti-tank weapons, the Soviet Union is beginning to deploy a tank designed to defeat such systems. The Chinese must run very fast to stay in the same place." See Angus M. Fraser, "Military Modernization in China," *Problems of Communism*, 28, no. 5–6 (September–December 1979): 49.

believe it does. Rather, Beijing sees the Soviet deployments opposite China as intended to serve as an instrument of geopolitical pressure on the PRC.

This pressure is exerted in two ways: (1) It is viewed as a "gun at the head" used by the Soviet Union to back up the Soviet bargaining position in the Sino-Soviet border talks, and to add credibility to the Soviet refusal to entertain certain Chinese demands. (2) It is now also a means for tacit coercion of China on behalf of Soviet geopolitical interests elsewhere in Asia. This second function of these Soviet military dispositions grew increasingly important toward the end of the 1970s with the growth of Soviet political ambitions in Asia, and it is now unlikely ever to disappear. In particular, the Soviet forces along the Sino-Soviet frontier have become a lever with which Moscow has sought to inhibit and constrain the scope of Chinese military reactions to Vietnamese operations in Indochina.

The Border Negotiation Process. Partly as a result of this growing military confrontation, the Sino-Soviet border negotiations have emerged over the last decade as an arena in which the whole spectrum of the incompatible interests of the two sides is brought into focus. The intractable nature of the issues involved has deadlocked these sporadic talks from the moment they began in October 1969 to the present day. These issues are intractable, however, precisely because they go far beyond questions of disputed territory, and involve the total perception each of the rival powers has of its opponent. The Soviets will not seriously consider the Chinese demands in these negotiations partly because they are thought to involve the surrender of important Soviet interests, but more generally because major concessions would be considered appeasement of an intransigent enemy and acceptance of a far-reaching defeat in a much broader struggle.

Similarly, the Chinese for their part adamantly adhere to the border claims over which the talks are stalemated not so much because of the importance they assign to the territory in question, and still less because they expect the Soviets ever to yield, but rather because the assertion of these claims is seen as a major instrument of political warfare against the antagonist. And if the present pragmatic Chinese leaders have thus far maintained this instrument—this border negotiating posture—intact as it was bequeathed to them by Mao, this is because they continue to perceive events everywhere as reinforcing their overall assessment of the Soviet Union as an implacable enemy of China that must be resisted on the broadest possible front.

The negotiating positions thus generated and defined have therefore remained essentially unchanged since they were first spelled out publicly at the outset of the negotiations eleven years ago.[9] In brief, the Chinese assert

---

9. See the Chinese Foreign Ministry Statement of October 8, 1969 (*Xinhua*, October 8, 1969).

that tsarist Russia and the Soviet Union have illegally occupied certain territories not granted to Russia even by the so-called unequal treaties of the nineteenth and twentieth centuries. These involve, primarily, a sizable stretch of territory in the Pamirs, in the west, and several hundred islands in the Amur and Ussuri rivers, in the east, prominently including the two large islands at the junction of the two rivers which the Soviets consider essential to the defense of Khabarovsk. The Chinese declare this territory to be "in dispute," and require that the Soviets evacuate all of it before negotiation of an agreed frontier. The Soviets adamantly refuse, and offer instead the palliative of a nonaggression treaty. This the Chinese contemptuously reject.[10]

Although there seems little prospect that this stalemate will soon be broken, both sides appear to consider the occasional meetings that reiterate the two positions to be useful, as representing a symbol of stability in the relationship that serves to some degree to moderate the tensions created by the growth of military forces along the border. By the same token, each would probably regard the unilateral termination of these talks by the opponent as a dangerous sign of unpredictable intent.

The Geopolitical Struggle. The third addition of the Brezhnev era—and particularly of the last decade—to the Sino-Soviet dispute has already been alluded to. This is the Chinese sense of being faced with an inescapable geopolitical contest, worldwide in scope, with an advancing and insatiable Soviet power. Although it will be argued below that a perceived conflict of national interests has always been the most important single ingredient in the Sino-Soviet quarrel, there is little doubt that for the Chinese this perception has been extraordinarily magnified in the 1970s.

The decade that began against the background of the Soviet invasion of Czechoslovakia in 1968 and the Soviet defeats administered to China in the fire fights of 1969 was to conclude with the Soviet invasion of Afghanistan. Between these events, the spectacular Soviet interventions in Africa from mid-decade on—successfully combining new long-range transport and logistic capabilities, the large-scale use of Cuban proxy forces, and Soviet military leadership—demonstrated the Soviet ability to project power on a scale and at a distance hitherto unseen, and gave impetus to the widespread impression of an advancing tide of Soviet activity and presence in the Third World. This impression was thereafter strongly reinforced, in a manner much more painful to Beijing, by the events in Indochina in the closing years of the decade.

In the wake of the U.S. expulsion from the Indochinese peninsula in

---

10. For a more detailed discussion of this subject, see Harry Gelman, "Outlook for Sino-Soviet Relations," *Problems of Communism*, 28, no. 5–6 (September–December 1979): 57–60.

1975, the Soviet Union achieved a major political breakthrough as a result of the Vietnamese decision to move toward the USSR for support against China and in pursuit of Hanoi's local ambitions. By signing a treaty of friendship with Vietnam in November 1978, the Soviet leadership provided Hanoi with an instrument of deterrence against China that set the stage for the Vietnamese blitzkrieg that overran China's client, Cambodia, in December and January. Although Cambodian resistance has since continued, and although Beijing in response staged a limited military incursion into Vietnam early in 1979, Hanoi with Soviet assistance has thus far made good its attempt to assert its domination over the peninsula.

Because Beijing has been prudently unwilling, in view of the Soviet threat posed on the Chinese border, to assume the risks latent in any attempt to carry an attack on Vietnam so far as to threaten the viability of the Vietnamese regime, China has been unable to prevent Indochina from being converted into a zone hostile to its influence. The Soviets, on the other hand, in return for their services to Hanoi have acquired military rights and benefits in the peninsula which, though fairly restricted in scope, are nevertheless unprecedented, and which are seen by Beijing as gradually growing.[11] China, meanwhile, has been left for the indefinite future with a second hostile frontier.

Soviet conduct in the 1970s has thus given new and concrete meaning to the frequently expressed Chinese assertion that the Soviets were seeking to "encircle" them, politically and militarily. To the north, and notably in Mongolia, Beijing perceives an unceasing accumulation of military force intended to intimidate. To the east, China finds a steady growth in Soviet naval forces in the Pacific, dramatized by the movement of those forces during the Sino-Vietnamese hostilities, and by the subsequent journey of the *Minsk* around Africa to Vladivostok in 1979.[12] To the south, the PRC encounters a pugnacious client of the USSR, supplied and supported by the Soviet Union, and furnishing military bases to the Soviets in China's vicinity. And to the west, in Afghanistan, the Chinese find an invading Soviet army engaged in a punitive war of conquest adjacent to Xinjiang. Most Chinese are likely to see this striking combination of geopolitical

11. Chinese commentaries throughout 1979 and 1980 repeatedly portrayed Soviet naval and air use of Vietnamese facilities—particularly at Camranh Bay—as gradually expanding, and as furnishing a "forward base" for Soviet operations through the Strait of Malacca into the Indian Ocean (for example, Beijing radio commentary: "Why Has the Soviet Union Taken a Fancy to Camranh Bay?" August 8, 1980).

12. Beijing radio on May 23, 1979, pointedly noted that "when the guns roared on the border between China and Vietnam, Soviet warships became active and caused trouble in the Beibu Gulf to support Vietnam, the small hegemonist."

realities as testifying to a momentum in Soviet policy not susceptible to influence by any Chinese bilateral concessions to the Soviet Union.

The Changing Triangle. The fourth great change in the Sino-Soviet relationship during the Brezhnev era has been, of course, the virtual reversal of China's alliances. This has occurred incrementally in the 1970s in tandem with the growth of the perceived Soviet geopolitical threat.

The emerging Chinese perception that the United States represented a receding threat to Chinese national interests, increasingly dwarfed by the Soviet threat, became a conviction during the first two years of the decade, the period in which that portion of the Chinese leadership that was the most reluctant to admit this was removed,[13] and in which Chinese dealings with the United States began. The subsequent U.S. withdrawal from Indochina then confirmed this judgment. Moreover, this local withdrawal was accompanied and followed by a variety of evidence elsewhere to confirm the broader Chinese dictum that the United States was in fact a retreating force in the world as a whole, in contrast to the broadly advancing force of Soviet "hegemonism."

Indeed, this trend of declining U.S. presence and influence soon passed the point of being reassuring to China as evidence of the nonthreatening character of U.S. policy, and became, in the Chinese view, much too much of a good thing. Having spent most of the Khrushchev era rebuking the Soviet Union for its inadequacies in the struggle against the United States, the PRC was to spend most of the 1970s exhorting the United States to halt its retreat before the Soviet Union and to struggle more vigorously and courageously against the "polar bear." This reversal in attitudes was accompanied, in the latter years of the decade, by a trend toward increasing Chinese political, economic, and military cooperation with the United States, a trend that was given impetus first by the simultaneous decay of the U.S. détente with the Soviet Union, and then by the completion of Chinese "normalization" of relations with the United States in December 1978.

Under these circumstances, the 1950 Sino-Soviet treaty of alliance, which had been the centerpiece of Chinese foreign policy in the early years when Mao was "leaning to one side" toward the Soviet Union, became an increasing anomoly in the world of the late 1970s. Although Beijing had already lived comfortably for many years with the fact that the treaty had become a dead letter, the PRC was now confronted by the circumstance that this thirty-year instrument would be automatically renewed unless

---

13. That is to say, Chen Boda and Lin Biao. This is not to imply that resistance to this view did not continue after 1971 from the Gang of Four, but that it was less effective after the new line regarding the United States had been broadly approved by Mao. See Zhang Mingyang, "An Analysis" (note 4 above).

formally renounced one year before its expiration in the spring of 1980. The Deng Xiaoping leadership was most reluctant to allow this to happen. In the event, the PRC used its own necessity for diplomatic advantage, and promised Japan, as one of the inducements for Japanese agreement in 1978 to a Sino-Japanese friendship treaty on terms sought by China and opposed by the Soviet Union, that China would announce intention to abrogate the Sino-Soviet treaty the following year.[14] When China carried out this promise in April 1979, another milestone had been passed in the Sino-Soviet relationship.

An important footnote to this episode was provided, however, when the Chinese coupled this termination of the treaty with a proposal to the Soviet Union that new talks be held about the fundamentals of the relationship. In retrospect, it seems likely that the purposes underlying this suggestion were entirely tactical. The Chinese leadership sought, on the one hand, to use these proposed talks to create distrust between the Soviet Union and its Vietnamese clients by implying the possibility of an amelioration of Sino-Soviet relations at the expense of Vietnam. The Soviet Union was evidently highly defensive about Vietnamese suspicions of such a possibility, and was at pains to rebut them.[15] At the same time, the Chinese evidently envisioned the creation of a new and additional series of ongoing Sino-Soviet contacts, similar to the stalemated border talks, in which the struggle against Soviet "hegemony" would be maintained and nothing of significance conceded, but whose existence might nevertheless serve to some degree to ease the tensions created by China's new two-front confrontation with the Soviets and their clients.

Thus, although Beijing now offered to hold these talks without the unacceptable prerequisites that had previously made such conversations impossible for Moscow, well before the talks began Chinese leaders had hinted that they intended to reinsert these demands during the negotiations themselves as a necessary condition for any progress.[16] In the event, this is

14. The prospect of such abrogation was an inducement to Japan because the Sino-Soviet treaty had singled out Japan as a prospective antagonist. Deng Xiaoping on several occasions in 1979 informed Japanese journalists that the treaty would be abrogated. Kyodo News Service (Tokyo), September 6, 1978.

15. An authoritative *Pravda* article (July 11, 1979) signed with the pseudonym "Aleksandrov" voiced suspicions that the Chinese were seeking to use the preliminary negotiations leading to the talks to "bring pressure on Vietnam," and insisted that such efforts were in vain.

16. As early as July, Vice-Foreign Minister Han Nianlong was quoted by a Japanese interviewer as stating that "during the talks, there is a strong possibility China will bring up the issue of a Soviet military withdrawal from Mongolia." See *Mainichi Shimbun* (Tokyo), July 15, 1979. In August, Vice-Premier Geng Biao was quoted in a similar interview as asserting that as long as the Soviet

what transpired. The Soviets discovered, when the talks convened in the fall of 1979, that the signing of a new document on the principles of the bilateral relationship, as desired by Moscow, required Soviet action first to cease all assistance to Vietnam, to evacuate its military forces from Mongolia, and to reduce Soviet force levels in Siberia to those of Khrushchev's day—in short, to eliminate totally and in advance all the forms of geopolitical pressure on China to which Beijing objected.[17] Since the Soviet Union has no intention of doing this, the first session of these talks ended without result. The holding of further sessions was then indefinitely postponed by China in the wake of the Soviet invasion of Afghanistan.[18]

The Economic Reorientation. The fifth and last major change in the relationship during the Brezhnev era represents the bringing to fruition of a fundamental shift in orientation begun in Khrushchev's time. This is the drastic turn in Chinese external economic relations from reliance primarily on a relationship with the Soviet Union to overwhelming emphasis on dealings with the West and Japan.

In broadest terms, this pivoting of China's foreign economic policy was accomplished in two half steps. The economic disengagement of China from the Soviet Union, like the political and military disengagement, was essentially a phenomenon of the Khrushchev era, precipitated by Khrushchev's sudden—and in Chinese eyes, treacherous—withdrawal of Soviet experts from China in 1960, and carried to fruition in the precipitous decline of the economic relationship during the Chinese depression of the early 1960s. The subsequent fundamental reorientation of Chinese foreign economic dealings toward the non-Soviet world was an accomplishment of the Brezhnev era, and particularly of the 1970s.

Despite the much greater caution in foreign purchasing shown by the PRC recently, and despite Beijing's new awareness of the grave difficulties it faces in assimilating modern advanced technology, the orientation of Chinese foreign trade toward the industrialized capitalist world is unlikely to change significantly over the next decade. Although there has been a modest revival of Chinese trade with the Soviet Union in the 1970s along

---

Union did not change its attitude toward the "hegemony" issue, the result of the talks would be "obvious."

17. See the interview with *People's Daily* commentator Tan Wenrui, *Der Spiegel* (Hamburg), February 18, 1980.

18. A Chinese Foreign Ministry spokesman in announcing this postponement made the unusual statement that the invasion of Afghanistan had menaced world peace "and the security of China as well." He asserted that it had also created "new obstacles" for Sino-Soviet normalization, presumably superimposed on those already cited by Tan Wenrui, above. See the *Beijing Review*, January 28, 1980.

with the overall growth of Chinese foreign trade, the Soviet economic connection represents a distinctly subordinate one for China today, subject to severe constraints, and is likely to remain so. This is true partly because of Soviet inability to compete with the West and Japan in most areas of civilian technology desired by China, and partly because of Chinese determination never again to allow the Soviet Union to reach a position where it could use economic relations with China for political leverage.

Nor has the increasing pragmatism of Chinese internal economic life significantly helped Soviet standing in China by improving the image of the Soviet economic model. The Soviets have clearly hoped that this would be the case—that the removal of the ideological impediments imposed by Mao and the Gang of Four on the use of material incentives and rational planning, together with the rehabilitation of many figures associated with the era when the USSR was closely involved with Chinese industrialization, would mean a rehabilitation of Soviet economic practice in Chinese eyes. Soviet commentators frequently allude, therefore, somewhat wistfully, to laudatory statements about the Soviet Union made at the Chinese Eighth Party Congress in 1956 as an example that the Chinese pragmatists should now emulate.

Despite obvious similarities between the USSR and the PRC in the structure of many of the central economic mechanisms earlier copied by China, the direction of change in China is again moving away from the Soviet example. Rejecting the bureaucratic rigidity, overcentralization, drastic overemphasis on military production and the sectors of heavy industry necessary to supply military industries, and habitual underemphasis on light industry and agriculture they associate with Soviet practice, Chinese leaders have turned instead to the Hungarian and Yugoslav examples. In their cautious exploration of limited decentralization of management, partial use of the market mechanism, and some worker participation in management,[19] the Chinese have taken steps, however modest, that many Soviet *apparatchiki* regard as anathema, and that violate shibboleths that have paralyzed effective reform in the Soviet Union for many years. In short, in its movement from left to right since Mao's death the PRC apparently has bypassed the USSR, and what was scorned revisionism for the Chinese leaders of one era has become scorned dogmatism for those of another.

19. The Chinese have proceeded by trial and error in these matters, and retreated considerably in late 1980 and early 1981 from their initial application of these reforms as a result of difficulties encountered in the enforcement of broad central priorities, particularly in resource allocation. Nevertheless, the reforms have not been abandoned, and continue to reflect pragmatic Chinese impulses that have long been stifled in the Soviet Union by an ideologically inspired immobilism.

THE METAMORPHOSIS

With the advent of these five new central realities of the Sino-Soviet relationship in the 1970s, what has become of the main features of the dispute as they were widely assumed to exist before the Cultural Revolution? Let us review three of these older features in their turn.

The Ideological Nature of the Dispute. The so-called ideological dispute has virtually disappeared, and the ostensibly ideological indictments hurled at the Soviet Union by China from April 1960 on have now been transformed into accusations of a very different kind, often contradicting those that went before.

1. The charge that pusillanimous Soviet policy, overintent on conciliating voracious "U.S. imperialism," was betraying the sacred cause of armed revolution by all the world's peoples has now been replaced by the charge that insatiably aggressive Soviet policy, pressing everywhere against a weakened and retreating United States, was threatening all the world's peoples with domination by the Soviet "hegemonists."

2. The charge that the cowardly Soviet Union was everywhere inhibiting revolutions has now been replaced by the charge that the insidious Soviet Union is everywhere plotting coups and "making trouble."[20]

3. The famous Maoist metaphor of the United States as a "paper tiger," outwardly strong but inwardly weak, which must be challenged rather than appeased, has long since disappeared; it has been replaced by a very similar message about the Soviet Union, minus the metaphorical imagery. Allusions to U.S. weakness are now never exulting in tone, and often regretful.

4. The call for the broadest possible united front of the world's peoples against "U.S. imperialism" has been replaced by a virtually identical call for broad unity against "Soviet hegemonism."

5. The assertion that world war can only be averted or postponed by steadfast united struggle against the United States has been replaced by a similar assertion regarding the Soviet Union. But the parallel Maoist claim that the consequences of such a war—should it nevertheless materialize—should not be feared has now been dropped by the Chinese, despite Soviet assertions that the Chinese continue to welcome the prospect of a world war.[21]

6. Finally, Beijing has also abandoned the claim that the USSR was

---

20. For example, the Chinese habitually attribute the 1978 coups in Aden and Kabul to Soviet instigation. See the *Beijing Review*, January 19, 1979.

21. In general, consistent with the Soviet effort to depict present Chinese foreign policy as remaining Maoist and aggressive in essence, Soviet propaganda tends to minimize the extent of the foreign policy doctrinal changes that have occurred.

seeking a "phony" or "goulash" communism by catering to selfish materialistic and individualistic tendencies at the expense of selfless ideological purpose. Instead, as already noted, the Chinese now portray the Soviet Union as dominated by a rigidly militarized economy in which military requirements, themselves evoked by external "hegemonic" ambitions, increasingly constrict the material well-being of the Soviet population.

In retrospect, it seems clear that the Chinese ideological accusations and demands of the 1960s, while indeed reflecting genuine prejudices of Mao and certain of his associates, nevertheless were also more or less consciously tailored to fit what were then assumed to be the foreign policy needs of the Chinese state in its confrontation with the United States in East Asia. The language used was also tailored to the unsuccessful Chinese effort in those years to harness the Soviet state and its international instruments—the so-called world communist movement and the Soviet-controlled international front organizations—to these Chinese national needs. Since then, a changing perception of Chinese national interests and the audiences to be addressed on behalf of those interests has produced the revolution described in the nature of Chinese rhetorical attacks on Moscow. This fundamental shift was itself facilitated by the disappearance of those individuals in the Chinese leadership most reluctant to change Chinese priorities.

The Location of the Arena of Dispute. As a corollary, the struggle between Beijing and Moscow in the world communist movement, which for a time in the late 1950s and early 1960s seemed the main arena of their political conflict, has long since ceased to be so. By 1966 Beijing had opted out of this struggle and had read itself out of the world fraternity, breaking party ties not only with the Communist Party of the Soviet Union but with all those parties still closely aligned with it. When China gradually reemerged from its self-imposed international isolation during the 1970s, its main endeavors in the political competition with the Soviet Union were channeled away from the old communist movement and toward the elite of the capitalist industrial world and the Third World, and remain so to this day.[22] Although the post-Mao leadership in China, determined to explore all options available in the universal struggle against Soviet influence, has cautiously resumed contacts with certain of the old communist parties that have shown a significant degree of independence from Moscow,[23] this

22. Zhang Mingyang, in the article cited in note 4 above, notes that Lin Biao and the Gang of Four had sought to sabotage this redirection by stressing revolutionary missionary activity to the detriment of the preservation of governmental contacts.

23. Notably through the renewal of contacts with the Italian Communist Party. Beijing was probably gratified when an Italian communist delegation's visit to China in the spring of 1980 evoked a strong reaction in the Soviet press.

remains a marginal aspect of that struggle. Thus, in venue as well as in rhetoric, the old quasi-religious conflict has been secularized.

The Dependence of the Conflict on Mao. A third major aspect of the old conflict that has been transformed, and one which may have implications for the future, concerns the role of personalities. To a considerable extent, the evolution of the quarrel in its early years between 1956 and 1964 had seemed impelled by the attitudes, prejudices, and egos of the leading actors, Mao and Khrushchev. The post-Khrushchev Soviet leadership, sensing this, attempted to find a basis for understanding with China in November 1964, immediately after Khrushchev's removal.[24] Both sides were apparently disappointed to discover that this was impossible, because the vested interests on each side were incompatible. Thereafter the Soviets for many years pinned hopes for some amelioration of relations—on terms acceptable to their interests—on an improvement in the status of Zhou Enlai, whom they had long correctly regarded as the most moderate of Mao's senior lieutenants. But when in the early 1970s Zhou did gain a somewhat freer hand in directing foreign policy, the USSR was again gravely disappointed, finding Chinese flexibility and competitive capabilities indeed greatly enhanced but Chinese antagonism toward the Soviet Union essentially undiminished. Soviet allusions to Zhou in the final years of his life were consequently often hostile, and betrayed Moscow's chagrin.

Subsequently, therefore, the Soviets resumed their long wait for the death of Mao, expecting no improvement in his lifetime but hoping for better things thereafter. When this event at last occurred in September 1976, Moscow immediately probed the attitude of his successors, but was at once again rebuffed.[25] In the four years since, Soviet hopes have remained unfulfilled. Thus far, a consensus unfavorable to Soviet desires persists, sustained to some degree by the memory of past Soviet injuries to China, and much more by that sense of continuing and growing Soviet geopolitical pressure on China already discussed. In sum, the conflict has indeed outlived the leading personalities who gave it its initial impetus, and is about to be handed on to a new generation in both countries.

THE NEXT DECADE

In view of the rapidity and magnitude of the changes in the Sino-Soviet relationship in the last two decades, it would surely be foolhardy to pos-

24. Through the exploratory visit by Zhou Enlai that month to Moscow. Both sides subsequently attributed the failure of this mission to the opponent's obduracy.

25. This probe took the form of a congratulatory message addressed to Hua Guofeng in his capacity as party chairman. The Chinese rejected this rather crude effort to test Beijing's willingness to reestablish party relations.

tulate a freezing of present trends over the next ten years to be inevitable. But although the durability of some aspects of the present equation remains to be demonstrated, at least one very powerful factor will almost certainly persist. We shall now review each of these considerations in turn.

Considerable uncertainty persists about three issues. One is the question of the degree of stability that may be expected of the Chinese leadership over the next decade; or put more precisely, the degree to which a continuation of factional struggle—likely in any event—may be expected to affect Chinese policy generally and policy toward the USSR in particular. One favorable aspect is the Chinese awareness of the damage that leadership turmoil has done to China in the past. Another is the likelihood that while some disagreements may persist, a considerably greater degree of foreign policy consensus exists in the Chinese leadership than existed in early 1976, or even in early 1979. In addition, the record to date suggests that Chinese national interests are so sharply and directly affected by the Soviet Union as to insulate the Soviet issue to a considerable extent from the changing fortunes of individuals. Nevertheless, in view of the demonstrated volatility of the Chinese leadership, it is not impossible that future shifts in the balance of power within that leadership, particularly after the demise of Deng Xiaoping, could affect the Chinese posture toward Moscow.

Second, it must be recognized that some uncertainty remains about the future continuity and consistency of U.S. policy toward both China and the USSR. The United States has yet to demonstrate a broad and lasting consensus governing U.S. policies affecting the PRC—whether on the extent of the evolving U.S. security relationship with Beijing, on U.S. policy toward Moscow on matters affecting Chinese interests, or even on the understanding previously reached over Taiwan. Even though the Chinese quarrel with the USSR derives from fundamental and self-sustained issues of Soviet behavior that Beijing will find difficult to evade regardless of U.S. conduct, it is conceivable that a radical change in U.S. behavior on a matter very important to Beijing could evoke a change in Chinese tactics toward the Soviet Union.

Third, some uncertainty about the future course of the Sino-Soviet conflict also flows from the already mentioned "contradiction" between China's public hostility to the Soviet neighbor and her inability to alter significantly a position of relative military weakness—or even, indeed, to avoid reducing the priority assigned to military spending. Thus far, despite the grave military imbalance and the paucity of Chinese resources, it apparently remains the Chinese leadership calculation that the PRC's nuclear deterrent, the deterrent to land invasion created by her vast territory and population, and whatever assistance in military technology can be procured from the United States will together suffice to make continued resistance to Soviet "hegemonism" sustainable and major concessions unnecessary.

The Soviets, who are well aware of China's weaknesses, undoubtedly hope that their own demonstrated willingness to take decisive military action, as recently displayed in Afghanistan, will ultimately have an intimidating effect on Beijing, and eventually induce a much more conciliatory Chinese attitude toward Moscow. It is indeed likely that the Soviet objection to U.S. transfers of military technology to China stems not so much from fear that the present Sino-Soviet military imbalance could thereby be reversed to favor China and thus threaten the Soviet Union—highly improbable under any circumstances—but rather from a belief that the intimidating effect of Soviet local superiority will be diluted.

Against all these factors making for uncertainty, one element seems to possess very strong momentum and resistance to change. This is the assertive dynamism of Soviet foreign policy, which is likely to endure along with the continued growth of Soviet military capabilities in the 1980s. As a consequence, there is likely to be an indefinite continuation of what the Chinese term the Soviet "offensive posture" in Asia as elsewhere, pressing further against U.S. and Chinese interests, and impelling both to respond.

SOVIET EXPECTATIONS

Looking to the future in their relations with China across the panorama of issues, the Soviet leaders are likely to be somewhat ambivalent. Some Soviet specialists on China may prefer to emphasize what they interpret as the hopeful aspects of Chinese behavior since Mao's death. They may draw modest encouragement from the greater degree of civility in the conduct of state-to-state relations that has characterized post-Mao China,[26] from the decline and disappearance of Chinese ideologically charged rhetoric, from the gradual dismantling of Mao's reputation, from the rehabilitation of certain old Chinese cadres who under different circumstances many years ago had favored a more moderate Chinese attitude toward the USSR,[27] and from the obvious divisions within the Chinese elite.

The Soviet decision makers are likely to retain a certain skepticism about all this, however. For its part, looking back over the past decade and a half, the aging Soviet leadership is likely to be impressed by the continuity of Chinese hostility toward the USSR despite frequent changes in the mix of dominant Chinese personalities and drastic shifts in the Chinese posture toward the rest of the world. The Brezhnev regime is not likely to admit,

26. Notable in this respect was Chinese willingness to compromise sufficiently with Moscow to permit conclusion of a river navigation agreement in 1977. See Neville Maxwell, "Why the Russians Lifted the Blockade at Bear Island," *Foreign Affairs* 57, no. 1 (Fall 1978): 138–45. It should be stressed that this minor agreement did not affect Chinese claims in the border dispute.

27. Notably the deceased former ambassador to the USSR, Wang Jiaxiang, rehabilitated in April 1979.

even to itself, the extent to which its own policies have conditioned and perpetuated this Chinese attitude. The Soviets instead appear to attribute this persistence of Chinese antagonism to a regrettable underlying nationalism that permeates even the most nearly "sober" and "healthy" sections of the Chinese elite and allegedly preserves the essence of "Maoism" in Chinese policy despite all appearances to the contrary.[28] Although the Soviet leaders have by no means abandoned hope for some eventual change in Beijing favorable to their interests, they have a vivid sense of the extent to which those interests now collide with Beijing's. They have no inclination to make fundamental sacrifices in these interests and ambitions to conciliate the PRC. They remain, as before, far more inclined to hope that intimidation and a favorable "correlation of forces" may eventually, somehow, bring China to heel. In the meantime, they are likely to continue to base their assumptions about China on a prudent pessimism.

Prospects for the 1980s

HUGH SETON-WATSON

Hostility between the Soviet Union and China was one of the main facts of world politics in 1980. The causes that produced and intensified it—ideological, economic, military, territorial—are fairly well known, though in-

28. "The possibility of a 'peaceful respite' which Beijing is promising the peoples is interpreted by certain well-wishers of neo-Maoism, particularly in the West, as an indication of 'constructive shifts' and 'softening' in China's foreign policy. . . . The Chinese strategy, as the facts indicate, remains the same as under Mao Zedong." See I. Aleksandrov, "Beijing: Following a Course of Whipping Up Tension," *Pravda*, May 26, 1980.

dividual commentators continue to disagree about the relative importance of each at different times. Its development through the strong fluctuations of Chinese internal politics in the 1970s, and the varying attitudes to the Soviet Union at successive stages of Mao, Lin Biao, the Gang of Four, Zhou Enlai, and Deng Xiaoping are fully explored in previous chapters. Two points, which emerged from our discussion, seem worth stressing.

One is that there is a difference in the nature of the hostility of each nation to the other. On the Soviet side there appears to be an almost hysterical dread of hordes of little yellow men along the Soviet empire's southern and eastern borders, threatening one day to pour into the comparatively empty lands of Siberia and the Transbaikal region. Folk memories of medieval Mongol invasions combine with deep-seated racial prejudices, and this mentality has been noted by visitors to the USSR among both working people and the well educated. There are of course Soviet specialists who understand and respect Chinese culture, but these do not seem to form public opinion. Soviet political thinking has been obsessed, ever since 1919, by the dread of capitalist encirclement, and a certain older Russian self-righteousness has always regarded any combination of other states in opposition to Russian policies as an unholy alliance against Holy Russia. But a combination between Western states and China is endowed in Soviet imagination with an altogether higher level of unholiness than anything hitherto known.

The Chinese view was thought to be more pragmatic. Russia had been one of the European nations that in the nineteenth century had exploited the weakness of China, but it was not regarded as intrinsically worse or better than the others. But whereas the others had given up their previous privileges, and the status of Hong Kong and Macao was for the time being acceptable, and the United States had given partial satisfaction with regard to Taiwan, the Soviet leaders refused to make even verbal amends for the seizure of much larger territories by Russia in 1860, or to discuss the status of the Amur Islands, and kept some forty divisions along China's frontier. If, however, a future Soviet government should show itself more accommodating, no deep-seated Chinese hatred would inhibit negotiations. The psychological obstacles on the Soviet side might be expected to be more serious.

The second significant point is that the conflict has lost its ideological content. Until the death of Mao, Soviet spokesmen had denounced the doctrines and regime of "Maoism," which they saw as a monstrous perversion of Marxism-Leninism. For their part the Chinese saw in the Soviet leaders "modern revisionists," "new tsars," renegades to Marxism who had become drunk with great-power chauvinism and aimed at a condominium over the peoples of the world with the American imperialists. But with the death of Mao, the ascendancy of Deng Xiaoping, the liquidation of the Cultural Revolution, and the arrest of the Gang of Four, polemics on these lines were no longer relevant. Deng could hardly denounce Soviet revisionism when he was sponsoring archrevisionist policies, and Soviet propaganda would be wasted if directed against a Maoism which was no longer there.

China under Deng Xiaoping has embarked on a policy of the "four modernizations." But there will have to be a priority of modernizations, and the history of other rapidly modernizing polities has shown that the choice of priorities is both difficult and painful. Russian history has long been, and is still, dominated by the dilemma that military power requires industrial efficiency, and that industrial progress requires diversion of resources from military purposes, thereby threatening to weaken the state in the face of a hostile world. This was equally true of the eras of Peter the Great, Nicholas I, Witte, and Stalin. The Chinese are faced with this problem. The days when the invocation of the Thought of Mao provided an answer (much as the quotation of Stalin's apophthegm "There are no fortresses that Bolsheviks cannot storm" served in an earlier period in Soviet history) are long past. It is possible that the Chinese, heirs to a culture more ancient and more sophisticated than Russian culture, may prove more adept at economic development: the extraordinary successes of the overseas Chinese suggest it. Deng is certainly not neglecting the military factor, but seeks to balance it with the economic. China's orientation to the West will depend on the extent to which the United States and NATO maintain credibility as a counterweight to Soviet power, and on the extent and kind of economic assistance that China gets from the West. Disappointment in these two respects could make a reappraisal of relations with the Soviet Union inescapable.

The Soviet leaders felt threatened by China's improved relations not only with the United States but with Japan. The Chinese-Japanese Treaty of August 12, 1978, included the clause about opposition to "hegemony" (the Chinese code word for Soviet expansionism) which the Japanese had hesitated for three years to accept, from fear of antagonizing the Soviet Union. Throughout this period the Japanese would have been willing to refuse the reference to "hegemony" if the Soviet government had been willing to return to Japan the four islands lying north of Hokkaido. In the last resort Moscow had apparently considered it of higher priority to uphold the abstract principle of immutability of Soviet frontiers, and to keep territory enabling them to intimidate Hokkaido from a few miles' distance, than to prevent Japanese agreement with China. One is reminded of the attitude in 1850 of Tsar Nicholas I, who was not interested in the annexation of the mouth of the Amur, but when informed that a Russian naval captain had established a Russian settlement there, declared: "Where once the Russian flag has flown, it must not be lowered again."

It is curious to note that in the last century and more, Russia's position in the Far East has been most secure in those periods when she had good, or at least correct, relations with Japan—from 1875 to 1895, from 1907 to 1916, and, thanks to Stalin's brilliant diplomatic success in the April 1941 treaty, from 1941 to 1945. The periods of predominant Russian influence in China—from 1895 to 1905 and from 1945 to 1960—brought only defeat or disillusionment. Failure to stop Japan's drift toward China may prove to be one of the greatest mistakes in Soviet history.

Another important Far Eastern state is Vietnam, which, as shown in an earlier chapter, has moved even closer to the Soviet Union. Yet with its population of some sixty million, its battle-trained armies and highly militarized society, accustomed for more than thirty years to wartime austerity, it must be considered an autonomous factor. The country most likely to become an object of Vietnamese imperialism is Thailand. Potentially important, though at present passive, is the most populous Muslim state in the world, the Indonesian archipelago with its 150 million people. To its northwest lies Malaysia, where Muslim Malays confront overseas Chinese in uneasy coexistence; to the northeast the Philippines, in whose southern islands Muslim militants are in revolt against the government based on the Christian majority. The Muslim resurgence on the Persian Gulf does not yet seem to have affected the Indies, but it may yet. Beyond Indonesia in turn is Australia. It is worth remembering that the Soviet aim of becoming a major naval power in the Indian Ocean requires communication, through the narrow seas of the island region, with its Far Eastern base of Vladivostok. Southeast Asia has been described as the Balkans of Asia; but the varieties and complexity of its ethnic groups and its cultures (Buddhism, Islam, Confucianism and Christianity meet in the peninsula and islands) far surpass those of the Balkans, and the population is about six times larger.

India can hardly be regarded as part of the Far Eastern scene. Although Indian leaders like to think of their country as a great power, their concern has been limited in practice to the subcontinent, and marginally to the seas surrounding it. Indian policy has long been obsessed with Pakistan. This obsession may lead India into support of the Soviet enterprise in Afghanistan, and the two powers may have a common interest in promoting the disintegration of Pakistan. China's support of Pakistan has been resented in India, but there is not much that China can do to help Pakistan, and neither India nor China can do each other much harm.

The Chinese-Soviet conflict can only benefit the West, provided that the good will toward the West now evident in China is soberly handled. Complacent assumptions that the United States can "play the China card" in whatever way it wishes would be as out of place as naïve enthusiasm for all things Chinese, similar to the *Schwärmerei* for the Soviet "new civilization" in the 1930s. As to military aid, it is necessary to be aware of the two opposite dangers: that the bear may be driven to desperate moves to break out of its encirclement, as ably suggested by Seweryn Bialer in an earlier chapter, or that American or European hesitancy in the face of Chinese requests may cause the Chinese to lose faith in the *Bündnisfahigkeit*, credibility as allies, of the West.

Although in the 1970s the military strength of the Soviet Union greatly increased, and was extended over large parts of the world that had not yet known it, so that it became for the first time truly a superpower, its leaders had cause to look with anxiety to the next decade, and their anxiety promised perilous times for the rest of us.

The Soviet Union still lagged behind the advanced industrial states of the West and Japan economically, and the discrepancy was probably widening. The rigid bureaucratic framework of the Five-year Plan inhibited innovation. The growth of the economy was slowing down, and this trend was expected to continue. Despite massive investments, agriculture remained backward: the kolkhoz system, sanctified by party dogma, was still a "fetter on production." Demographic trends promised serious shortages of labor in the RSFSR and most of the western republics. It was difficult to avoid the conclusion that it would soon no longer be possible simultaneously to maintain military expenditure, develop heavy industry, and increase the supply of consumer goods. One of the three would have to give, and judging by past Soviet history, and the presumed strength of the respective lobbies at the top of the pyramid of power, it would be the last of the three.

At this point one must ask what is likely to be the reaction of the Soviet working class. The simple answer, that they will do what they are told, and if they don't will be mercilessly repressed, will not do. These are not the workers of the 1930s, uprooted peasant children accustomed to miserable living conditions and cowed by the all-powerful security police. They are a skilled working class on the European level, their standard of living has been slowly but steadily rising for the last twenty years, and they have not known the rigors of factory discipline and police repression that were customary in Stalin's time. What is more, the security police themselves, though still very powerful, have not used for twenty years or more the methods of the Stalin era. There have been signs of working-class opposition in the 1970s: if the government has to impose a general lowering of the standard of living in the years ahead, it cannot count on easy submission by the workers. This is almost certainly a source of worry to the Soviet leaders. It would not deter them from imposing their policies, but it remains an important unpredictable factor. The events in Poland are a warning.

Another set of problems concerns the non-Russian nations of the Soviet Union. Brezhnev's statement in 1972 that the "national question" had been definitely solved is certainly not true. The regime has made some concessions to national cultures, allowing the Baltic nations to live their own lives, separate from the Russians in their midst, to a much greater extent than under Stalin or even Khrushchev, and Estonia in particular has a higher material and cultural level than the rest of the Union, giving to visitors the impression that they are still in Europe. The Georgians, and still more the Armenians, are allowed to run their own republics, with very little intrusion by the rather small Russian minorities, provided that they follow the general party line. Ukrainian nationalism, however, remains vigorously alive, and Ukrainian *samvydav*, the equivalent of Russian *samizdat*, continues to exist. How widespread and how strong is sympathy for Ukrainian nationalism among the people of the Ukrainian SSR, and among the Ukrainians in the RSFSR or Kazakh SSR, we do not know, and probably even the KGB does not know. The case of the Muslim peoples, which is linked with the wider problem of Islam in world politics, will be discussed later. What is certain is that nationalism, preceded always in Soviet polemics by the pejorative adjective "bourgeois" (which has nothing to do with the social origins or outlook of the persons therewith denounced), is taken seriously.

Then there are the problems of Eastern Europe. In the last months of 1980 the workers' movement in Poland, supported by both the Catholic Church and the democratic intelligentsia, was the object of worldwide attention. But though in the other states things remained quiet, the essential problem was the same. Stalin imposed on the states that his armies conquered an approximate copy of Soviet political and economic institutions, and interfered with their cultural life, censoring their past and present literature and reinterpreting their history to the glory not only of the Soviet regime but of earlier Russian policies. Under his successors the restraints have been modified and varied, but Soviet Russian domination remains a fact not only known but resented by almost all. Economic and educational progress in Eastern Europe has created new social and cultural elites, and in doing so has increased the volume and intensity of nationalism beyond what it was under the prewar regimes. The object against which this nationalism is directed is the Soviet Union, and the Soviet leaders know it. From time to time more or less serious movements of revolt break out, and are suppressed. The Soviet leaders know that the East Europeans hate them, they do not know where and how the next troubles will be, and meanwhile domination over Eastern Europe is very expensive in both manpower and material resources.

To an outside observer it might seem that it would be more to Soviet interest if they would treat these countries as they have treated Finland—that is, insist on control of their foreign policy but allow them internal sovereignty, to conduct their political and social life as they wish. But this is unacceptable for three reasons. The first is that so much hatred has accumulated during thirty-five years that if the pressure were removed, there would be a danger of explosion. Second, the Soviets are determined to keep Germany divided, and in order to maintain unimpeded communication with East Germany they must keep a much firmer grip over Poland than over Finland. The third reason is that if the East European nations enjoyed internal sovereignty, there would soon be demands for similar status from several of the Soviet republics. The bogy of a disintegration of the Soviet empire paralyzes any Soviet initiative in the direction of Finlandization.

If economic prospects are unfavorable, the future of the working class is uncertain, non-Russian nationalism is alarming, and East Europeans are a perpetual nuisance, the one undoubted strength of the Soviet Union is military power. This is however, extremely costly, and prevents the use of all the resources required in economic advancement. Meanwhile, although Soviet domination has extended to Angola, Ethiopia, Aden, and Afghanistan, the specter of encirclement in the west and east is still there. The combination of defensive and offensive hysteria exhibited by Soviet spokesmen strangely recalls that which was visible in Germany under William II, in which pathetic plaints about *Einkreisung* were combined with talk about the mailed fist, *Weltpolitik* and *Weltmacht*. The replacement of the ruthless but prudent Bismarck by the volatile William II and the ambitious Admiral von Tirpitz has its parallel in the replacement of the ruthless but prudent Stalin by the colorless Brezhnev and the ambitious Admiral Gorshkov, who insists that Soviet naval power must be seen on all the oceans of the world. A case could even be made for a comparison between the insatiable imperialism of the parvenu industrial magnates and professional class pundits of Wilhelminian Germany and the insatiable imperialism of the new class in Brezhnevian Russia.

All these dangerous uncertainties are made more acute by the succession crisis, which, as Bialer convincingly shows, may well be prolonged by the succession to Brezhnev of another elder citizen whose rule must be short. There cannot be a more stable situation until a new generation has come to power. I can add nothing to Bialer's analysis except a general proposition: in periods of succession rival teams are forced to seek popularity within the party, and to some extent even outside it, and there are really only two main causes that can have popular appeal—a better and more relaxed life for the people (that is, more consumer goods at the cost of other branches of the economy) and perhaps also a peaceful posture in world affairs; or emphasis on the glory and power of the Soviet empire (that is, guns before butter, and no concessions to the capitalist imperialists). In one form or another, polarization between these two is likely to grow in the succession years.

Two rather alarming points may be made. First, although the repeated attribution by Soviet media of all blame for East European troubles (1956, 1968, 1980) to Western imperialist intrigues is, in its crude form, false, and is probably not believed by Soviet spokesmen themselves, yet in a more profound sense there is truth in it. The NATO governments do not urge the East Europeans to revolt: this is the opposite of the truth. But the existence only a few hundred miles away from their borders of a system of political liberty and European culture, similar to their own repressed culture, is a source of undying hope and irrepressible aspiration to Poles, Czechs, Hungarians, Romanians, and even Bulgarians. As long as Western Europe is free, East Europeans will never (whatever NATO's presidents and premiers may say) accept the permanence of Soviet domination. Thus Soviet domination over Eastern Europe, and indirectly Soviet Russian domination over non-Russians in the Union, cannot be secure until Western Europe ceases to be free.

Second, if it becomes clear that the United States, with its undoubtedly superior technology, is going to make a major effort to recover and increase its lead in military power over the Soviet Union, the Soviet general staff will find itself in the same position as the German general staff before 1914 when faced with the firm resolve of a Russia much weakened by defeat in the Far East to achieve superiority over Germany by 1917. The German general staff's advice was to use German military power while it was still superior. The German general staff did not cause the war of 1914, but the advice that it had long been giving decisively affected the German government's decision in the crisis of 1914. The Soviet general staff does not decide Soviet foreign policy, but its advice will carry weight in the crises that will break out from time to time in Africa, the Middle East, or Southern Asia in the 1980s.

Defeatists will say, we lose either way. If we don't rearm, and don't arm China, the Soviets will slowly and surely win all over the world, and China will return to the Soviet camp. If we do rearm and do arm China, the Soviets will threaten force, or use force while they still have superiority. The realist will say, we can survive, and win, in the face of these two undoubted dangers, if we use our resources, our brains, and our courage to good effect.

Though the Muslim world has barely affected Soviet-Chinese relations to date, still the apparent revival of militant Islam, which potentially concerns part of the populations of both countries, and is also potentially a major factor in world politics, touching the Soviet Union, China, the United States, and Europe, deserves in this survey a more than summary discussion.

Islam is not only a set of religious beliefs but an all-embracing way of life and thought: the distinction between sacred and secular activities and institutions, characteristic of Christian polities since the Middle Ages, did not exist in the Muslim world until it came under Western domination, and it is questionable how far, even after a century or more (depending on the country concerned) of Western domination, the distinction has been implanted in the Muslim mind.

The Muslim world, the *'umma*, has always been regarded as a single community, though in fact it had broken up into numerous states within three hundred years of the death of the Prophet. At its first and greatest flowering, it not only stretched from Estremadura to Khwarazm, but was the frame within which a splendid civilization grew. The memory of this civilization is the basis of the historical mythology of Muslim revivalism and Arab nationalism: like all mythologies it is compounded of truth and fiction. There was indeed a great Arab civilization, but Islam, the Arabic language, and all-conquering Arab tribesmen were not its sole ingredients: it incorporated both the people and a great deal of the ancient cultural legacies of the eastern Mediterranean and Persia. After the decline of the Abbasid Caliphate, other great Muslim empires rose and fell—Fatimids and Mamluks in Egypt, Moguls in India, Safavids in Iran, and above all the great Ottoman Empire which stretched from Hungary to the Crimea and from Tunis to Basra; but although each of these aimed to include the whole *'umma*, none ever did.

The Crusades of Christian armies had only short-lived successes south and east of the Mediterranean, but triumphed in Spain and in the Volga valley. From mid-eighteenth century, the military expansion and the increasingly superior economic organization of European Christian states pressed even more harshly on the Muslim world, until by 1918 almost all was subject either to direct foreign rule or to some sort of protectorate, the only important exceptions being residual Turkey and Iran. Although the dominant Europeans seldom interfered with Muslim beliefs or social hierarchies, their rule inevitably brought not only a new and alien bureaucracy but also the miscellaneous economic and cultural dissolving forces which it has become fashionable to subsume under the quasi-magical word "modernization." This evident material superiority of the Westerners aroused helpless and relentless rage in Muslim minds. The natural order of things, in which the Muslim community was not only free from infidel interference but was the divinely ordained system superior to all others, had been monstrously outraged, and must be restored.

One way to do this seemed to be to learn from the enemy, to accept many of his discoveries and institutions, and to find a place for Muslims as equals within the new Western-created world. This was the way of nationalism, a doctrine and a movement derived from a Western model, in which the secular factors of language and of modern state power, and a secular interpretation of history, were treated as of equal importance with Muslim identity. In two cases this seemed to have been successful. In Turkey, Kemal Atatürk relegated Islam to the background and even persecuted Muslim ulema; made the Turkish language, printed in Latin script, the basis of a new, never before known, modern Turkish national consciousness; exalted the pre-Islamic cultures of Central Asia, whence the Turks had come, and of the Hittites in Anatolia, which the Turks had made their home; and imposed European dress and superficial social habits in a mechanical way that recalls Peter the Great in the Russia of his time. In Iran, Reza Shah took Kemal as his model. He was more careful and milder in his treatment of the learned men of Islam, but more ambitious in having himself made shah and heir to the Peacock Throne. His successor was less patient with the Muslim elite, and aroused resentment or derision by his emphasis on the pre-Islamic glories of Achaemenid Persia and by his apparent view of himself as a reincarnation of Xerxes. In the Arabic-speaking lands there was less possibility of unscrambling Islam and nationalism. The concept of an Arab nation stressed language and the culture based on language and history, and this made it possible for Christian Arabs to take part in Arab nationalism: many of its pioneers were indeed Christians or even atheists.[1] But Islam was itself claimed as a great creation of the Arabs, or it might be argued that Arab civilization was the finest expression of Islam: either way the two were difficult to separate. There was no question of Arab nationalists persecuting Islam, as Turkish and Iranian nationalists had been seen to do.

Within ten years of the end of the Second World War almost all Muslim peoples in the world were free of European rule, but the painful process of "modernization" continued, under the leadership of indigenous Muslim rulers advised by numerous self-important American or European specialists, whether "Western" or "Eastern." Muslim traditions, inseparable in most men's minds still from national culture, were increasingly trampled down by brash modernizers. This spectacle strengthened a second kind of reaction against Western dominance and forced modernization: militant Muslim fundamentalism. This was the predominant outlook in most of Arabia (even though members of princely families in oil-bearing states were not immune to the delights of infidel fleshpots); the Muslim Brotherhood, despite persecution in several Arab states, has probably recently increased its following in Egypt, Syria, and elsewhere; there was a marked revival of Muslim opposition to the secularist conventional wisdom of Kemalism in Turkey; and fundamentalism achieved its sensational triumph with the victory of the Shi'i ayatullah Khomeini over the shah of Iran.

To the Muslim fundamentalist all forms of "modernization" are equally abhorrent. In particular, the penetration of capitalism, more or less identified with America, and the expansion of Soviet-sponsored communism are but two variants of the Satanic force that comes from the West, once Christian and now largely godless. Free enterprise liberalism and Marxism-

---

1. For a persuasive argument that two of the patron saints of both Arab nationalism and pan-Islamism were atheists, see Elie Kedourie, *Afghani and 'Abduh: An Essay on Religious Unbelief and Political Activism in Modern Islam* (London: Cass, 1966).

Leninism are two related false doctrines. It is, however, much easier and involves much less risk of life and liberty to struggle against the American than the Soviet variant.

It is arguable that the resurgence of Muslim fundamentalism is part of a worldwide reaction against the self-complacent materialist hedonism that has long dominated at least the world of the media in all continents. Not least among the factors provoking this reaction is the mentality of social scientists in the West, described by Donald Treadgold, elsewhere in this volume, in relation to "ideology" in general: "the tendency . . . to assume a rigoristic, quasi-moralistic stance . . . , a readiness to explain it [ideology] away and reduce it to something quite different, on the grounds that those professing it must be hypocrites only masking their contemptible self-serving motives by high-flown rhetoric." Needless to say, Soviet Marxist social scientists do not lag behind their Western counterparts in contempt for religious beliefs and in the attribution of the lowest motives to those who profess them. But both are unwilling to admit that their own wisdom is shallow.

Some might say that the optimism of the great age of scientific discovery —that man was the triumphant master of his world, and had no need for a God who did not seem to be there—had become inappropriate to an age in which further scientific discovery, as well as historical events, had shown man as a helpless dwarf, desperately needing a God whom he could not find. This, of course, is no reason for believing that fanatical fundamentalists, whether Christian or Shi'i, would do better.

There was one important part of the Muslim world that had undergone a different experience, whose results were far from clear: the Muslim republics of the Soviet Union, the one remaining great European colonial empire. Here, in contrast to Western colonial systems, modernization—Marxist-Leninist version—had been systematically introduced by the central government, and carried out without regard to the preferences of its Muslim (or any other) subjects, in conscious and direct conflict with Islam.

After sixty years of Soviet rule, enormous progress had been achieved in industry and in education in Soviet Azerbaijan and in the five Central Asian Soviet Republics. In the process, new professional and administrative cadres (in Soviet terminology, a new "toiling intelligentsia") have been created. The Soviet press and publications, which in such matters always speak with one voice, assume that the social strata created by sixty years of modernization are inspired by boundless gratitude and love for both the Soviet government, its author, and the great Russian people, its executant. But the experience of other empires does not support such a hypothesis: on the contrary, the modern educated elites created by colonial modernization processes provided the leadership of the nationalist movements to whom the colonial rulers ultimately found themselves obliged to surrender power.

It is of course possible that, under the magic of "socialism" and the infallible Marxist-Leninist science of the Central Committee of the CPSU, the Law of Colonial Ingratitude does not apply. It is possible but not likely.

It is true that there is no indication of any separatist movements in Soviet Central Asia. This should not surprise us: Soviet methods of repression, and the will to employ them, are different in kind from those of European colonial powers in their last decades. There is also no evidence of Central Asian dissidents or *samizdat*. This, too, is not surprising. There is little reason to expect that Western democratic ideas, or Western kinds of heretical Marxism, which can awaken a response in Russians, Ukrainians, or Baltic peoples, among whom European cultural traditions have never been completely interrupted, would have much appeal to Central Asian Muslims, who have no such traditions. It seems from available evidence that the Central Asian elites tend to take "socialism" for granted. Acceptance of Russian domination, however, is another matter altogether. It seems far more likely that they take pride in the great progress achieved in their lands in sixty years but believe that they would have done much better if they had not had the Russians on their backs. There are enough Russsians in each republic, especially in the cities, to be a source of resentment, but not enough to impose their way of living or thinking. Urban Muslims meet Russians at their place of work, and get on as well as they can with them, but they go back to their own homes, to a Muslim cultural world. There is virtually no common social life, still less any intermarriage.

The evidence suggests that the Muslim cultural leaders have been skillful in adapting the essence of the Muslim way of life to the inescapable requirements of the Soviet system—exempting the faithful from such obligations as public prayer at times when the rhythm of factory production prohibits it, making the ritual obeisances to the greatness and generosity of the Soviet leadership, and the like. But the identity and cohesion of the Muslim community is preserved, and it is gently but firmly pushing the Russians back. The greatest weapon of the Muslims is their birthrate, far higher than the Russians'. Already the proportion of younger age groups is much greater in the Muslim than in the Russian population. Neither the sense of belonging to the Muslim community nor the high rate of natural increase seem significantly to diminish among urban Muslims in comparison with rural ones. It also appears that emigration from the Muslim lands, where the population is growing so fast, to places of work in the Urals or in Russian-populated Siberia, where there is beginning to be labor shortage, does not commend itself to Muslims.

Russian domination is still ensured by the presence of Russian officials in party and state, especially as second secretaries of republican or provincial party committees; but the pressure of the increasing, and increasingly well-educated, Muslim elite will prove ever more difficult to resist.

There is a piece of information in the first published results of the 1979 census that is relevant. The proportion of the population of four of the main Muslim nations of Central Asia and Transcaucasia who could speak Russian in 1970 varied between 15 and 20 percent, and had increased by 1979 to between 25 and 30 percent; but the proportion among the fourth and largest, the Uzbek, had increased from 14.5 to 49.3 percent.[2] If we take this extraordinary figure at its face value, it need not be interpreted as evidence that Uzbek culture is being assimilated into Russian culture (which is certainly not happening); rather it may mean that Uzbeks, precisely in order to maintain their identity the better, and in order to be able to rise in the administrative hierarchy and take over jobs hitherto held by Russians, are being encouraged by their cultural leaders to learn Russian.

Enough has been said to show that the Muslim peoples give serious cause for worry to any Soviet leaders trying to think a decade or two ahead. The fact remains, however, that we know far too little of these people, and many important questions have to remain unanswered. One is the priority Soviet Muslims give the three aspects of their identity. For example, how many Uzbeks would feel, "I am first a Soviet citizen, second an Uzbek, and third a Muslim," or would put Uzbek first, or Muslim? Another unanswerable question concerns the affinity, on the basis of language, between the Turkic peoples. There are nearly forty million Turks—in this broad linguistic sense —in Turkey, nearly forty million in the Soviet Union, and a substantial number more in Iran, Afghanistan, and China.[3] There is little sign today, inside or outside Turkey, of the Panturkism that was a growing trend before 1914 but was repudiated by Atatürk and not encouraged by his successors. But it would be rash to prophesy a decade or two ahead.

The fact that Muslim and Turkic peoples are found on both sides of the Sino-Soviet frontier makes these problems directly relevant to the main subject of this work. It is true that Chinese rule has been hard for Uigurs and Kazakhs, both before and since communist rule in China. I agree with Bialer and Aspaturian that Central Asian Muslims have no cause to love China. But the existence of the conflict could be of benefit to them, surely not less than it has been to the Romanians. Their own increasing numbers and the proximity of the Chinese border should raise the price that they can demand from Moscow. The possibilities in the next decades of Central Asian exploitation of Soviet-Chinese hostility, and also of intelligent Chinese propaganda and subversion in Soviet Central Asia, should not be underrated.

2. Figures are from *Vestnik statistiki*, no. 2, 1980.
3. At the latest census, the population of Turkey was 43.2 million, several million of whom were Kurds, while smaller minorities totaled some hundreds of thousands. Adding up the totals of peoples of Turkic language given in the Soviet census figures for 1979, I reached a total of 38.75 million.

It is also difficult to estimate the effect on these problems of the Soviet invasion of Afghanistan. Its immediate purpose was to remove a government that was oppressing Muslims, and both the troops and the civilian advisers whom Moscow sent in appear to have included a high proportion of Central Asians. It seemed possible that the Soviet Union could play the part of a protector of the Afghan Muslims, saving them from Hafizullah Amin, whose misdeeds were a monstrous deviation from true Marxism-Leninism. But it did not work out that way. The almost universal hostility of the Afghans to the Soviet invaders, and the obvious devotion of the resisters to Islam, created odium for the Soviet Union in the Muslim world—even though it seems not to have equaled the odium attaching to American support of Israel. As for the effect on Soviet Central Asian troops of seeing a Muslim nation's resistance to Soviet invasion, it remains a subject of mere conjecture.

To sum up, Muslim fundamentalism is equally opposed to capitalist democracy, Soviet communism, and Chinese culture whether traditional or communist; the Soviet Muslims appear to be pursuing their own aims, maintaining effectively their Muslim identity but concealing their thoughts and aspirations. None of them are likely to be in any sense pro-Western, but a community of interest may develop between them and the West, and in any case American policy will be more effective if it constantly bears them in mind. In particular, Western specialists both in Soviet affairs and in the Far East should pay more attention to the Soviet Muslims, and more systematic efforts should be made to study the considerable volume of information that is obtainable about them.

Let us now return to the Far East, and think irresponsibly but seriously about future prospects. We are all familiar with the controversy between Asia Firsters and Europe Firsters, dating from the Second World War and continuing, whether latent or active, in American thinking about foreign policy ever since.

Though a European by birth and culture, I am almost inclined to join the Asia Firsters. I am restrained by a doubt whether the word Asia, in a political context, has any real meaning. There is of course a great land mass, to which the atlases attach the name Asia. The extreme western peninsula of this land mass bears a name of its own, Europe. But does the land mass constitute any sort of unit—historical, political, economic, cultural? I should have thought not. There are some big and some small states with very little in common. There are lands of Muslim culture, of Hindu, of Buddhist, and of Confucian—or Legalist, a good point made by George Taylor in our discussion. Each of these was and is as different from the others as any of them were or are from Europe or North America.

But the concept of Asia Firsters is not empty, it refers to a reality, which

I think I can best approach by a historical excursion of a quasi-Toynbean kind. For some three thousand years the history of civilization was the history of the peoples living round one Mediterranean Sea, with an extension toward the Persian Gulf. China and India were far away, their existence barely known. The Mediterranean area was the scene of the great struggles between Egyptians and Mesopotamians, Hellenes and Persians, Rome and Carthage, Arabs and Franks, Spaniards and Ottomans. Then, nearly five hundred years ago, Europeans burst out into the oceans, centers of civilization were dispersed, and conflicts spread all over the world. But now the era that began with Columbus and Vasco da Gama is perhaps drawing to a close, and the great confrontations between dominant civilizations are once more becoming centered on a single Mediterranean sea. But it is a different Mediterranean. In the age of jet aircraft, space satellites, and intercontinental missiles, it is a bigger sea: the Pacific Ocean. The Asia Firsters should be called Pacific Firsters. Unfortunately, the adjective refers to geography rather than to probable human behavior.

In this Pacific Basin there are four actors. They can combine in various ways: three against one, two against two, two and one and one, or four separate and each against all. I should hope that the pattern will be three against one, and the behavior of one of the four does indeed seem designed to unite the other three against it.

But we must distinguish between two that stretch also to the other ocean, the Atlantic, and two that are confined to the Pacific. The relationship between these last two is perhaps the most important of all. In the immediate future what most alarms the Soviet rulers is the prospect of closer alliance between the United States and China; but looking a little further ahead, it is arguable that closer association between China and Japan is even more alarming. Perhaps it was the Chinese-Japanese treaty of 1978 that was the most important agreement made in the Pacific region since the Soviet-Japanese treaty of 1941. One attempt in this century at a Greater East Asia Co-Prosperity Sphere was a disastrous failure, but another version, with greater good will on both sides, may result quite differently. The recession of the last years has produced ominous grumbling in Europe about Japanese trade competition. Let us remember what were the consequences of the closing in the 1930s of European and North American markets to Japanese goods. Today, in contrast to the 1930s, China is no longer a helpless object of predatory powers: the giant has awakened, and is standing erect. Japan needs Chinese custom, and China needs Japanese skills. Let us look even further ahead. The Japanese economic miracle, beginning with the Meiji era, interrupted and then renewed in the last thirty years, is familiar to us all. It was followed by the South Korean economic miracle, but let us not forget the miracles of Hong Kong, Singapore, and Taiwan. When the people of mainland China achieve the level of entrepreneurship and skill that their kinsmen overseas have long displayed, the Japanese miracle would be dwarfed, and world trade transformed.

These are no more than fantasies, but in our century fantasies are liable to turn into realities at astonishing speed. And the Pacific quadrille with its four performers is already a reality. So the Pacific Firsters have a very strong case. Still, they should pause a moment to remember the extreme westerly promontory of the Asian land mass. Four hundred million people, with a level of skill and culture not surpassed anywhere in the world, inhabit what is conventionally called Europe. To the two northern members of the Pacific quadrille the fate of these four hundred million is of some importance. Neither can afford to let the other get hold of them all.

One hundred million are subject to one power, and three hundred million are essentially dependent on the protection of the other. The West Europeans are quarrelsome, ungrateful, and absurdly unwilling to look after their own defenses; yet America cannot afford, in its own interest, to let them go. Some Europeans may think that it would be nice to be Finlandized; but if they were, it would not be long before they were Czechoslovakized; and this would mean that their resources in manpower, skill, and material wealth would be at the disposal of their Soviet masters for use against America. Subordination of Western Europe to Moscow would not mean a future of neutrality for Europeans: on the contrary, they would become the front line of Moscow's worldwide struggle against America.

So we must conclude that the fates of the Pacific peoples and of the Europeans are inextricably bound up with each other. In particular, Americans, whose coasts are washed by two oceans, have to pay attention to those who live on the opposite side of each. This is not just a platitude to be ritually intoned, but a truth to be deeply felt and lived. It is our job, as a profession, to bring it home to citizens, politicians, and presidents. Perhaps our conference will have done something to this end.

Index

Abbasid Caliphate, 380
'Abd al-Samad, Ahmad, 261
Aden. *See* Yemen, People's Democratic Republic of
Aden, Gulf of, 253, 262
Adenauer, Konrad, 139, 142; and Khrushchev, 299–300
Adzhubei, Aleksei, 298, 300
Afghanistan, xix, 266; Soviet invasion of, 74, 82, 132, 133–34, 136, 143, 163, 167, 171, 207, 230–34, 238, 244, 247, 252, 289, 356, 361, 365, 378; communist coup (1978), 206, 228, 367; upheaval in, 228–34; U.S. refuses military support to, 229; Soviet arms to, 229, 230, 235; Marxism in, 229; party factions, 229; and Iran, 229; and Pakistan, 225, 229; and India, 375; Daoud returns to power, 229; treaty with USSR, 229; and Islamic fervor, 230–31; Fifth Five-Year Plan, 224; economic assistance to, 224, 235–36; foreign trade, 237; prospects for USSR in, 238–39; approached to join security system, 241; and Soviet strategy, 244–45; Turks in, 384; and Muslim question, 385
Africa, 213, 214, 218, 269, 287, 361, 362
Afro-Asian Solidarity Committee (Soviet), 261
Agriculture: difficulties in USSR, 95, 376; Chinese imports, 95; Korea and Japan, 95–96, 104; Chinese harvests, 96–97; world grain market, 99; Taiwan, 104; U.S., Canada, and Australia as exporters, 105
Aidit, D. N., 346
Aircraft: Mirage fighters, 247; Harrier jump jets, 307–8, 309, 310, 311, 319; in China, 108, 110; MIG-19, 110; MIG-23 and MIG-25, 107; MIG fighter planes, 224, 250, 262
Albania, 150, 273, 274, 275, 277, 329–30, 334, 337, 345, 348
Albanian Communist Party, 282, 284, 289
Albanian "dogmatism," xviii, 193
Alexandria, 250
Algeria, 251, 256
'Ali Nasir Muhammad, 265
Amalrik, Andrei, 40–41
"American card," 33, 36
Amin, Hafizullah, 229, 230, 385
Amman, 247
Amur region, xviii, 3, 331–32, 336, 361, 373, 374
Anatolia, 380
Angola, 134, 232, 378
Anti-Semitism, 136
Arab civilization, 380–81
Arab-Israeli conflict, 241, 248, 249
Arab League, 254
Arab nationalist newspaper, 258
Arab "oil weapon," 132
Arbatov, Georgii, 309, 310
"Arc of crisis," 131
Armenians, 377
Armaments: deals between China and Western Europe, 86; for China, 107–9; Soviet and U.S., 132–33, 138; NATO, 132–33; increase in Japan, 179; for Vietnam, 195–96; Chinese aid to Pakistan, 222, 235; Soviet to Bangladesh, 224; Soviet to Afghanistan, 229; Soviet to India, 233; West to Pakistan, 234; Soviet to South Asia, 235; French to Iraq, 247; Soviet to Syria, 247; Soviet to Egypt, 249; Chinese to Egypt, 250; Soviet to Libya, 250; Chinese to Tunisia, 251; Soviet to Ethiopia, 252; Soviet to

Index 389

Somalia, 252; Soviet to YAR, 253; Soviet to Arab states, 265; Soviet to PDRY, 260; Soviets in Eastern Europe, 285; British to China, 307–8, 309–11, 319; USSR and Western Europe, 309, 312; West European to China, 310–11, 319; nuclear, 298, 330, 342; prospects for 1980s, 379. *See also* Nuclear weapons
Arms control, 43, 49, 144; advocates of, 139–40; Chinese attitude to, 302
Arms race, 127, 173
Army, Soviet, 98, 132
Asad, Hafiz al-, 247, 248
ASEAN. *See* Association of Southeast Asian Nations
Asia Firsters, 385–87
Asian collective security system, 216, 224, 241
Asiatic mode of production, 340
Association of Southeast Asian Nations (ASEAN): and U.S., 141; and Sino-Soviet dispute, 185, 187; importance of, 186, 205; improvement of, 197; bloc building, 198; relations with Hanoi, 200; communist attitude to, 201–2; hope of U.S. assistance, 203; and regionalism, 204
Atatürk, Kemal, 380, 381, 384
Atlantic Alliance, 297, 313, 314, 317
Atomic cooperation, Sino-Soviet agreement on, xvii
Atomic weapons. *See* Nuclear weapons
Augustine, 333
Australia, 105, 375
Australian Communist Party, 145, 157, 171
"Autonomists" in Eastern Europe, 288
Awami League, 217, 218
Ayub Khan, 210, 217
Azcárate, Manuel, 161, 168
Azerbaijan, 382

Bab al-Mandab, 253
BACKFIREs, 133
Bahrein, 246, 255
Baikal-Amur Mainline railroad (BAM), 117–18, 119, 179
Baltic nations, 376–77
Baluchis, 239
Baluchistan, 244–45
Bandung, 346, 349
Bangladesh, 337; birth of, 207; crisis over (1971), 216–20; establishing new relations, 221, 223; recognized by Pakistan, 223; aid from USSR, 224; India's policy to, 224; agreements with India and Pakistan, 225; Sino-Bangladesh trade agreement, 226; economic assistance to, 235–36; foreign trade, 237
Barre, Siyad, 252
Ba'th, Iraqi, 247, 254, 255
Ba'th, Syrian, 254, 255
Battelle Research Center, xxi
Baybakov (Gosplan chairman), 118
Beijing Military Region, 60
Belgian Communist Party, 171
Bely, Andrei, 40
Bengal, Bay of, 220
Bengalis, 217, 218
Benedict, Ruth, 344
Berbera, 252, 253
Berlin Wall, 300
Berlinguer, Enrico, 154, 157, 163, 166, 167, 168; visit to China, 169–70
Bessarabia, 278
Bessborough, Lord, 319–20
Bhutan, 207
Bhutto, Zulfikar Ali, 221–22, 223, 225, 226
Bialer, Seweryn, 376, 378
Bismarck, 378
"Black September," 248
Boat people, 197, 202
Boffa, Guiseppe, 159, 169
Bolshevik party, 37
Border disputes: between China and India, 206, 212, 215, 220, 222, 227; India and Pakistan, 219–20, 234, 236; China and Vietnam, 197, 198; roots of Sino-Soviet conflict, 344–45; geographical study on borderlands, 350; status in 1964, 51; Soviet build-up beginning in 1965, 53, 58; on Amur and Ussuri rivers (1969), xviii, 7, 10, 13, 14, 55, 58, 64, 156, 221, 269, 296, 300, 304, 345, 355, 357, 359, 361, 373; Xinjiang, 19, 21, 55, 58, 296, 357, 361; helicopter incident (1974), 19, 21; negotiations, xix, xx, 14, 20, 74, 360–61; transfer of troops in China (early 1970s), 60; stirred up by China, xx; Soviet reluctance to make concessions, 36; Soviet initiatives, 46; possible disruption of Soviet economy by China, 118–19; Soviet troop build-up, 122, 127, 373; enticement of Kazakhs over the border, 330
Brambilla, Giovanni, 158
Brandt, Willy, 166, 297, 299, 300, 306
Brazil, 111
Brezhnev Doctrine, xix, 7, 54, 65, 188, 221, 232, 335, 337; discussed, 280–81
Brezhnev, Leonid, 86, 136, 335, 355–56; summit with Nixon, 18; "Khrushchevism without Khrushchev," 52; Siberian

train ride, 83; and Sino-Soviet rapprochement, 134; and détente, 139, 143, 144; and Vietnam, 140, 141; massive attack on Chinese, 156; Asian collective security system, 216, 224; and France, 298, 316; anti-Chinese campaign, 308–9; letters to West European leaders, 309, 310, 311, 312; consolidation of power, 356; as Stalin's replacement, 378
British Communist Party (CPGB), 149, 154, 157, 162, 163, 171, 279, 281
Brown, Roger, 13
Brussels, 303, 315
Brzezinski, Zbigniew, 83, 296, 310, 347–49, 350, 352
Bucharest Conference of 1960, 191, 328, 331
Budapest preparatory conference meeting (1968), 155, 156
Bulgaria, 275, 277, 278, 292, 379; "loyalists," 287
Bulgarian Communist Party, 280, 284
Bung di, 194
Burckhardt, Jakob, 134
Burma, xix, 327

Callaghan, James, 311, 319
Calvin, 333
Cambodia, 141, 334, 356, 362; invaded by Vietnam, 180; importance of Sino-Soviet dispute to, 187. *See also* Kampuchea
Cameron, Neil, 307
"Campaign to Criticize Lin Biao and Confucius," 18, 19
Camp David, 132, 248–49
Camranh Bay, 136, 202, 362
Canada, 105
Carrillo, Santiago, 160–61, 163, 171
Carter administration, 47, 48; military cooperation with China and Japan, 181; attitude to India, 227; nonproliferation policies of, 228; human rights policy of, 228; and invasion of Afghanistan, 143–44; foreign policy, 322
Carter, Jimmy, 310, 311, 322
Catholic Church, 377; Catholic forces in Western Europe, 165. *See also* Christianity, Roman Catholicism
Ceausescu, Nicolae, 275, 277, 282, 284, 288; visit to China, 157
Center for Contemporary Chinese and Soviet Studies, University of Washington, xx
Center-left foreign policy forces in Western Europe, 295, 313–20
Central Asia, 40; industrialization of, 117; Soviet Muslims in, 231; and Sino-Soviet conflict, 384
Central Asian Soviet Republics, 382–85
CGIL labor federation (Italy), 168
Chamberlin, W. H., 341
Chen Boda, 8–9, 357, 363
Chen Yun, 26
Chiang Kai-shek, 5, 106, 140, 343
Chieu Hoi camps, 196
"China card," 32, 47, 48, 49, 84, 272, 295, 298, 300, 315, 321, 375
China, People's Republic of (PRC), historical background, 3–4, 35; emperor's role, 3–4; "sovereignty" as central goal, 4; "nativists," 5; "selective modernizers," 5; "technology firsters," 5; domestic priorities and international relations, 6–7; politics of the 1970s, 7–28; war psychosis, 7–8, 13; Ninth Party Congress, 7–8; Lin Biao affair, 8–15; political mobilization, 10; championing popular revolutionary movements, 10; struggle between Zhou Enlai and Lin Biao, 12–15; military budget, 11–12, 15, 33, 54–55, 108–10, 370; greater involvement in international market, 15–16; Shanghai Communiqué, 16, 337; rehabilitation of Deng Xiaoping, 16, 17; struggle between nativists and modernizers, 16–22; radicals gain strength, 18–19; deficit in foreign trade, 19; Fourth National People's Congress, 19, 20; "four modernizations," 20, 24, 36, 374; military program in 1975, 20; Deng's activities in 1975–76, 21–22; anti-Mao demonstrations and purge of Deng, 22; Mao's death, 22; Gang of Four arrested, 22; post-Mao activities, 23–26; economic development emphasized, 22; Fifth National People's Congress, 24; economic conditions, 24–25; economic policy, 27–28, 61–62, 365–66; moral framework lacking, 27; modernization, 30–34, 47, 69; ideological changes, 31–32; Maoism, 32–35; market socialism, 33–34; leadership struggle, 34; ideology versus nationalism, 38; nuclear weapons capability, 54; troop build-up, 60; relation between domestic and foreign policy, 61–63; security and global strategy, 63–73; influence of Den Xiaoping, 69; war preparedness, 70–71, 124–25, 170; "military-bureaucratic dictatorship," 77; as a fascist state, 81–82; as a capitalist country, 85; heavy industry of, 92, 94, 97; technical assistance, 94, 104, 116, 125, 126; petro-

leum, 95, 104, 112, 119; agriculture, 21, 95–97, 99, 105; income, 97; trade with Hong Kong, 98, 99; world trade, 99–100, 105, 386–87; population growth, 102; port facilities, 105; railroads, 105; energy shortages, 105; availability of weapons, 107–9; first five-year plan, 113, 116; conservatism on rise, 132, 134, 137; target of nuclear weapons, 133; domestic problems, 136; international relations, 138, 270, 272; relations with independent communist parties, 147–71; international conference of parties (1969), 148–57; attacks on China at conference, 156–57; relations with Italian Communist Party, 157–71; and Eastern Europe, 268–94; criticized by Czech communists, 287; military weakness of, 327; future economic development, 374; and Pakistan, 374; Turks in, 384; Central Asian question, 384–85; outlook for future, 27–28, 69–73, 369–72, 374, 386–87; military confrontation, 358–60; border negotiations, 360–61

RELATIONS WITH THE WEST AND JAPAN: U.S., Japan, and Europe, xx, 174; Westernization, 6; rapprochement with U.S., 11, 12, 15, 17, 180, 326, 363; relations with imperialist countries, 30–31; "American card," 33, 36; impossible military alliance with U.S., 48–49, 132; American efforts to encircle, 56–67; benefits of "American connection," 66, 71–72; normalization of relations with U.S., 24, 69, 83, 86, 198; trade with U.S., 99, 104; future relations with U.S., 292, 375–76; need for Western technology, 120, 125, 126; economic ties with West, 126–27; Western Europe, 295–322; France, 298, 316; West Germany, 300; three world theory, 301–2; trade with Europe, 301, 303, 308; foreign policy toward Europe, 302–3; European Community, 303, 304; German reunification, 305–6; "two Chinas," 306; support of West European defense, 307; "grand design" of, 308–13; arms from Western Europe, 307–8, 309–11; and West European foreign policy, 313–20; in Western analyses, 325–55; relations with Japan, xx, 16, 174, 176, 179–80, 181–83, 374, 386; trade with Japan, 95, 98, 100, 119, 120, 177, 182

RELATIONS WITH MIDDLE EAST: Opposes Asian security system idea, 241; attitude to Middle East, 242–43; "contract laborers," 243; Iraq-Iran war, 247; PLO, 248, 249; Egypt, 250; Tunisia, 250–51; Algeria and Morocco, 251; Red Sea area, 251; Sudan, 252; Ethiopia, 252; YAR, 253; PDRY, 253, 255; Dhufar rebellion, 257–65; Middle East interests of, 265–67

RELATIONS WITH SOUTH ASIA: Pakistan, 206, 207, 215, 222, 226, 227, 238; U.S.-Pakistani alliance, 210, 218; India, 210, 212, 216, 226–27, 228, 234, 238; Tibet, 212; security interest in South Asia, 215; fear of Indo-Soviet collaboration, 219; assistance to Pakistan, 222–23, 235; actions at United Nations, 223; Sino-Bangladesh trade agreement, 226; economic assistance in South Asia, 235–36; foreign trade with South Asia, 237

RELATIONS WITH SOUTHEAST ASIA: Vietnam, 141; war with Vietnam (1979), 25, 74, 82, 168, 180, 181, 182, 197, 198; relations with Korea, 183–84; Southeast Asia, 186–205; Vietnam War, 194–97, 197; current view of Vietnam, 203

RELATIONS WITH THE SOVIET UNION: Border clashes, 7, 13–14, 53–54, 55, 58, 77; strategy toward USSR in relation to U.S., 10; Soviet expansionism and hegemonism, 25–26; revisionism, 25; Soviet spies (1974), 19; flexibility in relations with USSR (1974), 19–20; possibilities of improved relations, 26–28, 32, 36–37, 46–47; Soviet view of post-Mao policy, 29–35; Great Han expansionism, 30; intractability of the conflict, 35–42; Soviet legitimacy, 37; Russian dislike of the Chinese, 39–42; Khrushchev's views on the Chinese, 41–42; relations in the 1960s, 51–55; military threat of USSR, 56–60, 68; view of Soviet-U.S. relationship, 64–67; Soviet image of China during 1970s, 77–90; Soviet view of China's economy, 79–80; post-Mao Soviet initiatives, 82–83, 115; Sino-Soviet deterrence, 74, 87–90; trade, 92–98, 112–20; USSR as an economic model, 92, 114; GNP compared with USSR, 100–106; economics of military balance with USSR, 106–10, 120–23; encirclement of USSR, 131, 136; encirclement by USSR, 132, 140, 141; Soviet military build-up on borders, 136; challenges to Soviet economic model, 276–77; working against USSR in Eastern Europe, 278; on Soviet invasion of Czechoslovakia, 281; view of Russians, 373; prospects for

1980s, 42–47. *See also* Sino-Soviet conflict

China, Republic of (Taiwan), xvi, 182, 327, 332, 336, 342, 370, 373, 386; American support of, 56–57; growth of, 104; agriculture, 104; Chiang Kai-shek, 106

Chinese Communist Party (CCP), 268, 270, 272, 276, 341; emergence of (1949), xvi; Deng Xiaoping vice-chairman of, 20; Military Affairs Commission, 20; Hua Guofeng chairman of, 23, 70; factionalism in, 34; attitude of leadership in 1960s, 52; Lin Biao's strength in, 54; influence of Lenin, 75; as a Marxist-Leninist body, 79; criticized by Soviets, 79, 80; comprehensive history of (to be published in USSR), 80; victory in Chinese revolution, 92; dependence on USSR, 140; PCI defense of, 157; PCI relations with, 159, 167; conflict with CPSU, 283; criticized by East European communist parties, 287–89; prospects for in Eastern Europe, 291–94; Central Committee secret letter of 1960, 328; Eighth Congress (1956), 366; Ninth Congress (1969), 7–8, 13, 54; Tenth Congress (1973), 18, 60, 71; Eleventh Congress (1977), 71; Third Plenum of Eleventh Central Committee (1978), 24

Chingis Khan, 39, 346

Chirac, Jacques, 316

Chou En-lai. *See* Zhou Enlai

Christian Democratic Union/Christian Socialist Union alliance (CDU/CSU), 317, 318, 319

Christian Democrats (DC), Italian, 320

Christian Europe: "guilt culture," 344

Christianity, 334, 348, 350, 352–53, 382; Crusades, 380

CIA, 230; economic estimates, 120–21

Ci Xi, 5

Clubb, O. Edmund, 347

Coal, 120; in Yakutsk, 178

Colombo, Emilio, 304

Colonial era, end of, 267

Colonial Ingratitude, Law of, 383

Comecon, 99, 253, 281, 282, 285–86, 290, 303, 315

Cominform, 274, 282

Comintern, xvi, 75, 140, 342

Common Market. *See* European Community (EC)

Communist International. *See* Comintern

Communist movement: interparty relations, xv–xvi; world communist revolution, xv, xix; legitimacy within, 51; leadership of CPSU, xvi, 146, 150, 156, 161, 162, 168, 268–69, 270, 271, 273, 274, 278, 288; fragmentation of, 273; pluralism, 279; polycentrism, 192, 201, 272; "revisionism," "dogmatism," and "factionalism," 192–94; study of communism, 35–52; ranking of parties, 341; West European parties, 279, 281, 290, 292; Brezhnev Doctrine, 280–81; economic integration, 113–14; independent parties, 146–71; relations with socialists, 166; indoctrination in Vietnam, 189; and Ho Chi Minh, 190; in India, 212. *See also communist parties of specific countries,* Eurocommunism

Communist Party of the Soviet Union (CPSU), 348, 368, 383; authority in world communist movement, xvi, 146, 150, 156, 161, 162, 168, 268–69, 270, 271, 273, 274, 278, 288; domestic legitimacy of, 89, 333; Mao's role in discrediting Khrushchev, 51–52; leadership will be compelled to curtail expansive security role beyond its borders, 72; "Open Letter," 147; "Theses on the 100th Anniversary of the First International," 152–53; relations with European parties, 145; rift with Japanese Communist Party, 153; relations with French Communist Party, 164, 316; relations with Italian Communist Party, 157, 159, 165, 167, 169; Central Committee, 261; global power status, 271–73; criticized by Maoists, 279; and invasion of Czechoslovakia, 282–85; conflict with CCP, 283; and Eastern Europe, 275–80, 283–85, 287; Twentieth Congress (1956), xvii, 274, 279, 327, 330; Twenty-second Congress (1961), xviii, 329, 331, 345; Twenty-fourth Congress (1971), 75; Twenty-fifth Congress, 163; Twenty-sixth Congress, 118; and international conference, 154, 155; and pan-European conference (1980), 171

Confucianism, 349

Congresses, party: East European, 284; Moscow conference (November 1957), xvii; Moscow conference (1969), xix, 145, 148–57; 81-party conference (November 1960), 145, 147, 329, 331; East Berlin conference (1976), 283–84. *See also entries under parties of individual countries*

Congress Party (India), 226

Congress, U.S., 134, 135

Conservatism: on the rise in U.S., USSR, and China, 132, 134–37

Conservative foreign policy forces in Western Europe, 295, 313–20
Conservative Party (Great Britain), 314, 315
Constitution of the USSR (1924), xvi
"Contract laborers," 243
Cotton, 99
Council for Economic Mutual Assistance (CEMA), 113, 116
Chankshaw, Edward, 310
Crimea, 284
Cruise missiles (CMs), 132, 133, 309, 312
Crusades, 380
Cuba, 114, 195, 252, 258, 262, 264; troops in Third World, 135, 361; independent/neutralist, 150; at international conference, 157; missile crisis, 337, 339
Cultural Revolution, 39, 62, 77, 78, 103, 104, 137, 158, 196, 204, 216, 222, 242, 243, 244, 257, 258, 266, 277, 296, 298, 300, 334–35, 337, 340, 353, 354, 357, 367, 373; Sino-Soviet relations become more strained during, xviii; little sympathy for Maoist China, xix; end of, xxi; rejection of, 3; unleashed by Mao Zedong in 1966, 5, 154; disruptive influence, 7; purges, 8, 10–11, 24; heroes in jeopardy, 8; radicals' position near end of, 10, 16; Lin Biao and Zhou Enlai during, 12; rehabilitation of victims of, 16, 17, 24, 26; Deng's son and, 18; Chinese xenophobia during, 53; effects on economy, 55; disastrous legacy of, 136
Cyclists, 168
Cyprus, 246
Czechoslovak Communist Party, 145, 284
Czechoslovakia, 275, 276; Soviet invasion of (1968), xviii–xix, 7, 10, 13, 15, 64, 145, 155, 221, 232, 280–83, 299, 304, 337, 357, 361; invasion delays world communist conference, 155–56; liberalization of, 277; "loyalists," 270, 287; criticism of China, 287

Dake, Antonie C. A., 346
Dalai Lama, 219, 227
Dalyell, Mr., 320
Danang, 136
Daoud, Muhammad, 225, 228–29
De Gasperi, Alcide, 144
De Gaulle, Charles, 295, 296, 297, 300; "China card," 298; overtures to Moscow, 298–99
Demirel, Süleyman, 246
Democratic Kampuchea (DK), 202
Democratic Republic of South Yemen, 255. See also Yemen, People's Democratic Republic of
Democratic Republic of Vietnam (DRV). See North Vietnam
Deng Xiaoping, 141, 244, 301, 354, 355–56, 357, 358, 364, 370, 373; as a technology firster, 6, 335; rise of, 136–37; son of, 18; vice-premier and chief of staff of PLA, 20; policy in 1975, 20–21; actions toward USSR, 21; relation with radicals, 21; challenged by Jiang Qing, 21–22; drops from public view, 22; and demonstrations in Tiananmen Square, 22; purged by Mao (April 5, 1976), 22; rehabilitated, 16, 17, 23, 26; current approach of, 26; failure to develop moral justification for policies, 27; political attacks on, 61; and Gang of Four, 69; influence of, 69; on need for ties with West, 72; economic approach of successors, 105; and invasion of Afghanistan, 143; visit to U.S. and Japan, 180; and Indo-Pakistani dispute, 234; visit to France, 315; meeting with Schmidt, 305; and Soviet revisionism, 374
Desai, Morarji, 226, 227–28
Détente (use of term), 75, 321
Deterrence, 74, 87–90
Developing countries: support of China to reactionary regimes in, 31–32. See also Third World
Dhufar Liberation Front (DLF), 255, 257
Dhufar rebellion (case analysis), 254–65
Diego Garcia, 141, 260
Diet, Japanese, 175, 177
Dissident movement in USSR, 136
Djibouti, 253
"Dogmatism," 193–94, 348
Dominican Communist Party, 157
Double hégémonie, 139
Dracopoulos, Babis, 171
"Dual adversary" conception, 53
Dubček, Alexander, 145
Dulles, John Foster, 337
Durand Line, 233
Dutch Communist Party, 162, 171

East Bengal, 219, 220
East Berlin, 143, 162, 306; uprising (1953), 273
East Berlin Conference (1976), 283, 284
Eastern Europe, 126, 146, 154, 156, 163, 164, 348; Chinese trade with, 92; tables, 93; Soviet trade with, 98, 116; economic integration with communist countries, 113; Soviet troops in, 122, 293–94; threats to Soviet dominance in, 135–36; and détente, 142; economic assistance

to South Asia, 236; importance of oil to, 243, 285; impact of Sino-Soviet dispute on, 268–94; Soviet predominance in, 273; party congresses, 284; economic dependence on USSR, 285–86; prospects for, 289–94; overtures of West Germany to, 299; trade, 303, 315; no NEP, 335; and USSR, 377–79
Eastern Military Districts, 57
East German Communist Party, 284
East Germany, 146, 161, 275, 277, 280, 311, 378; rapprochement with West Germany, 143; "loyalists," 287; and reunification, 305–6
East Pakistan, 217, 219, 220, 221, 222. *See also* Pakistan
"Economics is in command," 200
Egypt, 242, 243, 254, 256, 263, 380; China's sole ambassador, 3; Soviet expulsion from, 133; Moscow-Cairo relations, 249–50
Eighth Party Congress, Chinese (1956), 366
81-party meeting in Moscow (1960), 145, 147, 149, 329, 331
Eisenhower, Dwight D., 139
Eleventh Five-Year Plan (1981–85), Soviet, 117–18, 123, 127
Eleventh Party Congress, Chinese (1977), 71
Encirclement, 56–57, 131–32, 134, 136, 140, 141, 296, 301, 344, 362, 373, 378
Energy shortages, 105
"Equidistance," policy of, 176, 179, 338
Eritrea, 247, 263
Estonia, 377
Ethiopia, 232, 243, 247, 250, 252, 253, 254, 266, 378; Soviet victory in, 134
Ethnic groups, 333, 375
Etorofu island, 175
Eurocommunism, 163, 164, 165, 167, 168, 171, 272, 282, 283, 284, 286, 287, 288, 291, 292, 316, 327; internationalizing of Sino-Soviet dispute, 144–45
"Euroleft," 166
Europe, China's new approach to, xx
European Community (EC), 295, 296, 301, 305, 314; ties with China, 303, 316, 317, 319, 320; Soviet attitude to, 303–4; third-force character of, 315
European Conservative Group, 319
European Economic Community (EEC), 165, 168
European Parliament, 165, 168, 303, 309, 314, 317, 319–20
"Eurostrategic" nuclear parity, 133
Exchange-rate conversions, 102–3

"Factionalism," 194
Fallaci, Oriana, 359
Far East: economic prospects of, 112; transportation delays in, 122; Western investment in, 124
Fascist state, China seen as, 81–82
Fatimids, 380
Fattah Isma'il, 'Abd al-, 265
Faure, Edgar, 297
FBS (forward-based system), 144
Fejtö, François, 150, 299, 345
Fertile Crescent, 241, 246–49
Fertilizer, Chinese imports of, 99
Fifteenth Congress (PCI), 168
Fifth National People's Congress, Chinese (1978), 24
Finland, 377, 378
Fishing rights, 180
"571 Document," 11
Five-year plans: Chinese, 113, 116; Soviet, 117–18, 123, 124, 127, 376; Afghanistan, 224
Floyd, David, 341–42
Foreign trade: China and USSR, 91–98, 112–20; tables, 93, 96, 114, 115; China in world trade, 99–100, 105, 365–66; China and Europe, 301, 303, 307–8, 309–11, 315, 316, 318, 320; residual in Soviet statistics, 112; Japan and USSR, 177–79; China and Japan, 177, 182; USSR and South Asia, 213, 236–37; USSR and India, 224, 228; East European, 285, 303
"Four modernizations," 20, 24, 36, 374
Fourth National People's Congress, Chinese (1975), 19, 20, 67
Fourth World, 269
France, 295; GNP of, 101; relations with U.S., 108, 132, 136; relations with USSR, 132; Moscow hostile to, 140; elections of 1968, 145; arms sales to Iraq, 247; and Algeria, 251; and Djibouti, 253; recognition of PRC, 297; trade agreement with USSR, 297; fascination with things Chinese, 298; de Gaulle and USSR, 298–99; de Gaulle and PRC, 300; trade with PRC, 308; as mediator, 311; and West European foreign policy, 313–20; Franco-Soviet amity, 316; relations with West Germany, 322
Franco regime, 161
French Communist Party (PCF), 145, 272, 281, 284, 287, 288, 314, 316; Central Committee denounces Chinese positions, 148; journalists and parliamentarians refused visas by China, 160; joins independent alliance, 162, 163;

Twenty-second Congress (1976), 163; neo-Leninist position of, 163; and death of Mao, 163–64; endorsement of Afghan invasion, 169; Paris conference (1980), 170
Fulbright Red Hoard intervention myth, 196

Gandhi, Indira: and normalization of relations with China, 216; attack on Pakistan, 220; agreement with Bhutto, 221, 223; overtures to China, 222; quoted, 224; and Indo-Pakistani relations, 225; 1971–72 election victory, 226; criticized by China, 227; and Afghan invasion, 233
Gang of Four, 31, 34, 82, 85, 100, 335, 357, 363, 366, 368, 373; Wang Hongwen, 18; arrested, 22, 69; end of time to focus on evils of (December 1978), 24; political attacks on, 61; oppositions to relations with external world, 62; obstruction and opposition of, 69, 70; purge of, 136; hostile to U.S. and USSR, 141
Garthoff, Raymond L., 350
Gas development, 120, 178
General Order Number One, 8
Geneva summit conference (1955), 139, 140
Geng Biao, 364
Georgians, 377
German Democratic Republic. *See* East Germany
German Social Democratic Party (SPD), 313
Germany, 273, 378, 379; Imperial, 131–32; reunification, 305–6, 317–18, 377–78. *See also* East Germany, West Germany
Germany, Federal Republic of. *See* West Germany
Gheorghiu-Dej, Gheorghe, 275
Gibbons, Edward, 333
Gierek, Edward, 287
Giscard d'Estaing, Valéry, 143, 296, 297, 307, 311, 314, 315, 316, 317, 322
Gittings, John, 342–43, 351, 352
Goethe, Johann von, 140
Gomulka, Wladyslaw, 276, 277
González, Felipe, 166
Gorshkov, Admiral, 378
Gosplan, 118, 123
Gottlieb, Thomas, 53, 64
Gramsci, Antonio, 144
Great Britain, 166, 314; dependence on U.S., 108; and USSR, 132, 311, 317; and China, 305, 307, 311, 317, 319; trade with China, 307–8, 309–11, 319; role in South Asia, 209, 211; and Kuwait, 246; in Middle East, 251; in Oman, 254; withdrawal from South Yemen, 257; military presence in Middle East, 260, 262; withdrawal from areas "east of Suez," 263; and West European foreign policy, 313–20
Greater East Asia Co-Prosperity Sphere, 386
Great Han (*veliko-khanskikh*) expansionism, 30
Great Leap Forward, 113, 298, 328, 331, 340; Moscow criticizes, xvii; massive mistake of, 104; attempt to proclaim a new, 31
Great Mosque in Mecca, 246
Great Russians, 136
Greece, 165, 209
Greek Communist Party, 171
Griffith, William E., 329–35, 339, 340, 341, 353, 354
Gromyko, Andrei, 176; visit to Tokyo, 84; and India, 228; visit to Bonn, 318
Gross domestic capital formation (GDCF), in China, 109
Gross domestic product (GDP), in China, 109
Gross national product (GNP); China and USSR compared, 100–106; in China, 108, 110; in USSR, 119, 120, 122
Ground-launched cruise missiles (CLCMs), 133
Guadeloupe summit meeting, 310
Guang Xu emperor, as an early technology firster, 6
Guevara, Ché, 258

Habomais, 175
Hadramout region, 255
Haile Selassie, 252
Hamrin, 255, 256
Han Nianlong, 364
Hardt, John, 117
Harrier jump jets, 307–8, 309, 310, 311, 319
Heath, Edward, 301, 314, 315
"Hegemonism," 25; in communist terminology, 194; "psychological," 313
Hegemony: of China, 31, 33, 35, 124, 187; of U.S. and USSR, 67; of USSR, 71, 72, 142, 180, 226, 244, 246, 266, 301, 305, 309, 364–65, 367, 368, 374; of USSR in Eastern Europe, 285, 290, 292; Brezhnev Doctrine seen as "outright doctrine of hegemony," 65; *double hégémonie*, 139; *egemonia* (Gramsci's term), 144; of Vietnam, 203

396 INDEX

Helicopter incident (1974), 19, 21
Helsinki accords, 301
Helsinki conference, 18
Heng Samrin, 202
Herder, Joann, 352
Himalayas, 212, 215, 220, 222, 227, 236
Hindu-Muslim conflict, 208–9
Hindus in Pakistan, 217
Hinton, Harold, 335–39
Hittites, 380
Ho Chi Minh: Comintern agent, 140; aid from Khrushchev, 140; relations with USSR, 140–41; mediation efforts by, 189, 190; last will and testament of, 190; efforts to unite communists, 194
Hokkaido, 175, 374
Hong Kong, 98, 99, 373, 386
Hoxha, Enver, 274, 277, 330; as archdogmatist, 193
Hua Guofeng, 136, 369; chosen to replace Deng, 22; joins modernizers, 22; congratulations from USSR, 23; named party chairman, 70; report to Eleventh Party Congress, 71; rejects Soviet bid, 83; East European trip, 83; visits Romania and Yugoslavia, 167; visits Tehran, 245; and Eastern Europe, 288; visits Western Europe, 167, 305–7, 308, 309, 312–13, 317, 318, 319; meeting with Carter, 322
Huang Hua, 219–20
Hundred Flowers policy, 328
Hungarian Revolution (1956), xvii, 344
Hungary, 146, 232, 273, 275, 277, 278, 280, 328; loyalty to Soviet line, 288; as an economic model, 366
Husayn, King (Jordan), 247, 248

ICBMs (intercontinental ballistic missiles), 107, 132–33, 328
Iceland, 171
Icelandic Communist Party, 281
Income: in China, 97, 102; in USSR, 101; wages of skilled workers, 109
India, xix, 103, 270, 327, 336, 337, 348; USSR as an economic model for, 92; importance to USSR, 140; Soviet attitude to border skirmishes, 140; Chinese policies toward, 206; border war of 1962, 206; policies of, 207; relations with USSR, 207, 214, 216, 227, 228, 233, 239; disputes with Pakistan, 66, 208–9, 210, 219–20, 236; British in, 209; wars in, 209; and Kashmir, 209; relations with China, 210, 212, 216, 226–27, 228, 234, 238; as a world power, 210–11; nonalignment of, 212, 219, 228; Nehru's view of USSR, 212; communists in, 212; and Tibet, 212; and state-controlled economic development, 212; nuclear weapons and missiles, 214, 215, 216; Bangladesh crisis, 216–20; fear of Sino-Pakistani-American axis, 219; treaty with USSR, 219; support from USSR, 219; policy toward Bangladesh, 224; trade with USSR, 224, 228, 237; heavy industry of, 225, 228, 235; agreements with Pakistan and Bangladesh, 225; and overthrow of Mujib, 225–26; elections in, 226; nuclear explosion (1974), 226; and Carter administration, 227; and invasion of Afghanistan, 233; arms from USSR, 233, 235; economic assistance to, 236; foreign trade, 237; attitude of USSR to, 332; prospects for 1980s, 375; Moguls, 380
Indian Ocean, 224, 244, 251, 260, 263, 264, 362, 375
Indochina, 87, 88, 136, 327, 360; as focus of Chinese expansionism, 81; U.S. expulsion from, 361–62; Ho Chi Minh's plans to dominate, 141; USSR in, 141; Vietnamese intervention in Kampuchea, 168; Sino-Soviet impact on, 185–205; likely federation of, 204; Hanoi's dominant role in, 214. *See also countries of the region*
Indonesia, 327, 337; flirtation with USSR, 187; prospects for 1980s, 375
Indonesian Communist Party (PKI), 346
Indo-Pakistani wars, 66, 208–9, 210, 219–20, 236
Indo-Soviet Treaty of Friendship and Cooperation, 219, 228
Institute of International Affairs (Italy), 168
Institute of Marxism-Leninism, 153
International Meeting of Communist and Workers Parties, Moscow (1969), 156–57; opposition to, 148–55
International Monetary Fund, 99, 126
Iran, 132, 259, 260, 262, 265, 267; relations with USSR, 214; relations with Afghanistan, 229; Islamic fervor in, 231; and U.S., 232; conflict with Iraq, 132, 238, 247; approached to join security system, 241; in Oman, 256; prospect of Soviet invasion of, 244–45; Soviet aid to, 245; shah's influence on Oman, 246; Islamic revival, 246; Safavids, 380; Khomeini, 245, 246, 381; Turks in, 384
Iraq, 238, 243, 249, 250, 251, 253, 256, 259, 263, 264, 265, 266; importance in region, 246–47; relations with USSR, 247; arms from France, 247; conflict with Iran, 132, 238, 247

IRBMs (intermediate range ballistic missiles), 133
Islam (Muslim world), 40, 334, 375, 377, 379–85; in USSR, 135; Hindu-Muslim conflict, 208–9; population of Pakistan, 210; and division of Pakistan, 218; in Pakistan, 216–17, 226; in Afghanistan, 230–31; population of Soviet Central Asia, 231; reaction to Afghan invasion, 232–33; Islamic revival, 246; in Lebanon, 248; in world politics, 377, 379–85; Muslim Brotherhood, 381; fundamentalism, 381–85
Israel, 106, 241, 248, 261; Arab "oil weapon" used against, 132; U.S. support of, 134, 385; "whipping boy" in Sino-Soviet conflict, 249; defeat of Egypt, 249; Sadat's trip to, 250
Italian Communist Party (PCI), 272, 279, 284, 287, 368; autonomous and reformist ideology of, 144; and Yugoslavia, 144–45; and USSR, 145; and China, 147, 157–71; statements on China, 157; antishowdown attitude, 148–49, 150; "unity in diversity and autonomy," 148; opposition to world conference, 148–55; Togliatti's comments to Central Committee plenum, 151; Yalta Memorandum, 151–52; announcement of conference, 155; participation at conference, 156–67; relations with CPSU, 159, 165, 167, 169; independent alliance, 162; and death of Mao, 163–64; and Jacoviello, 164–65; "new internationalism," 165–66; Central Committee, 165, 168, 169; Soviet grievance against, 166; normalization of relations with China, 167; Fifteenth Congress, 168; condemns invasion of Afghanistan, 169, 170; and Paris pan-European conference (1980), 170–71; and invasion of Czechoslovakia, 281; and West European foreign policy, 314
Italy, 295, 305, 307, 320; Soviet influence in, 146; foreign policy, 165
Izvestiia, 298

Jabal Akhdar, 254
"Jabalis," 255
Jackson amendment, 179
Jackson, W. A. Douglas, 350
Jacoviello, Alberto, 158–59, 164–65
Janata (People's) Party, 226, 228
Japan, 292, 301, 308, 309, 331, 336, 349, 354; invasion of China, xvi; China's new approach to, xx; normalization of relations with China, 16, 176, 179, 182; relations with China, 4, 26, 174, 179–80, 181–83, 364, 374, 386; role in China's modernization, 30; investment in China, 172; view of China, 174, 181; friendship treaty with China, 83; support of Zhou Enlai, 176; trade with China, 95, 97, 98, 117, 182; oil imports from China, 119; cooperation to develop Chinese and Soviet energy resources, 120; need for oil, 95, 134; dependence on Middle East oil, 238; petroleum imports, 95, 100; relations with USSR, 76, 83–84, 132, 136, 174–83, 213, 214; Siberian development, 84, 172, 173, 176, 178–79, 182; territorial disputes with USSR, 36, 84, 175–77, 182; Soviet fears of, 131; Soviet influence in, 145; trade with USSR, 177–79; foreign policy toward USSR, 181–83; concern about Soviet military presence in Vietnam, 203; close alliance with U.S., 173; attitude toward U.S., 136; U.S.-Japan Security Treaty, 176; effects of Sino-Soviet dispute on, 172–84; political-strategic role of, 173; economic strength of, 173, 376, 386; in world trade, 98, 100; growth rate of, 103, 104; economic issues, 177–79; technology of, 225; agriculture, 95, 104; as an imperialist power, 65; blunder of World War II, 67; revival of, 138; policy of "equidistance," 176, 179; increase in armaments, 179; approach to defense, 181, 183; influence in Southeast Asia, 92; and Korea, 175; and Nationalist China (1937–41), 106; "Manchukuo," 220; "shame culture," 344
Japanese Communist Party, 163; independent/neutralist, 153; rift with CPSU, 153
Jenkins, Roy, 304
Jewish intellectuals in U.S., 135
Jiang Qing, 5, 9, 69, 357; and nativists, 16; challenges Deng, 21–22. *See also* Gang of Four
Ji Pengfei, 259, 262
Johnson, Lyndon, 140
Joint Japanese-Soviet Economic Cooperation Committee, 178
Jordan, 247, 248
Jordanian Communist Party, 262
Journalists, 341–47
Jukes, Geoffrey, 349

Kádár, János, 275, 288
Kampuchea, 168, 195, 197, 200, 201, 202, 270, 289; future of, 202; Democratic Kampuchea (DK), 202; People's Republic of (PRK), 202; third force, 202

Kanapa, Jean, 164
Karachi, 225
Karakhan Declaration, 75
Karakorum, 346
Karmal, Babrak, 229, 230
Kashmir, 234; India's attitude to, 209; Pakistan's efforts to control, 210; Indian-Pakistani discussion of, 221
Katkov, Mikhail, 352
Katushev, K. F., 261
Kazakhs, 330, 333, 377, 384
Kemalism, 381
Kennan, George, 231
Kennet, Lord, 320
Khabarovsk, 361
Khalq (Masses) faction, 229, 230
Khartoum, 252
Khmer Rouge, 200
Khmer Serai, 202
Khomeini, Shi'i ayatullah, 245, 246, 381
Khrushchev, Nikita (1894–1971), 329, 331, 335, 341, 345, 348; assumes Soviet primacy in interparty relations, xvi; visits Beijing (1954), xvii; attitude toward Tito, xvii; and Romanian Communist Party, xvii; attacks Chinese policies through Albanian surrogate, xviii; views on the Chinese, 41–42; personalized dispute with Mao, 51, 336; Mao's response to ouster of, 51–52, 54; China's dissatisfaction with, 338; Beijing's excoriation of, 76–77; détente with U.S., 138, 139, 337; and Adenauer, 139, 142, 299; and Western Europe, 296, 298; and West Germany, 300; policy in Third World, 140; "collective mobilization" against the Chinese, 145; call for end to Sino-Soviet polemics, 149; and Yalta Memorandum, 152; resolve to have world conference, 151, 153; and Southeast Asia, 188, 189, 195; and South Asia, 214; and communist terminology, 193; mission to Belgrade (1955), 273; secret speech, 327, 328, 336, 340, 341, 342, 349; disillusionment with, 328; aid to underdeveloped areas, 332; recklessness of, 349; repairing Stalin's damage, 354; withdrawal of experts from China, 365; fall of (October 1964), xviii, 153, 336, 337, 356
"Khrushchevism without Khrushchev," 52
Kim Il Sung, 183–84
Kissinger, Henry, xix, 15, 65, 157, 218, 297, 336, 337; quoted, 66; in Pakistan, 218
Kohl, Helmut, 301, 305
Korea, 87; U.S. intervention in, 57; agriculture, 95, 104; growth rate, 103, 104; energy shortage, 105; most disliked nation by Japan, 175; effects of Sino-Soviet dispute on, 172; independence of, 173; relations with USSR, 183–84; key role in international affairs, 183. *See also* Korean War, North Korea, South Korea
Korean War, 57, 196, 327; Chinese entry into, 92
Kosygin, A. N., 355; visit to Beijing (1969), xix; visit to Beijing (1965), 337; accused of practicing "Khrushchevism without Khrushchev," 52; meetings with Zhou, 58; promises to Zhou (1969), 83; visit to Hanoi (1965), 190; Tashkent meeting (1966), 210
Kozharov, Asen, 165
Kravis method of price recalculation, 103
Kunashiri island, 175
Kuomintang, xvi, 80, 85
Kurile Islands, 175
Kuwait, 246, 255, 259
Kuznetsov, 341

Labor camps in USSR, 163
Labor unrest in USSR, 46
Labour Party (Great Britain), 166, 317, 319, 320
Laos, xiv, 141; importance of Sino-Soviet dispute to, 187
Latin America, 213
Lebanon, 248
Le Duan, 200
Lee Kuan Yew (Singapore leader), 188
Leftists in America, 135
Lenin, 345; attitude toward independence of fellow communists, xvi; influence on CCP, 75; quoted by Hua Guofeng, 71; and communist terminology, 193
Leo X, 333
Leopard tanks, 310
Liaotung Peninsula, 332
Libya, 250, 251, 252, 256, 266
Lin Biao (1908–1971), 357, 363, 368, 373; issues General Order Number One, 8; Lin Biao affair, 8–15, 16, 22; and Chen Boda, 9; secret document expressing his views, 11; and military budget, 11–12; relations with Zhou, 12–13, 14; relations with Mao, 14–15; plans to seize power, 14; "Campaign to Criticize Lin Biao and Confucius," 18, 19; commitment to "dual adversary" idea, 53; designation as Mao's successor, 54; strength in CCP, 54; triumph over Luo Ruiqing, 55; emphasis on military, 59; compared with Gang of Four, 62; hostile to U.S. and USSR, 141; fall of, 337

Li Qiang, 305; quoted, 62
Lister, Enrique, 160
Liu Shaoqi, 8, 357; "China's Khrushchev," 61
Longo, Luigi, 148, 149; decision to publish Yalta Memorandum, 152; rejects international conference, 153; conditions for conference participation, 155
Lon Nol government, 202
Low, Alfred D., 338–40
"Loyalists," 287
LRTNF (long-range theater nuclear forces), 133, 144
Luo Ruiqing, 55
Lushan plenum, 331
Luther, Martin, 333

Macao, 373
Macciocchi, Maria Antonietta, 158
Macedonia, 278
Malacca, Strait of, 362
Malaya, 327
Malaysia, 375; importance of Sino-Soviet dispute to, 187
Malenkov, G. M., 328, 341
Maltese Communist Party, 171
Mamluks, 380
Manchuria, 57, 174, 304, 332, 344
Maoism, 372, 373; reinterpretation of, 32, 35; "permanent revolution," 32; significant break with, 33; Soviet view of current Chinese attitudes, 34–35; "new stage" in 1975, 81, 83; in Western Europe, 279
Maoists, 282; and North Vietnam, 190; accuse Western communists of revisionism, 157; and U.S., 302; Soviet view of, 308
Mao Zedong (1893–1976), 270, 331, 335, 341, 342, 344, 346, 349, 373, 374; communist rural base, xvi; break with the Soviets, xvi–xvii; opinion of Tito, xvii; personal attacks on, xviii; on equality with Soviets, xix; shift in policies before and after his death, xx; as a "selective modernizer," 5; and nativists, 6, 7; and Chen Boda, 8–9; support for Zhou against Lin Biao, 12–13; conflict with Lin, 14–15; health failing, 16, 17; relations with modernizers and nativists, 16, 18, 20; and helicopter incident, 21; support for radicals, 21; purges Deng, 22; Khrushchev's attitude to, 42; personalized dispute with Khrushchev, 51; rejects "united action," 51; response to Khrushchev's ouster, 51–52, 54; and "dual adversary" concept, 53; quoted about U.S. involvement in Asia, 57, 67; suspicions of Soviets, 57; on military strategy, 59–60; international strategy cited, 66; quoted about danger of war, 70; and East-West nuclear relations, 77; Soviet view of, 78, 79, 80; "people's war," 106; militarism of, 124; determination for China to be superpower, 138; Quemoy and Matsu issue, 139; relations with Ho Chi Minh, 140; and "anti-imperialist unity of action" in support of North Vietnam, 154; and Vietnam War, 189; and supplies for Vietnam, 190; and principles of war applied to Vietnam, 192; on U.S. in Vietnam, 195; attitude to Western communist parties, 157; meeting with Schmidt, 305; meeting with Heath, 315; as a father of Marxism, 327; as Stalin's replacement, 328; as a professional revolutionary, 329; ideological superiority, 336; and revisionism, 337; claims to be senior communist leader, 338; purges of, 354, 357; dependence of conflict on, 369; and Soviet seizure of Chinese territory, 359; new line toward U.S., 363; ideological impediments, 366; death of, 22, 69, 221, 272, 283; post-Mao reaction, 23–28, 163–64; post-Mao Soviet initiatives, 82
Mao Zedong Thought, 8–9, 13, 77, 374
Marchais, Georges, 163, 167, 170, 288
Market socialism in China, 34
MaRV (maneuverable reentry vehicle), 132
Marxism-Leninism, 333, 373, 381–82, 383, 385; deviation from, 268–69, 271; "Yugoslav way," 274
Marxists: in Afghanistan, 229, 239; in Middle East, 255–57, 260, 265
Mecca, 246
Mediterranean civilization, 386
Mehnert, Klaus, 343–45
Mengistu Haile Mariam, Colonel, 252
Mery, Guy, 307
Mexican Communist Party, 171
Middle East: "arc of crisis," 131; instability of, 132, 134; priority to USSR, 213; defined, 240–41; Moscow's behavior in, 242–43; Chinese attitude to, 242–43; economic interests, 243, 265; role of ideology, 244; Persian Gulf, 244–46; Fertile Crescent, 246–49; North Africa, 249–51; Red Sea area, 251–54; Dhufar rebellion, 254–65; USSR and PRC in, 265–67. *See also the various countries of the region*
Middleton, Drew, 345, 346

MIG fighter planes, 224, 250, 262; MIG-19, 110; MIG-23 and 25, 107
Military aid. *See* Armaments
"Military-bureaucratic dictatorship," 77
Military confrontation, 358–60, 362
Military expenditures: China, 11–12, 15, 24–25, 33, 54–55, 59, 106–10, 120–23, 127, 370; Soviet Union, 106–10, 120–23
Military power: China, 53, 60; USSR, 293, 350, 356, 376; Soviet build-up in Far East, 82; Soviet dilemma, 374, 378
Military-strategic interests defined, 241–42
Military tactics: Russian generals who have traded territory for time, 106; Chiang Kai-shek, 106
Military technology: unverifiable, 132; American breakthroughs, 138; research and development in China, 107–8
Mirage fighters, 247
Missiles, 107, 132–33, 309, 310, 312, 313, 328; in India, 214, 215; Cuban crisis, 337, 339
Mitterand, François, 166
Modernizers. *See* Selective modernizers
Moguls (India), 380
Monetary methods: exchange-rate conversions, 102–3; Kravis method, 103
Mongolia, xvii, xviii, xix, 156, 336, 359, 362, 365, 373
Mongols, 40, 325, 333, 338, 346, 347
Morocco, 157, 251, 265
Moscow Conference of World Communist Parties (June 1969), xix, 145, 148–57
Mosely, Philip, vii–viii
Mujibar Rahman, Sheikh, 217, 223–24, 225, 226
Muller, Antonio, 167
Mullor, Angel, 168
Muscat, 256
Muslims. *See* Islam
MX (missile experimental), 132

Nagy, Imre, 344
Nasser, Fuad, 262
National Assembly, French, 316
National Council of the Fatherland Front, 287
National Democratic Front for the Liberation of Oman and the Arab Gulf (NDFLOAG), 254, 257
National Liberation Front of South Yemen, 255, 263
Nationalism, 194, 377; replaces ideological interests, 38; principal driving force in international politics, 145; in Japan and Korea, 173; role in international affairs, 183; current age of, 330, 332, 348, 352, 353; Islamic, 380–85

Nationalist Chinese government. *See* China, Republic of
National People's Congress (PRC): Fourth (1975), 19, 20, 67; Fifth (1978), 24, 83
"National question" in USSR, 376
"Nativists": defined, 5; and selective modernizers, 6, 16–22; and the military, 7; essentially radicals, 6, 10; gain strength in 1973, 18; Mao sides against in 1974, 20; oppose Deng's action, 21
NATO, 47, 122, 246, 306–7, 312, 313, 317, 318, 321, 374, 378; Soviet relations with, 18; China's relations with, 25, 26; armaments, 132–33; threat to USSR, 188
Natta, Alessandro, 152
Naval power, Soviet, 362, 378
Nazi Germany: comparison with China, 81–82
Nazi negotiations with USSR, 212–13
Nehru, Jawaharlal, 212
Nepal, 207; economic assistance to, 235–36; foreign trade, 237
Nerchinsk, Treaty of (1689), 331
Neutralization, 199
New China News Agency (NCNA), 257
New Economic Mechanism (NEM), 275
New Economic Policy (NEP), 335
New Economic Zones, 197, 201
"New internationlism," 165–66, 167, 171
New Life Movement, 5
Nhan Dan, 191
NICs (newly industrialized countries), 111
Nicholas I, 374
Ninth Party Congress, Chinese (April 1969), 7–8, 13, 54
Nixon, Richard, 297, 326; visit to China, xix, 180, 336, 337; and full normalization of relations with China, 18; Nixon-Brezhnev summit, 18; and Zhou Enlai, 337
Nixon Doctrine, 264
Nixon-Kissinger administration, 47
Nonalignment: in Southeast Asia, 188, 191, 199; of India, 212, 219, 228; of Afghanistan, 229; of Iraq, 247; Soviet support of, 214
Nonproliferation policies, 228. *See also* Nuclear weapons
North Africa, 241, 249–51
Northeast Asia, impact of Sino-Soviet dispute on, 172–84
North Korea, 334; Chinese control in, xvii, xviii, xix; Soviet influence in, 145; Japanese military captured in, 174; source of armaments, 183; no NEP, 335. *See also* Korea, Korean War

North Vietnam, xviii, 140, 334; supports invasion of Czechoslovakia, 13; independent/neutralist, 150; and global power struggle, 188; beginning of war, 189; communist leadership in, 190–91, 199–200; and balance between USSR and China, 191–92, 194; defectors to South, 195–96; aims of in Vietnam War, 196; aid from USSR and China, 195–96; economic factors, 200–201; no NEP, 335; communist party unity regarding, 154. *See also* Indochina, Vietnam, Vietnam War
North Yemen. *See* Yemen Arab Republic
Norwegian Communist Party, 157, 279, 281
Nuclear Nonproliferation Treaty, 216
Nuclear test ban treaty (1963), 139, 298, 302, 337, 348
Nuclear weapons, 342; Soviet and U.S., 132–33, 138, 144; China and USSR, 87, 330, 350; China, 54, 58, 127, 343; USSR, 193, 311–12; India, 214, 215, 216, 226–27; Pakistan, 226–27; East-West nuclear relations, 77; research, 107–8; nuclear war, 194, 308
Numayri, Jaafar al-, 251–52

OECD (Organization for Economic Cooperation and Development), 134, 138
Oil. *See* Petroleum
Oman, Sultanate of, 246, 254–65
OPEC (Organization of Petroleum Exporting Countries), 104, 111, 138, 178, 265, 285, 292; prices in late 1973, 19
Orthodox Christianity, 352
Ostellino, Piero, 313
Ottoman Empire, 380

Pacific Firsters, 386–87
Pajetta, Gian, 160, 161, 162, 167, 169, 170
Pakistan, xix, 270, 337; policies of, 207; ties with China, 206, 207, 215, 222, 226, 227, 238; civil war, 207; disputes with India, 208–9, 210, 236; wars in, 209; and Kashmir, 209, 210; alliance with U.S., 210, 213, 216; Muslim population of, 209, 210, 216–17; equality with India, 211; U.S. military assistance, 211; relations with USSR, 214, 216, 239; 1971 crisis in, 206, 216; Bangladesh crisis, 216–20; army of, 217; USSR steel mill in, 217, 225; war with India, 219–20; assistance with China, 222–23, 235; recognizes Bangladesh, 223; agreements with India and Bangladesh, 225; fears about Afghans, 225; elections of 1977, 226; Islamic coup, 226; U.S. aid cut, 228; relations with Afghanistan, 229; and invasion of Afghanistan, 233–34; economic assistance to, 235–36; foreign trade, 236–37; India's obsession with, 375
Palestine Liberation Organization (PLO), 248–49
Palestinian issue, 132
Pamirs, 361
Pan-European communist conference on peace and disarmament (Paris, April 1980), 170–71
Panturkism, 384
Paracel Islands, 19
Paraguayan Communist Party, 148
Parcham (Banner) faction, 229, 230
Paris Agreements of 1973, 191
Party congresses. *See* Congresses, party
Pavolini, Luca, 158, 159
PCE. *See* Spanish Communist Party
PCF. *See* French Communist Party
PCI. *See* Italian Communist Party
Peace Agreement of 1956, 175–76
"Peace policy," 75–76
Peasantry, Chinese, 6, 8
Peng Dehuai, 26, 331, 335
People's Army of Vietnam (PAVN), 189, 196
People's Democratic Party (PDP), Afghanistan, 229
People's Democratic Republic of Yemen (PDRY), 253–65, 266
People's Liberation Army (PLA), 7, 8, 13, 16; Deng Xiaoping chief of staff of, 20; and Tangshan earthquake relief, 22; and budget allocations, 24, 54. *See also* Lin Biao
People's Republic of China (PRC). *See* China, People's Republic of
People's Republic of Kampuchea (PRK), 202. *See also* Kampuchea
"People's war," 106
Pershing II missiles, 133, 309, 312
Persian Gulf, 238, 241, 244–46, 258, 260, 263, 264, 292, 386; American interest in, 46
Petroleum: USSR, 117–19, 122, 123, 178, 213; exported by USSR, 94, 95; need for by USSR, 134, 135; and Soviet priorities, 213; significance to USSR and Eastern Europe in Middle East, 243; Soviet shortages, 290; China, 119; imported by China, 94; exported by China, 95; Chinese production in 1979–81, 104; exaggerated Western expectations of China's potential, 112; Arab "oil weapon," 132; OPEC prices, 138; Japanese

need for, 134; West's dependence on Middle East, 238; Libya, 250; Algeria, 251. *See also* OPEC
Philippines, 327, 375; importance of Sino-Soviet dispute to, 187
Phosphate industry loan to Morocco, 251
PKI (Indonesian Communist Party), 346
Podgorny, Nikolai V., 297; and Pakistan, 217–18
Poland, 146, 273, 275, 276, 277, 328, 356; recent events, 135, 142, 238, 287–88, 376, 377; and Paris conference (1980), 170; Soviet control of, 377–78; in 1956, 344
Polish Communist Party, 280, 284, 287, 341
Polish United Workers' Party (PUWP), 277–78
Politburo: Chinese, 16, 18, 355; Soviet, 338, 355; North Vietnamese, 191, 192, 199–200, 204; French, 163, 164
Political interests defined, 242
Pol Pot regime, 168, 200, 202, 204
Polycentrism (of communism), 192, 201, 272
Pompidou, Georges, 301, 304, 314, 315, 316
Popular Front for the Liberation of Oman (PFLO), 256–57, 263
Popular Front for the Liberation of Oman and the Arab Gulf (PFLOAG), 255
Popular Front for the Liberation of the Occupied Arab Gulf (PFLOAG), 254–65
Population growth: China, 102; USSR, 101
Ports at Bangladesh cleared by USSR, 224
Portugal, 165
Portuguese Communist Party, 148
POW camps in South Vietnam, 195–96
Precision-guided munitions (PGMs), 132
"Preemptive breakout," 131–32
Presidency (U.S.), 134–35
Price structures, 102–3
Purges, Great, 335

Qabus, Sultan, 254, 255, 256, 257, 263
Qaddafi, Colonel Muammar al-, 250, 251
Qatar, 246, 255
Qiao Guanhua, 304
Quemoy crisis, xvii
Quemoy and Matsu, 139

Racist persecution in Southeast Asia, 197
"Radicals": equivalent to "nativists," 6; and United States, 10, 141; policy of, 10; and Lin Biao, 12–13; pitted against Zhou and his allies, 16; policy toward USSR, 17, 18, 141; upsurge in influence, 18–19; overplay their hand, 19; Deng's actions alarm, 21; support from Mao, 21; efforts to unseat Deng, 22; purge of, 22; Gang of Four, 18, 22; post-Mao attitude to, 23
Radio Moscow, 318
Railroads: Baikal-Amur Mainline (BAM), 117–18, 119, 179; in China, 105
Reagan, Ronald, 135
Red Army, 98, 132
Red Guards, 8, 18, 78
Red Sea area, 241, 251–54
Refugees: in Southeast Asia, 204; from Pakistan, 217; from Tibet, 219
Regionalism in Southeast Asia, 204–5
"Relational" strategic interest, 241–42, 246, 266
Religion: analogy to communism, 333–34, 339–40, 341; contempt for, 382; revival in U.S., 135
Ren Guping, 68
Reunion Communist Party, 157
Revisionism, 328, 337, 338, 348, 357, 373, 374; Mao's description of Soviet domestic policies, xvii; Mao's view of Tito, xvii; Chinese attacks on Yugoslavia, xviii; and Chinese policy toward USSR, 17; Mao's concerns about, 52, 61; China charges Soviets with, 65; China charges Togliatti with, 147; Moscow conference charges Yugoslavia with, 149; Maoists accuse Western communists of, 157; in Eastern Europe, 146; as viewed in North Vietnam, 192–94
River navigation agreement, 371
Rolls-Royce, 310
Roman Catholicism, 333, 334
Romania, 277, 278, 334, 384; and Soviet border disputes, 36; "autonomist," 270; Hua's trip to, 312
Romanian Communist Party (RCP), 145, 275, 278, 280, 284; Khrushchev and, xvii; relations with China, 147, 157, 167; boycott of meeting, 153; participation in Budapest meeting, 155; not part of attack on China, 156; as intermediary, 160; independent alliance, 162; and death of Mao, 164; and pan-European conference, 171; and invasion of Czechoslovakia, 282; relations with CPSU and CCP, 288, 289; party congress (1965), 355
Rubbi, Antonio, 165–66
"Russian" attitude to the Chinese, 39–42
Russian émigrés, 343
Russian Revolution, 341

Sadat, Anwar al-, 249–50, 263
Saddam Husayn, 247
Safavids, 380
Sa'id ibn Taymur, Sultan, 254, 255, 257
Sakhalin, 178
Salisbury, Harrison E., 345–46
SALT II (Strategic Arms Limitation Talks), 83, 232, 311
San'a, 253
San Francisco Peace Treaty of 1952, 174, 175
San Marino Communist Party, 157, 162, 171
Saudi Arabia, 256, 292; U.S. commitment to, 134; backing for Pakistan, 234; policy to USSR, 245–46; and YAR, 253
Scandinavia, 166
Scheel, Walter, 305
Schmidt, Helmut, 295, 306, 311, 318, 322; and détente, 143, 144; visit to China, 305
Scholarship on the Sino-Soviet dispute, 351–52, 382
Schwartz, Harry, 348
SEATO (Southeast Asia Treaty Organization), 205
Second World, 301, 306
Security: Chinese strategy, 63–73; problems in Persian Gulf and Red Sea areas, 241; definition of terms, 241–44
Sergre, Sergio, 168
"Selective modernizers": defined, 5; dominating Chinese politics, 6; struggle with nativists, 16–22; Hua Guofeng joins, 22; Wang Dongxing joins, 22; post-Mao influence of, 23; "development first," 71
Shah of Iran, 245, 259, 260, 267; influence in Oman, 246; Reza Shah, 381
Shanghai Communiqué (1972), 16, 337
Shastri, Lal Bahadur, 210
Shelepin, Alexander, 338
Shelu, 330
Shenyang Military Region, 60
Shiga, Yoshio, 153
Shikotan island, 175
Siberia, 269, 344, 345, 359, 365, 373, 383; Brezhnev's train ride, 83; joint USSR-Japanese development of resources, 84, 172, 173, 176, 178–79, 182; petroleum and gas resources, 95, 100; economic prospects of, 112; Soviet plans to industrialize, 117–18; transportation delays, 122; Western investment in, 124
Sibir, 345
Sihanouk, Prince, 202
Sikkim, 227
Simla Accord, 221
Singapore, 141, 188, 386

Sinkiang. *See* Xinjiang
Sino-Indian border disputes, 206, 212, 215, 227
Sino-Japanese treaties, 83, 180, 182
Sinologists (Soviet), 78–82, 85
Sino-Soviet conflict: intractability of, 35–42; historical basis for, 35; American strategy, 47–49; in the 1960s, 51–55; militarization of, 54, 132–33, 358–60, 362; Soviet military threat to China, 56–60; global strategy, 63–69; deterrence, 74, 87–90; Soviet image of China during 1970s, 77–90; relations during 1950-70, 76–77; psychological aspects, 35, 39–42, 81–82, 88–89, 373; possibility of war, 87–89; economic problems, 91–127; economics of military balance, 106–10, 120–23; international politics, 131–46; independent communist parties, 147–71; Soviet leadership in world communist movement, 146, 150, 156, 161, 162; impact on Northeast Asia, 172–84; shift to Asian emphasis, 174; impact on Southeast Asia, 185–205; Hanoi and, 188–92, 201–2; date for start of, 188, 327, 336, 345; benefits of to North Vietnam, 192; impact on South Asia, 206–39; and economic assistance and trade in South Asia, 235–37; effects on Middle East, 240–67; effects on Eastern Europe, 268–94; effects on Western Europe, 295–322; West European cleavages over, 313–20; alternative Western views of, 325–55; roots not in border disputes, 344; scholarship on, 351–55, 382; overview of conflict, 355–72; border negotiations, 360–61; economic reorientation, 365–66; ideological nature of, 367–68; dependence of the conflict on Mao, 369; benefit to West, 375; and Central Asians, 379–85; prospects for 1980s, 27–28, 42–49, 72–73, 107–11, 126–27, 203–5; 238–40; 265–67; 289–94; 321–22; 369–72, 372–87
Sino-Vietnamese war (1979), 25, 74, 82, 168, 180, 181, 182, 197, 198
Slovak press, 287
Snow, Edgar, 341
Soares, Mário, 166
Social-democratic forces in Western Europe, 165
Social Democratic Party, German (SPD), 313, 317–18
Socialist Group, 320
Socialist Republic of Vietnam (SRV), 203
Socialists: relations with communists, 166
Socialists, French, 317, 320

Somalia, 242, 243, 252–53, 263, 264
Sonnenfeldt Doctrine, 302
Sonnenfeldt, Helmut, 231
Son Sann forces, 202
South Africa, 134
South Asia, 244; impact of Sino-Soviet conflict on, 206–39; 1971 crisis in, 206, 216; and Soviet priorities, 213; Bangladesh crisis, 216–20; Afghan crisis, 228–34; economic assistance and trade in, 235–37; foreign trade, 236–37
Southeast Asia: U.S. military presence in, 51, 53, 54; USSR supplanting U.S. in, 68; China and USSR in, 86; influence of Japan, 92; Soviet containment of China in, 126–27; Soviet forces in, 136; Ho Chi Minh's plans for, 141; and U.S., 141; Sino-Soviet impact on, 185–205; trend toward regionalism in, 186–87, 204–5; nonalignment, 188, 191, 199; future of, 197–205; attitude to USSR, 214; Balkans of Asia, 375. *See also* Indochina
Southern Kuriles, 175
South Korea, 111; industrialized, 182; American support of, 184. *See also* Korea, Korean War
South Vietnam, 140, 141; collapse of, 68; and Paracel Islands, 19; POW camps, 195–96. *See also* Vietnam, Vietnam War
Southwest Asia: "arc of crisis," 131
South Yemen. *See* Yemen, People's Democratic Republic of
Soviet army in Eastern Europe, 98
Soviet-Nazi pact (1939), 212–13
Soviet-Vietnamese Treaty of Friendship and Cooperation, 180
Spain: GNP of, 101; and EEC, 165; Soviet influence in, 145; diplomatic relations between Franco regime and China, 161
Spanish Communist Party (PCE), 272, 284, 287; relations with USSR, 145; relations with China, 147, 157, 164, 167, 168, 171; intermediary between PCI and CCP, 160; visit to China, 160–61; independent alliance, 162; Soviet grievance against, 166; condemns invasion of Kampuchea, 168; condemns invasion of Afghanistan, 169; and pan-European conference, 171; reaction to invasion of Czechoslovakia, 281
Spey 202 engine, 310
Spies in China (Soviet), 19, 21
Sputnik I, 328
Sri Lanka, 207, 224; economic assistance to, 235–37

SS-20s, 132–33, 144
"Stages of growth," 353
Stalin, Joseph (1879–1953), 144, 273, 274, 279, 329, 332, 334, 335, 342, 348, 354, 377, 378; attitude toward independence of fellow communists, xvi; criticized by Khrushchev, xvii; Trotsky's challenge to, 38; and Tito, 146; birthday celebrated in Vietnam, 190; and communist terminology, 193; death of, 327, 336; funeral, 341; Khrushchev's secret speech, 328; and Japan, 375; quoted, 374
"Stalinist" growth model, 123
Starlinger, Wilhelm, 299
State, U.S. Department of, 231
Steel: foreign trade in, 97, 99; shortage in USSR, 122, 123; Japanese export to USSR, 177; USSR mill in Pakistan, 217, 224
Strauss, Franz Josef, 301, 318
Students expelled from China and Soviet Union, xviii
Subic Bay, 141
Sudan, 157, 251–52
Supreme Soviet (USSR), 118
Suslov Report, 149, 150; publication delayed by Romanians, 151
Sweden, 157, 162, 171
Swedish Communist Party, 279, 281
Switzerland, 157, 171, 300
Syria, 243, 247, 248, 250, 254, 265, 266

Tacitus, quoted, 136
Taiwan. *See* China, Republic of
Taiwan Strait, 328
Tanaka, Kakuei, 84
Tangshan earthquake, 22
Tariki, Nur Muhammad, 229, 230
Tashkent, 210, 225
TASS, 220
Tatar-Mongol yoke, 39
Taylor, George, 385
Technical aid: USSR to Libya, 250; preference for Western technology, 251; USSR to China, 94
Technology: China's ability to produce weapons, 107–10; aircraft, 107, 110; Soviet use of Western, 118, 120, 124; need in China and USSR, 119–20; Chinese use of Western, 125; Soviet need for, 221; Chinese purchase of, 309–10; India's need for, 225; East European need for, 285, 286; weapons, 132, 138
"Technology firsters": defined, 5; priority of economic development, 6, 71; struggle with nativists, 16–17; gain influence, 23–24, 25

Tenth Five-Year Plan (Soviet), 124, 127
Tenth Party Congress (CCP), 18, 60, 66, 71
"Terrible simplifiers," 134
Test ban treaty. *See* Nuclear test ban treaty
Tet offensive (1968), 190, 195
Thailand, 141, 199, 375
Thatcher, Margaret, 295, 308, 313, 315, 317, 319
Third-force foreign policy in Western Europe, 295, 313-20
Third Plenum of the Eleventh Central Committee (China), 24
Third World, 250, 251, 257, 258, 263, 266, 269, 301, 336, 356, 361, 368; China's policy in, xix; conflict between USSR and U.S. over, xx; Chinese policy toward, 10, 68; Soviet expansionism in, 37, 139-40; American interests in, 46; Chinese view of in 1960s, 53; as an independent force, 63; Soviet economic competition in, 114, 126; trade with USSR, 116; Cuban troops in, 135; political instability of, 134, 138; Khrushchev's policy in, 140
Thorez, Secretary-General, 148
Thornton, Richard C., 340-41
Three worlds, theory of, 301-2, 306
Tianamen Square, 22
Tibet: India's attitude to, 212, 214; revolt in, 212; Chinese-Indian dispute over, 215; China's fears about, 219, 227
Tirpitz, Admiral von, 378
Tisza, 352
Tito, Josip Broz (1892-1980), 282, 288, 349; break with USSR, xvi; Khrushchev's attitude to, xvii; Mao's opinion of, xvii; condemned by Togliatti, 144; decision to defy Stalin, 146; talks with Togliatti, 149; as archrevisionist, 193
TNF (theater nuclear forces), 133
Togliatti, Palmiro, 272; choses exile in Moscow, 144; condemns Tito, 144; differs with Moscow, 144; denounced by China, 147; "methods of excommunication," 147-48; visit to Belgrade, 149; criticism of China, 149-50; quoted about split in international movement, 151; Yalta Memorandum, 151-52
Tomahawk Cruise missiles, 312
Tortorella, Aldo, 159
Trade. *See* Foreign trade
Transbaikal region, 373
Transcaucasia, 384
Transylvania, 278
Treadgold, Donald, 382
Treaties; nuclear test ban, 139, 298, 337, 348; SALT II, 232; Nuclear Nonproliferation Treaty, 216; San Francisco Peace Treaty (1952), 174, 175; Peace Agreement of 1956, 175-76; Soviet-Japanese, 174, 176, 180; Sino-Japanese, 176, 180, 182, 364, 374, 386; Sino-Soviet (1950), 363-64; U.S.-Japanese, 176; Indo-Soviet, 219, 228; Soviet-Vietnamese, 180, 362; Soviet-Afghanistan, 229; Sadat abrogates treaty with USSR, 250; Soviet-PDRY, 253; Nerchinsk (1689), 331
Treitschke, 352
Trotskyites, 37-38
Trucial Oman principalities, 255
Tunisia, 250-51
Turkey, 209, 265, 380, 384; relations with USSR, 214; strains in Western ties, 246
Turks, 40, 333, 345; numbers of, 384
Twentieth Congress (CPSU), xvii, 279, 327, 330; Khrushchev's speech, 273-74
Twenty-second Congress (CPSU), xviii, 329, 331, 345
Twenty-second Congress (PCF), 163
Twenty-fourth Congress (CPSU), 75
Twenty-fifth Congress (CPSU), 163
Twenty-sixth Congress (CPSU), 118
Tyumen, 178, 179

Uigurs, 333, 384
Ukrainian nationalism, 377
Union of Soviet Socialist Republics (USSR): expansionism of, 11, 25, 37, 48, 131, 136, 206, 231; military build-up, 42-43, 45, 82, 131, 132-33, 135, 136, 356; foreign policy, 43, 75-76; world priorities, 213; specter of labor unrest, 46; petroleum, 94, 95, 100, 118, 119, 122, 123, 290; agriculture, 45, 95, 99, 116; challenge to legitimacy, 37; ideology versus nationlism, 38; impending turnover of leadership, 43-44, 46; population growth, 45, 101, 376, 384; economic problems, 44-46, 116-17, 127, 376; GNP, 100-106, 119, 120, 122; defense budget, 109; residual in Soviet statistics, 112; natural resources, 117-20, 122; recruitment of manpower, 117, 122; industrialization plans, 117-20; economic efficiency, 121, 123-24; development of Siberia and maritime provinces, 172, 173, 177-79, 182; research and development, 121-22, 123; economic policy, 123-26, 365; economic decline, 356; economic ties with West, 126; "arc of crisis" defensiveness, 131; fears of encirclement, 131-32, 134, 136;

406 INDEX

preemptive breakout, 131–32; conservatism on rise, 132, 134, 136; domestic problems, 135–36; and international politics, 137–46; détente, 136, 139, 142; Soviet bases, 141; and independent communist parties, 147–71; leadership in world communist movement, 146, 150, 156; Moscow conference (1969), 156–57; French Communist Party criticizes, 163; pan-European conference (1980), 170–71; and communist dogma, 193–94; and secessionist movements, 218; and Islamic fervor, 230–31; pluralization of Soviet society, 271; as a global power, 271; challenge to Soviet economic development model, 276, 292; Brezhnev Doctrine, 280–81; military capabilities, 293–94, 376, 378; dilemma of military power, 374; "national question," 376–77; Asian continental collective security system, 241; "universally recognized vanguard" of world communist movement, 329; in Western analyses, 325–55; military confrontation, 358–60, 368, 371; future of, 369–72. See also Sino-Soviet conflict

RELATIONS WITH CHINA: Border disputes, xviii, xx, 7, 13–14, 19, 20, 36, 46, 53–54, 55, 58, 77, 156, 360–61; relations in 1960s, 51–55; trade, 92–98, 112–20; Chinese attitude toward in relation to U.S., 9; attitudes of Lin Biao and Zhou Enlai to, 12; Chinese charges of revisionism, 17, 25; Chinese policy toward in 1973–74, 18–19; anti-Sovietism of Deng, 21; post-Mao relations, 23, 70–73, 82–83, 115; possibilities for improved ties, 26–28, 32; Soviet view of post-Mao China, 29–35; Great Han expansionism, 30; intractability of Sino-Soviet conflict, 35–42; military threat to China, 56–60, 64, 68; "special war economy" criticized by China, 62; seen by China as imperialist, 64–65; Chinese view of Soviet-U.S. relations, 64–66; image of China during 1970s, 77–90; view of China as a threat, 81; Nazi comparison, 81–82; as an Asian power, 86; use of Chinese threat to mobilize national solidarity, 89–90; economics of military balance with China, 106–10, 120–23; interpretation of China's economic future, 125–26; fear of the Chinese, 35, 39–42, 136, 373; encirclement of China, 140, 141; support of Chinese Himalayan border claims, 222; and overthrow of Mujib, 225–26; and Chinese "grand design" in Europe, 308–13;

prospects for Sino-Soviet relations in the 1980s, 42–47

GLOBAL RELATIONS: Afghanistan, 74, 82, 132, 133–34, 136, 224, 229–35, 238–39; Bangladesh, 224; Central Asia, 382–85; Eastern Europe, 98, 116, 146–47, 268–94, 377–79 (Czechoslovakia, xviii–xix, 7, 10, 13, 15, 280); Egypt, 249–50; Ethiopia, 252; France, 297–99; Germany, 305–6; India, 207, 210, 212, 214, 216, 219, 224, 227, 233, 235, 239; Iran, 214, 245, 247; Iraq, 247; Japan, 84, 100, 120, 173–83, 374–75; Korea, 183–84; Libya, 250; Middle East, 134, 240–67, 265–67; Morocco, 251; Pakistan, 210, 214, 216, 217, 225, 239; PDRY, 253; PLO, 248–49; Somalia, 252; South Asia, 206–39; Southeast Asia, 186–205; Sri Lanka, 224; Sudan, 251–52; Syria, 247; Third World, 134, 139–40; Tunisia, 250; Turkey, 214, 246; United States, xx, 29, 46, 84, 192, 195, 219, 221, 235, 332, 336; Vietnam, 140–41, 192, 194–97, 198, 201–3; Western Europe, 98, 142–45, 146, 295–322; YAR, 253–54

United Arab Amirates (UAA), 246, 255
United Kingdom, 295; and nuclear test ban treaty, 298; and South Asia, 208
United Nations, 179–80, 242, 269; admission of PRC, 244, 297; and Indo-Pakistani war, 219; China's actions in, 223; General Assembly, 304
United States: and strategic triangle, 15; Watergate affair, 18; attitude toward military balance, 43; policy on arms control, 43, 49; strategy regarding Sino-Soviet conflict, 47–49; military presence in Southeast Asia, 51, 53, 54; and "dual adversary" concept, 53; post-1949 involvement in Asia, 56–57; containment strategy, 57; agricultural exporter, 105; dependence of allies, 108; defense budget, 109; relations with Western Europe, 132; post-Vietnam withdrawal syndrome, 132; military capabilities, 132; conservatism on rise, 132, 134–35; and instability in Third World, 134; domestic problems, 134; religious revival, 135; and Vietnam, 140–41, 154; relations with West Germany, 143; alliance with Japan, 173; security treaty with Japan, 176; and Korea, 184; and Vietnam War, 188, 189, 195–97; and Hanoi Politburo, 191, 200; and ASEAN, 203; role in South Asia, 208; alliance with Pakistan, 210, 211, 213, 216; and Indo-Pakistani wars, 210, 220; and Bangla-

desh crisis, 216–20; relations with India, 227, 228; aid cut to Pakistan, 228; refuses military support to Afghans, 229; increase in defense spending, 232; importance in Middle East, 241; involvement in Middle East, 245; dominant power in Fertile Crescent, 249; and Red Sea area, 251; offered base in Somalia, 253; support of shah, 267; and France, 297, 298; nuclear test ban treaty, 298; Carter policy, 310; relations with Western Europe, 321–22; upsurge in strategic capabilities, 290; ability to control events in Asia, 346; weakness of, 367; future policy, 370; and Taiwan, 373; military power of, 379; support of Israel, 385; prospects for 1980s, 387

RELATIONS WITH CHINA: Sino-American conflict during Quemoy crisis, xvii; Kissinger visits China, xix, 15; no longer a threat to China, xx; Chinese attitude to, 9, 10, 12; rapprochement, 11, 12, 15, 17, 18, 24, 69, 136, 174, 180, 198, 301, 317, 322, 326; role in China's modernization, 30; "China card," 32, 47, 48, 49, 84; prospects for military alliance, 48–49, 132; Chinese view of passing American predominance in "imperialist camp," 52; efforts to encircle PRC, 56–57; Chinese view of "collusion" between U.S. and USSR, 64–65, 66, 68; benefits to China of "American connection," 66, 71–72; normalization of relations, 69, 83, 363; trade with China, 92, 97, 99, 104; military cooperation with Japan, 181; and Chinese aid to Pakistan, 222; and PRC in Middle East, 264; Maoist attitude to, 302; American attitudes toward China, 344; military aid to China, 375–76; future relations, 86, 292, 374, 375

RELATIONS WITH THE SOVIET UNION: Growing conflict, xx; contest for central focus of international relations, 29; and Soviet legitimacy, 37; Russian opinion of Americans, 39; confrontation, 40; military parity with, 42; Khrushchev's relations with U.S., 52; Moscow's attempt to project China as a common threat, 54; USSR "peace policy," 76; relations in late 1970s, 84–85; Soviet fears of encirclement by, 131; détente, 136, 139, 142, 221; Carter and Brezhnev, 143–44; view of Soviet arms build-up in Asia and Pacific, 173, 181; unwillingness to take part with Japan in economic development of USSR, 179; Soviet attitude toward U.S. in Vietnam, 192, 195; and Soviet invasion of Afghanistan, 232, 233, 234; Soviet and U.S. power compared, 235; Soviet attitude to U.S. in Middle East, 242, 244; competition in Middle East, 260, 265, 266; attitude of USSR to, 332, 336; American attitudes toward USSR, 344; future relations, 46–47

University of Washington Center for Contemporary Chinese and Soviet Studies, xx
Urals, 383
Ussuri River, xviii, 269, 300, 331–32, 336, 361
Ust-Ilimsk, 286
Ustinov, 83
Uzbeks, 384

Vajpayee, Atal Bihari, 228
Van Ness, Peter, 350
Vatican, 334
Viet Cong, 140
Vietnam, xix, 270, 337, 360, 364, 365; and Paracel Islands, 19; U.S. military involvement in, 51, 53, 54; and Soviet Union, 86, 92, 114, 134, 140–41, 214; Soviet forces in, 136; threat to China, 110; intervention in Kampuchea (1979), 168, 180, 289; Chinese attack on (1979), 168, 180, 181, 182; Sino-Soviet impact on, 185–205; importance of Sino-Soviet dispute to, 187; current relations with China, 203; ideological mission of, 203–4; Soviet friendship with, 362; prospects for 1980s, 197–205, 375. See also North Vietnam, South Vietnam, Vietnam War
Vietnam, Socialist Republic of (SRV), 203
Vietnam War, xviii, xxi, 136, 264, 335; and Sino-Soviet relations, 77, 194–97; start of, 189; political settlement of, 191–92, 196–97; peace agreement (February 1973), 18; aftermath of, 197–99
Vietnam war with China (February–March 1979), 25, 74, 82, 197, 198, 228, 270, 289
Vladivostok, 344, 362, 375
Vo Nguyen Giap, 195

Wang Dongxing, 22
Wang Hongwen, 18
Wang Jiaxiang, 371
Wang Zhen, 307
Warsaw Pact, 281, 282, 285, 290, 299, 304, 307
Watergate affair, 18
Water Margin, The, 21
Weapons technology: unverifiable, 132;

American breakthroughs, 138. *See also* Armaments, Missiles, Nuclear weapons
Wehner, Herbert, 313
West Berlin, 143, 296, 300
Western Europe, 279, 292; relations with USSR, 76, 221; armaments, 86, 133; and United States, 136, 321–22; revival of, 138; reaction to invasion of Czechoslovakia, 281; impact of Sino-Soviet dispute on, 295–322; conservative forces, 295, 313; center-left groups, 295, 313; third-force groups, 295, 313; defense of, 306–7; trade with PRC, 307–8, 310; and Chinese "grand design," 308–13; cleavages in foreign policy, 313–20; prospects for 1980s, 387. *See also* NATO *and entries for various countries and communist parties of Western Europe*
Western technology: for USSR, 118, 120, 124; for China, 120, 125
West Germany, 195, 295, 296, 307; role in China's modernization, 30; trade with China, 97, 99, 308; GNP of, 101; Soviet fears of, 131; relations with U.S., 132, 136, 143; relations with USSR, 132; relations with France, 322; revival of, 138; Soviet policy toward, 142; Ostpolitik, 143, 299–300, 306; and PRC, 300, 305; and Khrushchev, 300; Brandt policy, 300, 306; Schmidt policy, 306; reunification of Germany, 305–6, 317–18; Hua's visit, 313, 317; and West European foreign policy, 313–20. *See also* Germany
West Pakistan, 217, 218, 220, 222, 223, 236. *See also* Pakistan
"White papers" in Japan, 181
Wich, Richard, 13
Wilhelm of Wied, 329
William II, 378
Wittfogel, Karl A., 353
World Bank, 3, 99, 103, 126
World Federation of Trade Unions (1960), 328, 331

Xinjiang, 110, 362; helicopter incident in, 19, 21; border clashes, 58; proximity to India, 215
Xuan Mai, 189

Yahya Khan, 217, 218
Yakutsk, 178
Yalta Memorandum, 151–52
Ye Jianying, 21, 71, 357
Yemen Arab Republic, 253–54
Yemen, People's Democratic Republic of (PDRY), 232, 253–54, 255, 256, 257, 258, 367; Soviet domination, 378
Yermak, 345
Yokosuka, 141
Yom Kippur War (1973), 285
Yoshida, Shigeru, 175
Yuan Shikai, 5
Yugoslav Communist Party (LCY), 282, 284; relations with China, 147, 157, 167; charged with revisionism, xviii, 149, 193; relations with PCI, 144, 149; opposition to world conference, 149–50; independent/neutralist, 150–51; independent alliance, 162; and death of Mao, 164; and pan-European conference, 171; relations with CPSU and CCP, 288, 289
Yugoslavia, 146, 273, 274, 275, 277, 278, 330, 334; break with USSR (1948), xvi; Hua's trip to, 312; as an economic model, 366
Yu Zhan, 167, 168

Zagoria, Donald S., 326–29, 330, 350, 353
Zahir Shah, 228
Zarodov, Konstantin, 166
Zhang Chunqiao, 20
Zhang Wentian, 26
Zhenbao island (Damansky), xiii, 7, 345, 357
Zhivkov, Todor, 165, 275, 287
Zhou Enlai (1898–1976), 141, 328, 355, 357, 369, 373; departure from Twenty-second Congress of CPSU, xviii; as a technology firster, 6; strategy of, 10–11; rehabilitation of colleagues, 10–11; relations with USSR, 10–11; relations with Lin Biao, 12–13, 14, 16; health of, 16, 68; struggle with radicals, 16, 18–19; relations with U.S., 18; at Tenth Party Congress, 18, 60, 71; visit to Moscow, 52; and "dual adversary" concept, 53; calls USSR "social-imperialist state," 54; meetings with Kosygin (1969), 58; on military strategy, 59–60, 64; quoted, 60, 66–67; political attacks on, 61; international strategy of, 66–67; address to National People's Congress (1975), 67; and Gang of Four, 69; Kosygin's promises to, 83; desire for alliance with U.S., 137; support for Japanese position on northern territories, 176; and Pakistan, 218; and Yemen, 257; and France, 304; and Nixon administration, 337; death of, 22; "testament" of, 338; and Stalin's funeral, 341
Ziaur Rahman, General, 226

Contributors

William J. Barnds is a professional staff member of the Senate Foreign Relations Committee, and senior research fellow at the Council on Foreign Relations.

Seweryn Bialer is professor of political science, and director of the Research Institute on International Change, Columbia University.

Paul H. Borsuk is an analyst with the National Foreign Assessment Center, U.S. Central Intelligence Agency.

Kevin Devlin is an analyst with Radio Free Europe/Radio Liberty, Munich, Federal Republic of Germany.

Herbert J. Ellison is professor of history; chairman, Center for Contemporary Chinese and Soviet Studies; and chairman, Russian and East European Studies, University of Washington.

Harry Gelman is a senior staff member of the Social Science Department, Rand Corporation.

Trond Gilberg is director, Slavic & Soviet Language and Area Center, and professor of political science, Pennsylvania State University.

William E. Griffith is Ford Professor of Political Science, Massachusetts Institute of Technology.

Donald C. Hellmann is professor, School of International Studies and Department of Political Science, University of Washington.

Kenneth Lieberthal is professor of political science, Swarthmore College.

Dwight Perkins is professor of modern China studies and of economics, and director of the Harvard Institute of International Development, Harvard University.

Douglas Pike is director of the Center for Southeast Asian Studies, University of California, Berkeley.

Jonathan D. Pollack is a staff member of the Social Science Department, Rand Corporation.

Henry W. Schaefer is an international economist, U.S. Arms Control and Disarmament Agency.

Hugh Seton-Watson is professor of Russian history, School of Slavonic and East European Studies, University of London.

Bettie M. Smolansky is a member of the Sociology Department, and assistant dean, Moravian College.

Oles M. Smolansky is chairman, Department of International Relations, and professor, Department of Political Science, Lehigh University.

Donald W. Treadgold is chairman and professor, Department of History, University of Washington.

Joan Barth Urban is associate professor, Department of Politics, The Catholic University of America.